# Spurgeon's Own Hymn Book

CHRISTIAN
HERITAGE

When I was about twenty years old, I began reading one of C.H. Spurgeon's sermons almost every day. I kept up the practice until I had read over 600 of them. In his sermons, Spurgeon often quoted portions of hymns, many of which were unknown to me. Many of the hymns he quoted can be found in Spurgeon's hymnal. Even the hymns with which I was already familiar became more meaningful to me when I read and sang the stanzas which have been left out of modern hymnals. For example, read "All hail the pow'r of Jesus' name" as it appears in Spurgeon's hymnal. I had no idea of the flow and the depth of the text until I read the full version. Or read "Alas! and did my Savior bleed," and it may be that the last stanza will make sense to you for the first time, because the penultimate stanza is often omitted, even though it sets up the final quatrain. Be sure to read "How firm a foundation," especially if, like me, gray, or "hoary hairs" are adorning your temples. People frequently ask me how to get started reading poetry. Reading the rich texts found in this hymnal is a pretty good way to learn how to read and enjoy poetry, but it is an even better way to feed your soul with these beautiful Psalms and hymns.

JIM SCOTT ORRICK

PROFESSOR OF LITERATURE AND CULTURE, SOUTHERN BAPTIST THEOLOGICAL SEMINARY

# Spurgeon's Own Hymn Book

A COLLECTION OF

## PSALMS AND HYMNS

FOR

## PUBLIC, SOCIAL, AND PRIVATE WORSHIP

---

A NEW EDITION OF

*OUR OWN HYMN-BOOK*

---

COMPILED BY

## C.H. SPURGEON

Copyright © 2019 Doxology & Theology Press
Compiled by Charles Haddon Spurgeon
Edited by Chris Fenner & Matt Boswell
Foreword by Tom Nettles

ISBN 978-1-5271-0442-6

Published in 2019
in the Heritage imprint by
Christian Focus Publications Ltd,
Geanies House, Fearn, Ross-shire,
IV20 1TW, Great Britain.

www.christianfocus.com

Library of Congress Classification
BV459.S68

Cover design by Daniel Van Straatan

Interior design by Chris Fenner

Printed in the USA

# Contents

## Appendices

## Indices

*"My God is ever near at hand,*
*and therefore I will sing."*
C.H. SPURGEON
HYMN NO. 39

# Introduction

Hymns play an indispensable role in Christian spirituality. As portable doctrinal confessions, they both articulate and shape our theology. As doxological expressions, they provide language of praise, prayer, lament, and petition. Indeed, church history has bequeathed to us a storehouse of hymnody filled with truths and treasures to unearth. Our current practice of hymnwriting adds to the riches left by men and women who expressed both their doctrine and their piety using melody and meter, poetry and rhyme.

The hymnal of Charles Spurgeon is itself a storehouse of riches. His desire to curate a body of hymnody for the church—as an aid in worship and for the exposition of Scripture[1]—flowed from his pastoral heart. This conviction echoed that of the previous pastors who had gone before him. From the seminal work of Benjamin Keach (the "father of Baptist hymnody"), to the doctrinal psalm-singing of John Gill, to the industrious curation of John Rippon, to Spurgeon's own turn at publishing a hymnal, the Prince of Preachers stood in an unsurpassed line of singing shepherds contributing to the heritage of hymnody.

While many know of Spurgeon as a preacher, few are familiar with his deep love of hymnody—and the role it played in his life as a worshiper of Christ and a pastor of Christ's people. This hymnal, then, is a window into the pastoral theology of congregational singing and hymnody Spurgeon held dear as a preacher. "No matter on what topic I am preaching," Spurgeon once said, "I can even now, in the middle of any sermon, quote some verse of a hymn in harmony with the subject. The hymns have remained with me."[2] Our hope is that the hymns collected by the Singing Lion of London will remain also with you, giving rich expression to your praise of the Lord Jesus Christ.

*Matt Boswell*
Hymnwriter and Pastor
The Trails Church
Prosper, TX

---

1. See Spurgeon's preface, pp. 3-5 in this volume.

2. *The Autobiography of Charles H. Spurgeon*, vol. 1 (Chicago: Curts & Jennings, 1898), pp. 43-44.

CHARLES HADDON SPURGEON

*The Sword and the Trowel*
May 1868

# Foreword

## Spurgeon's Hymnody

Anything that detracted from the fullest participation in the music by the entire congregation, Spurgeon opposed as a heart aggravation, or even an "evil." The compilation of his hymn book arose from such a vexation of spirit. What should have been a time of simple and unhindered praise had become a cumbersome confusion. The offending evil lay in the congregation's tradition of using two hymn books regularly in the time of corporate worship, John Rippon's *Selection* and Isaac Watts' *Psalms and Hymns*. Making the situation even less manageable was the complex arrangement of each of the books. This would not do.

For the great congregation, filled with experienced saints as well as hundreds of newly-churched, and scores of never-churched, over which Spurgeon presided and led in worship, nothing would do but to have *Our Own Hymn-Book*. Starts and stops finally yielded in 1866 to completion of the ambitious project. A careful reviewer for *The Wesleyan Times* concluded, "At present we can honestly say, it is the largest, cheapest, and most accurate hymn-book in the English language."[1]

Spurgeon did not undertake this task of collecting and organizing a hymn book as a novice. Hymns had been a part of his life since before remembrance. His grandmother paid him to memorize hymns while his grandfather paid him to kill rats.[2] Learning hymns by heart clearly proved to be a more valuable experience. He would punctuate his sermons with apt quotes from hymns, sometimes a full verse, sometimes two lines, but always spot-on in their relevance. His sermons in *The Metropolitan Tabernacle Pulpit* contain thousands of quotations of hymns. For *Our Own Hymn-Book*, he wrote 24 new texts, and he sprinkled others throughout the massive corpus of his writings.

His consistent interest in the musical aspect of congregational worship shows up in the *The Sword & The Trowel*. He regularly reviewed new hymnals and other specimens of worship music. When reviewing *A Complete Compend of Revival Music*, Spurgeon called some of the inclusions "execrable," yet recognized that some people "sing them with gusto, and get good out of them."[3] Reluctantly, on the matter of music, he yielded to the old proverb "which bids us neither dispute with winds nor tastes." In a review of *The Psalmist*, published under the supervision of Ebenezer Prout, Spurgeon noted an infelicitous rejection of widely approved tunes for the sake of more recent ones: "Some of the tunes rejected should, we think, have been retained, and if they have been sacrificed to modern taste, so much the worse for modern taste."[4]

## Musical Leadership at the Tabernacle

Spurgeon opposed performance and professionalism as a substitute for robust, hearty music from the entire gathering of worship-

---

1. *The Wesleyan Times*, 10 Sept. 1866.
2. W.Y. Fullerton, *C.H. Spurgeon: A Biography* (London: Williams & Norgate, 1920), p. 11.
3. *The Sword and the Trowel* [S&T], Sept. 1882, p. 495.
4. S&T, April 1879, p. 193.

pers. "The institution of singers, as a separate order, is an evil," he bristled, "a growing evil, and ought to be abated and abolished."[5] He condemned the practice, writing, "Praise is comely for the upright," but not "from unpardoned professional singers." Rather, before God it is "a jewel of gold in a swine's snout. Crooked hearts make crooked music, but the upright are the Lord's delight."[6]

Likewise, to the leader of the congregational song, he warned, "The people come together not to see you as a songster, but to praise the Lord in the beauty of Holiness." He was not a soloist, but "a leader of others, many of whom know nothing of music." Not only must the leader avoid ostentation, but members of the congregation should avoid drawing attention to themselves. He saw self-appointed vocalists destroy the spirit of public worship by deploying themselves in such a way as to dominate the time of singing. "A band of godless men and women," he called them, "will often install themselves in a conspicuous part of the chapel, and monopolise the singing to the grief of the pastor, the injury of the church, and the scandal of public worship." Other times, a person with delusions about his own gifts, "with a miserable voice, will drag a miserable few after him in a successful attempt to make psalms and hymns hideous, or dolorous."[7] Yes, the obstacles to musical purity and simplicity were many.

The character of the music itself held a special place of importance for Spurgeon. Tunes should be easily learned by all so that "none in the assembly may be compelled to be silent while the Lord is extolled."[8] None should be defrauded of their part in the worship because of the exclusive taste of the leader. "Simple airs are best," Spurgeon opined, and "very few of the more intricate tunes are really musical."[9] Spurgeon pointed

to Psalm 136 as a popular hymn among the Lord's ancient people, for, like today, "Most hymns with a solid, simple chorus become favourites with congregations, and this is sure to have been one of the best beloved."[10] The power of the repetitious phrase, "For His lovingkindness endureth forever," gave it the character of nothing but praise. "It is tuned to rapture," he noted, "and can only be fully enjoyed by a devoutly grateful heart."

Careless selection of a tune is another impediment to worship. "You mock God," Spurgeon warned, "and injure the devotions of his people" by a careless offering of worship material that cost no thought or effort, no exercise of judgment. On the other hand, a well-selected harmony can help the pious heart to wing its way to heaven rather than "vex the godly ear by inappropriate or unmelodious airs, adapted rather to distract and dishearten, than to encourage intelligent praise."[11] Drowning worship in slow and dull tempos with monotonous droning in large assemblies vexed Spurgeon, as did hymns treated as jigs and dashed through at a gallop.

On Lord's Day worship, Spurgeon liked neither choirs, nor professional musicians, nor instruments. With obvious visceral annoyance, Spurgeon remarked, "What a degradation to supplant the intelligent song of the whole congregation by the theatrical prettinesses of a quartette, the refined niceties of a choir, or the blowing off of wind from inanimate bellows and pipes!"[12]

At the opening of the Metropolitan Tabernacle in 1861, Spurgeon explained what he desired to hear. The newly constructed building was to be consecrated fully to the glory of God in preaching and corporate worship. He insisted that the worship of the congregation consisted of their participation in the singing of hymns. Spurgeon delighted in the sound of voices lifted in praise to God. He

5. S&T, June 1870, p. 278.
6. C.H. Spurgeon, *Treasury of David*, expos. on Ps. 33:1.
7. S&T, June 1870, p. 278.
8. S&T, June 1870, p. 278.
9. S&T, June 1870, p. 278.

10. *Treasury of David*, introduction to Ps. 136.
11. S&T, June 1870, p. 278.
12. *Treasury of David*, exposition on Ps. 42:4.

wanted all to participate. "What a joyous thing it is to hear the thousands praise God at once; every man contributing to the song." Variety would make the sound more glorious. "The poor, coarse voice belonging to some of us, who never can learn music, let us try as much as we will; the flute-like voices of our sisters, the deep resounding mellow bass of the full-developed man; all the different tones, and notes, and voices, perhaps expressive of our different degrees and growths in grace, of our different trials and our different temperaments, all join to swell one common hymn which rolls upward to the throne of God." Every one that refuses to sing, every silent tongue, and every dumb lip mars the song. Complete participation with nothing to muffle the sound of the voice and the clarity of the words was his goal. "As often as we meet together here may the song roll up to heaven like the voice of many waters, and like great thunders."[13]

## The Influence of John Curwen

No matter how idyllic was the image of music rolling "up to heaven like the voice of many waters," the reality fell short of the massive wave it should have been. When John Curwen, a prominent music educator, visited the Tabernacle in 1866, he noted that "Mr. Spurgeon has a beautiful high voice," and easily "goes mounting aloft most happily, supremely unconscious that we miserable people are left to grope after some one of the ready-made and mutually discordant bass or contralto 'parts' which are growling below." He made a suggestion to help improve the singing: "If Mr. Spurgeon were to provide for his own congregation . . . a hymn and tune book in one . . . and if he introduced this new book with three seasons of singing classes and praise meetings, he would soon have the joy of hearing at least half as many people again joining in the song, and all singing more hap-

pily and better."[14] Curwen was probably not aware that Spurgeon's hymnal was already in the works, but it did not contain any tunes.

Spurgeon, perhaps sensitized to the issue by Curwen's analysis, later indicated to his congregation that the lack of vocal control detracted from joyous worship. He felt they sang best when they were most energized spiritually. In his sermon of March 8, 1868, he noted, "Last Monday night, the singing was very much better than it was on Sabbath evening." They kept "better time and better tune" because they "had come up to worship God with more solemnity than usual, and therefore there was no slovenly singing such as pains my ear and heart some times." On those particularly onerous occasions, some would "fall half a note behind the rest, others of you are singing quite a false note, and few make no sound of any kind." Those content merely to look and listen were not much better than the crowd that sought to dominate the singing. He looked to "everybody singing, singing his best, singing carefully and heartily." Artistic improvement would come when the voice followed the heart with due attention to the sound. "With a little care," Spurgeon encouraged, "the heart brings the art, and heart desiring to praise will by-and-by train the voice to time and tune." He wanted the service of song "to be of the best; . . . let us have the best and most orderly harmony we can make."[15]

His commentary on Psalm 33 reinforced his desire for an artistic expression of singing as an honorable goal in worship. Spurgeon advised that one should learn "to sing according to the rules of the art, so that he may keep time and tune with the congregation."[16] If leaders select fitting tunes, they must work to make sure they are not "growled out by discordant voices." With utter transparency, Spurgeon wrote, "It is wretched to hear God

---

13. *Metropolitan Tabernacle Pulpit* (MTP), vol. 7, 31 Mar. 1861 (no. 375), p. 218.

14. John Curwen, "Psalmody in London Churches," *The Christian Witness*, June 1866, p. 291.
15. MTP, vol. 14, 8 Mar. 1868 (no. 799), p. 141.
16. *Treasury of David*, exposition on Ps. 33:3.

praised in a slovenly manner."[17]

Spurgeon took practical steps. He determined that a singing school using the solfa method would expand the percentage of participation in the singing throughout the congregation, as well as enhance its quality. He arranged for Curwen to conduct the training, and they produced a tune book especially for the classes.[18] In the preface, Spurgeon expressed on behalf of the class "hearty and sincere thanks to Mr. Curwen for the benefits they have derived from his Tonic Sol-Fa Notation." Their object, Spurgeon explained, was "aiding our singing in the Public Congregation." The process of assembling the tune book led Spurgeon to discontinue the use of some tunes, "in consequence of the numerous repetitions in the melody and the breaking up of the words to suit the music," rendering them "unsuitable for public worship, where purity and simplicity are essentials to successful Psalmody." Such tunes would persevere briefly; but Spurgeon did not "in any way desire to perpetuate their use."

Curwen's son, John Spencer Curwen (his co-laborer in publishing and pedagogy), visited the Tabernacle at the watchnight service leading out of 1873 and on the first Sunday of 1874, about four years after his father had conducted the singing school, and almost eight years after the elder Curwen's influential article. At the watchnight service, Spurgeon commented that sometimes the devil made the congregation linger half a note behind the precentor. On the following Sunday, Curwen described the singing as "thoroughly enjoyable." Both size and earnestness made it so.[19]

At the coming of the first hymn, the 1650 Scotch rendering of Psalm 46 (No. 46b), Curwen likened the congregation's response to "a giant that needs a moment to arouse himself." After a note or two, the congregation "entered in full strength. Then the heavy tide of sound streamed forth from every part of the building." On the second hymn, "Thou hidden love of God" (No. 798), the people "sang as before." For the third, "Beneath Thy cross I lay me down" (No. 818), Curwen commented that "the people were warming to their work and the volume of sound poured forth more solid and powerful than before." Curwen had observed more cultivated singing in many congregations; nevertheless, "from the numbers engaged, no other singing touches the heart with such indefinable pleasure, and makes the frame glow with such a sense of worshipful sympathy." It was clear to Curwen that "Mr. Spurgeon takes delight in the service of song, and is anxious above all things that every man, woman, and child in the place should sing."[20]

Spurgeon's sermon on this occasion pointed to the "overflow of enjoyment" as a mark of "Life Abundant." To illustrate the point, he noted, "When churches are revived, what life there is in them, and then what singing! Never has a revival of religion come without a revival of singing!" The great reformers, preachers, and evangelists of the church, like Luther, Whitefield, the Wesleys, and Toplady, supplied hymns "for the people to sing, for they must show their joy, a joy born of life!"[21]

Although the younger Curwen's report was more affirming than the elder's, he still saw room for improvement. Hearing an "undisciplined company of untrained voices," Curwen noted that the singing was "breathy and whispering in effect," and lacked "that musical ring which comes from people who have learned to use their voices." Given the total effect, he suggested that improvement could be made without losing, but rather increasing, the obvious involvement of heart in the rush of musical sound. "They use their voices," he surmised, "if with a drawl, yet with a will. And no one can doubt that they

---

17. *Treasury of David*, exposition on Ps. 33:3.

18. *Tabernacle Tune Book* (London: unpublished, n.d.).

19. J. Spencer Curwen, *Studies in Worship Music*, 1st series, 3rd ed., enl. & rev. (London, 1901), p. 428.

20. Curwen, *Studies*, pp. 427-428.

21. MTP, vol. 20, 4 Jan. 1874 (no. 1150), p. 10.

sing as much from the heart as any congregation in the kingdom."[22]

Curwen also observed Spurgeon's practice of reading hymns verse by verse and felt it was unnecessary. "The reading takes up time, and is evidently wearisome to many," he reported.[23] Yet Spurgeon strongly defended his practice of reading before singing. No person should be made to listen to singing in which he cannot join. "It is wretched to go into chapels and tear through a hymn like mad, while you have no idea what the words may be which they are thus hurrying over."[24]

**The True Director of Worship**

Congregational praise held a place of supreme importance in the theology and practice of Spurgeon, for he saw Jesus as the great leader of such praise. Every redeemed person stands in a chorus with Jesus as the director; in singing praise to God, we join the words of praise that Jesus himself is giving. In a sermon entitled "Jesus the Example of Holy Praise,"[25] Spurgeon ruminated aloud concerning the phrase "In the midst of the congregation will I praise thee" (Ps. 22:22). Was it merely his imagination, he pondered, or did the text actually indicate that "the Lord Jesus Christ, as man, adores and worships the eternal God in heaven, and is, in fact, the great leader of the devotions of the skies?" Would it be a mistake to look to Jesus as our High Priest as adoring the Lord God

and as lifting up his voice in sacred Psalmody to him? If he does so indeed, shall we not join him? "Is He the chief musician of the sky, the Master of the sacred choir? Does He beat time for all the hallelujahs of the universe? I think so." Spurgeon stated with emphasis that "As God, He is praised forever: far above all worshipping, He is Himself forever worshipped." As man, however, as "the Head of redeemed humanity, the ever-living Priest of the Most High God, I believe," Spurgeon continued, "that He praises Jehovah in heaven." Surely the fit occupation for the Head is "to speak and to represent the holy joys and devout aspirations of the whole body which He represents."

While Christians join to sing praise to Christ the King, also they join with Christ the Prophet, Christ the Priest, in loving, adoring, and praising the God whose wisdom established the eternal covenant in accordance with which he himself "entered the holy place once for all [and] through the eternal Spirit offered Himself without blemish to God" (Hebrews 9:12,14). Thus it is, that through him, we "continually offer up a sacrifice of praise to God, that is, the fruit of lips that give thanks to his name" (Hebrews 13:15).

*Tom Nettles*
The Southern Baptist Theological Seminary
Louisville, KY

---

22. Curwen, *Studies*, pp. 429-430.
23. Curwen, *Studies*, p. 428.
24. S&T, December 1877, p. 575.
25. MTP, vol. 14, 8 Mar. 1868 (no. 799).

# Abbreviations

**3.2**
Stanza 3, Line 2

**C.H.S.**
Charles Haddon Spurgeon

**C.M.**
Common Metre (8.6.8.6.)

**CUR**
J. Spencer Curwen, "Metropolitan Tabernacle," *Studies in Worship Music*, 1st Series, 3rd Ed. (London: J. Curwen & Sons, 1901).

**Ed: / ed.**
Editorial note / Editor, Edition

**EE**
Charles Spurgeon, *Evening by Evening* (London: Passmore & Alabaster, 1868).

**FPN**
Charles Spurgeon, *Fac-Simile Pulpit Notes* (London: Passmore & Alabaster, 1894).

**Julian's Dictionary**
John Julian, ed., *A Dictionary of Hymnology*, (London: J. Murray, 1892; with suppl., 1907).

**L.M.**
Long Metre (8.8.8.8.)

**MBTS**
Sermon Notes, The Spurgeon Library, Midwestern Baptist Theological Seminary, Kansas City, Missouri.

**MM**
Charles Spurgeon, *Morning by Morning* (London: Passmore & Alabaster, 1865).

**MTP**
*Metropolitan Tabernacle Pulpit* (London: Passmore & Alabaster, 1861-1917).

**NPSP**
*New Park Street Pulpit* (London: Passmore & Alabaster, 1855-1860).

**rev.**
Revised

**S&T**
*The Sword and the Trowel* (London: Passmore & Alabaster, 1865-1966, 1980–).

**S.M.**
Short Metre (6.6.8.6)

**st./sts.**
Stanza/Stanzas

**TD**
*Treasury of David* (London: Passmore & Alabaster, 1870-1886).

# Our Own Hymn-Book

# Preface

OUR congregation has long used two hymn-books: namely, the comprehensive edition of Dr. Rippon's *Selection*,[1] and Dr. Watts's *Psalms and Hymns*.[2] Despite the judgment of many to the contrary, we believe that the store of spiritual songs contained in these two volumes is not excelled, even if equalled by any compilation extant, and we should most probably have been very well content with those books had it not been for difficulties connected with the remarkably complex arrangement of their contents. To strangers, it was no small task to discover the hymn selected for singing; for in the first place, there were two books, which was in itself an evil, but the matter was made far worse by the fact that these two volumes were each a puzzle to the uninstructed; Rippon with its parts innumerable, and Watts with first, second, and third books.

The providence of God brings very many new hearers within the walls of our place of worship, and many a time have we marked their futile researches and pitied the looks of despair with which they have given up all hope of finding the hymns, and so of joining intelligently in our words of praise. We felt that such ought not to be the state of our service of song and resolved if possible to reform it.

1. John Rippon, *A Selection of Hymns from the Best Authors*, Comprehensive Ed. (1844).

2. Isaac Watts, *Psalms of David Imitated in the Language of the New Testament* (1719), *Hymns and Spiritual Songs* (1707, rev. 1709), later published together.

None of the collections already published are exactly what our congregation needs, or we would have cheerfully adopted one of them. They are good in their way, but we need something more. Our congregation has distinctive features which are not suited by every compilation, not indeed by any known to us. We thought it best to issue a selection which would contain the cream of the books already in use among us, together with the best of all others extant up to the hour of going to press, and having sought a blessing upon the project, we set about it with all our might, and at last have brought it to a conclusion. Our best diligence has been given to the work, and we have spared no expense. May God's richest blessing rest upon the result of our arduous labours! Unto his glory we dedicate *Our Own Hymn-Book*.

The area of our researches has been as wide as the bounds of existing religious literature, American and British, Protestant and Romish, ancient and modern. Whatever may be thought of our taste, we have used it without prejudice, and a good hymn has not been rejected because of the character of its author, or the heresies of the church in whose hymnal it first occurred, so long as the language and the spirit commended the hymn to our heart we included it, and believe that we have enriched our collection thereby. The range of subjects is very extensive, comprising not only direct praise, but doctrine, experience, and exhortation, thus enabling the saints according to apostolical command to edify one another in their spiritual songs.

If any object that some of the hymns are penitential or doctrinal, and therefore unfit to be sung, we reply that we find examples of such in the Book of Psalms, which we have made our model in compiling our work; there we have Maschils as well as hosannas, and penitential odes as well as hallelujahs. We have not been able to fall in with modern scruples, but have rested content with ancient precedents. We have not cast about for models suggested by the transient fancy of the hour, but have followed the indications given us in the Word of God in the long-established usage of the universal church, desiring to be obedient to the sacred precept, "Let the word of Christ dwell in you richly in all wisdom: teaching and admonishing one another in psalms and hymns and spiritual songs, singing with grace in your hearts to the Lord."[3] We hope that in some few churches of the land we may be helpful to their service of sacred song, and aid them in praising the Lord.

The features which distinguish this hymn-book are such as to justify its issue, at least in the mind of the compiler, upon whom it has involved immense labour—a labour which has been its own reward. Those features are as follows:

1.    The hymns have been drawn from the original works of the authors, and are given as far as practicable just as they were written. This is so unusual a practice as to be almost a novelty, while the mangling of hymns has grown into a system—a system, however, to be most heartily deprecated. The very few alterations which we have personally made are either grammatical corrections or emendations which seemed to be imperatively demanded by the interests of truth, or were necessary in order to change the metre into such as could be sung.

2.    Subjects frequently passed over or pushed into a corner are here made conspicuously the themes of song; such, for instance, as the great doctrines of sovereign grace, the personal Advent of our Lord, and especially the sweetness of present communion with Him.

3.    Hymns suitable for revivals, prayer meetings, and earnest addresses to sinners, are given in larger numbers and greater variety than in any other selection known to the editor, and several popular verses whose poetic merit had not commended them to previous compilers have been adopted in deference to the Great Spirit who has so frequently blessed the use of them both to saints and sinners.

4.    The Psalms of David are here, by the aid of various writers, more especially, Watts, the English and Scotch versions, Mr. Lyte, and Miss Auber,[4] all presented, in whole or in part, in forms suitable for congregational singing, and our endeavour has been to preserve the devout spirit of that inspired book even where the Jewish expressions have been necessarily changed for Christian language.

Our deepest obligations are acknowledged to Mr. D. Sedgwick, of Sun Street, Bishopsgate, without whose diligent assistance our work could never have been accomplished. His large collection of hymn-books, and his marvellous acquaintance with hymnology, render him the indespensible helper of all hymn collectors who would have their work well done. For the authorship, dates, and general correctness of the text, we have relied mainly upon him and believe that he has enabled us to produce a volume altogether unique and unrivalled in value.

To very many proprieters of original hymns we tender earnest thanks for the liberal manner in which consent has invariably been given to us to use their copyrights. If

---

3. Colossians 3:16, KJV.

4. See the Index of Authors and Sources for full citations. For the "English versions," see Thomas Sternhold (1548, etc.), Wm. Wittingham (1556), John Hopkins (1562), and Tate & Brady (1696-1698).

by inadvertence we have used any compositions without permission, we trust the owners will extend to us the same courtesy as if we had written to them, which kind assent we will gladly acknowledge in a future issue.

In the large type edition of this collection will be found a complete list of all the authors to whom we are indebted, with the titles of their various works; but even in this small copy we are bound to acknowledge our obligations to the proprieters of the invaluable works of James Montgomery, Conder, Lyte, Kelly, Sir Edward Denny, Dr. Neale, and Miss Anna Shipton. We thank Rev. W. Hiley Bathurst for permission to use his excellent *Psalms and Hymns;* Thomas Davis, of Roundhay, for like liberty with his valuable *Hymns New and Old*; Dr. Horatius Bonar, for his choice *Hymns of Faith and Hope*; Rev. J.S. Monsell, for his most precious *Spiritual Songs*; Mr. Caswall for assent to use his hymns given through Mr. Stevenson; to Rev. James Kelly, for hymns from his selection; Mr. Edmeston, for several poetical odes; Rev. W. Reid, for aid through his noble *Praise Book*; Mr. Henry Bateman, for use of *Heart Melodies* and other works; Rev. Newman Hall for original pieces, and especially Mr. Albert Midlane for use of *Gospel Echoes*, and for several contributions specially written for our assistance. We are grateful to representatives of Dr. Reed for the use of his hymns, and to Rev. Denham Smith and others for the same favour; while to many friends we are thankful for valuable information as to authorship and dates.

We are thus indebted to all classes of Christians, and are furnished with another instance of the intimate fellowship of all saints in their prayers and praises; we pray that believers of all denominations may derive a blessing from the combined works of so many of the Lord's servants.

*C.H. Spurgeon*
September, 1866

## SPIRIT OF THE PSALMS.

—o—

**1**   PSALM 1.   C.M.

1 BLEST is the man who shuns the place
  Where sinners love to meet;
 Who fears to tread their wicked ways,
  And hates the scoffer's seat:

2 But in the statutes of the Lord
  Has placed his chief delight;
 By day he reads or hears the word,
  And meditates by night.

3 He, like a plant of gen'rous kind,
  By living waters set,
 Safe from the storms and blasting wind,
  Enjoys a peaceful state.

4 Green as the leaf, and ever fair,
  Shall his profession shine;
 While fruits of holiness appear
  Like clusters on the vine.

5 Not so the impious and unjust;
  What vain designs they form!
 Their hopes are blown away like dust,
  Or chaff before the storm.

6 Sinners in judgment shall not stand
  Amongst the sons of grace,
 When Christ, the Judge, at His right hand
  Appoints His saints a place.

7 His eye beholds the path they tread;
  His heart approves it well:
 But crooked ways of sinners lead
  Down to the gates of hell.

        *Isaac Watts*, 1719.

1

*Our Own Hymn-Book.* 1st ed. (1866).

# Spirit of the Psalms

**1** C.M.
*Psalm 1*

1 BLEST is the man who shuns the place
    Where sinners love to meet,
Who fears to tread their wicked ways
    And hates the scoffer's seat:

2 But in the statutes of the Lord
    Has placed his chief delight;
By day he reads or hears the Word,
    and meditates by night.

3 He, like a plant of gen'rous kind,
    By living waters set,
Safe from the storms and blasting wind,
    Enjoys a peaceful state.

4 Green as the leaf, and ever fair,
    Shall his profession shine,
While fruits of holiness appear
    Like clusters on the vine.

5 Not so the impious and unjust;
    What vain designs they form!
Their hopes are blown away like dust
    Or chaff before the storm.

6 Sinners in judgment shall not stand
    Amongst the sons of grace,
When Christ, the Judge, and his right hand
    Appoints His saints a place.

7 His eye beholds the path they tread,
    His heart approves it well,
But crooked ways of sinners lead
    Down to the gates of hell.

*Isaac Watts*, 1719

**2** 6.6.6.6.4.4.4.4.
*Psalm 2*

1 THOUGH sinners boldly join
Against the Lord to rise,
Against His Christ combine,
    Th' Anointed to despise;
        Though earth disdain
            And hell engage,
            Vain is their rage,
        Their counsel vain.

2 Jesus the Saviour reigns!
On Zion is His throne;
The Lord's decree sustains
His own begotten Son:
        Up from the grave
            He bids Him rise,
            And mounts the skies
        With power to save.

3 O serve the Lord with fear,
    And rev'rence His command;
With sacred joy draw near,
With solemn trembling stand;
        Kneel at His throne,
            Your homage bear,
            His pow'r declare,
        And kiss the Son.

*William Goode*, 1811

**3** L.M.
*Psalm 3*

1 THY promise, Lord, is perfect peace,
And yet my trials still increase;
Till fears at times my soul assail,
That Satan's rage must yet prevail.

2 Then, Saviour, then I fly to Thee,
And in Thy grace my refuge see;
Thou heard'st me from Thy holy hill,
And Thou wilt hear and help me still.

3 Beneath Thy wings secure I sleep;
What foe can harm while Thou dost keep?
I wake and find Thee at my side,
My omnipresent Guard and Guide!

4 O why should earth or hell distress,
With God so strong, so nigh to bless?
From Him alone salvation flows;
On Him alone, my soul, repose!

*Henry Francis Lyte*, [1836]

**4** C.M.
*Psalm 4*

1 LORD of my life, my hopes, my joys,
My never-failing Friend,
Thou hast been all my help till now;
O help me to the end!

2 While worldly minds impatient grow
More prosp'rous times to see,
*O* let the glories of Thy face
Shine *brighter*, Lord, on me!

3 So shall my heart o'erflow with joy
More lasting and more true
Than theirs, *possessed of all that they
So eagerly pursue.*

4 Then down in peace I'll lay my head
And take my needful rest:
No other guard *I ask or need,
Of Thee, O Lord,* possess'd.

[1 *Henry Francis Lyte*, 1836]
 2-4 *Tate and Brady*, 1696 [*alt. H.F. Lyte*]

   **2.3:** *Still* **2.4:** *brightly*
   **3.3-4:** *who stores of corn and wine
      successively renew.*
   **4.3-4:** *O Lord, I crave,
      Of Thy defence*
   **Ed:** From Tate & Brady's longer paraphrase,
      "O Lord that art my righteous judge."

**5** C.M.
*Psalm 5*

1 LORD, in the morning Thou shalt hear
My voice ascending high;
To Thee will I direct my prayer,
To Thee lift up mine eye,

2 Up to the hills where Christ is gone
To plead for all His saints,

Presenting at His Father's throne
Our songs and our complaints.

3 Thou art a God before whose sight
The wicked shall not stand;
Sinners shall ne'er be Thy delight,
Nor dwell at Thy right hand.

4 But to Thy house will I resort
To taste Thy mercies there;
I will frequent Thy holy court
And worship in Thy fear.

5 Oh may Thy Spirit guide my feet
In ways of righteousness!
Make every path of duty straight
And plain before my face.

*Isaac Watts*, 1719

**6** 7.7.7.7.
*Psalm 6*

1 GENTLY, gently lay Thy rod
On my sinful head, O God.
Stay Thy wrath, in mercy stay,
Lest I sink before its sway.

2 Heal me, for my flesh is weak;
Heal me, for Thy grace I seek;
This my only plea I make:
Heal me for Thy mercy's sake.

3 Who within the silent grave
Shall proclaim Thy power to save?
Lord, my trembling soul reprieve;
Speak, and I shall rise and live.

4 Lo! He comes! He heeds my plea!
Lo! He comes! the shadows flee!
Glory round me dawns once more;
Rise, my spirit, and adore!

*Henry Francis Lyte*, 1834 [*rev.* 1836]

**7** 7.7.7.7. Double
*Psalm 7*

1 LORD, my God, in Thee I trust;
Save, O save Thy trembling dust

From the roaring lion's power,
Seeking whom he may devour,
From a thousand waves that roll
Shipwreck o'er my sinking soul;
God omnipotent, I flee
From them all to Thee, to Thee.

2 Thou my inmost wish canst read,
Thou canst help my utmost need;
Let the world Thy goodness see;
Let them mark Thy grace in me.
Lay the wicked in the dust,
Raise the feeble, guide the just:
Searcher of the heart, I flee
From myself to Thee, to Thee.

*Henry Francis Lyte*, 1834 [*rev.* 1836]

# 8
C.M.
*Psalm 8*

1 O LORD, our Lord, how wondrous great
Is Thine exalted name!
The glories of Thine heav'nly state
Let men and babes proclaim.

2 When I behold Thy works on high,
The moon that rules the night,
And stars that well adorn the sky,
Those moving worlds of light:

3 Lord, what is man, or all his race,
Who dwells so far below,
That Thou shouldst visit him with grace
And love his nature so?

4 That Thine eternal Son should bear
To take a mortal form,
Made lower than His angels are,
To save a dying worm?

5 Let Him be crowned with majesty
Who bowed His head to death,
And be His honours sounded high
By all things that have breath.

6 Jesus, our Lord, how wondrous great
Is Thine exalted name!

The glories of Thy heav'nly state
Let the whole earth proclaim.

*Isaac Watts*, 1719

> **MM:** Hymns, Set 1 (Jan./Nov.), 1st Morn,
> DEDHAM / CORONATION
> **TD:** "It is not possible for us to honour Jesus too
> much; what our God delights to do, we may
> certainly do to our utmost. Oh for new crowns
> for the lofty brow which once was marred
> with thorns!" (Ps. 21:5; vol. 1, p. 353).

# 9
C.M.
*Psalm 9*

1 TO celebrate Thy praise, O Lord,
I will my heart prepare;
To all the list'ning world Thy works,
Thy wondrous works declare.

2 The thought of them shall to my soul
Exalted pleasure bring,
Whilst to Thy name, O Thou most high,
Triumphant praise I sing.

3 All those who have His goodness proved
Will in His truth confide,
Whose mercy ne'er forsook the man
That on His help relied.

4 His suff'ring saints, when most distress'd,
He ne'er forgets to aid;
Their expectation shall be crown'd,
Though for a time delay'd.

5 Sing praises, therefore, to the Lord
From Zion, His abode;
Proclaim His deeds, till all the world
Confess no other God.

*Tate and Brady*, 1696 [*rev.* 1698]

# 10
C.M.
*Psalm 10:17-18*

1 O GOD, the help of all Thy saints,
Our hope in time of ill,
We'll trust Thee, though Thy face be hid,
And seek Thy presence still.

2  All our desires to Thee are known;
    Thy help is ever near;
  O first prepare our hearts to pray,
    And then accept our prayer.

*Edward Osler*, 1836

# 11 L.M.
*Psalm 11*

1  WHEN all bespeaks a Father's love,
  Oh wherefore, fearful as the dove,
  Should we in times of peril flee
  To any refuge, Lord, but Thee?

2  In vain the wicked bend their bow
  And seek to lay the righteous low;
  Thou from Thine everlasting throne
  With watchful care regard'st Thine own.

3  Thy voice shall seal the sinner's fate;
  Just vengeance shall his crimes await,
  While the bright beams of grace divine
  Shall on Thy faithful servants shine.

*Harriet Auber*, 1829

# 12 C.M.
*Psalm 12*

1  LORD, when iniquities abound,
    And blesphemy grows bold,
  When faith is hardly to be found,
    And love is waxing cold,

2  Is not Thy chariot hast'ning on?
    Hast Thou not giv'n this sign?
  May we not trust and live upon
    A promise so divine?

3  "Yes," saith the Lord, "now will I rise
    And make oppressors flee;
  I shall appear to their surprise
    And set my servants free."

4  Thy Word, like silver sev'n times tried,
    Through ages shall endure;
  The men that in Thy truth confide
    Shall find Thy promise sure.

*Isaac Watts*, 1719

**Ed:** Taken from the longer paraphrase,
"Help, Lord, for men of virtue fail."

# 13 C.M.
*Psalm 13*

1  HOW long wilt Thou forget me, Lord?
    Must I forever mourn?
  How long wilt Thou withdraw from me,
    Oh! never to return?

2  O hear! and to my longing eyes
    Restore Thy wonted light;
  *Revive my soul, nor let me* sleep
    In everlasting night.

3  Since I have always placed my trust
    Beneath Thy mercy's wing,
  Thy saving health will come, and then
    My heart with joy shall spring.

4  Then shall my song, with praise inspired,
    To Thee, my God, ascend,
  Who to Thy servant in distress
    Such bounty didst extend.

*Tate and Brady*, 1696
[*alt. Edward Harland*, 1855]

  **2.3:** *And suddenly, or I shall*

# 14 7.6.7.6.
*Psalm 14:7*

1  O THAT the Lord's salvation
    Were out of Zion come,
  To heal His ancient nation,
    To lead His outcasts home.

2  How long the holy city
    Shall heathen feet profane?
  Return, O Lord, in pity;
    Rebuild her walls again.

3  Let fall Thy rod of terror;
    Thy saving grace impart;
  Roll back the veil of error;
    Release the fettered heart.

4  Let Israel home returning
    Her lost Messiah see;

Give oil of joy for mourning
    And bind Thy church to Thee.

*Henry Francis Lyte*, 1834

## 15 S.M.
*Psalm 15*

1 LORD, I would dwell with Thee
    On Thy most holy hill:
Oh shed Thy grace abroad in me
    To mould me to Thy will.

2 Thy gate of pearl stands wide
    For those who walk upright,
But those who basely turn aside
    Thou chasest from Thy sight.

3 Oh tame my tongue to peace
    And tune my heart to love;
From all reproaches may I cease,
    Made harmless as a dove.

4 The vile, though proudly great,
    No flatterer find in me;
I count Thy saints of poor estate
    Far nobler company.

5 Faithful, but meekly kind,
    Gentle, yet boldly true,
I would possess the perfect mind
    Which in my Lord I view.

6 But Lord, these graces all
    Thy Spirit's work must be;
To Thee, through Jesu's blood I call,
    Create them all in me.

*Charles H. Spurgeon*, 1866

## 16 L.M.
*Psalm 16*

1 PRESERVE me, Lord, in time of need;
For succour to Thy throne I flee,
But have no merits there to plead;
My goodness cannot reach to Thee.

2 Oft have my heart and tongue confess'd
How empty and how poor I am;

My praise can never make Thee bless'd,
Nor add new glories to Thy name.

3 Yet, Lord, Thy saints on earth may reap
Some profit by the good we do;
These are the company I keep,
These are the choicest friends I know.

4 Let others choose the sons of mirth
To give a relish to their wine;
I love the men of heav'nly birth,
Whose thoughts and language are divine.

*Isaac Watts*, 1719

> **TD:** "Our hope must ever be that [by chance] some poor child of God may be served by us, or the Great Father can never need our aid. Well may we sing the verses of Watts:
>   'Oft have my heart and tongue confess'd
>     How empty and how poor I am . . .'
> Poor believers are God's receivers, and have a warrant from the Crown to receive the revenue of our offerings in the King's name" (Ps. 16:3; vol. 1, p. 218).

## 17 L.M.
*Psalm 17*

1 WHAT sinners value, I resign;
Lord, 'tis enough that Thou art mine;
I shall behold Thy blissful face
And stand complete in righteousness.

2 This life's a dream, an empty show,
But the bright world to which I go
Hath joys substantial and sincere;
When shall I wake and find me there?

3 O glorious hour! O blest abode!
I shall be near and like my God,
And flesh and sin no more control
The sacred pleasures of my soul.

4 My flesh shall slumber in the ground,
'Til the last trumpet's joyful sound,
Then burst the chains with sweet surprise,
And in my Saviour's image rise.

*Isaac Watts*, 1719

> **Ed:** Taken from the longer paraphrase, "Lord, I am thine, but thou wilt prove."

# 18a C.M.
*Psalm 18, Version I*

1  O GOD, my strength and fortitude,
   Of force I must love Thee;
Thou art my castle and defence
   In my necessity.

2  My God, my rock, in whom I trust,
   The worker of my wealth,
My refuge, buckler, and my shield,
   The horn of all my health.

3  *In my distress I sought my God,*
   *I sought Jehovah's face;*
*My cry before Him came; He heard*
   Out of His holy place.

4  The Lord descended from above
   And bowed the heavens high,
And underneath His feet He cast
   The darkness of the sky.

5  On cherub and on cherubim
   Full royally He rode,
And on the wings of mighty winds
   Came flying all abroad.

6  And so deliver'd He my soul:
   Who is a rock but He?
He liveth—blessed be my Rock!
   My God exalted be!

*Thomas Sternhold*, 1561
[*alt. Psalms, Hymns, and Passages of
Scripture for Christian Worship*, 1853]

   **3.1-3:** *I thus beset with pain and grief*
   *Did pray to God for grace,*
   *And he forthwith did hear my plaint*

# 18b L.M.
*Psalm 18, Version II*

1  NO change of times shall ever shock
My firm affection, Lord, to Thee,
For Thou hast always been my rock,
A fortress, and defence to me.

2  Thou my deliv'rer art, my God;
My trust is in Thy mighty pow'r;

Thou art my shield from foes abroad,
At home my safeguard and my tow'r.

3  Let the eternal Lord be prais'd!
The rock on whose defence I rest;
O'er highest heav'ns His name be rais'd,
Who me with His salvation bless'd!

4  Therefore to celebrate His fame
My grateful voice to heav'n I'll raise,
And nations, strangers to His name,
Shall thus be taught to sing His praise.

*Tate and Brady*, 1696 [*rev.* 1698]

# 18c L.M.
*Psalm 18, Version III*

1  JUST are Thy ways and true Thy Word,
Great Rock of my secure abode.
Who is a God beside the Lord?
Or where's a refuge like our God?

2  'Tis He that girds me with His might,
Gives me His holy sword to wield:
And while with sin and hell I fight,
Spreads His salvation for my shield.

3  He lives (and blessed be my Rock),
The God of my salvation lives;
The dark designs of hell are broke;
Sweet is the peace my Father gives.

4  Before the scoffers of the age,
I will exalt my Father's name,
Nor tremble at their mighty rage,
But meet reproach and bear the shame.

5  To David and his royal seed
Thy grace forever shall extend:
Thy love to saints, in Christ their head,
Knows not a limit nor an end.

*Isaac Watts*, 1719

# 19 L.M.
*Psalm 19*

1  THE heavens declare Thy glory, Lord;
In ev'ry star Thy wisdom shines;

But when our eyes behold Thy Word,
We read Thy name in fairer lines.

2 Sun, moon, and stars convey Thy praise
Round the whole earth, and never stand,
So when Thy truth began its race,
It touch'd and glanc'd on every land.

3 Nor shall Thy spreading gospel rest,
Till through the world Thy truth has run,
Till Christ has all the nations blest
That see the light or feel the sun.

4 Great Sun of Righteousness, arise,
Bless the dark world with heavenly light;
Thy gospel makes the simple wise;
Thy laws are pure, Thy judgments right.

5 Thy noblest wonders here we view,
In souls renew'd and sins forgiv'n:
Lord, cleanse my sins, my soul renew,
And make Thy Word my guide to heaven.

*Isaac Watts*, 1719

## 20 L.M.
*Psalm 20*

1 JESUS, with Thy salvation blest,
We yield the glory to Thy name:
Fix'd in Thy strength our banners rest,
With joy Thy vict'ry we proclaim.

2 Jehovah hears, He hears Thy pray'r,
The pray'r on which our hope relies;
Thy cross salvation shall prepare;
From His right hand Thy vict'ries rise.

3 Let men the rattling chariot trust,
Or the swift steed, with courage stor'd;
In Thee our confidence we boast,
Jesus, Messiah, conq'ring Lord!

4 Safe shall we stand, nor yield to fear,
When sinners with their hopes shall fall;
Save, Lord, O King Messiah, hear,
Hear, mighty Saviour, when we call.

*William Goode*, 1811 [*rev.* 1813]

**Ed:** The second part of a longer paraphrase,
"The Lord Messiah's pray'r attends."

## 21 L.M.
*Psalm 21*

1 THY strength, O Lord, makes glad our King
Who once in weakness bow'd the head;
Salvation makes His heart to sing,
For Thou hast raised Him from the dead.

2 Thou hast bestow'd His heart's desires,
Shower'd on His path Thy blessings down;
His royal pomp all heaven admires;
Thou on His head hast set the crown.

3 A life eternal as Thy years,
A glory infinite like Thine,
Repays Him for His groans and tears
And fills His soul with joy divine.

4 O King, belovèd of our souls,
Thine own right hand shall find Thy foes;
Swift o'er their necks Thy chariot rolls,
And earth Thy dreadful vengeance knows.

5 As glowing oven is Thy wrath,
As flame by furious blast upblown,
With equal heat Thy love breaks forth,
Like wall of fire around Thine own.

6 Be Thou exalted, King of Kings;
In Thine own strength sit Thou on high;
Thy church Thy triumph loudly sings
And lauds Thy glorious majesty.

*Charles H. Spurgeon*, 1866

**MBTS:** 21 Dec. 1884 (No. 1827), MAINZER

## 22a C.M.
*Psalm 22, Part I*

1 MY God, my God, why leav'st Thou me
When I with anguish faint?
Oh, why so far from me remov'd,
And from my *sad* complaint?

2 All day, but all the day unheard,
To Thee do I complain;
With cries implore relief all night,
But cry all night in vain.

3 Withdraw not, *Lord*, so far from me,
When trouble is so nigh;

Oh, send me help! Thy help, on which
    I only can rely.

*Tate and Brady*, 1696 [*alt.*]

> **1.4:** *loud*    **3.1:** *then*
> **Ed:** The alteration at 1.4 dates to the late 1700s,
> but 1.4 and 3.1 are both found in Edward Har-
> land's *A Church Psalter and Hymnal* (1855).

# 22b L.M.
*Psalm 22, Part II*

1  NOW let our mournful songs record
    The dying sorrows of our Lord,
    When He complain'd in tears and blood,
    As one forsaken of His God.

2  They wound His head, His hands, His feet,
    Till streams of blood each other meet;
    By lot His garments they divide,
    And mock the pangs in which he died.

3  But God, His Father, heard His cry;
    Rais'd from the dead, He reigns on high;
    The nations learn His righteousness,
    And humble sinners taste His grace.

*Isaac Watts*, 1719

# 22c C.M.
*Psalm 22, Part III*

1  ALL ye that fear Him, praise the Lord,
    *His sacred name adore;*
    *And ye His chosen Israel,*
    *Praise Him forever more.*

2  *Let all* the glad converted world
    To *Him* their homage pay,
    And scatter'd nations of the earth
    One sov'reign Lord obey.

3  With humble worship to His throne
    *Let* all for aid resort;
    That pow'r, which first their beings gave,
    *Alone can give* support.

4  Let them, O Lord, Thy truth declare,
    And show Thy righteousness;

That children, yet unborn, may learn
    Thy glory to confess.

[1 *Thomas Sternhold*, 1561, *alt.*]
[2-3 *Tate and Brady*, 1696, *rev.* 1698, *alt.*]
[4 *William J. Hall*, ed., 1836]

> **1.2-4:** *Thou seed of Jacob honor Him;*
>     *And with all reverence possible,*
>     *Thou seed of Israel worship Him.*
> **2.1:** *Then shall*    **2.2:** *God*
> **3.2:** *They*    **3.4:** *Can only them*
> **Ed:** This composite paraphrase appeared in
> Hall's *Psalms and Hymns Adapted* (1836),
> with the same alterations. Sts. 2-3 are from the
> same paraphrase as 22a. The final stanza is
> likely by Hall or Edward Osler. Sedgwick had
> credited the hymn as "Compiled from Old and
> New Versions, 1562–1696."

# 23a C.M.
*Psalm 23, Version I*

1  MY Shepherd will supply my need;
    Jehovah is His name;
    In pastures fresh He makes me feed,
    Beside the living stream.

2  He brings my wandering spirit back
    When I forsake His ways,
    And leads me, for His mercy's sake,
    In paths of truth and grace.

3  When I walk through the shades of death,
    Thy presence is my stay;
    A word of Thy supporting breath
    Drives all my fears away.

4  Thy hand, in *spite* of all my foes,
    Doth still my table spread;
    My cup with blessings overflows;
    Thine oil anoints my head.

5  The sure provisions of my God
    Attend me all my days;
    O may Thy house be mine abode,
    And all my work be praise!

6  There would I find a settled rest,
    While others go and come;

No more a stranger or a guest,
 But like a child at home.

*Isaac Watts*, 1719 [*rev.* 1722]

 **4.1:** Originally *sight*; *spite* appeared in Watts' 3rd ed. (1722), then returned to *sight*, then back to *spite* btw. the 7th and 10th eds. (1729/1736).

# 23b C.M.
*Psalm 23, Version II*

1 THE Lord's my Shepherd, I'll not want;
 He makes me down to lie
In pastures green: He leadeth me
 The quiet waters by.

2 My soul He doth restore again,
 And me to walk doth make
Within the paths of righteousness,
 E'en for His own name's sake.

3 Yea, tho' I walk through death's dark vale,
 Yet will I fear no ill:
For Thou art with me, and Thy rod
 And staff me comfort still.

4 My table Thou hast furnishèd
 In presence of my foes;
My head Thou dost with oil anoint,
 And my cup overflows.

5 Goodness and mercy all my life
 Shall surely follow me;
And in God's house forever more
 My dwelling place shall be.

*Scotch Version*, [1650]

# 23c S.M.
*Psalm 23, Version III*

1 THE Lord my Shepherd is;
 I shall be well supplied;
Since He is mine, and I am His,
 What can I want beside?

2 He leads me to the place
 Where heavenly pasture grows,
Where living waters gently pass,
 And full salvation flows.

3 If e'er I go astray,
 He doth my soul reclaim,
And guides me in His own right way
 For His most holy name.

4 While He affords His aid,
 I cannot yield fear;
Tho' I should walk thru' death's dark shade,
 My Shepherd's with me there.

5 In spite of all my foes,
 Thou dost my table spread;
My cup with blessings overflows,
 And joy exalts my head.

6 The bounties of Thy love
 Shall crown my following days,
Nor from Thy house will I remove,
 Nor cease to speak Thy praise.

*Isaac Watts*, 1719

# 23d 8.8.8.8.8.8.
*Psalm 23, Version IV*

1 THE Lord my pasture shall prepare
And feed me with a Shepherd's care;
His presence shall my wants supply
And guard me with a watchful eye:
My noon-day walks He will attend,
And all my midnight hours defend.

2 Though in the paths of death I tread,
With gloomy horrors overspread,
My steadfast heart shall fear no ill,
For Thou, O Lord, art with me still:
Thy friendly crook shall give me aid
And guide me through the dreadful shade.

*Joseph Addison*, 1712

# 24 L.M.
*Psalm 24*

1 OUR Lord is risen from the dead;
Our Jesus is gone up on high;
The powers of hell are captive led—
Dragg'd to the portals of the sky.

2 There His triumphal chariot waits,
And angels chant the solemn lay—

"Lift up your heads, ye heavenly gates!
Ye everlasting doors, give way."

3 Loose all your bars of massy light,
And wide unfold the ethereal scene;
He claims those mansions as His right—
Receive the King of Glory in.

4 "Who is the King of Glory, who?"
The Lord, that all His foes o'ercame;
The world, sin, death, and hell o'erthrew,
And Jesus is the Conqueror's name.

5 Lo! His triumphal chariot waits,
And angels chant the solemn lay—
"Lift up your heads, ye heavenly gates!
Ye everlasting doors, give way."

6 "Who is the King of Glory, who?"
The Lord, of glorious power possess'd,
The King of saints and angels too:
God over all, forever blest!

*Charles Wesley*, [1743]

> **Ed:** Taken from the longer hymn,
> "The earth and all her fullness owns."
> **TD:** "The ancient gates . . . are called upon 'to lift
> up their heads,' as though with all their glory
> they were not great enough for the all-glorious
> King. Let all things do their utmost to honour
> so great a Prince; let the highest heaven put
> on unusual loftiness in honour of 'the King of
> Glory.' . . . Great and everlasting as they are,
> those gates of pearl are all unworthy of Him
> before whom the heavens are not pure, and
> who chargeth His angels with folly" (Ps. 24:7;
> vol. 1, p. 426).

# 25 S.M.
*Psalm 25*

1 MINE eyes and my desire
Are ever to the Lord;
I love to plead His promises
And rest upon His Word.

2 When shall the sovereign grace
Of my forgiving God
Restore me from those dangerous ways
My wandering feet have trod!

3 The tumult of my thoughts
Doth but enlarge my woe;
My spirit languishes; my heart
Is desolate and low.

4 With every morning light
My sorrow new begins;
Look on my anguish and my pain,
And pardon all my sins.

5 O keep my soul from death,
Nor put my hope to shame,
For I have placed my only trust
In my Redeemer's name.

6 With humble faith I wait
To see Thy face again;
Of Israel it shall ne'er be said,
"He sought the Lord in vain."

*Isaac Watts*, 1719

# 26 L.M.
*Psalm 26*

1 LORD, I delight to find my place
Within the temples of Thy grace,
Where all Thy heav'nly beauties dwell,
And earth's sublimest pomp excel.

2 There, where Thy saints Thy glory see,
Let my fix'd rest, my dwelling be;
Nor 'midst the ungodly race consign
The soul which loves Thy courts to join.

3 Fix'd in Thy ways, my feet shall stand,
And wait the guidance of Thy hand;
Then 'midst Thy church, with sweet accord,
I'll join my praise, all-gracious Lord!

*William Goode*, 1811

> **Ed:** From the second part of a longer paraphrase,
> "Judge me, O Lord, tho' men defame."

# 27 C.M.
*Psalm 27*

1 THE Lord of glory is my light
And my salvation too;

God is my strength; nor will I fear
    What all my foes can do.

2 One privilege my heart desires:
    O grant me an abode
Among the churches of Thy saints,
    The temples of my God!

3 There shall I offer my requests
    And see Thy beauty still,
Shall hear Thy messages of love,
    And there enquire Thy will.

4 When troubles rise and storms appear,
    There may His children hide;
God has a strong pavilion where
    He makes my soul abide.

5 Now shall my head be lifted high
    Above my foes around,
And songs of joy and victory
    Within Thy temple sound.

*Isaac Watts*, 1719

# 28 7.7.7.7.
*Psalm 28*

1 *LORD*, my strength, to Thee I pray;
Turn not Thou Thine ear away;
Gracious to my vows attend,
While the humble knee I bend.

2 On *Thy* long-experienced aid
See my hope forever stay'd:
*Thou my shield, my fortress art;*
*Thou the refuge of my heart.*

3 *Grant me*, Lord, Thy love to share;
Feed *me* with a Shepherd's care;
Save Thy people from distress,
And Thy *fold forever* bless!

*James Merrick*, 1765
[*alt. William J. Hall*, 1836]

    **1.1:** *God*   **2.1:** *His*
    **2.3-4:** *Let me thanks perpetual yield;*
      *He my strength, and He my shield.*
    **3.1:** *Give them*   **3.2:** *them*   **3.4:** *Patrimony*

# 29 C.M.
*Psalm 29*

1 *ASCRIBE to God, ye sons of men,*
    *Ascribe with one accord,*
*All praise and honour, might and strength,*
    *To Him*, the living Lord!

2 Give glory to His holy name
    And honour Him alone;
*Give worship to* His majesty
    *And bow before His* throne.

3 The Lord *doth sit upon* the floods,
    *Their fury to restrain;*
*He reigns above, both* Lord and King,
    *And evermore shall reign.*

4 The Lord *shall* give His people *strength*
    *And bid their sorrows cease;*
The Lord *shall* bless His chosen *race*
    With everlasting peace.

*Thomas Sternhold*, [*ca.* 1548]
[*rev. William Wittingham*, 1556]
[*alt. William J. Hall*, 1836]

    **1.1-4:** *Give to the Lord, ye potentates,*
    *Ye rulers of the world,*
    *Give ye all praise, honour, and strength*
    *Unto*   **2.3:** *Worship Him in*
    **2.4:** *Within His holy*   **3.1:** *was set above*
    **3.2:** *Ruling the raging sea*
    **3.3:** *So shall He reign as*
    **3.4:** *Forever and for aye*   **4.1:** *will / power*
    **4.2:** *In virtue to increase*   **4.3:** *will / folk*
    **Ed:** Italics indicate Hall's deviations from Wit-
    tingham's revision, which became the official
    text of the 1562 English psalter.

# 30 C.M.
*Psalm 30*

1 I WILL exalt Thee, Lord of hosts,
    For Thou'st exalted me;
Since Thou hast silenced Satan's boasts,
    I'll therefore boast in Thee.

2 My sins had brought me near the grave,
    The grave of black despair;

I look'd, but there was none to save
    Till I look'd up in prayer.

3 In answer to my piteous cries,
    From hell's dark brink I'm brought:
  My Jesus saw me from the skies,
    And swift salvation wrought.

4 All through the night I wept full sore,
    But morning brought relief;
  That hand, which broke my bones before,
    Then broke my bonds of grief.

5 My mourning He to dancing turns;
    For sackcloth joy He gives;
  A moment, Lord, Thine anger burns,
    But long Thy favour lives.

6 Sing with me then, ye favoured men,
    Who long have known His grace;
  With thanks recall the seasons when
    Ye also sought His face.

*Charles Spurgeon*, 1866

> **Ed:** In his *Treasury of David*, vol. 2, p. 53,
> Spurgeon reprinted this paraphrase and
> gave a brief explanation of his intent: "In the
> following verses I have endeavoured to give
> the spirit of the Psalm, and to preserve the
> frequent antitheses."

## 31 C.M. Double
*Psalm 31*

1 THE Lord who hath redeem'd our souls
    From death and endless woe,
  Whose wisdom each event controls,
    From whom all mercies flow,
  He hath decreed that even here
    His faithful sons shall prove,
  In weal and woe, 'midst toil and *fear*,
    The riches of His love.

2 But oh, when life's brief term is o'er,
    And heaven unfolds her gates,
  For them what blessings are in store,
    For them what glory waits!
  Praise, then, the Lord, all ye His saints,
    To him devote your hearts;

He hears, He pities your complaints,
    Health, strength, and joy imparts.

*Harriet Auber*, 1829 [*alt. C.H.S.*]

**1.7:** *care*

## 32 C.M.
*Psalm 32*

1 HAPPY the man to whom his God
    No more imputes his sin,
  But wash'd in the Redeemer's blood
    Hath made his garments clean!

2 Happy beyond expression he,
    Whose debts are thus discharg'd;
  And from the guilty bondage free,
    He feels his soul enlarg'd.

3 While I my inward guilt suppress'd
    No quiet could I find;
  Thy wrath lay burning in my breast
    And rack'd my tortur'd mind.

4 Then I confess'd my troubled thoughts,
    My secret sins reveal'd;
  Thy pard'ning grace forgave my faults;
    Thy grace my pardon seal'd.

5 This shall invite Thy saints to pray;
    When, like a raging flood,
  Temptations rise, our strength and stay
    Is a forgiving God.

*Isaac Watts*, 1719

## 33 C.M.
*Psalm 33*

1 LET all the just to God with joy
    Their cheerful voices raise,
  For well the righteous it becomes
    To sing glad songs of praise.

2 For faithful is the Word of God;
    His works with truth abound;
  He justice loves, and all the earth
    Is with His goodness crown'd.

3 By His almighty Word at first
    The heavenly arch was rear'd,
And all the beauteous hosts of light
    At his command appear'd.

4 Whate'er the Mighty Lord decrees
    Shall stand forever sure;
The settled purpose of His heart
    To ages shall endure.

5 How happy, then, are they to whom
    The Lord for God is known!
Whom He, from all the world besides,
    Has chosen for His own!

6 Our soul on God with patience waits;
    Our help and shield is He!
Then, Lord, let still our hearts rejoice,
    Because we trust in Thee.

7 The riches of Thy mercy, Lord,
    Do Thou to us extend,
Since we, for all we want or wish,
    On Thee alone depend.

*Tate and Brady,* 1696 [*rev.* 1698]

**MM:** Hymns, Set 1 (Jan./Nov.), 12th Morn,
MARLOW / BROWN

# 34a C.M.
*Psalm 34, Version I*

1 THROUGH all the changing scenes of life,
    In trouble and in joy,
The praises of my God shall still
    My heart and tongue employ.

2 Of His deliv'rance I will boast,
    Till all that are distress'd,
From my example comfort take,
    And charm their griefs to rest.

3 *Come* magnify the Lord with me;
    With me exalt His name;
When in distress to Him I call'd,
    He to my rescue came.

4 O make but trial of His love;
    Experience will decide

How bless'd *are they*, and only they,
    Who in His truth confide.

5 Fear Him, ye saints, and you will then
    Have nothing else to fear;
Make you His service your delight,
    He'll make your wants His care.

*Tate and Brady,* 1696 [*rev.* 1698]
[*alt. Thomas Cotterill,* 1812]

    **3.1:** *O*   **4.3:** *they are*

# 34b L.M.
*Psalm 34, Version II*

1 LORD, I will bless Thee all my days;
    Thy praise shall dwell upon my tongue;
My soul shall glory in Thy grace,
    While saints rejoice to hear the song.

2 Come, magnify the Lord with me;
    Come, let us all exalt His name;
I sought th' eternal God, and He
    Has not exposed my hope to shame.

3 I told Him all my secret grief;
    My secret groaning reach'd His ears;
He gave my inward pains relief
    And calm'd the tumult of my fears.

4 To Him the poor lift up their eyes,
    Their faces feel the heavenly shine;
A beam of mercy from the skies
    Fills them with light and joy divine.

5 His holy angels pitch their tents
    Around the men that serve the Lord;
O fear and love Him, all His saints;
    Taste of His grace and trust His Word.

*Isaac Watts,* 1719

# 35a 7.7.7.7.
*Psalm 35, Song I*

1 PLEAD my cause, O Lord of hosts;
    Earth and hell now make their boasts;
See, against my soul they strive,
    *Mischief seek, and plots contrive.*

2 Shield and buckler are with Thee;
   Hold them forth, O Lord, for me;
   "I am thy salvation," say,
   That shall all my foes dismay.

3 Inbred sin my soul annoys;
   Unbelief my peace destroys;
   Fiery darts the tempter flings;
   Ev'ry day its battle brings.

4 Jesus, when on earth He dwelt,
   Sharpest pangs of conflict felt;
   All the pow'rs of darkness warr'd
   With our great anointed Lord.

5 He has vanquish'd all His foes
   For himself, and all He chose;
   His salvation is complete;
   All shall worship at His feet.

6 Lord, I will rejoice in Thee;
   Thy salvation makes me free;
   Plead my cause and all is well;
   I shall ever with Thee dwell.

*Joseph Irons*, 1847 [*alt. C.H.S.*]

> **1.4:** *Only by thy grace I live.*
> **S&T:** "Before I ever entered a pulpit, the thought
> occurred to me that I should one day preach
> sermons which would be printed. While read-
> ing the penny sermons of Joseph Irons, which
> were great favourites with me, I conceived in
> my heart that one day I should have a penny
> pulpit of my own. The dream has come to
> pass" (Jan. 1875, p. 3).

# 35b C.M.
*Psalm 35, Song II*

1 O PLEAD my cause, *my* Saviour, plead;
   I trust it all to Thee;
   *O Thou who didst* for sinners bleed,
   A sinner save in me.

2 Assure my weak, desponding heart;
   My threatening foes restrain;
   O tell me Thou my helper art,
   And all their rage is vain.

3 When round Thy cross they rush'd to kill,
   How was their fury foiled:
   Their madness only wrought Thy will,
   And on themselves recoiled.

4 The great salvation there achieved
   My hope shall ever be;
   My soul has in her Lord believed,
   And He will rescue me.

*Henry Francis Lyte*, 1834

> **1.1:** *blest*   **1.3:** *Thou who didst once*
> **Ed:** Lyte revised this hymn in 1836 but his orig-
> inal text continued to be reprinted, as above.
> Footnotes indicate Lyte's revisions.

# 36a L.M.
*Psalm 36, Song I*

1 HIGH in the heavens, Eternal God,
   Thy goodness in full glory shines;
   Thy truth shall break through every cloud
   That veils and darkens Thy designs.

2 Forever firm Thy justice stands,
   As mountains their foundations keep;
   Wise are the wonders of Thy hands;
   Thy judgments are a mighty deep.

3 Thy providence is kind and large;
   Both man and beast Thy bounty share;
   The whole creation is Thy charge,
   But saints are Thy peculiar care.

4 My God! how excellent Thy grace,
   Whence all our hope and comfort springs!
   The sons of Adam, in distress,
   Fly to the shadow of Thy wings.

*Isaac Watts*, 1719

> **MM:** Hymns, 15th Lord's Day,
>    HEBRON / GRATITUDE

# 36b C.M.
*Psalm 36, Song II*

1 ABOVE these heavens' created rounds,
   Thy mercies, Lord, extend;

Thy truth outlives the narrow bounds
Where time and nature end.

2 From Thee, when creature-streams run low
And mortal comforts die,
Perpetual springs of life shall flow
And raise our pleasures high.

3 Though all created light decay
And death close up our eyes,
Thy presence makes eternal day,
Where clouds can never rise.

*Isaac Watts*, 1719

**Ed:** Taken from the longer paraphrase,
"While men grow bold in wicked ways."

# 37a C.M.
*Psalm 37, Song I*

1 O GOD of love, how blest are they
Who in Thy ways delight!
Thy presence guides them all the day
And cheers them all the night.

2 Whene'er they faint, a mighty arm
Is nigh them to uphold,
And sin or Satan cannot harm
The feeblest of Thy fold.

3 The Lord is wise, the Lord is just,
The Lord is good and true,
And they who on His promise trust
Will find it bear them through.

4 His Word will stay their sinking hearts;
Their feet shall never slide;
The heavens dissolve, the earth departs;
They safe in God abide.

*Henry Francis Lyte*, 1834

# 37b C.M.
*Psalm 37, Song II*

1 SET thou thy trust upon the Lord,
*Do good and know no care,*
*For* so thou in the *land* shalt dwell,
*And God thy food prepare.*

2 Delight thyself in God, He'll give
Thine heart's desire to thee;
*Commit thy way to God alone,*
It *brought* to pass shall *be.*

3 And like unto the light He shall
Thy righteousness display;
And He thy judgment shall bring forth,
Like noontide of the day.

*Scotch Version*, [1650], *alt. C.H.S.*

**Ed:** Taken from the longer paraphrase,
"For evil doers fret thou not."
**1.2:** *And be thou doing good*
**1.3:** *And / Lord*  **1.4:** *And verily have food.*
**2.3:** *Thy way to God commit, Him trust,*
**2.4:** *bring / He.*

# 38 C.M.
*Psalm 38*

1 AMIDST Thy wrath remember love;
Restore Thy servant, Lord,
Nor let a Father's chast'ning prove
Like an avenger's sword.

2 All my desire to Thee is known;
Thine eye counts every tear,
And every sigh and every groan
Is notic'd by Thine ear.

3 Thou art my God, my only hope;
My God will hear my cry;
My God will bear my spirit up
When Satan bids me die.

4 My God, forgive my follies past,
And be forever nigh;
O Lord of my salvation, haste,
Before Thy servant die.

*Isaac Watts*, 1719

# 39 C.M.
*Psalm 39*

1 BEHOLD, O Lord, my days are made
A handbreath at the most;
Ere yet 'tis noon my flower must fade,
And I give up the ghost.

2 Then teach me, Lord, to know mine end,
    And know that I am frail;
To heaven let all my thoughts ascend,
    And let not earth prevail.

3 What is there here that I should wait?
    My hope's in Thee alone;
When wilt Thou open glory's gate
    And call me to Thy throne?

4 A stranger in this land am I,
    A sojourner with Thee;
Oh be not silent at my cry,
    But show Thyself to me.

5 Though I'm exiled from glory's land,
    Yet not from glory's King,
My God is ever near at hand,
    And therefore I will sing.

*Charles H. Spurgeon*, 1866

**Ed:** An account from the Metropolitan Tabernacle,
1 Feb. 1892, following Spurgeon's death:
"In the evening, an immense prayer meeting
was held, one of the largest ever known, even
at the Tabernacle, and amidst the hush of
stricken hearts, God visited His people, and
spoke peace to many. Mr. Spurgeon's own
version of the thirty-ninth Psalm, often used
at these Memorial gatherings, was then sung
with deep feeling, for the first time (S&T, Mar.
1892, p. 136)."
    This hymn was also sung at the memorial
service held at Auckland Tabernacle, New
Zealand, where Thomas Spurgeon was pastor
(S&T, Apr. 1892, p. 207).

# 40 C.M.
*Psalm 40*

1 I WAITED patient for the Lord;
    He bow'd to hear my cry;
He saw me resting on His Word
    And brought salvation nigh.

2 He rais'd me from a horrid pit,
    Where mourning long I lay,
And from my bonds releas'd my feet,
    Deep bonds of miry clay.

3 Firm on a rock He made me stand
    And taught my cheerful tongue
To praise the wonders of His hand
    In a new thankful song.

4 How many are Thy thoughts of love!
    Thy mercies, Lord, how great!
We have not words nor hours enough,
    Their numbers to repeat.

5 When I'm afflicted, poor, and low,
    And light and peace depart,
My God beholds my heavy woe
    And bears me on His heart.

*Isaac Watts*, 1719

**EE:** Hymns, Set 1 (Jan./Nov.), 21st Eve,
STEPHENS / HENSBURY

# 41 7.7.7.7.
*Psalm 41*

1 JESUS, poorest of the poor!
Man of sorrows! Child of grief!
Happy they whose bounteous store
Minister'd to Thy relief.

2 Jesus, though Thy head is crown'd,
Crown'd with loftiest majesty,
In Thy members Thou art found,
Plunged in deepest poverty.

3 Happy they who wash Thy feet,
Visit Thee in Thy distress!
Honour great, and labour sweet,
For Thy sake the saints to bless!

4 They who feed Thy sick and faint,
For Thyself a banquet find;
They who clothe the naked saint,
Round Thy loins the raiment bind.

5 Thou wilt keep their soul alive;
From their foes protect their head;
Languishing their strength revive,
And in sickness make their bed.

6 Thou wilt deeds of love repay;
Grace shall gen'rous hearts reward

Here on earth, and in the day
When they meet their reigning Lord.

*Charles H. Spurgeon*, 1866

# 42a C.M.
*Psalm 42, Version I*

1 LIKE as the hart for water brooks
  In thirst doth pant and bray,
So pants my longing soul, O God,
  That come to Thee I may.

2 My soul for God, the living God,
  Doth thirst: when shall I near
Unto Thy countenance approach,
  And in God's sight appear?

3 My tears have unto me been meat,
  Both in the night and day,
While unto me continually,
  "Where is thy God?" they say.

4 My soul is pourèd out in me,
  When this I think upon,
Because that with the multitude
  I heretofore had gone:

5 With them into God's house I went,
  With voice of joy and praise;
Yea, with the multitude that kept
  The solemn holy days.

6 Oh why art thou cast down, my soul?
  Why in me so dismayed?
Trust God, for I shall praise Him yet;
  His countenance is mine aid.

7 My God, my soul's cast down in me;
  Thee therefore mind I will
From Jordan's land, the Hermonites,
  And e'en from Mizar's hill.

8 At *noise of Thy dread* waterspouts,
  Deep unto deep doth call;
Thy breaking waves pass over me,
  Yea, and Thy billows all.

9 O why art thou cast down, my soul?
  Why thus with grief oppress'd,

Art thou disquieted in me?
  In God still hope and rest:

10 For yet I know I shall Him praise,
  Who graciously to me,
The health is of my countenance,
  Yea, mine own God is He.

*Scotch Version*, [1650, *rev.* 1686], *alt. C.H.S.*

**8.1:** *the noise of the*   **TD:** "Thus faith closes
the struggle, a victor in fact by anticipation, and in
heart by firm reliance. The saddest countenance
shall yet be made to shine, if there be a taking
of God at His word and an expectation of His
salvation'" (Ps. 42:11; vol. 2, p. 305).

# 42b C.M.
*Psalm 42, Version II*

1 AS pants the hart for cooling streams,
  When heated in the chase,
So *pants* my soul, O God, for Thee,
  And Thy refreshing grace.

2 For Thee, my God, the living God,
  My thirsty soul doth pine;
O when shall I behold Thy face,
  Thou Majesty divine?

3 I sigh *to think of happier days,*
  *When Thou, O Lord, wert nigh,*
*When every heart was tuned to praise,*
  *And none more blest than I.*

4 *Oh why art thou* cast down, my soul?
  Hope still, and thou shalt sing
The praise of Him who is Thy God,
  Thy health's eternal spring.

*Tate and Brady*, 1696 [*rev.* 1698, *alt.*]

**1.3:** *longs*
**3.1-4:** *whene'er my musing thoughts*
    *Those happy days present,*
    *When I with troops of pious friends*
    *Thy temple did frequent.*
**4.1:** *Why restless, why*
**Ed:** This four-stanza reduction and rewritten
    third stanza are from Henry Lyte's *Spirit of the
    Psalms* (1834), repeated and altered slightly in
    Josiah Conder's *Congregational Hymn Book*

(1836), but both of these differ from the text
above. This exact combination of alterations
appeared in *The New Congregational Hymn
Book* (ca. 1859).
**MM:** Hymns, 11th Lord's Day, NAOMI / WIRTH

# 43 L.M.
*Psalm 43*

1 JUDGE me, O Lord; to Thee I fly;
New foes and fears my spirit try;
Plead Thou my cause, my soul sustain,
And let the wicked rage in vain.

2 The mourner's refuge, Lord, Thou art;
Wilt Thou not take Thy suppliant's part?
Wilt Thou desert and lay me low,
The scorn of each insulting foe?

3 Send forth Thy light and truth once more;
To Thy blest house my steps restore;
Again Thy presence let me see,
And find my joy in praising Thee.

4 Arise, my soul, and praise Him now;
The Lord is good, be faithful thou;
His nature changes not like thine;
Believe, and soon His face will shine.

*Henry Francis Lyte*, 1834

# 44 C.M.
*Psalm 44*

1 OUR ears have heard, O glorious God,
What work Thou didst of old,
And how the heathen felt Thy rod
Our fathers oft have told.

2 'Twas not Thy people's arm or sword,
But only Thy right hand,
Which scatter'd all the race abhor'd,
And gave Thy tribes their land.

3 Thou hadst a favour to the seed
Which sprang of Jacob's line,
And still on men afore decreed
Doth love electing shine.

4 These shall the heritage obtain,
And drive out every sin;

E'en death and hell shall rage in vain;
They must the conquest win.

5 From grace alone their strength shall spring,
Nor bow nor sword can save;
To God alone, their Lord and King,
Shall all their banners wave.

6 Awake, O Lord, of Thine elect,
Achieve Thy great design;
Thy saints from Thee alone expect
Salvation's light to shine.

7 In Thee alone we make our boasts
And glory all day long;
Arise at once, thou Lord of hosts,
And fill our mouth with song.

*Charles H. Spurgeon*, 1866

# 45a C.M.
*Psalm 45, Version I*

1 O THOU that art the mighty One,
Thy sword gird on Thy thigh,
E'en with Thy glory excellent,
And with Thy majesty.

2 For meekness, truth, and righteousness,
In state ride prosp'rously;
And Thy right hand shall Thee instruct
In things that fearful be.

3 Thine arrows sharply pierce the hearts
Of *foemen* of the King,
And under Thy *dominion's rule*
The people down do bring.

4 Forever and forever is,
O God, Thy throne of might;
The sceptre of Thy kingdom is
A sceptre that is right.

5 Thou lovest right and hatest ill;
For God, Thy God, *is He*,
Above Thy fellows hath, with oil
Of joy, anointed Thee.

6 Of aloes, myrrh, and cassia,
A smell Thy garments had,

Out of the ivory palaces
   Whereby they made Thee glad.

*Scotch Version*, [1650, *rev.* 1686], *alt. C.H.S.*

**3.2:** *th' enemies*   **3.3:** *subjection*
**5.2:** *most high*
**Ed:** Taken from the longer paraphrase,
   "My heart brings forth a goodly thing."
**MM:** Hymns, 4th Lord's Day, DEDHAM / LA MIRA

# 45b
7.6.7.6. Double
*Psalm 45, Version II*

1 WITH hearts in love abounding,
   Prepare we now to sing
A lofty theme, resounding
   Thy praise, Almighty King,
Whose love, rich gifts bestowing,
   Redeem'd the human race,
Whose lips, with zeal o'erflowing,
   Breathe words of truth and grace.

2 In majesty transcendent,
   Gird on Thy conquering sword;
In righteousness resplendent,
   Ride on, Incarnate Word.
Ride on, O King Messiah!
   To glory and renown;
Pierced by Thy darts of fire,
   Be every foe o'erthrown.

3 So reign, O God, in heaven,
   Eternally the same,
And endless praise be given
   To Thy almighty name.
Clothed in Thy dazzling brightness,
   Thy church on earth behold;
In robe of purest whiteness,
   In raiment wrought in gold.

4 And let each Gentile nation
   Come gladly in Thy train,
To share her great salvation
   And join her grateful strain:
Then ne'er shall note of sadness
   Awake the trembling string;
One song of joy and gladness
   The ransom'd world shall sing.

*Harriet Auber*, 1829

# 45c
8.7.8.7.4.7
*Psalm 45, Version III*

1 *WARM with love my heart's* inditing
   *Cherish'd thoughts on* sacred things;
With my tongue like ready writing,
   I'll extol the King of Kings,
     Of whose glory
Ev'ry saint and angel sings.

2 Thou, of all the sons, art fairest;
   Yea, Thy lips are fill'd with grace;
All Thy fullness, Lord, Thou sharest
   'Mongst Thy chosen ransom'd race,
     And in glory
They shall see Thee face to face.

3 O most mighty, O most blessèd,
   Gird Thy sword upon Thy thigh;
Be thy majesty confessèd,
   Bring Thy blood-bought trophies nigh;
     Let thy glory
All Thy stubborn foes defy.

4 Truth and righteousness and meekness
   Are the weapons of Thy hand;
All Thy foes shall know their weakness;
   None can Jesus' pow'r withstand;
     'Tis Thy glory,
Rebels bow at Thy command.

*Joseph Irons*, 1847, *alt. C.H.S.*

**1.1:** *My heart expands, of good*
**1.2:** *I must speak of*

# 45d
C.M.
*Psalm 45, Version IV*

1 HAIL, mighty Jesus, how divine
   Is Thy victorious sword!
The stoutest rebel must resign
   At Thy commanding Word.

2 Deep are the wounds *Thy* arrows give;
   They *pierce the hardest* heart;
Thy *smiles of grace the* slain revive,
   And *joy succeeds to smart.*

3 *Still gird* Thy sword upon Thy thigh;
   *Ride with majestic sway;*

*Go forth, sweet Prince, triumphantly,*
*And make Thy foes obey.*

4 And when Thy vict'ries are complete,
  When all the chosen race
Shall round the throne of glory meet
  To sing Thy conqu'ring grace,

5 O may my humble soul be found
  Among that favour'd band!
And I, with them, Thy praise will sound
  Throughout Immanuel's land.

1-3 *Benjamin Wallin*, 1750 [*alt. A.T.*, 1776]
4-5 *Augustus Toplady*, 1776

> **2.1:** *Thine*  **2.2:** *pierce, they kill the*
> **2.3:** *living words thy*
> **2.4:** *love unknown impart.*  **3.1:** *Gird now*
> **3.2-4:** *Most mighty Prince of Peace;*
> *Ride forth in full prosperity*
> *Nor let thy conquests cease.*
> **Ed:** Wallin's text was headed "The Conquering
> Saviour: Alluding to the Conversion of St.
> Paul. Acts ix 1-20." Toplady omitted a stanza of
> Wallin's, added two of his own, and retitled it
> "Converting Grace. Psalm xlv 3-5."

# 46a L.M.
*Psalm 46, Version I*

1 GOD is the refuge of His saints,
  When storms of sharp distress invade;
Ere we can offer our complaints,
  Behold Him present with His aid.

2 Let mountains from their seats be hurl'd
  Down to the deep, and buried there:
Convulsions shake the solid world;
  Our faith shall never yield to fear.

3 Loud may the troubled ocean roar,
  In sacred peace our souls abide;
While every nation, every shore,
  Trembles, and dreads the swelling tide.

4 There is a stream whose gentle flow
  Supplies the city of our God;
Life, love, and joy, still gliding through,
  And watering our divine abode.

5 That sacred stream, Thine holy Word,
  That all our raging fear controls:
Sweet peace Thy promises afford,
  And give new strength to fainting souls.

6 Zion enjoys her Monarch's love,
  Secure against a threat'ning hour;
Nor can her firm foundations move,
  Built on His truth and arm'd with pow'r.

*Isaac Watts*, 1719

# 46b C.M.
*Psalm 46, Version II*

1 GOD is our refuge and our strength,
  In straits a present aid;
Therefore, although the earth remove,
  We will not be afraid.

2 Though hills amidst the seas be cast,
  Though waters roaring make,
And troubled be; yea, though the hills
  By swelling seas do shake.

3 A river is, whose streams do glad
  The city of our God;
The holy place, wherein the Lord
  Most high hath His abode.

4 God in the midst of her doth dwell;
  Nothing shall her remove:
The Lord to her an helper will,
  And that right early, prove.

5 Our God, who is the Lord of hosts,
  Is still upon our side;
The God of Jacob, our *defence*,
  Forever will abide.

*Scotch Version*, [1650], *alt. C.H.S.*

> **5.3:** *refuge*  **CUR:** "The first hymn on Sunday
> morning last was 'God is our refuge and our
> strength,' to the tune 'Evan.' Mr. Spurgeon read
> it slowly through, then he announced the tune
> and read the first verse again. As the people
> stood up, the precentor advanced from the
> back of the platform and started the melody
> with a clear voice. Like a giant that needs a
> moment to arouse himself the congregation

allowed a note or two to pass before they entered in full strength. Then the heavy tide of sound streamed forth from every part of the building. Many churches have more cultivated congregational singing than Mr. Spurgeon's, but, from the numbers engaged, no other singing touches the heart with such an indefinable pleasure, and makes the frame glow with such a sense of worshipful sympathy" (p. 427, describing a service on 4 Jan. 1874). See also Nos. 798, 818.

# 46c C.M.
*Psalm 46, Version III*

1 GOD is our refuge, tried and proved,
　　Amid a stormy world:
　We will not fear though earth be moved
　　And hills in ocean hurled.

2 The waves may roar, the mountains shake,
　　Our comforts shall not cease;
　The Lord His saints will not forsake;
　　The Lord will give us peace.

3 A gentle stream of hope and love
　　To us shall ever flow;
　It issues from His throne above,
　　It cheers His church below.

4 When earth and hell against us came,
　　He spake and quelled their powers;
　The Lord of hosts is still the same;
　　The God of grace is ours.

*Henry Francis Lyte*, 1834

**MM:** Hymns, Set 1 (Jan./Nov.), 23rd Morn,
DUNDEE / BYEFIELD

# 47 C.M.
*Psalm 47*

1 OH for a shout of sacred joy,
　　To God, the sovereign King!
　Let every land their tongues employ
　　And hymns of triumph sing.

2 Jesus our God ascends on high;
　　His heavenly guards around

Attend Him rising through the sky,
　　With trumpet's joyful sound.

3 While angels shout and praise their King,
　　Let mortals learn their strains;
　Let all the earth His honour sing;
　　O'er all the earth He reigns.

4 Rehearse His praise with awe profound,
　　Let knowledge lead the song,
　Nor mock Him with a solemn sound
　　Upon a thoughtless tongue.

5 In Israel stood His ancient throne;
　　He loved that chosen race;
　But now He calls the world His own,
　　And heathens taste His grace.

6 The British Islands are the Lord's;
　　There Abraham's God is known;
　While powers and princes,
　　　　shields and swords,
　　Submit before His throne.

*Isaac Watts*, 1719

# 48 S.M.
*Psalm 48*

1 GREAT is the Lord our God,
　　And let His praise be great;
　He makes His churches His abode,
　　His most delightful seat.

2 These temples of His grace,
　　How beautiful they stand!
　The honours of our native place
　　And bulwarks of our land.

3 In Zion God is known,
　　A refuge in distress;
　How bright has His salvation shone
　　Through all her palaces!

4 Oft have our fathers told,
　　Our eyes have often seen,
　How well our God secures the fold
　　Where His own sheep have been.

5 In every new distress
　　We'll to His house repair;

We'll think upon His wondrous grace
And seek deliverance there.

*Isaac Watts*, 1719

## 49 C.M.
*Psalm 49*

1 JEHOVAH speaks; let man be awed,
  And deep attention give.
Ye sinners, hear the way to God!
  Ye dead, arise and live!

2 Trust not in earthly wealth and show;
  Vain, vain are they to save;
Gold cannot buy release from woe
  Or ransom from the grave.

3 Worlds cannot reach the mighty price
  Of one immortal soul;
No, Lord, Thy blood and sacrifice
  Alone can make us whole.

4 In Thee be our salvation sure;
  No other wealth we seek:
We're rich in Thee, however poor,
  And strong, however weak.

*Henry Francis Lyte*, 1834

## 50 C.M.
*Psalm 50*

1 THE Lord, the Judge before His throne,
  Bids the whole earth draw nigh,
The nations near the rising sun
  And near the western sky.

2 No more shall bold blasphemers say,
  "Judgment will ne'er begin";
No more abuse His long delay
  To impudence and sin.

3 Thron'd on a cloud our God shall come;
  Bright flames prepare His way;
Thunder and darkness, fire and storm,
  Lead on the dreadful day.

4 Heaven from above His call shall hear;
  Attending angels come,

And earth and hell shall know, and fear
  His justice and their doom.

*Isaac Watts*, 1719

## 51a L.M.
*Psalm 51, Version I*

1 SHOW pity, Lord; O Lord, forgive;
  Let a repenting rebel live;
Are not Thy mercies large and free?
  May not a sinner trust in Thee?

2 My crimes are great but don't surpass
  The power and glory of Thy grace;
Great God, Thy nature hath no bound,
  So let Thy pardoning love be found.

3 O wash my soul from every sin
  And make my guilty conscience clean;
Here, on my heart, the burden lies,
  And past offences pain my eyes.

4 My lips, with shame, my sins confess
  Against Thy law, against Thy grace.
Lord, should Thy judgment grow severe,
  I am condemn'd, but Thou art clear.

5 Should sudden vengeance seize my breath,
  I must pronounce Thee just in death;
And if my soul were sent to hell,
  Thy righteous law approves it well.

6 Yet save a trembling sinner, Lord,
  Whose hope, still hovering round Thy Word,
Would light on some sweet promise there,
  Some sure support against despair.

*Isaac Watts*, 1719

## 51b L.M.
*Psalm 51, Version II*

1 LORD I am vile, conceiv'd in sin,
  And born unholy and unclean,
Sprung from the man whose guilty fall
  Corrupts the race and taints us all.

2 Soon as we draw our infant breath,
  The seeds of sin grow up for death;

Thy law demands a perfect heart,
But we're defil'd in every part.

3 Behold, I fall before Thy face;
My only refuge is Thy grace;
No outward forms can make me clean;
The leprosy lies deep within.

4 No bleeding bird, nor bleeding beast,
Nor hyssop branch, nor sprinkling priest,
Nor running brook, nor flood, nor sea,
Can wash the dismal stain away.

5 Jesus, my God, Thy blood alone
Hath power sufficient to atone;
Thy blood can make me white as snow;
No Jewish types could cleanse me so.

*Isaac Watts*, 1719

# 51c L.M.
*Psalm 51, Version III*

1 O THOU that hear'st when sinners cry,
Though all my crimes before Thee lie,
Behold them not with angry look,
But blot their memory from Thy book.

2 Create my nature pure within
And form my soul averse to sin;
Let Thy good Spirit ne'er depart,
Nor hide Thy presence from my heart.

3 Though I have griev'd Thy Spirit, Lord,
His help and comfort still afford;
And let a wretch come near Thy throne
To plead the merits of Thy Son.

4 A broken heart, my God, my King,
Is all the sacrifice I bring;
The God of grace will ne'er despise
A broken heart for sacrifice.

5 My soul lies humbled in the dust
And owns Thy dreadful sentence just;
Look down, O Lord, with pitying eye,
And save the soul condemn'd to die.

6 Then will I teach the world Thy ways;
Sinners shall learn Thy sovereign grace;

I'll lead them to my Saviour's blood,
And they shall praise a pardoning God.

7 O may Thy love inspire my tongue!
Salvation shall be all my song,
And all my powers shall join to bless
The Lord, my strength and righteousness.

*Isaac Watts*, 1719

# 51d C.M.
*Psalm 51, Version IV*

1 O GOD of mercy, hear my call,
My loads of guilt remove;
Break down this separating wall
That bars me from Thy love.

2 Give me the presence of Thy grace,
Then my rejoicing tongue
Shall speak aloud Thy righteousness
And make Thy praise my song.

3 No blood of goats, nor heifer slain,
For sin could e'er atone;
The death of Christ shall still remain
Sufficient and alone.

4 A soul oppress'd with sin's desert,
My God will ne'er despise;
A humble groan, a broken heart,
Is our best sacrifice.

*Isaac Watts*, 1719

# 52 C.M.
*Psalm 52*

1 IN vain the powers of darkness try
To work the church's ill.
The Friend of sinners reigns on high
And *checks* them at His will.

2 Though mischief in their hearts may dwell,
And on their tongues deceit,
A word of His their pride can quell,
And all their *aims* defeat.

3 My trust is in His grace alone;
His *house shall be* my home.

How sweet His *mercies* past to own,
And hope for more to come!

*Henry Francis Lyte*, 1834

> **1.4:** *foils* **2.4:** *rage* **3.2:** *mercy is* **3.3:** *blessings*
> **Ed:** Lyte revised this text in 1836 but his original text continued to be reprinted, as above. Footnotes indicate Lyte's revisions.

## 53 C.M.
*Psalm 53*

1 THE foes of Zion quake for fright,
Where no fear was they quail;
For well they know that sword of might
Which cuts through coats of mail.

2 The Lord of old defiled their shields,
And all their spears He scorn'd;
Their bones lay scatter'd o'er the fields,
Unburied and unmourn'd.

3 Let Zion's foes be fill'd with shame;
Her sons are bless'd of God;
Though scoffers now despise their name,
The Lord shall break the rod.

4 Oh would our God to Zion turn,
God with salvation clad;
Then Judah's harps should music learn,
And Israel be glad.

*Charles H. Spurgeon*, 1866

> **TD:** "When will the opposition of the saints come to its close, and glory crown their heads? . . . Inasmuch as the yoke has been heavy, and the bondage cruel, the liberty will be gladsome, and the triumph joyous. The second advent and the restoration of Israel are our hope and expectation" (Ps. 53:6; vol. 3, p. 3).

## 54 7.5.7.5.7.7.
*Psalm 54*

1 SAVE me by Thy glorious name;
Lord, that name is love!
Help *from Thee* I humbly claim;
*Send it from* above;
Hear, O hear my suppliant voice;
Hear, and bid my heart rejoice.

2 Foes to Christ and every good
Fiercely throng on me;
Soon my soul must be subdued,
Without aid from Thee.
But with Thee to make me strong,
Lord, they shall not triumph long.

3 Lo, He comes, He takes my part;
All my struggles cease.
Rise in praise, my grateful heart,
Bless the Prince of Peace.
God Himself has set me free;
God my worship ever be!

*Henry Francis Lyte*, 1834

> **1.3:** *through Christ* **1.4:** *Help from Thee*
> **Ed:** Lyte revised this text in 1836 but his original text continued to be reprinted, as above. Footnotes indicate Lyte's revisions.

## 55 C.M.
*Psalm 55*

1 O GOD, my refuge, hear my cries,
Behold my flowing tears,
For earth and hell my hurt devise,
And triumph in my fears.

2 O were I like the feather'd dove,
And innocence had wings,
I'd fly, and make a long remove
From all these restless things.

3 Let me to some wild desert go
And find a peaceful home,
Where storms of malice never blow,
Temptations never come.

4 Vain hopes, and vain inventions all,
To 'scape the rage of hell!
The mighty God on whom I call
Can save me here as well.

5 God shall preserve my soul from fear,
Or shield me when afraid;
Ten thousand angels must appear
If He command their aid.

6 I cast my burdens on the Lord;

The Lord sustains them all;
My courage rests upon His word,
That saints shall never fall.

*Isaac Watts*, 1719

## 56 C.M.
*Psalm 56*

1 GOD counts the sorrows of His saints;
  Their groans affect His ears;
Thou hast a book for my complaints,
  A bottle for my tears.

2 When to Thy throne I raise my cry,
  The wicked fear and flee;
So swift is prayer to reach the sky,
  So near is God to me.

3 In Thee, most holy, just, and true,
  I have repos'd my trust,
Nor will I fear what man can do,
  The offspring of the dust.

4 Thy solemn vows are on me, Lord;
  Thou shalt receive my praise;
I'll sing, "How faithful is Thy Word,
  How righteous all Thy ways!"

5 Thou hast secur'd my soul from death;
  O set Thy pris'ner free!
That heart and hand, and life and breath,
  May be employ'd for Thee.

*Isaac Watts*, 1719

**Ed:** Taken from the longer paraphrase,
"O Thou whose justice reigns on high."
**TD:** "'The machinery of prayer is not always visible, but it is most efficient. God inclines us to pray, we cry in anguish of heart, He hears, He acts, the enemy is turned back. What irresistible artillery is this which wins the battle as soon as its report is heard! What a God is this who hearkens to the cry of his children, and in a moment delivers them from the mightiest adversaries!" (Ps. 56:9; vol. 3, p. 39).

## 57 L.M.
*Psalm 57*

1 My God, in whom are all the springs
  Of boundless love and grace unknown,
Hide me beneath Thy spreading wings,
  Till the dark cloud is overblown.

2 Up to the heavens I send my cry;
  The Lord will my desires perform;
He sends His angel from the sky
  And saves me from the threatening storm.

3 Be Thou exalted, O my God,
  Above the heavens, where angels dwell;
Thy power on earth be known abroad,
  And land to land Thy wonders tell.

4 My heart is fix'd, my song shall raise
  Immortal honours to Thy name;
Awake, my tongue, to sound His praise,
  My tongue, the glory of my frame.

5 High o'er the earth His mercy reigns
  And reaches to the utmost sky;
His truth to endless years remains,
  When lower worlds dissolve and die.

6 Be Thou exalted, O my God,
  Above the heavens, where angels dwell;
Thy power on earth be known abroad,
  And land to land Thy wonders tell.

*Isaac Watts*, 1719

## 58 L.M.
*Psalm 58*

1 LORD, make my conversation chaste,
  And all my understanding purge,
Lest with the wicked throng I haste,
  And down to hell my pathway urge.

2 They from the womb are all estranged;
  The serpent's poison fills each vein;
They're not by wise persuasion changed,
  But like the adder deaf remain.

3 As lion's teeth the hunters break,
  As angry torrents soon are dry,

So shall Thy bow swift vengeance take
Upon the proud who truth defy.

4 As melts the snail with slimy trail,
As thorns consume in rapid blaze,
Before Thy wrath Thy foes shall fail,
Thy whirlwinds shall their souls amaze.

5 O God, Thou judgest all the earth;
Thy justice cheers my cleansèd heart;
Restrain my soul from sinners' mirth,
Lest in their doom I bear a part.

*Charles H. Spurgeon*, 1866

# 59 7.7.7.7.
*Psalm 59*

1 I AM hated, Lord! by those
Who Thy holy truth despise;
Save me from my wicked foes;
Lord of hosts, arise, arise!

2 Thou'rt my rock and my defence;
Thou a tow'r unto Thy saints;
Thee I make my confidence;
Thee I'll trust, though nature faints.

3 Glad Thy mercies will I sing,
All Thy pow'r and love confess;
Thou hast been, O heav'nly King,
My safe refuge in distress!

4 Songs with every morning's light,
Lord, shall rise up to Thy throne;
All Thy saints shall praise Thy might,
And Thy mercy shall make known!

*William Allen*, 1835

# 60 L.M.
*Psalm 60*

1 O GOD, Thou hast cast off Thy saints;
Thy face Thou dost in anger hide;
And lo, Thy church for terror faints,
While breaches all her walls divide!

2 Hard things Thou hast upon us laid,
And made us drink most bitter wine,
But still Thy banner we've display'd,
And borne aloft Thy truth divine.

3 Our courage fails not, though the night
No earthly lamp avails to break,
For Thou wilt soon arise in might,
And of our captors captives make.

4 Thy right hand shall Thy people aid;
Thy faithful promise makes us strong;
We will Philistia's land invade,
And over Edom chant the song.

5 In Jesu's name we'll Shechem seize
And swift divide all Succoth's vale;
E'en Moab's sons shall bow their knees
And Jesu's conquering sceptre hail.

6 Through Thee we shall most valiant prove,
And tread the foe beneath our feet;
Through Thee our faith shall hills remove,
And small as chaff the mountains beat.

*Charles H. Spurgeon*, 1866

**TD:** "For the truth's sake, and because the true
God is on our side, let us in these modern days
of warfare emulate the warriors of Israel, and
unfurl our banners to the breeze with confi-
dent joy. Dark signs of present or coming ill
must not dishearten us; if the Lord had meant
to destroy us He would not have given us
the gospel; the very fact that he has revealed
Himself in Christ Jesus involves the certainty
of victory" (Ps. 60:4-5, vol. 3, p. 92).

# 61a S.M.
*Psalm 61, Song I*

1 WHEN overwhelm'd with grief,
My heart within me dies;
Helpless and far from all relief,
To heaven I lift mine eyes.

2 O lead me to the rock
That's high above my head,
And make the covert of Thy wings
My shelter and my shade.

3 Within Thy presence, Lord,
Forever I'll abide;
Thou art the tow'r of my defence,
The refuge where I hide.

4   Thou givest me the lot
     Of those that fear Thy name;
  If endless life be their reward,
     I shall possess the same.

*Isaac Watts*, 1719

## 61b C.M.
*Psalm 61, Song II*

1   HAIL, gracious source of every good,
     Our Saviour and defence;
  Thou art our glory and our shield,
     Our help and confidence.

2   When anxious fears disturb the breast,
     When threatening foes are nigh,
  To Thee we pour our deep complaint,
     To Thee for succour fly.

3   Blest tower of strength, exalted rock,
     Whence living waters flow,
  Jesus our Lord, the only hope
     Of fallen man below.

4   To Thee we heavy laden come,
     To Thee our sorrows bring;
  Oh hear! and save us from the storm,
     Beneath Thy sheltering wing.

*Harriet Auber*, 1829

## 62 C.M.
*Psalm 62*

1   WHEN dangers press and fears invade,
     O let us not rely
  On man, who in the balance weigh'd,
     Is light as vanity!

2   Riches have wings and fly away;
     Health's blooming cheek grows pale;
  Vigour and strength must soon decay,
     And worldly wisdom fail.

3   But God, our God, is still the same
     As at that solemn hour
  When thunders spake His awful name,
     His majesty, and power.

4   And still sweet mercy's voice is heard,
     Proclaiming from above
  That good and gracious is the Lord,
     And all His works are love.

5   Then trust in God and God alone;
     On Him in faith rely;
  For man and all his works are known
     To be but vanity.

*Harriet Auber*, 1829

## 63a C.M.
*Psalm 63, Song I*

1   EARLY, my God, without delay,
     I haste to seek Thy face;
  My thirsty spirit faints away
     Without Thy cheering grace.

2   So pilgrims on the scorching sand,
     Beneath a burning sky,
  Long for a cooling stream at hand,
     And they must drink or die.

3   I've seen Thy glory and Thy pow'r
     Through all Thy temple shine;
  My God, repeat that heavenly hour,
     That vision so divine.

4   Not all the blessings of a feast
     Can please my soul so well,
  As when Thy richer grace I taste,
     And in Thy presence dwell.

5   Not life itself, with all her joys,
     Can my best passions move,
  Or raise so high my cheerful voice
     As Thy forgiving love.

6   Thus, till my last expiring day,
     I'll bless my God and King;
  Thus will I lift my hands to pray
     And tune my lips to sing.

*Isaac Watts*, 1719

**MM:** Hymns, 22nd Lord's Day,
    DEDHAM / LANESBORO

## 63b C.M.
*Psalm 63, Song II*

1 O GOD of love, my God Thou art;
　　To Thee I early cry;
　Refresh with grace my thirsty heart,
　　For earthly springs are dry.

2 Thy power, Thy glory let me see,
　　As seen by saints above.
　'Tis sweeter, Lord, than life to me,
　　To share and sing Thy love.

3 I freely yield Thee all my powers,
　　Yet ne'er my debt can pay;
　The thought of Thee at midnight hours
　　Turns darkness into day.

4 Lord, Thou hast been my help, and Thou
　　My refuge still shalt be.
　I follow hard Thy footsteps now—
　　O when Thy face to see?

*Henry Francis Lyte*, 1834

## 63c L.M.
*Psalm 63, Song III*

1 O GOD, Thou art my God alone;
　　Early to Thee my soul shall cry,
　A pilgrim in a land unknown,
　　A thirsty land, whose springs are dry.

2 O that it were as it hath been,
　　When praying in the holy place;
　Thy power and glory I have seen,
　　And mark'd the footsteps of Thy grace.

3 Yet through this rough and thorny maze,
　　I follow hard on Thee, my God;
　Thine hand unseen upholds my ways;
　　I safely tread where Thou hast trod.

4 Thee, in the watches of the night,
　　When I remember on my bed,
　Thy presence makes the darkness light;
　　Thy guardian wings are round my head.

5 Better than life itself Thy love,
　　Dearer than all beside to me;

For whom have I in heaven above,
　　Or what on earth, compared with Thee?

6 Praise with my heart, my mind, my voice,
　　For all Thy mercy I will give;
　My soul shall still in God rejoice;
　　My tongue shall bless Thee while I live.

*James Montgomery*, 1822

> **MM:** Hymns, Set 1 (Jan./Nov.), 11th Morn,
> HAMBURG / ROLLAND

## 64 8.7.8.7.
*Psalm 64*

1 HEAR, O Lord, our supplication;
　　Let our souls on Thee repose!
　Be our *refuge, our* salvation,
　　'Mid ten thousand threatening foes.

2 Lord, Thy saints have many troubles;
　　In their path lies many a snare,
　But before Thy breath, like bubbles,
　　Melt they soon in idle air.

3 Cunning are the foe's devices;
　　Bitter are his words of gall;
　Sin on every side entices;
　　Lord, conduct us safe through all.

4 Be our foes by Thee confounded;
　　Let the world Thy goodness see;
　While by might and love surrounded,
　　We rejoice and trust in Thee.

*Henry Francis Lyte*, 1834

> **1.3:** *hope, our strong*
> **Ed:** Lyte revised this text in 1836, but the
> original continued to be printed, as above.
> Footnote indicates Lyte's revision.

## 65 C.M.
*Psalm 65*

1 GOOD is the Lord, the heavenly King,
　　Who makes the earth His care,
　Visits the pastures every spring,
　　And bids the grass appear.

2 The clouds, like rivers rais'd on high,
    Pour out at Thy command
Their wat'ry blessings from the sky
    To cheer the thirsty land.

3 The soften'd ridges of the field
    Permit the corn to spring;
The valleys rich provision yield,
    And the poor labourers sing.

4 The little hills on every side
    Rejoice at falling showers;
The meadows, dress'd in all their pride,
    Perfume the air with flowers.

5 The various months Thy goodness crowns;
    How bounteous are Thy ways?
The bleating flocks spread o'er the downs,
    And shepherds shout Thy praise.

*Isaac Watts*, 1719

# 66a C.M.
*Psalm 66, Song I*

1 SING, all ye nations, to the Lord,
    Sing with a joyful noise;
With melody of sound record
    His honours and your joys.

2 Say to the power that shakes the sky,
    "How terrible art Thou!
Sinners before Thy presence fly,
    Or at Thy feet they bow."

3 O bless our God and never cease;
    Ye saints, fulfill His praise;
He keeps our life, maintains our peace,
    And guides our doubtful ways.

4 Lord, Thou hast prov'd our suffering souls
    To make our graces shine;
So silver bears the burning coals,
    The metal to refine.

5 Through wat'ry deeps and fiery ways
    We march at Thy command,
Led to possess the promis'd place
    By Thine unerring hand.

*Isaac Watts*, 1719

# 66b L.M.
*Psalm 66, Song II*

1 O ALL ye lands, rejoice in God,
    Sing praises to His name;
Let the whole earth, with one accord,
    His wondrous acts proclaim.

2 And let His faithful servants tell,
    How, by redeeming love,
Their souls are saved from death and hell
    To share the joys above.

3 Tell how the Holy Spirit's grace
    Forbids their feet to slide,
And as they run the Christian race,
    Vouchsafes to be their guide.

4 *Sing, sing, ye saints*, and shout for joy,
    Ye ransom'd of the Lord;
Be grateful praise your sweet employ,
    His presence your reward.

*Harriet Auber*, 1829 [*alt. C.H.S.*]

    **4.1:** *O then rejoice*

# 67a S.M.
*Psalm 67, Song I*

1     TO bless Thy chosen race,
      In mercy, Lord, incline,
And cause the brightness of Thy face
      On all Thy saints to shine.

2     That so Thy wondrous ways
      May through the world be known,
Whilst distant lands their tribute pay
      And Thy salvation own.

3     Let diff'ring nations join,
      *Their Saviour to proclaim;*
Let all the world, O Lord, combine
      To praise Thy glorious name.

4     O let them shout and sing
      With joy and pious mirth,
For Thou, the righteous Judge and King,
      Shalt govern all the earth.

5     Then God upon our land
      Shall constant blessings show'r,

And all the world in awe shall stand
Of His resistless pow'r.

*Tate and Brady*, 1696 [*rev.* 1698]
[*alt. Henry Francis Lyte*, 1834]

**3.2:** *To celebrate Thy fame*

# 67b 7.7.7.7.7.7.
*Psalm 67, Song II*

1 GOD of mercy, God of grace,
Show the brightness of Thy face;
Shine upon us, Saviour, shine;
Fill Thy church with light divine,
And Thy saving health extend
Unto earth's remotest end.

2 Let the people praise Thee, Lord;
Be by all that live adored;
Let the nations shout and sing
Glory to their Saviour King;
At Thy feet their tributes pay
And Thy holy will obey.

3 Let the people praise Thee, Lord;
Earth shall then her fruits afford;
God to man His blessing give;
Man to God devoted live;
All below and all above,
One in joy, and light, and love!

*Henry Francis Lyte*, 1834

# 68a C.M.
*Psalm 68, Part I*

1 LET God arise, and scatterèd
Let all His enemies be,
And let all those that do Him hate
Before His presence flee.

2 As smoke is driv'n, so drive Thou them;
As fire melts wax away,
Before God's face let wicked men
So perish and decay.

3 But let the righteous all be glad,
Let them before God's sight
Be very joyful; yea, let them
Rejoice with all their might.

4 To God sing *praise, to God* sing praise;
Extol Him with your voice;
*He rides* on heav'n, by His name JAH;
Before His face rejoice.

*Scotch Verson* [1650], *alt. C.H.S.*

**4.1:** *to His name,* **4.3:** *That ride*

# 68b 7.7.7.7. Double
*Psalm 68, Part II*

1 As Thy chosen, people, Lord,
Once oppress'd, in numbers few,
Trusted to Thy steadfast Word,
And a mighty nation grew,
So Thy church on earth begun,
By Thy blessings shall increase,
While the course of time shall run,
Till Messiah's reign of peace.

2 Soon shall every scatter'd tribe
To her bosom be restored;
Every heart and tongue ascribe
Praise and glory to the Lord;
Militant awhile below,
Rest and joy shall soon be given;
Then in rapt'rous strains shall flow
Her triumphant song in heaven.

*Harriet Auber*, 1829

# 68c L.M.
*Psalm 68, Part III*

1 KINGDOMS and thrones to God belong;
Crown Him, ye nations, in your song;
His wondrous names and powers rehearse;
His honours shall enrich your verse.

2 Proclaim Him King, pronounce Him blest;
He's your defence, your joy, your rest;
When terrors rise and nations faint,
God is the strength of every saint.

*Isaac Watts*, 1719

**Ed:** Taken from the longer paraphrase,
"Let God arise in all His might."

## 69 C.M.
*Psalm 69*

1 LORD, I would stand with thoughtful eye
   Beneath Thy fatal tree,
And see Thee bleed, and see Thee die,
   And think, "What love to me!"

2 Dwell on the sight, my stony heart,
   Till every pulse within
Shall into contrite sorrow start,
   And hate the thought of sin.

3 Didst Thou for me, my Saviour, brave
   The scoff, the scourge, the gall,
The nails, the thorns, the spear, the grave,
   While I deserved them all?

4 O help me some return to make,
   To yield my heart to Thee,
And do and suffer for Thy sake
   As Thou didst then for me!

*Henry Francis Lyte*, 1834

## 70 L.M.
*Psalm 70*

1 MAKE haste, O God, my soul to bless!
My help and deliv'rer Thou;
Make haste, for I'm in deep distress,
My case is urgent; help me NOW.

2 Make haste, O God! Make haste to save!
For time is short and death is nigh;
Make haste ere yet I'm in my grave,
And with the lost forever lie.

3 Make haste, for I am poor and low,
And Satan mocks my prayers and tears;
O God, in mercy be not slow,
But snatch me from my horrid fears.

4 Make haste, O God, and hear my cries;
Then with the souls who seek Thy face,
And those who Thy salvation prize,
I'll magnify Thy matchless grace.

*Charles H. Spurgeon*, 1866

**TD:** "'Make haste unto me, O God.' This is written
instead of 'yet the Lord thinketh upon me,' in
Psalm 40, and there is a reason for the change,
since the key note of the Psalm frequently
dictates its close. Psalm 40 sings of God's
thoughts, and, therefore, ends therewith; but
the peculiar note of Psalm 70 is 'Make haste,'
and therefore, so it concludes" (Ps. 70:5; vol.
3, p. 290).

## 71a C.M.
*Psalm 71, Song I*

1 MY Saviour, my almighty Friend,
   When I begin Thy praise,
Where will the growing numbers end,
   The numbers of Thy grace?

2 Thou art my everlasting trust;
   Thy goodness I adore;
And since I knew Thy graces first,
   I speak Thy glories more.

3 My feet shall travel all the length
   Of the celestial road,
And march with courage in Thy strength
   To see my Father God.

4 When I am fill'd with sore distress
   For some surprising sin,
I'll plead Thy perfect righteousness
   And mention none but Thine.

5 How will my lips rejoice to tell
   The victories of my King!
My soul redeem'd from sin and hell
   Shall Thy salvation sing.

6 Awake, awake, my tuneful powers;
   With this delightful song
I'll entertain the darkest hours,
   Nor think the season long.

*Isaac Watts*, 1719

## 71b C.M.
*Psalm 71, Song II*

1 MY God, my everlasting hope,
   I live upon Thy truth;
Thine hands have held my childhood up
   And strengthen'd all my youth.

2 Still has my life new wonders seen,
  Repeated every year;
Behold my days that yet remain,
  I trust them to Thy care.

3 Cast me not off when strength declines,
  When hoary hairs arise,
And round me let Thy glory shine,
  Whene'er Thy servant dies.

*Isaac Watts*, 1719

  **EE:** Hymns, Set 2 (Feb./Dec.), 12th Eve,
    IRISH / BEDFORD

## 72a L.M. *Psalm 72, Song I*

1 JESUS shall reign where'er the sun
Does His successive journeys run;
His kingdom stretch from shore to shore,
Till moons shall wax and wane no more.

2 For Him shall endless pray'r be made
And praises throng to crown His head;
His name like sweet perfume shall rise
With every morning sacrifice.

3 People and realms of every tongue
Dwell on His love with sweetest song,
And infant voices shall proclaim
Their early blessings on His name.

4 Blessings abound where'er He reigns;
The prisoner leaps to lose his chains,
The weary find eternal rest,
And all the sons of want are blest.

5 Where He displays His healing power,
Death and the curse are known no more;
In Him the tribes of Adam boast
More blessings than their father lost.

6 Let every creature rise and bring
Peculiar honours to our King;
Angels descend with songs sgain,
And earth repeat the loud AMEN.

*Isaac Watts*, 1719

  **MM:** Hymns, 20th Lord's Day,
    DUKE STREET / ROLLAND

**EE:** "We know that the world, and all that is
  therein, is one day to be burnt up, and after-
  wards we look for new heavens and for a new
  earth; but we cannot read our Bibles without
  the conviction that 'Jesus shall reign where'er
  the sun does his successive journeys run.' . . .
  Happy are they who trust themselves with this
  conquering Lord, and who fight side by side
  with Him, doing their little in His name and by
  His strength!" (Dec. 24).

## 72b 7.7.7.7. *Psalm 72, Song II*

1 HASTEN, Lord, the glorious time,
  When, beneath Messiah's sway,
Every nation, every clime,
  Shall the gospel's call obey.

2 Then shall wars and tumults cease,
  Then be banish'd grief and pain;
Righteousness, and joy, and peace,
  Undisturb'd shall ever reign.

3 As when soft and gentle showers
  Fall upon the thirsty plain,
Springing grass and blooming flowers
  Clothe the wilderness again;

4 So Thy Spirit shall descend,
  Soft'ning every stony heart,
And its sweetest influence lend
  All that's lovely to impart.

5 Time shall sun and moon obscure,
  Seas be dried, and rocks be riven,
But His reign shall still endure,
  Endless as the days of heaven.

6 Bless we then our gracious Lord;
  Ever praise His glorious name;
All His mighty acts record;
  All His wondrous love proclaim.

*Harriett Auber*, 1829

## 73a L.M. *Psalm 73, Part I*

1 LORD, what a thoughtless wretch was I,
To mourn and murmur and repine,

To see the wicked placed on high,
In pride and robes of honour shine!

2 But O their end! their dreadful end!
Thy sanctuary taught me so:
On slippery rocks I see them stand,
And fiery billows roll below.

3 Now let them boast how tall they rise;
I'll never envy them again;
There they may stand with haughty eyes,
Till they plunge deep in endless pain.

4 Their fancied joys, how fast they flee!
Just like a dream when man awakes;
Their songs of softest harmony
Are but a preface to their plagues.

5 Now I esteem their mirth and wine
Too dear to purchase with my blood;
Lord, 'tis enough that Thou art mine,
My life, my portion, and my God.

*Isaac Watts*, [1707, *rev.* 1719]


# 73b C.M.
*Psalm 73, Part II*

1 GOD, my supporter and my hope,
My help forever near,
Thine arm of mercy held me up
When sinking in despair.

2 Thy counsels, Lord, shall guide my feet
Through this dark wilderness;
Thy hand conduct me near Thy seat
To dwell before Thy face.

3 Were I in heaven without my God
'Twould be no joy to me;
And whilst this earth is mine abode,
I long for none but Thee.

4 What if the springs of life were broke,
And flesh and heart should faint?
God is my soul's eternal rock,
The strength of every saint.

5 *Still* to draw near to Thee, my God,
Shall be my sweet employ;

My tongue shall sound Thy works abroad
And tell the world my joy.

*Isaac Watts*, 1719
[*alt. John Bickersteth*, 1819]

**5.1:** *But*


# 73c C.M.
*Psalm 73, Part III*

1 WHOM have we, Lord, in heaven but Thee,
And whom on earth beside?
Where else for succour shall we flee,
Or in whose strength confide?

2 Thou art our portion here below,
Our promised bliss above;
Ne'er *can* our souls an object know
So precious as Thy love.

3 When heart and flesh, O Lord, shall fail,
Thou wilt our spirits cheer;
Support us through life's thorny vale
And calm each anxious fear.

4 Yes, *Thou, our only* guide through life,
*Shalt* help and strength supply;
Support us in death's fearful strife,
*Then* welcome us on high.

*Harriet Auber*, 1829
[*alt. William J. Hall*, 1836]

**2.3:** *may* **4.1:** *Thou shalt be our*
**4.2:** *And* **4.4:** *And*
**MM:** Hymns, Set 1 (Feb./Dec.), 27th Morn,
BROWN / DEDHAM


# 74 C.M.
*Psalm 74*

1 OF every earthly stay bereft,
Beset by many an ill,
One hope, one precious hope, is left;
The Lord is faithful still.

2 His church through every past alarm
In Him has found a Friend;
And Lord, on Thine almighty arm
We now for all depend.

*Henry Francis Lyte*, 1834

## 75 8.8.6.8.8.6
*Psalm 75*

1 THAT Thou, O Lord, art ever nigh,
   Though veil'd in awful majesty,
      Thy mighty works declare;
   Thy hand this earthly frame upholds,
   Thine eye the universe beholds
      With providential care.

2 Thou settest up and pullest down;
   To Thee the monarch owes his crown,
      The conqueror his wreath;
   In Thee all creatures live and move;
   Thou reign'st supreme in heaven above
      And in the earth beneath.

3 Great King of Kings and Lord of Lords,
   Whose hand chastises and rewards,
      Thee only we adore;
   To Thee the voice of praise shall rise
   In hallelujahs to the skies,
      When time shall be no more.

*Harriet Auber*, 1829


## 76 S.M.
*Psalm 76*

1 GOD in His church is known;
      His name is glorious there;
   He there sets up His earthly throne
      And hears His people's prayer.

2 The powers of death and hell
      In vain her peace oppose;
   A word of His the storm can quell
      And scatter all her foes.

3 The Lord to judgment came;
      Earth trembled and was still.
   'Tis His, 'tis His, the proud to tame,
      And shield the meek from ill.

4 The fury of His foes
      Fulfills but His decree.
   Ye saints, on Him your hopes repose,
      And He your strength will be.

*Henry Francis Lyte*, 1834 [*rev.* 1836]


## 77 C.M.
*Psalm 77*

1 *WILL* God forever cast us off,
      *His love return no more?*
   *His promise, will it never give*
      *Its comfort as before?*

2 Can His *abundant* love forget
      Its wonted aids to bring?
   Has He in wrath shut up and seal'd
      His mercy's healing spring?

3 I'll call to mind His works of old,
      The wonders of His might;
   On them my heart shall meditate,
      *Them shall my tongue* recite.

4 *Thy people, Lord, long since have* Thee
      *A God of wonders* found;
   Long since hast Thou Thy chosen seed
      With strong deliv'rance crown'd.

*Tate and Brady*, 1696 [*rev.* 1698]
[*alt. William J. Hall*, 1836]

> **1.1:** *Has*
> **1.2-4:** *Withdrawn His favour quite?*
>    *Are both His mercy and His truth*
>    *Retir'd to endless night?*
> **2.1:** *Long-practis'd*
> **3.4:** *My tongue shall them recite.*
> **4.1:** *Long since a God of wonders*
> **4.2:** *Thy rescued people*
> **Ed:** Taken from the longer paraphrase,
> "To God I cried, who to my help."


## 78 C.M. Double
*Psalm 78*

1 O PRAISE our great and gracious Lord
      And call upon His name;
   To strains of joy tune every chord,
      His mighty acts proclaim.
   Tell how He led His chosen race
      To Canaan's promis'd land;
   Tell how His covenant of grace
      Unchanged shall ever stand.

2 He gave the shadowing cloud by day,
      The moving fire by night;
   To guide His Israel on their way,

He made their darkness light.
And have not we a sure retreat,
 A Saviour ever nigh?
The same clear light to guide our feet,
 The day-spring from on high?

3 We too have manna from above,
 "The bread that came from heaven";
To us the same kind hand of love
 Hath living waters given.
A rock we have, from whence the spring
 In rich abundance flows:
"That rock is Christ," our Priest, our King,
 Who life and health bestows.

4 O let us prize this blessed food
 And trust our heavenly guide;
So shall we find death's fearful flood
 Serene as Jordan's tide,
And safely reach that happy shore,
 The land of peace and rest,
Where angels worship and adore,
 In God's own presence bless'd.

*Harriet Auber*, 1829

## 79 S.M.
*Psalm 79*

1 THOU gracious God, and kind,
 Oh cast our sins away,
Nor call our former guilt to mind,
 Thy justice to display.

2 The tend'rest mercies show,
 Thy richest grace prepare,
Ere yet, with guilty fears laid low,
 We perish in despair.

3 Save us from guilt and shame,
 Thy glory to display;
And for the great Redeemer's name,
 Wash all our sins away.

4 So we Thy flock, Thy choice,
 The people of Thy love,
Through life shall in Thy care rejoice,
 But praise Thee best above.

*William Goode*, 1811

## 80 L.M.
*Psalm 80*

1 GREAT Shepherd of Thine Israel,
 Who didst between the cherubs dwell,
And lead the tribes, Thy chosen sheep,
 Safe through the desert and the deep:

2 Thy church is in the desert now;
 Shine from on high and guide us through;
Turn us to Thee, Thy love restore;
 We shall be saved and sigh no more.

3 Great God, whom heavenly hosts obey,
 How long shall we lament and pray
And wait in vain Thy kind return?
 How long shall Thy fierce anger burn?

4 Instead of wine and cheerful bread,
 Thy saints with their own tears are fed;
Turn us to Thee, Thy love restore;
 We shall be saved and sigh no more.

*Isaac Watts*, 1719

## 81 C.M.
*Psalm 81*

1 O GOD, our strength, to Thee the song
 With grateful hearts we raise;
To Thee, and Thee alone, belong
 All worship, love, and praise.

2 In trouble's dark and stormy hour,
 Thine ear hath heard our prayer,
And graciously Thine arm of power
 Hath saved us from despair.

3 And Thou, O ever gracious Lord,
 Wilt keep Thy promise still,
If, meekly hearkening to Thy Word,
 We seek to do Thy will.

4 Led by the light Thy grace imparts,
 Ne'er may we bow the knee
To idols, which our wayward hearts
 Set up instead of Thee.

5 So shall Thy choicest gifts, O Lord,
 Thy faithful people bless;

For them shall earth its stores afford,
    And heaven its happiness.

*Harriet Auber*, 1829

## 82 C.M.
*Psalm 82*

1 THE kings of earth are in the hands
    Of God who reigns on high;
  He in their council chamber stands
    And sees with watchful eye.

2 Though foolish princes tyrants prove
    And tread the godly down,
  Though earth's foundations all remove,
    He weareth still the crown.

3 They proudly boast a godlike birth;
    In death like men they fall;
  Arise, O God, and judge the earth,
    And rule the nations all.

4 When shall Thy Son, the Prince of Peace,
    Descend with glorious power?
  Then only shall oppression cease;
    Oh, haste the welcome hour.

*Charles H. Spurgeon*, 1866

## 83 L.M.
*Psalm 83*

1 O GOD, be Thou no longer still;
  Thy foes are leagued against Thy law;
  Make bare Thine arm on Zion's hill,
  Great Captain of our Holy War.

2 As Amalek and Ishmael
  Had war forever with Thy seed,
  So all the hosts of Rome and hell
  Against Thy Son their armies lead.

3 Though they're agreed in nought beside,
  Against Thy truth they all unite;
  They rave against the crucified
  And hate the gospel's growing might.

4 By Kishon's brook all Jabin's band
  At thy rebuke were swept away;

O Lord, display Thy mighty hand;
  A single stroke shall win the day.

5 Come, rushing wind, the stubble chase!
  Come, sacred fire, the forests burn!
  Come, Lord, with all Thy conquering grace,
  Rebellious hearts to Jesus turn!

6 That men may know at once that Thou,
  Jehovah, lovest truth right well;
  And that Thy church shall never bow
  Before the boastful gates of hell.

*Charles H. Spurgeon*, 1866

**TD:** "Thus has this soul-stirring lyric [Psalm 83]
risen from the words of complaint to those of
adoration; let us in our worship always seek
to do the same. National trouble called out
the nation's poet laureate, and well did he
discourse at once of her sorrows, and prayers,
and hopes. Sacred literature thus owes much
to sorrow and distress. How enriching is the
hand of adversity!" (Ps. 83; vol. 4, p. 52).

## 84a L.M.
*Psalm 84, Song I*

1 HOW pleasant, how divinely fair,
  O Lord of hosts, Thy dwellings are!
  With long desire my spirit faints
  To meet th' assemblies of Thy saints.

2 My flesh would rest in Thine abode;
  My panting heart cries out for God;
  My God! my King! why should I be
  So far from all my joys and Thee?

3 Blest are the saints who sit on high
  Around Thy throne of majesty;
  Thy brightest glories shine above,
  And all their work is praise and love.

4 Blest are the souls that find a place
  Within the temple of Thy grace;
  There they behold Thy gentler rays,
  And seek Thy face, and learn Thy praise.

5 Blest are the men whose hearts are set
  To find the way to Zion's gate;
  God is their strength, and through the road
  They lean upon their helper God.

6 Cheerful they walk with growing strength,
Till all shall meet in heaven at length,
Till all before Thy face appear
And join in nobler worship there.

*Isaac Watts*, 1719

**MM:** Hymns, 14th Lord's Day,
ROLLAND / UXBRIDGE

# 84b L.M.
*Psalm 84, Song II*

1 GREAT God, attend, while Zion sings
The joy that from Thy presence springs;
To spend one day with Thee on earth
Exceeds a thousand days of mirth.

2 Might I enjoy the meanest place
Within Thine house, O God of grace;
Not tents of ease, nor thrones of power,
Should tempt my feet to leave Thy door.

3 God is our sun, He makes our day;
God is our shield, He guards our way
From all th' assaults of hell and sin,
From foes without and foes within.

4 All needful grace will God bestow,
And crown that grace with glory too;
He gives us all things and withholds
No real good from upright souls.

5 O God, our King, whose sovereign sway
The glorious hosts of heaven obey,
And devils at Thy presence flee;
Blest is the man that trusts in Thee.

*Isaac Watts*, 1719

**MM:** Hymns, 9th Lord's Day,
FEDERAL STREET / HAMBURG

# 84c 6.6.6.6.4.4.4.4.
*Psalm 84, Song III*

1 LORD of the worlds above,
How pleasant and how fair
The dwellings of Thy love,
Thy earthly temples are!
    To Thine abode,
    My heart aspires

With warm desires
To see my God.

2 O happy souls that pray
Where God appoints to hear!
O happy men that pay
Their constant service there!
    They praise Thee still,
    And happy they
    That love the way
    To Zion's hill.

3 They go from strength to strength,
Through this dark vale of tears,
Till each arrives at length,
Till each in heaven appears;
    O glorious seat,
    When God our King
    Shall thither bring
    Our willing feet!

4 To spend one sacred day
Where God and saints abide
Affords diviner joy
Than thousand days beside:
    Where God resorts,
    I love it more
    To keep the door
    Than shine in courts.

5 God is our sun and shield,
Our light and our defence;
With gifts his hands are fill'd;
We draw our blessings thence:
    He shall bestow
    On Jacob's race
    Peculiar grace
    And glory too.

6 The Lord His people loves;
His hand no good withholds
From those His heart approves,
From pure and pious souls.
    Thrice happy he,
    O God of hosts,
    Whose spirit trusts
    Alone in Thee.

*Isaac Watts*, 1719

# 85 L.M.
*Psalm 85*

1 SALVATION is forever nigh
The souls that fear and trust the Lord,
And grace, descending from on high,
Fresh hopes of glory shall afford.

2 Mercy and truth on earth are met,
Since Christ the Lord
   came down from heav'n;
By His obedience so complete
Justice is pleas'd and peace is given.

3 Now truth and honour shall abound,
Religion dwell on earth again;
And heavenly influence bless the ground
In our Redeemer's gentle reign.

4 His righteousness is gone before
To give us free access to God;
Our wand'ring feet shall stray no more,
But mark His steps and keep the road.

*Isaac Watts*, 1719

# 86 L.M.
*Psalm 86*

1 THY listening ear, O Lord, incline:
Hear me, my God, distress'd and weak!
Preserve my soul, for I am Thine;
O save me, for Thine aid I seek!

2 To Thee ascend my daily cries:
Hear, Lord, in mercy hear my voice!
To Thee my soul for comfort flies;
O bid Thy servant's soul rejoice!

3 'Tis Thine in goodness to abound,
'Tis Thine to pity and forgive;
'Tis Thine to heal the bleeding wound
And grant the plaintive soul to live.

4 Hear, O Jehovah, when I pray!
Attend my voice, my suppliant cry!
I call Thee in affliction's day,
For Thou wilt listen, Thou reply.

5 And Thee *my* heart shall still extol,
Thy goodness chant, Thy praises tell;

For large Thy love, and Thou my soul
Hast rescued from the lowest hell.

*Richard Mant*, 1824 [*alt. C.H.S.*]

   **5.1:** *that*

# 87 L.M.
*Psalm 87*

1 GOD in His earthly temple lays
Foundations for His heavenly praise;
He likes the tents of Jacob well,
But still in Zion loves to dwell.

2 His mercy visits every house
That pay their night and morning vows,
But makes a more delightful stay
Where churches meet to praise and pray.

3 What glories were describ'd of old?
What wonders are of Zion told?
Thou city of our God below,
Thy fame shall Tyre and Egypt know.

4 Egypt and Tyre, and Greek and Jew,
Shall there begin their lives anew;
Angels and men shall join to sing
The hill where living waters spring.

5 When God makes up His last account
Of natives in His holy mount,
'Twill be an honour to appear
As one new-born or nourish'd there.

*Isaac Watts*, 1719

# 88 7.6.7.6. Double
*Psalm 88*

1 LORD God of my salvation,
   To Thee, to Thee I cry;
O let my supplication
   Arrest Thine ear on high.
Distresses round me thicken;
   My life draws nigh the grave;
Descend, O Lord, to quicken,
   Descend my soul to save.

2 Thy wrath lies hard upon me,
　　Thy billows o'er me roll,
My friends all seem to shun me,
　　And foes beset my soul.
Where'er on earth I turn me,
　　No comforter is near.
Wilt Thou too, Father, spurn me?
　　Wilt Thou refuse to hear?

3 No! banished and heart-broken
　　My soul still clings to Thee;
The promise Thou hast spoken
　　Shall still my refuge be.
So present ills and terrors
　　My future joy increase,
And scourge me from my errors
　　To duty, hope, and peace.

*Henry Francis Lyte*, 1834

# 89a C.M.
*Psalm 89, Part I*

1 MY never-ceasing songs shall show
　　The mercies of the Lord,
And make succeeding ages know
　　How faithful is His Word.

2 The sacred truths His lips pronounce
　　Shall firm as heaven endure;
And if He speak a promise once,
　　Th' eternal grace is sure.

3 How long the race of David held
　　The promis'd Jewish throne!
But there's a nobler covenant seal'd
　　To David's greater Son.

4 His seed forever shall possess
　　A throne above the skies;
The meanest subject of His grace
　　Shall to that glory rise.

5 Lord God of hosts, Thy wondrous ways
　　Are sung by saints above;
And saints on earth their honours raise
　　To Thine unchanging love.

*Isaac Watts*, 1719

# 89b C.M.
*Psalm 89, Part II*

1 O GREATLY blest the people are
　　The joyful sound that know;
In brightness of Thy face, O Lord,
　　They ever on shall go.

2 They in Thy name shall all the day
　　Rejoice exceedingly,
And in Thy righteousness shall they
　　Exalted be on high.

3 Because the glory of their strength
　　Doth only stand in Thee,
And in Thy favour shall our horn
　　And pow'r exalted be.

4 For God is our defence, and He
　　To us doth safety bring;
The Holy One of Israel
　　Is our almighty King.

*Scotch Version*, [1650]

> **Ed:** Taken from the longer paraphrase,
> "God's mercies I will ever sing."

# 90 C.M.
*Psalm 90*

1 OUR God, our help in ages past,
　　Our hope for years to come,
Our shelter from the stormy blast
　　And our eternal home,

2 Under the shadow of Thy throne
　　Thy saints have dwelt secure;
Sufficient is Thine arm alone,
　　And our defence is sure.

3 Before the hills in order stood
　　Or earth receiv'd her frame,
From everlasting Thou art God,
　　To endless years the same.

4 A thousand ages in Thy sight
　　Are like an evening gone,
Short as the watch that ends the night
　　Before the rising sun.

5 Time, like an ever-rolling stream,
  Bears all its sons away;
They fly forgotten, as a dream
  Dies at the opening day.

6 Like flow'ry fields the nations stand,
  Pleas'd with the morning light;
The flow'rs beneath the mower's hand
  Lie with'ring e'er 'tis night.

7 Our God, our help in ages past,
  Our hope for years to come,
Be Thou our guard while troubles last
  And our eternal home.

*Isaac Watts*, 1719

> **MM:** Hymns, Set 1 (Jan./Nov.), 14th Morn,
> AZMON / DEDHAM

# 91a L.M.
*Psalm 91, Song I*

1 HE that hath made his refuge God
Shall find a most secure abode,
Shall walk all day beneath His shade,
And there at night shall rest his head.

2 Then will I say, "My God, Thy power
Shall be my fortress and my tower;
I that am form'd of feeble dust
Make Thine almighty arm my trust."

3 Thrice happy man! thy Maker's care
Shall keep thee from the fowler's snare,
Satan, the fowler, who betrays
Unguarded souls a thousand ways.

4 Just as a hen protects her brood
From birds of prey that seek their blood,
Under her feathers, so the Lord
Makes His own arm His people's guard.

5 If vapours with malignant breath
Rise thick and scatter midnight death,
Israel is safe; the poison'd air
Grows pure, if Israel's God be there.

6 What though a thousand at thy side,
At thy right hand ten thousand died;

Thy God His chosen people saves
Amongst the dead, amidst the graves.

7 But if the fire, or plague, or sword,
Receive commission from the Lord
To strike His saints among the rest,
Their very pains and deaths are blest.

8 The sword, the pestilence, or fire,
Shall but fulfill their best desire;
From sins and sorrows set them free,
And bring Thy children, Lord, to Thee.

*Isaac Watts*, 1719

# 91b C.M.
*Psalm 91, Song II*

1 THERE is a safe and secret place
  Beneath the wings divine,
Reserved for all the heirs of grace—
  O be that refuge mine!

2 The *least, the* feeblest there may *hide*
  Uninjured and unawed;
While thousands fall on every side,
  He rests secure in God.

3 The angels watch him on his way
  And aid with friendly arm;
And Satan, roaring for his prey,
  May hate but cannot harm.

4 He feeds in pastures large and fair
  Of love and truth divine.
O child of God, O glory's heir,
  How rich a lot is thine!

5 A hand almighty to defend,
  An ear for every call,
An honoured life, a peaceful end,
  And heaven to crown it all!

*Henry Francis Lyte*, 1834 [*rev.* 1858]

> **2.1:** *least and / bide*  **Ed:** Footnote indicates
> Lyte's original text, which was changed post-
> humously in editions by J.R. Hogg.

# 91c C.M.
*Psalm 91, Song III*

1 YE sons of men, a feeble race,
　　Expos'd to every snare,
　Come, make the Lord your dwelling place,
　　And try, and trust His care.

2 He'll give His angels charge to keep
　　Your feet in all their ways,
　To watch your pillow while you sleep
　　And guard your happy days.

3 "Because on Me they set their love,
　　I'll save them," saith the Lord;
　"I'll bear their joyful souls above
　　Destruction and the sword.

4 "My grace shall answer when they call;
　　In trouble I'll be nigh;
　My power shall help them when they fall
　　And raise them when they die.

5 "Those that on earth My name have known,
　　I'll honour them in heaven;
　There My salvation shall be shown
　　And endless life be given."

*Isaac Watts*, 1719

# 92a L.M.
*Psalm 92, Part I*

1 SWEET is the work, my God, my King,
　To praise Thy name, give thanks, and sing,
　To show Thy love by morning light,
　And talk of all Thy truth at night.

2 Sweet is the day of sacred rest;
　No mortal cares shall seize my breast;
　O may my heart in tune be found,
　Like David's harp of solemn sound!

3 My heart shall triumph in *the* Lord,
　And bless His works, and bless His Word;
　Thy works of grace, how bright they shine!
　How deep Thy counsels! how divine!

4 Fools never raise their thoughts so high;
　Like brutes they live, like brutes they die;

Like grass they flourish, till Thy breath
Blast them in everlasting death.

5 But I shall share a glorious part
　When grace hath well refin'd my heart,
　And fresh supplies of joy are shed
　Like holy oil to cheer my head.

6 Sin (my worst enemy before)
　Shall vex my eyes and ears no more;
　My inward foes shall all be slain,
　Nor Satan break my peace again.

7 Then shall I see, and hear, and know
　All I desir'd or wish'd below;
　And every power find sweet employ
　In that eternal world of joy.

*Isaac Watts*, 1719 [*alt.*]

**3.1:** *my* **Ed:** A common variant dating from the
late 1700s.
**MM:** Hymns, 25th Lord's Day, UXBRIDGE
/ FEDERAL STREET / ROLLAND
**TD:** "Harp-strings soon get out of order and
need to be screwed up again to their proper
tightness, and certainly our heart-strings are
evermore getting out of tune. Let 'Selah' teach
us to pray, 'O may my heart in tune be found
like David's harp of solemn sound'" (Ps. 3:2;
vol. 1, p. 25).
　"In the church of Christ, at this hour, no
Psalm is more frequently sung upon the
Lord's day than the present. The delightful
version of Dr. Watts is familiar to us all—
'Sweet is the work, my God, my King . . .'
(Ps. 92; vol. 4, p. 263).

# 92b L.M.
*Psalm 92, Part II*

1 LORD, 'tis a pleasant thing to stand
　In gardens planted by Thine hand;
　Let me within Thy courts be seen,
　Like a young cedar, fresh and green.

2 There grow Thy saints in faith and love,
　Blest with Thine influence from above;
　Not Lebanon with all its trees
　Yields such a comely sight as these.

3 The plants of grace shall ever live
(Nature decays, but grace must thrive).
Time, that doth all things else impair,
Still makes them flourish strong and fair.

4 Laden with fruits of age, they show
The Lord is holy, just, and true;
None that attend His gates shall find
A God unfaithful or unkind.

*Isaac Watts, 1719*

## 93 L.M.
*Psalm 93*

1 JEHOVAH reigns; He dwells in light,
Girded with majesty and might;
The world created by His hands
Still on its first foundation stands.

2 But ere this spacious world was made,
Or had its first foundations laid,
Thy throne eternal ages stood,
Thyself the ever-living God.

3 Like floods, the angry nations rise,
And aim their rage against the skies;
Vain floods, that aim their rage so high!
At thy rebuke the billows die.

4 Forever shall Thy throne endure;
Thy promise stands forever sure,
And everlasting holiness
Becomes the dwellings of Thy grace.

*Isaac Watts, 1719*

## 94 L.M.
*Psalm 94*

1 CAN guilty man, indeed, believe
That he, who made and knows the heart,
Shall not th' oppressor's crimes perceive,
Nor take His injured servants' part?

2 Shall He who, with transcendent skill,
Fashion'd the eye and form'd the ear,
Who modell'd nature to His will,
Shall He not see? Shall He not hear?

3 Shall He, who fram'd the human mind
And bade its kindling spark to glow,
Who all its varied powers combin'd,
Oh mortal, say—shall He not know?

4 Vain hope! His eye at once surveys
Whatever fills creation's space;
He sees our thoughts and marks our ways;
He knows no bounds of time and place.

5 Surrounded by His saints, the Lord
Shall arm'd with holy vengeance come,
To each his final lot award,
And seal the sinner's fearful doom.

*Harriet Auber, 1829*

## 95a C.M.
*Psalm 95, Song I*

1 SING to the Lord Jehovah's name,
And in His strength rejoice;
When His salvation is our theme,
Exalted be our voice.

2 With thanks approach His awful sight,
And psalms of honour sing;
The Lord's a God of boundless might,
The whole creation's King.

3 Come, and with humble souls adore;
Come, kneel before His face;
O may the creatures of His power
Be children of His grace!

4 Now is the time: He bends His ear
And waits for your request;
Come, lest He rouse His wrath and swear,
"Ye shall not see my rest."

*Isaac Watts, 1719*

## 95b S.M.
*Psalm 95, Song II*

1 COME, sound His praise abroad,
And hymns of glory sing;
Jehovah is the sovereign God,
The universal King.

2 He form'd the deeps unknown;
　　He gave the seas their bound;
　The wat'ry worlds are all His own,
　　And all the solid ground.

3 Come, worship at His throne;
　　Come, bow before the Lord;
　We are His works, and not our own;
　　He form'd us by His word.

4 Today attend His voice,
　　Nor dare provoke His rod;
　Come, like the people of His choice,
　　And own your gracious God.

5 But if your ears refuse
　　The language of His grace,
　And hearts grow hard, like stubborn Jews,
　　That unbelieving race,

6 The Lord, in vengeance dress'd,
　　Will lift His hand and swear,
　"You that despise my promis'd rest
　　Shall have no portion there."

*Isaac Watts*, 1719

# 95c L.M.
*Psalm 95, Song III*

1 O COME, loud anthems let us sing;
　*Give* thanks to our Almighty King:
　For we our voices high should raise,
　When our salvation's Rock we praise.

2 *Yea, let us stand before His face*
　*To thank Him for His matchless grace;*
　To Him address in joyful songs
　The praise that to His name belongs.

3 For God the Lord, enthron'd in state,
　Is, with unrivall'd glory, great;
　The *strength* of earth *is* in His hand;
　*He made the sea and fix'd the land.*

4 O let us to His courts repair
　And bow with adoration there;
　Down on our knees devoutly all
　Before the Lord our Maker fall.

*Tate and Brady*, 1696 [*rev.* 1698], *alt.*

**1.2:** *Loud*　**2.1-2:** *Into His presence let us haste*
　*To thank Him for His favours past;*
**3.3:** *depths / are*
**3.4:** *That form'd and fix'd the solid land.*
**Ed:** The four-stanza reduction and alterations in
　stanzas 1 and 3 are from William J. Hall, 1836.
　The alterations in stanza 2 are by Spurgeon.

# 96 C.M.
*Psalm 96*

1 SING to the Lord, ye distant lands,
　　Ye tribes of every tongue;
　His new discover'd grace demands
　　A new and nobler song.

2 Say to the nations, "Jesus reigns,
　　God's own Almighty Son;
　His power the sinking world sustains,
　　And grace surrounds His throne."

3 Let heaven proclaim the joyful day,
　　Joy through the earth be seen;
　Let cities shine in bright array,
　　And fields in cheerful green.

4 Let an unusual joy surprise
　　The islands of the sea;
　Ye mountains sink, ye valleys rise;
　　Prepare the Lord His way.

5 Behold He comes, He comes to bless
　　The nations as their God,
　To show the world His righteousness
　　And send His truth abroad.

6 But when His voice shall raise the dead
　　And bid the world draw near,
　How will the guilty nations dread
　　To see their Judge appear?

*Isaac Watts*, 1719

# 97 L.M.
*Psalm 97*

1 JEHOVAH reigns! O earth, rejoice;
　Ye ransom'd isles, exalt your voice;
　Make every hill and vale around
　Responsive to the welcome sound.

2 Though far remov'd from mortal eye,
  He reigns in glorious majesty;
  Himself in awful clouds conceal'd,
  His truth, His justice stands reveal'd.

3 Yes, Jesus reigns! the gospel's light
  Beams with mild radiance on our sight;
  And fallen man, redeem'd, forgiven,
  May lift his heart, his hopes to heaven.

4 Oh then, obey His sacred Word,
  All ye who love and fear the Lord;
  Go, publish through His wide domains
  The glorious truth—Jehovah reigns!

*Harriet Auber,* 1829

# 98 C.M.
*Psalm 98*

1 SING to the Lord a new-made song,
  Who wondrous things has done;
  With His right hand and holy arm
  The conquest He has won.

2 The Lord has through th' astonish'd world
  Display'd His saving might
  And made His righteous acts appear
  In all the heathens' sight.

3 Of Israel's house His love and truth
  Have ever mindful been;
  Wide earth's remotest parts the pow'r
  Of Israel's God have seen.

4 Let therefore earth's inhabitants
  Their cheerful voices raise,
  And all with universal joy
  Resound their Maker's praise.

5 Clap, clap your hands, ye rolling floods,
  And toss your waves on high;
  And all ye hills, with all your woods,
  Shout to the echoing sky.

6 Jehovah comes, He takes His state,
  He comes to judge mankind:
  On His high throne shall justice wait,
  And truth His sentence bind.

1-4 *Tate and Brady,* 1696 [*rev.* 1698]
5-6 *Richard Mant,* 1824

> **Ed:** Sts. 5-6 are from Mant's paraphrase,
> "Sing to the Lord new songs, for He."

# 99 7.7.7.7.
*Psalm 99*

1 REIGNS Jehovah, King supreme,
  (Let the nations own His sway!)
  Thron'd between the cherubim,
  (Prostrate let the earth obey!)

2 High exalt Jehovah's name;
  *Fall* in worship at His feet;
  Wide our God's renown proclaim;
  Holy is Jehovah's seat!

3 Loud Jehovah's praise recount,
  Spread His glorious name abroad,
  Worship on His holy mount:
  Holy is Jehovah God!

*Richard Mant,* 1824 [*alt. C.H.S.*]

**2.2:** *Fall'n*

# 100a L.M.
*Psalm 100, Version I*

1 *BEFORE Jehovah's awful throne,*
  *Ye nations, bow with sacred joy.*
  Know that the Lord is God alone;
  He can create, and He destroy.

2 His sovereign power without our aid
  Made us of clay and form'd us men;
  And when like wandering sheep we stray'd,
  He brought us to His fold again.

3 We are His people, we His care,
  Our souls, and all our mortal frame;
  What lasting honours shall we rear,
  Almighty Maker, to Thy name?

4 We'll crowd Thy gates with thankful songs,
  High as the heavens our voices raise;
  And earth with her ten thousand tongues
  Shall fill Thy courts with sounding praise.

5 Wide as the world is Thy command;
   Vast as eternity Thy love;
   Firm as a rock Thy truth must stand,
   When rolling years shall cease to move.

*Isaac Watts*, [1707, *rev.* 1719]
[*alt. John Wesley*, 1737]

> **1.1-2:** *Nations, attend before this throne*
>    *With solemn fear,*
> **Ed:** Adapted from Watts' longer paraphrase,
>    "Sing to the Lord with joyful voice."

# 100b L.M.
*Psalm 100, Version II*

1 ALL people that on earth do dwell,
   Sing to the Lord with cheerful voice;
   Him serve with *mirth*, His praise forth tell;
   Come ye before Him and rejoice.

2 *Know that the Lord* is God indeed;
   Without our aid He did us make;
   We are His flock, He doth us feed,
   And for His sheep He doth us take.

3 O enter then His gates with praise;
   Approach with joy His courts unto;
   Praise, laud, and bless His name always,
   For it is seemly so to do.

4 For why? The Lord our God is good;
   His mercy is forever sure;
   His truth at all times firmly stood,
   And shall from age to age endure.

*William Kethe*, [1560]
[*alt. Scotch Version*, 1650]

> **1.3:** *fear*  **2.1:** *The Lord, ye know,*
> **Ed:** Sedgwick originally attributed this text to
>    John Hopkins, 1562; Hopkins did publish a
>    paraphrase of Psalm 100 that year in the En-
>    glish metrical psalter, but his began, "In God
>    the Lord, be glad and light." The authorship
>    was corrected in the 3rd ed. (1868).

# 100c L.M.
*Psalm 100, Version III*

1 WITH one consent let all the earth
   To God their cheerful voices raise;

Glad homage pay with awful mirth,
And sing before Him songs of praise.

2 Convinc'd that He is God alone,
   From whom both we and all proceed;
   We, whom He chooses for His own,
   The flock that He vouchsafes to feed.

3 O enter then His temple gate,
   Thence to His courts devoutly press,
   And still your grateful hymns repeat,
   And still His name with praises bless.

4 For He's the Lord, supremely good;
   His mercy is forever sure;
   His truth, which always firmly stood,
   To endless ages shall endure.

*Tate and Brady*, [1698]

> **TD:** "Nothing can be more sublime this side of
>    heaven than the singing of this noble psalm
>    by a vast congregation. Watts' paraphrase,
>    beginning 'Before Jehovah's awful throne,'
>    and the Scotch 'All people that on earth do
>    dwell,' are both noble versions; and even Tate
>    and Brady rise beyond themselves when they
>    sing— 'With one consent let all the earth to
>    God their cheerful voices raise.' In this divine
>    lyric we sing with gladness the creating power
>    and goodness of the Lord, even as before with
>    trembling we adored His holiness" (Ps. 100;
>    vol. 4, p. 397).

# 100d L.M.
*Psalm 100, Version IV*

1 YE nations round the earth, rejoice
   Before the Lord, your Sovereign King;
   Serve Him with cheerful heart and voice;
   With all your tongues His glory sing.

2 The Lord is God, 'tis He alone
   Doth life and breath and being give;
   We are His work, and not our own,
   The sheep that on His pastures live.

3 Enter His gates with songs of joy,
   With praises to His courts repair,
   And make it your divine employ
   To pay your thanks and honours there.

4  The Lord is good, the Lord is kind;
   Great is His grace, His mercy sure;
   And the whole race of man shall find
   His truth from age to age endure.

*Isaac Watts*, 1719

# 101 C.M.
*Psalm 101*

1  LORD, when I lift my voice to Thee,
   To whom all praise belongs,
   Thy justice and Thy love shall be
   The subject of my songs.

2  Let wisdom o'er my heart preside,
   To lead my steps aright,
   And make Thy perfect law my guide,
   Thy service my delight.

3  All sinful ways I will abhor,
   All wicked men forsake,
   And only those who love Thy law
   For my companions take.

4  Lord, that I may not go astray,
   Thy constant grace impart,
   When wilt Thou come to point my way
   And fix my roving heart?

*William Hiley Bathurst*, 1831

# 102a C.M.
*Psalm 102, Part I*

1  HEAR me, O God, nor hide Thy face,
   But answer, lest I die:
   Hast Thou not built a throne of grace
   To hear when sinners cry?

2  My days are wasted, like the smoke
   Dissolving in the air;
   My strength is dried, my heart is broke
   And sinking in despair.

3  Sense can afford no real joy
   To souls that feel Thy frown;
   Lord, 'twas Thy hand advanc'd me high,
   Thy hand hath cast me down.

4  But Thou forever art the same,
   O my eternal God;
   Ages to come shall know Thy name
   And spread Thy works abroad.

5  Thou wilt arise and show Thy face,
   Nor will my Lord delay
   Beyond th' appointed hour of grace,
   That long-expected day.

*Isaac Watts*, 1719

# 102b C.M.
*Psalm 102, Part II*

1  THOU shalt arise, and mercy have
   Upon Thy Zion yet;
   The time to favour her is come,
   The time that Thou hast set.

2  For in her rubbish and her stones
   Thy servants pleasure take;
   Yea, they the very dust thereof
   Do favour for her sake.

3  So shall the heathen people fear
   The Lord's most holy name,
   And all the kings on earth shall dread
   Thy glory and Thy fame.

4  When Zion by the mighty Lord
   Built up again shall be,
   *Then shall her gracious God appear*
   *In glorious majesty.*

*Scotch Version*, [1650], *alt. C.H.S.*

   **4.3-4:** *In glory then, and majesty*
     *To men appear shall He.*
   **Ed:** Taken from the longer paraphrase,
     "O Lord, unto my prayer give ear."

# 103a S.M.
*Psalm 103, Version I*

1  MY soul, repeat His praise,
   Whose mercies are so great,
   Whose anger is so slow to rise,
   So ready to abate.

2 God will not always chide,
  And when His strokes are felt,
His strokes are fewer than our crimes
  And lighter than our guilt.

3 High as the heavens are rais'd
  Above the ground we tread,
So far the riches of His grace
  Our highest thoughts exceed.

4 His power subdues our sins,
  And His forgiving love,
Far as the east is from the west,
  Doth all our guilt remove.

5 The pity of the Lord
  To those that fear His name
Is such as tender parents feel;
  He knows our feeble frame.

6 He knows we are but dust,
  Scatter'd with every breath;
His anger, like a rising wind,
  Can send us swift to death.

7 Our days are as the grass,
  Or like the morning flower;
If one sharp blast sweep o'er the field,
  It withers in an hour.

8 But Thy compassions, Lord,
  To endless years endure;
And children's children ever find
  Thy words of promise sure.

*Isaac Watts*, 1719

# 103b   C.M.
*Psalm 103, Version II*

1 O BLESS the Lord, my soul;
  Let all within me join
And aid my tongue to bless His name,
  Whose favours are divine.

2 O bless the Lord, my soul,
  Nor let His mercies lie
Forgotten in unthankfulness,
  And without praises die.

3 'Tis He forgives thy sins;
  'Tis He relieves thy pain;
'Tis He that heals thy sicknesses
  And makes thee young again.

4 He crowns thy life with love,
  When ransom'd from the grave;
He that redeem'd my soul from hell
  Hath sovereign power to save.

5 He fills the poor with good;
  He gives the sufferers rest;
The Lord hath judgments for the proud
  And justice for the oppress'd.

6 His wondrous works and ways
  He made by Moses known,
But sent the world His truth and grace
  By His belovèd Son.

*Isaac Watts*, 1719

 **MM:** Hymns, Set 1 (Jan./Nov.), 13th Morn,
 GOLDEN HILL / BOYLE

# 103c   8.7.8.7.4.7
*Psalm 103, Version III*

1 PRAISE, my soul, the King of heaven;
  To His feet thy tribute bring!
Ransomed, healed, restored, forgiven,
  Who like me His praise should sing?
   Praise Him! Praise Him!
  Praise the everlasting King!

2 Praise Him for His grace and favour
  To our fathers in distress!
Praise Him still the same *as* ever,
  Slow to chide and swift to bless!
   Praise Him! Praise him,
  Glorious in His fathfulness!

3 Father-like He tends and spares us;
  Well our feeble frame He knows.
In His hands He gently bears us,
  Rescues us from all our foes.
   Praise Him! Praise Him,
  Widely as His mercy flows!

4 Frail as summer's flower we flourish;
   Blows the wind, and it is gone.
But while mortals rise and perish,
   God endures unchanging on.
     Praise Him! Praise Him!
   Praise the High Eternal One!

5 Angels, help us to adore Him;
   Ye behold Him face to face;
Sun and moon, bow down before Him,
   Dwellers all in time and space.
     Praise Him! Praise Him!
   Praise with us the God of grace!

*Henry Francis Lyte*, 1834 [*rev.* 1864]

> **2.3:** *for* (1834-1841 eds.)
> **EE:** Hymns, Set 1 (Jan./Nov.), 20th Eve,
> VESPER / ROUSSEAU

# 104 10.10.11.11.
*Psalm 104*

1 O WORSHIP the King,
   All glorious above;
O gratefully sing
   His power and His love—
Our Shield and Defender,
   The Ancient of Days,
Pavilion'd in splendour
   And girded with praise.

2 O tell of His might,
   O sing of His grace,
Whose robe is the light,
   Whose canopy space,
*Whose* chariots of wrath
   *The* deep thunder-clouds form,
And dark is His path
   On the wings of the storm.

3 The earth with its store
   Of wonders untold,
Almighty! Thy power
   Hath founded of old,
Hath *stablish'd* it fast
   By a changeless decree,
And round it hath cast
   Like a mantle, the sea.

4 Thy bountiful care
   What tongue can recite?
It breathes in the air,
   It shines in the light:
*It* streams from the hills,
   It descends to the plain,
And sweetly distills
   In the dew and the rain.

5 Frail children of dust,
   And feeble as frail,
In Thee do we trust,
   Nor find Thee to fail;
Thy mercies how tender!
   How firm to the end!
Our Maker, Defender,
   Redeemer, and Friend!

6 O measureless might!
   Ineffable love!
While angels delight
   To hymn Thee above,
The humbler creation,
   Though feeble their lays,
With true adoration
   Shall lisp to Thy praise!

*Sir Robert Grant*, 1839 [*alt.*]

> **Ed:** This hymn appeared first in Edward Bick-
> ersteth's *Christian Psalmody* (1833), in 6
> groups of 4 full lines, with *His* (2.5), *The* (2.6),
> *establish'd* (3.5), and *It* (4.5). The hymn then
> appeared in H.V. Elliott's *Psalms and Hymns*
> (1835), in 3 groups of 8 full lines, with *His*,
> *The*, *stablish'd*, and *In*. Julian's *Dictionary of
> Hymnology* claimed, "From the preface to El-
> liott's *Psalms & Hymns* we find that the text
> in Bickersteth was not authorized" (p. 855),
> but no known ed. of Elliott's book included a
> preface. The hymn also appeared in a posthu-
> mous edition of Grant's work, *Sacred Poems*
> (1839), offering "a more correct and authentic
> version," in 6 groups of 8 short lines, with *His*,
> *stablish'd*, and *It*, minus *The*. Spurgeon's text
> mirrors the 1839 ed. with the exception of *His*.
> For this edition, we have re-inserted *The* at 2.6
> because it appears in the earliest sources and
> it is required of the metre.

# 105 C.M.
### *Psalm 105*

1 O RENDER thanks and bless the Lord;
   Invoke His sacred name;
Acquaint the nations with His deeds;
   His matchless deeds proclaim.

2 Sing to His praise, in lofty hymns
   His wondrous works rehearse;
Make them the theme of your discourse
   And subject of your verse.

3 Rejoice in His almighty name,
   Alone to be ador'd;
And let their hearts o'erflow with joy
   That humbly seek the Lord.

4 Seek ye the Lord, His saving strength
   Devoutly still implore;
And where He's ever present, seek
   His face forever more.

*Tate and Brady*, 1696 [*rev.* 1698]


# 106a L.M.
### *Psalm 106, Part I*

1 O RENDER thanks to God above,
   The fountain of eternal love,
   Whose mercy firm through ages past
   Has stood, and shall forever last.

2 Who can His mighty deeds express,
   Not only vast but numberless?
   What mortal eloquence can raise
   His tribute of immortal praise?

3 Extend to me that favour, Lord,
   Thou to Thy chosen dost afford;
   When Thou return'st to set them free,
   Let Thy salvation visit me.

4 O may I worthy prove to see
   Thy saints in full prosperity!
   That I the joyful choir may join
   And count Thy people's triumph mine.

*Tate and Brady*, 1696 [*rev.* 1698]


# 106b S.M.
### *Psalm 106, Part II*

1 GOD of eternal love,
   How fickle are our ways!
And yet how oft did Israel prove
   Thy constancy of grace!

2 They saw Thy wonders wrought,
   And then Thy praise they sung,
But soon Thy works of power forgot,
   And murmur'd with their tongue.

3 Now they believe His word,
   While rocks with rivers flow;
Now with their lusts provoke the Lord,
   And He reduced them low.

4 Yet when they mourn'd their faults,
   He harkenen'd to their groans,
Brought His own covenant to His thoughts,
   And call'd them still His sons.

5 Their names were in His book;
   He saved them from their foes;
Oft He chastised, but ne'er forsook
   The people that He chose.

6 Let Israel bless the Lord,
   Who loved their ancient race;
And Christians join the solemn word,
   Amen, to all the praise.

*Isaac Watts*, 1719

> **TD:** "They tested Him again and again, through-
> out forty years, though each time his work
> was conclusive evidence of his faithfulness.
> Nothing could convince them for long" (Ps.
> 95:9; vol. 4, p. 321).


# 107a 7.7.7.7.
### *Psalm 107, Song I*

1 O GIVE thanks unto the Lord;
   Praise His name with one accord;
   Tell the wonders of His pow'r;
   Praise His goodness ev'ry hour.

2 Let His ransom'd church begin,
   Whom He hath redeem'd from sin,

Gather'd from the east and west,
North and south, to enter rest.

3 Through the wilderness they stray,
In a solitary way;
Hungry, thirsty, tried, and faint,
God attends to their complaint.

4 Led by Him from day to day,
Right, although mysterious, way,
To His city they *shall* come,
Habitation, rest, and home.

5 O that men would praise the Lord,
While His goodness they record;
All His wondrous works rehearse,
Who redeem'd them from the curse.

*Joseph Irons*, 1847 [*alt. C.H.S.*]

> **4.3:** *all*   **Ed:** This change was made by Spurgeon, likely for theological reasons related to his convictions on election.

# 107b C.M.
*Psalm 107, Song II*

1 HOW are Thy servants blest, O Lord!
How sure is their defence!
Eternal wisdom is their guide,
Their help Omnipotence.

2 In foreign realms and lands remote,
Supported by Thy care,
Through burning climes *they pass* unhurt
And *breathe* in tainted air.

3 *When by the dreadful tempest borne*
High on the broken wave,
*They know Thou art* not slow to hear,
Nor impotent to save.

4 The storm *is* laid, the winds *retire*,
Obedient to Thy will;
The sea that *roars* at Thy command,
At Thy command *is* still.

5 In midst of dangers, fears, and *deaths*,
Thy goodness *we* adore;
*We* praise Thee for Thy mercies past
And humbly hope for more.

6 *Our life, while Thou preservest life,*
*A* sacrifice shall be;
And death, *when death shall be our lot,*
Shall join *our souls* to Thee.

*Joseph Addison*, 1712
[*alt.* John Rippon, 1787]

> **2.2:** *I pass'd*   **2.3:** *breath'd*
> **3.1:** *For tho' in dreadful whirles we hung*
> **3.3:** *I knew Thou wert*   **4.1:** *was / retir'd*
> **4.3:** *roar'd*   **4.4:** *was*   **5.1:** *death*   **5.2:** *I'll*
> **5.3:** *And*   **6.1:** *My life, if Thou preserv'st my life,*
> **6.2:** *Thy*   **6.3:** *if death must be my doom,*
> **6.4:** *my soul*

# 108 C.M.
*Psalm 108*

1 O GOD, my heart is fully bent
To magnify Thy name;
My tongue with cheerful songs of praise
Shall celebrate Thy fame.

2 To all the list'ning tribes, O Lord,
Thy wonders I will tell,
And to those nations sing Thy praise
That round about us dwell,

3 Because Thy mercy's boundless height
The highest heav'n transcends,
And far beyond th' aspiring clouds
Thy faithful truth extends.

4 Be Thou, O God, exalted high
Above the starry frame,
And let the world, with one consent,
Confess Thy glorious name.

*Tate and Brady*, 1696 [*rev.* 1698]

> **EE:** Hymns, Set 1 (Jan./Nov.), 17th Eve,
> ARLINGTON / LONDON

# 109 L.M.
*Psalm 109*

1 STRANGER and pilgrim here below,
I turn for refuge, Lord, to Thee.
Thou know'st my every want and woe;
O smite my foes and rescue me!

2  Thy name is love; for that name's sake
   Sustain and cheer my sinking soul.
   *Low as I am*, and poor, and weak,
   *One word of Thine can* make me whole.

3  Help, Lord! let all my foes perceive
   'Tis Thine to comfort or condemn.
   With Thee to bless me and relieve,
   I little heed reproach from them.

4  Arise then, on my soul arise!
   Thy sheltering wings around me cast!
   And all that now afflicts or tries
   Shall work my peace, O Lord, at last.

*Henry Francis Lyte*, 1834

> **2.3:** *Thou seest me low*
> **2.4:** *O speak the word, and*
> **Ed:** Lyte revised this text in 1836, but the original text continued to be reprinted, as above. Footnotes indicate Lyte's revisions.

# 110  7.7.7.7. Double
*Psalm 110*

1  JESUS, Lord, to Thee we sing,
   Thee our Saviour, Priest, and King,
   Who our guilt and woes sustain'd,
   And the cup of vengeance drain'd;
   Now Thou sitt'st enthroned on high,
   Crown'd with power and victory;
   All Thy foes shall prostrate fall,
   Ev'ry nation hear Thy call.

2  As at morning's youthful hour,
   Dewdrops gem each leaf and flower,
   So, O Lord, our sons unborn
   Shall Thy crowded courts adorn,
   Gladly own Thee for their King,
   Gladly free-will off'rings bring,
   Till Thy spreading empire prove
   Boundless as Thy wondrous love.

*Harriet Auber*, 1829

# 111  8.7.8.7.
*Psalm 111*

1  PRAISE the Lord; with exultation
   My whole heart my Lord shall praise;
   'Midst the upright congregation,
   Loftiest hallelujahs raise.

2  All His works are great and glorious;
   Saints review them with delight;
   His redemption all victorious
   We remember day and night.

3  Meat He gives to those who fear Him,
   Of His covenant mindful still;
   Wise are those who much revere Him
   And rejoice to do His will.

4  For His grace stands fast forever;
   His decrees the saints secure;
   From His oath He turneth never;
   Every promise standeth sure.

5  Therefore be His praise unceasing,
   Be His name forever blest;
   And with confidence increasing,
   Let us on His promise rest.

*Charles H. Spurgon*, 1866

# 112  8.7.8.7.4.7.
*Psalm 112*

1  BLESSED is the man that feareth
   And delighteth in the Lord;
   Wealth, the wealth which truly cheereth,
   God shall give Him for reward,
   And his children
   Shall be blest around his board.

2  He shall not be moved forever,
   Though with evil tidings tried;
   Nought from God his faith shall sever,
   Fix'd his heart shall still abide;
   For believers
   Are secured on every side.

3  To the upright light arises,
   Darkness soon gives place to day,
   While the man who truth despises
   And refuses to obey,
   In a moment,
   Cursed of God, shall melt away.

4 Therefore let us praise Jehovah,
　　Sound His glorious name on high,
　Sing His praises, and moreover
　　By our actions magnify
　　　Our Redeemer,
　　Who by blood has brought us nigh.

*Charles H. Spurgeon*, 1866

# 113 7.7.7.7.
*Psalm 113*

1 HALLELUJAH! Raise, oh raise
　To our God the song of praise;
　All His servants join to sing
　God our Saviour and our King.

2 Blessèd be forever more
　That dread name which we adore!
　Round the world His praise be sung,
　Through all lands, in every tongue.

3 O'er all nations God alone,
　Higher than the heavens His throne;
　Who is like to God most high,
　Infinite in majesty?

4 Yet to view the heavens He bends;
　Yea, to earth He condescends,
　Passing by the rich and great,
　For the low and desolate.

5 He can raise the poor to stand
　With the princes of the land;
　Wealth upon the needy shower;
　Set the meanest high in power.

6 He the broken spirit cheers,
　Turns to joy the mourner's tears;
　Such the wonders of His ways!
　Praise His name—forever praise.

*Josiah Conder*, [1836]

# 114 C.M.
*Psalm 114*

1 WHEN forth from Egypt's trembling strand
　　The tribes of Israel sped,
　And Jacob in the stranger's land
　　Departing banners spread;

2 Then One amidst their thick array
　　His kingly dwelling made,
　Who all along the desert way
　　Their guiding sceptre sway'd.

3 The sea beheld, and *struck* with dread,
　　Roll'd all its billows back,
　And Jordan, through his deepest bed,
　　Reveal'd their destined track.

4 What ail'd thee, O thou mighty *sea?*
　　*Why* roll'd thy waves in dread?
　What bade thy tide, O Jordan, flee,
　　And bare its deepest bed?

5 O earth, before the Lord, the God
　　Of Jacob, tremble still,
　Who makes the waste a water'd sod,
　　The flint a gushing rill.

*George Burgess*, [1840, *rev.* 1864, *alt.*]

**3.1:** *smit* **4.1-2:** *sea, and*
**Ed:** The variant at 3.1 appeared as early as 1845
　in *Psalms and Hymns for Christian Use and*
　*Worship*; 4.1-2 is by Spurgeon.
**TD:** "It was no slight miracle to divide a pathway
　through such a sea, and to make it fit for the
　traffic of a whole nation. He who did this can
　do anything, and must be God, the worthy
　object of adoration" (Ps. 66:6; vol. 3, p. 184).

# 115 6.6.8.6.8.8.
*Psalm 115*

1 ALL glory be to Thee,
　　Who dwellest high in heaven;
　Not to a feeble child of clay
　　Be praise or worship given;
　Thy hand the mightiest can o'erthrow,
　And dash their every idol low.

2 All glory, Lord, be Thine,
　　Our fortress and our shield;
　Whose arm upholds Thine Israel
　　And strengthens for the field;
　In Thee Thy faithful people trust,
　And lay the proudest in the dust.

3 Blest by Thy favour, Lord,
　　No foe can work us ill;

Supported by Thy gracious Word,
  We feel Thee present still;
And e'en in death and in the grave
  Shall own Thy power to help and save.

*Robert Allan Scott*, 1839

# 116a C.M.
*Psalm 116, Song I*

1 I LOVE the Lord; He heard my cries
    And pitied every groan;
  Long as I live, when troubles rise,
    I'll hasten to His throne.

2 I love the Lord; He bow'd His ear
    And chased my griefs away;
  O let my heart no more despair,
    While I have breath to pray!

3 My flesh declin'd, my spirits fell,
    And I drew near the dead,
  While inward pangs and fears of hell
    Perplex'd my wakeful head.

4 "My God," I cried, "Thy servant save,
    Thou ever good and just;
  Thy power can rescue from the grave;
    Thy power is all my trust."

5 The Lord beheld me sore distress'd,
    He bid my pains remove;
  Return, my soul, to God thy rest,
    For thou hast known His love.

6 My God hath sav'd my soul from death
    And dried my falling tears;
  Now to His praise I'll spend my breath
    And my remaining years.

*Isaac Watts*, 1719

# 116b C.M.
*Psalm 116, Song II*

1 WHAT shall I render to my God
    For all His kindness shown?
  My feet shall visit Thine abode,
    My songs address Thy throne.

2 Among the saints that fill Thine house,
    My offerings shall be paid;
  There shall my zeal perform the vows
    My soul in anguish made.

3 How much is mercy Thy delight,
    Thou ever-blessèd God!
  How dear Thy servants in Thy sight!
    How precious is their blood!

4 How happy all Thy servants are!
    How great Thy grace to me!
  My life, which Thou hast made Thy care,
    Lord, I devote to Thee.

5 Now I am Thine, forever Thine,
    Nor shall my purpose move;
  Thy hand hath loos'd my bands of pain
    And bound me with Thy love.

6 Here in Thy courts I leave my vow,
    And Thy rich grace record;
  Witness, ye saints, who hear me now,
    If I forsake the Lord.

*Isaac Watts*, 1719

**MM:** Hymns, 7th Lord's Day,
  MARLOW / CAMBRIDGE

# 116c L.M.
*Psalm 116, Song III*

1 REDEEM'D from guilt, redeem'd from fears,
  My soul enlarged, and dried my tears,
  What can I do, O love divine,
  What, to repay such gifts as Thine?

2 What can I do, so poor, so weak,
  But from Thy hands new blessings seek?
  A heart to feel my mercies more,
  A soul to know Thee and adore?

3 O teach me at Thy feet to fall,
  And yield Thee up myself, my all;
  Before Thy saints my debt to own,
  And live and die to Thee alone!

4 Thy Spirit, Lord, at large impart;
  Expand, and raise, and fill my heart;

So may I hope my life shall be
Some faint return, O Lord, to Thee.

*Henry Francis Lyte*, 1834

# 117a 7.7.7.7.
*Psalm 117, Song I*

1 ALL ye *nations*, praise the Lord;
   All ye lands, your voices raise;
Heaven and earth with loud accord,
   Praise the Lord, forever praise.

2 For His truth and mercy stand,
   Past, and present, and to be,
Like the years of His right hand,
   Like His own eternity.

3 Praise Him, ye who know His love;
   Praise Him from the depths beneath;
Praise Him in the heights above;
   Praise your Maker, all that breathe.

*James Montgomery*, 1822 [*alt.*]

   **1.1:** *Gentiles*   **Ed:** A common alteration, ap-
   pearing as early as 1826 in *Hymns for Public
   Worship, Selected for the Use of … Octagon
   Chapel, Norwich.*

# 117b L.M.
*Psalm 117, Song II*

1 FROM all that dwell below the skies
Let the Creator's praise arise;
Let the Redeemer's name be sung
Through every land, by every tongue.

2 Eternal are Thy mercies, Lord;
Eternal truth attends Thy Word;
Thy praise shall sound from shore to shore
Till suns shall rise and set no more.

*Isaac Watts*, 1719

# 117c S.M.
*Psalm 117, Song III*

1    THY name, Almighty Lord,
      Shall sound through distant lands;
Great is Thy grace, and sure Thy Word;
      Thy truth forever stands.

2    Far be Thine honour spread,
      And long Thy praise endure,
Till morning light and evening shade
      Shall be exchang'd no more.

*Isaac Watts*, 1719

# 118a 7.7.7.7.
*Psalm 118, Song I*

1 TO Jehovah hymn the lay,
   "Ever shall His love endure."
O let grateful Israel say,
   "Stands His love forever sure."

2 O let Aaron's house reply,
   "Evermore His love shall last."
All who fear Him, shout and cry,
   "Stands His love forever fast."

3 On the ever-living name,
   In distress on JAH I cried;
JAH to my deliverance came,
   And my prison open'd wide.

4 See Jehovah near me stand!
   What from mortals shall I dread?
See Jehovah lift the hand!
   Victor on my foes I tread.

5 Hark! the voice of joy and song
   Echoes from the faithful seed;
By His right hand firm and strong
   He hath done a mighty deed.

6 High Jehovah's hand is rais'd
   By the conquest He hath won.
Be Jehovah's right hand prais'd!
   He a mighty deed hath done.

*Richard Mant*, 1824

# 118b C.M.
*Psalm 118, Song II*

1 BEHOLD the sure foundation stone
   Which God in Zion lays
To build our heavenly hopes upon
   And His eternal praise.

2 Chosen of God, to sinners dear,
　　And saints adore the name;
　They trust their whole salvation here,
　　Nor shall they suffer shame.

3 The foolish builders, scribe and priest,
　　Reject it with disdain;
　Yet on this Rock the church shall rest,
　　And envy rage in vain.

4 What though the gates of hell withstood,
　　Yet must this building rise;
　'Tis *Thine* own work, Almighty God,
　　And wondrous in our eyes.

*Isaac Watts*, 1719 [*alt.*]

**4.3:** *Thy* **Ed:** This minor alteration was common in 19th century hymn books.

# 118c 7.7.7.7.
*Psalm 118, Song III*

1 THEE, Jehovah, will I bless;
　　Thou didst my request allow;
　Thee my Saviour I confess,
　　Author of my health art Thou.

2 Lo, the stone, which once aside
　　By the builders' hands was thrown,
　See it now the building's pride,
　　See it now the cornerstone!

3 Lo, we hail Jehovah's deed,
　　Strange and wondrous in our eyes!
　Lo, the day our God hath made!
　　Bid the voice of gladness rise.

4 Save, Hosanna! Lord, I pray!
　　Save, Hosanna, God of might!
　Lord, for us Thy pow'r display;
　　Lord, on us Thy favour light!

5 He, Jehovah, is our Lord;
　　He, our God, on us hath shined;
　Bind the sacrifice with cord,
　　To the hornèd altar bind.

6 Thee I bless, my God and King!
　　Thee, my God and King, I hail!

Hallelujah, shout and sing!
　Never shall His goodness fail.

*Richard Mant*, 1824

**Ed:** This paraphrase is a continuation of 118a.
**TD:** "'Bind the sacrifice with the cord, to the hornèd altar bind.' The word rendered 'cords' carries with it the idea of wreaths and boughs, so that it was not a cord of hard, rough rope, but a decorated band; even as in our case, though we are bound to the altar of God, it is with the cords of love and the bands of a man, and not by a compulsion which destroys the freedom of the will. . . . We bring ourselves to His altar, and desire to offer Him all that we have and are" (Ps. 118:27; vol. 5, p. 334).

# 119a C.M.
*Psalm 119, Song I*

1 O HOW I love Thy holy law!
　　'Tis daily my delight;
　And thence my meditations draw
　　Divine advice by night.

2 How doth Thy Word my heart engage!
　　How well employ my tongue!
　And in my tiresome pilgrimage
　　Yields me a heavenly song.

3 Am I a stranger, or at home,
　　'Tis my perpetual feast;
　Not honey dropping from the comb
　　So much allures the taste.

4 No treasures so enrich the mind,
　　Nor shall Thy Word be sold
　For loads of silver well-refin'd,
　　Nor heaps of choicest gold.

5 When nature sinks, and spirits droop,
　　Thy promises of grace
　Are pillars to support my hope,
　　And there I write Thy praise.

*Isaac Watts*, 1719

**EE:** Hymns, Set 1 (Jan./Nov.), 8th Eve, ABRIDGE / ANN'S

# 119b C.M.
*Psalm 119, Song II*

1 O THAT the Lord would guide my ways
   To keep His statutes still!
O that my God would grant me grace
   To know and do His will!

2 O send Thy Spirit down to write
   Thy law upon my heart!
Nor let my tongue indulge deceit,
   Nor act the liar's part.

3 From vanity turn off my eyes;
   Let no corrupt design
Nor covetous desires arise
   Within this soul of mine.

4 Order my footsteps by Thy Word
   And make my heart sincere;
Let sin have no dominion, Lord,
   But keep my conscience clear.

5 My soul hath gone too far astray,
   My feet too often slip;
Yet since I've not forgot Thy way,
   Restore Thy wand'ring sheep.

6 Make me to walk in Thy commands;
   'Tis a delightful road;
Nor let my head, or heart, or hands
   Offend against my God.

*Isaac Watts*, 1719

> **EE:** "The man who is cheerful in his service of
> God, proves that obedience is his element; he
> can sing, 'Make me to walk in Thy commands,
> 'tis a delightful road.' Reader, let us put this
> question—Do you serve the Lord with glad-
> ness? Let us show to the people of the world,
> who think our religion to be slavery, that it is
> to us a delight and a joy! Let our gladness pro-
> claim that we serve a good Master" (Jan. 9).

# 119c C.M.
*Psalm 119, Song III*

1 MY soul lies cleaving to the dust;
   Lord, give me life divine;
From vain desires and every lust
   Turn off these eyes of mine.

2 I need the influence of Thy grace
   To speed me in Thy way,
Lest I should loiter in my race
   Or turn my feet astray.

3 When sore afflictions press me down,
   I need Thy quickening powers;
Thy Word that I have rested on
   Shall help my heaviest hours.

4 Are not Thy mercies sovereign still,
   And Thou a faithful God?
Wilt Thou not grant me warmer zeal
   To run the heavenly road?

5 Does not my heart Thy precepts love
   And long to see Thy face?
And yet how slow my spirits move
   Without enlivening grace!

6 Then shall I love Thy gospel more
   And ne'er forget Thy Word,
When I have felt its quickening power
   To draw me near the Lord.

*Isaac Watts*, 1719

# 119d S.M.
*Psalm 119, Song IV*

1 MY soul lies grov'ling low,
   Still cleaving to the dust;
Thy quick'ning grace, O Lord, bestow,
   For in Thy Word I trust.

2 Make me to understand
   Thy precepts and Thy will;
Thy wondrous works on ev'ry hand
   I'll sing and talk of still.

3 My soul, oppress'd with grief,
   In heaviness melts down;
O strengthen me and send relief,
   And thou shalt wear the crown.

4 Remove from me the voice
   Of falsehood and deceit;
The way of truth is now my choice;
   Thy Word to me is sweet.

5 Thy testimony stands
    And never can depart;
  I'll run the way of Thy commands
    If Thou enlarge my heart.

*Joseph Irons*, 1847

## 119e C.M.
*Psalm 119, Song V*

1 CONSIDER all my sorrows, Lord,
    And Thy deliverance send;
  My soul for Thy salvation faints;
    When will my troubles end?

2 Yet I have found 'tis good for me
    To bear my Father's rod;
  Afflictions make me learn Thy law
    And live upon my God.

3 This is the comfort I enjoy
    When new distress begins;
  I read Thy Word, I run Thy way,
    And hate my former sins.

4 Had not Thy Word been my delight
    When earthly joys were fled,
  My soul, oppress'd with sorrow's weight,
    Had sunk amongst the dead.

5 I know Thy judgments, Lord, are right,
    Though they may seem severe;
  The sharpest sufferings I endure
    Flow from Thy faithful care.

6 Before I knew Thy chastening rod
    My feet were apt to stray;
  But now I learn to keep Thy Word,
    Nor wander from Thy way.

*Isaac Watts*, 1719

## 119f C.M.
*Psalm 119, Song VI*

1 O THAT Thy statutes every hour
    Might dwell upon my mind!
  Thence I derive a quickening power,
    And daily peace I find.

2 To meditate Thy precepts, Lord,
    Shall be my sweet employ;
  My soul shall ne'er forget Thy Word;
    Thy Word is all my joy.

3 How would I run in Thy commands,
    If Thou my heart discharge
  From sin and Satan's hateful chains,
    And set my feet at large!

4 My lips with courage shall declare
    Thy statutes and Thy name;
  I'll speak Thy Word, tho' kings should hear,
    Nor yield to sinful shame.

*Isaac Watts*, 1719

## 119g L.M.
*Psalm 119, Song VI*

1 FATHER, I bless Thy gentle hand;
  How kind was Thy chastising rod
  That forced my conscience to a stand
  And brought my wand'ring soul to God!

2 Foolish and vain, I went astray
  Ere I had felt Thy scourges, Lord;
  I left my guide and lost my way,
  But now I love and keep Thy Word.

3 'Tis good for me to wear the yoke,
  For pride is apt to rise and swell;
  'Tis good to bear my Father's stroke
  That I might learn His statutes well.

4 Thy hands have made my mortal frame,
  Thy Spirit form'd my soul within;
  Teach me to know Thy wondrous name
  And guard me safe from death and sin.

5 Then all that love and fear the Lord,
  At my salvation shall rejoice;
  For I have hopèd in Thy Word
  And made Thy grace my only choice.

*Isaac Watts*, 1719

# 120 C.M.
*Psalm 120*

1 WOE'S me that I in Mesech am
    A sojourner so long,
That I in tabernacles dwell
    To Kedar that belong.

2 My soul with him that hateth peace
    Hath long a dweller been;
I am for peace, but when I speak,
    For battle they are keen.

3 My soul distracted mourns and pines
    To reach that peaceful shore,
Where all the weary are at rest
    And troublers vex no more.

4 Fierce burning coals of juniper
    And arrows of the strong
Await those false and cruel tongues
    Which do the righteous wrong.

5 But as for me my song shall rise
    Before Jehovah's throne,
For He has seen my deep distress
    And harken'd to my groan.

1-2 *Scotch Version*, [1650]
3-5 *Charles H. Spurgeon*, 1866

> **Ed:** Sts. 1-2 are from the longer paraphrase,
> "In my distress to God I cried."
> **TD:** "Our poet [the Psalmist] felt himself to be
> as ill-at-ease among lying neighbors as if he
> had lived among savages and cannibals. . . .
> He cries, 'Woe is me!' . . . He had some hope
> from the fact that he was only a sojourner
> in Mesech; but as years rolled on, the time
> dragged heavily, and he feared that he might
> call himself a dweller in Kedar. The wander-
> ing tribes to whom he refers were constantly
> at war with one another, . . . with their hand
> against every man and every man's hand
> against them" (Ps. 120:5; vol. 6, p. 406).

# 121 C.M.
*Psalm 121*

1 TO heav'n I lift my waiting eyes;
    There all my hopes are laid;

The Lord that built the earth and skies
    Is my perpetual aid.

2 Their feet shall never slide to fall,
    Whom He designs to keep;
His ear attends the softest call;
    His eyes can never sleep.

3 He will sustain our weakest powers
    With His almighty arm,
And watch our most unguarded hours
    Against surprising harm.

4 Israel, rejoice, and rest secure;
    Thy keeper is the Lord;
His wakeful eyes employ His power
    For thine eternal guard.

5 Nor scorching sun nor sickly moon
    Shall have his leave to smite;
He shields thy head from burning noon,
    From blasting damps at night.

6 He guards thy soul, He keps thy breath,
    Where thickest dangers come;
Go and return, secure from death,
    Till God commands thee home.

*Isaac Watts*, 1719

# 122a C.M.
*Psalm 122, Song I*

1 HOW did my heart rejoice to hear
    My friends devoutly say,
"In Zion let us all appear
    And keep the solemn day!"

2 I love her gates, I love the road;
    The church adorn'd with grace
Stands like a palace built for God
    To show His milder face.

3 Up to her courts with joys unknown
    The holy tribes repair;
The Son of David holds His throne
    And sits in judgment there.

4 He hears our praises and complaints,
    And while His awful voice

Divides the sinners from the saints,
 We tremble and rejoice.

5 Peace be within this sacred place
 And joy a constant guest!
With holy gifts and heavenly grace
 Be her attendants blest!

6 My soul shall pray for Zion still
 While life or breath remains;
There my best friends, my kindred dwell;
 There God my Saviour reigns.

*Isaac Watts*, 1719

 **MM:** Hymns, 19th Lord's Day,
 CORONATION / BROWN
 **TD:** "Our own dwellings are very dear to us, but
 we must not prefer them to the assemblies of
 the saints; we must say of the church— 'Here
 my best friends, my kindred dwell; here God
 my Saviour reigns" (Ps. 87:2; vol. 4, p. 115).

# 122b C.M.
*Psalm 122, Song II*

1 PRAY that Jerusalem may have
 Peace and felicity;
Let them that love thee and thy peace
 Have still prosperity.

2 Therefore, I wish that peace may still
 Within thy walls remain,
And ever may thy palaces
 Prosperity retain.

3 Now for my friends' and brethren's sakes,
 Peace be in thee, I'll say;
And for the house of God, our Lord,
 I'll seek thy good alway.

*Scotch Version*, [1650]

 **Ed:** Taken from the longer paraphrase,
 "Joyed, when to the house of God."

# 123 7.7.7.7.
*Psalm 123*

1 UNTO Thee I lift my eyes,
Thou that dwellest in the skies;

At Thy throne I meekly bow;
Thou canst save, and only Thou.

2 As a servant marks his Lord,
As a maid her mistress' word,
So I watch and wait on Thee,
Till Thy mercy visit me.

3 Let Thy face upon me shine;
Tell me, Lord, that Thou art mine;
Poor and little though I be,
I have all in having Thee.

4 Here to be despised, forgot,
Is Thy children's common lot;
But with Thee to make it up,
Lord, I ask no better cup.

*Henry Francis Lyte*, 1834

# 124 L.M.
*Psalm 124*

1 HAD not the Lord, my soul may cry,
Had not the Lord been on my side;
Had He not brought deliv'rance nigh,
Then must my helpless soul have died.

2 Had not the Lord been on my side,
My soul had been by Satan slain;
And Tophet, op'ning large and wide,
Would not have gaped for me in vain.

3 *Lo*, floods of wrath and floods of hell,
In *fierce* impetuous *torrents* roll;
Had not the Lord defended well,
The waters had o'erwhelm'd my soul.

4 As when the fowler's snare is broke,
The bird escapes on cheerful wings;
My soul, set free from Satan's yoke,
With joy bursts forth,
  and *mounts*, and sings!

5 She sings the Lord her Saviour's praise,
Sings forth His praise with joy and mirth;
*To* Him her song in heaven she'll raise,
*To* Him that made both heav'n and earth!

*John Ryland*, [1771, *alt. C.H.S.*]

 **3.1:** *When* **3.2:** *an / stream did* **4.4:** *flees*
 **5.3-4:** *My help is in the name, she says, / Of*

# 125a C.M.
*Psalm 125, Song I*

1 UNSHAKEN as the sacred hill
    And firm as mountains be,
Firm as a rock the soul shall rest
    That leans, O Lord, on Thee.

2 Not walls nor hills could guard so well
    Old Salem's happy ground,
As those eternal arms of love
    That every saint surround.

3 Deal gently, Lord, with souls sincere,
    And lead them safely on
To the bright gates of Paradise,
    Where Christ their Lord is gone.

4 But if we trace those crooked ways
    That the old serpent drew,
The wrath that drove him first to hell
    Shall smite his followers too.

*Isaac Watts*, [1707, *rev.* 1719]

# 125b S.M.
*Psalm 125, Song II*

1 WHO in the Lord confide,
    And feel His sprinkled blood,
In storms and hurricanes abide
    Firm as the mount of God.

2 Steadfast and fixed and sure,
    His Zion cannot move;
His faithful people stand secure
    In Jesus' guardian love.

3 As round Jerusalem
    The hilly bulwarks rise,
So God protects and covers them
    From all their enemies.

4 On every side He stands,
    And for His Israel cares,
And safe in His almighty hands
    Their souls forever bears.

5 But let them still abide
    In Thee, all-gracious Lord,

Till ev'ry soul is sanctified
    And perfectly restor'd.

6 The men of heart sincere
    Continue to defend,
And do them good, and save them here,
    And love them to the end.

*Charles Wesley*, [1743]

# 126 C.M.
*Psalm 126*

1 WHEN God reveal'd His gracious name
    And chang'd my mournful state,
My rapture seem'd a pleasing dream,
    The grace appear'd so great.

2 The world beheld the glorious change,
    And did Thy hand confess;
My tongue broke out in unknown strains
    And sung surprising grace.

3 "Great is the work," my neighbors cried,
    And own'd the power divine;
"Great is the work," my heart replied,
    "And be the glory Thine."

4 The Lord can clear the darkest skies,
    Can give us day for night,
Make drops of sacred sorrow rise
    To rivers of delight.

5 Let *them* that sow in sadness wait
    Till the fair harvest come;
They shall confess their sheaves are great
    And shout the blessings home.

6 Though seed lie buried long in dust,
    It shan't deceive their hope;
The precious grain can ne'er be lost,
    For grace insures the crop.

*Isaac Watts*, 1719 [*alt. C.H.S.*]

**5.1:** *those* **TD:** "Ah me, what captives we have
been! . . . From multiplied troubles, from depression of spirit, from miserable backsliding,
from grievous doubt, we have been eman-
cipated, and we are not able to describe the
bliss which followed each emancipation"
(Ps. 126:1; vol 7, p. 13).

# 127 8.7.8.7.
*Psalm 127*

1 VAINLY through *the night the ranger*
*Keeps his* watch lest foes alarm;
*Still the city lies in danger*
But for God's protecting arm.

2 Vain were all our toil and labour
Did not God that labour bless;
Vain without His grace and favour,
Every talent we possess.

3 Vainer still the hope of heaven
That on human strength relies;
But to him shall help be given
Who in humble faith applies.

4 Seek we then the Lord's Anointed;
He shall grant us peace and rest;
Ne'er was suppliant disappointed
Who through Christ his prayer address'd.

*Harriett Auber*, 1829, *alt. C.H.S.*

**1.1:** *night's weary hours,*   **1.2:** *Keep we*
**1.3:** *Vain our bulwarks and our towers,*

# 128 L.M.
*Psalm 128*

1 HOW blest the man who fears the Lord,
Who walks by His unerring Word;
His labours find a full increase;
His days are crown'd with health and peace.

2 Domestic comfort builds her nest,
Beneath his roof, within his breast;
And earth's best blessings hourly rise
To cheer his pathway to the skies.

3 But earth's best gifts are poor to those
The Spirit on his soul bestows;
The earnest here of joys above,
The foretaste of eternal love.

4 Onward he goes, from strength to strength,
Till heaven's bright morning breaks at length
And calls him to his full reward—
How blest the man who fears the Lord!

*Henry Francis Lyte*, 1834

# 129 7.6.7.6. Double
*Psalm 129*

1 MANY times since days of youth,
May Israel truly say,
Foes devoid of love and truth
Afflict me day by day;
Yet they never can prevail;
God defends His people still;
Jesus' power can never fail
To save from all that's ill.

2 God hath Zion set apart
For His abiding place;
Sons of wrath and guileful art
He'll banish from His face;
God for Israel doth fight;
Israel, on thy God depend;
Christ shall keep thee day and night,
Till all thy troubles end.

*John Beaumont*, 1834

# 130 C.M.
*Psalm 130*

1 OUT of the depths of doubt and fear,
Depths of despair and grief,
I cry; my voice, O Jesus, hear,
And come to my relief!

2 Thy gracious ears, O Saviour, bow
To my distressful cries,
For who shall stand, O Lord, if Thou
Shouldst mark iniquities?

3 But why do I my soul distress?
Forgiveness is with Thee!
With Thee there is abundant grace,
That Thou may'st fearèd be.

4 Then for the Lord my soul shall wait,
And in His Word I hope;
Continue knocking at His gate,
Till He the door shall ope'.

5 Not weary guards, who watch for morn
And stand with longing eyes,
Feel such desires to see the dawn,
The joyful dawn arise!

6 They never feel such warm desires
    As those which in me move,
As those wherewith my soul aspires
    To see the God of love!

7 O God of mercy, let me not
    Then *hope for Thee* in vain;
Nor let me ever be forgot,
    And in despair remain!

*John Ryland*, [1771, alt. C.H.S.]

**7.2:** *for Thee hope*

# 131 7.7.7.7.7.7.
*Psalm 131*

1 QUIET, Lord, my froward heart;
Make me teachable and mild;
Upright, simple, free from art,
Make me as a weanèd child,
    From distrust and envy free,
    Pleas'd with all that pleases Thee.

2 What Thou shalt today provide,
Let me as a child receive;
What tomorrow may betide,
Calmly to Thy wisdom leave;
    'Tis enough that Thou wilt care.
    Why should I the burden bear?

3 As a little child relies
On a care beyond his own,
Knows he's neither strong nor wise,
Fears to stir a step alone:
    Let me thus with Thee abide,
    As my Father, Guard, and Guide.

4 Thus preserv'd from Satan's wiles,
Safe from dangers, free from fears,
May I live upon Thy smiles
Till the promis'd hour appears,
    When the sons of God shall prove
    All their Father's boundless love.

*John Newton*, 1779

# 132 C.M.
*Psalm 132*

1 ARISE, O King of grace, arise,
    And enter to Thy rest:
Lo! Thy church waits with longing eyes,
    Thus to be own'd and blest.

2 Enter with all Thy glorious train,
    Thy Spirit and Thy Word;
All that the ark did once contain
    Could no such grace afford.

3 Here, mighty God, accept our vows,
    Here let Thy praise be spread;
Bless the provisions of Thy house
    And fill Thy poor with bread.

4 Here let the Son of David reign,
    Let God's Anointed shine;
Justice and truth His court maintain,
    With love and power divine.

5 Here let Him hold a lasting throne,
    And as His kingdom grows,
Fresh honours shall adorn His crown,
    And shame confound His foes.

*Isaac Watts*, 1719

> **Ed:** Taken from the longer paraphrase,
> "No sleep, nor slumber to his eyes."

# 133 C.M.
*Psalm 133*

1 BEHOLD, how good a thing it is,
    And how becoming well,
Together such as brethren are
    In unity to dwell.

2 Like precious ointment on the head
    That down the beard did flow,
E'en Aaron's beard, and to the skirts
    Did of his garments go.

3 As Hermon's dew, the dew that doth
    On Zion's hills descend,
For there the blessing God commands,
    Life that shall never end.

*Scotch Version*, [1650]

## 134
7.7.7.7.7.7.
*Psalm 134*

1 PRAISE to God on high be given,
Praise from all in earth and heaven.
Ye that in His presence stand,
Ye that walk by His command,
Saints below and hosts above,
Praise, O praise the God of love!

2 Praise Him at the dawn of light;
Praise Him at returning night;
Strings and voices, hands and hearts,
In His praises bear your parts.
Thou that madest earth and sky,
Bless us in return from high!

*Henry Francis Lyte*, 1834

## 135a
C.M.
*Psalm 135, Version I*

1 O PRAISE the Lord with one consent
And magnify His name;
Let all the servants of the Lord
His worthy praise proclaim.

2 Praise Him all ye that in His house
Attend with constant care,
With those that to His outmost courts
With humble zeal repair.

3 For God His own peculiar choice
The Sons of Jacob makes;
And Israel's offspring for His own
Most valued treasure takes.

4 Let all with thanks His wondrous works
In Zion's courts proclaim.
Let them in Salem, where He dwells,
Exalt His holy name.

*Tate and Brady*, 1696 [*rev.* 1698]

## 135b
L.M.
*Psalm 135, Version II*

1 PRAISE ye the Lord, exalt His name,
While in His holy courts ye wait,
Ye saints, that to His house belong,
Or stand attending at His gate.

2 Praise ye the Lord; the Lord is good;
To praise His name is sweet employ;
Israel He chose of old, and still
His church is His peculiar joy.

3 The Lord himself will judge His saints;
He treats His servants as His friends;
And when He hears their sore complaints,
Repents the sorrow that He sends.

4 Through every age the Lord declares
His name and breaks th' oppressor's rod;
He gives His suffering servants rest
And will be known th' Almighty God.

5 Bless ye the Lord, who taste His love;
People and priests exalt His name;
Amongst His saints He ever dwells;
His church is His Jerusalem.

*Isaac Watts*, 1719

## 136a
7.7.7.7.
*Psalm 136, Song I*

1 LET us with a gladsome mind
Praise the Lord, for He is kind;
For His mercies *shall* endure,
Ever faithful, ever sure.

2 Let us *sound* His name abroad,
For of gods He is the God;
For His mercies *shall* endure,
Ever faithful, ever sure.

3 *He, with* all-commanding might,
*Fill'd* the new-made world with light;
For His mercies *shall* endure,
Ever faithful, ever sure.

4 All *things living* He doth feed;
*His* full hand supplies their need;
For His mercies *shall* endure,
Ever faithful, ever sure.

5 *He His chosen race* did bless
In the wasteful wilderness;
For His mercies *shall* endure,
Ever faithful, ever sure.

6 He hath, with a piteous eye,
   *Look'd upon* our misery;
   For His mercies *shall* endure,
   Ever faithful, ever sure.

7 Let us *then, with gladsome mind,*
   *Praise the Lord, for He is kind;*
   For His mercies *shall* endure,
   Ever faithful, ever sure.

*John Milton*, 1645 [*rev.* 1673, *alt.*]

**1.3, etc.:** *ay (aye)*  **2.1:** *blaze*  **3.1:** *Who by his*
**3.2:** *Did fill*  **4.1:** *living creatures*
**4.2:** *And with*  **5.1:** *His chosen people he*
**6.2:** *Beheld us in*  **7.1-2:** *therefore warble forth*
   *His mighty majesty and worth:*
**Ed:** Some of these alterations (1.3, 2.1, 3.2, 4.2)
   appeared as early as 1781 in Benjamin Williams'
   *Book of Psalms.* This particular version seems
   to have come from James Montgomery's
   *Christian Psalmist* (1825), which contained
   sts. 1, 3-7 above with identical wording.
**TD:** "Day unto day uttereth speech concerning
   the mercy of the Lord; every sunbeam is a
   mercy, for it falls on undeserving sinners who
   else would sit in doleful darkness, and find
   earth a hell. Milton puts it well:
      'He, the golden tressèd sun
      Caused all day his course to run;
      For His mercy shall endure,
      Ever faithful, ever sure'"
   (Ps. 136:8; vol. 7, p. 175).

# 136b L.M.
*Psalm 136, Song II*

1 GIVE to our God immortal praise;
   Mercy and truth are all His ways;
   Wonders of grace to God belong;
   Repeat His mercies in your song.

2 Give to the Lord of Lords renown;
   The King of Kings with glory crown;
   His mercies ever shall endure,
   When lords and kings are known no more.

3 He built the earth, He spread the sky,
   And fix'd the starry lights on high;
   Wonders of grace to God belong;
   Repeat His mercies in your song.

4 He fills the sun with morning light;
   He bids the moon direct the night;
   His mercies ever shall endure,
   When suns and moons shall shine no more.

5 The Jews He freed from Pharaoh's hand,
   And brought them to the promis'd land;
   Wonders of grace to God belong;
   Repeat His mercies in your song.

6 He saw the Gentiles dead in sin
   And felt His pity work within;
   His mercies ever shall endure,
   When death and sin shall reign no more.

7 He sent His Son with power to save
   From guilt and darkness and the grave;
   Wonders of grace to God belong;
   Repeat His mercies in your song.

8 Through this vain world He guides our feet
   And leads us to His heavenly seat;
   His mercies ever shall endure,
   When this vain world shall be no more.

*Isaac Watts*, 1719

# 137 S.M.
*Psalm 137*

1 FAR from my heavenly home,
   Far from my Father's breast,
   Fainting I cry, blest Spirit, come,
   And speed me to my rest!

2 Upon the willows long
   My harp has silent hung.
   How should I sing a cheerful song
   Till Thou inspire my tongue?

3 My spirit homeward turns
   And fain would thither flee;
   My heart, O Zion, droops and yearns
   When I remember thee.

4 To thee, to thee I press,
   A dark and toilsome road.
   When shall I pass the wilderness,
   And reach the saints' abode?

5   God of my life, be near!
     On Thee my hopes I cast.
     O guide me through the desert *drear*
     And bring me home at last!

*Henry Francis Lyte*, 1834 [*alt. C.H.S.*]

**5.3:** *here*

# 138 L.M.
*Psalm 138*

1  WITH all my powers of heart and tongue,
    I'll praise my Maker in my song;
    Angels shall hear the notes I raise,
    Approve the song, and join the praise.

2  I'll sing Thy truth and mercy, Lord;
    I'll sing the wonders of Thy Word;
    Not all Thy works and names below
    So much Thy power and glory show.

3  To God I cried when troubles rose;
    He heard me and subdued my foes;
    He did my rising fears control,
    And strength diffused through all my soul.

4  The God of heaven maintains His state,
    Frowns on the proud, and scorns the great;
    But from His throne descends to see
    The sons of humble poverty.

5  Amidst a thousand snares I stand,
    Upheld and guarded by *Thine* hand;
    Thy words my fainting soul revive
    And keep my dying faith alive.

6  Grace will complete what grace begins,
    To save from sorrows or from sins;
    The work that wisdom undertakes
    Eternal mercy ne'er forsakes.

*Isaac Watts*, 1719

**5.2:** *Thy*  **Ed:** A common variant in the 1800s.

# 139a L.M.
*Psalm 139, Song I*

1  LORD, Thou hast search'd and seen me thru';
    Thine eye commands with piercing view

My rising and my resting hours,
My heart and flesh, with all their powers.

2  My thoughts, before they are my own,
    Are to my God distinctly known;
    He knows the words I mean to speak,
    Ere from my opening lips they break.

3  Within Thy circling power I stand;
    On every side I find Thy hand;
    Awake, asleep, at home, abroad,
    I am surrounded still with God.

4  Amazing knowledge, vast and great!
    What large extent! what lofty height!
    My soul, with all the powers I boast,
    Is in the boundless prospect lost.

5  O may these thoughts possess my breast,
    Where'er I rove, where'er I rest!
    Nor let my weaker passions dare
    Consent to sin, for God is there.

*Isaac Watts*, 1719

# 139b C.M.
*Psalm 139, Song II*

1  LORD, when I count Thy mercies o'er,
    They strike me with surprise;
    Not all the sands that spread the shore
    To equal numbers rise.

2  My flesh with fear and wonder stands,
    The product of Thy skill,
    And hourly blessings from Thy hands
    Thy thoughts of love reveal.

3  These on my heart by night I keep;
    How kind, how dear to me!
    O may the hour that ends my sleep
    Still find my thoughts with Thee.

*Isaac Watts*, 1719

# 140 L.M.
*Psalm 140*

1  THE Christian, like his Lord of old,
    Must look for foes and trials here;

Yet may the weakest saint be bold,
With such a friend as Jesus near.

2  The lion's roar need not alarm,
O Lord, the feeblest of Thy sheep;
The serpent's venom cannot harm,
While Thou art nigh to watch and keep.

3  Before, when dangers round me spread,
I cried to Thee, Almighty Friend;
Thou covered'st my defenceless head;
And shall I not on Thee depend?

4  O refuge of the poor and weak,
Regard Thy suffering people's cry;
Humble the proud, uphold the meek,
And bring us safe to Thee on high.

*Henry Francis Lyte*, 1834

# 141 7.7.7.7.
*Psalm 141*

1  LORD, I daily call on Thee;
Hear my voice and answer me;
Save me, for in faith I pray;
Take, O take my sins away.

2  Let my prayer as incense rise,
Pure accepted sacrifice;
Let my life with virtue shine;
Fill my soul with love divine.

3  Keep, O keep my lips and heart;
Let me ne'er from Thee depart;
Holy, happy, may I be
Perfect, O my God, like Thee.

*John Beaumont*, 1834

# 142 L.M.
*Psalm 142*

1  BEHOLD me unprotected stand,
No friendly guardian at my hand,
No place of flight, no refuge near,
And none to whom my soul is dear.

2  But, Lord, to Thee I pour my vow;
My hope, my place of refuge Thou;

And whilst the light of life I see,
I still my portion find in Thee.

3  Then hear and heed my fervent cry,
For low, oppress'd with grief, I lie;
Against my foes Thy arm display,
For I am weak, and pow'rful they.

4  Come, loose my prison bands; set free
My soul that I may sing to Thee;
Then shall the righteous round me press
And join Thy bounteous love to bless.

*Richard Mant*, 1824

**Ed:** Taken from the longer paraphrase,
"To God my earnest voice I raise."

# 143 C.M.
*Psalm 143*

1  HEAR, O my God, with pity hear
My humble supplicating moan;
In mercy answer all my prayer,
And make Thy truth and goodness known.

2  And O let mercy still be nigh,
Should awful justice frown severe.
Before the terrors of Thine eye,
What trembling mortal can appear?

3  I call to mind the former days;
Thy ancient works declare Thy name,
Thy truth, Thy goodness, and Thy grace;
And these, O Lord, are still the same.

4  Come, Lord, on wings of mercy fly;
My spirit fails at Thy delay;
Hide not Thy face; I faint, I die,
Without Thy blissful healing ray.

5  Teach me to do Thy sacred will;
Thou art my God, my hope, my stay;
Let Thy good Spirit lead me still,
And point the safe, the upright way.

6  Thy name, Thy righteousness I plead;
O Lord, revive my drooping heart;
Let these distressing fears recede,
And bid my troubles all depart.

*Anne Steele*, 1760 [*rev.* 1780]

# 144 S.M.
*Psalm 144*

1 I'LL bless my Saviour God,
　Who doeth all things right;
Arm'd with His Spirit's two-edg'd sword,
　Against my foes I'll fight.

2 My goodness and high tower,
　My fortress and my shield;
Depending on His love and power,
　I'll boldly take the field.

3 My Saviour shall subdue
　The powers of earth and hell;
Behold He maketh all things new;
　He doeth all things well.

*John Beaumont*, 1834

# 145a C.M.
*Psalm 145, Part I*

1 LONG as I live I'll bless Thy name,
　My King, my God of love;
My work and joy shall be the same
　In the bright world above.

2 Great is the Lord, His power unknown,
　And let His praise be great;
I'll sing the honours of Thy throne,
　Thy works of grace repeat.

3 Thy grace shall dwell upon my tongue,
　And while my lips rejoice,
The men that hear my sacred song
　Shall join their cheerful voice.

4 Fathers to sons shall teach Thy name,
　And children learn Thy ways;
Ages to come Thy truth proclaim,
　And nations sound Thy praise.

5 Thy glorious deeds of ancient date
　Shall through the world be known;
Thine arm of power, Thy heavenly state,
　With public splendour shown.

6 The world is manag'd by Thy hands,
　Thy saints are rul'd by love,

And Thine eternal kingdom stands
　Though rocks and hills remove.

*Isaac Watts*, 1719

# 145b C.M.
*Psalm 145, Part II*

1 SWEET is the memory of Thy grace,
　My God, my heavenly King;
Let age to age Thy righteousness
　In sounds of glory sing.

2 God reigns on high, but not confines
　His goodness to the skies;
Through the whole earth His bounty shines
　And every want supplies.

3 With longing eyes Thy creatures wait
　On Thee for daily food;
Thy liberal hand provides their meat
　And fills their mouths with good.

4 How kind are Thy compassions, Lord!
　How slow Thine anger moves!
But soon He sends His pardoning word
　To cheer the souls He loves.

5 Creatures with all their endless race
　Thy power and praise proclaim,
But saints that taste Thy richer grace
　Delight to bless Thy name.

*Isaac Watts*, 1719

# 146a L.M.
*Psalm 146, Version I*

1 PRAISE ye the Lord; my heart shall join
　In work so pleasant, so divine,
Now while the flesh is mine abode,
　And when my soul ascends to God.

2 Praise shall employ my noblest powers,
　While immortality endures;
My days of praise shall ne'er be past,
　While life and thought and being last.

3 Happy the man whose hopes rely
　On Israel's God; He made the sky

And earth and seas with all their train,
And none shall find His promise vain.

4 His truth forever stands secure;
He saves th' oppress'd, He feeds the poor,
He sends the labouring conscience peace,
And grants the prisoner sweet release.

5 The Lord hath eyes to give the blind;
The Lord supports the sinking mind;
He helps the stranger in distress,
The widow and the fatherless.

6 He loves His saints; He knows them well,
But turns the wicked down to hell;
Thy God, O Zion, ever reigns;
Praise Him in everlasting strains.

*Isaac Watts*, 1719

# 146b 8.8.8.8.8.8.
*Psalm 146, Version II*

1 I'LL praise my Maker with my breath,
And when my voice is lost in death,
    Praise shall employ my nobler powers;
My days of praise shall ne'er be past,
While life and thought and being last,
    Or immortality endures.

2 Why should I make a man my trust?
Princes must die and turn to dust;
    Vain is the help of flesh and blood;
Their breath departs, their pomp and power,
And thoughts all vanish in an hour,
    Nor can they make their promise good.

3 Happy the man whose hopes rely
On Israel's God; He made the sky
    And earth and seas, with all their train;
His truth forever stands secure;
He saves th' oppress'd, He feeds the poor,
    And none shall find His promise vain.

4 The Lord hath eyes to give the blind;
The Lord supports the sinking mind;
    He sends the labouring conscience peace,
He helps the stranger in distress,
The widow and the fatherless,
    And grants the prisoner sweet release.

5 He loves His saints, He knows them well,
But turns the wicked down to hell;
    Thy God, O Zion, ever reigns;
Let every tongue, let every age,
In this exalted work engage;
    Praise Him in everlasting strains.

6 I'll praise Him while He lends me breath,
And when my voice is lost in death,
    Praise shall employ my nobler powers;
My days of praise shall ne'er be past,
While life and thought and being last,
    Or immortality endures.

*Isaac Watts*, 1719

# 147a L.M.
*Psalm 147, Song I*

1 O PRAISE the Lord; 'tis sweet to raise
The grateful heart to God in praise;
When fallen raised, when lost restored,
O it is sweet to praise the Lord!

2 Great is His power, divine His skill,
His love diviner, greater still;
The sinner's Friend, the mourner's stay,
He sends no suppliant sad away.

3 The lions roar to Him for bread;
The ravens by His hand are fed.
And shall His chosen flock despair?
Shall they mistrust their Shepherd's care?

4 His church is precious in His sight;
He makes her glory His delight;
His treasures on her head are pour'd;
O Zion's children, praise the Lord!

*Henry Francis Lyte*, 1834 [*rev. 1836*]

# 147b L.M.
*Psalm 147, Song II*

1 PRAISE ye the Lord; 'tis good to raise
Our hearts and voices in His praise;
His nature and His works invite
To make this duty our delight.

2 The Lord builds up Jerusalem
And gathers nations to His name;

His mercy melts the stubborn soul
And makes the broken spirit whole.

3 He form'd the stars, those heav'nly flames;
He counts their numbers, calls their names;
His wisdom's vast and knows no bound,
A deep where all our thoughts are drown'd.

4 Great is our Lord, and great His might,
And all His glories infinite;
He crowns the meek, rewards the just,
And treads the wicked to the dust.

*Isaac Watts*, 1719

# 148a L.M.
*Psalm 148, Song I*

1 LOUD hallelujahs to the Lord,
From distant worlds where creatures dwell;
Let heaven begin the solemn word,
And sound it dreadful down to hell.

2 The Lord! how absolute He reigns!
Let every angel bend the knee;
Sing of His love in heavenly strains,
And speak how fierce His terrors be.

3 Wide as His vast dominion lies,
Make the Creator's name be known;
Loud as His thunder shout His praise,
And sound it lofty as His throne.

4 Jehovah! 'tis a glorious word;
Oh may it dwell on every tongue!
But saints who best have known the Lord
Are bound to raise the noblest song.

5 Speak of the wonders of that love
Which Gabriel plays on every chord;
From all below and all above,
Loud hallelujahs to the Lord.

*Isaac Watts*, [1707, *rev.* 1719]

# 148b C.M. Double
*Psalm 148, Song II*

1 PRAISE ye Jehovah, shout and sing,
Extol His glorious name;

From day to day your praises bring,
His power and love proclaim.
All, all ye saints, wher'er ye be,
And angels round His throne,
Praise ye the Co-eternal Three,
The Great Mysterious One.

2 O sun and moon, your Maker praise,
And stars of feebler light;
O heav'n of heav'ns, in joyful lays,
Adore the God of might.
Let earth and water, fire and air,
Praise the Eternal King;
All, all ye creatures ev'rywhere,
Your constant praises sing.

*John Beaumont*, 1834

# 149a 10.10.11.11.
*Psalm 149, Version I*

1 O PRAISE ye the Lord
With heart and with voice;
His mercies record,
And round Him rejoice.
Ye children of Zion,
Your Saviour adore,
And learn to rely on
His grace evermore.

2 Repose on His arm,
Ye sheep of His fold.
What terror can harm
With Him to uphold?
His saints are His treasure,
Their peace *will He* seek,
And pour without measure
His gifts on the meek.

3 Go on in His might,
Ye men of the Lord;
His Word be your light,
His promise your sword.
The King of salvation
Your foes will subdue,
And their degradation
Bring glory to you.

*Henry Francis Lyte*, 1834 [*alt. C.H.S.*]

**2.6:** *He will*

# 149b
10.10.11.11.
*Psalm 149, Version II*

1 PREPARE a new song,
　　Jehovah to praise,
　Amidst the full throng,
　　His honours to raise;
　O Israel, forever
　　thy Maker adore;
　Exult in thy Saviour,
　　thy King evermore!

2 Encircling His throne
　　with sacred delight,
　Let Jesus alone
　　your praises invite;
　Your voices combining
　　touch ev'ry sweet string,
　In harmony joining,
　　the Saviour to sing.

3 Ye saints of the Lord,
　　as round Him ye stand,
　His two-edged sword,
　　His Word, in your hand,
　To sound His high praises
　　your voices employ;
　To vict'ry He raises,
　　and crowns you with joy.

4 In vengeance He comes;
　　the nations draw near;
　His throne He resumes;
　　His judgments appear;
　There kings shall adore Him,
　　nor princes rebel,
　And sinners before Him
　　sink trembling to hell.

5 Then, raised from the dust
　　His church shall proclaim,
　"Thy judgments are just,
　　and faithful Thy name."

This honour forever
　His saints shall attend;
　Let praise to the Saviour
　　in triumph ascend!

*William Goode*, 1811

# 150a
C.M.
*Psalm 150, Version I*

1 IN God's own house pronounce His praise;
　　His grace He there reveals;
　To heaven your joy and wonder raise,
　　For there His glory dwells.

2 Let all your sacred passions move
　　While you rehearse His deeds,
　But the great work of saving love
　　Your highest praise exceeds.

3 All that have motion, life, and breath
　　Proclaim your Maker blest;
　Yet when my voice expires in death,
　　My soul shall praise Him best.

*Isaac Watts*, 1719

# 150b
L.M.
*Psalm 150, Version II*

1 O PRAISE the Lord in that blest place,
　　From whence His goodness largely flows;
　Praise Him in heav'n, where He His face
　　Unveil'd in perfect glory shows.

2 Praise Him for all the mighty acts
　　Which He in our behalf has done;
　His kindness this return exacts,
　　With which our praise should equal run.

3 Let all that vital breath enjoy,
　　The breath He does to them afford;
　In just returns of praise employ;
　　Let every creature praise the Lord.

*Tate and Brady*, 1696 [*rev.* 1698]

# Doxologies:
## The Adorable Trinity in Unity

## 151 7.6.7.6. Double

1 MEET and right it is to sing,
    In every time and place,
Glory to our heavenly King,
    The God of truth and grace.
Join we then with sweet accord,
    All in one thanksgiving join;
Holy, holy, holy, Lord,
    Eternal praise be Thine!

2 Father, God, Thy love we praise,
    Which gave Thy Son to die;
Jesus, full of truth and grace,
    Alike we glorify;
Spirit, Comforter divine,
    Praise by all to Thee be given,
Till we in full chorus join
    And earth is turn'd to heaven.

*Charles Wesley*, 1749

## 152 L.M.

1 BLEST be the Father and His love,
To whose celestial source we owe
Rivers of endless joy above
And rills of comfort here below.

2 Glory to Thee, great Son of God,
From whose dear wounded body rolls
A precious stream of vital blood,
Pardon and life for dying souls.

3 We give *Thee*, sacred Spirit, praise,
Who in our hearts of sin and woe
Makes living springs of grace arise,
And into boundless glory flow.

4 Thus God the Father, God the Son,
And God the Spirit we adore;

That sea of life and love unknown,
Without a bottom or a shore.

*Isaac Watts*, [1707, *alt.*]

> **3.1:** *the* sacred Spirit praise,
> **Ed:** A common alteration since the late 1700s.

## 153 L.M.

1 PRAISE God, from whom all blessings flow;
Praise Him, all creatures here below;
Praise Him above, ye heavenly host;
Praise Father, Son, and Holy Ghost.

*Thomas Ken*, [1692, *rev.* 1709]

## 154 C.M.

1 GLORY to God the Father's name,
    Who, from our sinful race,
Chose out His fav'rites to proclaim
    The honours of His grace.

2 Glory to God the Son be paid,
    Who dwelt in humble clay,
And to redeem us from the dead
    Gave His own life away.

3 Glory to God the Spirit give,
    From whose almighty power
Our souls their heavenly birth derive,
    And bless the happy hour.

4 Glory to God that reigns above,
    Th' eternal Three *in* One,
Who by the wonders of His love
    Has made His nature known.

*Isaac Watts*, [1707, *alt.*]

> **4.2:** *and* **Ed:** A common alt. since the late 1700s.

# 155 10.10.11.11.

1 GIVE glory to God, ye children of men,
And publish abroad again and again,
The Son's glorious merit,
　　the Father's free grace,
The gifts of the Spirit, to Adam's lost race.

*Joseph Hart*, 1762

# 156 8.7.8.7.

1 GLORY to the Almighty Father,
　　Fountain of eternal love,
Who, His wandering sheep to gather,
　　Sent a Saviour from above.

2 To the Son all praise be given,
　　Who with love unknown before,
Left the bright abode of heaven,
　　And our sins and sorrows bore.

3 Equal strains of warm devotion
　　Let the Spirit's praise employ,
Author of each holy motion,
　　Source of wisdom, peace, and joy.

4 Thus while our glad hearts ascending
　　Glorify Jehovah's name,
Heavenly songs with ours are bleeding,
　　There the theme is still the same.

*William Hiley Bathurst*, 1831

> **Ed:** Taken from the longer hymn,
> "To the source of every blessing."

# 157 6.6.6.6.4.4.4.4.

1 TO Him that chose us first,
Before the world began,
To Him that bore the curse
To save rebellious man,
　　To Him that form'd
　　Our hearts anew
　　Is endless praise
　　And glory due.

2 The Father's love shall run
Through our immortal songs;
We bring to God the Son
Hosannas on our tongues;
　　Our lips address
　　The Spirit's name
　　With equal praise,
　　And zeal the same.

3 Let every saint above
And angel round the throne
Forever bless and love
The sacred Three in One:
　　Thus heaven shall raise
　　His honours high,
　　When earth and time
　　Grow old and die.

*Isaac Watts*, 1709

# 158 8.7.8.7. Double

1 FOR Thy free electing favour,
　　Thee, O Father, we adore!
Jesus, our atoning Saviour,
　　Thee we worship evermore!
Holy Ghost, from both proceeding,
　　Let Thy praise our breath employ;
Earnest of our future heaven,
　　Source of holiness and joy!

Toplady's *Psalms & Hymns*, 1776

> **Ed:** In Toplady's collection, these lines were the
> final stanza (st. 6) of "Sons of God by blest
> adoption." This hymn appeared in Joseph
> Hart's *Hymns* (with suppl., 1762) in 3 sts., not
> including the text above. Hart died in 1768.

# 159 8.7.8.7. Double

1 PRAISE the God of all creation;
　　Praise the Father's boundless love;
Praise the Lamb, our expiation,
　　Priest and King enthroned above.
Praise the Fountain of salvation,
　　Him by whom our spirits live;

Undivided adoration
  To the One Jehovah give.

*Josiah Conder*, 1837

# 160 7.7.7.7.7.7.

1 NOW with angels round the throne,
Cherubim and seraphim,
And the church, which still is one,
Let us swell the solemn hymn.
Glory to the great I AM!
Glory to the Victim-Lamb!

2 Blessing, honour, glory, might,
And dominion infinite,
To the Father of our Lord,
To the Spirit and the Word:
As it was all worlds before,
Is and shall be evermore.

*Josiah Conder*, 1824 [*rev.* 1836]

# 161 S.M.

1 GIVE to the Father praise,
  Give glory to the Son,
And to the Spirit of His grace
  Be equal honour done.

*Isaac Watts*, [1707]

# 162 7.7.7.7. Double

1 HOLY, holy, holy! Thee,
One Jehovah evermore,
Father, Son, and Spirit! we,
Dust and ashes, would adore:
Lightly by the world esteemed,
From that world by Thee redeemed,
Sing we here, with glad accord,
Holy, holy, holy Lord!

2 Holy, holy, holy! All
Heaven's triumphant choir shall sing
When the ransom'd nations fall
At the footstool of their King;

Then shall saints and seraphim,
Harps and voices, swell one hymn,
Round the throne with full accord,
Holy, holy, holy Lord.

*James Montgomery*, [1836, *rev.* 1853]

> **Ed:** *Taken from the longer hymn,*
> "Holy, holy, holy Lord."

# 163 7.7.7.7.

1 HALLELUJAH! joyful raise
Heart and voice our God to praise!
Praise the Father! Praise the Son!
Praise the Spirit! Three in One!

2 One to perfect all the plan
Of redeeming ruined man!
Triune God! to Thee be given
Praise on earth and praise in heaven!

*Newman Hall*, [1858]

> **Ed:** Newman Hall was part of a contingent of local pastors who attended a special service on 27 March 1861, for the dedication of the new Metropolitan Tabernacle. At the time, Hall was pastor of Surrey Chapel, which till that point "had been the largest Christian sanctuary south of the Thames." Rev. Hall "hoped there was not a worthy member of Surrey Chapel who did not rejoice that there was a sanctuary raised more than twice as large; and even should it lead to a decrease of the number of worshippers at Surrey Chapel, yet, if on the whole the cause of God were more advanced, it would be their duty and their pleasure to say, 'Herein do I rejoice, yes, and will rejoice'" (MTP, vol. 7, p. 198).
>
> Thirty-one years later, in the same building, Hall had the tender duty of praying to close the memorial service for his long-time colleague (S&T, Mar. 1892, p. 151).
>
> This hymn was composed for Surrey Chapel, 19 Nov. 1857, and published in 1858.

# 164 L.M.

1 TO God the Father, God the Son,
And God the Spirit, Three in One,
Be honour, praise, and glory giv'n
By all on earth and all in heav'n.

*Isaac Watts*, [1707]

# 165 C.M.

1 TO Father, Son, and Holy Ghost,
*One* God, whom we adore,
Be glory, as it was, is now,
And shall be evermore.

*Tate and Brady*, 1696 [*alt.*]

> **1.2:** *The*  **Ed:** This alteration did not appear
> in official printings of the *New Version*, but
> it appeared as early as 1702 in *Some of the
> Psalms of David in metre, done by J. Patrick,
> D.D. and by Mr Brady and Mr Tate*, and was
> repeated in other collections.

# 166 6.6.4.6.6.6.4.

1 COME, Thou Almighty King,
Help us Thy name to sing,
   Help us to praise!
Father all-glorious,
O'er all victorious,
Come and reign over us,
   Ancient of Days!

2 Jesus, our Lord, arise;
Scatter our enemies
   And make them fall;
Let Thine almighty aid
Our sure defence be made—
Our souls on Thee be stay'd—
   Lord, hear our call!

3 Come, Thou Incarnate Word,
Gird on Thy mighty sword—
   Our pray'r attend!
Come! and Thy people bless,

And give Thy word success;
Spirit of holiness,
   On us descend!

4 Come, Holy Comforter,
Thy sacred witness bear
   In this glad hour!
Thou, who almighty art,
Now rule in ev'ry heart,
And ne'er from us depart,
   Spirit of power!

5 To the Great One in Three
Eternal praises be,
   Hence—evermore!
His sov'reign majesty,
May we in glory see,
And to eternity
   Love and adore!

[George Whitefield's *Collection*,] 1757

> **Ed:** This hymn is sometimes credited to Charles
> Wesley on the basis of it being printed togeth-
> er with his hymn "Jesus, let thy pitying eye"
> in a leaflet that was appended to Whitefield's
> *Collection*, 6th–9th eds. (1757-1760), then in-
> corporated into the 10th ed. (1761). Sedgwick
> was a firm believer in Wesley's authorship,
> even though this text never appeared in the
> Wesleys' collections.

# 167 8.7.8.7.
*"Make a joyful noise."*

1 MUSIC, bring thy sweetest treasures,
   Dulcet melody and chord;
Link the notes with loveliest measures
   To the glory of the Lord.

2 Wing the praise from every nation;
   Sweetest instruments employ;
Raise the chorus of creation;
   Swell the universal joy.

3 Far away be gloom and sadness;
   Spirits with seraphic fire,
Tongues with hymns,
   and hearts with gladness,
Higher sound the chords and higher.

4 To the Father, to the Saviour,
   To the Spirit, source of light,
   As it was is now, and ever,
   Praise in heaven's supremest height.

*James Edmeston*, [1866]

> **Ed:** Dated 1837 by Sedgwick, apparently from
> Edmeston's manuscripts; first published in
> *Our Own Hymn-Book*. It did not appear, as
> Julian's *Dictionary* claimed (p. 322), in Ed-
> meston's *Sacred Poetry* (1848).

# 168 L.M. / *"The Father, the Word, and the Holy Ghost."*

1 FATHER of heav'n! whose love profound
  A ransom for our souls has found,
  Before Thy throne we sinners bend;
  To us Thy pard'ning love extend.

2 Almighty Son! Incarnate Word!
  Our Prophet–Priest–Redeemer–Lord!
  Before Thy throne we sinners bend;
  To us Thy saving grace extend.

3 Eternal Spirit! by whose breath
  The soul is rais'd from sin and death,
  Before Thy throne we sinners bend;
  To us Thy quick'ning pow'r extend.

4 Jehovah! Father, Spirit, Son—
  Mysterious Godhead—Three in One!
  Before Thy throne we sinners bend;
  Grace, pardon, life, to us extend.

[*Edward*] *Cooper*, [1805]

> **Ed:** Attributed by Sedgwick to "J. Cooper, 1812,"
> the date coming from its anonymous appear-
> ance in Thomas Cotterill's *Selection* (1812).

# 169 8.7.8.7.4.4.7. *"God be merciful unto us."*

1 LEAD us, heavenly Father, lead us
   O'er the world's tempestuous sea;
   Guard us, guide us, keep us, feed us,
   For we have no help but Thee;
      Yet possessing
      every blessing,
   If our God our Father be!

2 Saviour! breathe forgiveness o'er us;
   All our weakness Thou dost know;
   Thou didst tread this earth before us;
   Thou didst feel its keenest woe;
      Lone and dreary,
      faint and weary,
   Through the desert Thou didst go!

3 Spirit of our God, descending,
   Fill our hearts with heavenly joy,
   Love, with every passion blending,
   Pleasure that can never cloy.
      Thus provided,
      pardon'd, guided,
   Nothing can our peace destroy!

*James Edmeston*, [1821]

# 170 6.6.4.6.6.6.4. *"Let there be light."*

1 THOU, whose almighty word
   Chaos and darkness heard,
      And took their flight,
   Hear us, we humbly pray,
   And where the gospel's day
   Sheds not its glorious ray,
      Let there be light.

2 Thou, who didst come to bring
   On Thy *protecting* wing,
      Healing and sight,
   *Sight to the inly blind,*
   *Health to the sick in mind,*
   Oh! now to all mankind,
      Let there be light.

3 Spirit of truth and love,
   Life-giving holy Dove,
      Speed forth Thy flight;
   Move *o'er* the water's face
   *By Thine almighty grace,*
   And in earth's darkest place,
      Let there be light.

4 Blessèd and holy *Three*,
   Glorious Trinity,
      Wisdom, Love, Might,

Boundless as ocean's tide,
Rolling in fullest pride,
*O'er* the world, far and wide,
    Let there be light.

*John Marriott*, [1825, *alt.*]

**2.2:** *redeeming*  **2.4-5:** *Health … / Sight …*
**3.4:** *on* (July 1825); *oe'r* (1867)
**3.5:** *Bearing the lamp of grace*
**4.1:** *and*  **4.6:** *Through*
**Ed:** 1866 ed., attributed to "Thomas Marriott,
    1825," then changed to "John Marriott, 1813"
    in **1868?**. According to Julian's *Dictionary*

*of Hymnology*, pp. 715 & 1714, the hymn was
written ca. 1813, then printed "without his permission" in the *Evangelical Magazine* (June
1825). A different version appeared soon
after in *The Friendly Visitor* (July 1825). It
entered hymn collections as early as James H.
Stewart's *Selection*, 6th ed. (1830). A late but
notable printing is in *Lyra Britannica* (1867),
based on a manuscript supplied by Marriott's
son, and nearly identical to the July 1825 form.
Multiple variants of the text exist between
1825 and 1867; the version used by Spurgeon
appeared in Edward Bickersteth's *Christian
Psalmody* (1833; *rev.* 1834) and was repeated
in the Compr. Ed. of Rippon's *Selection* (1844).

# God the Father

## ADORATION OF GOD.

# 171 7.7.7.7.
*Praise the Lord.*

1  PRAISE the Lord, His glories show,
Saints within His courts below,
Angels round His throne above,
*All that see and* share His love.

2  Earth to heaven, *and heaven to earth,*
*Tell His wonders, sing His worth;*
Age to age and shore to shore,
Praise Him, praise Him evermore!

3  Praise the Lord, His *mercies* trace;
*Praise His providence and grace,*
All that He *for man hath* done,
All He sends us through His Son:

4  Strings and voices, hands and hearts,
In the concert bear your parts.
All that breathe, your Lord adore;
Praise Him, praise Him evermore!

*Henry Francis Lyte*, 1834 [*rev.* 1836]

**1.4:** *Praise Him all that*  **2.1:** *exalt the strain*
**2.2:** *Send it, heaven, to earth again;*
**3.1:** *goodness*  **3.2:** *All the wonders of His grace*
**3.3:** *hath borne and*
**Ed:** Lyte revised this text in 1836, but the origi-
    nal continued to printed, as above. Footnotes
    indicate Lyte's revisions.

# 172 8.7.8.7.
*"Praise ye the Lord."*

1  PRAISE the Lord, ye heav'ns, adore Him;
    Praise Him, angels, in the height;
Sun and moon, rejoice before Him;
    Praise Him, all ye stars *of* light.

2  Praise the Lord, for He hath spoken;
    Worlds His mighty voice obey'd;
Laws *that* never shall be broken,
    For their guidance *He hath* made.

3  Praise the Lord, for He is glorious;
    Never shall His promise fail;
God hath made His saints victorious;
    Sin and death shall not prevail.

4  Praise the God of our salvation;
    Hosts on high His power proclaim;

Heaven and earth and all creation
    Laud and magnify His name.

*[Psalms, Hymns, and Anthems, 1796, alt.]*

    **1.4:** *and*   **2.3:** *which*   **2.4:** *hath He*
    **Ed:** This specific combination of alterations
    appeared in many collections starting in 1825,
    as in *Psalms and Hymns, for the use of St.
    Mary's Chapel, Maidenhead,* and in Harriet
    Auber's *Spirit of the Psalms* (1829). Sedgwick
    credited the hymn to Richard Mant.

# 173
10.10.11.11.
*Praise in the sanctuary.*

1  O PRAISE ye the Lord,
    prepare your glad voice,
His praise in the great
    assembly to sing;
In our great Creator
    let Israel rejoice,
And children of Zion
    be glad in their King.

2  *Let all who adore*
    *Jehovah, our Lord,*
*With heart and with tongue*
    His praises express;
Who always takes pleasure
    His saints to *reward,*
And with His salvation
    the humble to bless.

3  With glory adorn'd,
    His people shall sing
To God, who their *heads*
    with safety doth shield;
*Such honour and triumph*
    *His favour doth bring;*
*Oh therefore, forever,*
    *all praise to Him yield.*

*Tate and Brady,* 1696 [rev. 1698], *alt.*

    **2.1-3:** *Let them His great name*
        *extol in the dance;*
        *With timbrel and harp*
    **2.6:** *advance*   **3.3:** *beds*
    **3.5-8:** *Their mouths fill'd with praises*

*of him their great King;*
    *Whilst a two-edged sword*
        *their right hand shall wield.*
    **Ed:** The alterations in st. 3 appeared as early as
    1785 in Richard Cecil's *The Psalms of David,*
    whereas the changes in st. 2 date to William J.
    Hall's *Psalms and Hymns* (1836). Spurgeon's
    source for this version is unclear; this text
    appears exactly as in *The New Congregational
    Hymn Book* (ca. 1859), save for one word at
    3.6: *doth/shall.*

# 174
7.7.7.7.
*Call to universal praise.*

1  SING, ye seraphs in the sky;
    Let your loftiest praises flow;
Swell the song with raptures high,
    All ye sons of men below.

2  With one soul, one heart, one voice,
    Heaven and earth alike we call
In His praises to rejoice,
    Who is past the praise of all.

3  Night and day His goodness tell;
    Earth, and sun, and moon, and star,
Winds and waves that sink and swell,
    Ceaseless spread His name afar.

4  Every living thing His hands,
    Which first made, sustain, supply;
Wide o'er all His love expands
    As the vast embracing sky.

5  Sin, which strove that love to quell,
    Woke yet more its wondrous blaze;
Eden, Bethlehem, Calvary, tell,
    More than all beside, His praise.

6  Sing, ye seraphs, in the sky;
    Let your loftiest praises flow;
Swell the song with raptures high,
    All ye sons of men below.

*Thomas Davis,* 1864

## 175
S.M.
*Stand up and bless the Lord.*

1 STAND up and bless the Lord,
Ye people of His choice;
Stand up and bless the Lord your God,
With heart and soul and voice.

2 Though high above all praise,
Above all blessing high,
Who would not fear His holy name,
And laud, and magnify?

3 O for the living flame
From His own altar brought,
To touch our lips, our minds inspire,
And wing to heaven our thought!

4 There with benign regard,
Our hymns He deigns to hear;
Though unreveal'd to mortal sense,
The spirit feels Him near.

5 God is our strength and song,
And His salvation ours;
Then be His love in Christ proclaim'd
With all our ransm'd powers.

6 Stand up and bless the Lord;
The Lord your God adore;
Stand up and bless His glorious name,
Henceforth forever more.

*James Montgomery*, 1825

> **Ed:** Line 1.2 was originally written as "Ye children of his choice" for the Sheffield Red Hill Wesleyan Sunday School Anniversary, 15 Mar. 1824, then revised for publication.

## 176
L.M.
*O sing unto the Lord a new song.*

1 UNTO the Lord, unto the Lord,
Oh, sing a new and joyful song!
Declare His glory, tell abroad
The wonders that to Him belong.

2 For He is great, for He is great;
Above all gods His throne is raised;

He reigns in majesty and state;
In strength and beauty *He is* praised.

3 Give to the Lord, give to the Lord
The glory due unto His name;
Enter His courts with sweet accord;
In songs of joy His grace proclaim.

4 For lo! He comes, for lo! He comes
To judge the earth in truth and love;
His saints in triumph leave their tombs
And shout His praise in heaven above.

*Sabbath Hymn Book*, 1858 [*alt. C.H.S.*]

> **2.4:** *is He*  **Ed:** In the 5th ed. of *OOHB*, Sedgwick attr. the hymn to Edwards A. Park, who had worked on the *Sabbath Hymn Book*. See Julian's *Dictionary*, p. 1585, for the assertion that the hymn is best regarded as anonymous.

## 177
10.10.11.11.
*Salvation to God and the Lamb.*

1 YE servants of God, your master proclaim,
And publish abroad His wonderful name;
The name all-victorious of Jesus extol;
His kingdom is glorious and rules over all.

2 God ruleth on high, almighty to save,
And still He is nigh, His presence we have;
The great congregation
His triumph shall sing,
Ascribing salvation to Jesus our King.

3 Salvation to God, who sits on the throne!
Let all cry aloud and honour the Son!
*The praises of Jesus* the angels proclaim,
Fall down on their faces,
and worship the Lamb.

4 Then let us adore and give Him His right,
All glory, and power,
and wisdom, and might,
All honour, and blessing,
with angels above,
And thanks never-ceasing *for* infinite love.

*Charles Wesley*, 1744

[*alt. A Collection of Hymns for the Use …
of the United Brethren*, 1789, *rev.* 1801]

**3.3:** *Our Jesus's praises* **6.4:** *and*

# 178 C.M.
*Praise our God, all ye His servants.*

1 HOW shall I praise Thee, O my God?
   How to Thy throne draw nigh?
I in the dust—and Thou array'd
   In might and majesty!

2 Praise Him, ye gladdening smiles of morn;
   Praise Him, O silent night;
Tell forth His glory, all the earth;
   Praise Him, ye stars of light!

3 Praise Him, ye stormy winds, that rise
   Obedient to His word;
Mountains and hills and fruitful trees,
   Join ye and praise the Lord!

4 Praise Him, ye heavenly host, for ye,
   With purer lips, can sing—
Glory and honour, praise and power,
   To Him, the Eternal King!

5 Praise Him, ye saints! who here rejoice
   To do His heavenly will,
The incense of whose prayers ascends
   Upon His altar still.

6 Praise Him, all works of His that own
   His Spirit's blest control!
O Lord my God, how great art Thou!
   Bless thou the Lord, my soul!

*Anna Shipton*, 1855 [*rev.* 1858, 1865]

# ATTRIBUTES OF GOD.

# 179 C.M.
*The perfections as a whole.*

1 HOW shall I praise th' eternal God,
   That infinite Unknown?
Who can ascend His high abode
   Or venture near His throne?

2 The great Invisible! He dwells
   Conceal'd in dazzling light;
But His all-searching eye reveals
   The secrets of the night.

3 Those watchful eyes that never sleep
   Survey the world around;
His wisdom is a boundless deep,
   Where all our thoughts are drown'd.

4 He knows no shadow of a change,
   Nor altars His decrees;
Firm as a rock His truth remains
   To guard His promises.

5 Justice upon a dreadful throne
   Maintains the rights of God;
While mercy sends her pardons down,
   Bought with a Saviour's blood.

6 Now to my soul, immortal King,
   Speak some forgiving word;
Then 'twill be double joy to sing
   The glories of my Lord.

*Isaac Watts*, 1709

# 180 L.M.
*Perfections as a Sovereign.*

1 JEHOVAH reigns, His throne is high;
   His robes are light and majesty;
His glory shines with beams so bright,
   No mortal can sustain the sight.

2 His terrors keep the world in awe;
   His justice guards His holy law;
His love reveals a smiling face;
   His truth and promise seal the grace.

3 Through all His works His wisdom shines
   And baffles Satan's deep designs;
His pow'r is sov'reign to fulfill
   The noblest counsels of His will.

4 And will this glorious Lord descend
   To be my Father and my Friend?
Then let my songs with angels join;
   Heav'n is secure if God be mine.

*Isaac Watts*, 1709

# 181 L.M.
*The Lord God omnipotent reigneth.*

1 THE Lord is King! Lift up Thy voice;
   O earth, and all ye heavens, rejoice!
   From world to world the joy shall ring:
   The Lord Omnipotent is King.

2 The Lord is King! Who then shall dare
   Resist His will, distrust His care,
   Or murmur at His wise decrees,
   Or doubt His royal promises?

3 The Lord is King! Child of the dust,
   The Judge of all the earth is just.
   Holy and true are all His ways;
   Let every creature speak His praise.

4 He reigns! Ye saints, exalt your strains;
   Your God is King, your Father reigns.
   And He is at the Father's side,
   The Man of love, the crucified.

5 Come, make your wants,
        your burdens known;
   He will present them at the throne;
   And angel bands are waiting there,
   His messages of love to bear.

6 Oh, when His wisdom can mistake,
   His might decay, His love forsake,
   Then may His children cease to sing,
   The Lord Omnipotent is King.

*Josiah Conder*, 1824

> **EE:** Hymns, Set 2 (Feb./Dec.), 10th Eve,
>    CHINA / PASCAL
> **MM:** Hymns, Set 2 (Feb./Dec.), 29th Morn,
>    OLD HUNDREDTH / DUKE STREET
> **TD:** "We who come to the church and its public
>    worship are charmed to come to the throne
>    of God, and to the throne of the reigning
>    Saviour. . . . To see God reigning in the Son of
>    David and evermore avenging the just cause
>    is a thing which is good for weeping eyes, and
>    cheering for disconsolate hearts. They sang of
>    old as they went towards the throne, and so
>    do we" (Ps. 122:5; vol. 6, p. 431).

# 182 C.M.
*God eternal and infinite.*

1 GREAT God! how infinite art Thou!
   What worthless worms are we!
   Let the whole race of creatures bow
   And pay their praise to Thee.

2 Thy throne eternal ages stood,
   Ere seas or stars were made;
   Thou art the ever-living God,
   Were all the nations dead.

3 Eternity, with all its years,
   Stands present in Thy view;
   To Thee there's nothing old appears;
   Great God! there's nothing new.

4 Our lives thru' various scenes are drawn,
   And vex'd with trifling cares,
   While Thine eternal thought moves on
   Thine undistrb'd affairs.

5 Great God, how infinite art Thou!
   What worthless worms are we!
   Let the whole race of creatures bow
   And pay their praise to Thee.

*Isaac Watts*, [1707]

> **NPSP:** "The highest science, the loftiest spec-
>    ulation, the mightiest philosophy which can
>    ever engage the attention of a child of God is
>    the name, the nature, the person, the work,
>    the doings, and the existence of the great God
>    whom he calls his Father. . . . It is a subject
>    so vast that all our thoughts are lost in its
>    immensity, so deep that our pride is drowned
>    in its infinity. . . . No subject of contempla-
>    tion will tend more to humble the mind than
>    thoughts of God. We shall be obliged to feel,
>    'Great God, how infinite art Thou, what worth-
>    less worms are we!'" (vol. 1, no. 1, p. 1).

# 183 L.M.
*The Ancient of Days.*

1 GREAT Former of this various frame,
   Our souls adore Thine awful name,
   And bow and tremble, while they praise
   The Ancient of eternal Days.

2 Before Thine infinite survey,
   Creation rose as yesterday;
And as tomorrow shall Thine eye
   See earth and stars in ruin lie.

3 Our days a transient period run,
   And change with ev'ry circling sun;
And while to lengthen'd years we trust,
   Before the moth we sink to dust.

4 But let the creatures fall around;
   Let death consign us to the ground;
Let the last gen'ral flame arise
   And melt the arches of the skies:

5 Calm as the summer's ocean, we
   Can all the wreck of nature see,
While grace secures us an abode,
   Unshaken as the throne of God.

*Philip Doddridge*, 1755
[*alt. Josiah Conder*, 1836]

> **2.1-2:** *Thou, Lord, with unsurpriz'd survey*
> *Saw'st nature rising yesterday;*
> **3:3-4.** *And in the firmest state we boast,*
> *A moth can crush us into dust.*

# 184 C.M.
*Omniscience.*

1 GREAT God! Thy penetrating eye
   Pervades my inmost powers;
With awe profound my wond'ring soul
   Falls prostrate and adores.

2 To be encompass'd *round* with God,
   *The* holy and the just,
Arm'd with omnipotence to save,
   Or *crush me into* dust!

3 Oh, how tremendous is the thought!
   Deep may it be impress'd,
And may the Spirit firmly 'grave
   This truth within my breast.

4 By Thee observ'd, by Thee upheld,
   *Let earth or hell oppose;*
*I'll press* with dauntless courage on
   *And dare the proudest foes.*

5 Begirt with Thee, my *fearless* soul
   The gloomy vale shall tread,
And Thou wilt bind th' immortal crown
   Of glory round my head.

*Elizabeth Scott*, 1764
[*alt. John Dobell*, 1806]

> **2.1:** *thus*   **2.2:** *Th'all*   **2.4:** *crumble me to*
> **4.2:** *I'll dare the proudest foes,*   **4.3:** *And march*
> **4.4:** *Tho' earth and hell oppose.*   **5.1:** *fearful*
> **Ed:** Written between 1740–1751 but not
> published until Jan. 1764 in *The Christian's*
> *Magazine,* and not included in a hymnal until
> John Dobell's *New Selection* (1806). 5.1 reads
> *fearful* in 1764, but *fearless* in 1806 and in the
> manuscript book held by Yale.

# 185 C.M.
*Omnipresence.*

1 IN all my vast concerns with Thee,
   In vain my soul would try
To shun Thy presence, Lord, or flee
   The notice of Thine eye.

2 Thy all-surrounding sight surveys
   My rising and my rest,
My public walks, my private ways,
   And secrets of my breast.

3 My thoughts lie open to the Lord,
   Before they're form'd within;
And ere my lips pronounce the word,
   He knows the sense I mean.

4 O wondrous knowledge, deep, and high!
   Where can a creature hide?
Within Thy circling arms I lie,
   Beset on every side.

5 So let Thy grace surround me still,
   And like a bulwark prove,
To guard my soul from every ill,
   Secur'd by sovereign love.

6 Lord, where shall guilty souls retire,
   Forgotten and unknown?
In hell they meet Thy dreadful fire,
   In heaven Thy glorious throne.

7 Should I suppress my vital breath
    To 'scape Thy wrath divine,
Thy voice would break the bars of death
    And make the grave resign.

8 If wing'd with beams of morning light,
    I fly beyond the west,
Thy hand, which must support my flight,
    Would soon betray my rest.

9 If o'er my sins I think to draw
    The curtains of the night,
Those flaming eyes that guard Thy law
    Would turn the shades to light.

10 The beams of noon, the midnight hour,
    Are both alike to Thee;
O may I ne'er provoke that power
    From which I cannot flee!

*Isaac Watts*, 1719

**FPN:** 17 July 1887 (No. 1973), MAGNUS

# 186 L.M.
*Divine glory.*

1 ETERNAL Power! whose high abode
Becomes the grandeur of a God;
Infinite lengths, beyond the bounds
Where stars revolve their little rounds.

2 The lowest step *around* Thy seat
Rises too high for Gabriel's feet;
In vain the tall archangel tries
To reach Thine height with wond'ring eyes.

3 Lord, what shall earth and ashes do?
We would adore our Maker too;
From sin and dust to Thee we cry,
The Great, the Holy, and the High.

4 Earth from afar has heard Thy fame,
And worms have learnt to lisp Thy name;
But O the glories of Thy mind
Leave all our soaring thoughts behind.

5 God is in heaven, and men below;
Be short our tunes, our words be few;
A sacred reverence checks our songs,
And praise sits silent on our tongues.

*Isaac Watts*, 1706 [*rev.* 1709]
[*alt. John Rippon*, 1787; *rev.* ca. 1805]

    **2.1:** *about* (1706), *above* (1787)
    **TD:** "In the height of His abode, none can be
    like Him. His throne, His whole character, His
    person, His being, everything about Him, is
    lofty, and infinitely majestic, so that none can
    be likened unto Him" (Ps. 113:5; vol. 5, p. 240).

# 187 L.M.
*Incomprehensible and Sovereign.*

1 CAN creatures to perfection find
Th' eternal, uncreated mind?
Or can the largest stretch of thought
Measure and search His nature out?

2 'Tis high as heav'n, 'tis deep as hell,
And what can mortals know or tell?
His glory spreads beyond the sky
And all the shining worlds on high.

3 God is a King of power unknown;
Firm are the orders of His throne;
If He resolve, who dare oppose,
Or ask Him why, or what He does?

4 He wounds the heart, and He makes whole;
He calms the tempest of the soul;
When He shuts up in long despair,
Who can remove the heavy bar?

5 He frowns, and darkness veils the moon;
The fainting sun grows dim at noon;
The pillars of heav'n's starry roof
Tremble and start at His reproof.

6 These are a portion of His ways,
But who shall dare describe His face?
Who can endure His light, or stand
To hear the thunders of His hand?

*Isaac Watts*, 1709

# 188 C.M.
*Holy and Reverend.*

1 HOLY and reverend is the name
    Of our eternal King;

"Thrice holy Lord," the angels cry,
"Thrice holy," let us sing!

2 The *deepest reverence* of the mind,
    *Pay O my soul, to God;*
Lift with thy hands a holy heart
    To His sublime abode.

3 With sacred awe pronouce His name,
    Whom words nor thoughts can reach;
A *contrite* heart shall please Him more
    Than *noblest* forms of speech.

4 Thou holy God! preserve my soul,
    From all pollution free;
The pure in heart are Thy delight,
    And they Thy face shall see.

*John Needham,* 1768
[*alt. Lowell Mason,* 1831]

> **2.1:** *veneration*  **2.2:** *My soul pay to thy God;*
> **3.3:** *broken*  **3.4:** *the best*
> **Ed:** The alterations at 2.1-2 date to Rippon's *Selection* (1787), but this reduction to 4 sts. and the additional alterations are from Mason.

# 189   7.7.7.7.
*Divine Purity and Holiness.*

1 HOLY, holy, holy Lord,
    God of hosts in heaven adored;
Earth with awe has heard Thy name;
    Men Thy majesty proclaim.

2 Just and true are all Thy ways;
    Great Thy works above our praise;
Humbled in the dust, we own,
    Thou art holy, Thou alone.

3 In Thy sight, the angel band
    Justly charged with folly stand;
Holiest deeds of creatures lie
    Meritless before Thine eye.

4 How shall sinners worship Thee,
    God of spotless purity?
To Thy grace all hope we owe;
    Thine own righteousness bestow.

*Basil Manly Jr.,* 1850

**Ed:** Spurgeon and Manly died on the same day, 31 Jan. 1892. Manly was a founding professor of The Southern Baptist Theological Seminary (Louisville, KY). In a letter to Manly's colleague John Broadus, C.H. Hudson noted the connection:

> "The daily papers of this morning announce the death of two eminently godly and useful men—Rev. Charles H. Spurgeon, of London, and Dr. Basil Manly, of Kentucky. The Baptist world mourns their loss. Their voices are now hushed in the sleep of death. Their words live on, and will continue to live, till they themselves shall awake to newness of life" (A.T. Robertson, *Life and Letters of John A. Broadus,* 1909, p. 400).

# 190   7.7.7.7.
*Holy, Holy, Holy.*

1 HOLY, holy, holy Lord,
    Be Thy glorious name ador'd;
Lord, Thy mercies never fail;
    Hail, celestial goodness, hail!

2 Though unworthy, Lord, Thine ear,
    *Deign our humble songs to* hear;
Purer praise we hope to bring,
    When around Thy throne we sing.

3 There no tongue shall silent be;
    All shall join in harmony;
That through heaven's *capacious* round
    *Praise to Thee* may ever sound.

4 Lord, Thy mercies never fail;
    Hail, celestial goodness, hail!
Holy, holy, holy Lord,
    Be Thy glorious name ador'd.

[*William Dodd,* 1766]
[*adapt.*] *Benjamin Williams,* 1778
[*alt. Universalists' Hymn Book,* 1821]

> **2.2:** *Our humble hallelujahs*
> **3.3:** *all-spacious*  **3.4:** *Thy praise, O God,*
> **Ed:** Williams adapted Dodd's antiphonal text into quatrains, as a hymn. Footnotes indicate deviations from the 1778 text.

# 191
**L.M.**
*The Truth of God the Promiser.*

1 PRAISE, everlasting praise, be paid
To Him that earth's foundation laid;
Praise to the God whose strong decrees
Sway the creation as He please.

2 Praise to the goodness of the Lord,
Who rules His people by His Word;
And there, as strong as His decrees,
He sets His kindest promises.

3 Firm are the words His prophets give,
Sweet words, on which His children live;
Each of them is the voice of God,
Who spoke and spread the skies abroad.

4 Each of them powerful as that sound
That bid the new-made world go round,
And stronger than the solid poles
On which the wheel of nature rolls.

5 O for a strong, a lasting faith,
To credit what th' Almighty saith!
T' embrace the message of His Son,
And call the joys of heaven our own.

6 Then should the earth's old pillars shake,
And all the wheels of nature break;
Our steady souls should fear no more
Than solid rocks when billows roar.

7 Our everlasting hopes arise
Above the ruinable skies,
Where th' eternal Builder reigns
And His own courts His power sustains.

*Isaac Watts,* [1707, *rev.* 1740]

# 192
**C.M. /** *Faithful and powerful in performing His promises.*

1 BEGIN, my tongue, some heav'nly theme,
And speak some boundless thing;
The mighty works, or mightier name,
Of our eternal King.

2 Tell of His wondrous faithfulness
And sound His power abroad;
Sing the sweet promise of His grace
And the performing God.

3 Proclaim salvation from the Lord,
For wretched, dying men;
His hand has writ the sacred Word
With an immortal pen.

4 Engrav'd as in eternal brass
The mighty promise shines;
Nor can the powers of darkness 'rase
Those everlasting lines.

5 He that can dash whole worlds to death
And make them when He please,
He speaks, and that almighty breath
Fulfills His great decrees.

6 His very word of grace is strong
As that which built the skies;
The voice that rolls the stars along
Speaks all the promises.

7 O might I hear Thine heav'nly tongue
But whisper, "Thou art mine,"
Those gentle words should raise my song
To notes almost divine.

8 How would my leaping heart rejoice
And think my heav'n secure!
I trust the all-creating voice,
And faith desires no more.

*Isaac Watts,* [1707, *rev.* 1709]

**MTP:** Spurgeon quoted this hymn in his last
sermon at the Metropolitan Tabernacle, 7
June 1891 (vol. 37, p. 315): "Yes, we have no
doubt about the result of our warfare. He that
is faithful to Christ shall be glorified with him.
That he will divide the spoil with the strong is
never a matter of question. 'The pleasure of the
Lord shall prosper in his hand.' The old truth by
which we stand shall never be blotted out.
'Engraved as in eternal brass
The mighty promise shines.
Nor shall the powers of darkness 'rase
Those everlasting lines.'"

# 193
**L.M.**
*Faithful and unchanging.*

1 HOW oft have sin and Satan strove
To rend my soul from Thee, my God?

But everlasting is Thy love,
And Jesus seals it with His blood.

2 The oath and promise of the Lord
Join to confirm the wondrous grace;
Eternal power performs the word
And fills all heaven with endless praise.

3 Amidst temptations sharp and long,
My soul to this dear refuge flies;
Hope is my anchor, firm and strong,
While tempests blow and billows rise.

4 The gospel bears my spirit up;
A faithful and unchanging God
Lays the foundation for my hope
In oaths, and promises, and blood.

*Isaac Watts*, 1709

# 194 L.M.
*Condescension.*

1 UP to the Lord that reigns on high
And views the nations from afar,
Let everlasting praises fly,
And tell how large His bounties are.

2 He that can shake the worlds he made,
Or with His word, or with His rod;
His goodness, how amazing great!
And what a condescending God!

3 God that must stoop to view the skies
And bow to see what angels do,
Down to our earth He casts His eyes
And bends His footsteps downward too.

4 He over-rules all mortal things
And manages our mean affairs;
On humble souls the King of Kings
Bestows His counsels and His cares.

5 Our sorrows and our tears we pour
Into the bosom of our God;
He hears us in the mournful hour
And helps us bear the heavy load.

6 O could our thankful hearts devise
A tribute equal to Thy grace,

To the third heav'n our songs should rise
And teach the golden harps Thy praise.

*Isaac Watts*, [1707, *rev.* 1709]

# 195 C.M.
*Condescension.*

1 MY God! how wonderful Thou art,
Thy majesty how bright,
How beautiful Thy mercy seat
In depths of burning light!

2 O how I fear Thee, living God!
With deepest, tenderest fears,
And worship Thee with trembling hope
And penitential tears.

3 Yet may I love Thee too, O Lord!
Almighty as Thou art,
For Thou hast stooped to ask of me
The love of my poor heart.

4 No earthly father loves like Thee,
No mother half so mild
Bears and forbears, as Thou hast done,
With me Thy sinful child.

5 Father of Jesus, love's reward!
What rapture will it be,
Prostrate before Thy throne to lie
*And ever gaze* on Thee!

*Frederick William Faber*, 1849
[*alt. Hymns Ancient & Modern*, 1861]

**5.4** *And gaze and gaze*

# 196 L.M.
*Loving kindness.*

1 AWAKE, my soul, in joyful lays,
And sing Thy great Redeemer's praise;
He justly claims a song from me;
His loving kindness, *O how* free!

2 He saw me ruin'd in the fall,
Yet lov'd me, notwithstanding all;
*He* sav'd me from my lost estate;
His loving kindness, *O how* great!

3 Though *numerous* hosts of *mighty* foes,
*Though* earth and hell my way oppose,
He safely leads my soul along;
His loving kindness, *O how* strong!

4 When trouble, like a gloomy cloud,
Has gather'd thick and thunder'd loud,
He near my soul has always stood;
His loving kindess, O how good!

5 Often I feel my sinful heart
Prone from my Jesus to depart,
*But though I have Him oft* forgot,
His loving kindness changes not.

6 *Soon shall I pass the* gloomy vale,
*Soon all my* mortal pow'rs *must* fail;
Oh! may my last expiring breath
His loving kindness sing in death.

7 Then *let me* mount and soar away
To the bright world of endless day;
*And sing, with rapture and* surprise,
His loving kindness in the skies.

1-3, 5-7 *Samuel Medley*, [1782, *rev.* 1785]
[*alt. John Rippon*, 1787]
4 John Rippon's *Selection*, 1787

**1.4, etc.:** *is so* **2.3:** *And* **3.1:** *mighty / cruel*
**3.2:** *Where* **5.3:** *And though I oft have Him*
**6.1:** *So when I pass death's*
**6.2:** *And life and / shall* **7.1:** *shall I*
**7.3:** *There shall I sing, with sweet*
**MM:** Hymns, Set 2 (Feb./Dec.), 10th Morn,
LOVING KINDNESS / ROLLAND
**FPN:** 5 Sept. 1889 (No. 2120), DERBY

# 197 8.7.8.7.
*Wisdom and love.*

1 GOD is love! His mercy brightens
All the path in which we rove;
Bliss He wakes, and woe He lightens;
God is wisdom! God is love!

2 Chance and change are busy ever;
Man decays and ages move;
But His mercy waneth never;
God is wisdom! God is love!

3 E'en the hour that darkest seemeth
Will His changeless goodness prove;
From the mist His brightness streameth;
God is wisdom! God is love!

4 He with earthly cares entwineth
Hope and comfort from above;
Everywhere His glory shineth;
God is wisdom! God is love!

*John Bowring*, 1825

# 198 C.M.
*All-sufficient in Grace.*

1 MY God, how cheerful is the sound!
How pleasant to repeat!
Well may that heart with pleasure bound,
Where God hath fix'd His seat.

2 What want shall not our God supply
From his redundant stores?
What streams of mercy from on high
An arm almighty pours!

3 From Christ the ever-living spring,
These ample blessings flow;
Prepare, my lips, His name to sing,
Whose heart hath lov'd us so.

4 Now to our Father and our God,
Be endless glory giv'n,
Through all the realms of man's abode,
And through the highest heav'n.

*Philip Doddridge*, 1755

# 199 C.M.
*Goodness of God.*

1 YE humble souls, approach your God
With songs of sacred praise,
For He is good, immensely good,
And kind are all His ways.

2 All nature owns His guardian care;
In Him we live and move;
But nobler benefits declare
The wonders of His love.

3 He gave His son, His only Son,
  To ransom rebel worms;
 'Tis here he makes His goodness known
  In its *diviner* forms.

4 To this dear refuge, Lord, we come;
  'Tis here our hope relies;
 A safe defence, a peaceful home,
  When storms of trouble rise.

5 *Thine* eye beholds with kind regard
  The souls who trust in Thee;
 Their humble hope Thou wilt reward
  With bliss divinely free.

6 Great God, to Thy almighty love,
  What honours shall we raise?
 Not all the raptur'd songs above
  Can render equal praise.

*Anne Steele*, 1760 [*rev.* 1780]
[*alt.* John Rippon, 1787]

  **3.4:** *divinest*  **5.1:** *Thy*

# 200 L.M.
*Goodness and kindness.*

1 GIVE thanks to God, He reigns above;
 Kind are His thoughts; His name is love;
 His mercy ages past have known,
 And ages long to come shall own.

2 Let the redeemèd of the Lord
 The wonders of His grace record;
 How great His works! how kind His ways!
 Let every tongue pronounce His praise.

*Isaac Watts*, 1719

# 201 11.11.11.11.
*The mercy of God.*

1 THY mercy, my God,
   is the theme of my song,
 The joy of my heart,
   and the boast of my tongue;
 Thy free grace alone,
   from the first to the last,
 Has won my affections
   and bound my soul fast.

2 Without Thy sweet mercy,
   I could not live here;
 Sin soon would reduce me
   to utter despair;
 But through Thy free goodness
   my spirits revive,
 And He that first made me
   still keeps me alive.

3 Thy mercy is more than
   a match for my heart,
 Which wonders to feel its
   own hardness depart;
 Dissolv'd by Thy *goodness*,
   I fall to the ground,
 And weep to the praise of
   the mercy I've found.

4 The *door* of Thy mercy
   *stands* open all day
 To th' poor and the needy,
   who knock by the way;
 *No sinner shall ever*
   *be empty sent back,*
 *Who comes seeking mercy*
   *for Jesus's sake.*

5 Thy mercy, in Jesus,
   exempts me from hell;
 *Its glories* I'll sing, *and*
   *its wonders* I'll tell;
 'Twas Jesus, my Friend, when
   He hung on the tree,
 That open'd the channel
   of mercy for me.

6 Great Father of mercies,
   Thy goodness I own,
 And the covenant love of
   Thy crucified Son;
 All praise to the Spirit,
   whose whisper divine
 Seals mercy, and pardon, and
   righeousness, mine.

*John Stocker*, 1776
[*alt.* John Rippon, 1787]

  **3.5:** *sun shine*  **4.1:** *doors*  **4.2:** *are*

**4.5-8:** *But those that bring cash in*
*the mouth of their sack,*
*The rich and the proud, shall*
*be empty sent back.*

**5.3:** *Of thy mercy* / of **5.4:** *thy mercy*

**Ed:** Julian, in his *Dictionary*, p. 1094, complained, "Sedgwick had no authority for saying that 'J.S.' was John Stocker; we have no authority for saying this is not so. There is no proof either way." In all fairness to Sedgwick, the May 1777 issue of *The Gospel Magazine* contained four hymns variously signed "John Stocker," "J. Stocker," and "J.S." If anyone could claim those initials in the March 1776 issue, it would be Stocker.

**MBTS:** 8 Feb. 1883 (No. 2564), MONTGOMERY

# 202   8.8.8.8.8.8.
*A pardoning God.*

1 GREAT God of wonders! all Thy ways
Are matchless, God-like, and divine,
But the fair glories of Thy grace
More God-like and unrivall'd shine.
    Who is a pard'ning God like Thee?
    Or who has grace so rich and free?

2 Crimes of such horror to forgive,
Such guilty, daring worms to spare;
This is thy grand prerogative,
And none shall in the honour share.
    Who is a pard'ning God like Thee?
    Or who has grace so rich and free?

3 In wonder lost, with trembling joy,
We take the pardon of our God,
Pardon for crimes of deepest dye,
A pardon bought with Jesus' blood.
    Who is a pard'ning God like Thee?
    Or who has grace so rich and free?

4 O may this strange, this matchless grace,
This God-like miracle of love,
Fill the wide earth with grateful praise,
And all th' angelic choirs above!
    Who is a pard'ning God like Thee?
    Or who has grace so rich and free?

*Samuel Davies,* 1769

# ACTS OF GOD: CREATION AND PROVIDENCE.

# 203   7.7.7.7.
*He is worthy to be praised.*

1 SONGS of praise the angels sang,
Heaven with hallelujahs rang,
When Jehovah's work begun,
When He spake, and it was done.

2 Songs of praise awoke the morn,
When the Prince of Peace was born;
Songs of praise arose, when He
Captive led captivity.

3 Heaven and earth must pass away;
Songs of praise shall crown that day;
God will make new heavens and earth;
Songs of praise shall hail their birth.

4 And shall man alone be dumb
Till that glorious kingdom come?
No—the church delights to raise
Psalms and hymns and songs of praise.

5 Saints below, with heart and voice,
Still in songs of praise rejoice,
Learning here, by faith and love,
Songs of praise to sing above.

6 Borne upon their latest breath,
Songs of praise shall conquer death;
Then, amidst eternal joy,
Songs of praise their powers employ.

*James Montgomery,* 1819

# 204   8.7.8.7.
*"Thou hast created all things."*

1 PRAISE to Thee, Thou great Creator!
    Praise be Thine from every tongue;
Join, my soul, with every creature,
    Join the universal song.

2 *Father! Source of* all compassion!
    Pure, unbounded *grace is Thine;*

*Hail the God of our salvation!*
   *Praise Him for His love divine.*

3 For ten thousand blessings given,
   For the *hope of future joy,*
Sound His praise through earth and heaven,
   Sound Jehovah's praise *on high.*

4 *Joyfully on earth adore Him,*
   *Till in heaven our song we raise;*
*There, enraptured fall before Him,*
   Lost in wonder, love, and praise.

1,3 *John Fawcett,* 1782, *alt.*
2,4 *Charles Wesley,* 1747, *alt.*

   **2.1:** *Jesus, Thou art*  **2.2:** *love Thou art;*
   **2.3-4:** *Visit us with Thy salvation;*
      *Enter every trembling heart.*
   **3.2:** *richest gifts bestow'd*  **3.4:** *aloud*
   **4.1-3:** *Chang'd from glory into glory,*
      *Till in heaven we take our place,*
      *Till we cast our crowns before Thee,*
   **Ed:** This text is a cross between Fawcett's "Lo!
   the bright, the rosy morning," and Wesley's
   "Love divine, all loves excelling," combined and
   altered for *Psalms and Hymns for Social and
   Private Worship* (1812).

# 205 C.M.
*"He that built all things is God."*

1 I SING th' almighty power of God
   That made the mountains rise,
That spread the flowing seas abroad
   And built the lofty skies.

2 I sing the wisdom that ordain'd
   The sun to rule the day;
The moon shines full at His command,
   And all the stars obey.

3 I sing the goodness of the Lord
   That fill'd the earth with food;
He form'd the creatures with His word
   And then pronounc'd them good.

4 There's not a plant or flower below
   But makes Thy glories known,
And clouds arise and tempests blow
   By order from Thy throne.

5 Creatures, as numerous as they be,
   Are subject to Thy care;
There's not a place where we can flee,
   But God is present there.

6 In heaven He shines with beams of love,
   With wrath in hell beneath;
'Tis on His earth I stand or move,
   And 'tis His air I breathe.

7 His hand is my perpetual guard;
   He guides me with His eye;
Why should I then forget the Lord,
   Who is forever nigh?

*Isaac Watts,* 1715

# 206 C.M.
*Creating and creating new.*

1 LET them neglect Thy glory, Lord,
   Who never knew Thy grace,
But our loud song shall still record
   The wonders of Thy praise.

2 We raise our shouts, O God, to Thee,
   And send them to Thy throne;
All glory to th' united Three,
   The undivided One.

3 'Twas He (and we'll adore His name)
   That form'd us by a word;
'Tis He restores our ruin'd frame;
   Salvation to the Lord!

4 Hosanna! let the earth and skies
   Repeat the joyful sound;
Rocks, hills, and vales reflect the voice
   In one eternal round.

*Isaac Watts,* [1707]

# 207 C.M.
*Divine pedestination.*

1 KEEP silence, all created things,
   And wait your Maker's nod;
*My soul* stands trembling while she sings
   The honours of her God.

2 Life, death, and hell, and worlds unknown
  Hang on His firm decree;
He sits on no precarious throne,
  Nor borrows leave to be.

3 Chain'd to His throne a volume lies,
  With all the fates of men,
With every angel's form and size
  Drawn by th' eternal pen.

4 His providence unfolds the book
  And makes His counsels shine;
Each opening leaf and every stroke
  Fulfills some deep design.

5 Here He exalts neglected worms
  To sceptres and a crown;
Anon the following page he turns
  And treads the monarchs down.

6 Not Gabriel asks the reason why,
  Nor God the reason gives,
Nor dares the favourite angel pry
  Between the folded leaves.

7 My God, I *would not long* to see
  My fate with curious eyes,
What gloomy lines are writ for me,
  Or what bright scenes *may* rise.

8 In Thy fair book of life and grace
  May I but find my name
Recorded in some humble place
  Beneath my Lord, the Lamb!

*Isaac Watts*, 1709
[*alt. John Rippon*, 1787]

  **1.3:** *The muse*  **7.1:** *never long'd*  **7.4:** *shall*

# 208 7.7.7.7.
*All our ways appointed.*

1 SOVEREIGN Ruler of the skies,
Ever gracious, ever wise!
All my times are in Thy hand,
All events at Thy command.

2 His decree, who form'd the earth,
Fix'd my first and second birth;

Parents, native place, and time,
All appointed were by Him.

3 He that form'd me in the womb,
He shall guide me to the tomb;
All my times shall ever be
Order'd by His wise decree.

4 Times of sickness, times of health,
Times of penury and wealth,
Times of trial and of grief,
Times of triumph and relief,

5 Times the tempter's power to prove,
Times to taste a Saviour's love:
All must come, and last, and end,
As shall please my heavenly Friend.

6 Plagues and deaths around me fly;
Till He bids, I cannot die;
Not a single shaft can hit
Till the God of love *thinks* fit.

7 O Thou gracious, wise, and just,
In Thy hands my life I trust;
Have I somewhat dearer still?
I resign it to Thy will.

8 May I always own Thy hand;
Still to the surrender stand;
Know that Thou art God alone;
I and mine are all Thine own.

9 Thee, at all times, will I bless;
Having Thee, I all possess;
How can I bereavèd be,
Since I cannot part with Thee?

*John Ryland*, 1787
[*alt. John Rippon's Selection*, 1828]

  **6.4:** *sees*  **Ed:** Dated 1 Aug. 1777 in his MSS, but
  first published in Rippon's *Selection* (1787).
  **TD:** "The Lord's prophets shall live on in the
  midst of famine, and war, and plague, and
  persecution, till they have uttered all the words
  of their prophecy; his priests shall stand at the
  altar unharmed till their last sacrifice has been
  presented before Him. No bullet will find its bil-
  let in our hearts till we have finished our alloted
  period of activity" (Ps. 118:17; vol. 5, p. 328).

# 209 L.M.
*Providence wise and good.*

1 *THY ways, O Lord! with* wise design,
Are fram'd upon *Thy* throne above,
And ev'ry dark *and* bending line
Meets in the centre of *Thy* love.

2 With feeble light and half obscure,
Poor mortals *Thy* arrangements view,
Not knowing that the least are sure,
And the mysterious just and true.

3 *Thy* flock, *Thy* own peculiar care,
*Though now they seem to roam uneyed,*
Are led or driven only where
*They* best and saftest *may abide.*

4 *They neither* know nor trace the way,
But trusting to *Thy* piercing eye,
None of their feet to ruin stray,
*Nor shall the weakest fail* or die.

5 My favour'd soul shall meekly learn
To lay her reason at *Thy* throne;
*Too* weak *Thy* secrets to discern,
*I'll* trust *Thee* for *my* guide alone.

*Ambrose Serle,* [1776]
[*alt. John Rippon,* 1787]

**1.1:** *Jehovah's ways, in* **1.2:** *His* **1.3:** *or*
**1.4:** *His* **2.2:** *His* **3.1:** *His / His*
**3.2:** *Simply though now they seem to roam,*
**3.4:** *He brings them, …, home*
**4.1:** *True, they nor* **4.2:** *His*
**4.4:** *None of them fail, or droop,* **5.2:** *His*
**5.3:** *And / His* **5.4:** *Shall / Him / her*

# 210 L.M.
*God's counsels wise and just.*

1 WAIT, O my soul, Thy Maker's will;
Tumultuous passions, all be still;
Nor let a murmuring thought arise;
His ways are just, His counsels wise.

2 He in the thickest darkness dwells,
Performs His work, the cause conceals;
And though His footsteps are unknown,
Judgment and truth support His throne.

3 In heaven and earth, in air and seas,
He executes His wise decrees;
And by His saints it stands confess'd,
That what He does is ever best.

4 *Wait, then,* my soul, submissive wait;
With reverence bow before His seat;
And 'midst the terrors of His rod,
Trust in a wise and gracious God.

*Benjamin Beddome,* [1787, *rev.* 1817]

**4.1:** *Then, oh* (1817)

# 211 C.M.
*God moves in a mysterious way.*

1 GOD moves in a mysterious way,
His wonders to perform;
He plants His footsteps in the sea
And rides upon the storm.

2 Deep in unfathomable mines
Of never-failing skill,
He treasures up His bright designs
And works His sov'reign will.

3 Ye fearful saints, fresh courage take;
The clouds ye so much dread
Are big with mercy and shall break
In blessings on your head.

4 Judge not the Lord by feeble sense,
But trust Him for His grace;
Behind a frowning providence
He hides a smiling face.

5 His purposes will ripen fast,
Unfolding every hour;
The bud may have a bitter taste,
But sweet will be the flower.

6 Blind unbelief is sure to err,
And scan His work in vain;
God is His own interpreter,
And He will make it plain.

*William Cowper,* 1774

**FPN:** 17 July 1887 (No. 1973), WINCHESTER
**Ed:** In 1844, when Spurgeon was about ten,

Richard Knill, an English missionary, made a famous prophesy over the young man:

"Mr. Knill took me on his knee, and said, 'This child will one day preach the gospel, and he will preach it to great multitudes. I am persuaded that he will preach in the chapel of Rowland Hill, where (I think he said) I am now the minister.' He spoke very solemnly, and called upon all present to witness what he said. Then he gave me sixpence as a reward if I would learn the hymn, 'God moves in a mysterious way, His wonders to perform.' I was made to promise that, when I preached in Rowland Hill's Chapel, that hymn should be sung. . . .

Years flew by. After I had begun for some little time to preach in London, Dr. Alexander Fletcher was engaged to deliver the annual sermon to children in Surrey Chapel; but as he was taken ill, I was asked in a hurry to preach to the children in his stead. 'Yes,' I replied, 'I will, if you will allow the children to sing "God moves in a mysterious way." I have made a promise, long ago, that hymn should be sung.' And so it was: I preached in Rowland Hill's Chapel, and the hymn was sung" (*Autobiography*, vol. 1, p. 34).

# 212 L.M.
*Providence to be trusted.*

1 LORD, we adore Thy vast designs,
Th' obscure abyss of Providence,
Too deep to sound with mortal lines,
Too dark to view with feeble sense.

2 Now Thou array'st Thine awful face
In angry frowns, without a smile;
We, through the cloud, believe Thy grace,
Secure of Thy compassions still.

3 Through seas and storms of deep distress
We sail by faith and not by sight;
Faith guides us in the wilderness,
Through all the briars and the night.

4 Dear Father, if Thy lifted rod
Resolve to scourge us here below,
Still we must lean upon our God;
Thine arm shall bear us safely through.

*Isaac Watts*, [1707]

**TD:** "This is grand faith which can trust the Lord even when he seems to have cast us off. Some can barely trust Him when He pampers them, and yet David relied upon Him when Israel seemed under a cloud and the Lord had hidden His face. O for more of this real and living faith" (Ps. 108:11; vol. 5, p. 150).

# 213 L.M.
*How unsearchable are Thy judgments.*

1 LORD, my weak tho't in vain would climb
To search the starry vault profound,
In vain would wing her flight sublime
To find creation's utmost bound.

2 But weaker yet that thought must prove
To search Thy great eternal plan,
Thy sovereign counsels, born of love,
Long ages ere the world began.

3 When my dim reason would demand
Why that or this Thou dost ordain,
By some vast deep I seem to stand,
Whose secrets I must ask in vain.

4 When doubts disturb my troubled breast,
And all is dark as night to me,
Here, as on solid rock, I rest;
That so it seemeth good to Thee.

5 Be this my joy, that evermore
Thou rulest all things at Thy will;
Thy sovereign wisdom I adore,
And calmly, sweetly, trust Thee still.

*Ray Palmer*, 1858

# 214 C.M.
*Gratitude for providence.*

1 WHEN all Thy mercies, O my God,
My rising soul surveys,
Transported with the view, I'm lost
In wonder, love, and praise.

2 O how shall words, with equal warmth,
The gratitude declare
That glows within my ravish'd heart?
But Thou canst read it there.

3 To all my weak complaints and cries
    Thy mercy lent an ear,
Ere yet my feeble thoughts had learnt
    To form themselves in prayer.

4 When in the slippery paths of youth
    With heedless steps I ran,
Thine arm unseen convey'd me safe,
    And led me up to man.

5 Through hidden dangers, toils, and deaths,
    It gently clear'd my way,
And through the pleasing snares of vice,
    More to be fear'd than they.

6 When worn with sickness, oft hast Thou
    With health renew'd my face,
And when in sins and sorrow sunk,
    Revived my soul with grace.

7 Through every period of my life
    Thy goodness I'll pursue;
And after death, in distant worlds,
    The glorious theme renew.

8 When nature fails, and day and night
    Divide Thy works no more,
My ever grateful heart, O Lord,
    Thy mercy shall adore.

9 Through all eternity to Thee
    A joyful song I'll raise;
*But* oh! eternity's too short
    To utter all Thy praise.

*Joseph Addison*, 1712, [*alt.*]

**9.3:** *For*   **Ed:** This minor alteration dates as
early as John H. Meyer's *Collection* (1782).
**TD:** "What gems are those two expressions, 'tender mercies and loving-kindnesses'! They are
the virgin honey of language; for sweetness no
words can excel them; but as for the gracious
favours which are intended by them, language
fails to describe them" (Ps. 25:6; vol. 1, p. 443).

# 215   C.M.
*The God of Bethel.*

1 O GOD of *Bethel*, by whose hand
    *Thy people* still *are* fed,

Who through this weary pilgrimage
    Hast all our fathers led:

2 Our vows, our pray'rs, we now present
    Before Thy throne of grace;
God of our fathers! be the God
    Of their succeeding race.

3 Through each perplexing path of life
    Our wand'ring foosteps guide;
Give us each day our daily bread,
    And raiment fit provide.

4 *O spread Thy cov'ring wings* around,
    Till *all* our wand'rings cease,
And at our Father's lov'd abode
    Our souls arrive in peace.

5 Such blessings from Thy gracious hand
    Our humble pray'rs implore,
And Thou shalt be our chosen God
    And portion evermore.

1,4 *Philip Doddridge*, 1755 [*alt. J.L.*, 1781]
[2,3,5 *John Logan*, 1781]

**1.1:** *Jacob*   **1.2:** *Thine Israel / is*
**4.1:** *If Thou wilt spread thy shield*   **4.2:** *these*
**MM:** Hymns, Set 2 (Feb./Dec.), 31st Morn,
MEAR / HELENA

# 216   C.M.
*Goodness of God in providence.*

1 SINCE all the downward tracts of time
    God's watchful eye surveys,
Oh! who so wise to choose our lot
    And regulate our ways?

2 Good when He gives, supremely good,
    Nor less when He denies;
E'en crosses from His sovereign hand
    Are blessings in disguise.

3 Since none can doubt His equal love,
    Unmeasurably kind,
To His unerring, gracious will
    Be ev'ry wish resign'd.

*James Hervey*, [1746]

**Ed:** The original order of stanzas was 1,3,2.

## 217 C.M.
*"He careth for you."*

1 OH, why despond in life's dark vale?
　　Why sink to fears a prey?
Th' almighty power can never fail,
　　His love can ne'er decay.

2 Behold the birds that wing the air,
　　Nor sow nor reap the grain;
Yet God, with all a Father's care,
　　Relieves when they complain.

3 Behold the lilies of the field:
　　They toil nor labour know,
Yet royal robes to theirs must yield,
　　In beauty's richest glow.

4 That God who hears the raven's cry,
　　Who decks the lily's form,
Will surely all your wants supply
　　And shield you in the storm.

5 Seek first His kingdom's grace to share,
　　Its righteousness pursue,
And all that needs your earthly care
　　Will be bestowed on you.

6 Why then despond in life's dark vale?
　　Why sink to fears a prey?
Th' almighty power can never fail;
　　His love can ne'er decay.

*Sabbath Hymn Book*, 1858

## Grace

## PREDESTINATION
## IN CONNECTION WITH GRACE.

## 218 C.M.
*Sovereign grace.*

1 WHEN the Eternal bows the skies
　　To visit earthly things,
With scorn divine He turns His eyes
　　From towers of haughty kings.

2 He bids His awful chariot roll
　　Far downward from the skies,
To visit every humble soul
　　With pleasure in His eyes.

3 Why should the Lord that reigns above
　　Disdain so lofty kings?
Say, Lord, and why such looks of love
　　Upon such worthless things?

4 Mortals, be dumb; what creature dares
　　Dispute His awful will?
Ask no account of His affairs,
　　But tremble and be still.

5 Just like His nature is His grace,
　　All sovereign and all free,
Great God, how searchless are Thy ways!
　　How deep Thy judgments be!

*Isaac Watts*, 1709

## 219 11.8.11.8.
*Gracious election.*

1 IN songs of sublime adoration and praise,
　　Ye pilgrims to Zion who press,
Break forth and extol the great
　　　　Ancient of Days,
　　His rich and distinguishing grace.

2 His love, from eternity fix'd upon you,
　　Broke forth and discover'd its flame,
When each with the cords of His
　　　　kindness He drew
　　And brought you to love His great name.

3 O had He not pitied the state you were in,
    Your bosoms His love had ne'er felt,
You all would have lived, would have
        died too in sin,
    And sunk with the load of your guilt.

4 What was there in you that could
        merit esteem
    Or give the Creator delight?
'Twas "even so, Father," you ever must sing,
    "Because it seem'd good in Thy sight."

5 'Twas all of Thy grace we were
        brought to obey,
    While others were suffer'd to go
The road which by nature we
        chose as our way,
    Which leads to the regions of woe.

6 Then give all the glory to His holy name;
    To Him all the glory belongs;
Be yours the high joy still to
        sound forth His fame,
    And crown Him in each of your songs.

*K—* in John Rippon's *Selection*, 1787

**Ed:** See the notes on No. 732.

# 220
7.6.7.6. Double
*Electing Love Acknowledged.*

1 'TIS not that I did choose Thee,
    For, Lord, that could not be;
This heart would still refuse Thee,
    But Thou hast chosen me;
*Thou* from the sin that stained me
    Washed me and set me free,
And to this end ordained me,
    That I should live to Thee.

2 'Twas sovereign mercy called me
    And taught my opening mind;
The world had else enthralled me,
    To heavenly glories blind.
My heart owns none above Thee;
    For Thy rich grace I thirst;
This knowing, if I love Thee,
    Thou must have loved me first.

*Josiah Conder,* [1842]
[*alt. Sabbath Hymn Book,* 1858]

**1.5:** *Hast*

# 221
8.7.8.7.4.7.
*Free Grace in Election.*

1 SONS we are through God's election,
    Who in Jesus Christ believe;
By eternal destination,
    *Sov'reign* grace we here receive;
       *Lord, Thy* mercy
    Does both grace and glory give.

2 Ev'ry *fallen soul, by* sinning,
    Merits everlasting pain;
But Thy love, without beginning,
    *Has restored Thy sons again;*
       Countless millions
    Shall in life, through Jesus, reign.

3 Pause, my soul! adore and wonder!
    Ask, "O why such love to me?"
Grace hath put me in the number
    Of the Saviour's family;
       Hallelujah!
    Thanks, *eternal thanks*, to Thee!

4 Since that love had no beginning,
    And shall never, never cease,
Keep, O keep me, Lord, from sinning!
    Guide me in the way of peace!
       Make me walk in
    All the paths of holiness.

5 When I quit this feeble mansion
    And my soul returns to Thee,
Let the pow'r of Thy ascension
    Manifest itself in me;
       Through Thy Spirit,
    Give the final victory!

6 When the angel sounds the trumpet,
    When my soul and body join,
When my Saviour comes to judgment,
    Bright in majesty divine,
       *Let me* triumph
    *In Thy* righteousness *as* mine.

7 When in that blest habitation,
   Which my God *has fore*-ordain'd,
When in glory's full possession,
   I with saints and angels stand;
      Free grace only
   Shall resound through Canaan's land.

*S—P—R—*, 1777
[*alt. John Rippon*, 1787]

   **1.4:** *Saving*  **1.5:** *Sov'reign*  **2.1:** *soul, by Adam's*
   **2.4:** *Form'd and fix'd the gracious plan;*
   **3.6:** *Eternal Love*  **6.5:** *I shall*  **6.6:** *For His / is*
   **7.2:** *for me*  **TD:** "Pause, my soul, at this *Selah*,
      and consider thine own interest in the salva-
      tion of God; and if by humble faith thou art
      enabled to see Jesus as thine by his own free
      gift of himself to thee, if this greatest of all
      blessings be upon thee, rise up and sing—
      'Rise, my soul! adore and wonder! . . .'" (Ps. 3:8;
      vol. 1, p. 27).

# 222 C.M.
*Election Love Adored.*

1 O GIFT of gifts! O grace of faith!
   My God! how can it be
That Thou, who hast discerning love,
   Shouldst give that gift to me?

2 How many hearts Thou might'st have had
   More innocent than mine!
How many souls more worthy far
   Of that *pure* touch of Thine!

3 Ah, grace! into unlikeliest hearts
   It is thy boast to come,
The glory of thy light to find
   In darkest spots a home.

4 Thy choice, O God of goodness! then
   I lovingly adore;
O give me grace to keep Thy grace,
   And grace to *long for* more!

*Frederick William Faber*, 1849
[*alt. Sabbath Hymn Book*, 1858]

   **2.4:** *sweet*  **4.4:** *merit*
   **Ed:** Taken from the longer hymn,
      "O faith! thou workest miracles."

# 223 L.M.
*Electing Love Immutable.*

1 WHO shall condemn to endless flames
   The chosen people of our God?
Since in the book of life their names
   Are fairly writ in Jesus' blood.

2 He, for the sins of all the elect,
   Hath a complete atonement made;
And Justice never can expect
   That the same debt should twice be paid.

3 Not tribulation, nakedness,
   The famine, peril, or the sword,
Not persecution, or distress,
   Can separate from Christ the Lord.

4 Nor life, nor death, nor depth, nor height,
   Nor powers below, nor powers above,
Nor present things, nor things to come,
   Can change His purposes of love.

5 His sovereign mercy knows no end,
   His faithfulness shall still endure;
And those who on His Word depend
   Shall find His Word forever sure.

*Benjamin Beddome*, [1787]

# 224 L.M.
*Everlasting Love.*

1 'Twas with an everlasting love
   That God His own elect embrac'd,
Before He made the worlds above,
   Or earth, on her huge columns plac'd.

2 Long ere the sun's refulgent ray
   Primeval shades of darkness drove,
They on His sacred bosom lay,
   Lov'd with an everlasting love.

3 Then, in the glass of His decrees,
   Christ and His bride appear'd as one;
Her sin, by imputation, His,
   Whilst she in spotless splendour shone.

4 O love, how high thy glories swell,
   How great, immutable, and free;
Ten thousand sins, as black as hell,
   Are swallowed up, O love, in thee.

5 Lov'd when a wretch defil'd with sin,
    At war with heaven, in league with hell,
A slave to ev'ry lust obscene,
    Who, living, lived but to rebel.

6 Believer, here thy comfort stands;
    From first to last, salvation's free;
And everlasting love demands
    An everlasting song from thee.

*John Kent,* 1803

## 225 L.M.
*Election in Christ.*

1 JESUS, we bless Thy Father's name;
Thy God and ours are both the same;
What heav'nly blessings from His throne
Flow down to sinners through His Son?

2 "Christ, be my first elect," He said,
Then chose our souls in Christ our head,
Before He gave the mountains birth
Or laid foundations for the earth.

3 Thus did eternal love begin
To raise us up from death and sin;
Our characters were then decreed,
"Blameless in love, a holy seed."

4 Predestined to be sons,
Born by degrees, but chose at once,
A new regenerated race,
To praise the glory of His grace.

5 With Christ our Lord we share our part
In the affections of His heart,
Nor shall our souls be thence remov'd
Till He forgets His first-belov'd.

*Isaac Watts,* [1707]

## 226 C.M.
*Love before atonement.*

1 'TWAS not to make Jehovah's love
    Towards the sinner flame,
That Jesus, from His throne above,
    A suff'ring man became.

2 'Twas not the death which He endur'd,
    Nor all the pangs He bore,
That God's eternal love procur'd,
    For God was love before.

3 He lov'd the world of His elect
    With love surpassing thought,
Nor will His mercy e'er neglect
    The souls so dearly bought.

4 The warm affections of His breast
    Towards His chosen burn;
And in His love He'll ever rest,
    Nor from His oath return.

5 Still to confirm His oath of old,
    See in the heav'ns His bow;
No fierce rebukes, but love untold
    Awaits His children now.

*John Kent,* 1803

# THE COVENANT.

## 227 6.6.6.6.8.8.
*The Covenant.*

1 WITH David's Lord, and ours,
    A cov'nant once was made,
Whose bonds are firm and sure,
    Whose glories ne'er shall fade,
Sign'd by the sacred Three in One,
In mutual love ere time begun.

2 Firm as the lasting hills,
    This cov'nant shall endure,
Whose potent 'shalls' and 'wills'
    Make every blessing sure;
When ruin shakes all nature's frame,
Its jots and tittles stand the same.

3 Here, when thy feet shall fall,
    Believer, thou shalt see
Grace to restore thy soul,
    And pardon, full and free;
Thee with delight shall God behold,
A *sheep restored to* Zion's fold.

4 And when through Jordan's flood
    Thy God shall bid thee go,
His arm shall thee defend
    And vanquish every foe;
And in this cov'nant thou shalt view
Sufficient strength to bear thee through.

*John Kent, 1803, alt. C.H.S.*

**3.6:** *chosen sheep in*

# 228 C.M.
*An Everlasting Covenant.*

1 MY God, the cov'nant of Thy love
    Abides forever sure,
And in its matchless grace I feel
    My happiness secure.

2 What though my house be not with Thee
    As nature could desire?
To nobler joys than nature gives
    Thy servants all aspire.

3 Since Thou, the everlasting God,
    My Father art become;
Jesus, my Guardian and my Friend,
    And heav'n my final home.

4 I welcome all Thy sovereign will,
    For all that will is love;
And when I know not what Thou dost,
    I'll wait the light above.

5 *Thy cov'nant the last accent claims*
    *Of this poor falt'ring tongue,*
*And that shall the first notes employ*
    *Of my celestial song.*

*Philip Doddridge, 1755*

**5:** *Thy cov'nant in the darkest gloom*
    *Shall heav'nly rays impart,*
*Which, when my eye-lids close in death,*
    *Shall warm my chilling heart.*
**Ed:** The 5th stanza is substituted from another
Doddridge hymn, "'Tis mine, the cov'nant
of His grace." This substitution was first em-
ployed by John Rippon (1787).

# 229 6.6.8.4. Double
*The Covenant God Extolled.*

1 THE God of Abrah'm praise,
    Who reigns enthron'd above,
Ancient of everlasting days,
    And God of love:
Jehovah, great I AM!
By earth and heav'n confest;
I bow and bless the sacred name,
    Forever blest.

2 The God of Abrah'm praise,
    At whose supreme command,
From earth I rise and seek the joys
    At His right hand.
I all on earth forsake,
    Its wisdom, fame, and power;
And Him my only portion make,
    My shield and tower.

3 The God of Abrah'm praise,
    Whose all-sufficient grace
Shall guide me all my happy days
    In all His ways.
He calls a worm His friend!
He calls Himself my God!
And He shall save me to the end,
    Through Jesu's blood.

4 He by Himself hath sworn,
    I on His oath depend;
I shall, on eagles' wings upborne,
    To heaven ascend;
I shall behold His face,
I shall His power adore,
And sing the wonders of His grace
    Forever more.

PART THE SECOND.

5 Though nature's strength decay,
    And earth and hell withstand,
To Canaan's bounds I urge my way
    At His command.
The wat'ry deep I pass,
With Jesus in my view,
And through the howling wilderness
    My way pursue.

6    The goodly land I see,
      With peace and plenty blest,
  A land of sacred liberty
      And endless rest:
    There milk and honey flow,
    And oil and wine abound,
  And trees of life forever grow
      With mercy crown'd.

7    There dwells the Lord our King,
      The Lord our righteousness,
  Triumphant o'er the world and sin,
      The Prince of Peace:
    On Zion's sacred height,
    His kingdom still maintains,
  And glorious with His saints in light,
      Forever reigns.

8    The whole triumphant host
      Give thanks to God on high;
  "Hail Father, Son, and Holy Ghost!"
      They ever cry;
    Hail, Abrah'm's God and mine!
    I join the heavenly lays;
  All might and majesty are Thine,
      And endless praise.

*Thomas Olivers*, 1772

# THE WORK OF GRACE
# AS A WHOLE.

## 230
6.6.6.6.8.8.
*All mercies traced to electing love.*

1 INDULGENT God! how kind
   Are all Thy ways to me,
  Whose dark benighted mind
    Was enmity with Thee;
  Yet now, subdu'd by sov'reign grace,
  My spirit longs for Thine embrace.

2 How precious are Thy thoughts
   That o'er my bosom roll;
  They swell beyond my faults
    And captivate my soul;
  How great their sum, how high they rise
  Can ne'er be known beneath the skies.

3 Preserv'd in Jesus, when
   My feet made haste to hell;
  And there should I have gone,
   But Thou dost all things well;
  Thy love was great, Thy mercy free,
  Which from the pit delivr'd me.

4 Before Thy hands had made
   The sun to rule the day,
  Or earth's foundation laid,
   Or fashion'd Adam's clay,
  What thoughts of peace and mercy flow'd
  In Thy dear bosom, O my God!

5 Oh! fathomless abyss,
   Where hidden myst'ries lie;
  The seraph finds his bliss
   Within the same to pry;
  Lord, what is man, Thy desp'rate foe,
  That Thou shouldst bless and love him so?

6 A monument of grace,
   A sinner sav'd by blood;
  The streams of love I trace
   Up to the fountain, God,
  And in His sacred bosom see
  Eternal thoughts of love to me.

*John Kent*, 1803

**FPN:** 17 July 1887 (No. 1973), DARWALL'S

## 231
C.M.
*Eternal love exalted.*

1 SAVED from the damning power of sin,
   The law's tremendous curse,
  We'll now the sacred song begin
   Where God began with us.

2 We'll sing the vast unmeasur'd grace
   Which from the days of old
  Did all *the chosen sons* embrace,
   As sheep within *the* fold.

3 The basis of eternal love
   Shall mercy's frame sustain;
  Earth, hell, or sin, the same to move,
   Shall all conspire in vain.

4 Sing, O ye sinners bought with blood;
    Hail the Great Three in One;
Tell how secure the cov'nant stood
    Ere time its race begun.

5 Ne'er had ye felt the guilt of sin,
    Nor sweets of pard'ning love,
Unless your worthless names had been
    Enroll'd to life above.

6 Oh what a sweet *exulting* song
    Shall rend the vaulted skies,
When, shouting grace,
        the blood-wash'd throng
Shall see the Top Stone rise.

*John Kent*, 1803, alt. C.H.S.

**2.3:** *his Son's elect*  **2.4:** *His*  **6.1:** *exalted*
**Ed:** This hymn was used at the opening of the
Metropolitan Tabernacle, 18 Mar. 1861, and
reprinted in MTP, vol. 7, p. 168.

# 232
C.M.
*The love that God hath to us.*

1 OH love beyond the reach of thought
    That formed the sovereign plan,
Ere Adam had our ruin wrought,
    Of saving fallen man!

2 God has so loved our rebel race
    As His own Son to give,
That whoso will, amazing grace!
    May look to Him and live.

3 Chosen in Christ, His ransomed flock
    The eternal purpose prove;
By nature of a sinful stock,
    Made blameless now in love.

4 Ransomed by price, by blood redeemed,
    Restored by power divine,
Though lightly by the world esteemed,
    They as the stars shall shine.

5 Bless'd be the Father of our Lord,
    From whom all blessings spring!
And bless'd be the Incarnate Word,
    Our Saviour and our King!

6 We know and have believed the love
    Which God through Christ displays;
And when we see His face above,
    We'll nobler anthems raise.

*Josiah Conder*, 1856

# 233
S.M.
*"Grace reigns."*

1 GRACE! 'tis a charming sound,
    Harmonious to *the* ear!
Heav'n with the echo shall resound,
    And all the earth shall hear.

2 Grace first contriv'd *the* way
    To save rebellious man,
And all the steps that grace display,
    Which drew the wondrous plan.

3 *Grace first inscrib'd* my name
    In *God's* eternal book;
'Twas grace that gave me to the Lamb,
    Who all my sorrows took.

4 Grace *led* my *roving* feet
    To tread the heav'nly road,
And new supplies each hour I meet
    While pressing on to God.

5 Grace taught my soul to pray
    And made my eyes o'erflow;
'Twas grace *that* kept me to this day
    And will not let me go.

6 Grace all the work shall crown,
    Through everlasting days;
It lays in heav'n the topmost stone
    And well deserves the praise.

1,2,4,6 *Philip Doddridge*, 1755
3,5 *Augustus Toplady*, 1776
[alt. *John Rippon*, 1800]

**1.2:** *my* (1755)  **2.1:** *a* (1755, 1776)
**3.1:** *'Twas grace that wrote* (1776)  **3.2:** *thy* (1776)
**4.1:** *taught / wand'ring* (1755)  *forc'd /
wand'ring* (1776)  **5.3:** *which* (1776, 1800)
*that* (Compr. Ed., 1844)

## 234 S.M.
*Grace most free*

1 NOT to myself I owe
    That I, O Lord, am Thine;
Free grace hath all the shades broke thru'
    And caus'd the light to shine.

2 Me Thou hast willing made
    Thy offers to receive;
Call'd by the voice that wakes the dead,
    I come to Thee and live.

3 Because Thy sov'reign love
    Was bent the worst to save,
Jesus, who reigns enthron'd above,
    The free salvation gave.

*Augustus Toplady*, 1759

## 235 C.M.
*All Due to Grace.*

1 ALL that I was—my sin, my guilt,
    My death, was all my own;
All that I am, I owe to Thee,
    My gracious God, alone.

2 The evil of my former state
    Was mine and only mine;
The good in which I now rejoice
    Is Thine and only Thine.

3 The darkness of my former state,
    The bondage all was mine;
The light of life in which I walk,
    The liberty is Thine.

4 Thy grace *that* made me feel my sin,
    It taught me to believe;
Then, in believing, peace I found,
    And now I live, I live.

5 All that I am, even here on earth,
    All that I hope to be,
When Jesus comes and glory dawns,
    I owe it, Lord, to Thee.

*Horatius Bonar*, [1845]
[*alt. Psalms and Hymns … for the Use of
the Baptist Denomination*, 1857]

    **4.1:** *first*

## 236 L.M.
*Salvation by grace in Christ.*

1 NOW to the power of God supreme
    Be everlasting honours giv'n;
He saves from hell (we bless His name);
    He calls our wand'ring feet to heav'n.

2 Not for our duties or deserts,
    But of His own abounding grace,
He works salvation in our hearts
    And forms a people for His praise.

3 'Twas His own purpose that begun
    To rescue rebels doom'd to die;
He gave us grace in Christ His Son
    Before He spread the starry sky.

4 Jesus the Lord appears at last
    And makes His Father's counsels known,
Declares the great transactions past,
    And brings immortal blessings down.

5 He dies, and in that dreadful night
    Did all the powers of hell destroy;
Rising, He brought our heaven to light
    And took possession of the joy.

*Isaac Watts*, 1709

## 237 C.M.
*Christ claims the glory.*

1 *NOT for the* works which we have done,
    Or shall hereafter do
Hath God decreed on sinful worms
    Salvation to bestow.

2 The glory, Lord, from first to last,
    Is due to Thee alone;
Aught to ourselves we dare not take,
    Or rob Thee of Thy crown.

3 Our glorious Surety undertook
    To satisfy for man,
And grace was given us, in Him,
    Before the world began.

4 This is Thy will, that in Thy love
    We ever should abide,

And lo, we earth and hell defy
To make Thy counsel void.

5 Not one of all the chosen race
But shall to heav'n attain;
Partake on earth the purpos'd grace,
And then with Jesus reign.

6 Of Father, Son, and Spirit, we
Extol the threefold care;
Whose love, whose merit, and whose power
Unite to lift us there.

*Augustus Toplady*, 1774 [*alt. C.H.S.*]

**1.1:** *But not for*
**Ed:** Taken from the longer hymn,
"How vast the benefits divine."

# 238 C.M.
*Sin subdued by grace.*

1 LORD, we confess our num'rous faults;
How great our guilt has been!
Foolish and vain were all our thoughts,
And all our lives were sin.

2 But O my soul! forever praise,
Forever love His name,
Who turns thy feet from dang'rous ways
Of folly, sin, and shame.

3 'Tis not by works of righteousness
Which our own hands have done,
But we are sav'd by sovereign grace
Abounding through His Son.

4 'Tis from the mercy of our God
That all our hopes begin;
'Tis by the water and the blood
Our souls are wash'd from sin.

5 'Tis through the purchase of His death
Who hung upon the tree,
The Spirit is sent down to breathe
On such dry bones as we.

6 Raised from the dead, we live anew,
And justified by grace,
We shall appear in glory too
And see our Father's face.

*Isaac Watts*, 1709

# 239 C.M.
*Salvation.*

1 SALVATION! O the joyful sound!
'Tis pleasure to our ears;
A sovereign balm for every wound,
A cordial for our fears.

2 Buried in sorrow and in sin,
At hell's dark door we lay,
But we arise by grace divine
To see a heavenly day.

3 Salvation! let the echo fly
The spacious earth around,
While all the armies of the sky
Conspire to raise the sound.

*Isaac Watts*, [1707, *rev.* 1709]

**EE:** Hymns, Set 2 (Feb./Dec.), 4th Eve,
ASHLEY / LONDON

# 240 C.M.
*The Unspeakable Gift.*

1 COME, happy souls, approach your God
With new melodious songs;
Come render to almighty grace
The tribute of your tongues.

2 So strange, so boundless was the love
That pitied dying men,
The Father sent His equal Son
To give them life again.

3 Thy hands, dear Jesus, were not arm'd
With *an avenging* rod,
No hard commission to perform
The vengeance of a God.

4 But all was mercy, all was mild,
And wrath forsook the throne,
When Christ on the kind errand came
And brought salvation down.

5 Here, sinners, you may heal your wounds
And wipe your sorrows dry;
Trust in the mighty Saviour's name
And you shall never die.

6   See, dearest Lord, our willing souls
      Accept Thine offer'd grace;
  We bless the great Redeemer's love
      And give the Father praise.

*Isaac Watts,* [1707, *rev.* 1709, *alt.*]

> **3.2:** *a revenging*   **Ed:** A common alteration, appearing as early as Thomas Jones' *A Selection of Psalms and Hymns* (1812).

# 241   S.M.
*The Messenger of Grace.*

1   RAISE your triumphant songs
      To an immortal tune;
  Let the wide earth resound the deeds
      Celestial grace has done.

2   Sing how eternal love
      Its chief beloved chose,
  And bid Him raise our wretched race
      From their abyss of woes.

3   His hand no thunder bears,
      Nor terror clothes His brow;
  No bolts to drive our guilty souls
      To fiercer flames below.

4   'Twas mercy fill'd the throne
      And wrath stood silent by,
  When Christ was sent with pardons down
      To rebels doom'd to die.

5   Now sinners, dry your tears,
      Let hopeless sorrows cease,
  Bow to the sceptre of His love,
      And take the offer'd peace.

6   Lord, we obey Thy call;
      We lay an humble claim
  To the salvation Thou hast brought,
      And love and praise Thy name.

*Isaac Watts,* [1707, *rev.* 1720]

# 242   L.M.
*"We will rejoice in His salvation."*

1  GOD of salvation, we adore
    Thy saving love, Thy saving pow'r;

And to our utmost stretch of thought,
Hail the redemption Thou hast wrought.

2  We love the stroke that breaks our chain,
The sword by which our sins are slain;
And while abas'd in dust we bow,
We sing the grace that lays us low.

3  Perish each thought of human pride;
Let God alone be magnified;
His glory let the heav'ns resound,
Shouted from earth's remotest bound.

4  Saints, who His full salvation know,
Saints, who but taste it here below,
Join with the angelic choir to raise
Transporting songs of deathless praise.

*Philip Doddridge,* 1755 [*rev.* 1839]

# 243   6.6.6.6.8.8.
*Grace immutable*

1  O MY distrustful heart,
    *How small thy faith appears!*
*But greater, Lord, Thou art*
    *Than all my doubts and fears:*
Did Jesus once upon *me* shine?
Then Jesus is forever *mine.*

2  *Unchangable* His will,
    Whatever *be my* frame;
His loving heart is still
    *Eternally* the same.
My soul through many changes goes;
His love no variation knows.

3  *Thou, Lord, wilt* carry on
    And perfectly perform
The work *Thou hast* begun
    In me, a sinful *worm.*
*'Midst all my fear, and sin, and woe,*
*Thy Spirit will not let me go.*

4  The bowels of *Thy* grace
    At first did freely move;
I still *shall see Thy* face
    And feel that God is love!
My soul into *Thine* arms I cast;
I know I shall be sav'd at last.

*William Hammond, 1745*
*[alt. Augustus Toplady, 1776]*

**1.2-4:** *What? Must I always doubt?*
    *Still must I feel this smart*
    *And thus be toss'd about?*
**1.5:** *Thee*   **1.6:** *Thine*   **2.1:** *Immutable*
**2.2:** *is Thy*   **2.4:** *Unchangeably*
**3.1:** *Will He not*   **3.3:** *He hath*   **3.4:** *worm?*
**3.5-6:** *Will God reveal his Son in me*
    *And cast me off eternally?*
**4.1:** *His*   **4.3:** *behold His*   **4.5:** *His*
**NPSP:** "I will be an infidel at once, when I can
believe that a saint of God can ever fall finally.
If God hath loved me once, then He will love
me forever. 'Did Jesus once upon me shine,
then Jesus is forever mine.' The objects of everlasting love never change" (vol. 1, no 1, p. 4).

# 244 C.M.
*Grace enjoyed.*

1 ARISE, my soul, my joyful powers,
    And triumph in my God;
Awake, my voice, and loud proclaim
    His glorious grace abroad.

2 He rais'd me from the deeps of sin,
    The gates of gaping hell,
And fix'd my standing more secure
    Than 'twas before I fell.

3 The arms of everlasting love
    Beneath my soul He plac'd,
And on the Rock of Ages set
    My slippery footsteps fast.

4 The city of my blest abode
    Is wall'd around with grace;
Salvation for a bulwark stands
    To shield the sacred place.

5 Satan may vent his sharpest spite,
    And all his legions roar;
Almighty mercy guards my life
    And bounds his raging power.

6 Arise, my soul, awake, my voice,
    And tunes of pleasure sing;
Loud hallelujahs shall address
    My Saviour and my King.

*Isaac Watts, [1707, rev. 1709]*

# 245 S.M.
*Grace completing its work.*

1 TO God the only wise,
    Our Saviour and our King,
Let all the saints below the skies
    Their humble praises bring.

2 *His tried* almighty love,
    His counsel, and His care,
Preserve us safe from sin and death
    And ev'ry hurtful snare.

3 He will present our souls
    Unblemish'd and complete
Before the glory of His face,
    With joys divinely great.

4 Then all the chosen seed
    Shall meet around the throne,
Shall bless the conduct of His grace,
    And make His wonders known.

5 To our Redeemer God
    Wisdom and pow'r belong,
Immortal crowns of majesty,
    And everlasting song.

*Isaac Watts, [1707], alt. C.H.S.*

**2.1:** *'Tis His*

# 246 C.M.
*Love unfailing.*

1 NOW shall my inward joys arise
    And burst into a song;
Almighty love inspires my heart,
    And pleasure tunes my tongue.

2 God in His thirsty Zion-hill
    Some mercy-drops has thrown,
And solemn oaths have bound His love
    To shower salvation down.

3 Why do we then indulge our fears,
    Suspicions, and complaints?
Is He a God, and shall His grace
    Grow weary of His saints?

4 Can a kind woman e'er forget
    The infant of her womb,

And 'mongst a thousand tender thoughts
Her suckling have no room?

5 "Yet," saith the Lord, "should nature change
And mothers monsters prove,
Zion still dwells upon the heart
Of everlasting love."

6 "Deep on the palms of both my hands
I have engrav'd her name;
My hands shall raise her ruin'd walls
And build her broken frame."

*Isaac Watts*, [1707]

# 247
7.7.7.7.7.7.
*Grace acknowledged.*

1 WHEN I stand before the throne
Dressed in beauty not my own,
When I see Thee as Thou art,
Love Thee with unsinning heart,
Then, Lord, shall I fully know—
Not till then—how much I owe.

2 Chosen not for good in me,
Waken'd up from wrath to flee,
Hidden in the Saviour's side,
By the Spirit sanctified.
Teach me, Lord, on earth to show,
By my love, how much I owe.

3 Oft I walk beneath the cloud,
Dark as midnight's gloomy shroud;
But when fear is at the height,
Jesus comes and all is light;
Blessèd Jesus! bid me show
Doubting saints how much I owe.

*Robert Murray M'Cheyne*, [1843]

**Ed:** Taken from the longer hymn, "When this passing world is done." In Spurgeon's *Lectures to My Students* (1875), p. 70, he quoted this description of M'Cheyne from his *Memoir and Remains* (1844):
"Anxious to give his people on the Sabbath what had cost him somewhat, he never,

without an urgent reason, went before them without much previous meditation and prayer. … Indeed, he could not neglect fellowship with God before entering the congregation. He needed to be bathed in the love of God."

# 248
C.M.
*Grace causing love.*

1 WE love Thee, Lord, because when we
Had err'd and gone astray,
Thou didst recall our wandering souls
Into the heavenward way.

2 When helpless, hopeless, we were lost
In sin and sorrow's *night*,
Thou didst send forth a guiding ray
Of Thy benignant light.

3 Because when we forsook Thy ways,
Nor kept Thy holy will,
Thou wert not the avenging Judge,
But gracious Father still:

4 Because we have forgot Thee, Lord,
But Thou hast not forgot—
Because we have forsaken Thee,
But Thou forsakest not.

5 Because, O Lord, Thou lovedst us
With everlasting love;
Because Thou *sent'st* Thy Son to die,
That we might live above;

6 Because, when we were heirs of wrath,
Thou gav'st *us* hope of heaven;
We love because we much have sinn'd
And much have been forgiven.

*Julia Anne Elliott*, 1835, [*alt.*]

**2.2:** *might*  **5.3:** *gav'st*  **6.2:** *the*
**Ed:** Taken from the longer hymn, "We love Thee, Lord! yet not alone." The alterations at 2.2 and 5.3 appeared as early as 1853 in *Psalms, Hymns, and Passages of Scripture for Christian Worship*; 6.2 is by Spurgeon.

# Our Lord Jesus

## HIS DEITY AND INCARNATION.

### 249
L.M.
*Deity and humanity of our Lord.*

1 ERE the blue heav'ns were stretch'd abroad,
From everlasting was the Word;
With God He was; the Word was God,
And must divinely be ador'd.

2 By His own pow'r were all things made;
By Him supported all things stand;
He is the whole creation's head,
And angels fly at His command.

3 Ere sin was born, or Satan fell,
He led the host of morning stars.
(Thy generation who can tell,
or count the number of Thy years?)

4 But lo, He leaves those heav'nly forms;
The Word descends and dwells in clay,
That He may hold converse with worms,
Dress'd in such feeble flesh as they.

5 Mortals with joy beheld His face,
Th' eternal Father's only Son;
How full of truth! how full of grace,
When thru' His eyes the Godhead shone!

6 Archangels leave their high abode
To learn new mysteries here, and tell
The loves of our descending God,
The glories of Immanuel.

*Isaac Watts*, [1707]

**FPN:** 10 Aug. 1890 (No. 2158), SAMSON
**TD:** "Our knowledge reaches but to a small fragment of the life of God, whose 'goings forth were of old, even from everlasting.' Well might the Jewish church hymn the eternal God, and well may we join therewith the adoration of the Great Firstborn: 'Ere sin was born, or Satan fell, He led the host of morning stars . . .'" (Ps. 68:33; vol. 3, 226).

### 250
L.M.
*His great love.*

1 THE *Lord* of glory, mov'd by love,
Descends in mercy from above;
And He, before whom angels bow,
Is found a man of grief below.

2 *Such* love is great, too great for thought;
Its length and breadth in vain are sought;
No tongue can tell its depth and height;
The love of *Christ* is infinite.

3 But though His love no measure knows,
The Saviour to His people shows
Enough to give them joy, when known,
Enough to make their hearts His own.

*Thomas Kelly*, 1809 [*alt.*]

**1.1:** *God*  **2.2:** *This*  **2.4:** *Christ*
**Ed:** Taken from the longer hymn, "The God of glory dwells on high." The alterations at 1.1 and 2.4 appeared as early as 1835 in the Synod of Relief *Hymns*; all three appeared in Basil Manly Jr.'s *Baptist Psalmody* (1850).

### 251
8.7.8.7. with Alleluias
*Praise to the Redeemer.*

1 MIGHTY God! while angels bless Thee,
May an infant lisp Thy name?
Lord of men as well as angels,
Thou art every creature's theme.
Hallelujah, hallelujah, hallelujah, amen.

2 Lord of every land and nation,
Ancient of eternal days;
Sounded through the wide creation
Be Thy just and lawful praise.
Hallelujah, hallelujah, hallelujah, amen.

3 For the grandeur of Thy nature,
Grand beyond a seraph's thought,
For created works of power,

Works with skill and kindness wrought,
Hallelujah, hallelujah, hallelujah, amen.

4 For Thy providence that governs
    Through Thine empire's wide domain;
Wings an angel, guides a sparrow;
    Blessèd be Thy gentle reign.
Hallelujah, hallelujah, hallelujah, amen.

5 But Thy rich, Thy free redemption,
    Dark through brightness all along;
Thought is poor, and poor expression;
    Who dare sing that awful song?
Hallelujah, hallelujah, hallelujah, amen.

6 Brightness of the Father's glory,
    Shall Thy praise unutter'd lie?
Fly, my tongue, such guilty silence!
    Sing the Lord who came to die.
Hallelujah, hallelujah, hallelujah, amen.

7 Did archangels sing Thy coming?
    Did the shepherds learn their lays?
Shame would cover me ungrateful,
    Should my tongue refuse to praise.
Hallelujah, hallelujah, hallelujah, amen.

8 From the highest throne in glory
    To the cross of deepest woe,
All to ransom guilty captives?
    Flow, my praise, forever flow.
Hallelujah, hallelujah, hallelujah, amen.

9 Go, return, immortal Saviour;
    Leave Thy footstool, take Thy throne;
Thence return, and reign forever;
    Be the kingdom all Thy own.
Hallelujah, hallelujah, hallelujah, amen.

*Robert Robinson*, 1778

**Ed:** According to Josiah Miller in *Singers and Songs of the Church* (1869), p. 267, Robinson's manuscripts indicate that he wrote the hymn in 1774 and it was initially printed on a broadsheet with music by "Dr. Randall." See also Joseph Belcher, *Historical Sketches of Hymns* (1859), p. 231.

# 252  8.7.8.7.
*Joy at Jesus' birth.*

1 LET us all, with grateful praises,
    Celebrate the happy day
When the lovely, loving Jesus
    First partook of human clay.

2 When the heavenly host assembled,
    Gazed with wonder from the sky;
Angels joy'd and devils trembled,
    Neither fully knowing why.

3 Long had Satan reign'd imperious,
    Till the woman's promised seed,
Born a babe, by birth mysterious,
    Came to bruise the serpant's head.

4 Crush, dear babe, his power within us,
    Break our chains, and set us free;
Pull down all the bars between us,
    Till we fly and cleave to Thee.

*Joseph Hart*, 1759

# 253  8.7.8.7.4.7.
*Good tidings.*

1 ANGELS! from the realms of glory,
    Wing your flight o'er all the earth;
Ye who sang creation's story
    Now proclaim Messiah's birth:
        Come and worship,
        Worship Christ, the new-born King.

2 Saints! before the altar bending,
    *Waiting* long *with* hope and fear,
Suddenly the Lord descending
    In His temple shall appear;
        Come and worship,
        Worship Christ, the new-born King.

3 Sinners, wrung with true repentance,
    Doom'd for guilt to endless pains,
Justice now *repeals* the sentence,
    Mercy calls you—break your chains;
        Come and worship,
        Worship Christ, the new-born King.

*James Montgomery*, [1816]

**2.2:** *Watching / in*   **3.3:** *revokes*

**Ed:** Montgomery revised this text for his *Christian Psalmist* (1825), but his original, as above, was popularized via Thomas Cotterill's *Selection* (8th ed., 1819). Footnotes indicate Montgomery's revisions.

# 254 C.M.
*Heaven's joy at incarnation.*

1 MORTALS, awake, with angels join,
   And chant the solemn lay;
Joy, love, and gratitude combine
   To hail th' auspicious day.

2 In heaven the rapt'rous song began,
   And sweet seraphic fire
Through all the shining legions ran,
   And strung and tun'd the lyre.

3 Swift through the vast expanse it flew,
   And loud the echo roll'd;
The theme, the song, the joy was new,
   'Twas more than heaven could hold.

4 Down *from* the portals of the sky
   Th' impetuous torrent ran,
And angels flew with eager joy
   To bear the news to man.

5 Hark! the cherubic armies shout,
   And glory leads the song;
Good will and peace are heard throughout
   Th' harmonious heavenly throng.

6 With joy the chorus *we* repeat,
   "Glory to God on high!
Good will and peace are now complete;
   Jesus was born to die!"

7 Hail, Prince of Life, forever hail!
   Redeemer, Brother, Friend!
Though earth and time and life should fail,
   Thy praise shall never end.

*Samuel Medley*, [1782, alt.]

4.1: *through*  6.1: *we'll*  **Ed:** The alteration at 4.1 is from John Rippon's *Selection* (1844); 6.1 is a common variant dating to the late 1700s.

# 255 7.7.7.7.
*Advent morning.*

1 BRIGHT and joyful is the morn,
   For to us a child is born;
From the highest realms of heaven,
   Unto us a Son is given.

2 On His shoulder He shall bear
   Power and majesty, and wear
On His vesture and His thigh
   Names most awful, names most high.

3 Wonderful in counsel He,
   The Incarnate Deity,
Sire of Ages ne'er to cease,
   King of Kings, and Prince of Peace.

4 Come and worship at His feet;
   Yield to Christ the homage meet;
From His manger to His throne,
   Homage due to God alone.

*James Montgomery*, [1825]

# 256 7.7.7.7.
*The Angels' song.*

1 HARK, *the herald angels sing*,
   Glory to the *new-born King*,
"Peace on earth and mercy mild,
   God and sinners reconcil'd."

2 Joyful, all ye nations, rise,
   Join the triumph of the skies;
Hail the heaven-born Prince of Peace!
   Hail the Sun of Righteousness!

3 Veil'd in flesh, the Godhead see;
   Hail th' incarnate Deity!
Pleas'd as man with men t' appear,
   Jesus, our Immanuel here!

4 Mild he lays His glory by,
   Born that men no more *might* die,
Born to raise the sons of earth,
   Born to give them second birth.

5 Come, Desire of Nations, come,
   Fix in us Thy humble home;

Rise, the woman's *promis'd* seed;
Bruise in us the serpent's head.

6 Glory to the new-born King!
Let us all the anthem sing,
"Peace on earth and mercy mild,
God and sinners reconciled."

1-5 *Charles Wesley*, 1739 [*alt.*]
[6 *John Rippon*, 1787]

**1.1:** *how all the welkin rings,*
**1.2:** *King of Kings,*   **4.2:** *may*   **5.3:** *conqu'ring*
**Ed:** The alterations at 1.1-2 are by George Whitefield (1753); the reduction of stanzas and other
alterations are by Rippon.

# 257 C.M.
*The Advent.*

1 HARK, the glad sound! the Saviour comes,
The Saviour promis'd long!
Let ev'ry heart prepare a throne,
And ev'ry voice a song.

2 On Him the Spirit, largely pour'd,
Exerts its sacred fire;
Wisdom and might and zeal and love
His holy breast inspire.

3 He comes, the pris'ners to release,
In Satan's bondage held;
The gates of brass before Him burst,
The iron fetters yield.

4 He comes, from thickest films of vice,
To clear the mental ray,
And on the eyeballs of the blind
To pour celestial day.

5 He comes, the broken heart to bind,
The bleeding soul to cure,
And with the treasures of His grace,
T' enrich the humble poor.

6 Our glad hosannas, Prince of Peace,
Thy welcome shall proclaim;
And heav'n's eternal arches ring
With Thy beloved name.

*Philip Doddridge,* [1745, *rev.* 1755]

# 258 C.M.
*Joy at His coming.*

1 JOY to the world, the Lord is come;
Let earth receive her King:
Let every heart prepare Him room,
And heaven and nature sing.

2 Joy to the earth, the Saviour reigns;
Let men their songs employ,
While fields and floods,
rocks, hills, and plains
Repeat the sounding joy.

3 No more let sins and sorrows grow,
Nor thorns infest the ground.
He comes to make His blessings flow
Far as the curse is found.

4 He rules the world with truth and grace
And makes the nations prove
The glories of His righteousness
And wonders of His love.

*Isaac Watts,* 1719

# 259 C.M.
*"He humbled himself."*

1 SAVIOUR of men and Lord of love,
How sweet Thy gracious name!
With joy that errand we review,
On which Thy mercy came.

2 While all Thy own angelic bands
Stood waiting on the wing,
Charm'd with the honour to obey
The word of such a King,

3 For us, mean, wretched, sinful men,
Thou laidst that glory by,
First in our mortal flesh to serve,
Then in that flesh to die.

4 Bought with Thy service and Thy blood,
We doubly, Lord, are Thine;
To Thee our lives we would devote,
To Thee our death resign.

*Philip Doddridge,* 1755

# 260
C.M.
*Jesus the Son of Man.*

1 IT is my sweetest comfort, Lord,
　　And will forever be,
　To muse upon the gracious truth
　　Of Thy humanity.

2 Oh joy! there sitteth in our flesh,
　　Upon a throne of light,
　One of a human mother born,
　　In *perfect* Godhead bright!

3 Though earth's foundations should be mov'd
　　Down to their lowest deep,
　Though *all the trembling* universe
　　Into destruction sweep—

4 Forever God, forever man,
　　My Jesus shall endure;
　And fix'd on Him, my hope remains
　　Eternally secure.

*Edward Caswall*, 1858 [*alt.*]

　　**2.4:** *blazing*　**3.3:** *the whole sunder'd*
　　**Ed:** The alteration at 3.3 is from *The Catholic
　　Hymnal* (1860); 2.4 is by Spurgeon.

# 261
L.M.
*Flesh of our flesh.*

1 JESUS, who pass'd the angels by,
　Assum'd our flesh to bleed and die,
　And still He makes it His abode;
　As man, He fills the throne of God.

2 Our next of kin, our Brother now,
　Is He to whom the angels bow;
　They join with us to praise His name,
　But we the nearest interest claim.

3 But ah! how faint our praises rise!
　Sure, 'tis the wonder of the skies
　That we, who share His richest love,
　So cold and unconcern'd should prove.

4 Oh glorious hour, it comes with speed!
　When we from sin and darkness freed,
　Shall see the God who died for man,
　And praise Him more than angels can.

*John Newton*, 1779

**Ed:** Taken from the longer hymn,
　　"Now let us join with hearts and tongues."

# OUR LORD'S LIFE ON EARTH.

# 262
L.M.
*His divine example.*

1 MY dear Redeemer and my Lord,
　I read my duty in Thy Word,
　But in Thy life the law appears
　Drawn out in living characters.

2 Such was Thy truth, and such Thy zeal,
　Such deference to Thy Father's will,
　Such love, and meekness so divine,
　I would transcribe and make them mine.

3 Cold mountains and the midnight air
　Witness'd the fervour of Thy pray'r;
　The desert Thy temptation knew,
　Thy conflict and Thy victory too.

4 Be Thou my pattern; make me bear
　More of Thy gracious image here;
　Then God the Judge shall own my name
　Amongst the followers of the Lamb.

*Isaac Watts*, 1709

　　**MM:** "No shepherd sitting beneath the cold
　　skies, looking up to the stars, could ever utter
　　such complaints, because of the hardness of
　　his toil, as Jesus Christ might have brought,
　　if He had chosen to do so, because of the
　　sternness of His service in order to procure
　　His spouse" (Nov. 22).

# 263
C.M.
*Imitation of Jesus.*

1 LORD, as to Thy dear cross we flee
　　And plead to be forgiven,
　So let Thy life our pattern be,
　　And form our souls for heaven.

2 Help us, through good report and ill,
　　Our daily cross to bear,
　Like Thee, to do our Father's will,
　　Our brethren's griefs to share.

3 Let grace our selfishness expel,
   Our earthliness refine,
And kindness in our bosoms dwell,
   As free and true as Thine.

4 If joy shall at Thy bidding fly,
   And grief's dark day come on,
We, in our turn, would meeekly cry,
   "Father, Thy will be done."

5 Kept peaceful in the midst of strife,
   Forgiving and forgiven,
O may we lead the pilrgim's life,
   And follow Thee to Heaven!

*John Hampden Gurney*, 1838

# 264 7.7.7.7.
*The mind of Christ.*

1 FATHER of eternal grace,
   *May we all resemble Thee;*
Meekly beaming in *our* face,
   May the world Thine image see.

2 Happy only in Thy love,
   Poor, unfriended, or unkown;
Fix *our* thoughts on things above;
   Stay *our* hearts on Thee alone.

3 Humble, holy, all resign'd
   To Thy will—Thy will be done!
Give *us*, Lord, the perfect mind
   Of Thy well-belovèd Son.

4 Counting gain and glory loss,
   May *we* tread the path He trod,
*Bear with Him on earth our* cross,
   Rise with Him to Thee, *our* God.

*James Montgomery*, [1812]
[*alt. A Selection of 600 Psalms & Hymns
for Public and Private Use*, 1823]

  **1.2:** *Glorify Thyself in me;*  **1.3:** *my*
  **2.3:** *my*  **2.4:** *my*  **3.3:** *me*  **4.2:** *I*
  **4.3:** *Die with Jesus on the*  **4.4:** *my*
  **Ed:** Montgomery first offered this hymn for
    William Gardiner's *Sacred Melodies*. His cor-
    respondance with Gardiner dates to 1807-1808
    and is included in Montgomery's *Memoirs*

(1855), vol. 2, pp. 145-148, but Gardiner's
publication does not date earlier than 1812
(see WorldCat and the Grove *Dictionary of
Music*, for example). In 1812, this hymn was
also published in Wm. Collyer's *Hymns*, with
some differences; this version was included
in Montgomery's collections, starting with
*The Christian Psalmist* (1825). The plural
alteration used by Spurgeon is an oddity, not
frequently published before 1866 nor included
in Montgomery's collections, yet incorporated
into editions of his *Poetical Works*—without
explanation—starting in 1870.

# 265 S.M.
*His love to souls.*

1    DID Christ o'er sinners weep,
      And shall our cheeks be dry?
Let floods of penitential grief
      Burst forth from every eye.

2    The Son of God in tears,
      Angels with wonder see!
Be thou astonish'd, oh my soul,
      He shed those tears for thee.

3    He wept that we might weep;
      Each sin demands a tear;
In heaven alone no sin is found,
      And there's no weeping there.

*Benjamin Beddome*, 1817

# 266 8.7.8.7.4.7.
*His fellowship with us.*

1 PILGRIMS here on earth and strangers,
   'Neath a weary load we bend.
O how sweet, 'mid toils and dangers,
   Still to have a heavenly friend!
     Christ has suffered,
   And to sufferers grace will send.

2 By as deadly foes assaulted,
   By as strong temptations tried,
Still His footsteps never halted,
   On from strength to strength He hied.
     What could move Him
   With Jehovah at His side?

3 To the shameful cross they nailed Him,
  And that cross became His throne;
In the tomb they laid and sealed Him;
  Lo, the *Saviour* bursts the stone,
    And ascending,
  Claims all empire as His own.

4 *Jesu*, from Thy heavenly glories
  Here an eye of mercy cast;
Make our path still plain before us,
  Smooth the wave, and still the blast.
    Thou hast helped us;
  Bear us safely home at last.

*Henry Francis Lyte*, 1834 [*rev.* 1858]

  **3.4:** *Godhead* **4.1:** *Saviour*
  **Ed:** Footnotes indicate the original text; this was
    edited by J.R. Hogg after Lyte's death.

**267** 8.7.8.7.4.7.
*His work as God's anointed.*

1 THUS saith God, of His Anointed:
  He shall let my people go;
'Tis the work for Him appointed,
  'Tis the work that He shall do;
    And my city
  He shall found, and built it too.

2 He whom man with scorn refuses,
  Whom the favour'd nation hates,
He it is Jehovah chooses,
  Him the highest place awaits;
    Kings and princes
  Shall do homage at His gates.

3 He shall humble all the scorners,
  He shall fill His foes with shame;
He shall raise and comfort mourners
  By the sweetness of His name.
    To the captives
  He shall liberty proclaim.

4 He shall gather those that wander'd;
  When they hear the trumpet's sound,
They shall join His sacred standard,
  They shall come and flock around;

He shall save them;
  They shall be with glory crown'd.

*Thomas Kelly*, 1809

**FPN:** 15 Sept. 1889 (No. 2333), ROUSSEAU

## JESUS' SUFFERING AND DEATH.

**268** C.M.
*Despised and rejected of men.*

1 REJECTED and despis'd of men,
  Behold a man of woe!
*And grief* His close companion still
  Through all His life below!

2 Yet all the griefs He felt were ours,
  Ours were the woes He bore;
Pangs, not His own, His spotless soul
  With bitter anguish tore.

3 We held Him as condemn'd *of* heaven,
  An outcast from His God;
While for our sins He groan'd, He bled
  Beneath His Father's rod.

4 His sacred blood hath wash'd our souls
  From sin's *polluting* stain;
His stripes have heal'd us, and His death
  Reviv'd our souls again.

*William Robertson*, [1745, *rev.* 1781]
[*alt. Sabbath Hymn Book*, 1858]

  **1.3:** *Grief was* **3.1:** *by* **4.2:** *polluted*
  **Ed:** Taken from the longer hymn,
    "How few receive with cordial faith."

**269** 7.7.7.7.7.7.
*A place called Gethsemane.*

1 GO to dark Gethsemane,
  Ye that feel the tempter's power;
Your Redeemer's conflict see;
  Watch with Him one bitter hour;
Turn not from His griefs away;
  Learn of Jesus Christ to pray.

2 Follow to the judgment hall,
  View the Lord of life arraign'd;

O the wormwood and the gall!
O the pangs His soul sustain'd!
Shun not suffering, shame, or loss;
Learn of Him to bear the cross.

3 Calvary's mournful mountain climb;
There, adoring at His feet,
Mark that miracle of time,
God's own sacrifice complete.
"It is finish'd!" hear Him cry;
Learn of Jesus Christ to die.

4 Early hasten to the tomb,
Where they laid His breathless clay;
All is solitude and gloom.
Who hath taken Him away?
Christ is risen—He meets our eyes;
Saviour, teach us so to rise.

*James Montgomery*, [1820, *rev.* 1825]

# 270 L.M.
*Gethsemane.*

1 COME, all ye chosen saints of God,
*Who* long to feel the cleansing blood;
In pensive pleasure join with me
To sing of sad Gethsemane.

2 Gethsemane, the olive-press!
(And why so call'd let Christians guess.)
Fit name! fit place! where vengeance strove,
And griped, and grappled hard with love.

3 'Twas here the Lord of life appear'd,
And sigh'd, and groan'd,
    and pray'd, and fear'd,
Bore all incarnate God could bear,
With strength enough—and none to spare.

4 And why, dear Saviour, tell me why
Thou *didst a bleeding sufferer lie?*
What mighty motive could Thee move?
The motive's plain: 'twas all for love.

5 For love of whom? Of sinners base,
A harden'd herd, a rebel race
That mock'd and trampled on Thy blood,
And wanton'd in the wounds of God.

6 O love of unexampled kind!
That leaves all thought so far behind,
Where length, and breadth,
    and depth, and height
Are lost to my astonish'd sight.

*Joseph Hart*, 1759, *alt. C.H.S.*

**1.2:** *That* **4.2:** *thus would'st suffer, bleed, and die?*

# 271 7.7.7.7.7.7.
*Gethsemane.*

1 MANY woes had He endur'd,
    Many sore temptations met,
Patient, and to pains inur'd,
    But the sorest trial yet
Was to be sustain'd in Thee,
Gloomy, sad Gethsemane.

2 Came at length the dreadful night;
    Vengeance with its iron rod
Stood, and with collected might
    Bruis'd the harmless Lamb of God.
See, my soul, thy Saviour see,
*Prostrate* in Gethsemane!

3 There my God bore all my guilt;
    This through grace can be believ'd;
But the horrors which He felt
    Are too vast to be conceiv'd.
None can penetrate through thee,
Doleful, dark Gethsemane.

4 Sins against a holy God;
    Sins against His righteous laws;
Sins against His love, His blood;
    Sins against His name and cause;
Sins immense as is the sea—
Hide me, O Gethsemane!

5 Here's my claim, and here alone;
    None a Saviour more can need;
Deeds of righteousness I've none;
    No, not one good work to plead;
Not a glimpse of hope for me;
Only in Gethsemane.

6 Father, Son, and Holy Ghost,
    One almighty God of love,

Hymn'd by all the heavenly host
  In Thy shining courts above,
We poor sinners, gracious Three,
  Bless Thee for Gethsemane.

*Joseph Hart*, 1759 [*alt.*]

> **2.6:** *Grov'ling*
> **Ed:** Taken from the longer hymn, "Jesus, while
> He dwelt below," with a common alteration,
> which appeared as early as 1815 in Samuel
> Worcester's *Christian Psalmody.*
> **FPN:** 19 Feb. 1888 (No. 2357), MADRID
> **TD:** "On every side He was beset with evils;
> countless woes environed the great Substitute
> for our sins. . . . The pains of divine penalty
> were beyond compute, and the Saviour's soul
> was so burdened with them, that He was sore
> amazed, and very heavy even unto a sweat of
> blood" (Ps. 40:12; vol. 2, p. 267).

# 272   8.8.6.8.8.6.   *Gethsemane.*

1 IMMANUEL, sunk with dreadful woe,
Unfelt, unknown to all below—
  Except the Son of God—
In agonizing pangs of soul,
Drinks deep of wormwood's bitterest bowl,
  And sweats great drops of blood.

2 "O Father, hear! this cup remove!
Save Thou the darling of Thy love
  (The prostrate victim cries)
From overwhelming fear and dread!
Though He must mingle with the dead—
  His people's sacrifice."

3 His earnest prayers, His deep'ning groans,
Were heard before angelic thrones;
  Amazement wrapt the sky;
 "Go, strengthen Christ!" the Father said;
Th' astonish'd seraph bow'd his head
  And left the realms on high.

4 Made strong in strength,
  renew'd from heav'n,
Jesus receives the cup as giv'n,
  And perfectly resign'd,
He drinks the wormwood mix'd with gall,

Sustains the curse—removes it all—
  Nor leaves a dreg behind.

John Rippon's *Selection*, 1800

# 273   7.7.7.7.   *"Thine unknown sufferings."*

1 MUCH we talk of Jesu's blood,
But how little's understood!
Of His suff'rings, so intense,
Angels have no perfect sense.

2 Who can rightly comprehend
Their beginning or their end?
'Tis to God and God alone
That their weight is fully known.

3 *See the suffering Son of God,*
*Panting, groaning, sweating blood!*
*Boundless depths of love divine!*
*Jesus, what a love was Thine!*

4 Though the wonders Thou hast done
Are as yet so little known,
Here we fix and comfort take,
Jesus died for sinners' sake.

*Joseph Hart*, 1759 [*alt. C.H.S.*]

> **3.1-2:** *Dearly are we bought; for God*
>   *Bought us with his own heart's blood.*
> **Ed:** The lines at 3:1-2 are also by Hart, but taken
> from his hymn "O ye sons of men, be wise," a
> substitution unique to *Our Own Hymn-Book.*

# 274   L.M.   *His Passion.*

1 SEE how the patient Jesus stands,
Insulted in His lowest case;
Sinners have bound th' Almighty's hands
And spit in their Creator's face.

2 With thorns His temples gor'd and gash'd
Send streams of blood from ev'ry part;
His back's with knotted scourges lash'd,
But sharper scourges tear His heart.

3 Nail'd naked to th' accursed wood,
Expos'd to earth and heav'n above,

A spectacle of wounds and blood,
A prodigy of injur'd love!

4 Hark! how His doleful cries affright
Affected angels, while they view;
His friends forsook Him in the night
And now His God forsakes Him too.

5 Behold that pale, that languid face,
That drooping head, those *languid* eyes!
Behold in sorrow and disgrace
Our conqu'ring Hero hangs and dies!

6 Ye that assume His sacred name,
Now tell me, what can all this mean?
What was it bruis'd God's harmless Lamb?
What was it pierc'd His soul but sin?

7 Blush, Christian blush; let shame abound;
If sin affects thee not with woe,
Whatever *life* is in thee found,
The *life* of Christ thou dost not know.

*Joseph Hart*, 1759 [*alt. C.H.S.*]

**5.2:** *cold dead*   **7.3:** *Spir't*   **7.4:** *Spir't*
**Ed:** Taken from the longer hymn,
"Now from the garden to the cross."
**MM:** "My soul, stand here and weep over his
poor, stricken body. Believer in Jesus, can you
gaze upon Him without tears, as He stands
before you the mirror of agonizing love? . . . As
we feel the sure and blessed healing which His
stripes have wrought in us, does not our heart
melt as once with love and grief?" (Mar. 31).

# 275   7.6.7.6. Double
*"A crown of thorns."*

1 O SACRED Head, *once* wounded,
With grief and *pain* weigh'd down,
*How* scornfully surrounded,
With thorns *Thine* only crown;
How *pale art Thou* with anguish,
With sore abuse and scorn;
How does that visage languish,
Which once was bright as morn.

2 O *Lord of life and glory,*
What bliss till now was Thine!

*I read the wondrous story;*
I joy to call Thee mine.
*Thy grief and Thy compassion*
*Were* all for sinners' gain;
Mine, mine was the transgression,
But Thine the deadly pain.

3 What language shall I borrow
To *praise* Thee, *Heavenly* Friend,
For this Thy dying sorrow,
Thy pity without end?
*Lord*, make me Thine forever,
*Nor let me faithless prove;*
*O* let me never, never
*Abuse such dying love.*

4 Be near *me, Lord, when* dying;
O show Thy cross to me!
And for my succour flying,
Come, Lord, to set me free.
These eyes, new faith receiving,
From Jesus shall not move,
For he who dies believing,
Dies safely, through Thy love.

[*Arnulf of Leuven*, 13th century]
*tr. Paul Gerhardt*, 1656
[*tr. James Alexander*, 1830, *alt.*]

**1.1:** *now*   **1.2:** *shame*   **1.3:** *Now*   **1.4:** *Thy*
**1.5:** *art Thou pale*   **2.1:** *sacred Head, what*
**2.3:** *Yet though despised and gory*
**2.5:** *What Thou, my Lord, hast suffer'd*
**2.6:** *was*   **3.2:** *thank / dearest*   **3.5:** *O*
**3.6:** *And should I fainting be,*   **3.7:** *Lord,*
**3.8:** *Outlive my love to Thee.*   **4.1:** *when I am*
**Ed:** From the Latin, "Salve caput cruentatum,"
often misattributed to Bernard of Clairvaux.
Translated as "O Haupt voll Blut und Wunden"
by Gerhardt, then translated from German
to English by Alexander. Some alts., such as
1.1-3, 2.5-6, 3.2-8, are from Thomas Hastings'
*Christian Psalmist* (1836). The first three sts.
appeared as above in *Hymns for Divine Worship* (1863), but not the fourth. This whole set
of alts. appeared in David Thomas' *Augustine
Hymn Book* (ca. 1862-65), except Thomas
changed "sacred head" to "blessed head."

# 276 C.M.
*Jesus wounded.*

1 *HOW clearly all His torturing wounds*
   The love of Jesus show,
   *Those wounds* from whence
              encrimson'd rills
   Of blood *atoning* flow.

2 How doth th' ensanguined thorny crown
   That beauteous brow transpierce!
   How do the nails those hands and feet
   Contract with tortures fierce!

3 He bows his head, and forth at last
   His loving spirit soars;
   Yet even after death His heart
   For us its tribute pours.

4 Oh, come all ye in whom are fix'd
   The deadly stains of sin!
   Come! wash in this all-saving blood,
   And ye shall be made clean.

5 Praise Him, who with the Father sits
   Enthron'd upon the skies,
   Whose blood redeems our souls from guilt,
   Whose Spirit sanctifies.

[*Breviarium Romanum*, 1827]
   *tr. Edward Caswall, 1849, alt. C.H.S.*

   **1.1:** *Hail wounds! which through eternal years*
   **1.3:** *Hail wounds!*  **1.4:** *forever*
   **Ed:** From the Latin, "Salvete Christi vulnera." See
   also No. 503.

# 277 7.7.7.7.
*Jesu's sorrow.*

1 SEE the destin'd day arise!
   See, a willing sacrifice;
   *Jesus, to redeem our* loss,
   *Hangs upon the shameful* cross!

2 Jesu, who but Thou had borne,
   Lifted on that tree of scorn,
   Every pang and bitter throe,
   Finishing Thy life of woe?

3 Who but Thou had dared to drain,
   Steep'd in gall, the cup of pain,

And with tender body bear
Thorns, and nails, and piercing spear?

4 Thence *the cleansing* water flow'd,
   Mingled from Thy side with blood,
   Sign to all attesting eyes
   Of the finished sacrifice.

5 Holy Jesus, grant us grace
   In that sacrifice to place
   All our trust for life renew'd,
   Pardon'd sin, and promised good.

[*Venantius Fortunatus*, 6th century]
   *tr. Richard Mant, 1837, alt.*

   **1.3:** *To redeem our fatal*
   **1.4:** *Jesus hangs upon the*  **4.1:** *pour'd forth*
   **Ed:** From the Latin, "Pange lingua gloriosi proeli-
   um certaminis" (the portion beginning "Lustra
   sex qui jam peracta").The alterations at 1.3-4
   appeared as early as 1846 in *Hymns for the
   Principal Fasts and Festivals of the Church*
   and also *Sacred Hymns and Anthems*; all
   three alts. can be found in *Hymns for the
   Public Worship of the Church* (1849).

# 278 L.M.
*"They crucified Him."*

1 OH come and mourn with me awhile!
   *Oh come ye to the Saviour's* side;
   Oh come, *together let us mourn*;
   Jesus, our *Lord*, is crucified.

2 Have we no tears to shed for Him,
   While soldiers scoff and Jews deride?
   Ah! look how patiently He hangs;
   Jesus, our *Lord*, is crucified!

3 How fast His hands and feet are nailed;
   His *throat with parching* thirst is *dried;*
   His failing eyes are *dimmed* with blood;
   Jesus, our *Lord*, is crucified!

4 A broken heart, a fount of tears
   Ask, and they will not be denied;
   *Lord Jesus, may we love and weep,*
   *Since Thou for us art crucified.*

*Frederick William Faber, 1849*
[*alt. Hymns Ancient & Modern, 1861*]

**1.2:** *See, Mary calls us to her*
**1.3:** *and let us mourn with her;* **1.4:** *Love*
**2.4:** *Love* **3.2:** *blessèd tongue with / tied*
**3.3:** *blind* **3.4:** *Love*
**4.3-4:** *A broken heart, Love's cradle is;*
*Jesus, our Love, is crucified!*

# 279 C.M.
*Weeping at the Cross.*

1 ALAS! and did my Saviour bleed?
  And did my Sovereign die?
Would he devote that Sacred head
  For such a worm as I?

2 Was it for crimes that I had done
  He groan'd upon the tree?
Amazing pity! grace unknown!
  And love beyond degree.

3 Well might the sun in darkness hide
  And shut his glories in,
When God, the mighty Maker died
  For man, the creature's sin.

4 Thus might I hide my blushing face,
  While His dear cross appears,
Dissolve my heart in thankfulness,
  And melt my eyes to tears.

5 But drops of grief can ne'er repay
  The debt of love I owe;
Here, Lord, I give myself away;
  'Tis all that I can do.

*Isaac Watts*, [1707]

# 280 C.M.
*The Attraction of the Cross.*

1 YONDER—amazing sight!—I see
  Th' incarnate Son of God
Expiring on th' accursed tree
  And welt'ring in His blood.

2 Behold, a purple torrent run
  Down from His hands and head;
The crimson tide puts out the sun;
  His groans awake the dead.

3 The trembling earth, the darken'd sky,
  Proclaim the truth aloud!
And with th' amaz'd centurion cry,
  "This is the Son of God!"

4 So great, so vast a sacrifice
  May well my hope revive;
If God's own Son thus bleeds and dies,
  The sinner sure may live.

5 O that these cords of love divine
  Might draw me, Lord, to Thee!
Thou hast my heart, it shall be Thine—
  Thine it shall ever be!

*Samuel Stennett*, [1782]

# 281 8.7.8.7.
*A view of Christ crucified.*

1 SWEET the moments, rich in blessing,
  Which before the cross I spend;
Life and health and peace possessing,
  From the sinner's dying Friend.

2 Here I'll sit forever viewing
  Mercy's streams in streams of blood;
Precious drops my soul bedewing
  Plead and claim my peace with God.

3 Truly blessèd in this station,
  Low before His cross to lie,
While I see divine compassion
  Floating in His languid eye.

4 Here it is I find my heaven,
  While upon the *cross* I gaze;
Love I much? I've more forgiven;
  I'm a miracle of grace.

5 Love and grief my heart dividing,
  With my tears His feet I'll bathe,
Constant still in faith abiding,
  Life deriving from His death.

6 May I still enjoy this feeling,
  In all need to Jesus go,
Prove His wounds each day more healing,
  And Himself more *fully* know.

*James Allen*, 1757
*adapt. Walter Shirley*, 1770
[*alt. A Collection of Hymns for the Use … of the United Brethren*, 1789, *rev.* 1801]

**4.2:** *Lamb* **6.4:** *deeply*
**Ed:** The original text by Allen began, "While my Jesus I'm possessing." Shirley's extensive reworking of the hymn is detailed in Julian's *Dictionary of Hymnology*, pp. 1274-75. The additional changes were made in 1789 (4.2) and 1801 (4.2 and 6.4).
**MM:** Hymns, Set 2 (Feb./Dec.), 25th & 26th Morn, SICILY / DISMISSION / GREENVILLE

# 282 L.M.
*Crucifixion to the world by the cross.*

1 WHEN I survey the wondrous cross
   On which the Prince of Glory died,
   My richest gain I count but loss,
   And pour contempt on all my pride.

2 Forbid it, Lord, that I should boast,
   Save in the death of Christ, my God;
   All the vain things that charm me most,
   I sacrifice them to His blood.

3 See from His head, His hands, His feet,
   Sorrow and love flow mingled down;
   Did e'er such love and sorrow meet?
   Or thorns compose so rich a crown?

4 His dying crimson, like a robe,
   Spreads o'er His body on the tree;
   Then am I dead to all the globe,
   And all the globe is dead to me.

5 Were the whole realm of nature mine,
   That were a present far too small;
   Love so amazing, so divine,
   Demands my soul, my life, my all.

*Isaac Watts,* [1707, *rev.* 1709]

**MM:** Hymns, Set 1 (Jan./Nov.), 9th Morn, WINDHAM / ZEPHYR
**FPN:** 15 Sept. 1889 (No. 2333), JOB

# 283 C.M.
*Love in agony.*

1 THE enormous load of human guilt
   Was on my Saviour laid;
   With woes, as with a garment, He
   For sinners was array'd.

2 And in the horrid pangs of death
   He wept, He pray'd for me,
   Lov'd and embrac'd my guilty soul
   When nailèd to the tree.

3 O love amazing! love beyond
   The reach of human tongue,
   Love which shall be the subject of
   An everlasting song.

*William Williams,* 1759

# 284 C.M. / *"The Lord hath laid on Him the iniquity of us all."*

1 IN Jesu's name, with one accord,
   Lift up a sacred hymn,
   And think what healing streams He pour'd
   From every bleeding limb.

2 O who can tell what woes He bore
   When that pure blood was spilt,
   What pangs His tortured bosom tore
   When loaded with our guilt?

3 'Twas not the insulting voice of scorn
   So deeply wrung His heart;
   The piercing nail, the pointed thorn,
   Caus'd not the saddest smart:

4 But every struggling sigh betray'd
   A heavier grief within,
   How on His burden'd soul was laid
   The weight of human sin.

5 O Thou who hast vouchsaf'd to bear
   Our sins' oppresive load,
   Grant us Thy righteousness to *wear*
   And lead us to our God.

*William Hiley Bathurst,* 1831 [*alt. C.H.S.*]

**5.3:** *share*

# 285

C.M.
*"He loved me."*

1 FOR me vouchsaf'd th' unspotted Lamb
    His Father's wrath to bear;
I see His feet, and read my name
    Engraven deeply there.

2 Forth from the Lord His gushing blood
    In purple currents ran,
And ev'ry wound proclaim'd aloud
    His wondrous love to man.

3 For me the Saviour's blood avails,
    Almighty to atone;
The hands He gave to piercing nails
    Shall lead me to His throne.

*Augustus Toplady*, 1759

**EE:** Hymns, Set 2 (Feb./Dec.), 27th Eve,
BEDFORD / HENSBURY
**Ed:** Taken from the longer hymn,
"Redeemed offender, hail the day."

# 286

8.7.8.7.4.7.
*A song for the foot of the cross.*

1 NOW, my soul, thy voice upraising,
    Sing aloud in mournful strain
Of the sorrows most amazing
    And the agonizing pain,
      Which our Saviour
Sinless bore, for sinners slain.

2 He the ruthless scourge enduring,
    Ransom for our sins to pay,
Sinners by His own stripes curing,
    Raising those who wounded lay,
      Bore our sorrows
And removed our pains away.

3 He to liberty restored us
    By the very bonds He bare,
And His nail-pierced limbs afford us
    Each a stream of mercy rare;
      *Lo! He draws us*
To the cross, and *keeps* us there.

4 When His painful life was ended,
    When the spear transfixed His side,

Blood and water thence descended,
    Pouring forth a double tide;
      This to cleanse us,
That to heal us, is applied.

5 *Jesus!* may Thy promised blessing
    Comfort to our souls afford;
May we, now Thy love possessing,
    And at length our full reward,
      Ever praise Thee
As our ever-glorious Lord.

[*Claude de Santeüil*, 1680]
 *tr. John Chandler*, 1837
[*alt. Sabbath Hymn Book*, 1858]

**3.5:** *Us they fasten*   **3.6:** *keep*   **5.1:** *Jesu,*
**Ed:** From the Latin, "Prone vocem, mens,
canoram."

# 287

S.M.
*A song at the foot of the cross.*

1 LET all our tongues be one,
    To praise our God on high,
Who from His bosom sent His Son
    To fetch us strangers nigh.

2 Nor let our voices cease
    To sing the Saviour's name;
Jesus, th' ambassador of peace,
    How cheerfully He came!

3 It cost Him cries and tears
    To bring us near to God;
Great was our debt, and He appears
    To make the payment good.

4 Look up, my soul, to Him
    Whose death was thy desert,
And humbly view the living stream
    Flow from His breaking heart.

5 There, on the cursèd tree,
    In dying pangs He lies,
Fulfills His Father's great decree,
    And all our wants supplies.

6 Lord, cleanse my soul from sin,
    Nor let Thy grace depart;

Great Comforter, abide within
And witness to my heart.

*Isaac Watts*, [1707]

# 288 C.M.
*The cleansing fountain.*

1 THERE is a fountain fill'd with blood,
   Drawn from Immanuel's veins,
And sinners plung'd beneath that flood
   Lose all their guilty stains.

2 The dying thief rejoic'd to see
   That fountain in his day;
*O may I there, though* vile as he,
*Wash* all my sins away.

3 Dear dying Lamb, Thy precious blood
   Shall never lose its pow'r,
Till all the ransom'd church of God
   Be sav'd to sin no more.

4 E'er since by faith I saw the stream
   Thy flowing wounds supply,
Redeeming love has been my theme
   And shall be till I die.

5 Then in a nobler, sweeter song,
   I'll sing thy pow'r to save,
When this poor, lisping,
      stammering tongue
   Lies silent in the grave.

*William Cowper*, [1772]
[*alt. John Rippon*, 1787]

**2.3:** *And there have I, as* **2.4:** *Wash'd*
**MM:** Hymns, Set 1 (Jan./Nov.), 26th Morn,
   FOUNTAIN / AZMON
**MM:** Hymns, Set 2 (Feb./Dec.), 3rd Morn,
   BALERMA / HELENA
**Ed:** From an account of the graveside service for
   C.H. Spurgeon, 11 Feb. 1892:
   "As the service proceeded, a little redbreast
   poured forth its liquid note all the while from
   a neighbouring tombstone; the redbreast made
   appropriate music, fabled as it was to have had
   its crimson coat ever since it picked a thorn
   from the Saviour's bleeding brow. Well, we do
   not believe that; but we believe what we sang

at the grave, the truth that the beloved Pastor
lived to preach, and died to defend:
   'Dear dying Lamb, Thy precious blood
      Shall never lose its power,
   Till all the ransomed church of God
      Be saved to sin no more'"
(S&T, Mar. 1892, pp.152-153).

# 289 L.M.
*Wonders of the cross.*

1 NATURE with open volume stands
   To spread her Maker's praise abroad,
And every labour of His hands
   Shows something worthy of a God.

2 But in the grace that rescued man
   His brightest form of glory shines;
Here on the cross 'tis fairest drawn
   In precious blood and crimson lines.

3 Here I behold His inmost heart,
   Where grace and vengeance strangely join,
Piercing His Son with sharpest smart
   To make the purchas'd pleasures mine.

4 O the sweet wonders of that cross,
   Where God the Saviour lov'd and died!
Her noblest life my spirit draws
   From His dear wounds and bleeding side.

5 I would forever speak His name
   In sounds to mortal ears unknown,
With angels join to praise the Lamb,
   And worship at His Father's throne.

*Isaac Watts*, [1707]

**FPN:** 20 Feb. 1890 (No. 2287), ROCKINGHAM

# 290 S.M.
*Depths of wisdom in the cross.*

1 AWAKE, my soul, and rise
   Amaz'd, and yonder see,
How hangs the mighty Saviour God
   Upon a cursèd tree!

2 Now gloriously fulfill'd
   Is that most ancient plan,

Contriv'd in the Eternal Mind
Before the world began.

3 Here depths of wisdom shine,
Which angels cannot trace;
The highest rank of cherubim
Still lost in wonder gaze.

4 Here free salvation reigns
And carries all before;
And this shall, for the guilty race,
Be refuge evermore.

5 Now Hell, in all her strength,
Her rage, and boasted sway,
Can never snatch a wand'ring sheep
From Jesus' arms away.

*William Williams*, 1772

## 291 S.M.
*The Shepherd smitten.*

1 LIKE sheep, we went astray
And broke the fold of God,
Each wand'ring in a different way,
But all the downward road.

2 How dreadful was the hour
When God our wand'rings laid,
And did at once His vengeance pour
Upon the Shepherd's head!

3 How glorious was the grace
When Christ sustain'd the stroke!
His life and blood the Shepherd pays,
A ransom for the flock.

4 His honour and His breath
Were taken both away,
Join'd with the wicked in His death,
And made as vile as they.

5 But God shall raise His head
O'er *sons of men to reign*,
And make Him see a num'rous seed
To recompense His pain.

6 "I'll give Him," saith the Lord,
"A portion with the strong;

He shall possess a large reward
And hold His honours long."

*Isaac Watts*, 1709, *alt. C.H.S.*

**5.2:** *all the sons of men,*

## 292 7.7.7.7.
*The three mountains.*

1 WHEN on Sinai's top I see
God descend in majesty,
To proclaim His holy law,
All my spirit sinks with awe.

2 When, in ecstacy sublime,
Tabor's glorious steep I climb,
At the too-transporting light,
Darkness rushes o'er my sight.

3 When on Calvary I rest,
God, in flesh made manifest,
Shines in my Redeemer's face,
Full of beauty, truth, and grace.

4 Here I would forever stay,
Weep and gaze my soul away;
Thou art heaven on earth to me,
Lovely, mournful Calvary.

*James Montgomery*, [1812, *rev. 1825*]

## 293 S.M. / "I, if I be lited up,
*Will draw all men unto me."*

1 BEHOLD th' amazing sight,
The Saviour lifted high!
Behold the Son of God's delight
Expire in agony!

2 For whom, for whom, my heart,
Were all these sorrows borne?
Why did He feel that piercing smart
And meet that various scorn?

3 For love of us He bled,
And all in torture died;
'Twas love that bow'd His fainting head,
And oped His gushing side.

4    I see and I adore
     In sympathy of love;
  I feel the strong attractive pow'r
     To lift my soul above.

5    Drawn by such cords as these,
     Let all the earth combine
  With cheerful ardour to confess
     The energy divine.

6    In Thee our hearts unite,
     Nor share Thy griefs alone,
  But from Thy cross pursue their flight
     To Thy triumphant throne.

*Philip Doddridge*, 1755

  **Ed:** Dated 8 May 1737 in Doddridge's manu-
    scripts, but not published until 1755.

# 294 8.7.8.7.
*His death.*

1 ON the wings of faith uprising,
     Jesus crucified I see;
  While His love, my soul surprising,
     Cries, "I suffer'd all for thee!"

2 Then, beneath the cross adoring,
     Sin doth like itself appear;
  When the wounds of Christ exploring,
     I can read my pardon there.

3 Who can think without admiring?
     Who can hear and nothing feel?
  See the Lord of life expiring,
     Yet retain a heart of steel?

4 Angels here may gaze and wonder
     What the God of love could mean,
  When He tore the heart asunder,
     Never once defil'd with sin!

*Joseph Swain*, 1792

# 295 7.7.7.7.
*"The love of Christ constraineth us."*

1 IN the Lord's atoning grief
     Be our rest and sweet relief;

Store we deep in heart's recess
All the shame and bitterness.

2 Thorns, and cross, and nails, and lance,
  Wounds, our treasure that enhance,
  Vinegar, and gall, and reed,
  And the pang His soul that freed:

3 May these all our spirits sate,
  And with love inebriate;
  In our souls plant virtue's root,
  And mature its glorious fruit.

4 Crucified, we Thee adore,
  Thee with all our hearts implore,
  Us with saintly bands unite
  In the realms of heav'nly light.

5 Christ! by coward hands betray'd,
  Christ! for us a captive made,
  Christ! upon the bitter tree,
  Slain for man, be praise to Thee!

[*St. Bonaventura*, 13th century]
[*tr. Frederick Oakeley*, 1842]

  **Ed:** From the Latin, "In passione Domini." Sedg-
    wick credited the hymn to John Mason Neale.

# 296 L.M.
*For me.*

1 THE Son of God, in mighty love,
  Came down to Bethlehem for me,
  Forsook His throne of light above,
  An infant upon earth to be.

2 In love, the Father's sinless child
  Sojourn'd at Nazareth for me;
  With sinners dwelt the Undefiled,
  The Holy One in Galilee.

3 Jesus, whom angel hosts adore,
  Became a man of griefs for me;
  In love, though rich, becoming poor,
  That I through Him enrich'd might be.

4 Though Lord of all, above, below,
  He went to Olivet for me;
  He drank my cup of wrath and woe,
  *And bled in dark* Gethsemane.

5 The ever-blessèd Son of God
  Went up to Calvary for me,
There paid my debt, there bore my load,
  In His own body on the tree.

6 Jesus, whose dwelling is the skies,
  Went down into the grave for me,
There overcame my enemies,
  There won the glorious victory.

7 'Tis finish'd all; the veil is rent,
  The welcome sure, the access free;
Now then we leave our banishment,
  O Father, to return to Thee.

*Horatius Bonar*, [1843]

> **4.4:** *When bleeding in* **Ed:** This alt. appeared in
> an obscure collection, *Hymns for Public and
> Private Use*, ca. 1860, but otherwise seems to
> have been proliferated via *OOHB*.
> **EE:** Hymns, Set 2 (Feb./Dec.), 5th Eve,
> ALFRED / MONTGOMERY

# 297   8.7.8.7. Double
*All for us.*

1 GREAT High Priest, we view Thee stooping,
  With our names upon Thy breast,
In the garden, groaning, drooping,
  To the ground with horrors press'd.
Weeping angels stood confounded
  To behold their Maker thus;
And can we remain unwounded
  When we know 'twas all for us?

2 On the cross Thy body broken
  Cancels ev'ry penal tie;
Tempted souls, produce this token,
  All demands to satisfy.
All is finish'd; do not doubt it,
  But believe your dying Lord;
Never reason more about it,
  Only take Him at His word.

3 Lord, we fain would trust Thee solely;
  'Twas for us Thy blood was spilt;
Bruisèd Bridegroom, take us wholly,
  Take and make us what Thou wilt.

Thou hast borne the bitter sentence
  Past on man's devoted race;
True belief and true repentence
  Are Thy gifts, Thou God of grace.

*Joseph Hart*, 1759

> **Ed:** This is the second part of a longer hymn,
> "Let us ask the important question."

# 298   7.7.7.7.
*Sin removed by the cross.*

1 SONS of peace, redeem'd by blood,
Raise your songs to Zion's God;
Made from condemnation free,
Grace triumphant sing with me.

2 Calv'ry's *wonders* let us trace,
*Justice magnified in* grace;
*Mark* the purple *streams* and say,
Thus my sins were *wash'd* away.

3 *Wrath divine no more* we dread;
*Vengeance smote our Surety's head;*
*Legal claims are fully met;*
*Jesus paid the dreadful debt.*

4 *Sin is lost beneath the* flood,
*Drown'd in the Redeemer's* blood;
Zion, O! how bless'd art thou,
Justified from all things now.

*John Kent*, 1803, *alt. C.H.S.*

> **2.1:** *summit*  **2.2:** *View the heights and depths*
> **2.3:** *Count drops*  **2.4:** *borne*
> **3.1:** *Now no more his wrath*
> **3.2-4:** *He hath thus to Zion said,*
> *"Since thy Surety paid thy score,*
> *I behold thy sins no more."*
> **4.1:** *Sunk as in a shoreless*
> **4.2:** *Lost as in a Saviour's*
> **EE:** Hymns, Set 2 (Feb./Dec.), 28th Eve,
> RATISBON / HART'S

# 299   S.M.
*Jehovah satisfied.*

1 MORE marr'd than any man's,
  The Saviour's visage see;

Was ever sorrow like to His
  Endured on Calvary?

2 O hear that piercing cry!
    What can its meaning be?
  "My God! my God! oh, why hast Thou
    In wrath forsaken me?"

3 O 'twas because our sins
    On Him by God were laid;
  He who Himself had never sinned,
    For sinners, sin was made.

4 Thus sin He put away
    By His one sacrifice,
  Then, conqueror over death and hell,
    *He mounted to the skies.*

5 Therefore let all men know
    That God is satisfied,
  And sinners all who Jesus trust,
    Through Him are justified.

*William Russell*, 1862 [*alt.*]

  **4.4:** *Triumphantly did rise.*
  **Ed:** This change originated with *OOHB*; whether
  it was a revision by Russell or an alteration by
  Spurgeon is unclear.
  **FPN:** 15 Sept. 1889 (No. 2333), AUGUSTINE

# 300  8.7.8.7.4.7.
*"It is finished."*

1 HARK! the voice of love and mercy
    Sounds aloud from Calvary!
  See! it rends the rocks asunder,
    Shakes the earth, and veils the sky!
      "It is finished!"
    Hear the dying Saviour cry!

2 "It is finished!" O what pleasure
    Do these charming words afford!
  Heav'nly blessings without measure
    Flow to us from Christ the Lord!
      "It is finished!"
    Saints, the dying words record.

3 Finish'd, all the types and shadows
    Of the ceremonial law!

Finish'd, all that God had promis'd;
    Death and hell no more shall awe.
      "It is finish'd!"
    Saints, from hence your comfort draw.

4 Tune your harps anew, ye seraphs;
    Join to sing the pleasing theme;
  All on earth and all in heaven,
    Join to praise Immanuel's name!
      Hallelujah!
    Glory to the bleeding Lamb!

*Jonathan Evans*, [1784]

# 301  7.7.7.7.
*Joy or sorrow.*

1 "IT is finish'd!"—Shall we raise
    Songs of sorrow or of praise;
  Mourn to see the Saviour die,
    Or proclaim His victory?

2 If of Calvary we tell,
    How can songs of triumph swell?
  If of man, redeem'd from woe,
    How shall notes of mourning flow?

3 Ours the guilt which pierced His side;
    Ours the sin for which He died;
  But the blood which flow'd *that day*
    Wash'd *our* sin and guilt away.

4 Lamb of God! Thy death hath giv'n
    *Pardon, peace, and hope* of heav'n.
  "It is finish'd!"—Let us raise
    Songs of *thankfulness* and praise!

[*A Collection of Psalms & Hymns for the
Use of St. Mary's, St. Giles's, and Trinity
Churches, Reading*, 1830, *rev. and alt.*]

  **3.3:** *today*  **3.4:** *that*  **4.2:** *High and joyous hopes*
  **4.4:** *glory, joy,*  **Ed:** The changes at 4.2 and 4.4
  appeared in the 3rd edition of the Reading
  *Collection* (1838). The author is quite possibly
  Henry Hart Milman, a skilled poet who was
  appointed to St. Mary's at Reading in 1818. He
  was later appointed canon of Westminster and
  rector of St. Margaret's in 1835; a collection of
  hymns for that congregation appeared there in
  1837 under Milman's name, not including this

hymn. The final altered form appeared in *The Winchester Church Hymn Book* in 1857; at the time, Milman was Dean of St. Paul's Cathedral, London, from 1849 to his death in 1868.

# 302 C.M.
*Christ's death, victory, and dominion.*

1 I SING my Saviour's wondrous death;
   He conquer'd when He fell;
"'Tis finish'd," said His dying breath,
   And shook the gates of hell.

2 "'Tis finish'd!" our Immanuel cries;
   The dreadful work is done;
Hence shall His sovereign throne arise;
   His kingdom is begun.

3 His cross a sure foundation laid
   For glory and renown,
When through the regions of the dead
   He pass'd to reach the crown.

4 Exalted at His Father's side
   Sits our victorious Lord;
To heaven and hell His hands divide
   The vengeance or reward.

5 The saints, from His propitious eye
   Await their several crowns,
And all the sons of darkness fly
   The terror of His frowns.

*Isaac Watts,* 1709

**FPN:** 19 Feb. 1888 (No. 2357), WINCHESTER
**FPN:** 9 Sept. 1888 (No. 2043), MAGNUS

# 303 C.M.
*The cup of wrath.*

1 ONCE it was mine, the cup of wrath,
   But Jesus drank it dry;
When on the cursèd tree transfix'd,
   He breathed th' expiring sigh.

2 No tongue can tell the wrath He bore,
   The wrath so due to me;
Sin's just desert; He bore it all
   To set the sinner free!

3 Now not a single drop remains;
   "'Tis finish'd" was His cry;
By one effectual draught, He drank
   The cup of wrath quite dry.

*Albert Midlane,* [1861]

# JESUS SEEN OF ANGELS.

# 304 C.M.
*Jesus seen of angels.*

1 BEYOND the glittering starry *skies*,
   Far as th' eternal hills,
There, in the boundless worlds of light,
   Our dear Redeemer dwells.

2 *Immortal* angels, *bright* and fair,
   In countless armies shine.
At His right hand, with golden harps,
   They offer songs divine.

3 *In all His toils and dangerous paths*
   They did His steps attend,
Oft *paused*, and wonder'd *how* at last
   This scene of love would end!

4 And when the powers of hell combin'd
   To fill His cup of woe,
*Their* pitying eyes beheld His tears
   In bloody anguish flow.

5 As on the *tottering tree* He hung,
   And darkness veil'd the sky,
They saw, aghast, that awful sight,
   The Lord of Glory die!

6 Anon He bursts the gates of death,
   Subdues the tyrant's power;
*They* saw th' illustrious Conqueror rise
   And hail'd the blessèd hour.

7 They brought His chariot from above
   To bear Him to His throne,
Clapp'd their triumphant wings, and cried,
   "The glorious work is done!"

8 My soul the joyful triumph feels,
   And thinks the moments long,

Ere she her Saviour's glory sees,
And joins *the* rapt'rous song.

1-3,7 *James Fanch*, [1776,] *alt.*
4-6,8 *Daniel Turner*, 1791, *alt.*

**1.1:** *globes,*   **2.1:** *Legions of / strong*
**3.1:** *Thru' all His travels here below,*
**3.3:** *gaz'd / where*   **4.3:** *Your*
**5.1:** *torturing cross*   **6.3:** *Ye*   **8.4:** *your*
**Ed:** The alteration at 1.1 appeared in Rowland
Hill's *Collection* (1787). 2.1 is by Turner. 3.1-3,
4.3, 6.3 and 8.4 are from Rippon's *Selection*,
27th ed. (c. 1828); 5.1 was changed in the
Comprehensive Ed. (1844). Turner's adaptation had been in circulation as early as March
1791, as mentioned in Rippon's *Baptist Annual Register*, vol. 3, p. 471 (1798-1801).
**FPN:** 9 Sept. 1888 (No. 2043), ARLINGTON

# 305   6.6.6.6.4.4.4.4.
*Jesus seen of angels.*

1  YE bright immortal throng
Of angels round the throne,
Join with our feeble song
To make the Saviour known:
    On earth ye knew
    His wondrous grace;
    His beauteous face
    In heaven ye view.

2  Ye saw the heaven-born child
In human flesh array'd,
Benevolent and mild,
While in the manger laid;
    And praise to God,
    And peace on earth,
    For such a birth
    Proclaim'd aloud.

3  Ye in the wilderness
Beheld the tempter spoil'd,
Well known in every dress,
In every combat foil'd;
    And joy'd to crown
    The Victor's head,
    When Satan fled
    Before His frown.

4  Around the bloody tree
Ye press'd with strong desire
That wondrous sight to see,
The Lord of life expire;
    And could your eyes
    Have known a tear,
    Had dropp'd it there
    In sad surprise.

5  Around His sacred tomb
A willing watch ye kept,
Till the blest moment came
To awaken Him that slept:
    Then roll'd the stone,
    And all adored
    Your rising Lord,
    With joy unknown.

6  When all array'd in light
The shining Conqueror rode,
Ye hail'd His rapturous flight
Up to the throne of God,
    And waved around
    Your golden wings,
    And struck your strings
    Of sweetest sound.

7  The warbling notes pursue,
And louder anthems raise,
While mortals sing with you
Their own Redeemer's praise;
    And thou, my heart,
    With equal flame,
    And joy the same,
    Perform thy part.

*Philip Doddridge*, 1755 [*rev.* 1839]

**Ed:** In the earlier editions of 1755-1766, this
hymn began, "O ye immortal throng."

# RESURRECTION AND ASCENSION OF OUR LORD.

# 306   7.7.7.7.
*The Lord is risen.*

1 "CHRIST the Lord is ris'n today,"
Sons of men and angels say;

Raise your joys and triumphs high;
Sing, ye heav'ns, and earth reply.

2 Love's redeeming work is done;
Fought the fight, the battle won;
Lo! *the* sun's eclipse is o'er;
Lo! He sets in blood no more.

3 Vain the stone, the watch, the seal;
Christ has burst the gates of hell!
Death in vain forbids His rise;
Christ hath open'd paradise!

4 Lives again our glorious King;
Where, O death, is now thy sting?
*Once He died our souls to save;*
*Where's* thy victory, *boasting* grave?

5 Soar we now where Christ has led,
Following our exalted head;
Made like Him, like Him we rise;
Ours the cross, the grave, the skies!

6 Hail the Lord of earth and heav'n!
Praise to Thee by both be giv'n;
Thee we greet triumphant now;
Hail the Resurrection Thou!

*Charles Wesley*, 1739 [*alt.*]

**2.2:** *our*   **4.3:** *Dying once he all doth save;*
**4.4:** *Where / O*   **Ed:** Wesley's hymn was based
loosely on the Latin "Surrexit Christus hodie"
(14th cen.) and the translation "Jesus Christ
is risen today" (1708). The alteration at 4.3 is
from Martin Madan's *Collection* (1760); the
others are from Rippon's *Selection* (1787).
**MM:** Hymns, 3rd & 12th Lord's Day,
NUREMBERG / HERNDON

# 307   7.7.7.7. with Alleluias
*"He is risen."*

1 ANGELS, roll the rock away;
Death, *resign thy* mighty prey;
*See the Saviour quit* the tomb,
Glowing with immortal bloom.
Hallelujah.

2 *Shout, ye seraphs! Gabriel*, raise
Fame's eternal trump of praise;

Let the earth's remotest bound
Hear the joy-inspiring sound.
Hallelujah.

3 *Saints on earth*, lift up your eyes,
Now to glory see Him rise;
*Troops of angels on the road*
*Hail and sing th' incarnate God.*
Hallelujah.

4 Heaven *unfolds its* portals wide;
Gracious hero, through them ride;
King of glory, mount Thy throne;
*Boundless empire is Thine* own.
Hallelujah.

5 Praise Him, *ye celestial* choirs,
Praise, and sweep your golden lyres;
Shout, O earth, in rapturous song;
Let the strains be sweet and strong!
Hallelujah.

6 Every note with wonder swell;
Sin o'erthrown, and captiv'd hell;
Where is hell's once dreaded king?
Where, O death, thy mortal sting?
Hallelujah.

*Thomas Scott*, 1769 [*alt.*]

**1.2:** *yield up thy*   **1.3:** *See! He rises from*
**2.1:** *'Tis the Saviour, angels,*
**3.1:** *Now, ye saints*
**3.3-4:** *In long triumph up the sky,*
      *Up to waiting worlds on high.*
**4.1:** *displays her*
**4.4:** *Thy great Father's and Thy*
**5.1:** *all ye heavenly*
**Ed:** These alterations, except 1.2 and 3.1, are by
Thomas Gibbons, from *The Gospel Magazine*
(Sept. 1775). 3.1 was changed in Gibbons'
*Hymns Adapted* (1784). 1.1–5.2 appeared
exactly as in Edward Williams' *Collection*
(1801). The entire hymn above appears as in
the Baptist *New Selection of Hymns* and its
successors (1828-1865).

# 308   6.6.6.6.4.4.4.4.
*Praise the risen Lord.*

1 YES, the Redeemer rose;
The Saviour left the dead,

And o'er our hellish foes
High rais'd His conqu'ring head;
   In wild dismay,
   The guards around
   Fell to the ground
   And sunk away.

2  Lo! the angelic bands
In full assembly meet
To wait His high commands
And worship at His feet:
   Joyful they come
   And wing their way
   From realms of day
   To *Jesus'* tomb.

3  Then back to heav'n they fly
And the glad tidings bear;
Hark! as they soar on high,
What music fills the air!
   Their anthems say,
   "Jesus, who bled,
   Hath left the dead;
   He rose today."

4  Ye mortals, catch the sound,
Redeem'd by Him from hell,
And send the echo round
The globe on which you dwell;
   Transported cry,
   "Jesus, who bled,
   Hath left the dead,
   No more to die."

5  All hail, triumphant Lord,
Who sav'st us with Thy blood!
Wide be Thy name ador'd,
Thou rising, reigning God!
   With Thee we rise,
   With Thee we reign,
   And empires gain
   Beyond the skies.

*Philip Doddridge*, 1755
[*alt.* John Rippon, 1787]

**2.8:** *such a*

# 309   S.M.
*"The Lord is risen indeed."*

1  "THE Lord is ris'n indeed";
   *Now* is His work perform'd;
*Now is the mighty Captive* freed,
   And *death's strong castle storm'd.*

2  "The Lord is ris'n indeed";
   *The grave* has lost *its* prey;
With Him is ris'n the ransom'd seed
   To reign in endless day.

3  "The Lord is ris'n indeed";
   He lives to die no more;
He lives, the sinner's cause to plead,
   Whose curse and shame He bore.

4  "The Lord is ris'n indeed";
   Attending angels hear;
Up to the courts of heav'n, with speed,
   The joyful tidings bear.

5  Then *tune* your golden lyres
   And strike each cheerful chord;
Join all *ye* bright celestial choirs
   To sing our risen Lord.

*Thomas Kelly*, [1802, *rev.* 1811], *alt.*

**1.2:** *Then*  **1.3:** *The captive surety now is*
**1.4:** *death our foe disarm'd.*
**2.2:** *Then hell / his*  **5.1** *take*  **5.3:** *the*
**Ed:** The alterations at 1.2, 1.3, and 2.2 appeared
in *The Sabbath Hymn Book* (1858); the rest
are by Spurgeon.
**FPN:** 20 Feb. 1890 (No. 2287), ST. MICHAEL'S

# 310   6.6.6.6.8.8.
*Captivity led captive.*

1  THE happy morn is come;
   *Triumphant o'er* the grave,
*The Saviour leaves the tomb,*
   *Omnipotent* to save;
Captivity is captive led,
*For* Jesus liveth that was dead.

2  Who now accuseth them,
   For whom their *ransom* died?
Who now shall those condemn

Whom God hath justified?
Captivity is captive led,
*For* Jesus liveth that was dead.

3 Christ hath the ransom paid;
    The glorious work is done;
On Him our help is laid;
    *By Him our victory* won;
Captivity is captive led,
*For* Jesus liveth that was dead.

1,3 *Thomas Haweis*, 1792 [*alt.* E.B.]
[2 Edward Bickersteth, 1833, *alt.*]

   **1.2:** *The Saviour leaves*
   **1.3:** *His glorious work is done,*
   **1.4:** *Almighty now*   **1.6, etc.:** *Since*
   **2.2:** *surety*   **3.4:** *The victory is*
   **Ed:** The alteration at 2.2 is from Stow & Smith,
   *The Psalmist* (1843), where this hymn was
   credited to Bickersteth's collection.

## 311   10.11.11.11.12.11.10.11.
*Death conquered.*

1 PRAISE the Redeemer, almighty to save;
Immanuel has triumphed o'er death and
    the grave!
Sing, for the door of the dungeon is open;
The Captive came forth at the dawn of
    the day.
How vain the precautions! the signet
    is broken;
The watchmen in terror have fled far away.
Praise the Redeemer, almighty to save;
Immanuel has triumphed o'er death and
    the grave!

2 Praise to the Conqueror; oh tell of His love!
In pity to mortals He came from above.
Who shall rebuild for the tyrant his prison?
The sceptre lies broken that fell from
    his hands;
His dominion is ended; the Lord *is* arisen;
The helpless shall soon be released from
    their bands.
Praise the Redeemer, almighty to save;
Immanuel has triumphed o'er death and
    the grave!

*William Groser*, [1838]
[*alt.* John Rippon's *Selection*, 1844]

   **2.5:** *has*

## 312   C.M.
*Comfort from the Resurrection.*

1 YE humble souls that seek the Lord,
    Chase all your fears away,
And bow with pleasure down to see
    The place where Jesus lay.

2 Thus low the Lord of Life was brought;
    Such wonders love can do;
Thus cold in death that bosom lay,
    Which throbb'd and bled for you.

3 A moment give a loose to grief,
    Let grateful sorrows rise,
And wash the bloody stains away
    With torrents from your eyes.

4 Then raise your hopes and tune your songs;
    The Saviour lives again!
Not all the bolts and bars of death
    The Conqu'ror could detain.

5 High o'er th' angelic bands He rears
    His once dishonour'd head,
And through unnumber'd years He reigns,
    Who dwelt among the dead.

6 With joy like His shall every saint
    His empty tomb survey,
Then rise with His ascending Lord
    To heaven's eternal day.

*Philip Doddridge*, 1755 [*rev.* 1839]

## 313   C.M.
*Resurrection and Ascension.*

1 HOSANNAH to the Prince of light,
    *Who* clothed himself in clay,
Enter'd the iron gates of death,
    And tore the bars away.

2 Death is no more the king of dread,
    Since our Immanuel rose;

He took the tyrant's sting away
　　And spoil'd our hellish foes.

3 See how the Conqueror mounts aloft
　　And to His Father flies,
With scars of honour in His flesh
　　And triumph in His eyes.

4 There our exalted Saviour reigns
　　And scatters blessings down;
*His Father well rewards His pains*
　　*And bids Him wear the crown.*

5 Bright angels, strike your loudest strings,
　　Your sweetest voices raise;
Let heaven and all created things
　　Sound our Immanuel's praise.

*Isaac Watts*, [1707, *rev.* 1709] *alt. C.H.S.*

**1.2:** *That*　**4.3-4:** *Our Jesus fills the middle seat*
*Of the celestial throne.*

# 314 C.M.
*He is gone.*

1 HE'S gone—the Saviour's work on earth,
　　His task of love is o'er;
And lo! this dreary desert knows
　　His gracious steps no more.

2 Oh 'twas a waste to Him indeed;
　　No rest on earth He knew;
No joy from its unhallow'd springs
　　His sorrowing spirit drew.

3 He's gone! and shall our truant feet
　　And ling'ring hearts delay
In a dark world that cast His love,
　　Like worthless dross, away.

4 Hopeless of joy in aught below,
　　We only long to soar,
The fullness of His love to feel,
　　And lose His smile no more.

5 His hand, with all the gentle power,
　　The sweet constraint of love,
Hath drawn us from this restless world
　　And fix'd our hearts above.

*Edward Denny*, 1848

# 315 8.7.8.7.7.7.
*Jesus victorious.*

1 "WHO is this that comes from Edom?"
　　All His raiment stain'd with blood,
To the slave proclaiming freedom,
　　Bringing and bestowing good;
Glorious in the garb He wears;
Glorious in the spoils He bears.

2 'Tis the Saviour, now victorious,
　　Travelling onward in His might;
'Tis the Saviour, O how glorious
　　To His people is the sight!
Jesus now is strong to save,
Mighty to redeem the slave.

3 Why that blood His raiment staining?
　　'Tis the blood of many slain;
Of His foes there's none remaining,
　　None the contest to maintain;
Fall'n they are no more to rise;
All their glory prostrate lies.

4 This the Saviour has effected,
　　By His mighty arm alone;
See the throne for Him erected;
　　'Tis an everlasting throne;
'Tis the great reward He gains,
Glorious fruit of all His pains.

5 Mighty Victor, reign forever,
　　Wear the crown, so dearly won;
Never shall Thy people, never
　　Cease to sing what Thou hast done;
Thou hast fought Thy people's foes;
Thou hast heal'd Thy people's woes.

*Thomas Kelly*, 1809

# 316 L.M.
*"Who is the King of glory?"*

1 REJOICE, ye shining worlds on high,
Behold the King of glory nigh;
Who can this King of glory be?
The mighty Lord, the Saviour's He.

2 Ye heav'nly gates, your leaves display
To make the Lord the Saviour way;

Laden with spoils from earth and hell,
The Conqueror comes with God to dwell.

3 Rais'd from the dead, He goes before;
He opens heaven's eternal door
To give His saints a blest abode,
Near their Redeemer and their God.

*Isaac Watts*, 1719

**Ed:** Taken from the longer paraphrase,
"This spacious earth is all the Lord's."

# 317
7.7.7.7. with Alleluias
*Sing, O heavens*

1 SING, O heavens! O earth, rejoice!
Angel harp and human voice,
Round Him, as He rises, raise
Your ascending Saviour's praise.
Alleluia!

2 Bruisèd is the serpent's head,
Hell is vanquished, death is dead,
And to Christ, gone up on high,
Captive is captivity.
Alleluia!

3 All His work and warfare done,
He into His heaven is gone,
And beside His Father's throne,
Now is pleading for His own,
Alleluia!

4 Asking gifts for sinful men,
That He may come down again,
And the fallen to restore,
In them dwell forever more.
Alleluia!

5 Sing, O heavens! O earth, rejoice!
Angel harp and human voice,
Round Him, in His glory, raise
Your ascended Saviour's praise.
Alleluia!

*John S.B. Monsell*, 1863

# 318
C.M.
*"I go to prepare a place for you."*

1 TH' eternal gates lift up their heads;
The doors are open'd wide;
The King of glory is gone up
Unto His Father's side.

2 Thou art gone in before us, Lord;
Thou hast prepared a place,
That we may be where now Thou art
And look upon Thy face.

3 And ever on our earthly path
A gleam of glory lies;
A light still breaks upon the cloud
That veils Thee from our eyes.

4 Lift up our *thoughts*, lift up our *songs*,
And let Thy grace be giv'n,
That while we linger yet below,
Our *hearts may* be in heav'n.

5 That where Thou art, at God's right hand,
Our hope, our love may be;
Dwell in us now, that we may dwell
Forever more in Thee.

*Cecil Frances Alexander*, 1852
[*alt. Sabbath Hymn Book*, 1858]

**4.1:** *hearts / minds*   **4.4:** *treasure*

# 319
S.M. Double
*Gone into Heaven.*

1 THOU art gone up on high
To mansions in the skies,
And round Thy throne unceasingly
The songs of praise arise.
But we are lingering here
With sin and care oppress'd;
Lord, send Thy promised Comforter
And lead us to *Thy* rest.

2 Thou art gone up on high,
But Thou didst first come down,
Through earth's most bitter *agony*
To pass unto Thy crown;

And girt with griefs and fears
Our onward course must be,
But only let that path of tears
Lead us, at last, to Thee!

3   Thou art gone up on high,
But Thou shalt come again,
With all the bright ones of the sky
Attendant in Thy train.
Oh! by Thy saving power,
So make us live and die,
That we may stand in that dread hour
At Thy right hand on high.

*Emma Toke*, 1852 [*alt. C.H.S.*]

**1.8:** *our*  **2.3:** *misery*
**MM:** Hymns, Set 2 (Feb./Dec.), 20th Eve,
PRAGUE / ST. MICHAEL'S
**Ed:** Spurgeon had divided this hymn into six
stanzas of four lines, but the proper structure
of the hymn is in sets of eight lines.

# 320   7.7.7.7.7.7.
*Glory to our King.*

1 GLORY, glory to our King!
Crowns unfading wreathe His head!
Jesus is the name we sing,
Jesus, risen from the dead,
Jesus, *spoiler of* the grave,
Jesus, mighty now to save.

2 Jesus is gone up on high;
Angels come to meet their King;
Shouts triumphant rend the sky,
While the Victor's praise they sing:
"Open now, ye heav'nly gates!
'Tis the King of glory waits."

3 Now behold Him high enthron'd!
Glory beaming from His face!
By adoring angels own'd,
*Lord* of holiness and grace!
O for hearts and tongues to sing,
"Glory, glory to our King!"

4 Jesus, on Thy people shine!
Warm our hearts and tune our tongues!
That with angels we may join,

Share their bliss and swell their songs.
Glory, honour, praise, and pow'r,
Lord, be Thine forever more!

*Thomas Kelly*, 1804 [*alt. C.H.S.*]

**1.5:** *conqu'ror o'er*  **3.4:** *God*

# 321   L.M.
*Our forerunner.*

1 JESUS the Lord, our souls adore,
A painful suff'rer now no more;
High on His Father's throne He reigns,
O'er earth and heaven's extensive plains.

2 His race forever is complete;
Forever undisturb'd His seat;
Myriads of angels round Him fly
And sing His well-gain'd victory.

3 Yet, 'midst the honours of His throne,
He joys not for Himself alone;
His meanest servants share their part,
Share in that royal tender heart.

4 Raise, raise, my soul, thy raptur'd sight
With sacred wonder and delight;
Jesus, thine own forerunner see
Enter'd beyond the veil for thee.

5 Loud let the howling tempest yell,
And foaming waves to mountains swell;
No shipwreck can my vessel fear,
Since hope hath fix'd her anchor here.

*Philip Doddridge*, 1755

**MM:** Hymns, Set 2 (Feb./Dec.), 8th Morn,
OLD HUNDREDTH / ROLLAND

# 322   L.M.
*"Lift up your heads."*

1 LIFT up your heads, ye gates, and wide
Your everlasting doors display;
Ye angel-guards, like flames divide,
And give the King of glory way.

2 Who is the King of glory?—He,
The Lord omnipotent to save,

Whose own right arm in victory
Led captive death and spoil'd the grave.

3 Lift up your heads, ye gates, and high
Your everlasting portals heave;
Welcome the King of glory nigh;
Him must the heaven of heavens receive.

4 Who is the King of glory?—Who?
The Lord of hosts, behold His name;
The kingom, power, and honour due,
Yield Him, ye saints, with glad acclaim.

*James Montgomery*, 1822 [*rev.* 1853]

# 323 8.7.8.7.
*All hail.*

1 JESUS, hail! enthron'd in glory,
There forever to abide;
All the heav'nly hosts adore Thee,
Seated at Thy Father's side.

2 There for sinners Thou art pleading;
*There Thou dost our place prepare,*
*Ever for us* interceding,
Till in glory *we* appear.

3 Worship, honour, pow'r, and blessing,
Thou art worthy to receive;
Loudest praises without ceasing,
Meet it is for us to give!

4 Help, ye bright, angelic spirits,
Bring your sweetest, noblest lays;
Help to sing our *Saviour's* merits,
Help to chant Immanuel's praise.

1,3 *John Bakewell*, 1757
[2,4 *Martin Madan's Collection*, 1760]
[*alt. Augustus Toplady*, 1776]

**2.2:** *"Spare them yet another year"*—
**2.3:** *Thou for saints art* **2.4:** *they* **4.3:** *Jesu's*
**Ed:** Taken from the longer hymn, "Hail, Thou
once despisèd Jesus." See also No. 419.

# 324 C.M.
*The Conqueror reigns.*

1 TRIUMPHANT, *Christ* ascends on high,
The glorious work complete;
Sin, death, and hell, low vanquish'd lie
Beneath His awful feet.

2 There, with eternal glory crown'd,
The Lord, the Conqueror reigns;
His praise the heavenly choirs resound,
In their immortal strains.

3 Amid the splendours of His throne,
Unchanging love appears;
The names He purchas'd for His own
Still on His heart He bears.

4 O the rich depths of love divine!
Of bliss, a boundless store;
Dear Saviour, let me call Thee mine;
I cannot wish for more.

5 On Thee alone my hope relies;
Beneath Thy cross I fall,
My Lord, my life, my sacrifice,
My Saviour, and my all.

*Anne Steele*, 1760
[*alt. Jeremiah Day*, 1845]

**1.1:** *He* **Ed:** Taken from the longer hymn,
"Come, heavenly love, inspire my song."
**EE:** Hymns, Set 1 (Jan./Nov.), 19th Eve,
MARTYRDOM / SMYRNA

# OUR LORD IN HEAVEN.

# 325 C.M.
*Prevalent intercession.*

1 AWAKE, sweet gratitude, and sing
Th' ascended Saviour's love;
Tell how He lives to carry on
His people's cause above.

2 With cries and tears He offer'd up
His humble suit below,
But with authority He asks,
Enthron'd in glory now.

3 For all that come to God by Him,
Salvation He demands,
Points to their names upon His breast,
And spreads His wounded hands.

4 His covenant and sacrifice
Give sanction to His claim;
"Father, I will that all my saints
Be with me where I am."

5 "By their salvation, recompense
The sorrows I endur'd;
Just to the merits of Thy Son
And faithful to Thy Word."

6 Eternal life, at His request,
To ev'ry saint is giv'n;
Safety on earth, and after death,
The plentitude of heav'n.

*Augustus Toplady,* 1771

# 326 L.M.
*"He ever liveth."*

1 HE lives, the great Redeemer lives,
(What joy the blest assurance gives!)
And now before His Father God
Pleads the full merit of His blood.

2 Repeated crimes awake our fears,
And justice arm'd with frowns appears,
But in the Saviour's lovely face
Sweet mercy smiles, and all is peace.

3 Hence, then, ye black despairing thoughts;
Above our fears, above our faults,
His pow'rful intercessions rise,
And guilt recedes, and terror dies.

4 In ev'ry dark, distressful hour,
When sin and Satan join their pow'r,
Let this dear hope repel the dart,
That Jesus bears us on His heart.

5 Great Advocate, Almighty Friend,
On Him our humble hopes depend;
Our cause can never, never fail,
For Jesus pleads and must prevail.

*Anne Steele,* 1760

MM: Hymns, Set 1 (Jan./Nov.), 22nd Morn,
ZEPHYR / RETREAT

# 327 L.M. / *Touched with a feeling of our infirmities.*

1 WHERE high the heavenly temple stands,
The house of God not made with hands,
A great High Priest our nature wears,
The Patron of mankind appears.

2 He, who for men their Surety stood
And pour'd on earth His precious blood,
Pursues in heav'n His mighty plan,
The Saviour and the Friend of man.

3 Though now ascended up on high,
He bends on earth a brother's eye;
Partaker of the human name,
He knows the frailty of our frame.

4 Our fellow suff'rer yet retains
A fellow feeling of our pains,
And still remembers in the skies
His tears, and agonies, and cries.

5 In ev'ry pang that rends the heart,
The Man of Sorrows had a part;
He sympathizes in our grief,
And to the suff'rer sends relief.

6 With boldness, therefore, at the throne,
Let us make all our sorrows known,
And ask the aid of heav'nly power
To help us in the evil hour.

*Michael Bruce,* [1781]

Ed: In 1781, this hymn was published in John
Logan's *Poems* and the Church of Scot-
land's *Translations and Paraphrases,* each
somewhat different. This version represents
a combination of both, as given in the Baptist
*New Selection* (1828).
MM: Hymns, Set 2 (Feb./Dec.), 5th Morn,
DUMBARTON / WARD

# 328 C.M.
*Christ's compassion to the weak.*

1 WITH joy we meditate the grace
Of our High Priest above;

His heart is made of tenderness;
    His bowels melt with love.

2 Touch'd with a sympathy within,
    He knows our feeble frame;
He knows what sore temptations mean,
    For He has felt the same.

3 But spotless, innocent, and pure,
    The great Redeemer stood,
While Satan's fiery darts He bore
    And did resist to blood.

4 He in the days of feeble flesh
    Pour'd out His cries and tears,
And in His measure feels afresh
    What every member bears.

5 Then let our humble faith address
    His mercy and His power;
We shall obtain delivering grace
    In the distressing hour.

*Isaac Watts*, 1709

**Ed:** In Spurgeon's first sermon at the Metropolitan Tabernacle, 25 Mar. 1861, while speaking on the divinity and humanity of Christ, he said (MTP, vol. 7, p. 170):

    "We must have a human Christ, and we must have one of real flesh and blood too; not of shadows or filmy fancies. We must have one to whom we can talk, one with whom we can walk, one 'Who in his measure feels afresh what every member bears,' who is so intimately connected with us in ties of blood, that he is with us one, the head of the family, first-born among many brethren."

# 329 L.M.
*Faith triumphant in her living Lord.*

1 WHO shall the Lord's elect condemn?
    'Tis God that justifies their souls;
And mercy like a mighty stream
    O'er all their sins divinely rolls.

2 Who shall adjudge the saints to hell?
    'Tis Christ that suffer'd in their stead;
And *their* salvation to fulfill,
    Behold Him rising from the dead.

3 He lives, He lives, and sits above,
    Forever interceding there;
Who shall divide us from His love?
    Or what should tempt us to despair?

4 Shall persecution, or distress,
    Famine, or sword, or nakedness?
He that hath loved us bears us through,
    And makes us more than conquerors too.

5 Faith hath an overcoming power;
    It triumphs in the dying hour;
Christ is our life, our joy, our hope,
    Nor can we sink with such a prop.

6 Not all that men on earth can do,
    Nor pow'rs on high, nor pow'rs below,
Shall cause His mercy to remove,
    Or wean our hearts from Christ, our love.

*Isaac Watts*, [1707, *alt.*]

**2.3:** *the* **Ed:** This variant dates to the early 1800s.

# 330 C.M.
*Preservation by His plea.*

1 THERE is a Shepherd kind and strong,
    Still watchful for His sheep;
Nor shall th' infernal lion rend,
    Whom He vouchsafes to keep.

2 Blest Jesus, intercede for us,
    That we may fall no more;
O raise us, when we prostrate lie,
    And comfort lost restore.

3 Thy secret energy impart,
    That faith may never fail;
But under showers of fiery darts,
    That temper'd shield prevail.

*Philip Doddridge*, 1755 [*rev.* 1839]

**Ed:** Taken from the longer hymn,
    "How keen the tempter's malice is!"
**EE:** Hymns, Set 2 (Feb./Dec.), 21st Eve,
    ARLINGTON / ANN'S

## 331 C.M.
*The power of the risen Lord.*

1 JESUS, the name high over all,
    In hell, or earth, or sky;
  Angels and men before it fall,
    And devils fear and fly.

2 Jesus, the name to sinners dear,
    The name to sinners given;
  It scatters all their guilty fear
    And turns their hell to heaven.

3 Jesus the prisoner's fetters breaks,
    And bruises Satan's head;
  Power into strengthless souls it speaks,
    And life into the dead.

4 His only righteousness I show,
    His saving truth proclaim;
  'Tis all my business here below
    To cry, "Behold the Lamb!"

5 Happy, if with my latest breath
    I may but gasp His name,
  Preach Him to all, and cry in death,
    "Behold, behold the Lamb!"

*Charles Wesley*, 1749

> **Ed:** Taken from the longer hymn,
> "Jesu, accept the grateful song."
> **TD:** "What wonders have been wrought in the
> name of the Lord! It is the battle-cry of faith,
> before which its adversaries fly apace. . . .
> Let us take care never to venture into the
> presence of the foe without first of all arming
> ourselves with this impenetrable mail. If we
> knew this name better, and trusted it more,
> our life would be more fruitful and sublime"
> (Ps. 118:12; vol. 5, p. 326).

## 332 C.M.
*He must reign.*

1 'TIS past—that agonizing hour
    Of torture and of shame;
  And Jesus is gone up with power,
    His promis'd throne to claim.

2 The Father heard Him when He cried
    From sorrow's deepest flood,
And gave Him those for whom He died,
    The purchase of His blood.

3 The first-fruits have been gather'd in,
    The work of love begun,
But brighter years shall soon begin
    Their glorious course to run.

4 The name of Jesus shall be known
    To earth's remotest bound;
Nations shall bow before His throne
    And hail the joyful sound.

5 His summons shall awake the dead
    And break the captive's chain,
Till o'er a ransom'd world shall spread
    Christ's universal reign.

*William Hiley Bathurst*, 1831

## 333 8.7.8.7.4.7.
*"He shall reign forever and ever."*

1 LOOK, ye saints, the sight is glorious;
    See the "Man of Sorrows" now;
From the fight return'd victorious;
    Every knee to Him shall bow;
      Crown Him, crown Him;
  Crowns become the Victor's brow.

2 Crown the Saviour; angels crown Him;
    Rich the trophies Jesus brings;
In the seat of pow'r enthrone Him,
    While the vault of heaven rings:
      Crown Him, crown Him,
  Crown the Saviour, "King of Kings!"

3 Sinners in derision crown'd Him,
    Mocking thus the Saviour's claim;
Saints and angels crowd around Him,
    Own His title, praise His name;
      Crown Him, crown Him;
  Spread abroad the victor's fame.

4 Hark, those bursts of acclamation!
    Hark, those loud triumphant chords!
Jesus takes the highest station;
    O what joy the sight affords!

Crown Him, crown Him,
"King of Kings and Lord of Lords."

*Thomas Kelly*, 1809

**MBTS:** 21 Dec. 1884 (No. 1827), VESPER

# 334
6.6.6.6.8.8.
*The kingdom of Christ.*

1 REJOICE, the Lord is King!
Your Lord and King adore;
Mortals, give thanks, and sing,
And triumph evermore:
Lift up *the* heart, lift up *the* voice,
Rejoice *aloud, ye saints*, rejoice.

2 Jesus the Saviour reigns,
The God of truth and love;
When He had purg'd our stains,
He took His seat above;
Lift up *the* heart, lift up *the* voice,
Rejoice *aloud, ye saints*, rejoice.

3 His kingdom cannot fail;
He rules o'er earth and heaven;
The keys of death and hell
Are to our Jesus given;
Lift up *the* heart, lift up *the* voice,
Rejoice *aloud, ye saints*, rejoice.

4 He all His foes shall quell,
Shall all our sins destroy,
And every bosom swell
With pure seraphic joy;
Lift up *the* heart, lift up *the* voice,
Rejoice *aloud, ye saints*, rejoice.

5 Rejoice in glorious hope;
Jesus, the Judge, shall come
And take His servants up
To their eternal home;
We soon shall hear th' archangel's voice;
The trump of God shall sound, rejoice.

*Charles Wesley*, 1746
[*alt. John Rippon*, 1787]

**1.5, etc.:** *your / your*   **1.6, etc.:** *again, I say,*

# 335
6.6.6.6.8.8.
*Reigning power.*

1 REJOICE! the Saviour reigns
Among the sons of men;
He breaks the pris'ners' chains
And makes them free again;
Let hell oppose God's only Son;
In spite of foes, His cause goes on.

2 The cause of righteousness,
Of truth and holy peace,
Design'd our world to bless,
Shall spread and never cease;
Gentile and Jew, their souls shall bow,
Allegiance due, with rapture, vow.

3 The baffled prince of hell
In vain new efforts tries,
Truth's empire to repel
By cruelty and lies;
Th' infernal gates shall rage in vain;
Conquest awaits the Lamb once slain.

4 He died, but soon arose
Triumphant o'er the grave;
And still Himself He shows
Omnipotent to save;
Let rebels kiss the victor's feet;
Eternal bliss His subjects meet.

5 All pow'r is in His hand,
His people to defend;
To His most high command
Shall millions more attend;
All heav'n with smiles approves His cause,
And distant isles receive His laws.

*John Ryland*, [1793, *rev.* 1828]

# 336
C.M.
*Christ glorified.*

1 THE head that once was crown'd
with thorns
Is crown'd with glory now;
A royal diadem adorns
The mighty Victor's brow.

2 The highest place that heaven affords
   Is His, is His by right,
"The King of Kings and Lord of Lords,"
   And heaven's eternal light.

3 The joy of all who dwell above,
   The joy of all below,
To whom He manifests His love
   And grants His name to know.

4 *We* suffer with *our* Lord below,
   *We* reign with Him above,
*Our* profit and *our* joy to know
   The myst'ry of His love.

5 The cross He bore is life and health,
   Though shame and death to Him,
His people's hope, His people's wealth,
   Their everlasting theme.

*Thomas Kelly*, 1820
[*alt. George Bird*, 1853]

   **4.1:** *They / their* **4.2:** *They* **4.3:** *Their / their*
   **MM:** Hymns, Set 2 (Feb./Dec.), 23rd Morn,
   DUNDEE / BROWN
   **NPSP:** "Do you see Him? 'The head that once
   was crowned with thorns is crowned with glory now . . .' Look at Him! Can your imagination
   picture Him? Behold His transcendent glory!"
   (vol. 2, no. 101, p. 383).

# 337 C.M.
*The glory of Christ in heaven.*

1 O THE delights, the heavenly joys,
   The glories of the place,
Where Jesus sheds the brightest beams
   Of His o'erflowing grace!

2 Sweet majesty and awful love
   Sit smiling on His brow,
And all the glorious ranks above
   At humble distance bow.

3 Those soft, those blessèd feet of His
   That once rude iron tore,
High on a throne of light they stand,
   And all the saints adore.

4 His head, the dear majestic head
   That cruel thorns did wound,
See what immortal glories shine,
   And circle it around.

5 This is the Man, th' exalted Man,
   Whom we unseen adore,
But when our eyes behold His face,
   Our hearts shall love Him more.

*Isaac Watts*, [1707, *rev.* 1709]

# 338 7.7.7.7.
*Our victorious Lord.*

1 CROWNS of glory ever bright
   Rest upon the *Conqu'ror's* head;
Crowns of glory are His right,
   His, "Who liveth and was dead."

2 He subdued the pow'rs of hell;
   In the fight He stood alone;
All His foes before Him fell,
   By His single arm o'erthrown.

3 His the *battle, His the* toil,
   His the honours of the day,
His the glory and the spoil;
   Jesus bears them all away!

4 Now proclaim His deed afar;
   Fill the world with His renown;
His alone the victor's car,
   His the everlasting crown.

*Thomas Kelly*, 1806 [*rev.* 1809]
[*alt. Sabbath Hymn Book*, 1858]

   **1.2:** *victor's* **3.1:** *fight, the arduous*

# 339 8.7.8.7.4.7.
*"In thy majesty ride properously."*

1 LET us sing the King Messiah,
   King of righteousness and peace;
Hail Him, all His happy subjects;
   Never let His praises cease;
      Ever hail Him,
   Never let His praises cease.

2 How transcendent are Thy glories,
    Fairer than the sons of men!
While Thy blessèd mediation
    Brings us back to God again.
      Blest Redeemer,
    How we triumph in Thy reign!

3 Gird Thy sword on, mighty Hero!
    Make the Word of truth Thy car!
Prosper in Thy course majestic!
    All success attend Thy war!
      Gracious Victor,
    Let mankind before Thee bow!

4 Majesty, combin'd with meekness,
    Righteousness and peace unite,
To insure Thy blessèd conquests;
    On, great Prince, assert Thy right!
      Ride triumphant,
    All around the conquer'd globe!

5 Blest are all that touch Thy sceptre;
    Blest are all that own Thy reign;
Freed from sin, that worst of tyrants,
    Rescued from its galling chain.
      Saints and angels,
    All who know Thee, bless Thy reign.

*John Ryland*, [1798, *rev.* 1828]

> **Ed:** Dated 31 July 1790 in Ryland's manuscripts, but not known to be published until 1798.

# 340   C.M.
*At the right hand of God.*

1 HE who on earth as man was known
    And bore our sins and pains,
Now seated on th' eternal throne,
    The God of glory reigns.

2 His hands the wheels of nature guide
    With an unerring skill,
And countless worlds, extended wide,
    Obey His sov'reign will.

3 While harps unnumber'd sound His praise
    In yonder world above,
His saints on earth admire His ways
    And glory in His love.

4 When troubles, like a burning sun,
    Beat heavy on their head,
To this almighty Rock they run
    And find a pleasing shade.

5 How glorious He! how happy they
    In such a glorious Friend!
Whose love secures them all the way
    And crowns them at the end.

*John Newton*, 1779

> **MM:** Hymns, Set 1 (Jan./Nov.), 30th & 31st Morn,
> LA MIRA / BYEFIELD / BALERMA /STEPHENS

# SECOND ADVENT: REIGN AND JUDGMENT.

# 341   8.7.8.7.
*He cometh.*

1 HARK! the cry, "Behold He cometh."
    Hark! the cry, "The Bridegroom's near."
These are accents falling sweetly
    On the ransomed sinner's ear.

2 Man may disbelieve the tidings,
    Or in anger turn away;
'Tis foretold there shall be scoffers
    Rising in the latter day;

3 But He'll come, the Lord from heaven,
    Not to suffer or to die,
But to take His waiting people
    To their glorious rest on high.

4 Happy they who stand expecting
    Christ, the Saviour, to appear;
Sad for those who do not love Him—
    Those who do not wish Him here.

5 But in mercy still He lingers,
    Lengthening out the day of grace,
Till He comes, inviting sinners
    To His welcome, fond embrace.

*Albert Midlane*, [1865]

# 342
8.7.8.7.4.7.
*The coming glory.*

1 'MID the splendours of the glory
 Which we hope ere long to share,
Christ our Head, and we His members,
 Shall appear, divinely fair.
  O how glorious!
 When we meet Him in the air!

2 From the dateless, timeless periods,
 He has loved us without cause,
And for all His blood-bought myriads,
 His is love that knows no pause.
  Matchless Lover!
 Changeless as the eternal laws!

3 Oh what gifts shall yet be granted,
 Palms, and crowns, and robes of white,
When the hope for which we panted
 Bursts upon our gladden'd sight,
  And our Saviour
 Makes us glorious through His might.

4 Bright the prospect soon that greets us
 Of that long'd-for nuptial day,
When our heavenly Bridegroom meets us
 On His kingly, conquering way;
  In the glory,
 Bride and Bridegroom reign for aye!

*William Reid*, 1863

# 343
C.M.
*The kingdom of Christ among men.*

1 LO! what a glorious sight appears
 To our believing eyes!
The earth and seas are pass'd away,
 And the old rolling skies.

2 From the third heaven where God resides,
 That holy, happy place,
The New Jerusalem comes down,
 Adorn'd with shining grace.

3 Attending angels shout for joy,
 And the bright armies sing,
"Mortals, behold the sacred seat
 Of your descending King.

4 "The God of glory down to men
 Removes His blest abode,
Men the dear objects of His grace,
 And He their loving God.

5 "His own soft hand shall wipe the tears
 From every weeping eye,
And pains, and groans, and griefs, and fears,
 And death itself shall die."

6 How long, dear Saviour! Oh how long
 Shall this bright hour delay?
Fly swifter round, ye wheels of time,
 And bring the welcome day.

*Isaac Watts*, [1707, *rev.* 1709]

# 344
8.7.8.7. Double
*Glory for the chosen.*

1 LORD, in love Thou didst receive us,
 Ere creation, as "thine own,"
And that love will never leave us,
 But will raise us to Thy throne.
Thou wilt come, and we shall meet Thee,
 Then the saints whom Thou wilt raise
Will, with those remaining, greet Thee,
 Joining in one song of praise.

2 Then shall we, Thine image bearing,
 Know thee, Lord, as we are known;
With our blood-wash'd robes, declaring
 What for us Thy death hath done.
Thus we all, our joy expressing,
 Shall forever praise Thy name;
"Glory, power, dominion, blessing,
 Be to God and to the Lamb."

*James Kelly*, 1849

# 345
S.M.
*"Come quickly."*

1 COME, Lord, and tarry not;
 Bring the long-look'd-for day;
Oh why these years of waiting here,
 These ages of delay?

2 Come, for Thy saints still wait;
 Daily ascends their sigh;

The Spirit and the bride say, come;
  Dost Thou not hear the cry?

3 Come, for creation groans
  Impatient of Thy stay,
Worn out with these long years of ill,
  These ages of delay.

4 Come, for the corn is ripe;
  Put in Thy sickle now;
Reap the great harvest of the earth,
  Sower and reaper Thou!

5 Come, in Thy glorious might,
  Come with the iron rod,
Scattering Thy foes before Thy face,
  Most mighty Son of God.

6 Come, and make all things new;
  Build up this ruin'd earth;
Restore our faded Paradise,
  Creation's second birth.

7 Come, and begin Thy reign
  Of everlasting peace;
Come, take the kingdom to Thyself,
  Great King of righteousness.

*Horatious Bonar*, 1857

**EE:** Hymns, Set 2 (Feb./Dec.), 22nd Eve,
ARRAN / SHIRLAND

# 346   7.7.7.7.
*Signs of the Second Advent.*

1 WHEN the gospel race is run,
When the Gentile day is done,
Signs and wonders there shall be
In the heaven, and earth, and sea.

2 Jesus, in that awful hour,
Every soul shall own Thy power,
Every eye the cloud shall scan,
Signal of the Son of man.

3 Lo! mid terror and mid tears,
Jesus in the cloud appears,
While the trump's tremendous blast
Peals, the loudest and the last.

4 East, and west, and south, and north,
Speeds each glorious angel forth,
Gathering in with glittering wing
Zion's saints to Zion's King.

5 Man nor angel knows that day,
Heaven and earth shall pass away;
Still shall stand the Saviour's Word,
Deathless as its deathless Lord.

*William Dickinson*, 1846

# 347   C.M.
*"Thy kingdom come."*

1 ISLES of the deep, rejoice! rejoice!
  Ye ransom'd nations, sing
The praises of your Lord and God,
  The triumphs of your King.

2 He comes—and at His mighty word,
  The clouds are fleeting *past*,
And o'er the land of promise, see,
  The glory breaks at last.

3 There He, upon His ancient throne
  His pow'r and grace displays,
While Salem, with its echoing hills,
  Sends forth the voice of praise.

4 Oh let His praises fill the earth
  While all the blest above,
In strains of loftier triumph still,
  Speak only of His love.

5 Sing, ye redeem'd! Before the throne,
  Ye white-robed myriads fall;
Sing—for the Lord of glory reigns,
  The Christ—the heir of all.

*Edward Denny*, 1848 [*alt. C.H.S.*]

**2.2:** *fast*

# 348   8.7.8.7.7.7.
*Welcome, Son of God.*

1 WELCOME sight! the Lord descending;
  Jesus in the clouds appears;
Lo! the Saviour comes, intending
  Now to dry His people's tears.

Lo! the Saviour comes to reign;
Welcome to His waiting train.

2 Long they mourn'd their absent Master;
    Long they felt like men forlorn;
Bid the seasons fly still faster,
    While they sigh'd for His return;
Lo! the period comes at last;
All their sorrows now are past.

3 Now from home no longer banish'd,
    They are going to their rest;
Tho' the heav'ns and earth *are* vanish'd,
    With their Lord they shall be blest;
Blest with Him His saints shall be,
Blest through all eternity!

4 Happy people! grace unbounded,
    Grace alone exalts you thus;
Be ashamed, and be confounded,
    Sing forever—"Not to us,
Not to us be glory giv'n,
Glory to the God of heav'n!"

*Thomas Kelly*, 1809 [*alt.*]

> **3.3:** *have*  **Ed:** This minor variant appears as
> early as 1830 in James H. Stewart's *Selection.*

# 349   8.7.8.7.4.7.
*"Behold, He cometh."*

1 LIFT your heads, ye friends of Jesus,
    Partners *of His sufferings* here;
Christ to all believers precious,
    Lord of lords shall soon appear;
    Mark the tokens
    Of His heavenly kingdom near!

2 Close behind the tribulation
    Of the last tremendous days,
See the flaming revelation,
    See the universal blaze!
    Earth and heaven
    Melt before the Judge's face!

3 Sun and moon are both confounded,
    Darken'd into endless night,
When with angel hosts surrounded,
    In His Father's glory bright

Beams the Saviour,
Shines the everlasting Light.

4 Lo! 'Tis He! our heart's desire,
    Come for His espous'd below,
Come to join us with His choir,
    Come to make our joys o'erflow;
    Palms of victory,
    Crowns of glory to bestow.

*Charles Wesley*, 1758
[*alt.* John Rippon's *Selection*, 1844]

> **1.2:** *in His patience*

# 350   L.M.
*"Come, Lord Jesus."*

1 WHEN shall Thy lovely face be seen?
When shall our eyes behold our God?
What lengths of distance lie between,
And hills of guilt, a heavy load!

2 Our months are ages of delay,
And slowly every minute wears;
Fly, wingèd time, and roll away
These tedious rounds of sluggish years.

3 Ye heavenly gates, loose all your chains;
Let the eternal pillars bow;
Blest Saviour, cleave the starry plains,
And make the crystal mountains flow.

4 Hark how Thy saints unite their cries,
And pray and wait the general doom;
Come, Thou the soul of all our joys,
Thou the Desire of Nations, come.

5 Put Thy bright robes of triumph on,
And bless our eyes, and bless our ears,
Thou absent Love, Thou dear unknown,
Thou fairest of ten thousand fairs.

*Isaac Watts*, 1706 [*rev.* 1737]

# 351   8.7.8.7.4.7.
*Reign of Christ.*

1 BRIGHT with all His crowns of glory,
    See the royal Victor's brow;

Once for sinners marr'd and gory—
　See the Lamb exalted now,
　　While before Him
　All His ransom'd brethren bow.

2 Blessèd morning! long expected,
　Lo! they fill the peopled air;
Mourners once by man rejected,
　They with Him, exalted there,
　　Sing His praises,
　And His throne of glory share.

3 Judah! Lo, thy royal Lion
　Reigns on earth, a conq'ring King;
Come, ye ransom'd tribes, to Zion,
　Love's abundant off'rings bring;
　　There behold Him,
　And His ceaseless praises sing.

4 King of kings! let earth adore Him,
　High on His exalted throne;
Fall, ye nations, fall before Him,
　And His righteous sceptre own;
　　All the glory
　Be to Him and Him alone!

*Edward Denny*, [1838]

　**Ed:** Credited to James Kelly in the 1866 ed. of
　*OOHB*; corrected in 1867.

# 352 C.M.
*The latter-day glory.*

1 BEHOLD! the mountain of the Lord
　In latter days shall rise
On mountain tops, above the hills,
　And draw the wond'ring eyes.

2 To this the joyful nations round,
　All tribes and tongues shall flow;
Up to the hill of God, they'll say,
　And to His house we'll go.

3 The beam that shines from Zion hill
　Shall lighten every land;
The King that reigns in Salem's tow'rs
　Shall all the world command.

4 Among the nations He shall judge;
　His judgments truth shall guide;

His sceptre shall protect the just
　And quell the sinner's pride.

5 No strife shall vex Messiah's reign
　Or mar those peaceful years;
To ploughshares men shall beat
　　their swords,
　To pruning hooks their spears.

6 No longer hosts encount'ring hosts
　Their millions slain deplore;
They hang the trumpet in the hall
　And study war no more.

7 Come then—O come from every land
　To worship at His shrine,
And, walking in the light of God,
　With holy beauties shine.

[*Church of Scotland*, 1745]
[*adapt.*] *Michael Bruce*, [ca. 1764]
[*alt. John Logan*, 1781]

　**Ed:** This hymn originally appeared with the first
　line "In latter days, the mount of God." The
　version given here is a cross between the ver-
　sions in Logan's *Poems* (1781) and the Church
　of Scotland's *Translations and Paraphras-
　es* (1781); John Logan had a hand in both
　editions. Some controversy surrounds Logan's
　use of Bruce's hymns. For a fuller discussion,
　see Julian's *Dictionary*, pp. 187-189, 564-565.

# 353 7.6.7.6. Double
*"His name shall endure forever."*

1 HAIL to the Lord's Anointed!
　Great David's greater Son;
Hail, in the time appointed,
　His reign on earth begun!
He comes to break oppression,
　To set the captive free,
To take away transgression,
　And rule in equity.

2 He shall come down, like showers
　Upon the fruitful earth;
*Love, joy, and hope,* like flowers,
　Spring in His path to birth:

Before Him, on the mountains,
    Shall peace, the herald, go;
And righteousness, in fountains,
    From hill to valley flow.

3 Arabia's desert ranger
    To Him shall bow the knee;
The Ethiopian stranger
    His glory come to see;
With offerings of devotion,
    Ships from the Isles shall meet,
To pour the wealth of ocean
    In tribute at His feet.

4 Kings shall fall down before Him,
    And gold and incense bring;
All nations shall adore Him,
    His praise all people sing;
For He shall have dominion
    O'er river, sea, and shore,
Far as the eagle's pinion,
    Or dove's light wing can soar.

5 For Him shall prayer unceasing
    And daily vows ascend;
His kingdom still increasing,
    A kingdom without end;
The mountain dews shall nourish
    A seed in weakness sown,
Whose fruit shall spread and flourish,
    And shake like Lebanon.

6 O'er every foe victorious,
    He on His throne shall rest;
From age to age more glorious,
    All blessing and all blest.
The tide of time shall never
    His covenant remove;
His name shall stand forever,
    That name to us is—Love.

*James Montgomery*, 1822 [*alt.*]

> **2.3:** *And love, joy, hope*  **Ed:** This simple
> alteration seems to have originated from
> J.C. Franks' *Christian Psalmody* (1834).

## 354

7.7.7.7. Double
*Hasten, Lord.*

1 SEE the ransomed millions stand,
    Palms of conquest in their hand;
This before the throne their strain,
    Hell is vanquished, death is slain;
Blessing, honour, glory, might
    Are the Conqueror's native right;
Thrones and powers before Him fall,
    Lamb of God, and Lord of all.

2 Hasten, Lord, the promised hour!
    Come in glory and in power!
Still Thy foes are unsubdued;
    Nature sighs to be renewed.
Time has nearly reached its sum.
    All things with Thy bride say, "Come!"
Jesus, whom all worlds adore,
    Come and reign forever more!

*Josiah Conder*, 1836

## 355

7.7.7.7. Double
*Universal reign of Christ.*

1 HARK! the song of Jubilee,
    Loud as mighty thunders roar,
Or the fullness of the sea,
    When it breaks upon the shore;
Hallelujah! for the Lord
    God omnipotent shall reign;
Hallelujah! let the word
    Echo round the earth and main.

2 Hallelujah!—hark! the sound,
    From the centre to the skies,
Wakes above, beneath, around,
    All creation's harmonies:
See Jehovah's banner furl'd,
    Sheathed His sword! He speaks—'tis done,
And the kingdoms of this world
    Are the kingdoms of His Son.

3 He shall reign from pole to pole,
    With illimitable sway;
He shall reign, when like a scroll,
    Yonder heavens have pass'd away;

Then the end—beneath His rod,
Man's last enemy shall fall;
Hallelujah! Christ in God,
God in Christ, is all in all.

*James Montgomery,* [1818, *rev.* 1825]

> **Ed:** Line 2.2, originally "From the depths unto
> the skies," was changed in 1825 to the form
> above, then back to the original in 1853; the
> 1825 form was retained in many collections,
> including *OOHB.*

## 356 C.M.
*"O Lord, how long?"*

1 TO Calv'ry, Lord, in spirit now,
    Our weary souls repair,
To dwell upon Thy dying love
    And taste its sweetness there.

2 Sweet resting-place of every heart
    That feels the plague of sin,
Yet knows that deep mysterious joy,
    The peace with God within.

3 There, through Thine hour of deepest woe,
    Thy suffering spirit pass'd;
Grace there its wondrous victory gain'd,
    And love endured its last.

4 Dear suffering Lamb! Thy bleeding wounds,
    With cords of love divine,
Have drawn our willing hearts to Thee
    And link'd our life with Thine.

5 Thy sympathies and hopes are ours;
    Dear Lord! we wait to see
Creation, all—below, above,
    Redeem'd and blest by Thee.

6 Our longing eyes would fain behold
    That bright and blessed brow,
Once wrung with bitterest anguish, wear
    Its crown of glory now.

7 Why linger then? Come, Saviour, come,
    Responsive to our call;
Come, claim Thine ancient power,

and reign
    The Heir and Lord of all.

*Edward Denny,* 1839

> **EE:** Hymns, Set 2 (Feb./Dec.), 9th Eve,
> MARTYRDOM / SMYRNA

## 357 C.M.
*Triumphs of the Saviour.*

1 GO forth, ye saints, behold your *King,*
    With radiant glory crown'd;
The wondrous progress of His Word
    Shall spread His fame around.

2 Where'er the sun begins its race
    Or stops its swift career,
Both east and west shall own His grace,
    And Christ be honoured there.

3 Ten thousand crowns encircling show
    The victories He has won;
Oh may His conquests ever grow
    While time its course shall run.

4 Ride forth, Thou mighty Conqueror, ride,
    And millions more subdue;
Destroy our *enmity* and pride,
    And we will crown Thee too.

*Benjamin Beddome,* [1800, *rev.* 1817]

> **1.1:** *Lord,*  **4.3:** *unbelief*  **Ed:** The text above
> is Beddome's 1817 version, except the two
> words in italics, which were retained from
> Rippon's *Selection* (1800), apparently pre-
> ferred by Spurgeon over Beddome's revision.

## 358 8.7.8.7. Double
*The Lord shall reign forever.*

1 ZION'S King shall reign victorious;
    All the earth shall own His sway;
He will make His kingdom glorious;
    He will reign through endless day.
What though none on earth assist Him?
    God requires not help from man.
What though all the world resist Him?
    God will realize His plan.

2 Nations now from God estrangèd,
　　Then shall see a glorious light;
Night to day shall then be changèd;
　　Heaven shall triumph in the sight:
See the ancient idols falling!
　　Worshipp'd once, but now abhorr'd;
Men on Zion's King are calling,
　　Zion's King by all ador'd.

3 Then shall Israel long-dispersèd,
　　Mourning seek the Lord their God,
Look on Him whom once they piercèd,
　　Own and kiss the chast'ning rod:
Then all Israel shall be savèd,
　　War and tumult then shall cease,
While the greater Son of David
　　Rules a conquer'd world in peace.

*Thomas Kelly*, 1806

# 359 C.M.
*The Jews restored.*

1 WAKE, harp of Zion, wake again,
　　Upon thine ancient hill,
On Jordan's long deserted plain,
　　By Kedron's lowly rill.

2 The hymn shall yet in Zion swell
　　That sounds Messiah's praise,
And Thy loved name, Immanuel!
　　As once in ancient days.

3 For Israel yet shall own her King,
　　For her salvation waits,
And hill and dale shall sweetly sing
　　With praise in all her gates.

4 Hasten, O Lord, these promised days,
　　When Israel shall rejoice;
And Jew and Gentile join in praise,
　　With one united voice.

*James Edmeston*, [1866]

> **Ed:** Dated 1846 by Sedgwick, apparently from
> Edmeston's manuscripts; first published in
> *Our Own Hymn-Book*. It did not appear, as
> Julian's *Dictionary of Hymnology* claimed (p.
> 322), in Edmeston's *Sacred Poetry* (1848).

# 360 C.M.
*The coming One.*

1 BEHOLD He comes! the glorious King
　　Whom once a cross upbore;
Let saints redeem'd His praises sing,
　　And angel hosts adore.

2 The reed, the purple, and the thorn
　　Are lost in triumph now;
His person, robes of light adorn,
　　And crowns of gold His brow.

3 Dear Lord, no more despised, disowned,
　　A victim bound and slain—
But in the power of God enthroned,
　　Thou dost return to reign.

4 To Thee—the world its treasure brings;
　　To Thee—its mighty bow;
To Thee—the church exulting springs,
　　Her Sovereign—Saviour Thou!

5 Beneath Thy touch, beneath Thy smile,
　　New heavens and earth appear;
No sin their beauty to defile,
　　Nor dim them with a tear.

6 Thrice happy hour! and those thrice-blest
　　That gather round Thy throne!
They share the honours of Thy rest,
　　Who have Thy conflict known.

*Joseph Tritton*, 1856

# 361 8.7.8.7.4.7.
*Judgment.*

1 LO! He comes with clouds descending,
　　Once for favour'd sinners slain!
Thousand thousand saints attending,
　　Swell the triumph of His train:
　　　　Hallelujah,
God appears on earth to reign!

2 Every eye shall now behold Him,
　　Rob'd in dreadful majesty;
Those who set at nought and sold Him,
　　Pierc'd, and nail'd Him to the tree,
　　　　Deeply wailing,
Shall the true Messiah see.

3 Ev'ry island, sea, and mountain,
 Heav'n and earth shall flee away!
All who hate Him must, *confounded*,
 Hear the trump proclaim *the* day:
  Come to judgment!
 *Come to judgment! come away!*

4 Now redemption long-expected,
 See, in solemn pomp appear;
All His *saints, by man rejected*,
 Now shall meet Him in the air.
  Hallelujah!
 *See the day of God appear!*

5 Answer Thine own bride and Spirit;
 Hasten, Lord, the gen'ral doom!
The new heav'n and earth t' inherit,
 Take Thy pining exiles home:
  All creation
 Travails, groans, and bids Thee come!

6 Yea, amen! let all adore Thee,
 High on Thine eternal throne;
Saviour, take the power and glory,
 Claim the kingdom for Thine own:
  *Oh come quickly!*
 Everlasting God, come down.

1-2,6 *Charles Wesley*, 1758 [*alt. M.M.*]
3-4 *John Cennick*, 1752 [*alt. M.M.*]
5 *Martin Madan*, 1760

 **3.3:** *ashamèd* **3.4:** *His*
 **3.6:** *Stand before the Son of Man!*
 **4.3:** *people, once despisèd,*
 **4.6:** *Now the promis'd Kingdom's come!*
 **6.5:** *Jah, Jehovah,*
 **Ed:** Cennick's hymn begins, "Lo! he cometh,
 countless trumpets," as in No. 363.
 **MM:** "Christian! if thou art in a night of trial,
 think of the morrow; cheer up thy heart with
 the thought of the coming day of thy Lord.
 Be patient, for 'Lo! He comes with clouds
 descending'" (May 13).

# 362
8.7.8.7.4.7.
*That great day.*

1 DAY of judgment, day of wonders!
 Hark! the trumpet's awful sound,

Louder than a thousand thunders,
 Shakes the vast creation round!
  How the summons
 Will the sinner's heart confound!

2 See the Judge our nature wearing,
 Clothed in majesty divine!
Ye who long for His appearing,
 Then shall say, "This God is mine!"
  Gracious Saviour,
 Own me in that day for Thine!

3 At His call the dead awaken,
 Rise to life from earth and sea;
All the pow'rs of nature shaken
 By His look prepares to flee:
  Careless sinner,
 What will then become of thee!

4 Horrors, past imagination,
 Will surprise your trembling heart,
When you hear your condemnation,
 "Hence, accursed wretch, depart!
  Thou with Satan
 And his angels, have thy part!"

5 But to those who have confessèd,
 Lov'd and serv'd the Lord below;
He will say, "Come near, ye blessed,
 See the kingdom I bestow:
  You forever
 Shall My love and glory know."

6 Under sorrows and reproaches,
 May this thought our courage raise!
Swiftly God's great day approaches;
 Sighs shall then be chang'd to praise;
  We shall triumph
 When the world is in a blaze.

*John Newton*, 1779

# 363
8.7.8.7.4.7.
*Lo, He cometh!*

1 LO! He cometh; countless trumpets
 Blow *to raise the sleeping dead;*
'Midst ten thousand saints and angels,
 See the *great exalted Head.*

Hallelujah!
Welcome, welcome, *Son of God.*

2 Now His merits, by the harpers,
    Through the eternal deep resounds!
Now resplendent shine His nail prints;
    Every eye shall see His wounds!
        They who pierc'd Him
    Shall at His appearance wail.

3 Full of joyful expectation,
    *Saints*, behold the Judge appear;
Truth and justice go before Him,
    Now the joyful sentence hear.
        Hallelujah,
Welcome, welcome, Judge divine.

4 "Come, ye blessèd of my Father,
    Enter into life and joy;
Banish all your fears and sorrows;
    Endless praise be your employ."
        Hallelujah,
    Welcome, welcome to the skies.

5 Now at once they rise to glory;
    Jesus brings them to the King;
There, with all the hosts of heaven,
    They eternal anthems sing:
        Hallelujah,
    Boundless glory to the Lamb.

1-2 John Cennick, 1752 [*alt.*]
3-5 Caleb Evans' *Collection*, 1769 [*alt.*]

**1.2:** *before His bloody sign!* **1.4:** *crucified shine,*
**1.6:** *bleeding Lamb!* **3.2:** *All*
**Ed:** The alteratons at 1.2-6 are from Caleb Evans'
*Collection*; the additional change to Evans is
from John Rippon's *Selection* (1787). Another
portion of Cennick's hymn is in No. 361.

# 364 L.M.
*The Lord shall come.*

1 THE Lord *shall* come! the earth shall quake,
*The mountains to their centre shake,*
And withering from the vault of night,
The stars *shall pale* their feeble light.

2 The Lord *shall* come! but not the same
As once in *lowliness* He came;

A silent lamb *before His foes,*
*A weary man, and full of woes.*

3 The Lord *shall* come! a dreadful form,
With *rainbow wreath* and robes of storm;
On cherub wings and wings of wind,
Appointed Judge of *all mankind.*

4 Can this be He who wont to stray
A pilgrim on the world's highway,
*Oppress'd by power* and mock'd by pride,
*The Nazarene*—the Crucified?

5 *While sinners in despair shall call,*
*"Rocks, hide us; mountains, on us fall!"*
*The saints, ascending from* the tomb,
Shall *joyful sing*, "The Lord is come!"

*Reginald Heber*, 1811 [*rev. 1827*]
*alt. Thomas Cotterill*, 1815 [*rev. 1819*]

**1.1:** *will* (1827)
**1.2:** *The hills their fixèd seat forsake;* (1811/1827)
**1.4:** *withdraw* (1827)  **2.1:** *will* (1827)
**2.2:** *lowly guise* (1811/1815); *lowly form* (1827)
**2.3:** *to slaughter led,* (1827)
**2.4:** *The bruis'd, the suffering, and the dead.* (1827)
**3.1:** *will* (1827)  **3.2:** *wreath of flame* (1827)
**3.4:** *human kind.* (1811/1827)
**4.3:** *By power oppress'd … pride?* (1827)
**4.4:** *Oh God! is this* (1811/1827)
**5.1-3:** *Go, tyrants! to the rocks complain!*
    *Go, seek the mountain's cleft in vain!*
    *But faith,* (1811/1827)
**5.3:** *victorious o'er* (1827)
**5.4:** *shouting sing* (1811); *sing for joy* (1827)
**NPSP:** In Spurgeon's return to the pulpit after
    the Surrey Gardens catastrophe (19 Oct.
    1856), he preached, "Let us consider, for a
    moment, that depth of degradation to which
    Christ descended, and then, my beloved, it will
    give you joy to think, that for that very reason
    His manhood was highly exalted. Do you see
    that man— 'The humble man before His foes,
    the weary man and full of woes?'" (vol. 2, no.
    101, p. 381).

# 365 S.M.
*An admonition.*

1 HOW will my heart endure
    The terrors of that day,

When earth and heav'n, before His face,
Astonish'd shrink away?

2   But ere that trumpet shakes
The mansions of the dead;
Hark, from the gospel's gentle voice,
What joyful tidings spread!

3   Ye sinners, seek His grace,
Whose wrath ye cannot bear;
Fly to the shelter of His cross
And find salvation there.

4   So shall that curse remove,
By which the Saviour bled,
And the last awful day shall pour
His blessings on your head.

*Philip Doddridge*, 1755

> **Ed:** Taken from the longer hymn,
> "And will the judge descend?"

# 366   8.8.6.8.8.6.
*A prayer.*

1   *WHEN Thou*, my righteous Judge,
        *shalt* come
To fetch *Thy* ransom'd people home,
        Shall I among them stand?
Shall such a worthless worm as I,
*Who sometimes am afriad* to die,
        Be found at Thy right hand?

2   I love to meet among them now,
Before *Thy gracious* feet to bow,
        Though *vilest of* them all;
But *can I* bear the piercing thought?
What if my name should be left out,
        When Thou for them shalt call!

3   *Prevent*, prevent it by Thy grace;
*Be Thou, dear Lord, my hiding place*
        In this *the accepted* day;
Thy pard'ning voice, oh! let me hear
To still my unbelieving fear,
        Nor let me *fall, I pray*.

4   *Let me among Thy saints* be found,
Whene'er th' archangel's trump
        shall sound,

To see Thy smiling face;
Then loudest of the crowd I'll sing,
*While* heav'n's resounding mansions ring
*With shouts of sovereign* grace.

[*The Collection of Hymns Sung in the
Countess of Huntingdon's Chapels*,] ca. 1774
[*alt. John Rippon*, 1787]

> **1.1:** *Oh! when / shall*   **1.2:** *His*
> **1.5:** *So sinful and unfit*   **2.2:** *Jehovah's*
> **2.3:** *viler than*   **2.4:** *who can*   **3.1:** *Dear Lord*
> **3.2:** *Oh! let me see Thy smiling face*
> **3.3:** *my gracious*   **3.6:** *fall away!*
> **4.1:** *Among Thy saints, let me*   **4.5:** *Till*
> **4.6:** *The riches of Thy*
> **Ed:** In Sedgwick's various collections, he had
> attributed this hymn at first to the Countess
> of Huntingdon, then to Charles Wesley. John
> Julian's assessment was blunt: "It is clear that
> these guesses of Sedgwick are worthless." —
> *Dictionary of Hymnology*, p. 854.

# NAMES AND TITLES
# OF THE LORD JESUS.

# 367   L.M.
*Advocate.*

1   LOOK up, my soul, with cheerful eye,
See where the great Redeemer stands;
The glorious Advocate on high,
With precious incense in His hands.

2   He sweetens every humble groan;
He recommends each broken prayer;
Recline Thy hope on Him alone,
Whose power and love forbid despair.

3   Teach my weak heart, O gracious Lord,
With stronger faith to call Thee mine;
Bid me pronounce the blissful word,
My Father God, with joy divine.

*Anne Steele*, [1780]

> **Ed:** Taken from the longer hymn,
> "Where is my God? Does He retire."
> **EE:** Hymns, Set 2 (Feb./Dec.), 14th Eve,
> WAREHAM / BARNSTAPLE

# 368
8.7.8.7. Double
*All in all.*

1 JESUS is our God and Saviour,
    Guide, and Counsellor, and Friend,
Bearing all our misbehaviour,
    Kind and loving to the end.
Trust Him; He will not deceive us,
    Though we hardly of Him deem;
He will never, never leave us,
    Nor will let us quite leave Him.

2 Nothing but Thy blood, O Jesus,
    Can relieve us from our smart;
Nothing else from guilt release us;
    Nothing else can melt the heart.
Law and terrors do but harden,
    All the while they work alone,
But a sense of blood-bought pardon
    Soon dissolves a heart of stone.

3 Jesus, all our consolations
    Flow from Thee, the sov'reign good.
Love, and faith, and hope, and patience
    All are purchas'd by Thy blood.
From Thy fullness we receive them;
    We have nothing of our own;
Freely Thou delight'st to give them
    To the needy, who have none.

*Joseph Hart,* 1759

# 369
C.M.
*Ambassador.*

1 JESUS, commission'd from above,
    Descends to men below
And shows from whence the springs of *love*
    In endless currents flow.

2 He, whom the boundless heav'n adores,
    Whom angels long to see,
Quitted with joy those blissful shores,
    Ambassador to me!

3 To me, a worm, a sinful clod,
    A rebel all forlorn,
A foe, a traitor to my God,
    And of a traitor born.

4 To me, who never sought His grace,
    Who mock'd His *sacred* word,
Who never knew or loved His face,
    But all His will abhorr'd.

5 To me, who could not even praise
    When His kind heart I knew,
But sought a thousand devious ways
    Rather than find the true;

6 Yet this redeeming Angel came
    So vile a worm to bless;
He took with gladness all my blame
    And gave His righteousness.

7 O that my languid heart might glow
    With ardour all divine,
And for more love than seraphs know,
    Like burning seraphs shine.

*Ambrose Serle,* [1776, *rev.* 1784]
[*alt.* John Rippon, 1787]

    **1.3:** *grace*   **4.2:** *holy*

# 370
S.M.
*Angel.*

1 THOU very Paschal Lamb,
    *Who didst for Israel bleed;*
Through whom we out of Egypt came,
    Thy ransom'd people lead.

2 Angel of gospel-grace,
    Fulfill Thy character,
To guard and feed the chosen race,
    In Israel's camp appear.

3 Throughout the desert way
    Conduct us by Thy light,
Be Thou a cooling cloud by day,
    A cheering fire by night.

4 Our fainting souls sustain
    With blessings from above,
And ever on Thy people rain
    The manna of Thy love.

*Charles Wesley,* 1745, *alt. C.H.S.*

    **1.2:** *Whose blood for us was shed,*

## 371 L.M.
*Bridegroom.*

1 JESUS, the heav'nly lover, gave
His life my wretched soul to save;
Resolv'd to make His mercy known,
He kindly claims me for His own.

2 Rebellious, I against Him strove,
Till melted and constrain'd by love;
With sin and self I freely part;
The heav'nly Bridegroom wins my heart.

3 My guilt, my wretchedness, He knows,
Yet takes and owns me for His spouse;
My debts He pays, and sets me free,
And makes His riches o'er to me.

4 My filthy rags are laid aside;
He clothes me as becomes His bride;
Himself bestows my wedding dress,
The robe of perfect righteousness.

5 Lost in astonishment I see,
Jesus, Thy boundless love to me;
With angels I Thy grace adore,
And long to love and praise Thee more.

6 Since Thou wilt take me for Thy bride,
O keep me, Saviour, near Thy side;
I fain would give Thee all my heart,
Nor ever from my Lord depart.

*John Fawcett*, 1782

## 372 6.6.6.6.4.4.4.4.
*Captain and conqueror.*

1 MY dear Almighty Lord,
My Conqueror and my King,
Thy sceptre and Thy sword,
Thy reigning grace I sing;
Thine is the power;
Behold, I sit
In willing bonds,
*Beneath* Thy feet.

2 Now let my soul arise
And tread the tempter down;
My captain leads me forth
To conquest and a crown;

A feeble saint
Shall win the day,
Tho' death and hell
Obstruct the way.

3 Should all the hosts of death
and powers of hell unknown
Put their most dreadful forms
Of rage and mischief on,
I shall be safe,
For Christ displays
Superior power
And guardian grace.

*Isaac Watts*, 1709 [*alt.*]

**1.8:** *Before* **Ed:** Taken from the longer hymn,
"Join all the glorious names." See also No. 383.
This alteration appeared in editions of Watts
after his death, starting with the 17th ed. (1751).

## 373 S.M.
*Christ of God.*

1 JESUS, the Lamb of God,
Who us from hell to raise
Hast shed Thy reconciling blood;
We give Thee endless praise.

2 God, and yet man, Thou art,
True God, true man, art Thou;
Of man, and of man's earth a part,
One with us Thou art now.

3 Great sacrifice for sin,
Giver of life for life,
Restorer of the peace within,
True ender of the strife:

4 To Thee, the Christ of God,
Thy saints exulting sing,
The bearer of our heavy load,
Our own anointed King.

5 True lover of the lost,
From heaven Thou camest down
To pay for souls the righteous cost,
And claim them for Thine own.

6  Rest of the weary, Thou!
   To Thee, our rest, we come;
   In Thee to find our dwelling now,
   Our everlasting home.

*Horatius Bonar*, [1864]

> **Ed:** Taken from the longer hymn,
> "Jesus, the Christ of God."

**374** 8.7.8.7. Double
*Consolation of Israel.*

1  COME, Thou long-expected Jesus,
   Born to set Thy people free;
   From our fears and sins *release* us;
   Let us find our rest in Thee;
   Israel's strength and consolation,
   Hope of all the saints Thou art;
   Dear desire of every nation,
   Joy of every longing heart.

2  Born Thy people to deliver,
   Born a child, and yet a King;
   Born to reign in us forever,
   Now Thy gracious kingdom bring;
   By Thine own eternal Spirit
   Rule in all our hearts alone;
   By Thine all-sufficient merit,
   Raise us to Thy glorious throne.

*Charles Wesley*, [1745]
[*alt. Martin Madan*, 1760]

> **1.3:** *relieve* **Ed:** Madan's alteration was later ad-
> opted by the Wesleys in the 1777 ed. of *Hymns
> for the Nativity of Our Lord.*

**375** 10.10.11.11.
*Fountain.*

1  THE fountain of Christ, assist me to sing,
   The blood of our Priest, our crucifed King,
   Which perfectly cleanses from sin and
      from filth
   And richly dispenses salvation and health.

2  This fountain from guilt not only
      makes pure,
   And gives, soon as felt, infallible cure,

But if guilt removèd return and remain,
Its pow'r may be provèd again and again.

3  This fountain, though rich, from charge is
      quite clear;
   The poorer the wretch, the welcomer here;
   Come *needy and* guilty, come loathsome
      and bare;
   You can't come too filthy—come just as
      you are.

4  This fountain in vain has never been tried;
   It takes out all stain whenever applied;
   The water flows sweetly with virtue divine
   To cleanse souls completely, though
      leprous as mine.

*Joseph Hart*, 1759
[*alt. John Rippon*, 1787]

> **3.3:** *needy, come*  **MM:** "Though dishonest as
> the thief, though unchaste as the woman who
> was a sinner, though fierce as Saul of Tarsas,
> though cruel as Manasseh, though rebellious
> as the prodigal, the great heart of love will
> look upon the man who finds himself to have
> no soundness in him, and will pronounce him
> clean, when he trusts in Jesus crucified. Come
> to Him, then, poor heavy-laden sinner, 'Come
> needy, come guilty, come loathsome and bare;
> you can't come too filthy—come just as you
> are'" (Sept. 29).

**376** 8.7.8.7.7.7.
*Friend.*

1  ONE there is, above all others,
   Well deserves the name of Friend;
   His is love beyond a brother's,
   Costly, free, and knows no end;
      They who once His kindness prove
      Find it everlasting love!

2  Which of all our friends to save us,
   Could or would have shed their blood?
   But our Jesus died to have us
   Reconcil'd in Him to God;
      This was boundless love indeed!
      Jesus is a friend in need.

3 When He liv'd on earth abasèd,
   Friend of sinners was His name;
   Now above all glory raisèd,
   He rejoices in the same;
       Still He calls them brethren, friends,
       And to all their wants attends.

4 Oh! for grace our hearts to soften!
   Teach us, Lord, at length to love;
   We, alas! forget too often,
   What a friend we have above;
       But when home our souls are brought,
       We *shall* love Thee as we ought.

*John Newton*, 1779, *alt.*

> **4.6:** *will* **Ed:** A common alt. that seems to have
> started with John Dobell's *New Selection* (1806).

# 377 L.M.
*Friend.*

1 O THOU, my soul, forget no more
   The friend who all thy misery bore;
   Let every idol be forgot,
   But O my soul, forget Him not.

2 *Jesus* for thee a body takes,
   Thy guilt assumes, thy fetters breaks,
   Discharging all thy dreadful debt;
   And canst thou ere such love forget?

3 Renounce thy works and ways with grief
   And fly to this most sure relief,
   Nor Him forget who left His throne,
   And for thy life gave up His own.

4 Infinite truth and mercy shine
   In Him, and He Himself is thine;
   And canst thou then, with sin beset,
   Such charms, such matchless
       charms forget?

5 Ah! no—till life itself depart,
   His name shall cheer and warm my heart;
   And lisping this, from earth I'll rise,
   And join the chorus of the skies.

6 Ah! no—when all things else expire
   And perish in the general fire,

This name all others shall survive,
And through eternity shall live.

*Krishnu Pal*
*tr. Joshua Marshman*, 1801
*alt. John Rippon*, 1827

> **2.1:** *Brumhu*, Hindu term for 'The One God.'
> **Ed:** Marshman, a missionary to India, translated
> this from Pal, the first Hindu baptized in Ben-
> gal. It is reported as being written in 1801, but
> its publication history is unclear. It appears as
> early as 18 Nov. 1820 in *The Christian Herald*,
> p. 448, and was adopted into the 27th ed. of
> Rippon's *Selection* (1827).

# 378 C.M.
*Friend.*

1 A FRIEND there is—your voices join,
   Ye saints, to praise His name!
   Whose truth and kindness are divine,
   Whose love's a constant flame.

2 When most we need His helping hand,
   This friend is always near;
   With heav'n and earth at His command,
   He waits to answer prayer.

3 His love no end or measure knows;
   No change can turn its course;
   Immutably the same it flows
   From one eternal source.

4 When frowns appear to veil His face,
   And clouds surround His throne,
   He hides the purpose of His grace
   To make it better known.

5 And if our dearest comforts fall
   Before His sov'reign will,
   He never takes away our all—
   Himself He gives us still!

6 Our sorrows in the scale He weighs,
   And measures out our pains;
   The wildest storm His word obeys;
   His word its rage restrains.

*Joseph Swain*, 1792

# 379 L.M.
*Friend.*

1 POOR, weak, and worthless though I am,
I have a rich almighty Friend;
Jesus, the Saviour, is His name;
He freely loves, and without end.

2 He ransom'd me from hell with blood,
And by His pow'r my foes controll'd;
He found me wand'ring far from God
And brought me to His chosen fold.

3 He cheers my heart, my wants supplies,
And says that I shall shortly be
Enthron'd with Him above the skies;
Oh! what a Friend is Christ to me.

4 But ah! my inmost spirit mourns,
And well my eyes with tears may swim
To think of my perverse returns;
I've been a faithless friend to Him.

5 Sure, were not I most vile and base,
I could not thus my friend requite!
And were not He the God of grace,
He'd frown and spurn me from His sight.

*John Newton*, 1779

# 380 C.M.
*Head of the Church.*

1 JESUS, I sing Thy matchless grace
That calls a worm Thine own,
Gives me among Thy saints a place
To make Thy glories known.

2 Allied to Thee, our vital Head,
We act, and grow, and thrive;
From Thee divided, each is dead
When most he seems alive.

3 Thy saints on earth, and those above,
Here join in sweet accord;
One body all in mutual love,
And Thou our common Lord.

4 Oh may my faith each hour derive
Thy Spirit with delight;
While death and hell in vain shall strive
This bond to disunite.

5 Thou the whole body wilt present
Before Thy Father's face,
Nor shall a wrinkle or a spot
Its beauteous form disgrace.

*Philip Doddridge*, 1755

# 381 L.M.
*Hiding place.*

1 AWAKE, sweet harp of Judah, wake;
Retune thy strings for Jesus' sake;
We sing the Saviour of our race,
The Lamb, our shield and hiding place.

2 When God's right arm is bared for war,
And thunders clothe His cloudy car,
Where, where, oh where shall man retire
To escape the horror of His ire?

3 'Tis He, the Lamb, to Him we fly,
While the dread tempest passes by;
God sees His well-belovèd's face
And spares us in our hiding place.

4 While yet we sojourn here below,
Pollutions still our hearts o'erflow;
Fallen, abject, mean—a sentenced race,
We deeply need a hiding place.

5 Yet courage—days and years will glide,
And we shall lay these clods aside;
Shall be baptiz'd in Jordan's flood,
And wash'd in Jesus' cleansing blood.

6 Then pure, immortal, sinless, freed,
We through the Lamb shall be decreed,
Shall meet the Father face to face,
And need no more a hiding place.

*Henry Kirke White*, 1807

# 382 C.M.
*High Priest.*

1 NOW let our cheerful eyes survey
Our great High Priest above,
And celebrate His constant care
And sympathetic love.

2 Though rais'd to a superior throne,
   Where angels bow around,
And high o'er all the shining train,
   With matchless honours crown'd,

3 The names of all His saints He bears
    Deep graven on His heart,
Nor shall the meanest Christian say
   That he hath lost his part.

4 Those characters shall fair abide,
   Our everlasting trust,
When gems and monuments and crowns
   Are moulder'd down to dust.

5 So, gracious Saviour, on my breast,
   May Thy dear name be worn,
A sacred ornament and guard
   To endless ages borne.

*Philip Doddridge*, 1755

**MM:** Hymns, Set 2 (Feb./Dec.), 11th Morn,
PETERBORO / AZMON

# 383
6.6.6.6.4.4.4.4.
*High Priest and Surety.*

1 JESUS, my great High Priest,
Offer'd His blood and died;
My guilty conscience seeks
No sacrifice beside.
   His powerful blood
   Did once atone,
   And now it pleads
   Before the throne.

2 To this dear Surety's hand
Will I commit my cause;
He answers and fulfills
His Father's broken laws;
   Behold my soul
   At freedom set!
   My Surety paid
   The dreadful debt.

3 My advocate appears
For my defence on high;
The Father bows His ear
And lays His thunder by.

Not all that hell
Or sin can say
Shall turn His heart,
His love away.

4 Immense compassion reigns
In my Immanuel's heart;
*He condescends* to act
A mediator's part;
   He is my friend
   And brother too,
   Divinely kind,
   Divinely true.

*Isaac Watts*, 1709 [*alt. C.H.S.*]

**4.3:** *When He descends*
**Ed:** Stanzas 1-3 are taken from the longer hymn,
   "Join all the glorious names." See also No. 372.
   Stanza 4 is from "With cheerful voice I sing."

# 384
7.7.7.7.
*Immanuel.*

1 SWEETER sounds than music knows
Charm me in Immanuel's name;
All her hopes my spirit owes
To His birth, and cross, and shame.

2 When He came the angels sung
"Glory be to God on high";
Lord, unloose my stamm'ring tongue;
Who should louder sing than I?

3 Did the Lord a man become
That He might the law fulfill,
Bleed and suffer in my room,
And canst thou, my tongue, be still?

4 No, I must my praises bring,
Though they worthless are, and weak,
For should I refuse to sing,
Sure the very stones would speak.

5 O my Saviour, Shield, and Sun,
Shepherd, Brother, Husband, Friend,
Ev'ry precious name in one,
I will love Thee without end.

*John Newton*, 1779

# 385 C.M.
*Jesus.*

1 JESUS, I love Thy charming name;
   'Tis music to mine ear;
Fain would I sound it out so loud
   That earth and heav'n should hear.

2 Yes, Thou art precious to my soul,
   My transport and my trust;
Jewels to Thee are gaudy toys,
   And gold is sordid dust.

3 All my capacious pow'rs can wish
   In Thee doth richly meet;
Nor to mine eyes is light so dear,
   Nor friendship half so sweet.

4 Thy grace still dwells upon my heart
   And sheds its fragrance there;
The noblest balm of all its wounds,
   The cordial of its care.

5 I'll speak the honours of Thy name
   With my last lab'ring breath;
Then speechless, clasp Thee in my arms,
   The antidote of death.

*Philip Doddridge,* [1747, *rev.* 1755]

**Ed:** Dated 23 Oct. 1717 in his manuscripts, but
not known to have been published until 1747.
**MM:** "Jesus! . . . It is the music with which the
bells of heaven ring; a song in a word; an
ocean of comprehension, although a drop for
brevity; a matchless oratorio in two syllables;
a gathering up of the hallelujahs of eternity in
five letters" (Feb. 8).

# 386 C.M.
*Jesus.*

1 HOW sweet the name of Jesus sounds
   In a believer's ear!
It soothes his sorrows, heals his wounds,
   And drives away his fear.

2 It makes the wounded spirit whole
   And calms the troubled breast;
'Tis manna to the hungry soul,
   And to the weary, rest.

3 Dear name! the rock on which I build,
   My shield, and hiding-place,
My never-failing treas'ry, fill'd
   With boundless stores of grace.

4 By Thee my pray'rs acceptance gain,
   Although with sin defil'd;
Satan accuses me in vain,
   And I am own'd a child.

5 Jesus! my Shepherd, Husband, Friend,
   My Prophet, Priest, and King;
My Lord, my Life, my Way, my End,
   Accept the praise I bring.

6 Weak is the effort of my heart,
   And cold my warmest thought;
But when I see Thee as Thou art,
   I'll praise Thee as I ought.

7 Till then I would Thy love proclaim
   With ev'ry fleeting breath,
And may the music of Thy name
   Refresh my soul in death.

*John Newton,* 1779

**MM:** Hymns, Set 1 (Jan./Nov.), 10th Morn,
ORTONVILLE / WIRTH

# 387 C.M.
*Jesus.*

1 JESUS! O word divinely sweet!
   How charming is the sound!
What joyful news! what heavenly sense
   In that dear name is found!

2 Our *souls, all* guilty and condemn'd,
   In hopeless fetters lay;
Our souls, with numerous sins deprav'd,
   To death and hell a prey.

3 Jesus, to purge away *our* guilt,
   A willing victim fell,
And on His cross triumphant broke
   The bands of death and hell.

4 Our foes were mighty to destroy;
   He mightier was to save;

He died, but could not long be held
    A pris'ner in the grave.

5 Jesus! who mighty art to save,
    Still push Thy conquests on,
    Extend the triumphs on Thy cross,
    Where'er the sun has shone.

6 O Captain of Salvation! make
    Thy power and mercy known;
    Till crowds of willing converts *come*
    *And worship at* Thy throne.

*Joseph Stennett*, 1709
[*alt. Caleb Evans*, 1769]

> **2.1:** *souls were* **3.1:** *this* **6.3:** *may*
> **6.4:** *Worship before*

# 388 C.M.
*Jesus.*

1 JESUS—in Thy transporting name,
    What blissful glories rise!
    Jesus, the angel's sweetest theme!
    The wonder of the skies!

2 Didst Thou forsake Thy radiant crown
    And boundless realms of day,
    Aside Thy robes of glory thrown,
    To dwell with feeble clay?

3 Victorious love! can language tell
    The wonders of Thy pow'r,
    Which conquered all the force of hell
    In that tremendous hour?

4 Is there a heart that will not bend
    To Thy divine control?
    Descend, O sov'reign love, descend,
    And melt that stubborn soul.

*Anne Steele*, 1760 [*rev.* 1769]

# 389 7.6.7.6.
*Jesus.*

1 EXULT all hearts with gladness
    At sound of Jesu's name;
    What other hath such sweetness
    Or such delight can claim?

2 O Jesu, health of sinners,
    Be present to our prayer;
    The wonderer's Guide become Thou,
    And us Thy people spare.

3 Thy name, may it defend us,
    Our stay in peril prove;
    And perfect us in blessing,
    And every stain remove.

4 For Thee, O Christ, all glory
    In this blest Name doth shine;
    Thy honour be our worship,
    O Jesu, Lord, benign.

[*Breviarium Sarum*, 1495]
  *tr. John David Chambers*, 1857, *alt.*

> **Ed:** Chambers' original text is "Let every heart
> exulting beat," translated from the 15th cen-
> tury Latin "Exultet cor precordiis." The text
> above is a complete reworking in a different
> meter by an unknown editor. It appeared in
> *Our Own Hymn-Book* and in the undated
> *Hymns of the Year*, which was also printed
> around 1866.

# 390 C.M.
*King of Saints.*

1 COME, ye that love the Saviour's name,
    And joy to make it known;
    The Sovereign of your heart proclaim,
    And bow before His throne.

2 Behold your King, your Saviour crown'd
    With glories all divine,
    And tell the wondering nations round
    How bright those glories shine.

3 Infinite power and boundless grace
    In Him unite their rays:
    You, that have e'er beheld His face,
    Can you forbear His praise?

4 When in His earthly courts we view
    The glories of our King,
    We long to love as angels do,
    And wish like them to sing.

5 And shall we long and wish in vain?
    Lord, teach our songs to rise!
Thy love can animate the strain
    And bid it reach the skies.

6 O happy period! glorious day!
    When heaven and earth shall raise,
With all their powers the raptur'd lay
    To celebrate Thy praise.

*Anne Steele*, [1769]

# 391   8.7.8.7.
*Light.*

1 LIGHT of those whose dreary dwelling
    Borders on the shades of death,
Come, and by Thyself revealing,
    Dissipate the clouds beneath:

2 The new heaven and earth's Creator,
    In our deepest darkness rise,
Scattering all the night of nature,
    Pouring *day upon* our eyes.

3 Still we wait for Thy appearing;
    Life and joy Thy beams impart,
Chasing all our fears, and cheering
    Every poor benighted heart.

4 Come, *extend Thy wonted* favour
    *To our ruin'd, guilty* race;
Come, Thou *dear exalted* Saviour,
    Come, *apply Thy saving* grace.

5 Save us in Thy great compassion,
    O Thou mild pacific Prince;
Give the knowledge of salvation,
    Give the pardon of our sins.

6 By Thine all-*sufficient* merit,
    Every burden'd soul release;
*By the teachings of Thy* Spirit,
    Guide *us into* perfect peace.

*Charles Wesley*, [1745]
[alt. *New Selection of Hymns*, 1828]

> **2.4:** *eyesight on*   **4.1:** *and manifest the*
> **4.2:** *God hath for our ransom'd*   **4.3:** *universal*
> **4.4:** *and bring the gospel*   **6.1:** *restoring*
> **6.3:** *Every weary wand'ring*   **6.4:** *into thy*

# 392   7.7.7.7.
*Melchizedek.*

1 KING of Salem, bless my soul!
Make a wounded sinner whole!
King of righteousness and peace,
Let not Thy sweet visits cease!

2 Come! refresh this soul of mine
With Thy sacred bread and wine!
All Thy love to me unfold,
Half of which cannot be told.

3 Hail, Melchizedek divine!
*Great High Priest, Thou* shalt be mine;
All my powers before Thee fall;
Take not tithe, but take them all!

*W—* in John Rippon's *Selection*, 1787 [*alt.*]

> **3.2:** *Thou, Great High Priest,*  **Ed:** This simple transposition dates to the early 1800s. Starting in the 6th ed. of *OOHB* (1873), Sedgwick credited the hymn to John Wingrove, 1785, but this source is unclear and could not be verified.

# 393   8.6.8.6.
*Melchizedek.*

1 THOU dear Redeemer, dying Lamb,
    We love to hear of Thee;
No *music's* like Thy charming name,
    *Nor* half so sweet *can* be.

2 O *may we* ever hear Thy voice;
    In mercy to *us* speak;
And in *our* Priest we will rejoice,
    *Thou* great Melchizedek.

3 *Our* Jesus shall be still *our* theme,
    While in this world *we* stay;
*We'll* sing *our* Jesu's lovely name
    When all things else decay.

4 When *we* appear in *yonder* cloud,
    With all His favour'd throng,
Then will *we* sing more sweet, more loud,
    And Christ shall be *our* song.

*John Cennick*, 1743, *alt.*

> **1.3:** *music*  **1.4:** *Is / to*  **2.1:** *let me*  **2.2:** *me*
> **2.3:** *my*  **2.4:** *My*  **3.1:** *My / my*  **3.2:** *I*

**3.3:** *I'll / my*  **4.1:** *I / yonder's*  **4.3:** *I*  **4.4:** *my*

**Ed:** The alterations in sts. 2-4 are from George Whitefield's *Collection* (1753); all of the alts. except 1.3 appeared in Martin Madan's *Collection* (1760); alt. 1.3 dates as early as *A Collection of Hymns for the Use of the Tabernacles in Scotland* (1800).

**TD:** "The King-Priest has been here and left His blessing upon the believing seed, and now He sits in glory in His complete character, atoning for us by the merit of His blood, and exercising all power on our behalf" (Ps. 110:4; vol. 5, p. 188).

8 *Behold me waiting*, in the way,
　　For Thee, the heavenly light;
　Command me to be brought, and say,
　　"Sinner, receive thy sight."

*Charles Wesley*, 1740, [*rev. 1786, alt.*]

**1.1:** *still Thou art*  **2.1:** *If*  **5.2:** *my*
**7.1:** *But / they say*  **8.1:** *Long have I waited*
**Ed:** The alteration at 8.1 appeared in eds. of the Wesleys' *Collection* starting ca. 1816; the other changes are apparently by Spurgeon.

# 394 C.M.
*Physician.*

1 JESUS, if *Thou art still* today
　　As yesterday the same,
　Present to heal, in me display
　　The virtue of Thy name.

2 *Since* still Thou goest about to do
　　Thy needy creatures good,
　On me, that I Thy praise may show,
　　Be all Thy wonders show'd.

3 Now, Lord, to whom for help I call,
　　Thy miracles repeat;
　With pitying eyes behold me fall
　　A leper at Thy feet.

4 Loathsome, and foul, and self-abhorr'd,
　　I sink beneath my sin,
　But if Thou wilt, a gracious word
　　Of Thine can make me clean.

5 Thou seest me deaf to Thy commands;
　　Open, O Lord, *mine* ear;
　Bid me stretch out my wither'd hand,
　　And lift it up in prayer.

6 Silent (alas! Thou know'st how long)
　　My voice I cannot raise;
　But O! when Thou shalt loose my tongue,
　　The dumb shall sing Thy praise.

7 *If* Thou, *my God*, art passing by,
　　O let me find Thee near;
　Jesus, in mercy hear my cry!
　　Thou, Son of David, hear!

# 395 C.M.
*Priest.*

1 JESUS, in Thee our eyes behold
　　A thousand glories more
　Than the rich gems and polish'd gold
　　The sons of Aaron wore.

2 They first their own burnt-offerings brought
　　To purge themselves from sin:
　Thy life was pure, without a spot,
　　And all Thy nature clean.

3 Fresh blood as constant as the day
　　Was on their altar spilt,
　But Thy one offering takes away
　　Forever all our guilt.

4 Their priesthood ran thru' several hands,
　　For mortal was their race;
　Thy never-changing office stands
　　Eternal as thy days.

5 Once in the circuit of a year,
　　With blood, but not his own,
　Aaron within the veil appears
　　Before the golden throne.

6 But Christ by His own pow'rful blood
　　Ascends above the skies,
　And in the presence of our God
　　Shows His own sacrifice.

7 Jesus, the King of Glory, reigns
　　On Sion's heavenly hill,
　Looks like a lamb that has been slain,
　　And wears His priesthood still.

8 He ever lives to intercede
    Before His Father's face:
    Give Him, my soul, thy cause to plead,
        Nor doubt the Father's grace.

*Isaac Watts*, 1709

> **MM:** Hymns, Set 2 (Feb./Dec.), 12th Morn,
> BROWN / DOWNS

# 396 C.M.
*Prince of Peace.*

1 LET saints on earth their anthems raise
    Who taste the Saviour's grace;
    *With those above*, proclaim His praise
        And crown Him Prince of Peace.

2 Praise Him who laid His glory by
    For man's apostate race;
    Praise Him who stoop'd to bleed and die,
        And crown Him Prince of Peace.

3 We soon shall reach the *heavn'ly* shore
    To view His lovely face,
    His name forever to adore,
        And crown him Prince of Peace.

*Jonathan Evans*, 1784
[*alt. Basil Manly Jr.*, 1850]

> **1.3:** *Let saints in Heav'n*  **3.1:** *blissful*

# 397 L.M.
*Righteousness.*

1 *JESUS*, Thy blood and righteousness
    My beauty are, my glorious dress;
    Midst flaming worlds, in these array'd,
    With joy shall I lift up my head.

2 When from the dust of death I rise
    To *take* my mansion in the skies,
    E'en then shall this be all my plea,
    "Jesus hath liv'd *and* died for me."

3 Bold shall I stand in *that* great day,
    For who aught to my charge shall lay?
.  *While through Thy blood absolved* I am
    From *sin's tremendous curse* and shame.

4 This spotless robe the same appears
    When ruin'd nature sinks in years;
    No age can change its *glorious* hue;
    *The robe of Christ is* ever new.

5 O let the dead now hear Thy voice!
    *Bid, Lord,* Thy banish'd ones rejoice;
    Their beauty this, their glorious dress,
    *Jesus, the Lord, our* righteousness.

*Nicolaus Ludwig von Zinzendorf*, 1739
*tr. John Wesley*, 1740 [*rev.* 1753]
[*alt. John Rippon*, 1787]

> **1.1:** *Jesu*  **2.2:** *claim*  **2.4:** *hath*  **3.1:** *Thy*
> **3.3:** *Fully absolved through these*
> **3.4:** *sin and fear, from guilt*
> **4.3:** *constant*  **4.4:** *Thy blood preserves it*
> **5.2:** *Now bid*  **5.4:** *Jesu, Thy blood and*
> **Ed:** Translated from the German, "Christi blut
> und gerechtigkeit."
> **TD:** "With Jesus as our complete and all-glorious
> righteousness we need not fear, though the
> day of judgment should commence at once,
> and hell open her mouth at our feet, but might
> joyfully prove the truth of our hymn writer's
> holy boast: 'Bold shall I stand in that great
> day . . .'" (Ps. 17:2; vol. 1, p. 243).

# 398 C.M.
*Our Righteousness.*

1 SAVIOUR divine, we know Thy name,
    And in that name we trust;
    Thou art the Lord our righteousness;
    Thou art Thine Israel's boast.

2 Guilty we plead before Thy throne,
    And low in dust we lie,
    Till Jesus stretch His gracious arm
    To bring the guilty nigh.

3 The sins of one most righteous day
    Might plunge us in despair,
    Yet all the crimes of num'rous years
    Shall our great Surety clear.

4 That spotless robe, which He hath wrought,
    Shall deck us all around;
    Nor by the piercing eye of God
    One blemish shall be found.

5 Pardon and peace and lively hope
    To sinners now are giv'n;
Israel and Judah soon shall change
    The wilderness for heav'n.

6 With joy we taste that manna now;
    Thy mercy scatters down;
We seal our humble vows to Thee
    And wait the promis'd crown.

*Philip Doddridge*, 1755

# 399
8.7.8.7.4.7.
*Saviour.*

1 JESUS is our great salvation,
    Worthy of our best esteem!
He has sav'd His fav'rite nation;
    Join to sing aloud to Him;
      He has sav'd us;
Christ alone *can* us redeem.

2 When involv'd in sin and ruin,
    And no helper there was found,
Jesus our distress was viewing;
    Grace did more than sin abound;
      He has call'd us
With salvation in the sound.

3 Save us from a mere profession;
    Save us from hypocrisy;
Give us, Lord, the sweet possession
    Of Thy righteousness and Thee;
      Best of favours,
None compared with this can be.

4 Free election, known by calling,
    Is a privilege divine;
Saints are kept from final falling;
    All the glory, Lord, be Thine!
      All the glory,
All the glory, Lord, is Thine.

*John Adams*, 1776
[*alt. A Selection of Hymns for the Use of Baptist Congregations*, 1845]

**1.6:** *could*

# 400
S.M.
*Shepherd.*

1 MY soul with joy attend,
    While Jesus silence breaks;
No angel's harp such music yields
    As what my Shepherd speaks.

2 "I know my sheep," He cries,
    "My soul approves them well;
Vain is the treach'rous world's disguise,
    And vain the rage of hell.

3 "I freely feed them now
    With tokens of My love,
But richer pastures I prepare,
    And sweeter streams above.

4 "Unnumber'd years of bliss
    I to My sheep will give,
And while My throne unshaken stands,
    Shall all My chosen live.

5 "This tried almighty hand
    Is rais'd for their defence;
Where is the pow'r shall reach them there?
    Or what shall force them thence?"

6 Enough, my gracious Lord,
    Let faith triumphant cry;
My heart can on this promise live,
    Can on this promise die.

*Philip Doddridge*, 1755

# 401
8.7.8.7.4.7.
*Shepherd.*

1 SHEPHERD of the chosen number,
    They are safe whom Thou dost keep;
Other shepherds faint and slumber
    And forget to watch the sheep;
      Watchful Shepherd!
Thou dost wake while others sleep.

2 When the lion came, depending
    On his strength to seize his prey,
Thou wert there, Thy sheep defending;
    Thou didst then Thy pow'r display;
      Mighty Shepherd!
Thou didst turn the foe away.

3 When the Shepherd's life was needful
 To redeem the sheep from death,
Of their safety ever heedful,
 Thou for them didst yield Thy breath.
  Faithful Shepherd!
 Love like Thine no other hath.

*Thomas Kelly*, 1809

# 402 7.7.7.7.
*Shepherd.*

1 LOVING Shepherd of Thy sheep,
Keep *me, Lord*, in safety keep;
Nothing can Thy power withstand;
None can pluck me from Thy hand.

2 Loving Shephered, Thou didst give
Thine own life that I might live;
May I love Thee day by day,
Gladly Thy sweet will obey.

3 Loving Shepherd, ever near,
Teach *me still* Thy voice to hear;
Suffer not my steps to stray
From the straight and narrow way.

4 Where Thou leadest may I go,
Walking in Thy steps below;
Then before Thy Father's throne,
Jesu, claim me for Thy own.

*Jane E. Leeson*, 1842 [*rev.* 1853, *alt. C.H.S.*]

 **1.2:** *Thy lamb*   **3.2:** *Thy lamb*

# 403 8.7.8.7.
*Sinner's Friend.*

1 FRIEND of sinners! Lord of glory!
 Lowly, mighty! Brother, King!
Musing o'er Thy wondrous story,
 Fain would I thy praises sing.

2 From Thy throne of light celestial,
 Moved with pity, Thou didst bend
To behold our woes terrestrial
 And become the sinner's Friend!

3 Sinner's Friend! O name most blessèd
 Unto those who mourn for sin;

By the devil sore distressèd,
 Foes without and fears within!

4 Friend to help us, cheer us, save us,
 In whom power and pity blend—
Praise we must, the grace which gave us
 Jesus Christ, the sinner's Friend.

*Newman Hall*, [1858]

 **Ed:** "Composed for the author's father, the writer
 of the well known tract, 'The Sinner's Friend.'
 Bolton Abbey, September 1857," as in Hall's
 *Hymns Composed at Bolton Abbey* (1858).
 See also the note at No. 163.

# 404 8.8.6.8.8.6.
*Substitute.*

1 FROM whence this fear and unbelief?
Hath not the Father put to grief
 His spotless Son for me?
And will the righteous Judge of men
Condemn me for that debt of sin,
 Which, Lord, was charg'd on Thee?

2 Complete atonement Thou hast made,
And to the utmost farthing paid,
 Whate'er Thy people owed;
Nor can His wrath on me take place
If shelter'd in Thy righteousness
 And sprinkled with Thy blood.

3 If Thou hast my discharge procur'd,
And freely in my room endur'd
 The whole of wrath divine,
Payment God cannot twice demand,
First at my bleeding Surety's hand,
 And then again at mine.

4 Turn then, my soul, unto thy rest;
The merits of thy great High Priest
 Have bought thy liberty;
Trust in His efficacious blood,
Nor fear thy banishment from God,
 Since Jesus died for thee.

*Augutus Toplady*, 1772

 **FPN:** 19 Feb. 1888 (No. 2357), PEMBROKE

# 405
8.8.6.8.8.6.
*Substitute.*

1 O THOU who didst Thy glory leave,
Apostate sinners to retrieve
From nature's deadly fall,
Me Thou hast purchas'd with a price,
Nor shall my crimes in judgment rise,
For Thou hast borne them all.

2 Jesus was punish'd in my stead,
Without the gate my Surety bled
To expiate my stain;
On earth the Godhead deign'd to dwell,
And made of infinite avail
The suff'rings of the man.

3 And was He for such rebels giv'n?
He was; th' incarnate King of Heav'n
Did for His foes expire;
Amaz'd, O earth, the tidings hear;
He bore, that we might never bear
His Father's righteous ire.

4 Ye saints, the Man of Sorrows bless,
The God for your unrighteousness
Deputed to atone;
Praise Him, till with the heaven'ly throng
Ye sing the never-ending song
And see Him on His throne.

*Augustus Toplady*, 1759

**TD:** "No fire consumes like God's anger, and no
anguish so troubles the heart as His wrath.
Blessed be that dear substitute, 'Who bore that
we might never bear His Father's righteous
ire'" (Ps. 90:7; vol. 4, p. 201).

# 406
7.7.7.7.
*Surety.*

1 CHRIST exalted is our song,
Hymn'd by all the blood-bought throng;
To His throne our shouts shall rise;
God with us by sacred ties.

2 Shout, believer, to thy God;
He hath once the winepress trod;
Peace procur'd by blood divine,
Cancell'd all thy sins and mine.

3 Here thy bleeding wounds are heal'd,
Sins condemn'd, and pardon seal'd;
Grace her empire still maintains;
*Love* without a rival reigns.

4 In thy Surety thou art free;
His dear hands were pierc'd for thee;
With His spotless vesture on,
Holy as the Holy One.

5 O! the heights and depths of grace,
Shining with meridian blaze;
Here the sacred records show
Sinners black, but comely too.

6 Saints dejected, cease to mourn;
Faith shall soon to vision turn;
Ye the kingdom shall obtain
And with Christ exalted reign.

*John Kent*, 1803, *alt. C.H.S.*

**3.4:** *Christ* **EE:** Hymns, Set 2 (Feb./Dec.), 23rd
Eve, KIEL / RATISBON. "The Christian knows
that God looks upon him as standing in union
with Jesus. Now, it is a sweet thing to know
that God accepts us, and to be able to sing . . .
'With my Saviour's vesture on, holy as the Holy
One'" (Aug. 11).

# 407
8.6.8.6.
*True Vine.*

1 JESUS immutably the same,
Thou true and living vine,
Around Thy all-supporting stem,
My feeble arms I twine.

2 Quicken'd by Thee and kept alive,
I flourish and bear fruit;
My life I from Thy sap derive,
My vigour from Thy root.

3 I can do nothing without Thee;
My strength is wholly Thine;
Wither'd and barren should I be,
If serv'd from the vine.

4 Upon my leaf, when parch'd with heat,
Refreshing dew shall drop;

The plant which Thy right hand hath set
    Shall ne'er be rooted up.

5 Each moment water'd by Thy care
    And fenc'd with pow'r divine,
Fruit to eternal life shall bear
    The feeblest branch of Thine.

*Augustus Toplady, 1771*

# 408 8.8.8.8.
*The Way.*

1 JESUS, my all, to heav'n is gone,
    He *whom I fix'd* my hopes upon;
His track I see, and I'll pursue
    The narrow way, till Him I view.

2 The way the holy prophets went,
    The road that leads from banishment,
The King's high way of holiness,
    I'll go, for all *His* paths are peace.

3 No stranger may proceed therein,
    No lover of the world and sin;
Wayfaring men, to Canaan bound,
    Shall only in the way be found.

4 This is the way I long have sought,
    And mourn'd, because I found it not;
My grief *and* burden long have been,
    Because I could not cease from sin.

5 The more I strove against its power,
    I sinn'd and stumbled but the more;
Till late I heard my Saviour say,
    "Come hither, soul! I am the Way!"

6 Lo! glad I come; and Thou, *blest* Lamb,
    Shalt take me to Thee, as I am:
Nothing but sin *have I to* give;
    *Nothing but love shall I receive.*

7 *Now will I tell to* sinners round,
    What a dear Saviour I have found;
I'll point to Thy redeeming blood
    And say, "Behold the way to God!"

*John Cennick, 1743, alt.*

**1.2:** *that I plac'd* **2.4:** *the* **4.3:** *my*
**6.1:** *dear* **6.3:** *I Thee can*

**6.4:** *Yet help me, and thy praise I'll live.*
**7.1:** *I'll tell to all poor*
**Ed:** The alterations at 1.2, 2.4, 6.1, 6.4, and 7.1
    are from Martin Madan's *Collection* (1760); 4.3
    appears as early as 1816 in *The Evangelical*
    *Magazine*; 6.3 appears as early as 1817 in *The*
    *Methodist Pocket Hymn-book.* Spurgeon's
    source for this combination of stanzas and
    alterations is unclear.

# 409 8.6.8.6.
*The Way, the Truth, and the Life.*

1 THOU art the Way—to Thee alone
    From sin and death we flee,
And he who would the Father seek,
    Must seek Him, Lord, by Thee.

2 Thou art the Truth—Thy word alone
    *Sound* wisdom can impart;
Thou only canst inform the mind
    And purify the heart.

3 Thou art the Life—the rending tomb
    Proclaims Thy conq'ring arm,
And those who put their trust in Thee
    Nor death nor hell shall harm.

4 Thou art the Way, the Truth, the Life—
    Grant us that Way to know,
That Truth to keep, that Life to win,
    Whose joys eternal flow.

*George W. Doane, [1824]*
*[alt. A Collection of Hymns and Liturgy*
*for the Use of Evangelical Lutheran*
*Churches, 1848]*

**2.2:** *True*

# PRAISE TO THE LORD JESUS.

# 410 L.M.
*Praise to the Redeemer.*

1 NOW to the Lord that makes us know
    The wonders of His dying love,
Be humble honours paid below
    And strains of nobler praise above.

2 'Twas He that cleans'd our foulest sins
　　And wash'd us in His richest blood;
　　'Tis He that makes us priests and kings
　　And brings us rebels near to God.

3 To Jesus our atoning Priest,
　　To Jesus our superior King,
　　Be everlasting power confess'd,
　　And every tongue His glory sing.

4 Behold! on flying clouds He comes,
　　And every eye shall see Him move;
　　Though with our sins we pierc'd Him once,
　　*Now* He displays His pard'ning love.

5 The unbelieving world shall wail,
　　While we rejoice to see the day;
　　Come, Lord, nor let Thy promise fail,
　　Nor let Thy chariots long delay.

*Isaac Watts*, [1707, *alt.*]

　　**4.4:** *Then*　**Ed:** This minor variant was especially
　　common in American collections, including
　　editions of Watts' hymns as early as 1806.

# 411 C.M.
*Praise to the Redeemer.*

1 TO Him that lov'd the souls of men
　　And wash'd us in His blood,
　　To royal honours rais'd our head
　　And made us priests to God,

2 To Him let ev'ry tongue be praise
　　And every heart be love!
　　All grateful honours paid on earth
　　And nobler songs above!

3 Behold, on flying clouds He comes!
　　His saints shall bless the day,
　　While they that pierc'd Him sadly mourn
　　In anguish and dismay.

4 *Thou art* the first, and *Thou* the last;
　　Time centres all in *Thee*,
　　Th' Almighty God, who was, and is,
　　And evermore shall be!

[*Church of Scotland*, 1745]
[*alt. John Estlin*, 1806]

**4.1:** *I am / I*　**4.2:** *me*　**Ed:** Sedgwick attributed the hymn to "Isaac Watts, 1709; Scripture
Songs, 1751," the latter of which probably
refers to the Church of Scotland's 1751
collection. The hymn does have a very minor
resemblance to Watts' text at No. 410 (see
especially line 3.1).

# 412 C.M.
*A new song to the Lamb.*

1 BEHOLD the glories of the Lamb
　　Amidst His Father's throne;
　　Prepare new honours for His name,
　　And songs before unknown.

2 Let elders worship at His feet,
　　The church adore around,
　　With vials full of odours sweet,
　　And harps of sweeter sound.

3 Those are the prayers of the saints,
　　And these the hymns they raise;
　　Jesus is kind to our complaints;
　　He loves to hear our praise.

4 Eternal Father, who shall look
　　Into Thy secret will?
　　Who but the Son shall take that book
　　And open every seal?

5 He shall fulfil Thy great decrees;
　　The Son deserves it well;
　　Lo! in His hand the sov'reign keys
　　Of heav'n, and death, and hell.

6 Now to the Lamb that once was slain
　　Be endless blessings paid;
　　Salvation, glory, joy, remain
　　Forever on Thy head.

7 Thou hast redeem'd our souls with blood,
　　Hast set the pris'ners free,
　　Hast made us kings and priests to God,
　　And we shall reign with Thee.

8 The worlds of nature and of grace
　　Are put beneath Thy pow'r;
　　Then shorten these delaying days
　　And bring the promis'd hour.

*Isaac Watts*, [1707]

# 413
C.M.
*Worthy the Lamb.*

1 COME, let us join our cheerful songs
    With angels round the throne;
Ten thousand thousand are their tongues,
    But all their joys are one.

2 "Worthy the Lamb that died," they cry,
    "To be exalted thus."
"Worthy the Lamb," our lips reply,
    "For He was slain for us."

3 Jesus is worthy to receive
    Honour and power divine;
And blessings more than we can give
    Be, Lord, forever Thine.

4 Let all that dwell above the sky,
    And air, and earth, and seas,
Conspire to lift Thy glories high
    And speak Thine endless praise.

5 The whole creation join in one
    To bless the sacred name
Of Him that sits upon the throne,
    And to adore the Lamb.

*Isaac Watts,* [1707]

> **Ed:** In Spurgeon's first sermon at the Metropol-
> itan Tabernacle, 25 Mar. 1861, while speaking
> on the divinity and humanity of Christ, he said
> (MTP, vol. 7, p. 170):
>     "He was either one of two things, very
> God of very God, or else an arch-deceiver
> of the souls of men, for He made many of
> them believe He was God, and brought upon
> Himself the consequences of what they call
> blasphemy; so that if He were not God, He
> was the greatest deceiver that ever lived. But
> God He is; and here, in this house, we must
> and will adore Him. With the multitude of His
> redeemed, we will sing—
>     Jesus is worthy to receive
>       Honour and power divine,
>     And blessings more than we can give
>       Be, Lord, forever thine."

# 414
L.M.
*Christ's humiliation and exaltation.*

1 WHAT equal honours shall we bring
    To Thee, O Lord our God, the Lamb,
When all the notes that angels sing
    Are far inferior to Thy name?

2 Worthy is He that once was slain,
    The Prince of Peace that groan'd and died;
Worthy to rise, and live, and reign
    At His Almighty Father's side.

3 Power and dominion are His due
    Who stood condemn'd at Pilate's bar;
Wisdom belongs to Jesus too,
    Tho' He was charg'd with madness here.

4 All riches are His native right,
    Yet He sustain'd amazing loss;
To Him ascribe eternal might,
    Who left His weakness on the cross.

5 Honour immortal must be paid,
    Instead of scandal and of scorn,
While glory shines around His head,
    And a bright crown without a thorn.

6 Blessings forever on the Lamb,
    Who bore the curse for wretched men;
Let angels sound His sacred name,
    And every creature say, "Amen."

*Isaac Watts,* [1707, *rev.* 1709]

# 415
C.M.
*"Worthy is the Lamb."*

1 WORTHY art Thou, O dying Lamb!
    Worthy, O bleeding Lord;
Eternal, infinite, I AM,
    Ceaseless to be ador'd!

2 Fullness of riches is in Thee!
    From Thee all mercies spring;
And grace and love, divine and free,
    And pow'r enlivening!

3 Out of the deep of ev'ry heart,
    Let praise to Thee ascend,

Till Thou to heav'n shalt us translate
Where praises never end!

4 Thither, O thither, quickly bring
Thy remnant, Lord, in peace;
We there with all Thy hosts will sing,
Nor ever, ever cease!

*John Cennick*, 1742

**Ed:** Taken from the longer hymn,
"To Jesus blessing and renown."
**EE:** Hymns, Set 2 (Feb./Dec.), 15th Eve,
MOUNT PLEASANT / BELGIUM

# 416 6.6.4.6.6.6.4.
*"Worthy is the Lamb."*

1 GLORY to God on high!
*Let earth and skies reply,*
Praise ye His name!
*His love and grace* adore,
Who all our sorrows bore;
*Sing aloud* evermore,
Worthy the Lamb.

2 Jesus, our Lord and God,
Bore sin's tremendous load;
Praise ye His name;
Tell what His arm hath done,
What spoils from death He won;
Sing His great name alone;
Worthy the Lamb.

3 *While* they around the throne
Cheerfully join in one,
Praising His name!
*Those* who have felt His blood
Sealing *their* peace with God,
*Sound* His dear fame abroad;
Worthy the Lamb.

4 Join all *ye ransom'd* race,
Our *holy Lord* to bless;
Praise ye His name!
In Him we will rejoice,
And make a *joyful* noise,
*Shouting* with heart and voice,
Worthy the Lamb.

5 *What though we* change our place,
*Yet we* shall never cease
Praising His name!
To Him *our songs we* bring,
*Hail* Him our gracious King,
And without ceasing sing,
Worthy the Lamb.

6 Then let the hosts above,
In realms of endless love,
Praise His dear name!
To Him ascribèd be
Honour and majesty;
Through all eternity:
Worthy the Lamb.

1,3-5 *James Allen*, 1761 [*alt. J.R.*]
[2,6 *John Rippon*, 1787]

**1.2:** *Let praises fill the sky;*
**1.4:** *Angels His name*  **1.6:** *And saints cry*
**3.1:** *All*  **3.4:** *We*  **3.5:** *our*  **3.6:** *Spread*
**4.1:** *the human*  **4.2:** *Lord and God*  **4.5:** *cheerful*
**4.6:** *And say*  **5.1:** *Though we must*
**5.2:** *Our souls*  **5.4:** *we'll tribute*  **5.5:** *Laud*

# 417 C.M.
*Crown Him.*

1 ALL hail the pow'r of *Jesus*' name,
Let angels prostrate fall;
Bring forth the royal diadem
*And* crown Him Lord of all.

2 Crown Him, ye martyrs of *our* God.
Who from His altar call;
Extol the stem of Jesse's rod,
And crown Him Lord of all.

3 Ye *chosen seed of Israel's* race,
*A remnant weak and small,*
Hail Him who saves you by His grace,
And crown Him Lord of all.

4 *Ye Gentile sinners*, ne'er forget
The wormwood and the gall,
Go—spread your trophies at His feet,
And crown Him Lord of all.

5 Babes, men, and sires, who know His love,
    Who feel your sin and thrall,
Now joy with all the hosts above
    And crown Him Lord of all.

6 Let every kindred, every tribe
    On this terrestrial ball,
To Him all majesty ascribe,
    And crown Him Lord of all.

7 O that with yonder sacred throng
    We at His feet may fall;
We'll join the everlasting song,
    And crown Him Lord of all.

1-4 *Edward Perronet*, 1779-80 [*alt. J.R.*]
[5-7 *John Rippon*, 1787]

    **1.1:** *Jesu's*   **1.4:** *To*   **2.1:** *your*
    **3.1:** *seed of Israel's chosen*
    **3.2:** *Ye ransom'd of the fall,*
    **4.1:** *Sinners! whose love can*
    **TD:** "He is strong to smite the foes of his peo-
    ple. Oppressors have been great breakers,
    but their time of retribution shall come, and
    they shall be broken themselves. Sin, Satan,
    and all our enemies must be crushed by the
    iron rod of King Jesus. We have, therefore,
    no cause to fear, but abundant reason to
    sing— 'All hail the power of Jesus' name!'"
    (Ps. 72:4; vol. 3, p. 317).

# 418 S.M.
*Crown Him.*

1 CROWN Him with many crowns,
    The Lamb upon His throne;
Hark! how the heavenly anthem drowns
    All music but its own!

2 Awake, my soul, and sing
    Of Him who died for thee,
And hail Him as thy matchless King
    Through all eternity.

3 Crown Him the Lord of Love!
    Behold His hands and side,
Rich wounds, yet visible above
    In beauty glorified.

4 Crown Him the Lord of Peace!
    Whose power a sceptre sways
From pole to pole, that wars may cease,
    Absorb'd in prayer and praise:

5 His reign shall know no end,
    And round His piercèd feet
Fair flowers of Paradise extend
    Their fragrance ever sweet.

6 All hail! Redeemer, hail!
    For Thou hast died for me:
Thy praise shall never, never fail
    Throughout eternity.

*Matthew Bridges*, [1851]

# 419 8.7.8.7. Double
*"Hail, King of the Jews."*

1 HAIL, thou once despisèd Jesus;
    Hail, thou Galilean King!
Thou didst suffer to release us,
    *Thou* didst free salvation bring!
Hail, thou *agonizing* Saviour,
    *Bearer of* our sin and shame;
By Thy merits we find favour;
    Life is given through Thy name!

2 Paschal Lamb, by God appointed,
    All our sins were on Thee laid;
By almighty love anointed,
    Thou hast full atonement made;
*All Thy people are* forgiven
    Through the virtue of Thy blood;
Open'd is the gate of heaven;
    Peace is made 'twixt man and God.

3 Jesus, hail! enthron'd in glory,
    There forever to abide;
All the heav'nly hosts adore Thee,
    Seated at Thy Father's side;
There for sinners Thou art pleading;
    *There Thou dost our place prepare;*
*Ever for us* interceding
    Till in glory *we* appear.

4 Worship, honour, pow'r, and blessing,
    *Thou art* worthy to receive;

Loudest praises without ceasing,
    Meet it is for us to give!
Help, ye bright angelic spirits,
    Bring your sweetest, noblest lays,
Help to sing our *Saviour's* merits;
    Help to chant Immanuel's praise!

1, 3:1-4 *John Bakewell*, 1757
[2, 3:5-8, 4 Martin Madan's *Collection*, 1760]
[*alt. Augutus Toplady*, 1776]

  **1.4:** *Who*   **1.5:** *universal*   **1.6:** *Who hast borne*
  **2.5:** *Ev'ry sin may be*
  **3.6:** *"Spare them yet another year"*—
  **3.7:** *Thou for saints art*   **3.8:** *they*
  **4.2:** *Christ is*   **4.7:** *Jesu's*
  **Ed:** Parts of this hymn are also given at No. 323.
  **MM:** Hymns, Set 1 (Jan./Nov.), 3rd Morn,
    AUTUMN / NETTLETON

# 420 C.M.
*"Not unto us."*

1 NOT unto us, to Thee alone,
    Bless'd Lamb, be glory giv'n!
Here shall Thy praises be begun
    But carried on in heav'n!

2 The hosts of spirits now with Thee
    Eternal anthems sing;
To imitate them here, lo! we
    Our hallelujahs bring.

3 Had we our tongues like them inspir'd,
    Like theirs our songs should rise;
Like them we never should be tir'd,
    But love the sacrifice.

4 Till we the veil of flesh lay down,
    Accept our weaker lays;
And when we reach Thy Father's throne,
    We'll join in nobler praise!

*John Cennick*, [1742]

  **Ed:** Taken from the longer hymn,
    "Let us, the sheep in Jesus nam'd."

# 421 C.M.
*"Altogether lovely."*

1 TO Christ the Lord let every tongue
    Its noblest tribute bring;
When He's the subject of the song,
    Who can refuse to sing?

2 Survey the beauties of His face
    And on His glories dwell;
Think of the wonders of His grace,
    And all His triumphs tell.

3 Majestic sweetness sits enthron'd
    Upon His awful brow;
His head with radiant glories crown'd,
    His lips with grace o'erflow.

4 No mortal can with Him compare
    Among the sons of men;
Fairer He is than all the fair
    That fill the heavenly train.

5 He saw me plung'd in deep distress;
    He *flew* to my relief;
For me He bore the shameful cross
    And carried all my grief.

6 To heaven, the place of His abode,
    He brings my weary feet,
Shows me the glories of my God,
    And makes my joys complete.

*Samuel Stennett*, [1782, *alt.* Rippon, ca. 1805]

  **5.2:** *fled*

# 422 C.M.
*Rejoicing in Jesus.*

1 O FOR a thousand tongues to sing
    My *great* Redeemer's praise!
The glories of my God and King,
    The triumphs of His grace!

2 My gracious Master and my God,
    Assist me to proclaim,
*And* spread through all the earth abroad
    The honours of Thy name.

3 Jesus! the name that charms our fears,
    That bids our sorrows cease;

'Tis music in the sinner's ears,
  'Tis life, and health, and peace!

4 He breaks the power of cancell'd sin,
  He sets the prisoner free;
  His blood can make the foulest clean,
  His blood avail'd for me.

*Charles Wesley*, 1740 [*alt.*]

  **1.2:** *dear*  **2.3:** *To*  **Ed:** From the longer hymn,
  "Glory to God, and praise, and love," shortened
  in 1753 to begin as above. The alts. at 1.2 and
  2.3 date to the early 1800s.

# 423 C.M.
*Redeeming Love.*

1 TO our Redeemer's glorious name,
  Awake the sacred song!
  O may His love (immortal flame!)
  Tune ev'ry heart and tongue.

2 His love, what mortal thought can reach?
  What mortal tongue display?
  Imagination's utmost stretch
  In wonder dies away.

3 Let wonder still with love unite,
  And gratitude and joy;
  Jesus be our supreme delight,
  His praise our blest employ.

4 Jesus, who left His throne on high,
  Left the bright realms of bliss,
  And came to earth to bleed and die—
  Was ever love like this?

5 O may the sweet, the blissful theme,
  Fill ev'ry heart and tongue,
  Till strangers love Thy charming name
  And join the sacred song.

*Anne Steele*, 1760 [*rev.* 1769]

# 424 L.M.
*Tribute for King Jesus.*

1 JESUS, Thou everlasting King,
  Accept the tribute which we bring;

Accept the well-deserv'd renown,
And wear our praises as Thy crown.

2 Let every act of worship be
  Like our espousals, Lord, to Thee;
  Like the dear hour when from above
  We first receiv'd Thy pledge of love.

3 The gladness of that happy day,
  Our hearts would wish it long to stay;
  Nor let our faith forsake its hold,
  Nor comfort sink, nor love grow cold.

4 Each following minute *while it stays*,
  *Improve our joys, increase Thy praise*,
  Till we are rais'd to sing Thy name
  At the great supper of the Lamb.

5 O that the months would roll away
  And bring *the* coronation day!
  The King of Grace shall fill the throne,
  With all His Father's glories on.

*Isaac Watts*, [1707], *alt. C.H.S.*

  **4.1:** *as it flies*,  **5.2:** *that*
  **4.2:** *Increase thy praise, improve our joys*,
  **Ed:** Taken from the longer hymn, "Daughters of
  Zion, come, behold."

# 425 L.M.
*Christ's glorious person.*

1 NOW to the Lord a noble song!
  Awake my soul, awake my tongue;
  Hosanna to th' eternal name,
  And all His boundless love proclaim.

2 See where it shines in Jesus' face,
  The brightest image of His grace;
  God, in the person of His Son
  Has all His mightiest works outdone.

3 The spacious earth and spreading flood
  Proclaim the wise and powerful God,
  And Thy rich glories from afar
  Sparkle in every rolling star.

4 But in His looks a glory stands,
  The noblest labour of Thine hands;

The pleasing lustre of His eyes
Outshines the wonders of the skies.

5 Grace, 'tis a sweet, a charming theme;
My thoughts rejoice at Jesus' name;
Ye angels, dwell upon the sound;
Ye heav'ns, reflect it to the ground!

*Isaac Watts*, [1707, *rev. 1709*]

## 426 L.M.
*Christ's sufferings and glory.*

1 NOW for a tune of lofty praise
To great Jehovah's equal Son!
Awake, my voice, in heavenly lays!
Tell the loud wonders He hath done.

2 Sing how He left the worlds of light
And the bright robes He wore above;
How swift and joyful was His flight
On wings of everlasting love!

3 Down to this base, this sinful earth,
He came to raise our nature high;
He came t' atone almighty wrath;
Jesus, the God, was born to die.

4 Deep in the shades of gloomy death
Th' almighty Captive prisoner lay;
Th' almighty Captive left the earth
And rose to everlasting day.

5 Lift up your eyes, ye sons of light,
Up to His throne of shining grace;
See what immortal glories sit
Round the sweet beauties of His face.

6 Amongst a thousand *hearts* and songs,
Jesus, the God, exalted reigns;
His sacred name fills all their tongues
And echoes through the heavenly plains.

*Isaac Watts*, [1707, *rev. 1709, alt.*]

**6.1:** *harps* **Ed:** This variant appeared in an 1855
edition of Watts' *The Psalms of David . . . with
Hymns and Spiritual Songs* but otherwise is
unique to *Our Own Hymn-Book.*

## 427 L.M.
*Song of songs.*

1 COME, let us sing the song of songs;
*The saints in heaven began the strain,*
The homage which to Christ belongs:
"Worthy the Lamb, for He was slain!"

2 Slain to redeem us by His blood,
To cleanse from every sinful stain,
And make us kings and priests to God,
"Worthy the Lamb, for He was slain!"

3 To Him who suffer'd on the tree,
Our souls at His soul's price to gain,
Blessing, and praise, and glory be:
"Worthy the Lamb, for He was slain!"

4 To Him, enthroned by filial right,
All power in heaven and earth procaim,
Honour and majesty and might:
"Worthy the Lamb, for He was slain!"

5 *Long as we live, and when we die,*
*And while in heaven* with Him *we* reign,
*This song* our song of songs *shall be*:
"Worthy the Lamb, for He was slain!"

*James Montgomery*, 1853
[*alt. Sabbath Hymn Book*, 1858]

**1.2:** *The song which saints in glory sing;*
**5.1:** *Yea, in eternity of bliss*
**5.2:** *If call'd through grace / to*
**5.3:** *Our song— / be this,*
**Ed:** This hymn was dated 1841 in Montgomery's
manuscripts, but not published until 1853.
**EE:** Hymns, Set 2 (Feb./Dec.), 17th Eve,
PASCAL / OLD HUNDREDTH

## 428 C.M.
*Praise to the Redeemer.*

1 PLUNG'D in a gulf of dark despair
We wretched sinners lay,
Without one cheerful beam of hope
Or spark of glimmering day.

2 With pitying eyes, the Prince of Grace
Beheld our helpless grief;

He saw, and (O amazing love)
   He ran to our relief.

3 Down from the shining seats above
   With joyful haste He fled,
Enter'd the grave in mortal flesh,
   And dwelt among the dead.

4 He spoil'd the powers of darkness thus
   And broke our iron chains;
Jesus has freed our captive souls
   From everlasting pains.

5 O for this love let rocks and hills
   Their lasting silence break,
And all harmonious human tongues
   The Saviour's praises speak.

6 Yes, we will praise Thee, dearest Lord;
   Our souls are all on flame;
Hosanna round the spacious earth
   To Thine adored name.

7 Angels, assist our mighty joys,
   Strike all your harps of gold,
But when you raise your highest notes,
   His love can ne'er be told.

*Isaac Watts*, [1707]

# 429 S.M.
*The passion and exaltation of Christ.*

1 COME, all harmonious tongues,
   Your noblest music bring;
'Tis Christ the everlasting God,
   And Christ the man we sing.

2 Tell how He took our flesh
   To take away our guilt;
Sing the dear drops of sacred blood
   That hellish monsters spilt.

3 The waves of swelling grief
   Did o'er His bosom roll,
And mountains of almighty wrath
   Lay heavy on His soul.

4 Down to the shades of death
   He bow'd His awful head,

Yet He arose to live and reign
   When death itself is dead.

5 No more the bloody spear,
   The cross and nails no more,
For hell itself shakes at His name,
   And all the heav'ns adore.

6 There the Redeemer sits
   High on the Father's throne;
The Father lays His vengeance by
   And smiles upon His Son.

7 There His full glories shine
   With uncreated rays
And bless His saints' and angels' eyes
   To everlasting days.

*Isaac Watts*, [1707]

# 430 L.M. / *The humiliation and triumphs of Christ.*

1 PROCLAIM inimitable love;
Jesus, the Lord of worlds above
Puts off the beams of bright array
And veils the God in mortal clay.

2 He that distributes crowns and thrones
Hangs on a tree and bleeds and groans:
The Prince of Life resigns His breath;
The King of Glory bows to death.

3 But see the wonders of His pow'r;
He triumphs in His dying hour;
And whilst by Satan's rage He fell,
He dash'd the rising hopes of hell.

4 Thus were the hosts of death subdued,
And sin was drown'd in Jesus' blood:
Then He arose, and reigns above,
And conquers sinners by His love.

*Isaac Watts*, [1736]

> **Ed:** Taken from the longer hymn,
> "The mighty frame of glorious grace."

# 431 L.M.
*Longing to praise Jesus better.*

1 LORD, when my thoughts with wonder roll
  O'er the sharp sorrows of Thy soul,
  And read my Maker's broken laws,
  Repair'd and honour'd by Thy cross,

2 When I behold death, hell, and sin,
  Vanquish'd by that dear blood of Thine,
  And see the Man that groan'd and died
  Sit glorious by His Father's side,

3 My passions rise and soar above,
  I'm wing'd with faith and fired with love;
  Fain would I reach eternal things
  And learn the notes that Gabriel sings.

*Isaac Watts*, [1707, *rev.* 1709, 1720, 1731]

> **EE:** Hymns, Set 2 (Feb./Dec.), 19th Eve,
>   NEAPOLIS / DUKE STREET

# 432 C.M.
*Extol the Son of God.*

1 THE Son of God! the Lord of Life!
  How wondrous are His ways;
  Oh for a harp of thousand strings
  To sound abroad His praise.

2 How passing strange to leave the seat
  Of heaven's eternal throne,
  And hosts of glittering seraphim,
  For guilty man alone.

3 And did He bow His sacred head
  And die a death of shame?
  Let men and angels magnify
  And bless His holy name.

4 Oh let us live in peace and love
  And cast away our pride,
  And crucify our sins afresh,
  As He was crucified.

5 He rose again; then let us rise
  From sin, and Christ adore,
  And dwell in peace with all mankind,
  And tempt the Lord no more.

6 The Son of God! the Lord of Life!
  How wondrous are His ways!
  Oh for a harp of thousand strings
  To sound abroad His praise!

*George Mogridge*, [1849]

> **Ed:** Taken from the longer hymn,
>   "I sing the coming of the Lord."
> **MM:** Hymns, Set 2 (Feb./Dec.), 20th Morn,
>   BALERMA / NAOMI

# 433 C.M.
*"He is our peace."*

1 DEAREST of all the names above,
  My Jesus and my God,
  Who can resist Thy heavenly love
  Or trifle with Thy blood?

2 'Tis by the merits of Thy death
  The Father smiles again;
  'Tis by Thine interceding breath
  The Spirit dwells with men.

3 Till God in human flesh I see,
  My thoughts no comfort find;
  The holy, just, and sacred Three
  Are terrors to my mind.

4 But if Immanuel's face appear,
  My hope, my joy begins;
  His name forbids my slavish fear;
  His grace removes my sins.

5 While Jews on their own law rely,
  And Greeks of wisdom boast,
  I love th' incarnate mystery,
  And there I fix my trust.

*Isaac Watts*, 1709

# 434 7.7.7.7.
*"He is become my salvation."*

1 I WILL praise Thee ev'ry day;
  Now Thine anger's turn'd away!
  Comfortable thoughts arise
  From the bleeding sacrifice.

2 Here, in the fair gospel field,
Wells of free salvation yield
Streams of life, a plenteous store,
And my soul shall thirst no more.

3 Jesus is become at length
My salvation and my strength,
And His praises shall prolong,
While I live, my pleasant song.

4 Praise ye then His glorious name;
Publish His exalted fame!
Still His worth your praise exceeds;
Excellent are all His deeds.

5 Raise again the joyful sound;
Let the nations roll it round!
Zion shout, for this is He;
God the Saviour dwells in thee.

*William Cowper*, 1779

> **MM:** Hymns, Set 1 (Jan./Nov.), 2nd Morn,
> NUREMBERG
> **TD:** "Now hearken to the music which faith
> makes in the soul. . . . Sweet is the music
> which sounds from the strings of the heart.
> But this is not all; the voice joins itself in the
> blessed work, and the tongue keeps tune with
> the soul, while the writer declares, . . . 'I will
> praise thee every day' (Ps. 13:6; vol. 1, p. 171).

# 435 S.M.
*Blessed be His name.*

1 I BLESS the Christ of God,
I rest on love divine,
And with unfaltering lip and heart
I call this Saviour mine.

2 His cross dispels each doubt;
I bury in His tomb
Each thought of unbelief and fear,
Each lingering shade of gloom.

3 I praise the God of grace;
I trust His truth and might;
He calls me His, I call Him mine,
My God, my joy, my light.

4 In Him is only good,
In me is only ill;
My ill but draws His goodness forth,
And me He loveth still.

5 'Tis He who saveth me
And freely pardon gives;
I love because He loveth me;
I live because He lives.

6 My life with Him is hid,
My death has passed away,
My clouds have melted into light,
My midnight into day.

*Horatius Bonar*, 1864

> **Ed:** Taken from the longer hymn,
> "Not what these hands have done."

# 436 C.M.
*Infinitely excellent.*

1 INFINITE excellence is Thine,
Thou lovely Prince of Grace;
Thy uncreated beauties shine
With never fading rays.

2 Sinners from earth's remotest end
Come bending at Thy feet;
To Thee their prayers and vows ascend;
In Thee their wishes meet.

3 Thy name, as precious ointment shed,
Delights the church around;
Sweetly the sacred odours spread
Through all Immanuel's ground.

4 Millions of happy spirits live
On Thy exhaustless store;
From Thee they all their bliss receive,
And still Thou givest more.

5 Thou art their triumph and their joy;
They find their all in Thee;
Thy glories will their tongues employ
Through all eternity.

*John Fawcett*, 1782

## 437
7.7.7.7.
*Blessed be His name.*

1 BRETHREN, let us join to bless
*Christ our peace and righteousness;*
Let our praise to Him be giv'n,
High at God's right hand in heav'n!

2 *Son of God,* to Thee we bow;
Thou art Lord, and only Thou;
Thou the *woman's promised* seed;
*Thou who didst for sinners bleed.*

3 Thee the angels ceaseless sing;
Thee we praise, our Priest and King;
Worthy is Thy name of praise,
Full of glory, full of grace.

4 Thou hast the glad tidings brought,
Of salvation fully wrought;
Wrought, *O Lord, alone by Thee,*
*Wrought to set Thy people free.*

5 *Thee, our Lord, would we* adore,
*Serve and follow more and more,*
*Praise and bless Thy matchless* love
Till we join *Thy saints* above.

*John Cennick,* 1742, *alt.*

**1.2:** *Jesus Christ, our joy and peace;*
**2.1:** *Master see* **2.3:** *blessed Virgin's*
**2.4:** *Glory of Thy church, and head!*
**4.3:** *for all Thy church! and we*
**4.4:** *Worship in their company!*
**5.1:** *We Thy little flock*
**5.2:** *Thee the Lord forever more!*
**5.3:** *Ever with us show thy* **5.4:** *with those*
**Ed:** The alts. at 2.1, 4.4, and 5.4 date to Thomas
Cotterill's *Selection* (1810); 1.2, 2.3-4, and 5.1-2
are from Josiah Conder's *Congregational Hymn
Book* (1836). The final form is by Spurgeon.
**MM:** Hymns, Set 2 (Feb./Dec.), 18th Morn,
NUREMBERG / FULTON

## 438
8.8.6.8.8.6.
*I will sing of my beloved.*

1 O COULD I speak the matchless worth,
O could I sound the glories forth
Which in my Saviour shine!
I'd soar and touch the heavenly strings
And vie with Gabriel while he sings
In notes almost divine.

2 I'd sing the precious blood He spilt,
My ransom from the dreadful guilt
Of sin and wrath divine;
I'd sing His glorious righteousness
In which all perfect, heavenly dress
My soul shall ever shine.

3 I'd sing the character He bears
And all the forms of love He wears,
Exalted on His throne;
In loftiest songs of sweetest praise,
I would to everlasting days
Make all His glories known.

4 Well, the delightful day will come
When *my* dear Lord will bring me home,
And I shall see His face;
Then with my Saviour, Brother, Friend,
A blest eternity I'll spend,
Triumphant in His grace.

*Samuel Medley,* [1800, *alt.*]

**4.2:** *He,* dear Lord, **Ed:** Taken from the longer
hymn, "Not of terrestrial mortal themes." 4.2
is a common variant, as early as 1807 in *Select
Hymns for the Use of Hoxton Academy.*

## 439
7.7.7.7.
*Jesus' love.*

1 SWEET the theme of Jesus' love!
Sweet the theme, all themes above;
Love, unmerited and free,
Our triumphant song shall be.

2 Love, so vast that nought can bound;
Love, too deep for thought to sound;
*Love, which made the Lord of all
Drink the wormwood and the gall.*

3 Love, which led Him to the cross,
Bearing there unutter'd loss;
Love, which brought Him to the gloom
Of the cold and darksome tomb.

4 Love, which made Him hence arise
  Far above the starry skies,
  There with tender, loving care,
  All His people's griefs to share.

5 Love, which will not let Him rest
  Till His chosen all are blest,
  Till they all for whom He died
  Live rejoicing by His side.

*Albert Midlane, 1864, alt. C.H.S.*

> **2.3-4:** *Love, which led God's only Son*
>   *To become the suffering One.*
> **FPN:** 20 Oct. 1889 (No. 2341), REDHEAD

# 440 7.7.7.7.
*Redeeming love.*

1 NOW begin the heav'nly theme;
  Sing aloud in *Jesus*' name!
  Ye, who *His salvation* prove,
  Triumph in redeeming love.

2 Ye, who see the Father's grace
  Beaming in the Saviour's face,
  As to Canaan on ye move,
  Praise and bless redeeming love.

3 Mourning souls, dry up your tears,
  Banish all your guilty fears;
  See your guilt and curse remove,
  Cancell'd by redeeming love.

4 Ye, alas! who long have been
  Willing slaves to death and sin,
  Now from bliss no longer rove;
  Stop—and taste redeeming love.

5 Welcome all by sin oppress'd,
  Welcome to His sacred rest;
  Nothing brought Him from above,
  Nothing but redeeming love.

6 When His Spirit leads us home,
  When we to His glory come,
  We shall all the fullness prove
  Of our Lord's redeeming love.

7 He subdued th' infernal pow'rs,
  His tremendous foes and ours,

From their cursèd empire drove,
Mighty in redeeming love.

8 Hither then your music bring;
  Strike aloud each cheerful string;
  Mortals, join the hosts above,
  Join to praise redeeming love.

1-5,7-8 Madan's *Collection*, 1763, [*alt. J.R.*]
[6 *John Rippon, 1787*]

> **1.2:** *Jesu's*   **1.3:** *Jesu's kindness*

# 441 6.6.6.6.8.8.
*"Thou art worthy."*

1 SHALL hymns of grateful love
  Through heaven's high arches ring,
  And all the hosts above
  Their songs of triumph sing?
  And shall not we take up the strain
  And send the echo back again?

2 Shall every ransomed tribe
  Of Adam's scattered race
  To Christ all power ascribe,
  Who saved them by His grace?
  And shall not we take up the strain
  And send the echo back again?

3 Shall they adore the Lord
  Who bought them by His blood,
  And all the love record
  That led them home to God?
  And shall not we take up the strain
  And send the echo back again?

4 O *spread the joyful* sound!
  The Saviour's love proclaim,
  And publish all around
  Salvation through His name;
  Till the *whole earth* take up the strain
  And send the echo back again!

*James J. Cummins,* [1839, *alt. C.H.S.*]

> **4.1:** *let us spread the*   **4.5:** *wide world*

# 442

11.11.11.11.
*Glory to the Lamb.*

1 COME, saints, and adore Him,
  come bow at His feet,
*Come*, give Him the glory,
  the praise that is meet;
Let joyful hosannas unceasing arise,
And join the *full* chorus
  that gladdens the skies.

2 To the Lamb that was slain
  all honour be paid;
Let crowns without number
  encircle His head;
Let blessing and glory
  and riches and might
Be ascribed evermore by angels of light.

1 *Maria de Fleury*, 1791 [*alt.*]
[2 *Edward Bickersteth*, 1833]

> **1.2:** *O* **1.4:** *grand* **Ed:** St. 1 is taken from the
> longer text, "Thou soft flowing Kedron, by thy
> silver stream." The alt. at 1.2 is by Bickersteth;
> 1.4 is from William Collyer's *Hymns* (1812).

# 443

11.11.11.11.
*Hosanna.*

1 THY triumphs, Redeemer of men,
  we proclaim,

Be boundless Thine empire,
  eternal Thy name;
We'll praise Thee on earth,
  and in glory again,
Sing loud hallelujahs, forever, Amen.

John Rippon's *Selection*, 1844

> **Ed:** Starting in the 6th ed. (1873), Sedgwick cred-
> ited this hymn to Richard Cope, 1813, but this
> source is unclear, and no source earlier than
> 1844 could be located or confirmed.

# 444

S.M.
*Hosanna.*

1 HOSANNA to the King
  That for our guilt was slain;
Let every soul its tribute bring
  And swell th' exulting strain.

2 Hosanna to the King,
  Who sitting high in heav'n
Bids sinners lost and wandering,
  Return and be forgiv'n.

3 Hosanna to the King
  Who ever lives and reigns;
Let heav'n and earth His praises sing,
  In loud and lofty strains!

*Thomas Hastings*, 1850

# The Holy Spirit

# 445

C.M.
*The promised Comforter.*

1 OUR blest Redeemer, ere He breathed
  His tender, last farewell,
A Guide, a Comforter, bequeath'd
  *With us on earth to dwell.*

2 He *comes, the mystic heavenly* Dove,
  With sheltering wings outspread,

The holy balm of peace and love
  *On chosen hearts to shed.*

3 He *comes*, sweet influence to impart,
  A gracious, willing guest,
Where He can find one humble heart
  *Wherein to make His rest.*

4 And His that gentle voice we hear,
  Soft as the breath of eve,

That checks each fault, that calms each fear,
*And bids us cease to grieve.*

5 And every virtue we possess,
And every victory won,
And every thought of holiness
*Are His, and His alone.*

6 Spirit of purity and grace,
Our weakness pitying see;
O make our hearts Thy dwelling place,
*Yea, make them meet for Thee.*

*Harriet Auber*, 1829, *alt. C.H.S.*

> **1.4:** *With us to dwell*
> **2.1:** *came in semblance of a*
> **2.4:** *On earth to shed*   **3.1:** *came*
> **3.4:** *Wherein to rest.*   **4.4:** *And speaks of Heaven.*
> **5.4:** *Are His alone.*   **6.4:** *And worthier Thee.*
> **Ed:** The original hymn is 8.6.8.4; it was modified
> to fit Common Meter tunes.

# 446   7.7.7.7.
*The Comforter.*

1 JESUS is gone up on high,
But His promise still is here;
"I will all your wants supply;
I will send the Comforter."

2 Let us now His promise plead;
Let us to His throne draw nigh;
Jesus knows His people's need;
Jesus hears His people's cry.

3 Send us, Lord, the Comforter,
Pledge and witness of Thy love,
Dwelling with Thy people here,
Leading them to joys above.

4 Till we reach the promis'd rest,
Till Thy face unveil'd we see,
Of this blessèd hope possess'd,
Teach us, Lord, to live to Thee.

*Thomas Kelly*, 1806 [*rev.* 1826]

# 447   L.M.
*Work of the Holy Spirit.*

1 ETERNAL Spirit, we confess
And sing the wonders of Thy grace;
Thy power conveys our blessings down
From God the Father and the Son.

2 Enlighten'd by Thine heavenly ray,
Our shades and darkness turn to day;
Thine inward teachings make us know
Our danger and our refuge too.

3 Thy power and glory work within
And break the chains of reigning sin,
Do our imperious lusts subdue,
And form our wretched hearts anew.

4 The troubled conscience knows Thy voice;
Thy cheering words awake our joys;
Thy words allay the stormy wind
And calm the surges of the mind.

*Isaac Watts*, 1709

> **MM:** Hymns, Set 2 (Feb./Dec.), 28th Morn,
> UXBRIDGE / MEROE

# 448   C.M.
*Regeneration.*

1 NOT all the outward forms on earth,
Nor rites that God has giv'n,
Nor will of man, nor blood, nor birth,
Can raise a soul to heav'n.

2 The sovereign will of God alone
Creates us heirs of grace,
Born in the image of His Son,
A new peculiar race.

3 The Spirit, like some heavenly wind,
Blows on the sons of flesh,
*Creates a new, a heavenly* mind,
And forms the man afresh.

4 Our quicken'd souls awake and rise
From the long sleep of death;
On heavenly things we fix our eyes,
And praise employs our breath.

*Isaac Watts*, 1709, *alt. C.H.S.*

> **3.3:** *New models all the carnal*

# 449
C.M.
*Pentecost.*

1 GREAT was the day, the joy was great,
When the divine disciples met;
Whilst on their heads the Spirit came
And sat like tongues of cloven flame.

2 What gifts, what miracles He gave!
And power to kill, and power to save!
Furnish'd their tongues with
    wondrous words,
Instead of shields, and spears, and swords.

3 Thus arm'd, He sent the champions forth,
From east to west, from south to north:
"Go, and assert your Saviour's cause;
Go, spread the mystery of His cross."

4 These weapons of the holy war,
Of what almighty force they are,
To make our stubborn passions bow
And lay the proudest rebel low!

5 Nations, the learnèd and the rude,
Are by these heavenly arms subdued,
While Satan rages at his loss
And hates the doctrine of the cross.

6 Great King of Grace, my heart subdue;
I would be led in triumph too,
A willing captive to my Lord,
And sing the victories of His Word.

*Isaac Watts, 1709*

# 450
S.M.
*Waiting for the promise of the Father.*

1 LORD God, the Holy Ghost,
In this accepted hour,
As on the day of Pentecost,
Descend in all Thy power.

2 We meet with one accord
In *one* appointed place,
And wait the promise of our Lord,
The Spirit of all grace.

3 Like mighty rushing wind
Upon the waves beneath,

Move with one impulse every mind,
One soul, one feeling breathe.

4 The young, the old inspire
With wisdom from above,
And give us hearts and tongues of fire,
To pray, and praise, and love.

5 Spirit of Light, explore,
And chase our gloom away,
With lustre shining more and more
Unto the perfect day.

6 Spirit of Truth, be Thou
In life and death our Guide;
O Spirit of Adoption, now
May we be sanctified!

*James Montgomery, 1819 [rev. 1825]*

**2.2:** *our* **Ed:** This alteration appeared in a series
of collections published in Dublin, as early as
1839, before being adopted by Spurgeon.

# 451
S.M.
*The Holy Ghost is here.*

1 THE Holy Ghost is here,
Where saints in prayer agree,
As Jesu's parting gift He's near
Each pleading company.

2 Not far away is He,
To be by prayer brought nigh,
But here in present majesty,
As in His courts on high.

3 He dwells within our soul,
An ever welcome Guest;
He reigns with absolute control
As Monarch in the breast.

4 Our bodies are His shrine,
And He th' indwelling Lord;
All hail, thou Comforter divine,
Be evermore adored.

5 Obedient to Thy will,
We wait to feel Thy power;
O Lord of life, our hopes fulfill,
And bless this hallow'd hour!

*Charles H. Spurgeon, 1866*

# 452 C.M.
*A prayer for His operations.*

1 ENTHRON'D on high, Almighty Lord,
 The Holy Ghost send down!
Fulfill in us Thy faithful word,
 And all Thy mercies crown.

2 Though on our heads no tongues of fire
 Their wondrous powers impart,
Grant, Saviour, what we more desire,
 Thy Spirit in our heart.

3 Spirit of life, and light, and love,
 Thy heav'nly influence give!
Quicken our souls, born from above,
 In Christ that we may live.

4 To our benighted minds reveal
 The glories of His grace,
And bring us where no clouds conceal
 The brightness of His face.

5 His love, within us shed abroad,
 Life's ever-springing well!
Till God in us, and we in God,
 In love eternal dwell.

*Thomas Haweis*, 1792

# 453 S.M.
*The Holy Spirit invoked.*

1 COME, Holy Spirit, come!
 With energy divine,
And on this poor benighted soul
 With beams of mercy shine.

2 From the celestial hills,
 *Life, light,* and joy dispense;
And may I daily, hourly feel
 Thy quickening influence.

3 *Melt*, melt this frozen heart;
 This stubborn will subdue;
Each evil passion overcome,
 And form me all anew.

4 *Mine will the profit be,*
 But Thine shall be the praise;

*And unto* Thee I will devote
 The remnant of my days.

*Benjamin Beddome*, 1800

**2.2:** *Light, life,* **3.1:** *Oh*
**4.1:** *The profit will be mine,* **4.3:** *Cheerful to*
**Ed:** This text appeared in a revised form in
 Beddome's *Hymns* (1817), indicated here
 by the footnotes, but the version in Rippon's
 *Selection* (1800) has had greater influence.

# 454 C.M.
*The Holy Spirit.*

1 COME, Holy Spirit, heavenly Dove,
 With all Thy quickening powers,
Kindle a flame of sacred love
 In these cold hearts of ours.

2 Look how we grovel here below,
 Fond of these trifling toys;
Our souls can neither fly nor go
 To reach eternal joys.

3 In vain we tune our formal songs;
 In vain we strive to rise;
Hosannas languish on our tongues,
 And our devotion dies.

4 Dear Lord! and shall we ever lie
 At this poor dying rate?
Our love so faint, so cold to Thee,
 And Thine to us so great?

5 Come, Holy Spirit, heavenly Dove,
 With all Thy quickening powers,
Come shed abroad a Saviour's love,
 And that shall kindle ours.

*Isaac Watts*, [1707, *rev.* 1709]

# 455 C.M.
*Come, Holy Ghost.*

1 COME, Holy Ghost, our hearts inspire;
 Let us Thine influence prove,
Source of the old prophetic fire,
 Fountain of light and love.

2 Come, Holy Ghost (for mov'd by Thee
 The prophets wrote and spoke),

Unlock the truth, Thyself the key,
Unseal the sacred book.

3 Expand Thy wings, celestial Dove;
Brood o'er our nature's night;
On our disorder'd spirits move,
And let there now be light.

4 God, through Himself, we then shall know,
If Thou within us shine,
And sound, with all Thy saints below,
The depths of love divine.

*Charles Wesley*, 1740 [*rev.* 1743]

**EE:** Hymns, Set 2 (Feb./Dec.), 18th Eve,
TIVERTON / FARRANT

# 456 S.M.
*His indwelling sought.*

1 COME, Holy Spirit, come,
Let Thy bright beams arise,
Dispel the darkness from our minds,
And open all our eyes.

2 Cheer our desponding hearts,
Thou heav'nly Paraclete;
Give us to lie, with humble hope,
At our Redeemer's feet.

3 'Tis Thine to cleanse the heart,
To sanctify the soul,
To pour fresh life on ev'ry part,
And new-create the whole.

4 Dwell, therefore, in our hearts;
Our minds from bondage free;
Then shall we know, and praise, and love
The Father, Son, and Thee.

*Joseph Hart*, 1759

**MM:** Hymns, Set 1 (Jan./Nov.), 28th Morn,
ST. THOMAS / STATE STREET

# 457 L.M.
*Spiritual power desired.*

1 COME, dearest Lord, descend and dwell
By faith and love in every breast;

Then shall we know, and taste, and feel
The joys that cannot be express'd.

2 Come fill our hearts with inward strength;
Make our enlargèd souls possess,
And learn the height, and breadth,
and length
Of Thine unmeasurable grace.

3 Now to the God, whose power can do
More than our thoughts or wishes know,
Be everlasting honours done
By all the church, through Christ His Son.

*Isaac Watts*, 1709

**MM:** Hymns, 10th Lord's Day,
ROLLAND / DUKE STREET

# 458 S.M.
*Love longed for.*

1 DESCEND, immortal Dove;
Spread Thy kind wings abroad;
And wrapt in flames of holy love,
Bear all my soul to God.

2 Jesus, my Lord, reveal
In charms of grace divine,
And be Thyself the sacred seal,
That pearl of price is mine.

3 Behold, my heart expands
To catch the heav'nly fire;
It longs to feel the gentle bands
And groans with strong desire.

4 Thy love, my God, appears,
And brings salvation down,
My cordial through this vale of tears,
In paradise my crown.

*Philip Doddridge*, 1755

**Ed:** Dated 11 Sept. 1737 in his manuscripts.

# 459 7.7.7.7.
*The Spirit's work requested.*

1 HOLY Spirit, from on high,
Bend on us a pitying eye;

Animate the drooping heart;
Bid the power of sin depart.

2 Light up every dark recess
Of our hearts' ungodliness;
Show us every devious way
Where our steps have gone astray.

3 Teach us with repentant grief
Humbly to implore relief,
Then the Saviour's blood reveal
All our deep disease to heal.

4 Other groundwork should we lay,
Sweep those empty hopes away;
Make us feel that Christ alone
Can for human guilt atone.

5 May we daily grow in grace
And pursue the heavenly race,
Train'd in wisdom, led by love,
Till we reach our rest above.

*William Hiley Bathurst*, 1831

# 460 7.7.7.7.
*His operations invited.*

1 HOLY Ghost, with light divine,
Shine upon this heart of mine,
Chase the shades of night away,
Turn the darkness into day.

2 Holy Ghost, with power divine,
Cleanse this guilty heart of mine;
Long has sin without control
Held dominion o'er my soul.

3 Holy Ghost, with joy divine,
Cheer this sadden'd heart of mine;
Bid my many woes depart;
Heal my wounded, bleeding heart.

4 Holy Spirit, all divine,
Dwell within this heart of mine,
Cast down every idol throne,
Reign supreme, and reign alone.

*Andrew Reed*, 1817

**EE:** Hymns, Set 2 (Feb./Dec.), 16th Eve,
MILAN / KIEL

# 461 C.M.
*Nature helpless—the Spirit working.*

1 HOW helpless guilty nature lies,
Unconscious of its load!
The heart unchang'd can never rise
To happiness and God.

2 Can aught beneath a power divine
The stubborn will subdue?
'Tis Thine, *Eternal Spirit*, Thine
To form the heart anew.

3 'Tis Thine the passions to recall,
And upwards bid them rise,
And make the scales of error fall
From reason's darken'd eyes.

4 To chase the shades of death away,
And bid the sinner live!
A beam of heaven, a vital ray,
'Tis Thine alone to give.

5 O change these wretched hearts of ours
And give them life divine!
Then shall our passions and our powers,
Almighty Lord, be Thine.

*Anne Steele*, [1769]

**2.3:** *almighty Saviour*
**Ed:** Footnote indicates a change made in Steele's
posthumous *Miscellaneous Pieces* (1780).

# 462 8.7.8.7.
*Comforter.*

1 HOLY Ghost, dispel our sadness,
Pierce the clouds of sinful night;
Come, thou source of sweetest gladness,
Breathe Thy life and spread Thy light!

2 Author of the new creation,
Come with unction and with pow'r;
Make our hearts Thy habitation;
On our souls Thy graces show'r.

*Paul Gerhardt*, 1648
*tr. J.C. Jacobi*, 1725 [*rev.* 1732]
*adapt. Augustus Toplady*, 1776

**Ed:** From the German, "O du allersüsste Freude," and adapted from Jacobi's translation, "O Thou sweetest source of gladness!" The original order of Toplady's lines in stanza 2 was *Come / On / Author / Make.* All three texts are significantly longer than this abridgement.

# 463 C.M.
*Divine drawings implored.*

1 IF Thou hast drawn a thousand times,
    Oh draw me, Lord, again;
*Around me cast Thy Spirit's bands,*
    *And all my powers constrain.*

2 Draw me from all created good,
    *From self,* the world, and sin,
To the dear fountain of Thy blood,
    And make me pure within.

3 Oh lead me to Thy mercy seat;
    Attract me nearer still;
Draw me, like Mary, to Thy feet
    To sit and learn Thy will.

4 Oh draw me all the desert through
    With cords of heavenly love,
And when prepar'd for going hence,
    Draw me to dwell above.

1,4 John Rippon's *Selection,* 1828 [*alt. C.H.S.*]
[2-3 *Benjamin Beddome, 1817, alt. J.R.*]

> **1.3-4:** *Thy Spirit, Word, and Providence*
> *Cannot attract in vain.* **2.2:** *Myself*
> **Ed:** Sts. 2-3 are from Beddome's hymn, "Jesus, my Saviour, bind me fast." Starting in the 6th ed. (1873), Sedgwick credited the hymn erroneously to "Beddome and Rippon, 1800."

# 464 C.M.
*The Holy Spirit invoked.*

1 SPIRIT divine! attend our prayers,
    And make this house Thy home;
Descend with all Thy gracious powers;
    O come—great Spirit—come!

2 Come as the light—to us reveal
    Our emptiness and woe;

And lead us in those paths of life
    Where all the righteous go.

3 Come as the fire—and purge our hearts
    Like sacrifical flame;
Let our whole soul an offering be
    To our Redeemer's name.

4 Come as the dew—and sweetly bless
    This consecrated hour;
May barrenness rejoice to own
    Thy fertilizing power.

5 Come as the dove—and spread Thy wings,
    The wings of peaceful love,
And let Thy church on earth become
    Blest as the church above.

6 Come as the wind—with rushing sound
    And pentecostal grace,
That all of woman born may see
    The glory of Thy face.

7 Spirit divine! attend our prayers,
    Make a lost world Thy home,
Descend with all Thy gracious powers;
    O come—great Spirit—come!

*Andrew Reed,* [1829]

# 465 C.M.
*His operations sought.*

1 *SPIRIT of Truth, Thy grace impart,*
    To guide our doubtful way;
Thy *beams* shall scatter every cloud
    And make a glorious day.

2 Light in Thy light, O may *we* see,
    Thy grace and mercy prove,
Revived, and cheer'd, and bless'd by Thee,
    *Spirit of peace and* love!

3 'Tis Thine to soothe the sorrowing *mind,*
    With *guilt and fear* oppress'd;
'Tis Thine to bid the dying live
    And give the weary rest.

4 Subdue the power of every sin,
    Whate'er that sin may be,

That we, in singleness of heart,
   May worship only Thee.

[1 *John Needham*, 1768, *alt.*]
[2 *Charles Wesley*, 1762, *alt.*]
3-4 *Thomas Cotterill*, [1810] *alt.*

  **1.1:** *Father of lights! Thy Spirit grant* **1.3:** *truth*
  **2.1:** *I*   **2.4:** *The God of pard'ning*   **3.1:** *soul,*
  **3.2:** *Satan's yoke*
  **Ed:** Taken from Needham's hymn, "Thy influence, mighty God! is felt," Wesley's hymn,
  "Eternal Sun of righteousness," and Cotterill's
  hymn, "Eternal Spirit! Source of truth!" This
  combination of stanzas and alterations appeared as early as ca. 1840 in James Haldane
  Stewart's *Selection*, 15th ed. Sedgwick had
  attributed the entire hymn to Cotterill.

## 466   L.M.
*The Spirit entreated not to depart.*

1 STAY, Thou insulted Spirit, stay,
  Though I have done Thee such despite;
  *Cast not a* sinner quite away,
  Nor take Thine everlasting flight.

2 Though I have most unfaithful been,
  Of all who e'er Thy grace receiv'd,
  Ten thousand times Thy goodness seen,
  Ten thousand times Thy goodness griev'd,

3 Yet O! the chief of sinners spare,
  In honour of my great High Priest,
  Nor in Thy righteous anger swear
  T' exclude me from Thy people's rest.

4 *Now, Lord,* my weary soul release,
  Upraise me by Thy gracious hand;
  *Guide me* into Thy perfect peace,
  And bring me to the promis'd land.

*Charles Wesley*, 1749, *alt.*

  **1.3:** *Nor cast the*  **4.1:** *From now*  **4.3:** *And guide*
  **Ed:** The alterations at 1.3 and 4.3 appeared in

John Rippon's *Selection* (1787); 4.1 appeared as
early as 1801 in Edward Williams' *Collection*.

## 467   7.7.7.7.
*Peace prayed for.*

1 CALMER of my troubled heart,
  Bid my unbelief depart;
  Speak, and all my sorrows cease;
  Speak, and all my soul is peace.

2 Comfort me, whene'er I mourn,
  With the hope of Thy return,
  And till I thy glory see,
  *Help me to* believe in Thee.

*Charles Wesley*, 1762 [*alt.*]

  **2.4:** *Bid me still*   **Ed:** This alteration appears as
  early as 1835 in John Bulmer's *Hymns*.
  **EE:** Hymns, Set 1 (Jan./Nov.), 18th Eve,
  GERMAN HYMN / HART'S

## 468   C.M. / *Divine sealing*
*and witnessing sought.*

1 WHY should the children of a King
  Go mourning all their days?
  Great Comforter, descend and bring
  Some tokens of Thy grace.

2 Dost Thou not dwell in all the saints
  And seal the heirs of heav'n?
  When wilt Thou banish my complaints
  And show my sins forgiv'n?

3 Assure my conscience of her part
  In the Redeemer's blood,
  And bear Thy witness with my heart
  That I am born of God.

4 Thou art the earnest of His love,
  The pledge of joys to come,
  And Thy soft wings, celestial Dove,
  Will safe convey me home.

*Isaac Watts*, 1709

## 469 C.M.
*Original sin.*

1 BACKWARD with humble shame we look
   On our original;
How is our nature dash'd and broke
   In our first father's fall!

2 To all that's good averse and blind,
   But prone to all that's ill,
What dreadful darkness veils our mind!
   How obstinate our will!

3 Wild and unwholesome as the root
   Will all the branches be.
How can we hope for living fruit
   From such a deadly tree?

4 What mortal pow'r from things unclean
   Can pure productions bring?
Who can command a vital stream
   From an infected spring?

5 Yet, mighty God, Thy wondrous love
   Can make our nature clean,
While Christ and grace prevail above
   The tempter, death, and sin.

6 The second Adam shall restore
   The ruins of the first;
Hosanna to *the* sov'reign pow'r
   That new-creates our dust.

*Isaac Watts*, [1707, *alt.*]

**6.3:** *that*

## 470 C.M.
*The distemper and madness of sin.*

1 SIN, like a venomous disease,
   Infects our vital blood;
The only balm is soveriegn grace,
   And the physician, God.

2 Our beauty and our strength are fled,
   And we draw near to death,

But Christ the Lord recalls the dead
   With His almighty breath.

3 Madness by nature reigns within;
   The passions burn and rage,
Till God's own Son, with skill divine,
   The inward fire assuage.

*Isaac Watts*, 1709

## 471 C.M.
*Need of the Atonement.*

1 HOW is our nature spoil'd by sin,
   Yet nature ne'er hath found
The way to make the conscience clean
   Or heal the painful wound.

2 In vain we seek for peace with God
   By methods of our own;
Jesus, there's nothing but Thy blood
   Can bring us near the throne.

3 The threat'nings of *Thy* broken law
   Impress our souls with dread;
If God His sword of vengeance draw,
   It strikes our spirits dead.

4 But Thine illustrious sacrifice
   Hath answer'd these demands,
And peace and pardon from the skies
   Come down by Jesus' hands.

5 Here all the ancient types agree,
   The altar and the Lamb,
And prophets in their visions see
   Salvation through His name.

6 'Tis by Thy death, we live, O Lord;
   'Tis on Thy cross we rest;
Forever be Thy love ador'd,
   Thy name forever blest.

*Isaac Watts*, [1729]

**3.1:** *the*   **Ed:** This variant dates to the late 1700s.

# 472
C.M.
*Our unconverted state.*

1 GREAT King of glory and of grace,
    We own with humble shame
How vile is our degenerate race
    And our first father's name.

2 From Adam flows our tainted blood;
    The poison reigns within,
Makes us averse to all that's good
    And willing slaves to sin.

3 Daily we break Thy holy laws
    And then reject Thy grace,
Engag'd in the old serpent's cause
    Against our Maker's face.

4 We live estrang'd afar from God
    And love the distance well;
With haste we run the dang'rous road
    That leads to death and hell.

5 And can such rebels be restor'd,
    Such natures made divine!
Let sinners see Thy glory, Lord,
    And feel this pow'r of Thine.

6 We raise our Father's name on high,
    Who His own Spirit sends
To bring rebellious strangers nigh
    And turn His foes to friends.

*Isaac Watts*, 1709

# 473
L.M.
*Mourning over transgressors.*

1 ARISE, my tend'rest thoughts, arise;
To torrents melt my streaming eyes,
And Thou, my heart, with anguish feel
Those evils which thou canst not heal.

2 See human nature sunk in shame;
See scandals pour'd on Jesus' name;
The Father wounded through the Son;
The world abus'd, and souls undone.

3 See the short course of vain delight
Closing in everlasting night,
In flames that no abatement know,
Though briny tears for ever flow.

4 My God, I feel the mournful scene;
My bowels yearn o'er dying men;
And fain my pity would reclaim,
And snatch the firebrands from the flame.

5 But feeble my compassion proves,
And can but weep where most it loves;
Thy own all-saving arm employ,
And turn these drops of grief to joy.

*Philip Doddridge*, 1747 [*rev.* 1759, 1839]

> **Ed:** Based on a sermon Doddridge preached on
> 13 June 1739 at Leicester, on Psalm 119:158,
> "I beheld the transgressors, and was grieved,
> because they kept not thy law."

# 474
C.M.
*Faith in Christ for cleansing.*

1 HOW sad our state by nature is!
    Our sin, how deep it stains!
And Satan binds our captive minds
    Fast in his slavish chains.

2 But there's a voice of sovereign grace
    Sounds from the sacred Word:
"Ho, ye despairing sinners, come,
    And trust upon the Lord."

3 My soul obeys th' almighty call
    And runs to this relief;
I would believe Thy promise, Lord;
    Oh, help my unbelief.

4 To the dear fountain of Thy blood,
    Incarnate God, I fly;
Here let me wash my spotted soul
    From crimes of deepest dye.

5 Stretch out Thine arm, victorious King,
    My reigning sins subdue;
Drive the old dragon from his seat,
    With all his hellish crew.

6 A guilty, weak, and helpless worm,
    On Thy kind arms I fall;
Be Thou my strength and righteousness,
    My Jesus, and my all.

*Isaac Watts*, [1707, *rev.* 1709]

# 475
C.M.
*The whole head is sick.*

1 PHYSICIAN of my sin-sick soul,
   To Thee I bring my case;
My raging malady control,
   And heal me by Thy grace.

2 Pity the anguish I endure;
   See how I mourn and pine;
For never can I hope a cure
   From any hand but Thine.

3 I would disclose my whole complaint,
   But where shall I begin?
No words of mine can fully paint
   That worst distemper, sin.

4 It lies not in a single part,
   But through my frame is spread,
A burning fever in my heart,
   A palsy in my head.

5 Lord, I am sick; regard my cry
   And set my spirit free:
Say, canst Thou let a sinner die,
   Who longs to live to Thee?

*John Newton*, 1779

# 476
L.M.
*Jesus delivering the lost ones.*

1 BURIED in shadows of the night,
We lie, till Christ restores the light;
Wisdom descends to heal the blind
And chase the darkness of the mind.

2 Our guilty souls are drown'd in tears
Till His atoning blood appears,
Then we awake from deep distress
And sing, "The Lord our Righteousness."

3 Our very frame is mix'd with sin;
His Spirit makes our natures clean;
Such virtues from His suff'rings flow,
At once to cleanse and pardon too.

4 Poor helpless worms in Thee possess
Grace, wisdom, power, and righteousness;
Thou art our Mighty All, and we
Give our whole selves, O Lord, to Thee.

*Isaac Watts*, 1709

**MBTS:** 8 Feb. 1883 (No. 2564), EDEN

# 477
C.M.
*Distinguishing love to man.*

1 DOWN headlong from their native skies
   The rebel angels fell,
And thunderbolts of flaming wrath
   Pursued them deep to hell.

2 Down from the top of earthly bliss
   Rebellious man was hurl'd,
And Jesus stoop'd beneath the grave
   To reach a sinking world.

3 O love of infinite degree!
   Immeasurable grace!
Must heaven's eternal darling die
   To save a traitorous race?

4 Must angels sink forever down
   And burn in quenchless fire,
While God forsakes His shining throne
   To raise us wretches higher?

5 O for this love let earth and skies
   With hallelujahs ring,
And the full choir of human tongues
   All hallelujahs sing.

*Isaac Watts*, [1707]

# The Holy Scriptures

## 478 C.M.
*Most excellent.*

1 LADEN with guilt and full of fears,
   I fly to Thee, my Lord,
And not a glimpse of hope appears
   But in Thy written Word.

2 The volume of my Father's grace
   Does all my griefs assuage;
Here I behold my Saviour's face
   Almost in every page.

3 This is the field where hidden lies
   The pearl of price unknown;
That merchant is divinely wise
   Who makes the pearl his own.

4 Here consecrated water flows
   To quench my thirst of sin;
Here the fair tree of knowledge grows,
   Nor danger dwells therein.

5 This is the judge that ends the strife,
   Where wit and reason fail,
My guide to everlasting life
   Through all this gloomy vale.

6 O may Thy counsels, mighty God,
   My roving feet command,
Nor I forsake the happy road
   That leads to Thy right hand.

*Isaac Watts*, 1709

   **TD:** "Every precept is a judgment of the highest
   court upon a point of action, an infallible and
   immutable decision upon a moral or spiritual
   question. The Word of God is a code of justice
   from which there is no appeal" (Ps. 119:20;
   vol. 6, p. 51).

## 479 C.M.
*The Bible, the light of the world.*

1 A GLORY gilds the sacred page,
   Majestic, like the sun;

It gives a light to ev'ry age;
   It gives but borrows none.

2 The hand that gave it still supplies
   The gracious light and heat;
*Its* truths upon the nations rise;
   They rise but never set.

3 Let everlasting thanks be Thine!
   For such a bright display,
As makes a world of darkness shine
   With beams of heav'nly day.

4 My soul rejoices to pursue
   The steps of Him I love,
Till glory breaks upon my view
   In brighter worlds above.

*William Cowper*, 1779 [*alt.*]

   **2.3:** *His*   **Ed:** Taken from the longer hymn,
   "The Spirit breathes upon the Word." 2.3 is a
   common variant, dating to the early 1800s.

## 480 C.M.
*The guide of youth.*

1 HOW shall the young secure their hearts
   And guard their lives from sin?
Thy Word the choicest rules imparts
   To keep the conscience clean.

2 When once it enters to the mind,
   It spreads such light abroad;
The meanest souls instruction find
   And raise their thoughts to God.

3 'Tis like the sun, a heavenly light,
   That guides us all the day,
And through the dangers of the night,
   A lamp to lead our way.

4 The men that keep Thy law with care
   And meditate Thy Word
Grow wiser than their teachers are
   And better know the Lord.

5 Thy precepts make me truly wise;
   I hate the sinner's road;
   I hate mine own vain thoughts that rise,
   But love Thy law, my God.

6 Thy Word is everlasting truth;
   How pure is every page!
   That holy Book shall guide our youth
   And well support our age.

*Isaac Watts*, 1719

# 481 C.M.
*Our heritage.*

1 LORD, I have made Thy Word my choice,
   My lasting heritage;
   There shall my noblest powers rejoice,
   My warmest thoughts engage.

2 I'll read the histories of Thy love
   And keep Thy laws in sight,
   While through the promises I rove
   With ever fresh delight.

3 'Tis a broad land of wealth unknown,
   Where springs of life arise,
   Seeds of immortal bliss are sown,
   And hidden glories lie.

4 The best relief that mourners have,
   It makes our sorrows blest;
   Our fairest hope beyond the grave
   And our eternal rest.

*Isaac Watts*, 1719

# 482 C.M.
*Heavenly teaching.*

1 FATHER of mercies, in Thy Word
   What endless glory shines!
   Forever be Thy name ador'd
   For these celestial lines.

2 Here may the wretched sons of want
   Exhaustless riches find;
   Riches, above what earth can grant
   and lasting as the mind.

3 Here the fair tree of knowledge grows
   And yields a free repast;
   Sublimer sweets than nature knows
   Invite the longing taste.

4 Here the Redeemer's welcome voice
   Spreads heav'nly peace around,
   And life, and everlasting joys,
   Attend the blissful sound.

5 O may these heav'nly pages be
   My ever dear delight,
   And still new beauties may I see,
   And still increasing light.

6 Divine Instructor, gracious Lord,
   Be Thou forever near;
   Teach me to love Thy sacred Word
   And view my Saviour there.

*Anne Steele*, 1760

# The Gospel

## GOSPEL EXCELLENCE.

**483** C.M.
*The different success of the gospel.*

1 CHRIST and His cross is all our theme;
  The mysteries that we speak
Are scandal in the Jews' esteem,
  And folly to the Greek.

2 But soul enlightened from above
  With joy receive the Word;
They see what wisdom, power, and love
  Shine in their dying Lord.

3 The vital savour of His name
  Restores their fainting breath,
But unbelief perverts the same
  To guilt, despair, and death.

4 Till God diffuse His graces down
  Like showers of heavenly rain,
In vain Apollos sows the ground,
  And Paul may plant in vain.

*Isaac Watts*, 1709

**484** L.M.
*Power of the gospel.*

1 THIS is the word of truth and love,
Sent to the nations from above;
Jehovah here resolves to show
What His almighty grace can do.

2 This remedy did wisdom find
To heal diseases of the mind;
This sovereign balm, whose virtues can
Restore the ruin'd creature, man.

3 The gospel bids the dead revive;
Sinners obey the voice and live;

Dry bones are rais'd and cloth'd afresh,
And hearts of stone are turn'd to flesh.

4 Lions and beasts of savage name
Put on the nature of the Lamb,
While the *wide* world esteem it strange,
Gaze and admire and hate the change.

5 May but this grace my soul renew;
Let sinners gaze and hate me too;
The word that saves me does engage
A sure defence from all their rage.

*Isaac Watts*, 1709, *alt.*

> **4.3:** *wild* **Ed:** This alteration appeared in post-
> humous editions of Watts, starting in 1751.

**485** S.M.
*Blessedness of gospel times.*

1 HOW beauteous are their feet
  Who stand on Zion's hill,
Who bring salvation on their tongues
  And words of peace reveal!

2 How charming is their voice!
  How sweet the tidings are!
"Zion, behold thy Saviour King;
  He reigns and triumphs here."

3 How happy are our ears
  That hear this joyful sound,
Which kings and prophets waited for,
  And sought but never found!

4 How blessèd are our eyes
  That see this heavenly light;
Prophets and kings desir'd it long,
  But died without the sight!

5 The watchmen join their voice
  And tuneful notes employ;
Jerusalem breaks forth in songs,
  And deserts learn the joy.

6   The Lord makes bare His arm
     Through all the earth abroad;
     Let ev'ry nation now behold
     Their Saviour and their God.

*Isaac Watts*, [1707]

**FPN:** 18 Aug. 1889 (No. 2327), HUDDERSFIELD

# 486 L.M.
*Excellence of the Gospel.*

1  LET everlasting glories crown
     Thy head, my Saviour and my Lord;
     Thy hands have brought salvation down
     And writ the blessings in Thy Word.

2  What if we trace the globe around
     And search from Britain to Japan,
     There shall be no religion found
     So just to God, so safe for man.

3  In vain the trembling conscience seeks
     Some solid ground to rest upon;
     With long despair the spirit breaks
     Till we apply to Christ alone.

4  How well Thy blessèd truths agree!
     How wise and holy Thy commands!
     Thy promises, how firm they be!
     How firm our hope and comfort stands!

5  Should all the forms that men devise
     Assault my faith with treacherous art,
     I'd call them vanity and lies,
     And bind the gospel to my heart.

*Isaac Watts*, 1709

# GOSPEL INVITATIONS.

# 487 6.6.6.6.8.8.
*The Jubilee Trumpet.*

1  BLOW ye the trumpet, blow
     The gladly solemn sound;
     Let all the nations know
     To earth's remotest bound;

     The year of jubilee is come;
     Return, ye ransom'd sinners, home!

2  Extol the Lamb of God,
     The *sin*-atoning Lamb;
     Redemption in His blood
     Throughout the world proclaim;
     The year of jubilee is come;
     Return, ye ransom'd sinners, home!

3  Ye who have sold for nought
     The heritage above,
     *Receive* it back unbought,
     The gift of Jesu's love:
     The year of jubilee is come;
     Return, ye ransom'd sinners, home.

4  Ye slaves of sin and hell,
     Your liberty receive,
     And safe in Jesus dwell,
     And blest in Jesus live:
     The year of jubilee is come;
     Return, ye ransom'd sinners, home.

5  Ye bankrupt debtors know
     The sovereign grace of heaven;
     Though sums immense ye owe,
     A free discharge is given:
     The year of jubilee is come;
     Return, ye ransomed sinners, home.

6  The gospel trumpet hear,
     The news of heavenly grace;
     And sav'd from earth appear
     Before your Saviour's face:
     The year of jubilee is come;
     Return, ye ransomed sinners, home.

7  Jesus, our great High Priest,
     Hath full atonement made;
     Ye weary spirits, rest;
     Ye mournful souls, be glad!
     The year of jubilee is come;
     Return, ye ransom'd sinners, home.

1-4,6 *Charles Wesley*, 1750, *alt.*
[5 *John Rippon*, ca. 1805]
[7 *Augustus Toplady*, 1776]

    **2.2:** *all*   **3.3:** *Shall have*

**Ed:** The alteration at 2.2 is by Toplady and reflects the dispute between him and the Wesleys regarding the extent of the atonement. 3.3 appeared in an edition of the Wesleys' *Collection* in 1831 and was repeated thereafter.

## 488 C.M.
*Mercy's invitation.*

1 LET ev'ry mortal ear attend
　　And ev'ry heart rejoice;
The trumpet of the gospel sound
　　With an inviting voice.

2 Ho, all ye hungry, starving souls
　　That feed upon the wind
And vainly strive with earthly toys
　　To fill an empty mind,

3 Eternal Wisdom has prepared
　　A soul-reviving-feast,
And bids your longing appetites
　　The rich provision taste.

4 Ho, ye that pant for living streams,
　　And pine away, and die,
Here you may quench your raging thirst
　　With springs that never dry.

5 Rivers of love and mercy here
　　In a rich ocean join;
Salvation in abundance flows
　　Like floods of milk and wine.

6 Come naked, and adorn your souls
　　In robes prepar'd by God,
Wrought by the labours of His Son
　　And dyed in His own blood.

7 *Great* God, the treasures of Thy love
　　Are everlasting mines,
Deep as our helpless miseries are,
　　And boundless as our sins.

8 The happy gates of gospel grace
　　Stand open night and day;
Lord, we are come to seek supplies
　　And drive our wants away.

*Isaac Watts,* [1707, *rev.* 1709]

**7.1:** *Dear* **Ed:** A common variant, as early as 1822 in *A Selection of Psalms and Hymns for Public Worship.*

## 489 C.M.
*Promises of grace.*

1 IN vain we lavish out our lives
　　To gather empty wind;
The choicest blessings earth can yield
　　Will starve a hungry mind.

2 Come, and the Lord shall feed our souls
　　With more substantial meat,
With such as saints in glory love,
　　With such as angels eat.

3 Come, and He'll cleanse our spotted souls
　　And wash away our stains
In the dear fountain that His Son
　　Pour'd from His dying veins.

4 Our guilt shall vanish all away
　　Though black as hell before;
Our sins shall sink beneath the sea
　　And shall be found no more.

5 And lest pollution should o'erspread
　　Our inward pow'rs again,
His Spirit shall bedew our souls
　　Like purifying rain.

6 Our heart, that flinty, stubborn thing
　　That terrors cannot move,
That fears no threatenings of His wrath,
　　Shall be dissolv'd by love:

7 Or He can take the flint away
　　That would not be refin'd,
And from the treasures of His grace
　　Bestow a softer mind.

8 There shall His sacred Spirit dwell,
　　And deep engrave His law;
And every motion of our souls
　　To swift obedience draw.

9 Thus will He pour salvation down,
　　And we shall render praise,

THE GOSPEL: ITS INVITATIONS

We the dear people of His love,
    And He our God of grace.

*Isaac Watts*, [1707, *rev.* 1709]

# 490   6.6.6.6.8.8.
*"Yet there is room."*

1    YE dying sons of men,
    Immerg'd in sin and woe,
    The gospel's voice attend,
    While Jesus sends to you;
    Ye perishing and guilty, come;
    In Jesu's arms there yet is room.

2    No longer now delay,
    Nor vain excuses frame;
    He bids you come today,
    Though poor, and blind, and lame.
    All things are ready; sinners come,
    For ev'ry trembling soul there's room.

3    Believe the heav'nly word
    His messengers proclaim;
    He is a gracious Lord,
    And faithful is His name;
    Backsliding souls, return and come;
    Cast off despair; there yet is room.

4    Compell'd by bleeding love,
    Ye wand'ring sheep, draw near;
    Christ calls you from above;
    His charming accents hear!
    Let whosoever will, now come;
    In mercy's breast there still is room.

*James Boden*, 1777 [*rev.* 1801]

# 491   C.M.
*"I am Alpha and Omega."*

1  O WHAT amazing words of grace
    Are in the gospel found!
  Suited to every sinner's case
    Who knows the joyful sound.

2  Here Jesus calls, and He's a true,
    A kind, a faithful friend;
  He's Alpha and Omega too,
    Beginning and the end.

3  Come, then, with all your wants
      and wounds;
    Your every burden bring;
  Here love, eternal love, abounds—
    A deep celestial spring.

4  "Whoever *wills*,"—O gracious word!—
    "Shall of this stream partake";
  Come, thirsty souls, and bless the Lord,
    And drink for Jesus' sake.

5  This spring with living waters flows,
    And living joy imparts;
  Come, thirsty souls, your wants disclose,
    And drink with thankful hearts.

6  To sinners poor, like me and you,
    He saith He'll freely give;
  Come, thirsty souls, and prove it true;
    Drink and forever live.

*Samuel Medley*, 1789 [*alt. C.H.S.*]

> **4.1:** *thirsts* **Ed:** Both "thirsts" and "wills" reflect
> the text of Rev. 22:17, but Spurgeon's change
> imitates the final phrase, "whosoever will, let
> him take the water of life freely" (KJV).

# 492   8.7.8.7.4.7.
*Come and welcome.*

1  COME, ye sinners, poor and wretched,
    Weak and wounded, sick and sore;
  Jesus ready stands to save you,
    Full of pity join'd with pow'r.
      He is able,
    He is willing: doubt no more.

2  *Come*, ye needy; come, and welcome;
    God's free bounty glorify;
  True belief and true repentance,
    Ev'ry grace that brings us nigh,
      Without money,
    Come to Jesus Christ and buy.

3  Let not conscience make you linger,
    Nor of fitness fondly dream;
  All the fitness He requireth,
    Is to feel your need of Him:
      This He gives you;
    'Tis the Spirit's rising beam.

4 Come, ye weary, heavy laden,
    Bruis'd and mangled by the fall;
  If you tarry till you're better,
    You will never come at all.
      Not the righteous,
    Sinners Jesus came to call.

5 View Him *prostrate* in the garden;
    *On the ground your Maker* lies!
  On the bloody tree behold Him;
    Hear Him cry before He dies,
      "It is finish'd!"
    Sinner, will not this suffice?

6 Lo! th' incarnate God, ascended,
    Pleads the merit of His blood:
  Venture on Him, venture wholly,
    Let no other trust intrude;
      None but Jesus
    Can do helpless sinners good.

7 Saints and angels join'd in concert
    Sing the praises of the Lamb;
  While the blissful seats of heaven
    Sweetly echo with His name.
      Hallelujah!
    Sinners here may sing the same.

*Joseph Hart*, 1759
[*alt. Augustus Toplady*, 1776]

**2.1:** *Ho!* **5.1:** *grov'ling*
**5.2:** *Lo! your Maker prostrate*
**MM:** "Believe on Jesus, thou outcast of the
    world's society! Jesus calls thee, and such as
    thou art. 'Not the righteous, not the righteous;
    Sinners Jesus came to call'" (June 6).

# 493   8.7.8.7.4.7.
*Come to Jesus.*

1 COME, ye souls, by sin afflicted,
    Bow'd with fruitless sorrow down;
  By the broken law convicted,
    Through the cross behold the crown!
      Look to Jesus—
    Mercy flows through Him alone.

2 Take His easy yoke and wear it;
    Love will make obedience sweet;

Christ will give you strength to bear it,
    While His wisdom guides your feet
      Safe to glory—
    Where His ransom'd captives meet.

3 Blessèd are the eyes that see Him;
    Blest the ears that hear His voice;
  Blessèd are the souls that trust Him
    And in Him alone rejoice;
      His commandments
    Then become their happy choice.

*Joseph Swain*, 1792

  **MM:** Hymns, 26th Lord's Day,
    GREENVILLE / NETTLETON

# 494   C.M.
*"Now is the accepted time."*

1 COME, guilty souls, and flee away
    Like doves to Jesu's wounds;
  This is the welcome gospel day
    Wherein free grace abounds.

2 God loved the church and gave His Son
    To drink the cup of wrath;
  And Jesus says He'll cast out none
    That come to Him by faith.

*Joseph Humphreys*, 1743

# 495   L.M.
*Jesus invites.*

1 "COME hither, all ye weary souls;
    Ye heavy laden sinners, come;
  I'll give you rest from all your toils
    And raise you to my heav'nly home.

2 "They shall find rest that learn of me;
    I'm of a meek and lowly mind;
  But passion rages like a sea,
    And pride is restless as the wind.

3 "Blest is the man whose shoulders take
    My yoke and bear it with delight;
  My yoke is easy to his neck;
    My grace shall make the burden light."

4 Jesus, we come at Thy command;
With faith, and hope, and humble zeal,
Resign our spirits to Thy hand
To mould and guide us at Thy will.

*Isaac Watts*, 1709

# 496 C.M.
*The Saviour calls.*

1 THE Saviour calls—let ev'ry ear
Attend the heav'nly sound;
Ye doubting souls, dismiss your fear;
Hope smiles reviving round.

2 For ev'ry thirsty, longing heart,
Here streams of bounty flow,
And life and health and bliss impart
To banish mortal woe.

3 Ye sinners, come, 'tis mercy's voice,
The gracious call obey;
Mercy invites to heav'nly joys—
And can you yet delay?

4 Dear Saviour, draw reluctant hearts,
To Thee let sinners fly,
And take the bliss Thy love imparts,
And drink, and never die.

*Anne Steele*, 1760

# 497 8.7.8.7.4.7.
*"Come unto me."*

1 HARK! the voice of Jesus calling—
"Come, thou laden, come to me;
I have rest and peace to offer,
Rest, poor labouring one, for thee;
Take salvation;
Take it now, and happy be."

2 Yes, though high in heavenly glory,
Still the Saviour calls to thee;
Faith can hear His gracious accents—
"Come, thou laden, come to me;
Take salvation;
Take it now, and happy be."

3 Soon that voice will cease its calling;
Now it speaks, and speaks to thee;

Sinner, heed the gracious message—
To the blood for refuge flee;
Take salvation;
Take it now, and happy be.

4 Life is found alone in Jesus;
Only there 'tis offered thee—
Offered without price or money;
'Tis the gift of God, sent free;
Take salvation;
Take it now, and happy be.

*Albert Midlane*, [1861, *rev.* 1865]

# 498 7.6.7.6. Double
*Seeking souls encouraged.*

1 SINNER, hear the Saviour's call,
He now is passing by;
He has seen thy grievous thrall
And heard thy mournful cry.
He has pardons to impart
*And grace to save from fears*;
See the love that fills his heart,
And wipe away thy tears.

2 Why art thou afraid to come
And tell Him all thy case?
He will not pronounce thy doom,
Nor frown thee from His face.
Wilt thou fear Immanuel?
*Or* dread the Lamb of God,
Who, to save thy soul from hell,
Has shed His precious blood?

3 Raise thy downcast eyes and see
What throngs His throne surround!
These, though sinners once like thee,
Have full salvation found.
Yield not then to unbelief!
*He* says, "there yet is room";
Though of sinners thou art chief,
Since Jesus calls thee, come.

*John Newton*, 1779
[*alt.* John Rippon's *Selection*, 1844]

**1.6:** *Grace to save thee from thy fears*
**2.6:** *Wilt thou*  **3.6:** *While He*
**Ed:** The original meter was 7.6.7.6.7.7.7.6.

# 499
7.7.7.7.
*"Seek, and ye shall find."*

1 COME, poor sinner, come and see,
All thy strength is found in Me;
I am waiting to be kind,
To relieve thy troubled mind.

2 Dost thou feel thy sins a pain?
Look to Me and ease obtain;
All my fullness thou may'st share
And be always welcome there.

3 Boldly come; why dost thou fear?
I possess a gracious ear;
I will never tell thee nay,
While thou hast a heart to pray.

4 Try the freeness of My grace;
Sure, 'twill suit thy trying case;
Mourning souls *will* ne'er complain,
Having sought My face in vain.

5 Knock, and cast all doubt behind;
Seek, and thou shalt surely find;
Ask, and I will give thee peace,
And thy confidence increase.

6 Will not this encourage thee,
Vile and poor, to come to Me?
Sure, thou canst not doubt My will?
Come and welcome, sinner, still.

[William Parkinson's *Selection*, 1809]

> **4.3:** *shall*
> **Ed:** Sedgwick credited this text to "Hewett,
> 1850," an allusion to Basil Manly Jr.'s *Baptist
> Psalmody*, No. 344. Parkinson credited the
> hymn to an unknown *New Selection*.

# 500
C.M.
*The gospel feast.*

1 COME, sinner, to the gospel feast;
O come without delay;
For there is room in Jesus' breast
For all who will obey.

2 There's room in God's eternal love
To save thy precious soul,

Room in the Spirit's grace above
To heal and make thee whole.

3 There's room within the church, redeem'd
With blood of Christ divine,
Room in the white-robed throng convened
For that dear soul of thine.

4 There's room in heaven among the choir,
And harps and crowns of gold,
And glorious palms of victory there,
And joys that ne'er were told.

5 There's room around thy Father's board
For thee and thousands more;
O come and welcome to the Lord;
Yea, come this very hour.

Stow & Smith, *The Psalmist*, 1843

# 501
C.M.
*"Come to the ark."*

1 COME to the ark! Come to the ark!
To Jesus come away;
The pestilence walks forth by night,
The arrow flies by day.

2 Come to the ark! the waters rise,
The seas their billows rear;
While darkness gathers o'er the skies,
*Behold a refuge near.*

3 Come to the ark—all—all that weep
Beneath the sense of sin;
Without, "deep calleth unto deep,"
But *all* is peace within.

4 Come to the ark! ere yet the flood
Your lingering steps oppose;
*Come, for the door which* open stood
Is now about to close.

[*The Child's Own Hymn Book*, 1836]
[alt. *The Village Psalmist*, 1844]

> **2.4:** *There yet is safety there.*   **3.4:** *there*
> **4.3:** *The door—which long hath*
> **Ed:** Sedgwick credited the hymn to John Cole-
> man's *Collection* (1846); it had also appeared
> in H.W. Beecher's *Plymouth Collection* (1855).

# 502
8.7.8.7.
*Come now.*

1 COME, poor *sinners*, come to Jesus,
　　Weary, heavy laden, weak;
　None but Jesus Christ can ease us;
　　Come ye all, His mercy seek.

2 "Come," it is His invitation;
　　"Come to Me," the Saviour says;
　Why, O why such hesitation,
　　Gloomy doubts, and base delays?

3 Do *you fear* your own unfitness,
　　Burdened as you are with sin?
　'Tis the Holy Spirit's witness;
　　Christ invites you—enter in.

4 Do your sins and your distresses
　　*'Gainst this sacred record plead?*
　Know that Christ most kindly blesses
　　Those who feel the most their need.

5 Hear His words, so true and cheering,
　　Fitted just for the distress'd;
　Dwell upon the sound endearing:
　　"Mourners, I will give you rest."

6 Stay not pond'ring on your sorrow;
　　Turn from your own self away;
　Do not linger till tomorrow;
　　Come to Christ without delay.

*William F. Lloyd*, [1826, *rev.* 1851, *alt.*]

　**1.1:** *sinner* (1826/1851)
　**3.1:** *ye fear* (1826); *you feel* (1851)
　**4.2:** *Urge that you will not succeed?* (1851)
　**Ed:** The minor shift from singular to plural in 1.1
　　predates *OOHB* but is rare.

# 503
C.M. Double
*All ye who seek a sure relief.*

1 ALL ye who seek a *sure relief*
　　In trouble or distress,
　Whatever sorrow vex the mind,
　　Or guilt the soul oppress,
　Jesus, who gave Himself for *us*
　　Upon the cross to die,
　*Unfolds* to *us* His sacred heart—

Oh to that heart draw nigh!

2 Ye hear how kindly He invites,
　　Ye hear His words so blest:
　"All ye that labour, come to Me,
　　And I will give you rest."
　O *Jesu, joy* of saints on high!
　　Thou hope of sinners here!
　Attracted by these loving words,
　　To Thee I lift my prayer.

3 Wash Thou my wounds in that dear blood
　　Which forth from Thee did flow;
　New grace, new hope inspire; a new
　　And better life bestow.
　Praise Him, who with the Father sits
　　Enthroned upon the skies,
　Whose blood redeems our souls from guilt,
　　Whose Spirit sanctifies.

[*Breviarium Romanum*, 1786]
　*tr. Edward Caswall*, 1849, *alt.*

　**1.1:** *certain cure*　**1.5:** *you*
　**1.7:** *Opens / you*　**2.5:** *Heart! thou*
　**FPN:** 18 Aug. 1889 (No. 2327), BELMONT
　**Ed:** Translated from the 18th century Latin,
　　"Quicunque certum quaeritis," except 3:5-8,
　　which are from "Hail wounds! which through
　　eternal years," translated by Caswall from
　　"Salvete Christi vulnera." See also No. 276.
　　The alteration at 2.5 appeared in the *Hymnal
　　for the Scottish Church* (1857), otherwise
　　this combination of texts and alterations was
　　printed in *OOHB* and *Hymns for the Year*; the
　　former likely drew from the latter.

# 504
S.M.
*"All things are ready."*

1 "ALL things are ready," come,
　　Come to the supper spread;
　Come rich and poor, come old and young,
　　Come and be richly fed.

2 "All things are ready," come,
　　The invitation's given
　Through Him who now in glory sits
　　At God's right hand in heaven.

3 "All things are ready," come,
    The door is open wide;
O feast upon the love of God,
    For Christ, His Son, has died.

4 "All things are ready," come,
    All hindrance is removed,
And God, in Christ, His precious love,
    To fallen man has proved.

5 "All things are ready," come,
    Tomorrow may not be;
O sinner, come, the Saviour waits
    This hour to welcome thee!

*Albert Midlane*, [1861]

# 505 L.M.
*None that come cast out.*

1 HARK! 'tis the Saviour's voice I hear;
Come, trembling soul, dispel thy fear;
He saith, and who His Word can doubt?
He will in no wise cast you out!

2 Doth Satan fill you with dismay
And tell you Christ will cast away?
It is a truth, why should you doubt?
He will in no wise cast you out!

3 Approach your God, make no delay;
He waits to welcome you today;
His mercy try, nor longer doubt;
He will in no wise cast you out!

4 Lord, at Thy call, behold, I come,
A guilty soul, lost and undone;
On Thy rich blood I now rely;
O pass my vile transgressions by.

[— *Smith*, 1806]

> **Ed:** Sedgwick attributed the hymn to Samuel F.
> Smith, 1850, but the hymn is much older and
> belongs to another unknown Smith.

# 506 8.7.8.7. Double
*Look unto Him.*

1 SEE the blessèd Saviour dying
    On the cross for ruin'd man;

There the willing, spotless victim,
    Working out redemption's plan;
Listen to His loving accents:
    "Father, O forgive," He cries.
Hark, again He speaks, "'Tis finish'd,"
    Ere He bows His head and dies.

2 With this cruel death before Him,
    Every insult, pang foreseen,
Nought could move Him from His purpose,
    No dismay could intervene;
Yea, and through the contradiction,
    Nothing could His calmness move;
O the wondrous depths eternal
    Of His own almighty love,

3 Love which made Him "Prince of Glory,"
    Come to die, the "Sinner's Friend,"
Love beyond the reach of mortals'
    Deepest thoughts to comprehend.
Sinner, make this love thy portion;
    Slight not love so vast and free;
Still unblest, if unforgiven,
    Come, the Saviour calleth thee.

*Albert Midlane*, 1865

# 507 7.7.7.7.
*Come and see.*

1 SINNERS! come, the Saviour see;
Hands, feet, side, and temples view;
See Him bleeding on the tree;
See His heart on fire for you!

2 View awhile, then haste away,
Find a thousand more, and say:
Come, ye sinners! come with me;
View Him bleeding on the tree.

3 Who would still such mercy grieve?
Sinners! hear instruction mild,
Doubt no more, but now believe;
Each become a simple child.

4 Artful doubts and reasonings be
Nail'd with Jesus to the tree;
*Mourning souls, who* simple are,
Surely shall the blessing share.

*Nicolaus Ludwig von Zinzendorf*, 1739
*tr. Charles Kinchin*, 1742
[*alt. A Collection of Hymns … of the
United Brethren*, 1789]

**4.3:** *Souls who truly*
**Ed:** From the German, "Kommt, Sünder, und
blicket dem ewigen Sohne." Said to be "written
in Aug. 1736 at Bernau," according to Julian's
*Dictionary of Hymnology*, p. 1303. Sedgwick
initially attr. the German to Frederick Neisser;
this was corrected in the 6th ed. (1873).

## 508 7.7.7.7.7.7.
*Come and welcome.*

1 FROM the cross uplifted high,
Where the Saviour deigns to die,
What melodious sounds I hear,
Bursting on my ravish'd ear!
Love's redeeming work is done;
Come and welcome, sinner, come.

2 Sprinkled now with blood the throne,
Why beneath thy burdens groan?
On My piercèd body laid,
Justice owns the ransom paid.
Bow the knee and kiss the Son;
Come and welcome, sinner, come.

3 Spread for thee the festal board;
See with richest dainties stored;
To thy Father's bosom press'd,
Yet again a child confess'd,
Never from His house to roam,
Come and welcome, sinner, come.

4 Soon the days of life shall end;
Lo, I come, your Saviour, Friend,
Safe your spirit to convey
To the realms of endless day.
Up to My eternal home,
Come and welcome, sinner, come.

*Thomas Haweis*, 1792

## 509 8.7.8.7.4.7.
*Come and welcome.*

1 COME, and welcome to the Saviour;
He in mercy bids thee come;

Come, be happy in His favour;
Longer from Him do not roam;
Come, and welcome,
Come to Jesus, sinner, come!

2 Come, and welcome; start for glory,
Leave the wretched world behind;
Christ will spread His banner o'er thee;
Thou in Him a friend shalt find;
Come, and welcome,
To a Saviour good and kind.

3 Come, and welcome; do not linger;
Make thy happy choice today;
True thou art a wretched sinner,
But He'll wash thy sins away;
Come, and welcome;
Time admits of no delay.

*Albert Midlane*, 1865

## 510 7.7.7.7.7.7.
*Take the peace the gospel brings.*

1 YE that in His courts are found,
List'ning to the joyful sound,
Lost and helpless as ye are,
Sons of sorrow, sin, and care,
Glorify the King of Kings;
Take the peace the gospel brings.

2 Turn to Christ your longing eyes;
View His bloody sacrifice;
See in Him your sins forgiv'n,
Pardon, holiness, and heav'n;
Glorify the King of Kings;
Take the peace the gospel brings.

*Rowland Hill*, [1765]

## 511 7.7.7.7.7.7.
*Wanderers invited.*

1 WEARY souls, who wander wide
From the central point of bliss,
Turn to Jesus crucified,
Fly to those dear wounds of His,
Sink into the purple flood,
Rise into the life of God!

2 Find in Christ the way of peace,
   Peace unspeakable, unknown;
By His pain He gives you ease,
   Life by His expiring groan;
Rise, exalted by His fall;
Find in Christ your all-in-all.

3 O believe the record true,
   God to you His Son hath giv'n!
Ye may now be happy too,
   Find on earth the life of heav'n;
Live the life of heav'n above,
All the life of glorious love.

*Charles Wesley*, 1747 [*rev.* 1780]

# 512 8.7.8.7. Double
*Mercy calls.*

1 'TIS the voice of mercy calls thee,
   Wanderer from the Father's home;
'Tis not God, in voice of thunder,
   'Tis a Father calls, thee, "Come";
Yea, His loving heart still waiteth,
   And canst thou refuse Him still?
Nay, with contrite heart relenting,
   Say, "Arise and come, I will."

2 Come, in all thy filthy garments,
   Tarry not to cleanse or mend;
Come, in all thy destitution,
   As thou art, and He'll befriend.
By the tempter's vain allurements,
   Be no longer thou beguiled;
God the Father waits to own thee
   As His dear adopted child.

*Albert Midlane*, 1865

# 513 8.7.8.7.4.7.
*Grace abounding.*

1 SCRIPTURE says, "Where sin abounded,
   There did grace much more abound."
Thus has Satan been confounded,
   And his own discomfit found.
      Christ has triumphed!
Spread the glorious news around.

2 Sin is strong, but grace is stronger,
   Christ than Satan more supreme;
Yield, oh yield to sin no longer;
   Turn to Jesus, yield to Him—
      He has triumphed!
Sinners, henceforth Him esteem.

*Albert Midlane*, 1865

# 514 C.M.
*The successful resolve.*

1 COME, humble sinner, in whose breast
   A thousand thoughts revolve;
Come, with your guilt and fear oppress'd,
   And make this last resolve:

2 "I'll go to Jesus, though my sin
   Hath like a mountain rose;
I know His courts, I'll enter in,
   Whatever may oppose.

3 "Prostrate I'll lie before His throne,
   And there my guilt confess;
I'll tell Him I'm a wretch undone,
   Without His sovereign grace.

4 "I'll to the gracious King approach,
   Whose sceptre pardon gives;
Perhaps He may command my touch,
   And then the suppliant lives.

5 "Perhaps He will admit my plea,
   Perhaps will hear my prayer,
But if I perish, I will pray
   And perish only there.

6 "I can but perish if I go;
   I am resolved to try;
For if I stay away, I know
   I must forever die.

7 "But if I die with mercy sought,
   When I the King have tried,
This were to die (delightful thought!)
   As sinner never died."

*Edmund Jones*, 1787 [*rev.*]

**Ed:** St. 7 was added between the 10th and 15th
eds. of Rippon's *Selection* (ca. 1800–1805).

# GOSPEL EXPOSTULATIONS.

## 515 L.M.
*The stranger at the door.*

1 BEHOLD! a stranger's at the door!
He gently knocks, has knock'd before,
Has waited long, is waiting still;
You treat no other friend so ill.

2 But will He prove a friend indeed?
He will; the very friend you need:
The Man of Nazareth, 'tis He!
With garments dyed at Calvary.

3 O lovely attitude! He stands
With melting heart and laden hands;
O matchless kindness! and He shows
This matchless kindness to His foes.

4 Rise, touch'd with gratitude divine,
Turn out His enemy and thine,
That hateful, hell-born monster, sin,
And let the heavenly stranger in.

5 Admit Him, ere His anger burn,
His feet *depart, and* ne'er return.
Admit Him, or the hour's at hand
When at His door denied you'll stand.

6 Admit Him, for the human breast
Ne'er entertain'd so kind a guest;
Admit Him, *for* you can't expel;
Where'er He comes, He comes to dwell.

7 Yet know (nor of the terms complain)
*Where* Jesus comes, He comes to reign,
To reign, and with no partial sway;
Thoughts must be slain that disobey.

8 Sov'reign of souls! Thou Prince of Peace!
O may Thy gentle reign increase!
Throw wide the door, each willing mind,
And be His empire all mankind!

*Joseph Grigg,* 1765

**5.2:** *departed,* **6.3:** *and* **7.2:** *If*
**Ed:** The alteration at 7.2 appeared in *The Poetical
Monitor* (1792) and was reprinted in successive
editions into the 1830s. 5.2 and 6.3 appeared in
Roundell Palmer's *Book of Praise* (1863).
**EE:** "When our renewed heart struggles against
our natural heaviness, we should be grateful to
sovereign grace for keeping a little vitality within the body of this death. Jesus will hear our
hearts, will help our hearts, will visit our hearts;
for the voice of the wakeful heart is really the
voice of our Beloved saying, 'Open to me.' Holy
zeal will surely unbar the door" (Sept. 24).

## 516 S.M.
*Despising the riches of goodness.*

1 AND canst thou, sinner, slight
The call of love divine?
Shall God with tenderness invite
And gain no thought of thine?

2 Wilt thou not cease to grieve
The Spirit from thy breast,
Till He thy wretched soul shall leave
With all thy sins oppress'd?

3 Today a pard'ning God
Will hear the suppliant pray;
Today a Saviour's cleansing blood
Will wash thy guilt away.

4 But grace so dearly bought,
If yet thou wilt despise,
Thy fearful doom with vengeance fraught
Will fill thee with surprise.

*Ann Beadley Hyde,* [1824]

## 517 7.7.7.7.7.7.
*Holy meltings.*

1 HEART of stone, relent, relent,
Break, by Jesu's cross subdued;
See His body, mangled, rent,
Cover'd with a gore of blood!
Sinful soul, what hast thou done?
*Crucified* God's *only* Son!

2 Yes, *thy* sins have done the deed,
*Driv'n* the nails that fix'd Him *there,*
Crown'd with thorns His sacred head,
*Plung'd into His side the* spear,

Made His soul a sacrifice,
*While for* sinful *man* He dies.

3 *Can I put my Lord to pain?*
Still to death *my Lord pursue?*
Open *all* His wounds again?
*And the shameful cross renew?*
No, with all *my* sins *I'll* part;
*Break, O break my bleeding* heart!

*Charles Wesley, 1745, alt.*

**1.6:** *Murder'd / eternal* **2.1:** *our*
**2.2:** *Drove / here*
**2.4:** *Pierc'd Him with the soldier's*
**2.6:** *For a / world*
**3.1:** *Shall we let Him die in vain?*
**3.2:** *pursue our God?* **3.3:** *tear*
**3.4:** *Trample on his precious blood?*
**3.5:** *our / we* **3.6:** *Saviour, take my broken*
**Ed:** These alterations are by Thomas Hastings,
from *Spiritual Songs for Social Worship*
(1831), except Hastings' rendering of 1.6 was
"Crucified th'incarnate Son!" and 3.1 was "Wilt
thou let Him bleed in vain?" The subsequent
change to 3.1 is by Spurgeon, while 1.6 appeared as early as John Henshaw's *Selection
of Hymns*, 5th ed. (1832).

# 518 8.7.8.7.4.7.
*Hear and live.*

1 SINNERS, will you scorn the message
Sent in mercy from above?
Ev'ry sentence, O how tender!
Ev'ry line is full of love!
Listen to it;
Every line is full of love!

2 Hear the heralds of the gospel
News from Zion's King proclaim:
*"Pardon to each rebel sinner;*
Free forgiveness in His name."
How important!
"Free forgiveness in His name."

3 Tempted souls, they bring you succour;
Fearful hearts, they quell your fears,
And with news of consolation,
Chase away the falling tears.

Tender heralds!
Chase away the falling tears.

4 Who hath our report believèd?
Who receiv'd the joyful word?
Who embrac'd the news of pardon
*Spoken* to you by the Lord?
Can you slight it,
*Spoken* to you by the Lord?

5 O ye angels! hov'ring round us,
Waiting spirits, speed your way;
*Haste ye* to the court of heaven,
Tidings bear without delay:
"Rebel sinners,
Glad the message will obey."

[Richard Pearsall Allen's *Hymns*], 1801, *alt.*

**2.3:** *To each rebel sinner—"Pardon*
**4.4:** *Offer'd* **4.6:** *Offer'd* **5.3:** *Hasten*
**Ed:** "What authority Sedgwick had for this
ascription [to Jonathan Allen] we cannot
determine. It is through him that it has gained
currency." —William T. Brooke in Julian's
*Dictionary of Hymnology*, p. 50.
The name "Allen" appeared in many early
collections because the hymn is from Richard
Allen's *Hymns*, where it was given without
attribution. The alterations at 2.3 and 5.5
appeared in Lowell Mason's *Church Psalmody*
(1831); 4.4 and 4.6 are apparently by Spurgeon.

# 519 8.7.8.7.4.7.
*The gospel message.*

1 SINNERS, you are now addressèd
In the name of Christ our Lord;
He hath sent a message to you;
Pay attention to His Word;
He hath sent it;
Pay attention to His Word.

2 Think what you have all been doing;
Think what rebels you have been;
You have spent your lives in nothing
But in adding sin to sin:
All your actions—
One continued scene of sin.

3 Yet your long-abusèd Sovereign
    Sends to you a message mild,
Loth to execute His vengeance,
    Prays you to be reconcil'd:
      Hear Him woo you—
Sinners now be reconcil'd.

4 Pardon now is freely publish'd
    Through the Mediator's blood,
Who hath died to make atonement
    And appease the wrath of God!
      Wondrous mercy!
See, it flows through Jesus' blood!

5 In His name, you are entreated
    To accept this act of grace;
This the day of your acceptance,
    Listen to the terms of peace:
      O delay not,
Listen to the terms of peace.

6 Having thus, then, heard the message,
    All with heav'nly mercy fraught,
Go, and tell the gracious Jesus
    If you will be saved or not:
      Say, poor sinner,
Will you now be saved or not?

*John Fountain*, 1800

# 520 7.7.7.7.
*Hasten, sinner.*

1 HASTEN, sinner, to be wise;
    Stay not for the morrow's sun;
Longer wisdom you despise,
    Harder is she to be won.

2 Hasten, mercy to implore;
    Stay not for the morrow's sun,
Lest thy season should be o'er,
    Ere this evening's stage be run.

3 Hasten, sinner, to return;
    Stay not for the morrow's sun,
Lest thy lamp should fail to burn,
    Ere salvation's work is done.

4 Hasten, sinner, to be blest;
    Stay not for the morrow's sun,

    Lest perdition thee arrest,
    Ere the morrow is begun.

5 Lord, do Thou the sinner turn!
    Rouse him from his senseless state;
Let him not Thy counsel spurn,
    Rue his fatal choice too late!

1-4 *Thomas Scott*, 1773
[5 John Rippon, 1800, *alt.*]

> **Ed:** Rippon's version of the hymn was expanded
> to long meter; his additional stanza has been
> reduced to fit Scott's original meter, a practice
> that dates to the 1830s.

# 521 L.M.
*Return, O wanderer.*

1 RETURN, O wanderer, return,
    And seek an injured Father's face;
Those warm desires that in thee burn
    Were kindled by reclaiming grace.

2 Return, O wanderer, return,
    And seek a Father's melting heart,
Whose pitying eyes thy grief discern,
    Whose hand can heal thine inward smart.

3 Return, O wanderer, return;
    He heard thy deep repentant sigh;
He saw thy soften'd spirit mourn
    When no intruding ear was nigh.

4 Return, O wanderer, return;
    Thy Saviour bids thy spirit live;
Go to His bleeding feet, and learn
    How freely Jesus can forgive.

5 Return, O wanderer, return,
    And wipe away the falling tear;
'Tis God who says, "No longer mourn,"
    'Tis mercy's voice invites thee near.

6 Return, O wanderer, return;
    Regain thy lost, lamented rest;
Jehovah's melting bowels yearn
    To clasp His Ephraim to His breast.

*William Collyer*, 1812

# 522

8.6.8.6.4.
*Return, O wanderer.*

1 RETURN, O wand'rer, to thy home;
   Thy Father calls for thee;
No longer now an exile roam
   In guilt and misery;
      Return, return!

2 Return, O wand'rer, to thy home;
   'Tis Jesus calls for thee;
The Spirit and the bride say, "come";
   Oh now for refuge flee;
      Return, return!

3 Return, O wand'rer, to thy home;
   'Tis madness to delay;
There are no pardons in the tomb,
   And brief is mercy's day.
      Return, return!

*Thomas Hastings*, [1831]

# 523

S.M.
*The day of grace.*

1 YE sinners, fear the Lord,
   While yet 'tis called today;
Soon will the awful voice of death
   Command your souls away.

2 Soon will the harvest close,
   The summer soon be o'er;
*O sinners! then your injur'd God*
   Will *heed* your *cries* no more.

3 Then while 'tis call'd today,
   O hear the gospel's sound;
Come sinner, haste, O haste away,
   While pardon may be found.

1-2 *Timothy Dwight*, 1800
[*alt. Thomas Hastings*, 1836]
[3 Stow & Smith, *The Psalmist*, 1843]

   **2.3:** *And soon your injur'd, angry God*
   **2.4:** *hear / prayers*
   **Ed:** Sts. 1-2 are from Dwight's longer paraphrase
      of Psalm 88, "Stretch'd on the bed of grief."

# 524

7.7.7.7.
*What hope have you?*

1 SINNER! what hast thou to show
Like the joys believers know?
Is thy path of fading flow'rs
Half so bright, so sweet as ours?

2 Doth a skillful, healing friend
On thy daily path attend,
And where thorns and stings abound,
Shed a balm on ev'ry wound?

3 When the tempests roar on high,
Hast thou still a refuge nigh?
Can, oh can thy dying breath
Summon one more strong than death?

4 Canst thou, in that awful day,
Fearless tread the gloomy way,
Plead a glorious ransom giv'n,
Burst from *earth* and soar to heav'n?

*Charlotte Elizabeth Tonna*, 1829
[*alt.* Stow & Smith, *The Psalmist*, 1843]

   **4.4:** *flesh*

# 525

7.7.7.7. Double
*"Prepare to meet thy God."*

1 SINNER, art thou still secure?
Wilt thou still refuse to pray?
Can thy heart or hands endure
In the Lord's avenging day?
See, His mighty arm is bared!
Awful terrors clothe His brow!
For His judgment stand prepar'd;
Thou must either break or bow.

2 At His presence nature shakes;
Earth affrighted hastes to flee;
Solid mountains melt like wax;
What will then become of thee?
Who His advent may abide?
You that glory in your shame,
Will you find a place to hide
When the world is wrapt in flame?

3 Then the rich, the great, the wise,
Trembling, guilty, self-condemn'd,
Must behold the wrathful eyes
Of the Judge they once blasphem'd.
Where are now their haughty looks?
Oh their horror and despair!
When they see the open'd books
And their dreadful sentence hear!

4 Lord, prepare us by Thy grace!
Soon we must resign our breath,
And our souls be call'd to pass
Through the iron gate of death:
Let us now our day improve;
Listen to the gospel voice;
Seek the things that are above;
Scorn the world's pretended joys.

5 Oh! when flesh and heart shall fail,
Let Thy love our spirits cheer;
Strengthen'd thus, we shall prevail
Over Satan, sin, and fear;
Trusting in Thy precious name,
May we thus our journey end;
Then our foes shall lose their aim,
And the Judge will be our friend.

*John Newton*, 1779

# 526 C.M.
*Treasuring up wrath.*

1 UNGRATEFUL sinners, whence this scorn
    Of long-extended grace?
And whence this madness that insults
    Th' Almighty to His face?

2 Is it because His patience waits,
    And pitying bowels move,
You multiply audacious crimes
    And spurn His richest love?

3 Is all the treasured wrath so small
    You labour still for more,
Though not eternal rolling years
    Can e'er exhaust the store?

4 Alarm'd and melted at Thy voice,
    Our conquer'd hearts would bow,

And to escape the Thund'rer then,
    Embrace the Saviour now.

*Philip Doddridge*, 1755

# 527 7.7.7.7.
*Appeal to conscience.*

1 SINNER, is thy heart at rest?
Is thy bosom void of fear?
Art thou not by guilt oppress'd?
Speaks not conscience in *thy* ear?

2 Can this world afford thee bliss?
Can it chase away thy gloom?
Flattering, false, and vain it is—
Tremble at the worldling's doom.

3 Long the gospel thou hast spurn'd,
Long delay'd to *love* thy God,
Stifled conscience, nor hast turn'd,
Wooed though by a Saviour's blood.

4 Think, O sinner, on thy end;
See the judgment day appear!
Thither must thy spirit wend;
There thy righeous sentence hear.

5 Wretched, ruin'd, helpless soul,
To a Saviour's blood apply;
He alone can make thee whole;
Fly to Jesus, sinner, fly!

*Jared Bell Waterbury*, [1830, *alt.*]

**1.4:** *thine*  **3.2:** *seek*  **Ed:** The alteration at 3.2
is from John Rippon's *Selection* (1844); 1.4 is a
minor variant introduced by Spurgeon.
**TD:** "Let the clamorous world be still awhile,
and let thy poor soul plead with thee to
bethink thyself before thou seal its fate, and
ruin it forever! *Selah.* O sinner! pause while I
question thee awhile in the words of a sacred
poet: 'Sinner, is thy heart at rest? . . .'" (Ps. 4:4;
vol. 1, p. 39).

# 528 L.M.
*Against self-destruction.*

1 SINNER, O why so thoughtless grown?
Why in such dreadful haste to die?

Daring to leap to worlds unknown,
Heedless against thy God to fly?

2 Wilt thou despise eternal fate,
Urged on by sin's fantastic dreams,
Madly attempt th' infernal gate,
And force thy passage to the flames?

3 Stay, sinner, on the gospel plain;
Behold the God of love unfold
The glories of His dying pains,
Forever telling, yet untold.

*Isaac Watts*, 1706
adapt. *John Rippon*, 1787

> **Ed:** Rippon's extensive alterations, yielding an
> almost new hymn, are detailed in Julian's
> *Dictionary of Hymnology*, p. 1060.

# 529
8.8.6.8.8.6.
*Prayer for thoughtfulness.*

1 THOU God of glorious majesty,
To Thee, against myself, to Thee,
A worm of earth I cry;
A half-awaken'd child of man,
An heir of endless bliss or pain,
A sinner born to die.

2 Lo! on a narrow neck of land,
'Twixt two unbounded seas, I stand;
*Yet how* insensible;
A point of *time*, a moment's space,
Removes me to *yon* heavenly place,
Or shuts me up in hell.

3 O God, *my* inmost soul convert,
And deeply on my thoughtful heart
Eternal things impress;
Give me to feel their solemn weight,
And *trembling* on the brink of fate,
*Wake me* to righteousness.

4 Before me place, in dread array,
The pomp of that tremendous day,
When Thou with clouds shalt come
To judge the nations at Thy bar;
And tell me, Lord, shall I be there
To meet a joyful doom?

5 Be this my one great business here,
With *holy trembling, holy* fear,
*To make my calling sure!*
Thine utmost counsel to fulfill,
And suffer all Thy righteous will,
And to the end endure.

6 Then, Saviour, then my soul receive,
Transported from *this* vale to live
And reign with Thee above,
Where faith is sweetly lost in sight,
And hope in full supreme delight,
And everlasting love.

*Charles Wesley*, 1749, *alt.*

> **2.3:** *Secure,*   **2.4:** *life*   **2.5:** *that*
> **3.1:** *mine*   **3.5:** *tremble*   **3.6:** *And wake*
> **5.2:** *serious industry and*
> **5.3:** *My future bliss t' insure,*   **6.2:** *the*
> **Ed:** These alterations are from John Rippon's
> *Selection* (1787, 1800), but Rippon's version
> of 3.5 reads "And save me ere it be too late"
> in every edition (1787-1844). The form of 3.5
> used here appears as early as 1777 in *A Col-
> lection of Hymns for the Use of the Hearers
> of the Apostles*, repeated in other scattered
> collections, and seemingly combined with
> Rippon's version for the first time in *OOHB*.

# THE GOSPEL STATED.

# 530
C.M.
*Justification by faith, not by works.*

1 VAIN are the hopes the sons of men
On their own works have built;
Their hearts by nature are unclean,
And all their actions guilt.

2 Let Jew and Gentile stop their mouths
Without a murm'ring word,
And the whole race of Adam stand
Guilty before the Lord.

3 In vain we ask God's righteous law
To justify us now,
Since to convince and to condemn
Is all the law can do.

4 Jesus, how glorious is Thy grace
　　When in Thy name we trust!
　　Our faith receives a righteousness
　　　That makes the sinner just.

*Isaac Watts*, 1709

# 531 C.M.
*The gospel worthy of all acceptation.*

1 JESUS, th' eternal Son of God,
　　Whom seraphim obey,
　　The bosom of the Father leaves
　　And enters human clay.

2 Into our sinful world He comes,
　　The Messenger of grace,
　　And on the bloody tree expires,
　　A victim in our place.

3 Transgressors of the deepest stain
　　In Him salvation find;
　　His blood removes the foulest guilt;
　　His Spirit heals the mind.

4 That Jesus saves from sin and hell
　　Is truth divinely sure,
　　And on this rock our faith may rest
　　Immovably secure.

5 O let these tidings be receiv'd
　　With universal joy,
　　And let the high angelic praise
　　Our tuneful pow'rs employ!

6 "Glory to God, who gave His Son
　　To bear our shame and pain;
　　Hence peace on earth, and grace to men,
　　In endless blessings reign."

*Thomas Gibbons*, 1769

**FPN:** 10 Aug. 1890 (No. 2158), DUBLIN

# 532 6.6.6.6.8.8.
*Himself He could not save.*

1 HIMSELF He could not save;
　　He on the cross must die,
　　Or mercy cannot come
　　To ruined sinners nigh;

Yes, Christ, the Son of God, must bleed
That sinners might from sin be freed.

2 Himself He could not save,
　　For justice must be done;
　　And sin's full weight must fall
　　Upon a sinless one;
For nothing less can God accept
In payment for the fearful debt.

3 Himself He could not save,
　　For He the surety stood
　　For all who now rely
　　Upon His precious blood;
He bore the penalty of guilt
When on the cross His blood was spilt.

4 Himself He could not save,
　　Yet now a Saviour He;
　　Come, sinner, to Him, come;
　　He waits to welcome thee;
Believe in Him, and thou shalt prove
His saving power, His deathless love.

*Albert Midlane*, 1865

# 533 8.8.8.8. Double
*Faith conquering.*

1 THE moment a sinner believes,
　　And trusts in his crucified God,
　　His pardon at once he receives,
　　Redemption in full through His blood;
　　Though thousands and thousands of foes
　　　Against him in malice unite,
　　Their rage he through Christ can oppose,
　　　Led forth by the Spirit to fight.

2 The faith that unites to the Lamb
　　And brings such salvation as this
　　Is more than mere notion or name;
　　The work of God's Spirit it is;
　　A principle, active and young,
　　　That lives under pressure and load,
　　That makes out of weakness more strong,
　　　And draws the soul upward to God.

3 It treads on the world, and on hell,
　　It vanquishes death and despair,

And (what *is still* stranger to tell)
    It overcomes heaven by pray'r,
Permits a vile worm of the dust
    With God to commune as a friend,
To hope His forgiveness as just,
    And look for His love to the end.

4 It says to the mountains, "Depart,"
    That stand betwixt God and the soul,
It binds up the broken in heart
    And makes wounded consciences whole,
Bids sins of a crimson-like dye
    Be spotless as snow, and as white,
And makes such a sinner as I
    As pure as an angel of light.

*Joseph Hart*, 1759 [*rev.* 1763]

# 534   7.7.7.7.
*The work is done.*

1 CHRIST has done the mighty work;
Nothing left for us to do
But to enter on His toil;
Enter on His triumph too.

2 He has sowed the precious seed,
Nothing left for us unsown;
Ours it is to reap the fields,
Make the harvest joy our own.

3 His the pardon, ours the sin;
Great the sin, the pardon great;
His the good and ours the ill;
His the love and ours the hate.

4 Ours the darkness and the gloom,
His the shade-dispelling light;
Ours the cloud and His the sun;
His the dayspring, ours the night.

5 His the labour, ours the rest;
His the death and ours the life;
Ours the fruits of victory,
His the agony and strife.

*Horatius Bonar*, [1864]

# 535   8.7.8.7. Double
*Believe and live.*

1 WHEN the Saviour said, "'Tis finish'd,"
    Everything was fully done;
Done, as God Himself would have it—
    Christ the victory fully won.
Vain and futile the endeavour
    To improve, or add thereto;
God's free grace is thus commended—
    To "believe" and not "to do."

2 All the doing is completed;
    Now 'tis "look, believe, and live";
None can purchase His salvation;
    Life's a gift that God must give;
Grace, through righteousness, is reigning,
    Not of works, lest man should boast;
Man must take the *mercy freely*,
    Or eternally be lost.

*Albert Midlane*, [1865, *alt. C.H.S.*]

**2.7:** *proffered mercy*

# 536   7.7.7.7.7.7.
*Substitution.*

1 SURELY Christ thy griefs hath borne;
Weeping soul, no longer mourn;
View Him bleeding on the tree,
Pouring out His life for thee;
There thy ev'ry sin He bore;
Weeping Soul, lament no more.

2 Cast thy guilty soul on Him;
Find Him mighty to redeem;
At His feet thy burden lay;
Look thy doubts and cares away;
Now by faith the Son embrace;
Plead His promise, trust His grace.

3 Lord, Thy arm must be reveal'd
Ere I can by faith be heal'd;
Since I scarce can look to Thee,
Cast a gracious eye on me!
At thy feet myself I lay;
Shine, O shine my fears away!

*Augustus Toplady*, 1759 [*rev.* 1774]

# 537 C.M.
*"Jesus only."*

1 WHEN wounded sore the stricken soul
    Lies bleeding and unbound,
One only hand, a piercèd hand,
    Can salve the sinner's wound.

2 When sorrow swells the laden breast
    And tears of anguish flow,
One only heart, a broken heart,
    Can feel the sinner's woe.

3 When penitence has wept in vain
    Over some foul dark spot,
One only stream, a stream of blood,
    Can wash away the blot.

4 'Tis Jesus' blood that washes white,
    His hand that brings relief,
His heart that's touch'd with all our joys,
    And feeleth for our grief.

5 Lift up Thy bleeding hand, O Lord;
    Unseal that cleansing tide;
We have no shelter from our sin
    But in Thy wounded side.

*Cecil Frances Alexander*, 1858

# 538 Irregular.
*The life-look.*

1 THERE is life for a look at the
    Crucified One;
There is life at this moment for thee;
Then look, sinner, look unto Him and
    be saved,
Unto Him who was nailed to the tree.

2 It is not thy tears of repentance or prayers,
But the blood that atones for the soul;
On Him, then, who shed it, *believing*
    at once,
Thy weight of iniquities roll.

3 His anguish of soul on the cross hast
    thou seen?
His cry of distress hast thou heard?
Then why, if the terrors of wrath

He endured,
Should pardon to thee be deferred?

4 We are heal'd by His stripes; wouldst thou
    add to the word?
And He is our righteousness made;
The best robe of heaven He bids thee
    put on;
Oh! couldst thou be better array'd?

5 Then doubt not thy welcome, since God
    has declared,
There remaineth no more to be done;
That once in the end of the world
    He appeared
And completed the work He begun.

6 But take, with rejoicing, from Jesus
    at once
The life everlasting He gives;
And know, with assurance, thou never
    canst die,
Since Jesus, thy righteousness, lives.

7 There is life for a look at the Crucified One;
There is life at this moment for thee;
Then look, sinner, look unto Him and
    be saved,
And know thyself spotless as He.

  *Amelia Matilda Hull*, 1860
[*alt. Richard Burnet*, 1864]

> **2.3:** *thou mayest*  **Ed:** Whether Burnet made the
> alteration, or Hull supplied a revised version
> to Burnet and Spurgeon, is unclear.

# 539 C.M.
*The brazen serpent.*

1 SO did the Hebrew prophet raise
    The brazen serpent high;
The wounded felt immediate ease,
    The camp forebore to die.

2 "Look upward in the dying hour
    And live," the prophet cries,
But Christ performs a nobler cure
    When faith lifts up her eyes.

3 High on the cross the Saviour hung;
　　High in the heav'ns He reigns;
　Here sinners, by th' old serpent stung,
　　Look and forget their pains.

4 When God's own Son is lifted up,
　　A dying world revives;
　The Jew beholds the glorious hope;
　　Th' expiring Gentile lives.

*Isaac Watts*, 1709

# 540 Irregular.
*"What must I do to be saved?"*

1 NOTHING, either great or small,
　　Nothing, sinner, no;
　Jesus did it, did it all,
　　Long, long ago.

2 When He from His lofty throne
　　Stoop'd to do and die,
　Everything was fully done;
　　Hearken to His cry—

3 "It is finish'd!" Yes, indeed,
　　Finish'd every jot;
　Sinner, this is all you need;
　　Tell me, is it not?

4 Weary, working, plodding one,
　　Why toil you so?
　Cease your doing; all was done
　　Long, long ago.

5 Till to Jesus' work you cling
　　By a simple faith,
　"Doing" is a deadly thing;
　　"Doing" ends in death.

6 Cast your deadly "doing" down,
　　Down at Jesus' feet;
　Stand in Him, in Him alone,
　　Glorious complete!

*James Procter*, 1858

**FPN:** 18 Aug. 1889 (No. 2327), INTROIT
**Ed:** Sedgwick's index of authors gave the source
　as "Original Hymn, 1858." Portions of the text
　appeared in *Friends' Review*, vol. XV (1862),

p. 351; Spurgeon quoted it in his sermon "A
hearer in disguise," *Sermons of Rev. C.H.
Spurgeon*, vol. 8 (1865). In *Cheering Words*
(Jan. 1864) and Edward Hammond's *Praises
of Jesus* (1865) the hymn included this note:
　"The author, the late Rev. Mr. Procter of
Scotland, says: 'Since I first discovered Jesus
to be the end of the law for righteousness to
every one that believeth, I have more than
once met with a poor sinner seeking peace at
the foot of Sinai instead of Calvary; and I have
heard him, now and again, in bitter disappoint-
ment and fear, groaning out: "What must I do?"
I have said to him: "Do! Do! What can you do?
What do you need to do?"'"

# 541 7.7.7.7.
*Grace is free.*

1 GRACE! how good, how cheap, how free;
　Grace, how easy to be found!
　Only let your misery
　In the Saviour's blood be drown'd!

2 Wishful lie before His throne;
　Say, "I never will be gone,
　Never, till my suit's obtain'd,
　Never, till the blessing's gain'd."

*Nicolaus Ludwig von Zinzendorf*, 1739
*tr. Charles Kinchin*, 1742

　**Ed:** Translated from stanza 5 of the German,
　　"Geschwister vir geben uns Herzen und Hände."

# 542 8.7.8.7.4.7.
*Why those fears?*

1 WHY those fears, poor trembling sinner?
　　Why those anxious, gloomy fears?
　Doubts and fears can never save thee;
　　Life is never won by tears;
　　　'Tis believing,
　　Which the soul to Christ endears.

2 Tears, though flowing like a river,
　　Never can one sin efface;
　Jesus' tears would not avail thee—
　　Blood alone can meet thy case;
　　　Fly to Jesus!
　　Life is found in His embrace.

3 Songs of triumph then resounding
    From thy happy lips shall flow;
In the knowledge of salvation
    Thou true happiness shalt know.
        Look to Jesus!
    He alone can life bestow.

*Albert Midlane,* 1865

## 543   8.7.8.7.
*Hope for sinners.*

1 SINNER, where is room for doubting?
    Has not Jesus died for sin?
Did He not in resurrection
    Victory over Satan win?

2 Hear Him on the cross exclaiming—
    "It is finish'd," ere He died;
See Him in His mercy saving,
    One there hanging by His side.

3 'Twas for sinners that He suffered
    Agonies unspeakable;
Canst thou doubt thou art a sinner?
    If thou canst—then hope farewell!

4 But believing what is written—
    "All are guilty"—"dead in sin,"
Looking to the Crucified One,
    Hope shall rise thy soul within.

5 Hope and peace and joy unfailing,
    Through the Saviour's precious blood,
All thy crimson sins forgiven,
    And thy soul brought nigh to God.

*Albert Midlane,* [1861, *rev.* 1865]

## 544   C.M.
*Mercy for the guilty.*

1 MERCY is welcome news indeed
    To those that guilty stand;
Wretches that feel what help they need
    Will bless the helping hand.

2 Who rightly would his alms dispose
    Must give them to the poor;
None but the wounded patient knows
    The comforts of his cure.

3 We all have sinn'd against our God;
    Exception none can boast;
But he that feels the heaviest load
    Will prize forgiveness most.

4 No reck'ning can we rightly keep,
    For who the sums can know?
Some souls are fifty pieces deep,
    And some five hundred owe.

5 But let our debts be what they may,
    However great or small,
As soon as we have nought to pay,
    Our Lord forgives us all.

6 'Tis perfect poverty alone
    That sets the soul at large;
While we can call one mite our own,
    We have no full discharge.

*Joseph Hart,* 1759

## 545   8.8.8.6.
*Just as thou art.*

1 JUST as thou art—without one trace
Of love, or joy, or inward grace,
Or meetness for the heavenly place,
    O guilty sinner, come.

2 Thy sins I bore on Calvary's tree;
The stripes, thy due, were laid on Me,
That peace and pardon might be free—
    O wretched sinner, come.

3 Burdened with guilt, wouldst thou be blest?
Trust not the world, it gives no rest;
I bring relief to hearts oppress'd—
    O weary sinner, come.

4 Come, leave thy burden at the cross;
Count all thy gains but empty dross;
My grace repays all earthly loss—
    O needy sinner, come.

5 Come, hither bring thy boding fears,
Thy aching heart, thy bursting tears;
'Tis mercy's voice salutes thine ears;
    O trembling sinner, come.

6 "The Spirit and the Bride say 'come.'"
Rejoicing saints re-echo, "come."
Who faints, who thirsts, who will,
    may come;
Thy Saviour bids thee come.

*Russell S. Cook*, 1850


# THE GOSPEL RECEIVED BY FAITH.


# 546   8.8.8.6.
*Just as I am.*

1 JUST as I am—without one plea,
But that Thy blood was shed for me,
And that Thou bidd'st me come to Thee—
    O Lamb of God, I come!

2 Just as I am—and waiting not
To rid my soul of one dark blot,
To Thee, whose blood can cleanse
    each spot—
    O Lamb of God, I come!

3 Just as I am—though toss'd about
With many a conflict, many a doubt,
Fightings *within, and fears* without,
    O Lamb of God, I come!

4 Just as I am—poor, wretched, blind;
Sight, riches, healing of the mind,
Yea, all I need, in Thee to find,
    O Lamb of God, I come!

5 Just as I am—Thou wilt receive,
Wilt welcome, pardon, cleanse, relieve;
Because Thy promise I believe,
    O Lamb of God, I come!

6 Just as I am—Thy love unknown
Has broken every barrier down;
Now, to be Thine, yea, Thine alone,
    O Lamb of God, I come!

7 Just as I am—of that free love,
The breadth, length, depth, and height
    to prove,

Here for a season, then above—
    O Lamb of God, I come!

*Charlotte Elliott*, [1841]

**3.3:** *and fears, within,*   **Ed:** The first publication contained only 6 sts.; the seventh was added in or before 1849. This common alteration at 3.3 appeared as early as Aug. 1845 in *The Baptist Record.*

**MM:** Hymns, Set 2 (Feb./Dec.), 16th Eve, WOODWORTH / ZEPHYR. "If the Holy Spirit shall enable thee from thy heart to cry, 'Just as I am, without one plea But that Thy blood was shed for me…' thou shalt rise from reading this morning's portion with all thy sins pardoned; and though thou didst wake this morning with every sin that man hath ever committed on thy head, thou shalt rest tonight accepted in the Beloved" (June 6).


# 547   L.M.
*Just as Thou art.*

1 JUST as Thou art—how wondrous fair,
Lord Jesus, all Thy members are!
A life divine to them is given—
A long inheritance in heaven.

2 Just as I was I came to Thee,
An heir of wrath and misery;
Just as Thou art before the throne,
I stand in righteousness Thine own.

3 Just as Thou art—how wondrous free,
Loosed by the sorrows of the tree;
Jesus! the curse, the wrath were Thine,
To give Thy saints this life divine.

4 Just as Thou art—nor doubt, nor fear,
Can with Thy spotlessness appear;
O timeless love! as Thee, I'm seen,
The "righteousness of God in Him."

5 Just as Thou art—Thou Lamb divine!
Life, light, and holiness are Thine:
Thyself their endless source I see,
And they, the life of God, in me.

6 Just as Thou art—O blissful ray
That turned my darkness into day!

That woke me from my death of sin
To know my perfectness in Him.

7 O teach me, Lord, this grace to own,
That self and sin no more are known;
That love—Thy love—in wondrous right,
Hath placed me in its spotless light!

8 Soon, soon, 'mid joys on joys untold,
Thou wilt this grace and love unfold,
Till worlds on worlds adoring see
The part Thy members have in Thee.

*Joseph Denham Smith*, 1860

## 548 8.8.8.6.
*The prodigal's welcome.*

1 THE wanderer no more will roam;
The lost one to the fold hath come;
The prodigal is welcom'd home;
    O Lamb of God, in Thee!

2 Though cloth'd with shame, by sin defil'd,
The Father hath embrac'd His child;
And I am pardon'd, reconcil'd,
    O Lamb of God, in Thee!

3 It is the Father's joy to bless;
His love provides for me a dress,
A robe of spotless righteousness,
    O Lamb of God, in Thee!

4 Now shall my famish'd soul be fed;
A feast of love for me is spread;
I feed upon the children's bread,
    O Lamb of God, in Thee!

5 Yea, in the fulness of His grace,
He put me in the children's place,
Where I may gaze upon His face,
    O Lamb of God, in Thee!

6 I cannot half His love express,
Yet, Lord! with joy my lips confess;
This blessèd portion I possess;
    O Lamb of God, in Thee!

7 It is Thy precious name I bear;
It is Thy spotless robe I wear;

Therefore, the Father's love I share,
    O Lamb of God, in Thee!

8 And when I in Thy likeness shine,
The glory and the praise be Thine;
That everlasting joy is mine,
    O Lamb of God, in Thee!

*Mary Jane Walker*, [1855]

## 549 8.8.8.8.8.8.
*The Solid Rock.*

1 MY hope is built on nothing less
Than Jesus' blood and righteousness;
I dare not trust the sweetest frame,
But wholly lean on Jesus' name.
    On Christ the solid rock I stand;
    All other ground is sinking sand.

2 When darkness veils His lovely face,
I rest *on His* unchanging grace;
In every *high* and stormy gale,
My anchor holds within the veil.
    On Christ the solid rock I stand;
    All other ground is sinking sand.

3 His oath, His cov'nant, and His blood
Support me in the sinking flood;
When all around my soul gives way,
He then is all my hope and stay.
    On Christ the solid rock I stand;
    All other ground is sinking sand.

4 When *the last awful trump shall sound*,
O may I then *in Him be found*,
Dress'd in His righteousness alone,
Faultless to stand before the throne.
    On Christ the solid rock I stand;
    All other ground is sinking sand.

*Edward Mote*, 1824 [*rev.* 1836], *alt.*

**2.2:** *upon*  **2.3:** *rough*
**4.1:** *I shall launch in worlds unseen,*
**4.2:** *be found in Him,*
**Ed:** Taken from the longer hymn, "Not earth,
    nor hell my soul can move." The hymn was
    truncated to start with "My hope is built on
    nothing less" in John Rees' *Collection* (1826).

The alterations at 2.2–2.3 are from Rees; 4.1–4.2, which imitate lines from an older hymn, "Guide of my youth, to Thee I cry," appeared together with 2.2–2.3 in Jonathan Whittemore's *Supplement* (1850).

# 550
6.6.4.6.6.6.4.
*"Be not afraid, only believe."*

1 MY faith looks up to Thee,
  Thou Lamb of Calvary,
    Saviour divine!
  Now hear me while I pray;
  Take all my guilt away;
  O let me from this day
    Be wholly Thine.

2 May Thy rich grace impart
  Strength to my fainting heart,
    My zeal inspire;
  As Thou hast died for me,
  Oh may my love to Thee,
  Pure, warm, and changeless be,
    A living fire.

3 While life's dark maze I tread,
  And griefs around me spread,
    Be Thou my guide;
  Bid darkness turn to day,
  Wipe sorrow's tears away,
  Nor let me ever stray
    From Thee aside.

4 When ends life's transient dream,
  When death's cold, sullen stream
    Shall o'er me roll,
  Blest Saviour, then in love,
  Fear and distrust remove;
  O bear me safe above—
    A ransom'd soul.

*Ray Palmer*, [1831]

> **Ed:** The following review of Palmer's *Voices of Hope and Gladness* (1881) appeared in S&T, June 1881, p. 287:
> "When we saw that this was a volume of poems by the author of the hymn 'My faith looks up to thee,' we reckoned not merely upon poetical beauty, but spiritual quicken-

ing therein: nor have we been disappointed. These poems throb with spiritual life, and in language forceful and chaste they make their power and beauty felt."

# 551
7.7.7.7. Double
*Christ is all.*

1 JESU, lover of my soul,
  Let me to Thy bosom fly,
  While the nearer waters roll,
  While the tempest still is high!
  Hide me, O my Saviour, hide,
  Till the storm of life be past;
  Safe into the haven guide;
  O receive my soul at last.

2 Other refuge have I none;
  Hangs my helpless soul on Thee;
  Leave, ah! leave me not alone;
  Still support and comfort me.
  All my trust on Thee is stay'd;
  All my help from Thee I bring;
  Cover my defenceless head
  With the shadow of Thy wing.

3 Thou, O Christ, art all I want;
  More than all in Thee I find:
  Raise the fallen, cheer the faint,
  Heal the sick, and lead the blind:
  Just and holy is Thy name;
  I am all unrighteousness;
  False and full of sin I am;
  Thou art full of truth and grace.

4 Plenteous grace with Thee is found,
  Grace to cover all my sin;
  Let the healing streams abound,
  Make and keep me pure within;
  Thou of life the fountain art;
  Freely let me take of Thee;
  Spring Thou up within my heart;
  Rise to all eternity!

*Charles Wesley*, 1740

> **TD:** "All the world tastes of his sparing mercy, those who hear the gospel partake of his inviting mercy, the saints live by his saving mercy,

and preserved by his upholding mercy, are cheered by his consoling mercy, and will enter heaven through his infinite and everlasting mercy" (Ps. 103:8; vol. 4, p. 452).

# 552
7.7.7.7.7.7.
*Rock of Ages.*

1 ROCK of Ages, cleft for me,
Let me hide myself in Thee!
Let the water and the blood,
From Thy riven side which flow'd,
Be of sin the double cure;
Cleanse me from its guilt and pow'r.

2 Not the labours of my hands
Can fulfill Thy law's demands;
Could my zeal no respite know,
Could my tears forever flow;
All for sin could not atone;
Thou must save, and Thou alone.

3 Nothing in my hand I bring,
Simply to Thy cross I cling;
Naked, come to Thee for dress;
Helpless, look to Thee for grace;
Foul, I to the fountain fly;
Wash me, Saviour, or I die!

4 *Whilst* I draw this fleeting breath,
When my eye-strings break in death,
When I soar *through tracts* unknown,
See Thee on Thy judgment throne,
Rock of Ages, cleft for me,
Let me hide myself in Thee!

*Augustus Toplady*, 1775-76

> **4.1:** *While*   **4.3:** *to worlds*   **Ed:** The version above appeared in *The Gospel Magazine*; the footnotes indicate his revisions in *Psalms & Hymns* (1776), which were not always observed by hymnal compilers.

# 553
C.M.
*Jesus died for me.*

1 GREAT God, when I approach Thy throne
And all Thy glory see,

This is my stay, and this alone,
That Jesus died for me.

2 How can a soul condemn'd to die
Escape the just decree?
A vile, unworthy wretch am I,
But Jesus died for me.

3 Burden'd with sin's oppressive chain,
O how can I get free?
No peace can all my efforts gain,
But Jesus died for me.

4 My course I could not safely steer
Through life's tempestuous sea,
Did not this truth relieve my fear,
That Jesus died for me.

5 And Lord, when I behold Thy face,
This must be all my plea;
Save me by Thy almighty grace,
For Jesus died for me.

*William Hiley Bathurst*, 1831

# 554
L.M.
*Christ and His righteousness.*

1 NO more, my God, I boast no more
Of all the duties I have done;
I quit the hopes I held before
To trust the merits of Thy Son.

2 Now for the love I bear His name;
What was my gain I count my loss;
My former pride I call my shame,
And nail my glory to His cross.

3 Yes, and I must and will esteem,
All things but loss for Jesus' sake;
Oh may my soul be found in Him,
And of His righteousness partake!

4 The best obedience of my hands
Dares not appear before Thy throne,
But faith can answer my demands
By pleading what my Lord has done.

*Isaac Watts*, 1709

# 555 
S.M.
*The true scapegoat.*

1   NOT all the blood of beasts
On Jewish altars slain
Could give the guilty conscience peace
Or wash away the stain.

2   But Christ, the heavenly Lamb,
Takes all our sins away;
A sacrifice of nobler name,
And richer blood than they.

3   My faith would lay her hand
On that dear head of Thine,
While like a penitent I stand
And there confess my sin.

4   My soul looks back to see
The burdens Thou didst bear
When hanging on the cursèd tree,
And hopes her guilt was there.

5   Believing, we rejoice
To see the curse remove;
We bless the Lamb with cheerful voice
And sing His bleeding love.

*Isaac Watts,* 1709

# 556 
L.M.
*The only plea.*

1   JESU, the sinner's Friend, to Thee,
Lost and undone, for aid I flee;
Weary of earth, myself, and sin—
Open Thine arms and take me in.

2   Pity and heal my sin-sick soul;
'Tis Thou alone canst make me whole;
Fall'n, till in me Thine image shine,
And *lost* I am till Thou art mine.

3   At last I own it cannot be
That I should fit myself for Thee;
Here, then, to Thee I all resign;
Thine is the work, and only Thine.

4   What Shall I say Thy grace to move?
Lord, I am sin—but Thou art love:

I give up every plea beside;
Lord, I am *lost*—but Thou hast died!

*Charles Wesley,* 1739 [*alt.*]

> **2.4:** *curs'd*  **4.4:** *damn'd*  **Ed:** These changes appeared in the Wesleys' *Collection*, posthumously, as early as 1804.

# 557 
C.M.
*"Remember me."*

1   JESUS! *Thou art the sinner's* Friend;
*As such,* I look to Thee;
Now, in the *fullness* of Thy love,
*O* Lord, remember me.

2   Remember Thy pure word of grace,
Remember *Calvary,*
Remember all Thy dying groans,
And then remember me.

3   Thou wondrous Advocate with God,
I yield *myself* to Thee;
While Thou art *sitting* on Thy throne,
Dear Lord, remember me.

4   *Lord! I am* guilty, *I am* vile,
*But* Thy salvation's free;
Then, in *Thine* all-abounding grace,
Dear Lord, remember me.

5   And when I close my eyes in death,
*When creature-helps all* flee,
Then, *O* my dear *Redeemer-God!*
*I pray,* remember me.

*Richard Burnham,* 1796, *alt.*

> **1.1:** *my kind and gracious*  **1.2:** *simply*
> **1.3:** *bowels*  **1.4:** *Dear*  **2.2:** *Calv'ry's tree*
> **3.2:** *my soul*  **3.3:** *pleading*
> **4.1:** *I own I'm / own I'm*  **4.2:** *Yet*  **4.3:** *Thy*
> **5.2:** *And human help shall*
> **5.3:** *then, / redeeming God,*  **5.4:** *O then*
> **Ed:** This altered form of Burnham's hymn, except 4.1-4.2, was published in William Parkinson's *Selection* (1809), where it was credited to an unknown *New Selection*; 4.1-4.2 appeared as early as 1843 in the Presbyterian *Church Psalmist.*

## 558
8.7.8.7.4.7.
*Divine indwelling desired.*

1 WELCOME, welcome, *great* Redeemer,
    Welcome to this heart of mine;
Lord, I make a full surrender;
    Every pow'r and thought be Thine,
        Thine entirely,
    Through eternal ages Thine.

2 Known *to* all to be Thy mansion,
    Earth and hell will disappear,
Or in vain attempt possession,
    When they find the Lord *is* near;
        Shout, O Zion;
    Shout, ye saints, the Lord is here.

[*William Mason*, 1794]

> **1.1:** *dear*  **2.1:** *by*  **2.4:** *so*  **Ed:** The alterations
> at 2.1-2.4 are from Asahel Nettleton's *Village
> Hymns* (1824); these were repeated, adding
> 1.1, in John Campbell's *Comprehensive Hymn
> Book* (1837), the 8th ed. of which was in Spur-
> geon's personal library. Sedgwick attributed
> the hymn to Thomas Hastings, 1842, but the
> hymn is much older.

## 559
7.6.7.6.
*The burden bearer.*

1 I LAY my sins on Jesus,
    The spotless Lamb of God;
He bears them all and frees us
    From the accursed load.
I bring my guilt to Jesus
    To wash my crimson stains,
White in His blood most precious,
    Till not a spot remains.

2 I lay my wants on Jesus;
    All fullness dwells in Him;
He *healeth* my diseases;
    He doth my soul redeem.
I lay my griefs on Jesus,
    My burdens and my cares;
He from them all releases—
    He all my sorrows shares.

3 I rest my soul on Jesus—
    This weary soul of mine;

His right hand me embraces;
    I on His breast recline.
I love the name of Jesus,
    Immanuel, Christ the Lord;
Like fragrance on the breezes,
    His name abroad is poured.

4 I long to be like Jesus,
    Meek, loving, lowly, mild;
I long to be like Jesus,
    The Father's Holy Child;
I long to be with Jesus,
    Amid the heavenly throng,
To sing with saints His praises,
    To learn the angels' song.

*Horatius Bonar*, [1843, *alt.*]

> **2.3:** *heals all*  **Ed:** This minor variant appeared
> as early as 3 May 1851 in *The Church of En-
> gland Magazine.*

## 560
C.M.
*The voice of Jesus.*

1 I HEARD the voice of Jesus say,
    "Come unto Me and rest;
Lay down, thou weary one, lay down
    Thy head upon My breast."
I came to Jesus as I was,
    Weary, and worn, and sad;
I found in Him a resting place,
    And He has made me glad.

2 I heard the voice of Jesus say,
    "Behold, I freely give
The living water—thirsty one,
    Stoop down, and drink, and live."
I came to Jesus and I drank
    Of that life-giving stream;
My thirst was quench'd, my soul revived,
    And now I live in Him.

3 I heard the voice of Jesus say,
    "I am this dark world's light;
Look unto Me, thy morn shall rise,
    And all thy day be bright."
I looked to Jesus and I found
    In Him my star, my sun;

And in that light of life I'll walk
  Till travelling days are done.

*Horatius Bonar*, [1846]

# 561 C.M.
*The great sight.*

1  IN evil long I took delight,
    Unaw'd by shame or fear,
  Till a new object struck my sight
    And stopp'd my wild career.

2  I saw One hanging on a tree,
    In agonies and blood,
  Who fix'd His languid eyes on me,
    As near His cross I stood.

3  Sure, never till my latest breath
    Can I forget that look;
  It seem'd to charge me with His death,
    Though not a word He spoke.

4  My conscience felt and own'd the guilt
    And plunged me in despair;
  I saw my sins His blood had spilt,
    And help'd to nail Him there.

5  Alas! I knew not what I did,
    But now my tears are vain.
  Where shall my trembling soul be hid?
    For I the Lord have slain.

6  A second look He gave, which said,
    "I freely all forgive;
  This blood is for thy ransom paid;
    I die that thou may'st live."

7  Thus while His death my sin displays
    In all its blackest hue
  (Such is the mystery of grace),
    It seals my pardon too.

8  With pleasing grief and mournful joy,
    My spirit now is fill'd,
  That I should such a life destroy,
    Yet live by Him I kill'd.

*John Newton*, 1779

# 562 7.7.7.7.
*Blessed be the Lord.*

1  WE were lost, but we are found;
  Dead, but now alive are we;
  We were sore in bondage bound,
  *But our Jesus sets* us free.

2  Strangers, and He takes us in;
  Naked, He becomes our dress;
  Sick, and He from stain of sin
  Cleanses with His righteousness.

3  Therefore will we sing His praise,
  Who His lost ones hath restored;
  Hearts and voices both shall raise
  Halleujahs to the Lord.

*John S.B. Monsell*, 1863 [*alt. C.H.S.*]

**1.4:** *Till He came to set*
**Ed:** Taken from the longer hymn,
  "Glory be to God on high."
**EE:** Hymns, Set 2 (Feb./Dec.), 3rd Eve,
  KIEL / THEODORA

# 563 8.8.6.8.8.6.
*Grace exalted.*

1  LET Zion in her songs record
  The honours of her dying Lord,
    Triumphant over sin;
  How sweet the song, there's none can say,
  But *those* whose sins are wash'd away,
    Who feels the same within.

2  We claim no merit of our own,
  But self-condemn'd, before Thy throne,
    Our hopes on Jesus place;
  *Though once in heart* and life deprav'd,
  *We now can sing as sinners* sav'd,
    And praise redeeming grace.

3  We'll sing the same while life shall last,
  And *when, at the* archangel's blast,
    Our sleeping dust shall rise,
  Then in a song forever new,
  The glorious theme we'll still pursue
    Throughout the azure skies.

4 Prepar'd of old, at God's right hand,
  Bright everlasting mansions stand
    For all the blood-bought race;
  And till we reach those seats of bliss,
  We'll sing no other song but this,
    *Salvation all of* grace.

*John Kent*, 1803, alt. C.H.S.

  **1.5:** *he*  **2.4:** *In heart, in lip,*
  **2.5:** *Our theme shall be a sinner*
  **3.2:** *when the great*  **4.6:** *A sinner sav'd by*

# 564 8.6.8.6. / *"The Lord hath laid on Him the iniquity of us all."*

1 CHARG'D with the complicated load
    Of *our enormous* debt,
  By faith, I see the Lamb of God
    Expire beneath its weight.

2 *My numerous sins, transferr'd* to Him,
    Shall never more be found,
  Lost in His blood's atoning stream,
    *Where every crime is* drown'd!

3 My mighty sins to Thee are known,
    But mightier still is He
  Who laid His life a ransom down
    *And* pleads His death for me.

4 O may my life, while here below,
    *Bear witness to Thy* love,
  Till I *before Thy footstool bow*
    And chant Thy praise above.

1-2 *Augustus Toplady*, 1776 [*alt.*]
3 *Charles Wesley*, 1762 [*alt. A.T.*]
[4 *Collection of Psalms & Hymns*, 1794, alt.]

  **1.2:** *all His people's*
  **2.1:** *My guilt, transferr'd from me*
  **2.4:** *And in that fountain*  **3.4:** *Who*
  **4.2:** *Be one return of*
  **4.3:** *behold Thee as Thou art*
  **Ed:** Wesley's original hymn began, "Of my
    transgressions numberless." Toplady's version
    included his two stazas, plus the stanza of
    Wesley's, with the minor alteration at 3.4.
    This combination of all four stanzas, with
    the changes at 1.2 and 3.4, appeared unat-
    tributed in the 1794 *Collection.* 2.1, 2.4, and
    4.3 appeared as early as 1809 in Thomas
    Biddulph's *Portions of the Psalms of David*,
    except his version of 2.1 reads, "My heinous
    guilt transferr'd." The full range of alterations
    above appeared as early as 1849 in *Covenant
    Hymns*, repeated in the 1850 edition of *The
    Invalid's Hymn Book*, which was part of Spur-
    geon's personal library.
  **EE:** "Believer, do you remember that rapturous
    day when you first realized pardon through
    Jesus the sin-bearer? . . . Blessed discovery!
    Eternal solace of a grateful heart! 'My numer-
    ous sins transferred to Him, shall never more
    be found . . .'" (Apr. 13).

# 565 6.6.8.6. *"We have peace with God."*

1 IN Christ I have believed,
    And through the spotless Lamb
  Grace and salvation have received;
    In Him complete I am!

2 This hope divine uplifts
    My soul amid distress;
  "Without repentance" are His gifts
    Who thus vouchsafes to bless.

3 My sins, my crimson stains,
    Are blotted out, each one;
  No condemnation now remains!
    God views me in His Son.

4 Then come what may to me,
    It will, it must be blest!
  Home, in the distance, I can see;
    There I shall be at rest!

*Charlotte Elliott*, [1845]

  **Ed:** Taken from the longer hymn,
    "What though my strength decline."

# 566 8.7.8.7. Double *I am pardoned.*

1 NOW, O joy! my sins are pardoned;
    Now I can and do believe;
  All I have, and am, and shall be,
    To my precious Lord I give;

He aroused my deathly slumbers,
  He dispersed my soul's dark night,
Whispered peace, and drew me to Him—
  Made Himself my chief delight.

2 Let the babe forget its mother;
  Let the bridegroom slight his bride;
True to Him, I'll love none other,
  Cleaving closely to His side.
Jesus, hear my soul's confession;
  Weak am I, but strength is Thine.
On Thine arms for strength and succour,
  Calmly may my soul recline.

*Albert Midlane*, [1861]

> **Ed:** Taken from the longer hymn,
> "Once I sang, but not in earnest."

# 567 L.M.
*Jesus pleads for me.*

1 BEFORE the throne of God above,
  I have a strong, a perfect plea,
  A great High Priest, whose name is Love,
  Who ever lives and pleads for me.

2 My name is graven on His hands;
  My name is written on His heart;
  I know that while in heaven He stands,
  No tongue can bid me thence depart.

3 When Satan tempts me to despair,
  And tells me of the guilt within,
  Upward I look and see Him there,
  Who made an end of all my sin.

4 Because the sinless Saviour died,
  My sinful soul is counted free;
  For God, the Just, is satisfied
  To look on Him and pardon me.

5 Behold Him there! the bleeding Lamb!
  My perfect, spotless Righteousness,
  The great unchangeable I AM,
  The King of glory and of grace.

6 One with Himself I cannot die;
  My soul is purchased by His blood;
  My life is hid with Christ on high,
  With Christ, my Saviour and my God.

*Charitie Lees Smith*, 1863

> **Ed:** Dated by Sedgwick as 1863, credited to
> her "Original Hymns, 1861–1863" in the List
> of Works. She married Arthur E. Bancroft in
> 1869; she is known often by that name. Arthur
> died in 1881; she married Frank De Cheney
> and divorced after emigrating to California.
>   Spurgeon quoted this hymn in his last
> address to his friends who had gathered to
> worship with him in Menton, France, 31 Dec.
> 1891 & 1 Jan. 1892 (S&T, Feb. 1892, p. 51):
>   "Though I have preached Christ crucified for
> more than forty years, and have led many to
> my Master's feet, I have at this moment no ray
> of hope but that which comes from what my
> Lord Jesus has done for guilty men.
>   'Behold him there! the bleeding Lamb!
>   My perfect, spotless Righteousness,
>   The great unchangeable "I AM,"
>   The King of glory and of grace.'"

## CONTRITE CRIES.

**568** 7.7.7.7. Double
*Depth of mercy.*

1 DEPTH of mercy! can there be
Mercy still reserv'd for me?
Can my God His wrath forbear?
Me, the chief of sinners, spare?
I have long withstood His grace,
Long provok'd Him to His face,
Would not hearken to His calls,
Griev'd Him by a thousand falls.

2 Kindled His relentings are;
Me He *still* delights to spare;
Cries, "How shall I give thee up?"
Lets the lifted thunder drop.
There for me the Saviour stands,
Shows His wounds, and spreads His hands;
God is love; I know, I feel
Jesus *pleads*, and loves me still.

3 Jesus, answer from above:
Is not all Thy nature love?
Wilt Thou not the wrong forget?
Suffer me to kiss Thy feet?
If I rightly read Thy heart,
If Thou all compassion art,
Bow Thine ear, in mercy bow;
Pardon and accept me now.

4 Pity from Thine eye let fall;
By a look my soul recall;
Now the stone to flesh convert;
Cast a look, and break my heart.
Now incline me to repent;
Let me now my fall lament;
Now my foul revolt deplore;
Weep, believe, and sin no more!

*Charles Wesley*, 1740 [*rev. 1780, alt.*]

> **2.2:** *now* **2.8:** *weeps* **Ed:** The alteration at 2.2 appeared as early as 1831 in Lowell Mason's *Church Psalmody*; 2.8 appeared as early as 1829 in *A Selection of Hymns … in Union Chapel, Calcutta*. This form of the hymn, in 4 stanzas of 8 lines, with the changes, appeared in *Psalms and Hymns … for the Use of the Parish Churches of Islington*, Enl. Ed. (1862).

**569** 7.7.7.7.7.7.
*The long-suffering of God.*

1 LORD, and am I yet alive,
Not in torments, not in hell!
Still doth Thy good Spirit strive,
With the chief sinners dwell!
  *Tell it unto sinners, tell,*
  *I am, I am out of hell!*

2 Yes, I still lift up *mine* eyes,
Will not of Thy love despair;
Still in spite of sin I rise,
Still *I bow to Thee in prayer.*
  *Tell it unto sinners, tell,*
  *I am, I am out of hell!*

3 O the length and breadth of love!
Jesus, Saviour, can it be?
All Thy mercy's height I prove;
All *the* depth is seen in me!
  *Tell it unto sinners, tell,*
  *I am, I am out of hell!*

4 See a bush that burns with fire,
Unconsumed amidst the flame!
Turn aside *the* sight t' admire;
I the living wonder AM!
  *Tell it unto sinners, tell,*
  *I am, I am out of hell!*

5  See a stone that hangs in air!
    See a spark in *ocean live!*
    Kept alive with death so near,
    *I to God the glory give.*
        *Ever tell—to sinners tell,*
        *I am, I am out of hell.*

*Charles Wesley*, [1742]
[*alt. John Rippon*, 1787]

> **2.4:** *to call Thee mine I dare.*  **3.4:** *its*
> **4.3:** *a*  **5.2:** *oceans dwell!*
> **5.4:** *I am, I am out of hell!*
> **Ed:** Wesley's original text was in 3 stanzas of 8
>     lines. The refrain was added by Rippon.
> **TD:** "When David speaks of his showing forth all
>     God's praise, he means that, in his deliverance
>     grace in all its heights and depths would be
>     magnified. Just as our hymn puts it:
>         O the length and breadth of love!
>         Jesus, Saviour, can it be?
>         All Thy mercy's height I prove,
>         All the depth is seen in me"
>     (Ps. 9:14; vol. 1, p. 111).

# 570 C.M.
*Confessing and pleading.*

1  BY Thy victorious hand struck down,
    Here prostrate, Lord, I lie,
   And *faint* to see my Maker frown,
    Whom once I *dared* defy.

2  With heart unshaken I have heard
    Thy dreadful thunders roar;
   When grace in all its charms appear'd,
    I only sinn'd the more.

3  With impious hands from off Thy head
    I've sought to pluck the crown,
   And insolently dared to tread
    Thy royal honour down.

4  Confounded, Lord, I wrap my face
    And hang my guilty head,
   Asham'd of all my wicked ways,
    The hateful life I've led.

5  I yield, by mighty love subdued;
    Who can resist its charms?

And throw myself, by wrath pursued,
    Into my Saviour's arms.

6  My wand'rings, Lord, are at an end;
    I'm now return'd to Thee;
   Be Thou my Father and my Friend;
    Be all in all to me.

*Simon Browne*, 1720 [*alt. C.H.S.*]

> **1.3:** *shake*  **1.4:** *did*  **Ed:** "This cento, as
>     given in Spurgeon's *OOHB*, 1866, No. 570, is
>     composed of stanzas from various hymns in
>     S. Browne's *Hymns and Spiritual Songs*,
>     1720, as follows: st. i from No. 10; ii from No.
>     9; iii from No. 13; iv from No. 11; v and vi from
>     No. 16. It is a most successful arrangement
>     of the stanzas selected, and well adapted to
>     its purpose." —John Julian's *Dictionary of*
>     *Hymnology*, p. 199.

# 571 S.M.
*"Lord, to whom shall we go?"*

1  AH! whither should I go,
    Burden'd, and sick, and faint?
   To whom should I my trouble show
    And pour out my complaint?

2  My Saviour bids me come;
    Ah! why do I delay?
   He calls the weary sinner home,
    And yet from Him I stay.

3  What is it keeps me back,
    From which I cannot part,
   Which will not let my Saviour take
    Possession of my heart?

4  Jesu, the hindrance show,
    Which I have feared to see;
   Yet let me now consent to know
    What keeps me out from Thee.

5  Searcher of hearts, in mine
    Thy trying power display;
   Into its darkest corners shine,
    And take the veil away.

*Charles Wesley*, [1742, *rev.* 1780]

# 572

S.M.
*Prayer for repentance.*

1 O THAT I could repent,
    With all my idols part,
And to Thy gracious eye present
    A humble, contrite heart.

2 A heart with grief oppress'd,
    For having grieved my God,
A troubled heart that cannot rest
    Till sprinkled with Thy blood.

3 Jesus, on me bestow
    The penitent desire;
With true sincerity of woe,
    My aching breast inspire.

4 With softening pity look,
    And melt my hardness down;
Strike with Thy love's resistless stroke,
    And break this heart of stone.

*Charles Wesley,* 1749 [*rev.* 1780]

# 573

L.M.
*The stony heart.*

1 OH! for a glance of heav'nly day
To take this stubborn stone away
And thaw with beams of love divine
This heart, this frozen heart of mine.

2 The rocks can rend, the earth can quake,
The seas can roar, the mountains shake;
Of feeling all things show some sign,
But this unfeeling heart of mine.

3 To hear the sorrows Thou hast felt,
Dear Lord, an adamant would melt,
But I can read each moving line,
And nothing move this heart of mine.

4 Thy judgments, too, unmov'd I hear,
(Amazing thought!) which devils fear;
Goodness and wrath in vain combine
To stir this stupid heart of mine.

5 But something yet can do the deed,
And that dear something much I need;

Thy Spirit can from dross refine,
And move and melt this heart of mine.

*Joseph Hart,* 1762

# 574

7.6.7.6. Double
*I need Thee, Jesus.*

1 I NEED Thee, precious Jesus!
    For I am full of sin;
My heart is dark and guilty;
    My heart is dead within;
I need the cleansing fountain,
    Where I can always flee—
The blood of Christ most precious,
    The sinner's perfect plea.

2 I need Thee, *blessèd* Jesus!
    For I am very poor;
A stranger and a pilgrim,
    I have no earthly store;
I need the love of Jesus
    To cheer me on my way,
To guide my doubting footsteps,
    To be my strength and stay.

3 I need Thee, *blessèd* Jesus!
    I need a friend like Thee,
A friend to soothe and sympathize,
    A friend to care for me.
I need the heart of Jesus
    To feel each anxious care,
To tell my every want to
    And all my sorrows share.

4 I need Thee, *blessèd* Jesus!
    And hope to see Thee soon,
Encircled with the rainbow
    And seated on Thy throne;
There, with Thy blood-bought children,
    My joy shall ever be,
To sing Thy *praise, Lord* Jesus,
    To gaze, my Lord, on Thee.

*Frederick Whitfield,* [1855, *alt. C.H.S.*]

**2.1, 3.1, 4.1:** *precious*  **4.7:** *praises,*
**Ed:** The date 1855 refers to a broadsheet. The
    hymn's first appearance in a hymnal was J.C.

Ryle's *Hymns for the Church* (1860), then in Whitfield's *Sacred Poems and Prose* (1861).

# 575 8.8.6.8.8.6.
*The rebel's surrender.*

1 LORD, Thou hast won, at length I yield;
My heart, by mighty grace compell'd,
  Surrenders all to Thee;
Against Thy terrors long I strove,
But who can stand against Thy love?
  Love conquers even me.

2 If Thou hadst bid Thy thunders roll,
And lightnings flash to blast my soul,
  I still had stubborn been;
But mercy has my heart subdued;
A bleeding Saviour I have view'd,
  And now I hate my sin.

3 Now, Lord, I would be Thine alone;
Come, take possession of Thine own,
  For Thou hast set me free;
Released from Satan's hard command,
See all my *members* waiting stand,
  To be employ'd by Thee.

*John Newton*, 1779 [*alt. C.H.S.*]

  **3.5:** *powers*

# 576 7.7.7.7.7.7.
*Invitation accepted.*

1 AM I called? And can it be!
Has my Saviour chosen me?
Guilty, wretched as I am,
Has He named my worthless name?
Vilest of the vile am I;
Dare I raise my hopes so high?

2 Am I called? I dare not stay;
May not, must not disobey;
Here I lay me at Thy feet,
Clinging to the mercy seat;
Thine I am and Thine alone;
Lord, with me Thy will be done.

3 Am I called? What shall I bring
As an offering to my King?

Poor, and blind, and naked I,
Trembling at Thy footstool lie;
Nought but sin I call my own,
Nor for sin can sin atone.

4 *Am I called? An heir* of God!
Washed, redeemed, by precious blood!
*Father, lead* me in Thy hand,
Guide me to that better land,
Where my soul shall be at rest,
Pillow'd on my Saviour's breast.

*Jane Gray*, [1834]
[*alt.* Presbyterian *Psalms & Hymns*, 1843]

  **4.1:** *Heir of bliss, a child*   **4.3:** *Ever hold*
  **Ed:** The fourth stanza here is a conflation of
  Gray's original stanzas 4 and 6.

# 577 L.M.
*"God be merciful to me."*

1 O LORD, my God, in mercy turn,
In mercy hear a sinner mourn!
To Thee I call, to Thee I cry;
O leave me, leave me not to die!

2 O pleasures past, what are ye now
But thorns about my bleeding brow!
Spectres that hover round my brain
And aggravate and mock my pain.

3 For pleasure I have given my soul;
Now, justice, let Thy thunders roll!
Now vengeance *smite*, and with a blow,
Lay the rebellious ingrate low.

4 Yet, Jesus, Jesus! there I'll cling;
I'll crowd beneath His sheltering wing;
I'll clasp the cross, and holding there,
Even me, oh bliss! His wrath may spare.

*Henry Kirke White*, 1807

  **3.3:** *smile*  **Ed:** The original version in his
  posthumous *Remains* (1807) reads "smile," as
  does its appearance in Wm. Collyer's *Hymns*
  (1812); "smite," a common variant, stems from
  an 1825 ed. of the *Remains*.

# 578 C.M.
*The penitent.*

1 PROSTRATE, dear Jesus, at Thy feet,
  A guilty rebel lies,
And upwards to Thy mercy seat
  Presumes to lift His eyes.

2 O let not justice frown me hence;
  Stay, stay, the vengeful storm;
Forbid it that Omnipotence
  Should crush a feeble worm.

3 If tears of sorrows would suffice
  To pay the debt I owe,
Tears should from both my weeping eyes
  In ceaseless torents flow.

4 But no such sacrifice I plead
  To expiate my guilt;
No tears, but those which Thou hast shed,
  No blood, but Thou hast spilt.

5 Think of Thy sorrows, dearest Lord,
  And all my sins forgive;
Justice will well approve the word
  That bids the sinner live.

*Samuel Stennett*, 1787

# 579 7.6.7.6.
*Sin wounding Jesus.*

1 MY sins, my sins, my Saviour!
  How sad on Thee they fall;
Seen through Thy gentle patience,
  I tenfold feel them all.

2 I know they are forgiven,
  But still, their pain to me
Is all the grief and anguish
  They laid, my Lord, on Thee.

3 My sins, my sins, my Saviour!
  Their guilt I never knew
Till, with Thee, in the desert
  I near Thy passion drew,

4 Till with Thee in the garden
  I heard Thy pleading prayer,

And saw the sweat drops bloody
  That told Thy sorrow there.

*John S.B. Monsell*, 1863

# 580 C.M. Double
*I crucified Him.*

1 MY Jesus! say what wretch has dared
  Thy sacred hands to bind?
And who has dared to buffet so
  Thy face so meek and kind?
'Tis I have thus ungrateful been,
  Yet, Jesus! pity take!
Oh spare and pardon me, my Lord,
  For Thy sweet mercy's sake!

2 My Jesus! who with spittle vile
  Profaned Thy sacred brow?
Or whose unpitying scourge has made
  Thy precious blood to flow?
'Tis I have thus ungrateful been,
  Yet, Jesus! pity take!
Oh spare and pardon me, my Lord,
  For Thy sweet mercy's sake!

3 My Jesus! whose the hands that wove
  That cruel thorny crown?
Who made that hard and heavy cross
  That weighs Thy shoulders down?
'Tis I have thus ungrateful been,
  Yet, Jesus! pity take!
Oh spare and pardon me, my Lord,
  For Thy sweet mercy's sake!

4 My Jesus! who has mocked Thy thirst
  With vinegar and gall?
Who held the nails that pierced Thy hands,
  And made the hammer fall?
'Tis I have thus ungrateful been,
  Yet, Jesus! pity take!
Oh spare and pardon me, my Lord,
  For Thy sweet mercy's sake!

5 My Jesus! say, who dared to nail
  Those tender feet of Thine,
And whose the arm that raised the lance
  To pierce that heart divine?
'Tis I have thus ungrateful been,

Yet, Jesus! pity take!
Oh spare and pardon me, my Lord,
For Thy sweet mercy's sake!

6 And, *Father!* who has murdered thus
Thy loved and only One?
Canst Thou forgive the blood-stained hand
That robbed Thee of Thy Son?
'Tis I have thus ungrateful been
To Jesus and to Thee;
Forgive me, *Lord, for His sweet* sake,
And *mercy grant to* me.

*Alphonso M. Liguori*, 1769
*tr. Robert A. Coffin*, 1854 [*alt. C.H.S.*]

**6.1:** *Mary,* **6.7:** *for thy Jesus'*
**6.8:** *pray to Him for*
**Ed:** From the Italian, "Gesù mio, con dure funi."

# 581 C.M. / *"Look on Him whom they pierced, and mourn."*

1 INFINITE grief! amazing woe!
Behold my bleeding Lord:
Hell and the Jews conspir'd His death
And used the Roman sword.

2 Oh the sharp pangs of smarting pain
My dear Redeemer bore,
When knotty whips and rugged thorns
His sacred body tore!

3 But knotty whips and rugged thorns
In vain do I accuse;
In vain I blame the Roman bands
And the more spiteful Jews.

4 'Twas you, my sins, my cruel sins,
His chief tormenters were;
Each of my crimes became a nail,
And unbelief the spear.

5 'Twas you that pull'd the vengeance down
Upon His guiltless head;
Break, break my heart, oh burst mine eyes!
And let my sorrows bleed.

6 Strike, mighty grace, my flinty soul,
Till melting waters flow,

And deep repentance drown mine eyes
In undissembled woe.

*Isaac Watts*, [1707, *alt.*]

**4.1:** *'Twere* **5.1:** *'Twere* **Ed:** This common
variant appeared in posthumous eds. of Watts'
*Hymns* as early as 1768.

# 582 C.M. *Repentance at the cross.*

1 O IF my soul were form'd for woe,
How would I vent my sighs!
Repentance should like rivers flow
From both my streaming eyes.

2 'Twas for my sins my dearest Lord
Hung on the cursèd tree
And groan'd away a dying life
For thee, my soul, for thee.

3 Oh how I hate those lusts of mine
That crucified my God,
Those sins that pierc'd and nail'd His flesh
Fast to the fatal wood.

4 Yes, my Redeemer, they shall die,
My heart has so decreed;
Nor will I spare the guilty things
That made my Saviour bleed.

5 Whilst with a melting, broken heart,
My murder'd Lord I view,
I'll raise revenge against my sins
And slay the murderers too.

*Isaac Watts*, [1707]

# 583 S.M. *Confession and pardon.*

1 MY sorrows like a flood,
Impatient of restraint,
Into Thy bosom, O my God,
Pour out a long complaint.

2 This impious heart of mine
Could once defy the Lord,
Could rush with violence on to sin
In presence of Thy sword.

3   How often have I stood
     A rebel to the skies,
*And yet, and yet, O matchless grace!*
*   Thy thunder silent lies.*

4   O shall I never feel
     The meltings of Thy love?
Am I of such hell-harden'd steel
   That mercy cannot move?

5   O'ercome by dying *love*,
     Here at Thy cross I lie,
And throw my flesh, my soul, my all,
   And weep, and love, and die.

6   *"Rise," says the Saviour, "rise,*
*    Behold my wounded veins;*
*Here flows a sacred crimson flood*
*   To wash away thy stains."*

7   *See, God is reconcil'd;*
*    Behold His smiling face!*
*Let joyful cherubs clap their wings*
*   And sound aloud His grace.*

  *Isaac Watts*, 1706 [*rev.* 1709]
  [*alt. John Rippon*, 1787]

    **3.3-4:** *The calls, the tenders of a God,*
*      And mercy's loudest cries!*
    **5.1:** *love I fall,*
    **6.1-4:** *"Rise," says the Prince of Mercy, "rise,"*
*      With joy and pity in his eyes;*
*      "Rise and behold my wounded veins;*
*      Here flows the blood to wash thy stains."*
    **7.1-4:** *"See my great Father reconcil'd,"*
*      He said, and lo the Father smil'd;*
*      The joyful cherubs clapt their wings*
*      And sounded grace on all their strings.*
    **Ed:** Taken from the longer hymn, "Alas, my
    aching heart!" Watts' metre was inconsistent,
    at st. 5 giving Common Metre, and at sts.
    6-7 giving Long Metre. The 1st ed. of Rippon
    repeated the inconsistency at 5; this was cor-
    rected in the 2nd ed. (ca. 1790).

# 584  C.M.
*"Jesus, master, have mercy on us."*

1 LORD, at Thy feet *we sinners lie*
   And knock at mercy's door,

With heavy heart and downcast *eye*
   Thy favour *we* implore.

2 On *us*, the vast extent display
   Of Thy forgiving love;
Take all *our* heinous guilt away;
   This heavy load remove.

3 'Tis mercy—mercy *we* implore;
   *We* would Thy *pity* move;
Thy grace is an exhaustless store,
   And Thou thyself art love.

4 Oh! for Thine own, for Jesus' sake,
   *Our numerous* sins forgive;
Thy grace *our* rocky *hearts* can break,
   *Our* breaking *hearts* relieve.

5 Thus melt *us* down, thus make *us* bend,
   And Thy dominion own,
Nor let a rival *dare* pretend
   To repossess Thy throne.

  *Simon Browne*, 1720 [*alt.*]
  [*alt. John Rippon*, 1787]

    **1.1:** *a sinner lies,*   **1.3:** *eyes*   **1.4:** *to*
    **2.1:** *me*   **2.3:** *mine*   **3.1:** *I*   **3.2:** *I / bowels*
    **4.2:** *My many*   **4.3:** *my / heart*   **4.4:** *My / heart*
    **5.1:** *me / me*   **5.3:** *more*
    **Ed:** The alterations at 1.1-3.1, 4.3, and 5.1, espe-
    cially the shift from singular to plural, are by
    John Rippon (1787); 3.2 and 4.2 appeared as
    early as 1827 in J. Curtis' *Union Collection*.
    This exact form of the hymn appeared in *The*
    *New Congregational Hymn Book* (ca. 1859).

# 585  7.7.7.7.7.7.
*At Jesus' feet.*

1 LORD, we lie before Thy feet;
  Look on all our deep distress;
Thy rich mercy may we meet;
  Clothe us with Thy righteousness;
Stretch forth Thy almighty hand;
  Hold us up, and we shall stand.

2 Oh that closer we could cleave
  To thy bleeding, dying breast!
Give us firmly to believe,

And to enter into rest.
Lord, increase, increase our faith!
Make us faithful unto death.

3 Let us trust Thee evermore;
   Ev'ry moment on Thee call
For new life, new will, new pow'r;
   Let us trust Thee, Lord, for all.
May we nothing know beside
Jesus and Him crucified!

*Joseph Hart*, 1759

# 586 C.M.
*Pleading the promise.*

1 APPROACH, my soul, the mercy seat
   Where Jesus answers pray'r;
There humbly fall before His feet,
   For none can perish there.

2 Thy promise is my only plea;
   With this I venture nigh;
Thou callest burden'd souls to Thee,
   And such, O Lord, am I.

3 Bow'd down beneath a load of sin,
   By Satan sorely press'd,
By war without and fears within,
   I come to Thee for rest.

4 Be Thou my shield and hiding place!
   That, shelter'd near Thy side,
I may my fierce accuser face
   And tell Him Thou hast died.

5 Oh wondrous love! to bleed and die,
   To bear the cross and shame,
That guilty sinners such as I
   Might plead Thy gracious name.

6 "Poor tempest-tossèd soul, be still,
   My promis'd grace receive,"
'Tis Jesus speaks—I must, I will,
   I can, I do believe.

*John Newton*, 1779

**MM:** Hymns, Set 2 (Feb./Dec.), 19th Eve,
AZMON / HELENA

# 587 8.7.8.7.
*Supplicating.*

1 JESUS, full of all compassion,
   Hear Thy humble suppliant's cry;
Let me know Thy great salvation;
   See, I languish, faint, and die.

2 Guilty, but with heart relenting,
   Overwhelm'd with helpless grief,
Prostrate at Thy feet repenting,
   Send, oh send me quick relief!

3 Whither should a wretch be flying,
   But to Him who comfort gives?
Whither, from the dread of dying,
   But to Him who ever lives?

4 While I view Thee, wounded, grieving,
   Breathless on the cursèd tree,
Fain I'd feel my heart believing
   That Thou suffered'st thus for me.

5 Hear, then, blessèd Saviour, hear me;
   My soul cleaveth to the dust;
Send the Comforter to cheer me;
   Lo! in Thee I put my trust.

6 On the Word Thy blood hath sealèd
   Hangs my everlasting all;
Let *Thy* arm be now revealèd;
   Stay, O stay me, lest I fall!

7 In the world of endless ruin,
   Let it never, Lord, be said,
"Here's a soul that perish'd, suing
   For the boasted Saviour's aid!"

8 Sav'd—the deed shall spread new glory
   Through the shining realms above;
Angels sing the pleasing story,
   All enraptur'd with Thy love!

*Daniel Turner*, [1769, *alt.*]

**6.3:** *Thine* **Ed:** This minor variant dates to the
early 1800s, including some editions of Rippon's *Selection*, but it is not in the Compr. Ed.
that Spurgeon used with his congregation.

# 588
C.M.
*"Save, Lord."*

1 O JESUS, Saviour of the lost,
   My rock and hiding place,
By storms of sin and sorrow toss'd,
   I seek Thy sheltering grace.

2 Guilty, forgive me, Lord, I cry;
   Pursued by foes I come;
A sinner, save me, or I die;
   An outcast, take me home.

3 Once safe in Thine almighty arms,
   Let storms come on amain;
There danger never, never harms—
   There death itself is gain.

4 And when I stand before Thy throne,
   And all Thy glory see,
Still be my righteousness alone
   To hide myself in Thee.

*Edward Henry Bickersteth*, [1852]

# 589
L.M.
*Desiring to submit.*

1 OH! that my load of sin were gone!
Oh! that I could at last submit
At Jesu's feet to lay it down,
To lay my soul at Jesu's feet.

2 When shall mine eyes behold the Lamb?
The God of my salvation see?
Weary, O Lord, Thou know'st I am;
Yet still I cannot come to Thee.

3 Rest for my soul I long to find;
Saviour *divine*, if mine Thou art,
Give me Thy meek and lowly mind,
And stamp Thine image on my heart.

4 Break off the yoke of inbred sin,
And fully set my spirit free;
I cannot rest till pure within,
Till I am wholly lost in Thee.

5 Come, Lord, the drooping sinner cheer,
Nor let Thy chariot wheels delay;

Appear in my poor heart, appear;
My God, my Saviour, come away.

*Charles Wesley*, 1742, *alt. C.H.S.*

**3.2:** *of all*  **Ed:** This alteration almost certainly
was made to reflect Spurgeon's theological
convictions.

# 590
L.M.
*"Come to me."*

1 WITH tearful eyes I look around;
Life seems a dark and stormy sea,
Yet 'mid the gloom, I hear a sound,
A heav'nly whisper, "Come to Me."

2 It tells me of a place of rest;
It tells me where my soul may flee;
Oh! to the weary, faint, oppress'd,
How sweet the bidding, "Come to Me!"

3 "Come, for all else must fail and die;
Earth is no resting place for thee;
*To heaven* direct thy weeping eye;
I am thy portion; come to Me."

4 O voice of mercy! voice of love!
In conflict, grief, and agony,
Support me, cheer me, from above!
And gently whisper—"Come to me."

*Charlotte Elliott*, 1834 [*rev.* 1841]
[*alt.* Sabbath Hymn Book, 1858]

**3.3:** *Heav'nward*

# 591
7.7.7.7. Double
*"Strong crying and tears."*

1 SAVIOUR, when in dust to Thee
Low we bow th' adoring knee;
When, repentant, to the skies
Scarce we lift our weeping eyes;
O! by all Thy pains and woe
Suffer'd once for man below,
Bending from Thy throne on high,
*Hear, oh hear our humble cry!*

2 By Thy helpless infant years,
By Thy life of want and tears,

By Thy days of sore distress,
In the savage wilderness,
By the dread, mysterious hour
Of th' insulting tempter's pow'r,
Turn, O turn a favouring eye;
*Hear, oh hear our humble cry!*

3 By Thine hour of dire despair,
By Thine agony of pray'r,
By the cross, the nail, the thorn,
Piercing spear, and torturing scorn,
By the gloom that veil'd the skies
O'er the dreadful sacrifice,
Listen to our humble *sigh!*
*Hear, oh hear our humble cry!*

4 By Thy deep expiring groan,
By the sad sepulchral stone,
By the vault whose dark abode
Held in vain the rising God;
O! from earth to heav'n restor'd,
Mighty re-ascended Lord,
Listen *from Thy throne on high;*
*Hear, oh hear our humble cry!*

*Robert Grant, 1815 [rev. 1839], alt.*

**1.8, 2.8, 3.8:** *Hear our solemn litany!*
**3.7:** *cry!* **4.7:** *listen to the cry*
**4.8:** *Of our solemn litany!*
**Ed:** Similar to No. 104, John Julian claimed
that H.V. Elliott's *Psalms and Hymns* (1835)
included the hymn, with a "protest in the
preface against its mutilation … and the
declaration that the text in that collection was
pure" (p. 997). Elliott did include the hymn—
identical to its 1815 form except for one word
in a stanza that has been omitted here—but no
known edition of Elliott's collection contains
a preface. The alterations to the repeated
phrase at 1.8 etc. are from *The Sabbath Hymn
Book* (1858); the others are by Spurgeon.

# 592 7.7.7.7.7.7.
*"Manifest thyself to me."*

1 SON of God, to Thee I cry!
By the holy mystery
Of Thy dwelling here on earth,
By Thy pure and holy birth;

Lord, Thy presence let me see;
Manifest Thyself to me!

2 Lamb of God, to Thee I cry;
By Thy bitter agony,
By Thy pangs, to us unknown,
By Thy Spirit's parting groan,
Lord, Thy presence let me see,
Manifest Thyself to me!

3 Prince of Life, to Thee I cry;
By Thy glorious majesty,
By Thy triumph o'er the grave,
Meek to suffer, strong to save,
Lord, Thy presence let me see,
Manifest Thyself to me!

4 Lord of Glory, God Most High,
Man exalted to the sky,
With Thy love my bosom fill;
Prompt me to perform Thy will;
*Then Thy glory I shall see;*
*Thou wilt bring me home to Thee.*

*Richard Mant, [1828] alt.*

**Ed:** Taken from the longer hymn, "Saviour, who,
exalted high." Mant's original stanzas of 13 lines
were condensed into sets of 6 lines, closing
with two completely new lines, for William
Cooke and William Denton's *Church Hymnal*
(1853), except their version began "Son of Man,
to Thee we cry" and had other alterations. This
was adopted into the enlarged ed. of S.P.C.K.'s
*Psalms and Hymns* (1863), but with corrections respecting Mant's original, while keeping
the final two lines from Cooke & Denton.

# 593 L.M.
*Be merciful to me.*

1 WITH broken heart and contrite sigh,
A trembling sinner, Lord, I cry;
Thy pardoning grace is rich and free;
O God, be merciful to me.

2 I smite upon my troubled breast,
With deep and conscious guilt oppress'd;
Christ and His cross my only plea;
O God, be merciful to me.

3 Far off I stand with fearful eyes,
   Nor dare uplift them to the skies;
   But Thou dost all my anguish see;
   O God, be merciful to me.

4 Nor alms, nor deeds that I have done
   Can for a single sin atone;
   To Calvary alone I flee;
   O God, be merciful to me.

5 And when, redeemed from sin and hell,
   With all the ransomed throng I dwell,
   My raptured song shall ever be,
   God has been merciful to me.

*Cornelius Elven*, [1857]

> **EE:** Hymns, Set 2 (Feb./Dec.), 7th Eve,
> ULVERSTONE / DOVERSDALE
> **Ed:** Samuel Duffield, in his *English Hymns*
> (1886), pp. 617-618, relayed the testimony of
> G.J. Stevenson, who said, "This hymn came to
> the author as an inspiration, whilst holding a
> series of revival services in the Baptist Chapel,
> Bury St. Edmonds, in January, 1852. . . .
> [Elven] was a true and devoted friend of
> Rev. C.H. Spurgeon, who wrote a sketch of
> him when he died, in July 1873, and says that
> he was a man of homely attainments, pre-emi-
> nently practical as a pastor and preacher, and
> full of faith and the Holy Ghost. The bulk of
> his body was stupendous, but his heart was
> large in proportion to his body, and it was full
> of kindness. He preached occasionally for Mr.
> Spurgeon, who loved him."
> The hymn was not published until 1857.

# 594 8.7.8.7.
*Deliver me.*

1 MERCY, mercy, God the Father;
   God the Son, be Thou my plea;
   God the Holy Spirit, comfort;
   Triune God, deliver me.

2 Not my sins, O Lord, remember;
   Not Thine own avenger be;
   But for Thy great tender mercies,
   Saviour God, deliver me.

3 By Thy cross and by Thy passion,
   Bloody sweat and agony,

By Thy precious death and burial,
   Saviour God, deliver me.

4 By Thy glorious resurrection,
   Thine ascent in heaven to be,
   By *the* Holy Spirit's coming,
   Saviour God, deliver me.

5 In all time of tribulation,
   In all time of wealth, in the
   Hour of death and day of judgment,
   Saviour God, deliver me.

*John S.B. Monsell*, [1861, *alt. C.HS.*]

> **4.3:** *Thy*  **EE:** Hymns, Set 2 (Feb./Dec.), 6th
> Eve, MARINER'S / MUNICH

# 595 8.7.8.7.4.7.
*Pity me, O Lord.*

1 PITY, Lord, a wretched creature,
   One whose sins for vengeance cry,
   Groaning 'neath his heavy burden,
   Throbbing breast, and heavy sigh!
     Oh! my Saviour,
   Canst Thou *let a sinner die?*

2 No, Thou canst not: Thou hast promis'd
   To attend unto his prayer;
   *Still* he cries in falt'ring accents,
   Jesus, oh! in mercy spare.
     Spare a sinner!
   Jesus, oh! in mercy spare.

3 Oh! how swift Divine compassion
   Runs to meet the mourning soul,
   And by words of consolation
   Makes the wounded spirit whole.
     "I'm thy Saviour";
   Let this truth thy mind console.

4 Groans and sighs are turn'd to praises;
   Doubts and fears are chas'd away;
   Now with saints his voice he raises;
   Jesus hears the pious lay.
     *Glory, glory,*
   Hallelujahs close the day.

5 Angels that were hovering o'er him
    Spread their wings and leave the place,
*Bear to heaven the* joyful tidings
    Of a sinner sav'd by grace.
       Myriads listen!
    Heaven rings with shouts of praise.

[*John Stamp, 1838, rev. 1845, alt.*]

**1.6:** *pass the sinner by?* **2.3:** *While*
**4.5:** *Hallelujah!* **5.3:** *Bearing with them*
**Ed:** The hymn seems to have first appeared in
*The Primitive Methodist Magazine*, Aug.
1838, with the signature "Cambridge. J.L."
From there it was given unattributed in *The
Christian's Spiritual Song Book* (1845), compiled by John Stamp, a Primitive Methodist,
with the changes above, except 2.3, which appeared in a few collections 1860-1861 before it
was adopted by Spurgeon. Sedgwick credited
the hymn to the 1845 collection; Julian,
p. 1590, credited the hymn directly to Stamp.

# 596   8.7.8.7.8.7.
*"Love us freely."*

1 LOVE us freely, blessèd Jesus,
    For we have not aught to pay;
Saviour Thou, and we poor sinners,
    Is alone what we can say;
Love us freely, blessèd Jesus,
    For we have not aught to pay.

2 Love us ever, blessèd Jesus;
    We are changing as the wind;
If Thy love on us depended,
    We should ne'er salvation find;
Love us ever, blessèd Jesus,
    We are changing as the wind.

3 Love and help us, blessèd Jesus,
    Help us to be wholly Thine;
Every idol and enchantment,
    For Thy glory to resign;
Love and help us, blessèd Jesus;
    Help us to be wholly Thine.

4 Love and keep us, blessèd Jesus,
    Keep us from denying Thee;
Keep our wayward feet from straying
    Into paths of vanity;

Love and keep us, blessèd Jesus,
    Keep us from denying Thee.

*Albert Midlane, 1865*

# 597   7.7.7.7.
*Confession of sin.*

1 SOVEREIGN Ruler, Lord of all,
Prostrate at Thy feet I fall;
Hear, oh hear my *earnest* cry;
Frown not, lest I faint and die!

2 Vilest of the sons of men,
*Chief of sinners* I have been!
Oft *have sinn'd before* Thy face,
Trampled on Thy richest grace.

3 Justly might Thy *fatal* dart
Pierce this *bleeding, broken* heart;
Justly might Thy *angry breath*
Blast me in eternal *death.*

4 Jesus, save my dying soul;
Make my broken spirit whole;
Humbled in the dust I lie;
Saviour, leave me not to die.

1-3 *Thomas Raffles, 1812, alt.*
4 *Thomas Hastings, 1831*

**1.3:** *ardent* **2.2:** *Worst of rebels*
**2.3:** *abus'd Thee to* **3.1:** *vengeful*
**3.2:** *broken, bleeding* **3.3:** *kindled ire*
**3.4:** *fire* **Ed:** The alterations at 1.3, 2.2, and
3.2-3.4 appeared as early as 1831 in Thomas
Hastings' *Spiritual Songs*, and Hastings' hymn
"Jesus, save my dying soul" appeared in an
1833 ed. This exact form of the hymn, combining Hastings' work and adding the other
alts., appeared in Stow & Smith, *The Psalmist*
(1843), and was repeated in Basil Manly's
*Baptist Psalmody* (1850), which was part of
Spurgeon's personal library. See also No. 601.

# 598   L.M.
*Think of Jesus.*

1 WHEN at Thy footstool, Lord, I bend,
And plead with Thee for mercy there,
Think of the sinner's dying Friend,
And for His sake receive my prayer!

2 O think not of my shame and guilt,
My thousand stains of deepest dye;
Think of the blood *for sinners* spilt,
And let that blood my pardon buy.

3 Think, Lord, how I am still *Thine* own,
The trembling creature of Thy hand;
Think how my heart to sin is prone,
And what temptations round me stand.

4 O think not of my doubts and fears,
My strivings with Thy grace divine;
Think upon *Jesu's* woes and tears,
And let His merits stand for mine.

5 Thine eye, Thine ear, they are not dull;
Thine arm can never shortened be;
Behold me *now*—my heart is full—
Behold, and spare, and succour me.

*Henry Francis Lyte*, 1833
[*alt. Thomas Davis*, 1864]

**2.3:** *which Jesus* **3.1:** *Thy* **4.3:** *Jesus'* **5.3:** *here*

# 599 L.M.
*Relying upon grace.*

1 WHY droops my soul, with grief oppress'd?
*Whence* these wild tumults in my breast?
Is there no balm to heal my wound?
No kind physician to be found?

2 Raise to the cross thy tearful eyes;
Behold! the Prince of Glory dies!
He dies extended on the tree
*And* sheds a sov'reign balm for *thee*.

3 *Blest* Saviour, at Thy feet I lie,
Here to receive a cure or die,
But grace forbids that painful fear,
*Almighty grace, which* triumphs here.

4 Thou wilt *withdraw* the poison'd dart,
Bind up and heal the *wounded* heart,
With blooming health my face adorn,
And *change* the gloomy night *to* morn.

*Elizabeth Scott*, 1763, *alt.*

**1.2:** *Why* **2.4:** *Thence / me!* **3.1:** *Dear*

**3.4:** *Infinite grace that* **4.1:** *extract*
**4.2:** *broken* **4.4:** *chase / with*
**Ed:** Written before 1750 and preserved in her
manuscripts at Yale. The alterations at 4.2
and 4.4 appeared in Caleb Evans' *Collection*
(1769); all except 3.1 appeared in Lowell
Mason's *Church Psalmody* (1831); this final
form appeared in Stow & Smith, *The Psalmist* (1843), and was repeated in Basil Manly's
*Baptist Psalmody* (1850).

# 600 8.7.8.7. / *"Wash me, and I shall be whiter than snow."*

1 JESUS, who on Calvary's mountain
Poured Thy precious blood for me,
Wash me in its flowing fountain,
That my soul may spotless be.

2 I have sinn'd, but oh, restore me,
For unless Thou smile on me,
Dark is all the world before me,
Darker yet eternity!

3 In Thy Word I hear Thee saying,
"Come, and I will give you rest";
*Glad* the gracious call obeying,
See, I hasten to Thy breast.

4 Grant, oh grant Thy Spirit's teaching,
That I may not go astray,
Till the gate of heaven reaching,
Earth and sin are passed away.

*H.W. Beecher's Plymouth Collection*, 1855
[*alt. Sabbath Hymn Book*, 1858]

**3.3:** *And*

# 601 7.7.7.7.
*Pleading for mercy.*

1 JESUS, full of every grace,
Now reveal Thy smiling face;
Grant the joys of sin forgiven,
Foretaste of the bliss of heaven.

2 All my guilt to Thee is known;
Thou art righteous, Thou alone;
All my help is from Thy cross;
All beside I count but loss.

3 Lord, in Thee I now believe;
  Wilt Thou—wilt Thou not forgive?
  Helpless at Thy feet I lie;
  Saviour, leave me not to die.

*Thomas Hastings*, [1833]

> **Ed:** From the longer hymn, "Jesus, save my
> dying soul." For the first stanza, see No. 597.

# 602 7.7.7.7.
*"Jesus! Master!"*

1 JESUS! Master! hear my cry;
  Save me, heal me with a word;
  Fainting at Thy feet I lie,
  Thou my whispered plaint hast heard.

2 Jesus! Master! mercy show;
  Thou art passing near my soul;
  Thou my inward grief dost know;
  Thou alone canst make me whole.

3 Jesus! Master! as of yore
  Thou didst bid the blind man see,
  Light upon my soul restore;
  Jesus! Master! heal Thou me.

*Anna Shipton*, [1858]

> **EE:** (Aug. 10) "He can breathe into thy soul at
> this very moment a peace with God which
> passeth all understanding, which shall spring
> from perfect remission of thy manifold
> iniquities. Dost thou believe that? I trust thou
> believest it. Mayst thou experience now the
> power of Jesus to forgive sin! Waste no time in
> applying to the Physician of souls, but hasten
> to Him with words like these:
> > Jesus! Master, hear my cry;
> > Save me, heal me with a word;
> > Fainting at Thy feet I lie,
> > Thou my whispered plaint hast heard."

# 603 8.6.8.6.
*"Jehovah Rophi."*

1 HEAL us, Emmanuel; here we are,
  Waiting to feel Thy touch;
  Deep-wounded souls to Thee repair,
  And, Saviour, we are such.

2 Our faith is feeble, we confess;
  We faintly trust Thy word;
  But wilt Thou pity us the less?
  Be that far from Thee, Lord!

3 Remember him who once applied
  With trembling for relief;
  "Lord, I believe," with tears he cried,
  "O help my unbelief."

4 She, too, who touch'd Thee in the press,
  And healing virtue stole,
  Was answered, "Daughter, go in peace,
  Thy faith hath made thee whole."

5 Conceal'd amid the gath'ring throng,
  She would have shunn'd Thy view,
  And if her faith was firm and strong,
  Had strong misgivings too.

6 Like her, with hopes and fears, we come
  To touch Thee if we may;
  Oh! send us not despairing home,
  Send none unheal'd away.

*William Cowper*, 1779

# 604 8.8.8.6.
*Plead for me!*

1 O THOU, the contrite sinner's Friend!
  Who loving, lov'st *him* to the end;
  On this alone my hopes depend,
  That Thou wilt plead for me.

2 When, weary in the Christian race,
  Far off appears my resting place,
  And fainting I mistrust Thy grace,
  Then, Saviour, plead for me!

3 When I have err'd and gone astray,
  Afar from Thine and wisdom's way,
  And see no glimmering, guiding ray,
  Still, Saviour, plead for me!

4 And when my dying hour draws near,
  *Then to preserve my soul from* fear,
  *Lord*, to my *fading* sight appear,
  Pleading in heaven for me.

*Charlotte Elliott*, 1835
[*alt. Thomas Davis*, 1864]

**1.2:** *them* **4.2:** *Darken'd with anguish, guilt, and*
**4.3:** *Then to my fainting*

# 605
8.6.8.6.
*"Let us return."*

1 COME, let us to the Lord our God
    With contrite hearts return;
  Our God is gracious, nor will leave
    The desolate to mourn.

2 His voice commands the tempest forth
    And stills the stormy wave,
  And though His arm be strong to smite,
    'Tis also strong to save.

3 Long hath the night of sorrow reign'd;
    The dawn shall bring us light;
  God shall appear, and we shall rise
    With gladness in His sight.

4 Our hearts, if God we seek to know
    Shall know Him and rejoice;
  His coming like the morn shall be,
    Like morning songs His voice.

5 As dew upon the tender herb,
    Diffusing fragrance round,
  As show'rs that usher in the spring
    And cheer the thirsty ground,

6 So shall His presence bless our souls
    And shed a joyful light;
  That hallow'd morn shall chase away
    The sorrows of the night.

*John Morrison*, 1781

**MM:** Hymns, Set 1 (Jan./Nov.), 24th Morn,
  EVAN / LA MIRA
**Ed:** See Julian's *Dictionary of Hymnology*, p.
  249, for the assertion that Morrison's text had
  been altered before it went to press.

# 606
7.7.7.7.
*Give me Christ.*

1 GRACIOUS Lord, incline Thine ear,
  My *requests* vouchsafe to hear;

*Hear my never-ceasing cry;*
  Give me Christ, or else I die.

2 Wealth and honour I disdain;
  Earthly comforts all are vain;
  These can never satisfy;
  Give me Christ, or else I die.

3 Lord, deny me what Thou wilt;
  Only ease me of my guilt;
  Suppliant at Thy feet I lie;
  Give me Christ, or else I die.

4 All unholy, all unclean,
  I am nothing else but sin;
  On Thy mercy I rely;
  Give me Christ, or else I die.

5 Thou dost freely save the lost!
  Only in Thy grace I trust;
  With my earnest suit comply;
  Give me Christ, or else I die.

6 Thou hast promis'd to forgive
  All who in Thy Son believe;
  Lord, I know Thou canst not lie;
  Give me Christ, or else I die.

7 Father, dost Thou seem to frown?
  I take shelter in *Thy* Son;
  *Jesus*, to Thy arms I fly;
  Save me, Lord, or else I die.

*William Hammond*, 1745
[*alt. John Rippon*, 1787]

**1.2:** *complaint* **1.3:** *Faint and sick of love am I*
**7.2:** *the* **7.3:** *Jesu*

# 607
8.8.8.8.3. / *"Bless me,*
*even me also, O my Father!"*

1 LORD, I hear of showers of blessing
  Thou art scattering full and free;
  Showers, the thirsty land refreshing;
  Let some droppings fall on me,
    Even me.

2 Pass me not, O gracious Father!
  Sinful though my heart may be;

Thou might'st curse me, but the rather,
Let Thy mercy light on me,
   Even me.

3 Pass me not, O tender Saviour!
Let me love and cling to Thee;
I am longing for Thy favour;
When Thou comest, call for me,
   Even me.

4 Pass me not, O mighty Spirit!
Thou canst make the blind to see;
Witnesser of Jesus' merit,
Speak the word of power to me,
   Even me.

5 Have I long in sin been sleeping,
Long been slighting, grieving Thee?
Has the world my heart been keeping?
Oh forgive and rescue me,
   Even me.

6 Love of God, so pure and changeless,
Blood of God, so rich and free,
Grace of God, so strong and boundless,
Magnify them all in me,
   Even me.

7 Pass me not, this lost one bringing,
Satan's slave Thy child shall be,
All my heart to Thee is springing;
Blessing others, oh bless me,
   Even me.

*Elizabeth Codner*, [1866]

> **Ed:** The hymn was dated 1860 in Codner's man-
> uscript, which had been sent to Sedgwick in
> the summer of 1866 and published in *OOHB*,
> according to Julian's *Dictionary*, p. 690.
> **MBTS:** 8 Feb. 1883 (No. 2564), EVEN ME
> **TD:** "It may be that under a sense of unwor-
> thiness the writer [of Psalm 119] feared lest
> mercy should be given to others, and not to
> himself; he therefore cries, 'Bless me, even
> me also, O my Father.' Viewed in this light
> the words are tantamount to our well-known
> verse— '. . . showers the thirsty land refresh-
> ing; let some droppings fall on me, even me.'
> (Ps. 119:41; vol. 6, p. 113).

# 608
8.6.8.6.
*Jesus, save me.*

1 JESUS, Thy pow'r I fain would feel,
   *For Thy sweet love I faint;*
O let Thine ears consider well
   The voice of my complaint.

2 Thou see'st me yet a slave to sin
   And destitute of God;
O purify *my soul within*
   By Thine all-cleansing blood.

3 O Jesus, undertake for me
   Thy peace to me be giv'n,
For while I stand away from Thee,
   I stand away from heav'n.

4 Reject not, Lord, my humble pray'rs,
   Nor yet my soul destroy;
Thine only Son hath sown in tears
   That I might reap in joy.

*Augustus Toplady*, 1759, *alt. C.H.S.*

> **1.2:** *Thy love is all I want;*
> **2.3:** *and make me clean*

# 609
8.6.8.6.
*Substitution pleaded.*

1 THE spotless Saviour liv'd for me
   And died upon the mount;
Th' obedience of His life and death
   Is plac'd to my account.

2 Canst Thou forget that awful hour,
   That sad, tremendous scene,
When Thy dear blood on Calvary
   Flow'd out at ev'ry vein?

3 No, Saviour, no; Thy wounds are fresh;
   E'en now they intercede;
Still, in effect, for guilty man
   Incessantly they bleed.

4 Thine ears of mercy still attend
   A contrite sinner's cries;
A broken heart that groans for God
   Thou never wilt despise.

5  O love incomprehensible
   That made Thee bleed for me!
  The judge of all hath suffer'd death
   To set His pris'ner free!

*Augustus Toplady*, 1759

   **FPN:** 20 Feb. 1890 (No. 2287), SPOHR
   **Ed:** Taken from the longer hymn,
     "From Thy supreme tribunal, Lord."

# 610   8.8.6.8.8.6.
*Pleading the blood.*

1  REMEMBER, Lord, that Jesus bled,
  That Jesus bow'd His dying head
   And sweated bloody sweat;
  He bore Thy wrath and curse for me
  In His own body on the tree,
   And more than paid my debt.

2  Surely He hath my pardon bought,
  A perfect righteousness wrought out,
   His people to redeem;
  O that His righteousness might be
  By grace imputed now to me,
   As were my sins to Him!

*Augustus Toplady*, 1759

   **Ed:** The second part of a longer hymn,
     "O might my groans as incense rise."

# 611   8.8.8.8.8.8.
*Sheltering at the cross.*

1  REDEEMER, whither should I flee,
  Or how escape the wrath to come?
  The weary sinner flies to Thee
  For shelter from impending doom;
  Smile on me, dearest Lord, and show
  Thyself the friend of sinners now.

2  Beneath the shadow of Thy cross
  My heavy laden soul finds rest;
  Let me esteem the world as dross,
  So I may be of Thee possess'd!
  I borrow ev'ry joy from Thee,
  For Thou art life and light to me.

3  Close to my Saviour's bloody tree
  My soul, untir'd, shall ever cleave;
  Both scourg'd and crucified with Thee,
  With Christ resolv'd to die and live;
  My pray'r, my great ambition this,
  Living and dying, to be His.

4  O nail me to the sacred wood;
  There tie me with Thy Spirit's chain;
  There seal me with Thy fast'ning blood,
  Nor ever let me loose again;
  There let me bow my suppliant knee
  And own no other Lord but Thee!

*Augustus Toplady*, 1759

# 612   7.7.7.7.
*Penitential sighs.*

1  FATHER, at Thy call I come;
  In Thy bosom there is room
  For a guilty soul to hide,
  Press'd with grief on every side.

2  Here I'll make my piteous moan;
  Thou canst understand a groan;
  Here my sins and sorrows tell;
  What I feel Thou knowest well.

3  Ah! how foolish I have been
  To obey the voice of sin,
  To forget Thy love to me,
  And to break my vows to Thee.

4  Darkness fills my trembling soul;
  Floods of sorrow o'er me roll;
  Pity, Father, pity me;
  All my hope's alone in Thee.

5  But may such a wretch as I,
  Self-condemn'd and doom'd to die,
  Ever hope to be forgiven,
  And be smil'd upon by Heaven?

6  May I round Thee cling and twine,
  Call myself a child of Thine,
  And presume to claim a part
  In a tender Father's heart?

7  Yes, I may; for I espy
  Pity trickling from Thine eye;

'Tis a Father's bowels move,
Move with pardon and with love.

8 Well I do remember too,
What His love hath deign'd to do,
How He sent a Saviour down,
All my follies to atone.

9 Has my elder Brother died?
And is justice satisfied?
Why, O why should I despair
Of my Father's tender care?

*Samuel Stennett*, 1787

# 613 6.6.6.6.
*"My Spirit longeth for Thee."*

1 MY spirit longeth for Thee
   Within my troubled breast,
Although I be unworthy
   Of so divine a guest.

2 Of so divine a guest
   Unworthy though I be,
Yet has my heart no rest
   Unless it come from Thee.

3 Unless it come from Thee,
   In vain I look around;
In all that I can see,
   No rest is to be found.

4 No rest is to be found
   But in Thy blessèd love;
O! let my wish be crown'd,
   And send it from above!

*John Byrom*, 1773

> **Ed:** The first stanza deviates from the overall
> metre of the piece, but this can be remedied
> by replacing "longeth" with "longs" and
> "although" with "though."

# 614 S.M.
*Rest in Jesus.*

1   O MAY I never rest
    Till I find rest in Thee,

Till of my pardon here possess'd
   I feel Thy love to me!

2   Turn not Thy face away;
    Thy look can make me clean;
Me in Thy wedding robe array,
    And cover all my sin.

3   Tell me, my God, for whom
    Thy precious blood was shed;
For sinners? Lord, as such I come,
    For such the Saviour bled.

4   Then raise a fallen wretch;
    Display Thy grace in me;
I am not out of mercy's reach,
    Nor too far gone for Thee.

*Augustus Toplady*, 1759

# 615 7.7.7.7. Double
*"We would see Jesus."*

1 JESUS, God of love, attend;
   From Thy glorious throne descend;
Answer now some waiting heart;
   Now some harden'd soul convert;
To our Advocate we fly;
   Let us feel Immanuel nigh;
Manifest Thy love abroad;
   Make us now the sons of God.

2 Prostrate at Thy mercy seat,
   Let us our Belovèd meet;
Give us in Thyself a part,
   Deep engraven on Thine heart;
Let us hear Thy pard'ning voice;
   Bid the broken bones rejoice;
Condemnation do away;
   O make this the perfect day!

*Augustus Toplady*, 1759

## CONFLICT AND ENCOURAGEMENT.

**616** C.M.
*Penitence and hope.*

1 DEAR Saviour, when my thoughts recall
  The wonders of Thy grace,
Low at Thy feet asham'd I fall
  And hide this wretched face.

2 Should love like Thine be thus repaid?
  Ah, vile, ungrateful heart!
By earth's low cares detain'd, betray'd,
  From Jesus to depart.

3 From Jesus, who alone can give
  True pleasure, peace, and rest,
When absent from my Lord, I live
  Unsatisfied, unblest.

4 But He, for His own mercy's sake,
  My wandering soul restores;
He bids the mourning heart partake
  The pardon it implores.

5 O while I breathe to Thee, my Lord,
  The penitential sigh,
Confirm the kind, forgiving word
  With pity in Thine eye!

6 Then Shall the mourner at Thy feet
  Rejoice to seek Thy face,
And grateful own how kind! how sweet!
  Thy condescending grace.

*Anne Steele*, [1780]

**617** C.M.
*Sins and sorrows laid before God.*

1 O THAT I knew the secret place
  Where I might find my God!
I'd spread my wants before His face
  And pour my woes abroad.

2 I'd tell Him how my sins arise,
  What sorrows I sustain,
How grace decays and comfort dies
  And leaves my heart in pain.

3 He knows what arguments I'd take
  To wrestle with my God;
I'd plead for His own mercy's sake
  And for my Saviour's blood.

4 My God will pity my complaints
  And heal my broken bones;
He takes the meaning of His saints,
  The language of their groans.

5 Arise, my soul, from deep distress,
  And banish every fear;
He calls thee to His throne of grace
  To spread thy sorrows there.

*Isaac Watts*, [1721]

**618** C.M.
*Will God cast off?*

1 WILL *God* forever cast me off?
  His promise ever fail?
Has He forgot His tender love?
  Shall anger still prevail?

2 I *call His* mercies to my mind,
  Which I enjoy'd before;
And will the Lord no more be kind?
  His face appear no more?

3 But I forbid this hopeless thought,
  This dark, despairing frame,
Rememb'ring what His hand hath wrought;
  *His* hand is still the same.

*Isaac Watts*, 1719 [*alt. C.H.S.*]

  **1.1:** *He*  **2.1:** *called Thy*  **3.4:** *Thy*
  **Ed:** From the longer paraphrase of Psalm 77,
    "To God I cried with mournful voice."

**619** C.M.
*Backslidings and returns.*

1 WHY is my heart so far from Thee,
  My God, my chief delight?
Why are my thoughts no more by day
  With Thee, no more by night?

2 Why should my foolish passions rove?
  Where can such sweetness be

As I have tasted in Thy love,
    As I have found in Thee?

3 Trifles of nature, or of art,
    With fair deceitful charms,
Intrude into my thoughtless heart
    And thrust me from Thy arms.

4 Then I repent, and vex my soul,
    That I should leave Thee so;
Where will those wild affections roll
    That let a Saviour go?

5 Sin's promised joys are turn'd to pain,
    And I am drown'd in grief,
But my dear Lord returns again;
    He flies to my relief.

6 Seizing my soul with sweet surprise,
    He draws with loving bands,
Divine compassion in His eyes,
    And pardon in His hands.

7 Wretch that I am, to wander thus
    In chase of false delight!
Let me be fasten'd to Thy cross
    Rather than lose Thy sight.

8 Make haste, my days, to reach the goal,
    And bring my heart to rest
On the dear centre of my soul,
    My God, my Saviour's breast.

*Isaac Watts*, [1707, *rev.* 1709]

# 620   C.M.
*Walking with God.*

1 O FOR a closer walk with God,
    A calm and heav'nly frame,
A light to shine upon the road
    That leads me to the Lamb!

2 Where is the blessedness I knew
    When first I saw the Lord?
Where is the soul-refreshing view
    Of Jesus and His Word?

3 What peaceful hours I then enjoy'd;
    How sweet their mem'ry still!

But *now I find* an aching void
    The world can never fill.

4 Return, O holy Dove; return,
    Sweet messenger of rest!
I hate the sins that made Thee mourn
    And drove Thee from my breast.

5 The dearest idol I have known,
    Whate'er that idol be,
Help me to tear it from Thy throne
    And worship only Thee.

6 So shall my walk be close with God,
    Calm and serene my frame;
So purer light shall mark the road
    That leads me to the Lamb.

*William Cowper*, [1772]
[*alt. John Rippon*, 1787]

    **3.3:** *they have left*

# 621   C.M.
*Sufficiency of pardon.*

1 WHY does your face, ye humble souls,
    Those mournful colours wear?
What doubts are these that waste your faith
    And nourish your despair?

2 What though your numerous sins exceed
    The stars that fill the skies,
And aiming at th' eternal throne,
    Like pointed mountains rise;

3 What though your mighty guilt beyond
    The wide creation swell,
And has its cursed foundation laid
    Low as the deeps of hell;

4 See here an endless ocean flows
    Of never-failing grace;
Behold a dying Saviour's veins
    The sacred flood increase:

5 It rises high and drowns the hills,
    *Has* neither shore nor bound:
Now if we search to find our sins,
    Our sins can ne'er be found.

6 Awake, our hearts, adore the grace
 That buries all our faults,
And pardoning blood that swells above
 Our follies and our thoughts.

*Isaac Watts,* [1707, *rev.* 1709, *alt.*]

 **5.2:** *'T has* **Ed:** This minor variant occured as
 early as 1759, and has appeared in editions of
 Watts since 1768 (25th ed.).

# 622 C.M.
*Making God a Refuge.*

1 DEAR refuge of my weary soul,
 On Thee, when sorrows rise,
On Thee, when waves of trouble roll,
 My fainting hope relies.

2 To Thee I tell each rising grief,
 For Thou alone canst heal;
Thy Word can bring a sweet relief
 For ev'ry pain I feel.

3 But oh! when gloomy doubts prevail,
 I fear to call Thee mine;
The springs of comfort seem to fail,
 And all my hopes decline.

4 Yet, gracious God, where shall I flee?
 Thou art my only trust;
And still my soul would cleave to Thee,
 Though prostrate in the dust.

5 Hast Thou not bid me seek Thy face?
 And shall I seek in vain?
And can the ear of sov'reign grace
 Be deaf when I complain?

6 No, still the ear of sov'reign grace
 Attends the mourner's pray'r;
O may I ever find access
 To breathe my sorrows there.

7 Thy mercy-seat is open still;
 Here let my soul retreat,
With humble hope attend Thy will,
 And wait beneath Thy feet.

*Anne Steele,* 1760

# 623 L.M.
*Life of the soul.*

1 WHEN sins and fears prevailing rise,
 And fainting hope almost expires,
Jesus, to Thee I lift mine eyes,
 To Thee I breathe my soul's desires.

2 Art Thou not mine, my living Lord?
 And can my hope, my comfort die,
Fix'd on Thy everlasting Word,
 That Word which built the earth and sky?

3 If my immortal Saviour lives,
 Then my immortal life is sure;
His Word a firm foundation gives;
 Here let me build and rest secure.

4 Here let my faith unshaken dwell;
 Immoveable the promise stands;
Not all the pow'rs of earth or hell
 Can e'er dissolve the sacred bands.

5 Here, O my soul, thy trust repose;
 If Jesus is forever mine,
Not death itself, that last of foes,
 Shall break a union so divine.

*Anne Steele,* 1760

# 624 L.M. Double
*Faith struggling.*

1 ENCOMPASS'D with clouds of distress,
 Just ready all hope to resign,
I pant for the light of Thy face
 And fear it will never be mine.
Dishearten'd with waiting so long,
 I sink at Thy feet with my load;
All plaintive I pour out my song
 And stretch forth my hands unto God.

2 Shine, Lord, and my terror shall cease,
 The blood of atonement apply,
And lead me to Jesus for peace,
 The rock that is higher than I.
Speak, Saviour, for sweet is Thy voice,
 Thy presence is fair to behold;
I thirst for Thy Spirit with cries
 And groanings that cannot be told.

3 If sometimes I strive, as I mourn,
  My hold of Thy promise to keep,
The billows more fiercely return,
  And plunge me again in the deep.
While harass'd and cast from Thy sight,
  The tempter suggests with a roar,
"The Lord hath forsaken thee quite:
  Thy God will be gracious no more."

4 Yet, Lord, if Thy love hath design'd
  No covenant-blessing for me,
Ah tell me, how is it I find
  Some sweetness in waiting for Thee?
Almighty to rescue Thou art;
  Thy grace is my only resource;
If e'er Thou art Lord of my heart,
  Thy Spirit must take it by force.

*Augustus Toplady*, 1772

# 625 C.M.
*"Remember me."*

1 O THOU, from whom all goodness flows,
  I lift my *soul* to Thee;
In all my sorrows, conflicts, woes,
  *Good* Lord! remember me.

2 When, *on my groaning*, burden'd heart,
  My sins lie heavily,
My pardon speak, new peace impart;
  In love remember me.

3 *When trials* sore obstruct my way,
  And ills I cannot flee,
O give me strength, Lord, as my day,
  For good remember me.

4 Distress'd with pain, disease, and grief,
  This feeble body see;
Grant patience, rest, and kind relief;
  Hear and remember me.

5 If on my face for Thy dear name
  Shame and reproaches be,
All hail reproach, and welcome shame,
  If Thou remember me!

6 The hour is near, consign'd to death;
  I own the just decree;

Saviour, with my last parting breath
  I'll cry, "Remember me!"

*Thomas Haweis*, [1791, *rev.* 1792, *alt.*]

**1.2:** *heart*  **1.4:** *Dear*
**2.1:** *groaning on my*  **3.1:** *Temptations*
**MM:** Hymns, Set 1 (Jan./Nov.), 5th Morn,
  AZMON / GAZER
**Ed:** These alterations are by James Montgomery,
  made for Cotterill's *Selection*, 8th ed. (1819),
  except his 2.1 has "on my aching," plus other
  alterations not repeated here. Spurgeon's
  source for this version is unclear.

# 626 7.7.7.7.
*Seeking guidance.*

1 HEAVENLY Father! to whose eye
Future things unfolded lie;
Through the desert where I stray,
Let Thy counsels guide my way.

2 Lead me not, for flesh is frail,
Where fierce trials would assail;
Leave me not, in darkened hour,
To withstand the tempter's power.

3 Lord! uphold me day by day;
Shed a light upon my way;
Guide me through perplexing snares:
Care for me in all my cares.

4 Should Thy wisdom, Lord, decree
Trials long and sharp for me,
Pain or sorrow, care or shame,
Father! glorify Thy name.

5 Let me neither faint nor fear,
Feeling still that Thou art near;
In the course my Saviour trod,
Tending still to Thee, my God!

*Josiah Conder*, 1836

**MM:** Hymns, Set 2 (Feb./Dec.), 21st Morn,
  FULTON / PLEYEL'S HYMN

# 627 L.M.
*Pleading divine faithfulness.*

1 GOD of my life, to Thee I call;
Afflicted at Thy feet I fall;
When the great water floods prevail,
Leave not my trembling heart to fail!

2 Friend of the friendless and the faint,
Where should I lodge my deep complaint?
Where, but with Thee, whose open door
Invites the helpless and the poor?

3 Did ever mourner plead with Thee,
And Thou refuse the mourner's plea?
Does not *Thy* Word still fix'd remain,
That none shall seek Thy face in vain?

4 That were a grief I could not bear,
Didst Thou not hear and answer pray'r ;
But a pray'r-hearing, answ'ring God
Supports me under ev'ry load.

5 Fair is the lot that's cast for me!
I have an Advocate with Thee;
They whom the world caresses most,
Have no such privilege to boast.

6 Poor though I am, despis'd, forgot,
Yet God, my God, forgets me not;
And he is safe, and must succeed,
For whom the Lord vouchsafes to plead.

*William Cowper*, 1779

**3.3:** *the*  **Ed:** This variant dates to the late 1700s.

# 628 L.M.
*Contention within.*

1 JESUS, our souls' delightful choice,
In Thee believing we rejoice;
Yet still our joy is mix'd with grief,
While faith contends with unbelief.

2 Thy promises our hearts revive
And keep our fainting hopes alive,
But guilt, and fears, and sorrows rise,
And hide the promise from our eyes.

3 O let not sin and Satan boast
While saints lie mourning in the dust,
Nor see that faith to ruin brought,
Which Thy own gracious hand hath wro't.

4 Do Thou the dying spark inflame;
Reveal the glories of Thy name,
And put all anxious doubts to flight
As shades dispersed by op'ning light.

*Philip Doddridge*, 1755

> **Ed:** Dated 7 Sept. 1735 in Doddridge's MSS. In
> the 6th ed. of *OOHB* (1873), Sedgwick errone-
> ously changed to author to "Watts and Rippon,
> 1706–1787."

# 629 C.M.
*Trust in God.*

1 DEAR Lord! why should I doubt Thy love
Or disbelieve Thy grace?
Sure Thy compassions ne'er remove,
Although Thou hide Thy face.

2 Thy smiles have freed my heart from pain;
My drooping spirits cheer'd;
And wilt Thou not apear again
Where Thou hast once appear'd?

3 Hast Thou not form'd my soul anew
And told me I am Thine?
And wilt Thou now Thy work undo
Or break Thy word divine?

4 Dost Thou repent? Wilt Thou deny
The gifts Thou hast bestow'd?
Or are those streams of mercy dry,
Which once so freely flow'd?

5 Lord! let no groundless fears destroy
The mercies now possess'd;
I'll praise for blessings I enjoy
And trust for all the rest.

John Rippon's *Selection*, 1800

# 630 C.M.
*"Fear not, I am with thee."*

1 AND art Thou with us, gracious Lord,
To dissipate our fear?
Dost Thou proclaim Thyself our God,
Our God forever near?

2 Dost Thou a Father's bowels feel
    For all Thy humble saints?
And in such tender accents speak
    To soothe their sad complaints?

3 Why droop our hearts? Why flow our eyes
    While such a voice we hear?
Why rise our sorrows and our fears
    While such a friend is near?

4 To all Thine other favours add
    A heart to trust Thy Word,
And death itself shall hear us sing
    While resting on the Lord.

*Philip Doddridge*, 1755

    **Ed:** Stanzas 3-4 are from Doddridge's hymn,
    "Viler than dust, O Lord, are we."

# 631 8.7.8.7.4.7.
*Hoping in God.*

1 O MY soul, what means this sadness?
    Wherefore art thou thus cast down?
Let thy griefs be turn'd to gladness;
    Bid thy restless fears be gone;
      Look to Jesus,
    And rejoice in His dear name.

2 What though Satan's strong temptations
    Vex and tease thee day by day?
And thy sinful inclinations
    Often fill thee with dismay?
      Thou shalt conquer
    Through the Lamb's redeeming blood.

3 Though ten thousand ills beset thee
    From without and from within,
Jesus saith, He'll ne'er forget thee,
    But will save from hell and sin;
      He is faithful
    To perform His gracious Word.

4 Though distresses now attend thee,
    And thou tread'st the thorny road,
His right hand shall still defend thee;
    Soon He'll bring thee home to God!
      Therefore praise Him;
Praise the great Redeemer's name.

5 O that I could now adore Him,
    Like the heav'nly hosts above,
Who forever bow before Him
    And unceasing sing His love!
      Happy songsters!
When shall I your chorus join?

*John Fawcett*, 1782

# 632 8.6.8.6.
*Confidence in the promises.*

1   WHY should I sorrow more?
    I trust a Saviour slain,
And safe beneath His shelt'ring cross,
    Unmoved I shall remain.

2   Let Satan and the world
    Now rage or now allure;
The promises *in Christ are* made
    *Immutable* and sure.

3   *The oath infallible*
    *Is now my spirit's* trust;
*I know that He who spake the word*
    Is faithful, *true, and* just.

4   He'll bring me on my way
    Unto my journey's end;
He'll be my Father and my God,
    My Saviour and my Friend.

5   So all my doubts and fears
    Shall wholly flee away,
And every mournful night of tears
    Be turn'd to joyous day.

6   All that remains for me
    Is but to love and sing,
And wait until the angels come
    To bear me to the King.

2-4 *William Williams*, 1772, *alt. C.H.S.*
1,5-6 *Charles Spurgeon*, 1866

    **2.3:** *are wholly*   **2.4:** *Immoveable*
    **3.1:** *And in the Word divine,*   **3.2:** *Infallible, I*
    **3.3:** *For He that promised is true*   **3.4:** *and is*

# 633
8.6.8.6.
*"Fear not."*

1 YE trembling souls, dismiss your fears,
  Be mercy all your theme;
  Mercy, which like a river flows
  In one perpetual stream.

2 Fear not the powers of earth and hell;
  God will these powers restrain;
  His arm shall all their rage repel
  And make their efforts vain.

3 Fear not the want of outward good;
  For His He will provide;
  Grant them supplies of daily food
  And give them heaven beside.

4 Fear not that He will e'er forsake
  Or leave His work undone;
  He's faithful to His promises
  And faithful to His Son.

5 Fear not the terrors of the grave
  Or death's tremendous sting;
  He will from endless wrath preserve,
  To endless glory bring.

*Benjamin Beddome,* [1787, *rev.* 1817]

# 634
8.6.8.6. / *Comfort in the covenant made with Christ.*

1 OUR God, how firm His promise stands,
  E'en when He hides His face;
  He trusts in our Redeemer's hands
  His glory and His grace.

2 Then why, my soul, these sad complaints,
  Since Christ and we are one?
  Thy God is faithful to His saints,
  Is faithful to His Son.

3 Beneath His smiles my heart has liv'd,
  And part of heaven possess'd;
  I praise His name for grace receiv'd
  And trust Him for the rest.

*Isaac Watts,* [1707]

# 635
8.6.8.6.
*O why so heavy, O my soul?*

1 *O WHY* so heavy, O my soul?
  (Thus to myself I said—)
  *O why* so heavy, O my soul,
  and so disquieted?

2 Hope thou in God; He still shall be
  Thy glory and thy praise;
  His saving grace shall comfort thee
  Through everlasting days.

3 His goodness made thee what thou art,
  And yet will thee redeem;
  *O be thou of a steadfast* heart
  And put thy trust in Him.

*Edward Caswall,* 1858 [*alt.*]

**1.1:** *Wherefore*   **1.3:** *Wherefore*
**3.3:** *Only be thou of a good*
**Ed:** These alterations appeared in *Hymns for the
Year,* which was printed without a publication
date but likely precedes Spurgeon's hymnal.

# HOLY ANXIETY.

# 636
L.M.
*The almost Christian.*

1 BROAD is the road that leads to death,
  And thousands walk together there,
  But wisdom shows a narrower path,
  With here and there a traveller.

2 "Deny thyself and take thy cross,"
  Is the Redeemer's great command;
  Nature must count her gold but dross
  If she would gain *the* heav'nly land.

3 The fearful soul that tires and faints
  And walks the ways of God no more
  Is but esteem'd almost a saint
  And makes his own destruction sure.

4 Lord, let not all my hopes be vain;
  Create my heart entirely new,

Which hypocrites could ne'er attain,
Which false apostates never knew.

*Isaac Watts*, 1709

**2.4:** *this* **Ed:** This minor variant dates to the 1700s.

# 637 L.M.
*Self-examination.*

1 WHAT strange perplexities arise?
What anxious fears and jealousies?
What crowds in doubtful light appear?
How few, alas! approved and clear!

2 And what am I?—My soul, awake,
And an impartial prospect take.
Does no dark sign, no ground of fear,
In practice or in heart appear?

3 What image does my spirit bear?
Is Jesus form'd and living there?
Say, do His lineaments divine
In thought and word and action shine?

4 Searcher of hearts, O search me still;
The secrets of my soul reveal;
My fears remove; let me appear
To God, and my own conscience, clear.

5 Scatter the clouds that o'er my head
Thick glooms of dubious terrors spread;
Lead me into celestial day
And to my self my self display.

6 May I at that blest world arrive,
Where Christ through all my soul shall live
And give full proof that He is there,
Without one gloomy doubt or fear.

*Samuel Davies*, 1769

# 638 C.M.
*The contrite heart.*

1 THE Lord will happiness divine
On contrite hearts bestow;
Then tell me, gracious God, is mine
A contrite heart or no?

2 I hear, but seem to hear in vain,
Insensible as steel;
If aught is felt, 'tis only pain
To find I cannot feel.

3 I sometimes think myself inclin'd
To love Thee, if I could,
But often feel another mind,
Averse to all that's good.

4 My best desires are faint and few;
I fain would strive for more;
But when I cry, "My strength renew,"
Seem weaker than before.

5 Thy saints are comforted, I know,
And love Thy house of pray'r;
I *sometimes* go where others go,
But find no comfort there.

6 O make this heart rejoice or ache;
Decide this doubt for me;
And if it be not broken, break,
And heal it, if it be.

*William Cowper*, 1779
[*alt. John Rippon*, 1787]

**5.3:** *therefore*

# 639 C.M.
*"Lovest thou me?"*

1 DO not I love Thee, O my Lord?
Behold my heart and see,
And turn each odious idol out
That dares to rival Thee.

2 Do not I love Thee from my soul?
Then let me nothing love:
Dead be my heart to ev'ry joy,
When Jesus cannot move.

3 Is not Thy name melodious still
To mine attentive ear?
Doth not each pulse with pleasure bound
My Saviour's voice to hear?

4 Hast Thou a lamb in all Thy flock
I would disdain to feed?

Hast Thou a foe, before whose face
　I fear Thy cause to plead?

5　Would not my ardent spirit vie
　　With angels round the throne
　To execute Thy sacred will
　　And make Thy glory known?

6　Would not my heart pour forth its blood
　　In honour of Thy name,
　And challenge the cold hand of death
　　To damp th' immortal flame?

7　Thou know'st I love Thee, dearest Lord;
　　But O! I long to soar
　Far from the sphere of mortal joys,
　　And learn to love Thee more.

*Philip Doddridge*, 1755

# 640 C.M.
*Love asserting herself.*

1　AND have I, Christ, no love for Thee,
　　No passion for Thy charms?
　No wish my Saviour's face to see,
　　And dwell within His arms?

2　Is there no spark of gratitude
　　In this cold heart of mine,
　To Him whose generous bosom glow'd
　　With friendship all divine?

3　Can I pronounce His charming name,
　　His acts of kindness tell,
　And while I dwell upon the theme,
　　No sweet emotion feel?

4　Such base ingratitude as this
　　What heart but must detest!
　Sure Christ deserves the noblest place
　　In every human breast.

5　A very wretch, Lord, I should prove,
　　Had I no love for Thee;
　Rather than not my Saviour love,
　　O may I cease to be!

*Samuel Stennett*, 1787 [*rev. ca.* 1805]

# 641 C.M.
*"Search me, O Lord!"*

1　SEARCHER of hearts, before Thy face
　　I all my soul display,
　And conscious of its innate arts,
　　Entreat Thy strict survey.

2　If lurking in its inmost folds,
　　I any sin conceal,
　O let a ray of light divine
　　That secret guile reveal.

3　If tinctur'd with that odious gall
　　Unknowing I remain,
　Let grace, like a pure silver stream,
　　Wash out th' accursed stain.

4　If in these fatal fetters bound,
　　A wretched slave I lie,
　Smite off my chains and wake my soul
　　To light and liberty.

5　To humble penitence and pray'r
　　Be gentle pity giv'n;
　Speak ample pardon to my heart
　　And seal its claim to heav'n.

*Philip Doddridge*, 1755

# 642 L.M. with refrain
*Was it for me?*

1　WAS it for me, dear Lord, for me,
　Thou didst endure such pain and grief,
　For me, the direful agony
　That knew not limit or relief?
　　Was it for me? Was it for me?

2　Was it for me, the mocking scorn,
　While love perfumed Thy passing breath,
　The rude contumely, meekly borne,
　Thy soul desertion, unto death?
　　Was it for me? Was it for me?

3　Was it for me, Thou Lord of light,
　Thy path through darkness to the grave,
　For me, the triumph infinite,
　When Thou didst rise and live to save?
　　Was it for me? Was it for me?

4 Was it for me, Lord Christ! for me,
  Ascending high, Thy mission done,
  Saviour to all eternity,
  In heaven Thou didst resume Thy throne?
  Was it for me? Was it for me?

*Henry Bateman*, 1862

## 643 8.7.8.7.4.7.
*The strait gate.*

1 STRAIT the gate, the way is narrow,
  To the realms of endless bliss;
  Sinful men and vain professors,
  Self-deceived, the passage miss;
  Rushing headlong,
  Down they sink the dread abyss.

2 Sins and follies unforsaken,
  All will end in deep despair;
  Formal prayers are unavailing;
  Fruitless is the worldling's tear;
  Small the number
  Who to wisdom's path repair.

3 Thou who art Thy people's guardian,
  Condescend my guide to be;
  By Thy Spirit's light unerring,
  Let me Thy salvation see;
  May I never
  Miss the way that leads to Thee.

*Benjamin Beddome*, 1817

## 644 S.M.
*The evil heart.*

1 ASTONISHED and distressed,
  I turn *mine* eyes within;
  My heart with loads of guilt oppressed,
  The seat of every sin.

2 What crowds of evil thoughts,
  What vile affections there!
  Envy and pride, deceit and guile,
  Distrust and slavish fear.

3 Almighty King of saints,
  These tyrant lusts subdue;

Drive the old serpent from his seat,
  And all my powers renew.

4 This done, my cheerful voice
  Shall loud hosannas raise;
  My soul shall glow with gratitude;
  My lips proclaim Thy praise.

*Benjamin Beddome*, [1787, *rev.* 1817]

**1.2:** *my* (1817)

# DESIRES AFTER HOLINESS.

## 645 C.M.
*Longing for a pure heart.*

1 O FOR a heart to praise my God,
  A heart from sin set free!
  A heart that always feels Thy blood
  So freely spilt for me!

2 A heart resign'd, submissive, meek,
  My great Redeemer's throne,
  Where only Christ is heard to speak,
  Where Jesus reigns alone;

3 A humble, lowly, contrite heart,
  Believing, true, and clean,
  Which neither life nor death can part
  From Him that dwells within;

4 A heart in every thought renew'd
  And full of love divine,
  Perfect, and right, and pure, and good,
  A copy, Lord, of Thine.

5 Thy nature, gracious Lord, impart;
  Come quickly from above;
  Write Thy new name upon my heart,
  Thy new, best name of love.

*Charles Wesley*, 1742 [*rev.* 1753, 1780]

**MM:** Hymns, Set 2 (Feb./Dec.), 15th Morn,
BALERMA / AZMON

# 646 L.M.
*Longing to love Christ.*

1 I THIRST, Thou wounded Lamb of God,
   To wash me in Thy cleansing blood,
   To dwell within Thy wounds, then pain
   Is sweet, and life or death is gain.

2 Take my poor heart, and let it be
   Forever closed to all but Thee!
   Seal Thou my breast, and let me wear
   That pledge of love forever there.

3 How blest are they who still abide
   Close shelter'd in Thy bleeding side!
   Who life and strength from thence derive,
   And by Thee move, and in Thee live!

4 What are our works but sin and death,
   Till Thou Thy quick'ning Spirit breathe!
   Thou giv'st the power Thy grace to move:
   O wondrous grace! O boundless love!

5 How can it be, Thou heavenly King,
   That Thou shouldst us to glory bring?
   Make slaves the partners of Thy throne,
   Deck'd with a never-fading crown.

6 Hence our hearts melt, our eyes o'erflow,
   Our words are lost, nor will we know,
   Nor will we think of aught beside,
   "My Lord, my Love, is crucified."

7 Ah, Lord! enlarge our scanty thought,
   To know the wonders Thou hast wrought;
   Unloose our stamm'ring tongues, to tell
   Thy love, immense, unsearchable!

8 First-born of many brethren Thou!
   To Thee, lo! all our souls we bow.
   To Thee, our hearts and hands we give;
   Thine may we die; Thine may we live.

1-2,7 *Nicolaus Ludwig von Zinzendorf*, 1738
3-6 *Johann Nitschmann*, 1738
8 *Anna Nitschmann*, 1738
*tr. John Wesley*, 1740

> **Ed:** Sts. 1-2 were translated from "Ach! mein
> verwundter Fürste!"; sts. 3-6 from "Du blutiger
> Versühner!"; st. 7 from "Der Gott von unserm

Bunde," and st. 8 from "Mein König deine Liebe." These were published together in the 7th appendix to Zinzendorf's *Gesang-Buch*.

# 647 C.M.
*Love constraining to obedience.*

1 NO strength of nature can suffice
   To serve the Lord aright,
   And what she has she misapplies
   For want of clearer light.

2 How long beneath the law I lay
   In bondage and distress!
   I toil'd the precept to obey,
   But toil'd without success.

3 Then to abstain from outward sin
   Was more than I could do;
   Now if I feel its pow'r within,
   I feel I hate it too.

4 Then all my servile works were done
   A righteousness to raise;
   Now, freely chosen in the Son,
   I freely choose His ways.

5 "What shall I do," was then the word,
   "That I may worthier grow?"
   "What shall I render to the Lord?"
   Is my inquiry now.

6 To see the law by Christ fulfill'd
   And hear His pard'ning voice,
   Changes a slave into a child
   And duty into choice.

*William Cowper*, 1779

# 648 L.M.
*Holiness and grace.*

1 SO let our lips and lives express
   The holy gospel we profess;
   So let our works and virtues shine
   To prove the doctrine all divine.

2 Thus shall we best proclaim abroad
   The honours of our Saviour God,
   When His salvation reigns within
   And grace subdues the power of sin.

3 Our flesh and sense must be denied,
　Passion and envy, lust and pride,
　While justice, temperance, truth, and love
　Our inward piety approve.

4 The gospel bears our spirits up,
　While we expect that blessèd hope,
　The bright appearance of the Lord,
　And faith stands leaning on His Word.

*Isaac Watts*, 1709

# 649 C.M.
*Holy principles desired.*

1 I WANT a principle within
　　Of jealous, godly fear,
　A sensibility of sin,
　　A pain to feel it near.

2 I want the first approach to feel
　　Of pride, or fond desire,
　To catch the wanderings of my will
　　And quench the kindling fire.

3 That I from Thee no more may part,
　　No more Thy goodness grieve,
　The filial awe, the fleshy heart,
　　The tender conscience, give.

4 Quick as the apple of an eye,
　　O God, my conscience make;
　Awake, my soul, when sin is nigh,
　　And keep it still awake.

5 If to the right or left I stray,
　　That moment, Lord, reprove;
　And let me weep my life away
　　For having griev'd Thy love.

6 O may the least omission pain
　　My well-instructed soul
　And drive me to the blood again,
　　Which makes the wounded whole.

*Charles Wesley*, 1749 [*rev.* 1780]

**FPN:** 23 May 1889 (No. 2313), TIVERTON
**Ed:** This hymn originally began "Almighty God
of truth and love," in 5 stanzas of 8 lines, but
was reduced to this form in 1780.

**EE:** "A heart of flesh is known by its tenderness
concerning sin. To have indulged a foul imagination, or to have allowed a vile desire to tarry
even for a moment, is quite enough to make a
heart of flesh grieve before the Lord. . . . A tender heart is the best defence against sin, and
the best preparation for heaven" (Aug 15).

# 650 8.7.8.7. Double
*Conformity to Christ.*

1 LOVE divine, all loves excelling,
　　Joy of heaven to earth come down;
　Fix in us Thy humble dwelling,
　　All Thy faithful mercies crown;
　Jesus, Thou art all compassion;
　　Pure, unbounded love Thou art;
　Visit us with Thy salvation;
　　Enter every trembling heart.

2 Come, almighty to deliver,
　　Let us all Thy grace receive;
　Suddenly return, and never,
　　Never more Thy temples leave;
　Thee we would be always blessing,
　　Serve Thee as Thy hosts above,
　Pray, and praise Thee, without ceasing;
　　Glory in Thy perfect love.

3 Finish, then, Thy new creation;
　　Pure and spotless let us be;
　Let us see Thy great salvation,
　　Perfectly restored in Thee;
　Changed from glory into glory,
　　Till in heaven we take our place,
　Till we cast our crowns before Thee,
　　Lost in wonder, love, and praise.

*Charles Wesley*, 1747 [*rev.* 1780]

# 651 C.M.
*"Sanctified by the Spirit of our God."*

1 NOT the malicious or profane,
　　The wanton or the proud,
　Nor thieves, nor slanderers shall obtain
　　The kingdom of our God.

2 Surprising grace! and such were we
　　By nature and by sin;

Heirs of immoral misery,
    Unholy and unclean.

3 But we are wash'd in Jesus' blood,
    We're pardon'd through His name,
And the good Spirit of our God
    Has sanctified our frame.

4 O for a persevering power
    To keep Thy just commands!
We would defile our hearts no more,
    No more pollute our hands.

*Isaac Watts*, 1709

# 652 C.M.
*Prayer for holiness.*

1 O MAY my heart, by grace renew'd,
    Be my Redeemer's throne,
And be my stubborn will subdued,
    His government to own.

2 Let deep repentance, faith, and love
    Be join'd with godly fear,
And all my conversation prove
    My heart to be sincere.

3 Preserve me from the snares of sin
    Through my remaining days,
And in me let each virtue shine
    To my Redeemer's praise.

4 Let lively hope my soul inspire,
    Let warm affections rise,
And may I wait with strong desire
    To mount above the skies.

*John Fawcett*, 1782

**Ed:** Taken from the longer hymn,
"Religion is the chief concern."

# 653 C.M.
*Holiness desired.*

1 LORD, I desire to live as one
    Who bears a blood-bought name,
As one who fears but grieving Thee
    And knows no other shame,

2 As one by whom Thy walk below
    Should never be forgot,
As one who fain would keep apart
    From all Thou lovest not.

3 I want to live as one who knows
    Thy fellowship of love,
As one whose eyes can pierce beyond
    The pearl-built gates above,

4 As one who daily speaks to Thee,
    And hears Thy voice divine
With depths of tenderness declare,
    "Belovèd! Thou art mine."

*Charitie Lees Smith*, [1863]

**Ed:** Dated by Sedgwick as 1861, and credited to
    her "Original hymns, 1861-1863"; published
    as early as 1 Dec. 1863 in *The Evangelical
    Witness*. See also the notes for No. 567.
**EE:** "You are God's priest; act as such. You are
    God's king; reign over your lusts. . . . Heaven
    is your portion; live like a heavenly spirit, so
    shall you prove that you have true faith in
    Jesus, for there cannot be faith in the heart
    unless there be holiness in the life" (June 26).

# RENUNCIATION OF THE WORLD.

# 654 C.M.
*Old things are passed away.*

1 LET worldly minds the world pursue;
    It has no charms for me;
Once I admir'd its trifles too,
    But grace has set me free.

2 Its pleasures now no longer please,
    No more content afford;
Far from my heart be joys like these,
    Now I have seen the Lord.

3 As by the light of op'ning day
    The stars are all conceal'd,
So earthly pleasures fade away,
    When Jesus is reveal'd.

4 Creatures no more divide my choice;
    I bid them all depart;
    His name, and love, and gracious voice
    Have fix'd my roving heart.

5 Now, Lord, I would be Thine alone
    And wholly live to Thee,
    But may I hope that Thou wilt own
    A worthess worm like me!

6 Yes, though of sinners I'm the worst,
    I cannot doubt Thy will,
    For if Thou hadst not lov'd me first,
    I had refus'd Thee still.

*John Newton*, [1772]

# 655   6.6.6.6.8.8.
*Renouncing the world.*

1 COME, my fond fluttering heart,
    Come, struggle to be free;
    Thou and the world must part,
    However hard it be.
My trembling spirit owns it just
But *still lies cleaving* to the dust.

2 Ye tempting sweets, forbear;
    Ye dearest idols, fall;
    My love ye must not share,
    Jesus shall have it all.
*Though painful and acute the smart,*
*His love can heal the bleeding heart!*

3 Ye fair, enchanting throng!
    Ye golden dreams, *adieu!*
    Earth has prevail'd too long;
    *Too long I've cherished you;*
*Aid me, dear Saviour, set me free;*
*My all I will resign to Thee.*

4 O may I feel Thy worth
    And let no idol dare;
    No vanity of earth
    With Thee, my Lord, compare;
Now bid all *earthly* joys depart,
And reign *unrivall'd* in my heart!

*Jane Taylor*, 1812, *alt.*

**1.6:** *cleaves yet closer*
**2.5-6:** *'Tis bitter pain, 'tis cruel smart,*
    *But ah! thou must consent, my heart!*
**3.2:** *farewell!*   **3.4:** *And now I break the spell;*
**3.5-6:** *Ye cherish'd joys of early years—*
    *Jesus, forgive these parting tears.*
**4.5:** *worldly*   **4.6:** *supremely*
**Ed:** These alterations appeared as early as 1827
    in J. Curtis' *Union Collection.*

# 656   L.M.
*Escaping from the current of sin.*

1 I SEND the joys of earth away;
    Away, ye tempters of the mind,
    False as the smooth deceitful sea,
    And empty as the whistling wind.

2 Your streams were floating me along
    Down to the gulf of black despair,
    And whilst I listen'd to your song,
    Your streams had e'en convey'd me there.

3 Lord, I adore Thy matchless grace
    That warn'd me of that dark abyss,
    That drew me from those treacherous seas
    And *bade* me seek superior bliss.

4 Now to the shining realms above
    I stretch my hands and glance *my* eyes;
    O for the pinions of a dove
    To bear me to the upper skies!

5 There from the bosom of my God,
    Oceans of endless pleasure roll;
    There would I fix my last abode
    And drown the sorrows of my soul.

*Isaac Watts*, [1707, *alt.*]

**3.4:** *bid*   **4.2:** *mine*
**Ed:** These minor variants date to the early 1800s.

# 657   C.M.
*Choosing the pearl.*

1 YE glittering toys of earth, adieu,
    A nobler choice be mine;
    A real prize attracts my view,
    A treasure all divine.

2 Be gone, unworthy of my cares,
  Ye specious baits of sense;
Inestimable worth appears,
  The pearl of price immense.

3 Jesus, to multitudes unknown,
  O name divinely sweet!
Jesus, in Thee, in Thee alone,
  Wealth, honour, pleasure meet.

4 Should both the Indies at my call,
  Their boasted stores resign,
With joy I would renounce them all,
  For leave to call Thee mine.

5 Should earth's vain treasures all depart,
  Of this dear gift possess'd,
I'd clasp it to my joyful heart
  And be forever bless'd.

6 Dear Sovereign of my soul's desires,
  Thy love is bliss divine;
Accept the wish that love inspires,
  And bid me call Thee mine.

*Anne Steele*, [1769]

# DEDICATION TO GOD.

**658** L.M.
*The heart given to God.*

1 O HAPPY day that fix'd my choice
  On Thee, my Saviour and my God!
Well may this glowing heart rejoice
  And tell its raptures all abroad.

2 'Tis done; the great transaction's done;
  I am my Lord's, and He is mine;
He drew me, and I follow'd on,
  Charm'd to confess the voice divine.

3 Now rest, my long-divided heart,
  Fix'd on this blissful centre, rest;
With ashes who would grudge to part,
  When call'd on angels' bread to feast?

4 High heav'n, that heard the solemn vow,
  That vow renew'd shall daily hear,

Till in life's latest hour I bow,
  And bless in death a bond so dear.

*Philip Doddridge*, 1755

**659** 8.7.8.7. Double / *"We have left all and have followed Thee."*

1 JESUS, I my cross have taken,
  All to leave and follow Thee;
Destitute, despised, forsaken,
  Thou, from hence, my all shalt be.
Let the world despise and leave me—
  They have left my Saviour too—
Human hearts and looks deceieve me;
  Thou art not, like them, untrue.

2 Man may trouble and distress me;
  'Twill but drive me to Thy breast.
Life with trials hard may press me;
  Heav'n will bring me sweeter rest.
O 'tis not in grief to harm me,
  While Thy love is left to me!
O 'twere not in joy to charm me,
  Were that joy unmix'd with Thee.

3 Take, my soul, thy full salvation;
  Rise o'er sin, and fear, and care;
Joy to find in every station
  Something still to do or bear!
Soon shall close thy earthly mission,
  *Soon* shall pass thy pilgrim days;
Hope shall change to glad fruition,
  Faith to sight, and prayer to praise.

*Henry Francis Lyte*, [1824, *rev.* 1833]

  **3.6:** *Swift* (1833)

**660** C.M. / *"My Beloved is mine, and I am His."*

1 WHEN I had wander'd from His fold,
  His love the wand'rer sought;
When slave-like into bondage sold,
  His blood my freedom bought.

2 Therefore that life, by Him redeem'd,
  Is His through all its days,

And as with blessings it hath teem'd,
 So let it teem with praise.

3 For I am His and He is mine,
 The God whom I adore!
My Father, Saviour, Comforter,
 Now and forever more!

4 When sunk in sorrow, I despair'd,
 And changed my hopes for fears;
He bore my griefs, my burden shared,
 And wiped away my tears.

5 Therefore the joy by Him restored,
 To Him by right belongs,
And to my gracious loving Lord,
 I'll sing through life my songs.

6 For I am His, and He is mine,
 The God whom I adore!
My Father, Saviour, Comforter,
 Now and forever more!

*John S.B. Monsell*, 1863

> **FPN:** 9 Feb. 1890 (No. 2275), BEDFORD
> **Ed:** This hymn was originally printed in 4 sts. of 12 lines (C.M. triple), with the last four lines being a refrain. Spurgeon split two of these sts. into quatrains, 1-3, 4-6, but each set of twelve lines should be read or sung together in order to follow the sense of the text.

# 661 C.M.
*"The Lord is my portion."*

1 FROM pole to pole let others roam
 And search in vain for bliss;
My soul is satisfied at home;
 The Lord my portion is.

2 Jesus, who on His glorious throne
 Rules heav'n, and earth, and sea,
Is pleas'd to claim me for His own
 And give Himself to me.

3 His person fixes all my love,
 His blood removes my fear,
And while He pleads for me above,
 His arm preserves me here.

4 His Word of promise is my food;
 His Spirit is my guide;
Thus daily is my strength renew'd
 And all my wants supplied.

5 For Him I count as gain each loss;
 Disgrace, for Him, renown;
Well may I glory in His cross,
 While He prepares my crown!

*John Newton*, 1779

# 662 L.M.
*Choosing the better part.*

1 BESET with snares on ev'ry hand,
In life's uncertain path I stand;
Saviour divine, diffuse Thy light,
To guide my doubtful footsteps right.

2 Engage this roving, treach'rous heart
To fix on Mary's better part,
To scorn the trifles of a day
For joys that none can take away.

3 Then let the wildest storms arise;
Let tempests mingle earth and skies;
No fatal shipwreck shall I fear,
But all my treasures with me bear.

4 If Thou, my Jesus, still be nigh,
Cheerful I live, and joyful die;
Secure, when mortal comforts flee,
To find ten thousand worlds in Thee.

*Philip Doddridge*, 1755

# 663 7.7.7.7.
*Jesus, I am Thine!*

1 JESUS, spotless Lamb of God,
Thou hast bought *me* with Thy blood—
*I* would value nought beside
Jesus—Jesus crucified.

2 *I am* Thine and Thine alone;
This *I* gladly, fully own;
And in all my works and ways,
Only now would seek Thy praise.

3 Help *me* to confess Thy name,
   Bear with joy Thy cross and shame,
   Only seek to follow Thee,
   Though reproach *my* portion be.

4 When Thou shalt in glory come,
   And I reach my heav'nly home,
   Louder still *my* lips shall own
   *I am* Thine and Thine alone.

*James George Deck*, [1838, alt. C.H.S.]

   **1.2:** *us*  **1.3:** *We*  **2.1:** *We are*  **2.2:** *we*
   **3.1:** *us*  **3.4:** *our*  **4.3:** *our*  **4.4:** *We are*

# 664 C.M.
*Safety and consecration.*

1 HOW can I sink with such a prop
   As my eternal God,
   Who bears the earth's huge pillars up
   And spreads the heav'ns abroad?

2 How can I die while Jesus lives,
   Who rose and left the dead?
   Pardon and grace my soul receives
   From mine exalted Head.

3 All that I am and all I have
   Shall be forever Thine;
   Whate'er my duty bids me give,
   My cheerful hands resign.

4 Yet if I might make some reserve,
   And duty did not call,
   I love my God with zeal so great
   That I should give Him all.

*Isaac Watts*, 1709

> **TD:** "While the pillars stand, and stand they
> must for God upholds them, the house will
> brave out the storm. In the day of the Lord's
> appearing a general melting will take place,
> but in that day our covenant God will be the
> sure support of our confidence" (Ps. 75:3; vol.
> 3, p. 391).

# LONGINGS FOR
# PERSEVERANCE IN GRACE.

# 665 8.7.8.7.4.7.
*Keep us, Lord.*

1 KEEP us, Lord, O keep us ever!
   Vain our hope if left by Thee;
   We are Thine, O leave us never!
   Till Thy face in heav'n we see,
   There to praise Thee
   Through a bright eternity.

2 All our strength at once would fail us,
   If deserted, Lord, by Thee;
   Nothing then could aught avail us;
   Certain our defeat would be;
   Those who hate us
   Thenceforth their desire would see.

3 But we look to Thee as able,
   Grace to give in time of need;
   Heav'n, we know, is not more stable
   Than the promise which we plead;
   'Tis Thy promise
   Gives Thy people hope indeed.

*Thomas Kelly*, 1815

# 666 C.M.
*"Will ye also go?"*

1 WHEN any turn from Zion's way,
   (Alas! what numbers do!)
   Methinks I hear my Saviour say,
   "Wilt thou forsake Me too?"

2 Ah, Lord! with such a heart as mine,
   Unless Thou hold me fast,
   I feel I must, I shall decline,
   And prove like them at last.

3 Yet Thou alone hast pow'r, I know,
   To save a wretch like me;
   To whom or whither could I go
   If I should turn from Thee?

4 Beyond a doubt, I rest assur'd
   Thou art the Christ of God,

Who has eternal life secur'd
By promise and by blood.

5 The help of men and angels join'd
Could never reach my case,
Nor could I hope relief to find
But in Thy boundless grace.

6 No voice but Thine can give me rest
And bid my fears depart;
No love but Thine can make me blest
And satisfy my heart.

7 What anguish has that question stirr'd,
If I will also go?
Yet, Lord, relying on Thy Word,
I humbly answer, "No!"

*John Newton, 1779*

# 667 8.7.8.7.4.7.
*Leave Thee—never.*

1 LEAVE Thee! No, my dearest Saviour,
Thee whose blood my pardon bought;
Slight Thy mercy, scorn Thy favour,
Perish such an impious thought;
Leave Thee—never;
Where for peace could I resort?

2 Be offended at Thee—never,
Thee to whom my all I owe;
Rather shall my heart endeavour
With unceasing love to glow;
Leave Thee—never;
Where for safety could I go?

3 Thou alone art my salvation;
There is none can save but Thee;
Thou, through Thy divine oblation,
From my guilt hast set me free;
Leave Thee—never;
Thou who deign'dst to die for me!

4 But, O Lord, Thou know'st my weakness,
Know'st how prone I am to stray;
God of love, of truth, of meekness,
Guide and keep me in Thy way;

Blest Redeemer,
Let me never from Thee stray.

*John Stamp, 1845*

# 668 L.M.
*Let us not fall.*

1 LORD, through the desert drear and wide,
Our erring footsteps need a guide;
Keep us, oh keep us near Thy side.
Let us not fall. Let us not fall.

2 We have no fear that Thou shouldst lose
One whom eternal love could choose,
But we would ne'er this grace abuse.
Let us not fall. Let us not fall.

3 Lord, we are blind, and halt, and lame;
We have no stronghold but Thy name;
Great is our fear to bring it shame.
Let us not fall. Let us not fall.

4 Lord, evermore Thy face we seek;
Tempted we are, and poor, and weak;
Keep us with lowly hearts, and meek.
Let us not fall. Let us not fall.

5 All Thy good work in us complete,
And seat us daily at Thy feet;
Thy love, Thy words, Thy name, how sweet!
Let us not fall. Let us not fall.

*Mary (Bowly) Peters, 1847*

**FPN:** 23 May 1889 (No. 2313), WINCHESTER
**Ed:** Peters' collection, *Hymns Intended to Help
the Communion of Saints* (1847), appears
to be no longer extant, and no other suitable
source could be identified for proofing.
**EE:** "How joyfully may we encounter toils, and
how cheerfully may we endure sufferings,
when we can lay hold upon celestial strength.
Divine power will rend asunder all the toils
of our enemies, confound their politics, and
frustrate their knavish tricks; he is a happy
man who has such matchless might engaged
upon his side" (Aug. 19).

## 669
L.M.
*None but Christ.*

1 THOU only Sov'reign of my heart,
My refuge, my almighty Friend—
And can my soul from Thee depart,
On whom alone my hopes depend?

2 Whither, ah! whither shall I go,
A wretched wand'rer from my Lord?
Could this dark world of sin and woe
One glimpse of happiness afford?

3 Eternal life Thy words impart;
On these my fainting spirit lives;
Here sweeter comforts cheer my heart
Than all the round of nature gives.

4 Let earth's alluring joys combine;
While Thou art near, in vain they call;
One smile, one blissful smile of Thine,
My gracious Lord, outweighs them all.

5 Low at Thy feet my soul would lie;
Here safety dwells, and peace divine;
Still let me live beneath Thine eye,
For life, eternal life, is Thine.

*Anne Steele,* 1760

# COURAGE AND CONFIDENCE.

## 670
C.M.
*Not ashamed of the Gospel.*

1 I'M not asham'd to own my Lord,
Or to defend His cause,
Maintain the honour of His Word,
The glory of His cross.

2 Jesus, my God; I know His name;
His name is all my trust;
Nor will He put my soul to shame,
Nor let my hope be lost.

3 Firm as His throne His promise stands,
And He can well secure
What I've committed to His hands,
Till the decisive hour.

4 Then will He own my worthless name
Before His Father's face;
And in the New Jerusalem
Appoint my soul a place.

*Isaac Watts,* 1709

> TD: "The sovereignty of God in all things is an
> unfailing ground for consolation; He rules and
> reigns whatever happens, and therefore all is
> well" (Ps. 102; vol. 4, p. 422).
> FPN: 23 May 1889 (No. 2313), MARTYRDOM
> 5 Sept. 1889 (No. 2120), MARTYRDOM
> 9 Feb. 1890 (No. 2275), ARLINGTON

## 671
C.M.
*Holy fortitude.*

1 AM I a soldier of the cross,
A follower of the Lamb?
And shall I fear to own His cause
Or blush to speak His name?

2 Must I be carried to the skies
On flow'ry beds of ease,
While others fought to win the prize
And sail'd through bloody seas?

3 Are there no foes for me to face?
Must I not stem the flood?
Is this vile world a friend to grace,
To help me on to God?

4 Sure I must fight if I would reign;
Increase my courage, Lord;
I'll bear the toil, endure the pain,
Supported by Thy Word.

*Isaac Watts,* [1729]

## 672
S.M. / *The Christian warrior
exhorted to perseverance.*

1 SOLDIERS of Christ, arise,
And put your armour on,
Strong in the strength which God supplies
Through His eternal Son;

2 Strong in the Lord of Hosts
And in His mighty power,

Who in the strength of Jesus trusts
Is more than conqueror.

3   Stand, then, in His great might,
With all His strength endued,
But take, to arm you for the fight,
The panoply of God.

4   To keep your armour bright,
Attend with constant care,
Still walking in your Captain's sight
And watching unto prayer.

5   In fellowship, alone,
To God with faith draw near;
Approach His courts, besiege His throne
With all the power of prayer.

6   From strength to strength go on,
Wrestle, and fight, and pray,
Tread all the powers of darkness down,
And win the well-fought day.

*Charles Wesley*, [1742, *rev.* 1780]

   **MM:** "Fear not; you shall overcome; for who
   can defeat Omnipotence? Fight on, 'looking
   unto Jesus;' and though long and stern be the
   conflict, sweet will be the victory, and glorious
   the promised reward" (June 2).

# 673  7.7.7.7.
*"A good soldier of Jesus Christ."*

1  *OFT* in sorrow, oft in woe,
Onward, Christians, onward go;
Fight the fight, *maintain the* strife,
*Strengthen'd with* the bread of life.

2  Let your drooping hearts be glad;
March in heavenly armour clad;
Fight, nor think the battle long;
*Soon shall victory* tune your song.

3  Let not sorrow dim your eye;
Soon shall every tear be dry;
Let not fears your course impede;
Great your strength, if great your need.

4  Onward, then, to *glory* move;
More than conquerors ye shall prove;

Though opposed by many a foe,
Christian soldiers, onward go.

1 *Henry Kirke White*, [1812]
2-4 *Frances Fuller-Maitland*, 1827
[*alt. William Hall*, 1836]
   **1.1:** *Much*  **1.3:** *and worn*  **1.4:** *Steep with tears*
   **2.4:** *Victory soon shall*  **4.1:** *battle*
   **Ed:** Upon White's death in 1806, this hymn was
   left unfinished, with just two and a half stanzas; William Collyer attempted to complete
   it in 1812, followed by this version in 1827.
   William Hall changed the opening phrase to
   read "Oft in danger," but this was not retained
   by Spurgeon. Edward Bickersteth's revision
   was reported by Julian (p. 774) as appearing
   before Hall's (1833), but it did not actually
   appear until his enlarged edition (1841).

# 674  7.6.7.6. Double
*Stand up for Jesus.*

1  STAND up! stand up for Jesus!
Ye soldiers of the cross;
Lift high His royal banner;
It must not suffer loss.
From victory unto victory
His army shall He lead,
Till every foe is vanquish'd
And Christ is Lord indeed.

2  Stand up! Stand up for Jesus!
The trumpet call obey;
Forth to the mighty conflict
In this His glorious day;
"Ye that are men, now serve Him,"
Against unnumber'd foes;
*Your* courage rise with danger,
And strength to strength oppose.

3  Stand up! stand up for Jesus!
Stand in His strength alone;
The arm of flesh will fail you;
Ye dare not trust your own.
Put on the gospel armour,
*And watching unto* prayer,
Where duty calls, or danger,
Be never wanting there!

4 Stand up! Stand up for Jesus!
    The strife will not be long;
This day the noise of battle,
    The next the victor's song.
To Him that overcometh
    A crown of life shall be;
He with the King of Glory
    Shall reign eternally.

*George Duffield*, 1858

**2.7:** *Let* (1868) **3.6:** *Each piece put on with* (1868)
**FPN:** 9 Feb. 1890 (No. 2275), MISSIONARY
    9 Sept. 1888 (No. 2043), MISSIONARY
**Ed:** The first printing is regarded to be in the
    supplement to the Presb. *Church Psalmist*
    (1858); this version had only 3 sts. That same
    year, it appeared in *The Sabbath Hymn Book*
    with 4 sts. as above; this was in Spurgeon's li-
    brary. The 1868 printing in Charles Cleveland's
    *Lyra Sacra Americana* contained 6 sts., some
    changes, and a historical note on p. 298.

# 675 L.M.
*"Be strong, fear not."*

1 NOW let the feeble all be strong
And make Jehovah's arm their song;
His shield is spread o'er every saint;
And thus supported, who shall faint?

2 What though the hosts of hell engage
With mingled cruelty and rage?
A faithful God restrains their hands
And chains them down in iron bands.

3 Bound by His Word, He will display
A strength proportion'd to our day;
And when united trials meet,
Will show a path of safe retreat.

4 Thus far we prove that promise good,
Which Jesus ratified with blood;
Still He is gracious, wise, and just,
And still in Him let Israel trust.

*Philip Doddridge*, 1755

**FPN:** 5 Sept. 1889 (No. 2120), SAMSON
**Ed:** Dated 24 June 1739 in Doddridge's MSS.

**MM:** "O Thou who art my God and my strength,
I can believe that this promise shall be fulfilled
['I will strengthen thee,' Isaiah 41:10], for the
boundless reservoir of Thy grace can never
be exhausted, and the overflowing storehouse
of Thy strength can never be emptied by Thy
friends or rifled by Thine enemies" (Dec. 22).

# 676 L.M.
*God is all sufficient.*

1 AWAKE, our souls, away, our fears;
Let every trembling thought be gone;
Awake, and run the heavenly race,
And put a cheerful courage on.

2 True, 'tis a straight and thorny road,
And mortal spirits tire and faint,
But they forget the mighty God
That feeds the strength of every saint.

3 Thee, mighty God, whose matchless pow'r
Is ever new and ever young,
And firm endures, while endless years
Their everlasting circles run.

4 From Thee, the overflowing spring,
Our souls shall drink a fresh supply,
While such as trust their native strength
Shall melt away, and droop, and die.

5 Swift as an eagle cuts the air,
We'll mount aloft to Thine abode;
On wings of love our souls shall fly,
Nor tire amidst the heavenly road.

*Isaac Watts*, [1707]

# 677 C.M.
*Be of good courage.*

1 WHENCE do our mournful thoughts arise,
And where's our courage fled?
Have resltess sin and raging hell
Struck all our comforts dead?

2 Have we forgot th' Almighty Name
That form'd the earth and sea?
And can an all-creating arm
Grow weary or decay?

3 Treasures of everlasting might
    In our Jehovah dwell;
  He gives the conquest to the weak
    And treads their foes to hell.

4 Mere mortal power shall fade and die,
    And youthful vigour cease,
  But we that wait upon the Lord
    Shall feel our strength increase.

5 The saints shall mount on eagles' wings
    And taste the promis'd bliss,
  Till their unwearied feet arrive
    Where perfect pleasure is.

*Isaac Watts*, [1707, *rev.* 1709]

# 678 L.M.
*The Christian warfare.*

1 STAND up, my soul, shake off thy fears,
  And gird the gospel armour on;
  March to the gates of endless joy,
  Where thy great Captain-Saviour's gone.

2 Hell and thy sins resist thy course,
  But hell and sin are vanquish'd foes;
  Thy Jesus nail'd them to the cross
  And sung the triumph when He rose.

3 What though thine inward lusts rebel?
  'Tis but a struggling gasp for life;
  The weapons of victorious grace
  Shall slay thy sins and end the strife.

4 Then let my soul march boldly on,
  Press forward to the heavenly gate;
  There peace and joy eternal reign,
  And glittering robes for conquerors wait.

5 There shall I wear a starry crown
  And triumph in almighty grace,
  While all the armies of the skies
  Join in my glorious Leader's praise.

*Isaac Watts*, [1707, *rev.* 1709]

  **TD:** "The defeat of the nations who fought with
  King David was so utter and complete that they
  were like powders pounded in a mortar; their
  power was broken into fragments and they

became weak as dust before the wind, and as
mean as the mire of the roads. . . . Arise, O my
soul, and meet thine enemies, for they have
sustained a deadly blow, and will fall before thy
bold advance" (Ps. 18:42; vol. 1, p. 278).

# 679 S.M.
*Our victorious Lord.*

1 JESU'S tremendous name
  Puts all our foes to flight!
Jesus, the meek, the angry Lamb,
  A Lion is in fight.

2 By all hell's host withstood,
  We all hell's host o'erthrow,
And conquering them, thru' Jesus's blood,
  We still to conquer go.

3 Our Captain leads us on;
  He beckons from the skies,
And reaches out a starry crown,
  And bids us take the prize.

4 "Be faithful unto death,
  Partake my victory,
And thou shalt wear this glorious wreath,
  And thou shalt reign with me."

*Charles Wesley*, 1749

  **Ed:** Taken from the longer hymn,
  "Hark, how the watchmen cry!"
  **EE:** "Who shall fight against the people who
  have such power vested in their Captain? O
  my soul, what can destroy thee if Omnipotence be thy helper? If aegis of the Almighty
  cover thee, what sword can smite thee? Rest
  thou secure. If Jesus is thine all-prevailing
  King, and hath trodden thine enemies beneath
  His feet; if sin, death, and hell are all vanquished by Him, and thou art represented in
  Him, by no possibility canst thou be destroyed" (April 21).

# 680 S.M.
*More than conqueror.*

1 HIS be the victor's name!
  *Who* fought our fight alone!
Triumphant saints no honour claim;
  *His conquest was* His own.

2     He hell in hell laid low;
      *Made sin, He* sin o'erthrew;
  Bow'd to the grave, *destroy'd* it so,
    And death, by dying, slew.

3     What though th' accuser roar
      Of ills that we have done,
  We know them well, and thousands more;
    Jehovah findeth none.

4     Sin, *Satan,* Death *appear*
      To harass and appal—
  *Yet since the gracious Lord is near,*
    Backward they go, and fall.

5     *We meet them face to* face,
      *Through Jesus' conquest blest;*
  March in the triumph of His grace,
    *Right onward to our* rest.

6     Bless, bless the Conq'ror slain,
      Slain in His victory,
  Who lived, who died, who lives again—
    For thee, His church, for thee!

*Samuel Gandy,* [1823, *alt.*]

**1.2:** *He*   **1.4:** *Their conquests are*
**2.2:** *He sin by sin*   **2.3:** *and kill'd*
**4.1:** *hell, and / press near*
**4.3:** *Let but my bleeding God appear,*
**5.1:** *I, waving in their*
**5.2:** *My captain's crimson vest,*
**5.4:** *And push my way to*
**Ed:** This hymn was attributed to Samuel Gandy
by Sedgwick, Julian (p. 1565), and others, and
it did appear in Wigram's *Hymns for the Poor
of the Flock* (1838), as they claimed. It was
unattributed there and printed in two distinct
parts, the first beginning "What though th'
accuser roar," in 5 sts., the second, "His be 'the
victor's name,'" in 4 sts. The text had actually
appeared earlier in Robert Carne's *Collection*
(1823), unattributed, beginning "Sin, hell, and
death press near," in 9 sts.; st. 3 above was
part of a different hymn altogether, "Now,
now the valleys rise." The 1838 edition, then,
is an alteration of what appeared in 1823, and
Spurgeon's version is a rearrangement of 1838.
Gandy's name did not appear in either collection, but his authorship was widely attested in
the late 1800s.

# 681  L.M.
*Christ our strength.*

1 LET me but hear my Saviour say,
  "Strength shall be equal to thy day,"
  Then I rejoice in deep distress,
  Leaning on all-sufficient grace.

2 I glory in infirmity,
  That Christ's own pow'r may rest on me;
  When I am weak, then I am strong;
  Grace is my shield, and Christ my song.

3 I can do all things, or can bear
  All suff'rings, if my Lord be there;
  Sweet pleasures mingle with the pains,
  While His left hand my head sustains.

4 But if the Lord be once withdrawn,
  And we attempt the work alone,
  When new temptations spring and rise,
  We find how great our weakness is.

*Isaac Watts,* [1707]

**MM:** "Are you mourning over your own weakness? Take courage, for there must be a
consciousness of weakness before the Lord
will give thee victory. Your emptiness is but
the preparation for your being filled, and your
casting down is but the making ready for your
lifting up" (Nov. 4).

# 682  C.M.
*Sufficient grace.*

1 KIND are the words that Jesus speaks
  To cheer the drooping saint;
  "My grace sufficient is for you,
  Though nature's powers may faint."

2 "My grace its glories shall display,
  And make your griefs remove;
  Your weakness shall the triumphs tell
  Of boundless power and love."

3 What though my griefs are not remov'd,
  Yet why should I despair?
  While my kind Saviour's arms support,
  I can the burden bear.

4 Jesus, my Saviour and my Lord,
    'Tis good to trust Thy name;
Thy pow'r, Thy faithfulness, and love
    Will ever be the same.

5 Weak as I am, yet through Thy grace
    I all things can perform;
And smiling, triumph in Thy name,
    Amidst the raging storm.

*John Needham, 1768*

# 683 L.M.
*Jesus still the same.*

1 HOW frail and fallible am I!
What weakness marks my changing frame!
Yet there is strength and comfort nigh,
For Jesus, Thou art still the same.

2 Thy love, immortal and divine,
    No coldness damps, no time destroys;
Through countless ages it will shine,
    Bright source of everlasting joys.

3 On Thy sure mercy I depend
    In all my trials, wants, and woes,
For Thou art an unchanging Friend;
    Sweet is the peace Thy hand bestows.

4 Hast Thou protected me thus far,
    To leave me in the dangerous hour?
Shall Satan be allow'd to mar
    Thy work, or to resist Thy power?

5 O never wilt Thou leave the soul
    That flies for refuge to Thy breast;
Thy love, which once hath made me whole,
    Shall guide me to eternal rest.

6 Though stars be from their courses hurl'd,
    Though mighty ruin should descend,
Wide o'er a desolated world,
    The love of Jesus knows no end.

*William Hiley Bathurst, 1831*

    **EE:** Hymns, Set 2 (Feb./Dec.), 2nd Eve,
        WINCHESTER / NEAPOLIS

# 684 L.M.
*My heart is fixed.*

1 NOW I have found the ground, wherein
    Sure my soul's anchor may remain;
The wounds of Jesus, for my sin,
    Before the world's foundation slain,
Whose mercy shall unshaken stay
When heaven and earth are fled away.

2 O love, thou bottomless abyss!
    My sins are swallow'd up in thee;
Cover'd is my unrighteousness,
    Nor spot of guilt remains on me.
While Jesu's blood, thru' earth and skies,
Mercy, free, boundless mercy cries.

3 With faith I plunge me in this sea;
    Here is my hope, my joy, my rest;
Hither, when hell assails, I flee,
    I look into my Saviour's breast;
Away, sad doubt, and anxious fear!
Mercy is all that's written there.

4 Though waves and storms go o'er my head,
    Though strength, and health,
        and friends be gone,
Though joys be wither'd all, and dead,
    Though every comfort be withdrawn,
On this my stedfast soul relies;
Father, Thy mercy never dies.

5 Fix'd on this ground will I remain,
    Though my heart fail, and flesh decay;
This anchor shall my soul sustain,
    When earth's foundations melt away;
Mercy's full power I then shall prove,
Lov'd with an everlasting love.

*Johann Andreas Rothe,* [1727]
*tr. John Wesley, 1740* [*rev. 1753*]

    **Ed:** From the German, "Ich habe nun den Grund
    gefunden." The only change between 1740 and
    1753 was in 2.4, originally "*in* me."
    **MM:** "The love of Christ in its sweetness, its
    fullness, its greatness, its faithfulness, passeth
    all human comprehension. . . . Well might the
    poet say, 'O love, thou fathomless abyss!' for
    this love of Christ is indeed measureless and
    fathomless; none can attain unto it" (Mar. 28).

# 685

S.M.
*Be of good courage.*

1 YOUR harps, ye trembling saints,
  Down from the willows take;
Loud to the praise of love divine,
  Bid ev'ry string awake.

2 Though in a foreign land,
  We are not far from home,
And nearer to our house above
  We ev'ry moment come.

3 His grace will to the end
  Stronger and brighter shine;
Nor present things, nor things to come,
  Shall quench the spark divine.

4 The people of His choice,
  He will not cast away;
Yet do not always here expect
  On Tabor's mount to stay.

5 When we in darkness walk,
  Nor feel the heav'nly flame,
Then is the time to trust our God
  And rest upon His name.

6 Soon shall our doubts and fears
  Subside at His control;
His loving-kindness shall break through
  The midnight of the soul.

7 Wait till the shadows flee;
  Wait thy appointed hour;
Wait till the Bridegroom of thy soul
  Reveals His *sovereign* pow'r.

8 Tarry His leisure then,
  Although He seem to stay;
A moment's intercourse with Him,
  Thy grief will overpay.

9 Blest is the man, O God,
  That stays himself on Thee!
Who wait for Thy salvation, Lord,
  Shall Thy salvation see.

*Augustus Toplady,* 1772 [*alt.* C.H.S.]

**7.4:** *love with*   **TD:** "Hitherto, all has been
mournful and disconsolate, but now, 'Your
harps, ye trembling saints, down from the
willows take.' Ye must have your times of
weeping, but let them be short. Get ye up, get
ye up from your dunghills! Cast aside your
sackcloth and ashes! Weeping may endure for
a night, but joy cometh in the morning" (Ps.
6:8; vol. 1, p. 65).

# 686

S.M.
*The Christian encouraged.*

1 GIVE to the winds thy fears;
  Hope, and be undismay'd;
God hears thy sighs and counts thy tears;
  God shall lift up thy head.

2 Through waves, and clouds, and storms,
  He gently clears thy way;
Wait thou His time; so shall *the* night
  Soon end in joyous day.

3 *He* ev'rywhere *hath* sway,
  And all things serve *His* might;
*His* ev'ry act pure blessing is;
  *His* path unsullied light.

4 When *He makes bare His arm,*
  What shall His work withstand?
When *He His people's cause defends,*
  Who, who shall stay His hand?

5 Leave to His sov'reign sway
  To choose and to command;
*With wonder fill'd, thou then shalt own*
  How wise, how strong His hand.

6 *Thou comprehend'st Him not,*
  Yet *earth and heaven tell,*
*God sits as Sovereign on His* throne;
  *He* ruleth all things well.

7 Thou seest our weakness, Lord;
  Our hearts are known to Thee;
O lift Thou up the sinking hand;
  Confirm the feeble knee!

8 Let us in life *and* death
  Thy stedfast truth declare,
And publish with our latest breath
  Thy love and guardian care.

*Paul Gerhardt,* [1653]
*tr. John Wesley,* 1739
[*alt. A Collection of Hymns for the Use …
of the United Brethren,* 1801]

**2.3:** *this* **3.1:** *Thou / hast* **3.2:** *Thy* **3.3:** *Thy*
**3.4:** *Thy* **4.1:** *Thou arisest, Lord,*
**4.3:** *all thy children want, Thou giv'st;*
**5.3:** *So shalt thou wondering own, his way*
**6.1:** *What tho' Thou rulest not?*
**6.2:** *Heav'n and earth and hell*
**6.3:** *Proclaim, God sitteth on the*
**6.4:** *And* **8.1:** *in*
**MM:** Hymns, Set 2 (Feb./Dec.), 22nd Morn,
LABAN / OLMUTZ
**Ed:** From the German, "Befiehl du deine Wege,"
and taken from the longer translation "Commit thou all thy griefs."

# 687  7.6.7.6. / *Weakness confessed,*
*but security enjoyed.*

1 I THOUGHT that I was strong, Lord,
 And did not need Thine arm;
 Though troubles throng'd around me,
 My heart felt no alarm.

2 I thought I nothing needed—
 Riches, nor dress, nor sight—
 And on I walked in darkness,
 And still I thought it light.

3 But Thou hast broke the spell, Lord,
 And waked me from my dream;
 The light has burst *upon me*
 With bright unerring beam.

4 *I* know Thy blood has cleans'd *me,*
 *I* know that I'm forgiven,
 And all the roughest *pathways*
 Will surely end in heaven.

5 *I* know that I am Thine, Lord,
 *And* none can pluck away
 The feeblest sheep that ever yet
 Did make Thine arm its stay.

*Joseph Denham Smith,* 1860 [*alt. C.H.S.*]

**3.3:** *into my soul* **4.1:** *For I / my soul*
**4.2:** *And I* **4.3:** *paths on earth* **5.1:** *For I*

**5.2:** *And that* **Ed:** The alterations here mostly
reflect the normalization of Smith's irregular
metre. In the 1st ed. of *OOHB,* 5.2 read *And
that*; this was changed to *And* in 1867.

# PEACEFUL TRUST.

# 688  8.6.8.6.
*Delight in God.*

1 O LORD, I would delight in Thee,
 And on Thy care depend;
 To Thee in every trouble flee,
 My best, my only friend.

2 When all created streams are dried,
 Thy fullness is the same;
 May I with this be satisfied,
 And glory in Thy name.

3 Why should the soul a drop bemoan,
 Who has a fountain near,
 A fountain which will ever run
 With waters sweet and clear?

4 No good in creatures can be found,
 But may be found in Thee;
 I must have all things and abound,
 While God is God to me.

5 O that I had a stronger faith
 To look within the veil,
 To credit what my Saviour saith,
 Whose word can never fail.

6 He that has made my heaven secure
 Will here all good provide;
 While Christ is rich, can I be poor?
 What can I want beside?

7 O Lord, I cast my care on Thee,
 I triumph and adore;
 Henceforth my great concern shall be
 To love and please Thee more.

*John Ryland,* [1787, *rev. ca.* 1805]

**Ed:** Dated 3 Dec. 1777 in his manuscript.

## 689

7.7.7.7.
*"Trust ye in the Lord forever."*

1 WHEN we cannot see our way,
Let us trust and still obey;
He who bids us forward go
Cannot fail the way to show.

2 Though *enwrapt in gloomy* night,
*We perceive* no ray of light;
Since the Lord Himself is *here*,
'Tis not meet that we should fear.

3 Night with Him is never night;
Where He is, there all is light;
When He calls us, why delay?
They are happy who obey.

4 Be it ours, then, while we're here,
Him to follow without fear;
Where He calls us, there to go;
What He bids us, that to do.

*Thomas Kelly*, 1815, *alt. C.H.S.*

   **2.1:** *it seems the gloom of*   **2.2:** *Though we see*

## 690

L.M.
*Confidence in God.*

1 MY spirit looks to God alone;
My rock and refuge is His throne;
In all my fears, in all my straits,
My soul on His salvation waits.

2 Trust Him, ye saints; in all your ways,
Pour out your hearts before His face;
When helpers fail and foes invade,
God is our all-sufficient aid.

*Isaac Watts*, 1719

## 691

C.M.
*Freedom from care.*

1 I *BOW me to Thy will, O* God,
And all Thy ways adore;
And every day I live, *I'll seek*
To *please* Thee more and more.

2 I love to kiss each print where *Christ*
*Did* set *His pilgrim* feet;
*Nor can I* fear *that* blessèd *path*
*Whose traces are* so sweet.

3 When obstacles and trials seem
Like prison walls to be,
I do the little I can do
And leave the rest to Thee.

4 I have no cares, O blessèd *Lord*,
For all my cares are Thine;
I live in triumph, *too*, for Thou
Hast made Thy triumphs mine.

5 And when it seems no chance nor change
From grief can set me free,
Hope finds its strength in helplessness,
And, *patient*, waits on Thee.

6 *Lead on*, *lead on* triumphantly,
O blessèd Lord, lead on!
Faith's pilgrim-sons behind Thee *seek*
The road that Thou hast gone.

*Frederick W. Faber*, 1849
[*alt. William Reid*, 1863]

   **1.1:** *worship thee, sweet will of*   **1.3:** *I seem*
   **1.4:** *love*   **2.1:** *thou*   **2.2:** *Hast / thine unseen*
   **2.3:** *I cannot / thee / Will!*   **2.4:** *Thine empire is*
   **4.1:** *Will!*   **4.3:** *Lord!*   **5.4:** *gaily*
   **6.1:** *Ride on, ride on*   **6.2:** *Thou glorious Will!*
   *ride on;*   **6.3:** *Take*
   **Ed:** In the first ed. of *OOHB* (1866), "From
   the Latin, W. Reid's Hymns of Praise, 1865,"
   changed to Faber 1852 in the 2nd ed. (1867),
   corrected to Faber 1849 in the 4th ed. (1869),
   but then curiously changed to Faber 1835 in
   the 6th ed. (1873); Faber is not known to have
   published hymns before 1849.

## 692

C.M.
*Trust for the future.*

1 ALMIGHTY Father of mankind,
On Thee my hopes remain,
And when the day of trouble comes,
I shall not trust in vain.

2 In early days Thou wast my guide,
And of my youth the friend;

And as my days began with Thee,
 With Thee my days shall end.

3 I know the power in whom I trust,
 The arm on which I lean;
 He will my Saviour ever be,
 Who has my Saviour been.

4 My God, who causèdst me to hope,
 When life began to beat,
 And when a stranger in the world,
 Didst guide my wandering feet.

5 Thou wilt not cast me off when age
 And evil days descend;
 Thou wilt not leave me in despair
 To mourn my latter end.

6 Therefore in life I'll trust to Thee,
 In death I will adore,
 And after death I'll sing Thy praise,
 When time shall be no more.

*Michael Bruce*, 1781

# 693
C.M.
*Dependence on God.*

1 *ETERNAL God! we look to Thee,*
 *To Thee for help we fly;*
 *Thine eye alone our wants can see;*
 *Thy hand alone supply.*

2 *Lord! let Thy fear within us dwell,*
 *Thy love our footsteps guide;*
 *That love will all vain love expel,*
 *That fear all fear beside.*

3 Not what *we* wish, but *what we* want,
 *Oh, let Thy grace supply;*
 *The good unask'd, in mercy* grant;
 *The* ill, though ask'd, deny.

 *James Merrick*, [1763]
[*alt. Thomas Cotterill*, 1810]

 **1.1-3:** *Author of good, to Thee I turn;*
 *Thy ever-wakeful eye*
 *Alone can all my wants discern,*
 **2.1:** *O / me* **2.2:** *my* **2.3:** *shall vainer loves*
 **3.1:** *my / to my* **3.2:** *Do Thou thy gifts apply*

 **3.3:** *Unask'd, what good thou knowest,*
 **3.4:** *What* **Ed:** Taken from the longer hymn,
 "Behold yon new-born infant grieved."

# CHRISTIAN ZEAL.

# 694
C.M.
*Running the Christian race.*

1 AWAKE, my soul, stretch ev'ry nerve,
 And press with vigour on;
 A heav'nly race demands thy zeal
 And an immortal crown.

2 'Tis God's all-animating voice
 That calls thee from on high;
 'Tis His own hand presents the prize
 To thine aspiring eye.

3 A cloud of witnesses around
 Hold thee in full survey,
 Forget the steps already trod,
 And onward urge thy way.

4 Blest Saviour, introduc'd by Thee,
 Have *we our* race begun;
 And crown'd with vict'ry, at Thy feet
 *We'll* lay *our* honours down.

 *Philip Doddridge*, 1755
[*alt. Caleb Evans*, 1769]

 **4.2:** *I my* **4.4:** *I'll / mine*
 **FPN:** 5 Aug. 1888 (No. 2037), MAGNUS

# 695
L.M.
*Zeal in duty.*

1 AWAKE my zeal, awake my love
 To serve my Saviour here below
 In works which *perfect* saints above
 *And* holy angels cannot do.

2 Awake my charity, *to* feed
 The hungry soul and clothe the poor;
 In heav'n are found no sons of need;
 There all these duties are no more.

3 Subdue thy passions, O my soul;
 Maintain the fight, thy work pursue;

Daily thy rising sins control,
And be thy vict'ries ever new.

4 The land of triumph lies on high;
There are no fields of battle there;
Lord, I would conquer till I die
And finish all the glorious war.

5 Let every flying hour confess
I gain Thy gospel fresh renown;
And when my life and labours cease,
May I possess the promis'd crown.

*Isaac Watts*, [1729]
[*alt. James Winchell*, 1820]

**1.3:** *all the*  **1.4:** *Which*  **2.1:** *and*
**Ed:** Winchell's alteration was repeated in a
combined ed. of Watts with Rippon's Comprehensive Ed. (1844).

## PATIENCE AND RESIGNATION.

# 696 C.M.
*The request.*

1 *FATHER*, whate'er of earthly bliss
Thy sovereign *will* denies,
Accepted at Thy throne of grace,
Let this petition rise:

2 "Give me a calm, a thankful heart,
From ev'ry murmur free;
The blessings of Thy grace impart,
And *make* me live to Thee.

3 "Let the sweet hope that Thou art mine
My life and death attend;
Thy presence through my journey shine,
And *crown my journey's* end."

*Anne Steele*, 1760
[*alt. Augustus Toplady*, 1776]

**1.1:** *And O*  **1.2:** *hand*  **2.4:** *let*
**3.4:** *bless its happy*
**MM:** Hymns, Set 2 (Feb./Dec.), 7th Morn,
NAOMI / LA MIRA
**Ed:** Taken from the longer hymn, "When I survey
life's varied scene," and truncated in this form
by Toplady.

# 697 7.7.7.7.
*"Give us day by day our daily bread."*

1 DAY by day the manna fell;
Oh to learn this lesson well!
Still by constant mercy fed,
Give me, Lord, my daily bread.

2 "Day by day," the promise reads;
Daily strength for daily needs.
Cast foreboding fears away;
Take the manna of today.

3 Lord! my times are in Thy hand;
All my sanguine hopes have plann'd
To Thy wisdom I resign,
And would make Thy purpose mine.

4 Thou my daily task shalt give;
Day by day to Thee I live.
So shall added years fulfill,
Not mine own—my Father's will.

5 Fond ambition, whisper not;
Happy is my humble lot.
Anxious, busy cares, away;
I'm provided for today.

6 Oh to live exempt from care,
By the energy of prayer;
Strong in faith, with mind subdued,
Yet elate with gratitude!

*Josiah Conder*, [1836]

**EE:** Hymns, Set 2 (Feb./Dec.), 13th Eve,
HART'S / PENTONVILLE

# 698 C.M.
*Submission.*

1 O LORD! my best desire fulfill,
And help me to resign
Life, health, and comfort to Thy will,
And make Thy pleasure mine.

2 Why should I shrink at Thy command,
Whose love forbids my fears?
Or tremble at the gracious hand
That wipes away my tears?

3 No, let me rather freely yield
    What most I prize to Thee,
Who never hast a good withheld,
    Nor wilt withhold, from me.

4 Thy favour all my journey through
    Thou art engaged to grant;
What else I want, or think I do,
    'Tis better still to want.

5 But ah! my inmost spirit cries,
    Still bind me to Thy sway;
Else the next cloud that veils my skies
    Drives all these thoughts away.

*William Cowper*, 1779

# 699
8.8.8.4.
*"Not as I will, but as Thou wilt."*

1 MY God and Father! while I stray
Far from my home, in life's rough way,
Oh! teach me from my heart to say,
    "Thy will be done!"

2 If Thou shouldst call me to resign
What most I prize—it ne'er was mine;
I only yield Thee what was Thine.
    "Thy will be done!"

3 If but my fainting heart be blest
With Thy sweet Spirit for its guest,
My God! to Thee I leave the rest—
    "Thy will be done!"

4 Renew my will from day to day;
Blend it with Thine, and take away
All that now makes it hard to say,
    "Thy will be done!"

5 Then when on earth I breathe no more
The prayer oft mix'd with tears before,
I'll sing upon a happier shore,
    "Thy will be done!"

*Charlotte Elliott*, 1834

# 700
C.M.
*"Yet what I shall choose I wot not."*

1 *LORD*, it belongs not to my care
    Whether I die or live;
To love and serve Thee is my share,
    And this Thy grace must give.

2 If life be long I will be glad,
    That I may long obey;
If short—yet why should I be sad,
    *To soar to endless day?*

3 Christ leads me through no darker rooms
    Than He went through before;
He that into God's kingdom comes
    Must enter by this door.

4 Come, Lord, when grace hath made
    me meet,
    Thy blessèd face to see;
For if Thy work on earth be sweet,
    What will Thy glory be?

5 Then I shall end my sad complaints,
    And weary, sinful days,
And join with the triumphant saints
    That sing Jehovah's praise.

6 My knowledge of that life is small,
    The eye of faith is dim,
But *'tis* enough that Christ knows all,
    And I shall be with Him.

*Richard Baxter*, 1681 [*alt.*]

**1.1:** *Now*   **2.4:** *That shall have the same pay.*
**6.3:** *it's*  **Ed:** Taken from the longer hymn,
"My whole, though broken heart, O Lord."
James Montgomery seems to be responsible
for truncating the hymn, in his *Christian Poet*
(1827), along with the changes at 1.1 and 6.3.
2.4 appeared as early as Jan. 1851 in *The Baptist Reporter*. Spurgeon probably adopted this
version via *The Sabbath Hymn Book* (1858).
**EE:** "Our weak eyes could not endure windows of
transparent glass to let in the Master's glory, but
when they are dimmed with weeping, the beams
of the Sun of Righteousness are tempered, and
shine through the windows of agate [Is. 54:12]
with a soft radiance inexpressibly soothing to
tempted souls" (Dec. 13).

# 701
S.M.
*"My times are in Thy hand."*

1    OUR times are in Thy hand;
*Father, we* wish them there;
*Our life, our soul, our all, we* leave
Entirely to Thy care.

2    *Our* times are in Thy hand,
Whatever they may be,
Pleasing or painful, dark or bright,
As best may seem to Thee.

3    *Our* times are in Thy hand;
Why should *we* doubt or fear?
*A* Father's hand will never cause
His child a needless tear.

4    *Our* times are in Thy hand,
Jesus, the Crucified!
*The hand our many* sins had pierced
*Is* now *our* guard and guide.

5    *Our* times are in Thy hand;
*We'll* always trust in Thee;
*Till we have left this weary land,*
*And all Thy glory see.*

*William Freeman Lloyd,* [1824, rev. 1851]
[*alt. George Wigram,* 1838]

**1.1, etc.** *My*   **1.2:** *My God, I*
**1.3:** *My life, my friends, my soul I*   **3.2:** *I*
**4.3:** *Those hands my cruel*   **4.4:** *Are / my*
**5.2:** *I'll*   **5.3:** *And after death at thy right hand*
**5.4:** *I shall forever be.*

# 702
C.M.
*Resignation.*

1 MY times of sorrow and of joy,
Great God, are in Thy hand;
My choicest comforts come from Thee
And go at Thy command.

2 *If Thou shouldst take them all away,*
Yet would I not repine;
Before they were *possess'd by me,*
They were entirely Thine.

3 Nor would I drop a murmuring word,
*Though the whole* world were gone,

But seek *enduring* happiness
In Thee and Thee alone.

4 What is the world with all its store?
'Tis but a bitter sweet;
When I attempt to pluck the rose,
A pricking thorn I meet.

5 Here perfect bliss can ne'er be found;
The honey's mix'd with gall;
Midst changing scenes and dying friends,
Be Thou my all in all.

*Benjamin Beddome,* [1787]

**2.1:** *Oh Lord, shouldst thou withhold them all,*
**2.3:** *by me possessed,*   **3.2:** *If all the*
**3.3:** *substantial*   **Ed:** Written on 4 Jan. 1778
for a sermon on Ps. 31:15, also the same day
as the death of his son. Footnotes indicate
revisions in Beddome's *Hymns* (1817); the
original version was retained by Spurgeon.

# 703
S.M.
*"He shall choose our inheritance for us."*

1    THY way, not mine, O Lord,
However dark it be!
*O* lead me by Thine own *right* hand;
Choose out the path for me.

2    Smooth let it be or rough,
It will be still the best;
Winding or straight, it matters not,
It leads me to Thy rest.

3    I dare not choose my lot;
I would not, if I might;
*But* choose Thou for me, O my God,
So shall I walk aright.

4    Take Thou my cup, and it
With joy or sorrow fill;
As *ever* best to Thee may seem,
Choose Thou my good and ill.

5    Choose Thou for me my friends,
My sickness, or my health;
Choose Thou my *joys and* cares for me,
My poverty or wealth.

6   Not mine, not mine the choice
    In things or great or small;
    Be Thou my guide, *my guard*, my strength,
    My wisdom, and my all.

*Horatius Bonar*, 1857
[*alt. Psalms and Hymns … for the Use of
the Baptist Denomination*, 1857]

    **EE:** Hymns, Set 1 (Jan./Nov.), 11th Eve,
      ST. MICHAEL'S / MT. EPHRAIM
    **TD:** "Cast away anxiety, resign thy will, submit
      thy judgment, leave all with the God of all.
      Our destiny shall be joyfully accomplished if
      we confidently entrust all to our Lord. We may
      serenely sing— 'Thy way, not mine, O Lord,
      however dark it be . . .'" (Ps. 37:5; vol. 2, p. 190).
    **Ed:** Bonar's original was written predominantly
      in 6.6.6.6; italics indicate text added in the
      Baptist collection to fill 6.6.8.6. Whether the
      revisions are by Bonar or the Baptist editors
      is unclear.

# HUMILITY.

**704**  7.7.7.7.
*A prayer for humility.*

1  LORD, if Thou *Thy* grace impart,
   Poor in spirit, meek in heart,
   I shall as my Master be,
   Rooted in humility.

2  Simple, teachable, and mild,
   Awed into a little child,
   *Pleas'd with all the Lord provides,*
   *Wean'd from all the world besides.*

3  *Father, fix my* soul on Thee;
   *Every evil let me flee;*
   Nothing want, beneath, above;
   *Happy only* in Thy love!

4  O that all might seek and find
   Ev'ry good in Jesus join'd;
   Him let Israel still adore;
   Trust Him, praise Him evermore!

*Charles Wesley*, [1743], *alt.*

    **1.1:** *the*  **2.3-4:** *Quiet now without my food,*
      *Wean'd from ev'ry creature-good.*
    **3.1:** *Hangs my newborn*  **3.2:** *Kept from all*
      *idolatry,*  **3.4:** *Happy, happy*
    **Ed:** The alterations at 2.3-4 and 3.1-2 are from
      Martin Madan's *Collection* (1760); 1.1 dates
      to the United Brethren's *Liturgy and Hymns*
      (1849); 3.4 to *The Book for All Ages* (1860),
      perhaps earlier.

**705**  S.M. / *"Blessed are the pure in
heart, for they shall see God."*

1  BLESS'D are the pure in heart,
   For they shall see our God;
   The secret of the Lord is theirs;
   Their soul is Christ's abode.

2  The Lord, who left the *heavens*,
   Our life and peace to bring,
   *To dwell* in lowliness with men,
   Their Pattern and their King;

3  *He* to the lowly soul
   *Doth still* Himself impart,
   And for His *dwelling* and His throne
   Chooseth the pure in heart.

4  Lord, we Thy presence seek;
   *May ours* this blessing be;
   *Give us a* pure and lowly heart,
   A temple meet for Thee!

5  All glory, Lord, to Thee,
   Whom heaven and earth adore,
   To Father, Son, and Holy Ghost,
   One God forever more.

1,3 *John Keble*, 1827, *alt.*
[2,4 Wm. Hall's *Psalms & Hymns*, 1836, *alt.*]
[5 S.P.C.K. *Psalms & Hymns*, 1863]

    **2.1:** *sky*  **2.3:** *And dwelt*  **3.1:** *Still*
    **3.2:** *He doth*  **3.3:** *cradle*  **4.2:** *Ours may*
    **4.3:** *O give the*  **Ed:** The alterations except 4.3
      are from Francis Murray's *Hymnal* (1852);
      These were repeated in the S.P.C.K. edition,
      plus 4.3 and the doxology. The 1836 text could
      be by Hall or Edward Osler.

# 706
C.M.
*The mind of Jesus.*

1 JESUS! exalted far on high,
  To whom a name is given,
  A name surpassing every name
  That's known in earth or heaven,

2 Before whose throne shall every knee
  Bow down with one accord,
  Before whose throne shall every tongue
  Confess that Thou art Lord.

3 Jesus! who in the form of God
  Didst equal honour claim,
  Yet to redeem our guilty souls
  Didst stoop to death and shame.

4 Oh! may that mind in us be form'd
  Which shone so bright in Thee!
  May we be humble, lowly, meek,
  From pride and evny free!

5 May we to others stoop, and learn
  To emulate Thy love;
  So shall we bear Thine image here,
  And share Thy throne above!

*Thomas Cotterill*, 1812

## SACRED GRATITUDE.

# 707
7.7.7.7.7.7.
*Sweet songs from saved souls.*

1 WHO can praise the blessèd God
  Like a sinner saved by grace?
  Angels cannot sing so loud,
  Though they see Him face to face—
  Sinless angels ne'er can know
  What a debt saved sinners owe.

2 Where iniquity's forgiven,
  There the grateful strains arise;
  He who knows the love of heaven
  Sings the songs which grace supplies;
  Precious songs of sins forgiven,
  Sweetest melody of heaven.

*Albert Midlane*, [1865]

# 708
C.M.
*"Return unto thy rest."*

1 MY heart is resting, O my God;
  I will give thanks and sing;
  My heart is at the secret source
  Of every precious thing.

2 Now the frail vessel Thou hast made
  No hand but Thine shall fill—
  The waters of the earth have failed,
  And I am *thirsting* still.

3 I thirst for springs of heavenly life,
  And here all day they rise—
  I seek the treasure of Thy love,
  And close at hand it lies.

4 And a new song is in my mouth,
  To long-loved music set—
  Glory to Thee for all the grace
  I have not tasted yet.

5 I have a heritage of joy
  That yet I must not see;
  The hand that bled to make it mine
  Is keeping it for me.

6 *My heart is resting* on His truth,
  Who hath made all things mine,
  *Who* draws my captive will to Him
  And makes it one with Thine.

*Anna Letitia Waring*, [1854], *alt.*

**2.4:** *thirsty* **6.1:** *A prayer reposing* **6.3:** *That*
**Ed:** This selection of 6 stanzas and the alteration at 6.1 appeared in George Bubier's *Hymns* (1855); this was repeated, adding 2.4 and 6.3, in *Psalms and Hymns … for the Use of the Baptist Denomination* (1857).
**TD:** "David lived a life of dangers and hair-breadth 'scapes, yet was he always safe. In the retrospect of his very many deliverances he feels that he must praise God, and looking upon the mercy which he sought as though it were already received, he sang this song over it— 'And a new song is in my mouth, to long-loved music set . . .'" (Ps. 54:7; vol. 3, p. 11).

# 709 C.M.
*"What shall I render?"*

1 FOR mercies countless as the sands,
    Which daily I receive
From Jesus my Redeemer's hands,
    My soul, what canst thou give?

2 Alas! from such a heart as mine,
    What can I bring Him forth?
My best is stain'd and dyed with sin;
    My all is nothing worth.

3 Yet this acknowledgment I'll make
    For all He has bestow'd:
Salvation's sacred cup I'll take,
    And call upon my God.

4 The best return for one like me,
    So wretched and so poor,
Is from His gifts to draw a plea,
    And ask Him still for more.

5 I cannot serve Him as I ought,
    No works have I to boast,
Yet would I glory in the thought
    That I should owe Him most.

*John Newton*, 1779

# 710 C.M.
*Gratitude for daily mercy.*

1 LORD, in the day Thou art about
    The paths wherein I tread,
And in the night, when I lie down,
    Thou art about my bed.

2 While others in God's prisons lie,
    Bound with affliction's chains,
I walk at large, secure and free
    From sickness and from pain.

3 *'Tis Thou dost crown my hopes and plans*
    With good success *each day*;
This crown, together with myself,
    At Thy blest feet I lay.

4 *O let* my house a temple be,
    *That* I and mine *may* sing

Hosannas to Thy majesty,
    And praise our heavenly King.

*John Mason*, 1683
*adapt. John Hampden Gurney*, 1851

> **3.1:** *But Thou hast crown'd my actions, Lord,*
> **3.2:** *today*  **4.1:** *Then shall*  **4.2:** *Then / shall*
> **MM:** Hymns, Set 1 (Jan./Nov.), 6th Morn,
>    HELENA / NAOMI
> **Ed:** This hymn is drawn from several portions
>    of separate hymns by Mason, as detailed in
>    Julian's *Dictionary of Hymnology*, p. 690.

# JOY AND PEACE.

# 711 C.M.
*God's presence is light in darkness.*

1 MY God, the spring of all my joys,
    The life of my delights,
The glory of my brightest days,
    And comfort of my nights;

2 In darkest shades if He appear,
    My dawning is begun;
He is my soul's sweet morning star,
    And He my rising sun.

3 The opening heavens around me shine
    With beams of sacred bliss,
While Jesus shows His heart is mine,
    And whispers "I am His."

4 My soul would leave this heavy clay
    At that transporting word,
Run up with joy the shining way
    T' embrace my dearest Lord.

5 Fearless of hell and ghastly death,
    I'd break through every foe;
The wings of love and arms of faith
    Should bear me conqueror through.

*Isaac Watts*, [1707]

> **MM:** Hymns, Set 1 (Jan./Nov.), 25th Morn,
>    HENRY / STEPHENS

## 712 S.M.
*Christ unseen but beloved.*

1 NOT with our mortal eyes
  Have we beheld the Lord,
Yet we rejoice to hear His name
  And love Him in His Word.

2 On earth we want the sight
  Of our Redeemer's face,
Yet, Lord, our inmost thoughts delight
  To dwell upon Thy grace.

3 And when we taste Thy love,
  Our joys divinely grow
Unspeakable, like those above,
  And heav'n begins below.

*Isaac Watts*, 1709

## 713 8.7.8.7.
*Sing, ye saints.*

1 SING, ye saints, admire and wonder,
  Jesu's matchless love adore;
Sing, for Sinai's awful thunder
  Shall upon you burst no more.

2 Sing, in spite of Satan's lying;
  Sing, though sins are black and large;
Sing, for Jesus, by His dying,
  Set you free from every charge.

3 Sing, though sense and carnal reason
  Fain would stop the joyful song;
Sing, and count it highest treason
  For a saint to hold his tongue.

4 Sing ye loud, whose holy calling
  Your election plainly shows;
Sing, nor fear a final falling;
  Jesu's love no changes knows.

5 Sing, for you shall heav'n inherit;
  Sing, and ne'er the song have done;
Sing to Father, Son, and Spirit,
  One in Three, and Three in One.

*John Ryland*, [1771]

## 714 C.M.
*The ransomed of the Lord.*

1 SING, ye redeemèd of the Lord,
  Your great Deliv'rer sing;
Pilgrims for Zion's city bound,
  Be joyful in your King.

2 A hand divine shall lead you on
  Through all the blissful road,
Till to the sacred mount you rise
  And see your similing God.

3 There garlands of immortal joy
  Shall bloom on ev'ry head,
While sorrow, sighing, and distress,
  Like shadows, all are fled.

4 March on in your Redeemer's strength,
  Pursue His footsteps still,
And let the prospect cheer your eye
  While lab'ring up the hill.

*Philip Doddridge*, 1755

## 715 C.M.
*A gracious God.*

1 MY soul, arise in joyful lays,
  Renounce this earthly clod,
Tune all thy pow'rs to sweetest praise,
  And sing, thy gracious God.

2 When in my heart His heav'nly love
  He sweetly sheds abroad,
How joyfully He makes me prove
  He is my gracious God.

3 When Jesus to my sinful soul
  Applies His precious blood,
To pardon, cleanse, and make me whole,
  I sing, my gracious God.

4 In all my trials here below,
  I'll humbly kiss His rod,
For this through grace, I surely know
  He's still my gracious God.

*Samuel Medley*, 1789

**FPN:** 20 Oct. 1889 (No. 2341), HENSBURY

# 716

7.6.7.6.
*Joy and peace in believing.*

1 SOMETIMES a light surprises
    The Christian while he sings;
It is the Lord who rises
    With healing in His wings.
When comforts are declining,
    He grants the soul again
A season of clear shining
    To cheer it after rain.

2 In holy contemplation,
    We sweetly then pursue
The theme of God's salvation
    And find it ever new.
Set free from present sorrow,
    We cheerfully can say,
E'en let th' unknown tomorrow
    Bring with it what it may.

3 It can bring with it nothing
    But He will bear us through;
Who gives the lilies clothing
    Will clothe His people too;
Beneath the spreading heavens
    No creature but is fed,
And He who feeds the ravens
    Will give His children bread.

4 *Though* vine nor fig tree neither
    Their wonted fruit should bear,
Though all the field should wither,
    Nor flocks, nor herds be there,
Yet God the same abiding,
    His praise shall tune my voice,
For while in Him confiding,
    I cannot but rejoice.

*William Cowper*, 1779 [*alt.*]

**4.1:** *The*  **Ed:** This minor variant appeared in
eds. of *Olney Hymns* starting ca. 1818.

# 717

7.7.7.7.
*Rejoicing in hope.*

1 CHILDREN of the heav'nly King,
    As ye journey, sweetly sing;
Sing your Saviour's worthy praise!
Glorious in His works and ways!

2 We are trav'lling home to God,
    In the way the fathers trod;
They are happy now, and *ye*
Soon their happiness shall see!

3 O ye banish'd seed, be glad!
    Christ our Advocate is made;
Us to save our flesh assumes,
Brother to our soul becomes.

4 Shout, ye little flock! and blest,
    You on Jesu's throne shall rest;
There your seat is now prepar'd;
There your kingdom and reward!

5 Fear not, brethren! joyful stand
    On the borders of your land;
Jesus Christ, your Father's Son,
Bids you undismay'd go on.

6 Lord, obediently we go,
    Gladly leaving all below;
Only thou our leader be,
And we still will follow thee.

*John Cennick*, 1742
[*alt. Martin Madan*, 1760]

**2.3:** *we*  **MM:** Hymns, Set 2 (Feb./Dec.),
    30th Morn, FULTON / PLEYEL'S HYMN

# 718

S.M.
*The meek beautified with salvation.*

1 YE humble souls, rejoice,
    And cheerful triumphs sing;
Wake all your harmony of voice,
    For Jesus is your King.

2 That meek and lowly Lord,
    Whom here your souls have known,
Pledges the honour of His word
    T' avow you for His own.

3 He brings salvation near,
    For which His blood was paid;
How beauteous shall your souls appear,
    Thus sumptuously array'd!

4   Sing, for the day is nigh,
     When near your Leader's seat,
  The tallest sons of pride shall lie,
     The footstoool of your feet.

5   Salvation, Lord, is Thine,
     And all Thy saints confess
  The royal robes, in which they shine,
     Were wrought by sov'reign grace.

*Philip Doddridge*, 1755

# 719 C.M.
*Gratitude and hope.*

1  MY soul, triumphant in the Lord,
     Shall tell its joys abroad
  And march with holy vigour on,
     Supported by its God.

2  Through all the winding maze of life,
     His hand hath been my guide,
  And in that long-experienc'd care
     My heart shall still confide.

3  His grace through all the desert flows,
     An unexhausted stream;
  That grace on Zion's sacred mount
     Shall be my endless theme.

4  Beyond the choicest joys of earth
     These distant courts I love;
  But O! I burn with strong desire
     To view Thy house above.

5  Mingled with all the shining band,
     My soul would there adore,
  A pillar in Thy temple fix'd,
     To be remov'd no more.

*Philip Doddridge*, 1755

# 720 S.M.
*Heavenly joys on earth.*

1  COME, we that love the Lord,
     And let our joys be known;
  Join in a song with sweet accord,
     And thus surround the throne.

2  The sorrows of the mind
     Be banish'd from the place;
  Religion never was design'd
     To make our pleasure less.

3  Let those refuse to sing
     That never knew our God,
  But favourites of the heavenly King
     May speak their joys abroad.

4  The God that rules on high
     And thunders when He please,
  That rides upon the stormy sky
     And manages the seas:

5  This awful God is ours,
     Our Father and our love;
  He shall send down His heav'nly pow'rs
     To carry us above.

6  There shall we see His face,
     And never, never sin;
  There from the rivers of His grace
     Drink endless pleasures in.

7  Yes, and before we rise
     To that immortal state,
  The thoughts of such amazing bliss
     Should constant joys create.

8  The men of grace have found
     Glory begun below;
  Celestial fruits on earthly ground
     From faith and hope may grow.

9  The hill of Zion yields
     A thousand sacred sweets,
  Before we reach the heav'nly fields
     Or walk the golden streets.

10  Then let our songs abound,
     And every tear be dry;
  We're marching thru' Immanuel's ground
     To fairer worlds on high.

*Isaac Watts*, [1707, *rev.* 1709]

**MBTS:** 21 Dec. 1884 (No. 1827), FALCON STREET

## 721 C.M.
*Spiritual apparel.*

1 AWAKE, my heart; arise, my tongue;
　　Prepare a tuneful voice;
In God, the life of all my joys,
　　Aloud will I rejoice.

2 'Twas he adorn'd my naked soul
　　And made salvation mine!
Upon a poor polluted worm
　　He makes His graces shine.

3 And lest the shadow of a spot
　　Should on my soul be found,
He took the robe the Saviour wrought
　　And cast it all around.

4 How far the heavenly robe exceeds
　　What earthly princes wear!
These ornaments, how bright they shine!
　　How white the garments are!

5 The Spirit wrought my faith and love,
　　And hope, and every grace,
But Jesus spent His life to work
　　The robe of righteousness.

6 Strangely, my soul, art thou array'd
　　By the great Sacred Three;
In sweetest harmony of praise
　　Let all thy powers agree.

*Isaac Watts*, [1707, *rev.* 1709]

> **EE:** "See with what matchless generosity the
> Lord provides for His people's apparel. They
> are so arrayed that the divine skill is seen
> producing an unrivalled broidered work, in
> which every attribute takes its part and every
> divine beauty is revealed. No art like the art
> displayed in our salvation, no cunning work-
> manship like that beheld in the righteousness
> of the saints" (Dec. 21).

## 722 C.M. / *Doubts scattered,*
*or spiritual joy restored.*

1 HENCE from my soul, sad thoughts,
　　be gone,
And leave me to my joys;

My tongue shall triumph in my God
　　And make a joyful noise.

2 Darkness and doubts had veil'd my mind
　　And drown'd my head in tears,
Till sov'reign grace with shining rays
　　Dispell'd my gloomy fears.

3 O what immortal joys I felt,
　　And raptures all divine,
When Jesus told me I was His,
　　And my beloved mine.

4 In vain, the tempter frights my soul
　　And breaks my peace in vain;
One glimpse, dear Saviour, of Thy face
　　Revives my joys again.

*Isaac Watts*, [1707]

## 723 C.M.
*God speaking peace to His people.*

1 UNITE, my roving thoughts, unite
　　In silence soft and sweet,
And thou, my soul, sit gently down
　　At thy great Sov'reign's feet.

2 Jehovah's awful voice is heard,
　　Yet gladly I attend;
For lo! the everlasting God
　　Proclaims Himself my friend.

3 Harmonious accents to my soul
　　The sounds of peace convey;
The tempest at His word subsides,
　　And winds and seas obey.

4 By all its joys, I charge my heart
　　To grieve His love no more,
But charm'd by melody divine
　　To give its follies o'er.

*Philip Doddridge*, 1755

## 724 C.M.
*The power of faith.*

1 FAITH adds new charms to earthly bliss
　　And saves me from its snares;

Its aid in every duty brings
    And softens all my cares.

2 The wounded conscience knows its power
    The healing balm to give;
That balm the saddest heart can cheer
    And make the dying live.

3 Wide it unveils celestial worlds,
    Where deathless pleasures reign,
And bids me seek my portion there,
    Nor bids me seek in vain,

4 Shows me the precious promise, seal'd
    With the Redeemer's blood,
And helps my feeble hope to rest
    Upon a faithful God.

5 There, there unshaken would I rest
    Till this vile body dies,
And then, on faith's triumphant wings,
    At once to glory rise.

*Daniel Turner*, [1769]

**725** C.M.
*Spiritual emotions.*

1 OUR country is Immanuel's land;
    We seek that promised soil;
The songs of Zion cheer our hearts
    While strangers here we toil.

2 Oft do our eyes with joy o'erflow,
    And oft are bathed in tears,
Yet nought but heaven our hopes can raise,
    And nought but sin our fears.

3 We tread the path our Master trod,
    We bear the cross He bore,
And every thorn that wounds our feet,
    His temples pierced before.

4 Our powers are oft dissolved away
    In ecstasies of love,
And while our bodies wander here,
    Our souls are fix'd above.

5 We purge our mortal dross away,
    Refining as we run,

But while we die to earth and sense,
    Our heaven is *here* begun.

*Anna Laetitia Barbauld*, [1792]
[*alt. William Collyer*, 1812]

> **Ed:** Taken from the longer hymn, "Lo, where a
> crowd of pilgrims toil." The extra word *here*
> in 5.4 assumes that *heaven* should be elided
> as one syllable, as in 2.3, but if taken as two
> syllables it isn't necessary. Barbauld's original
> uses the full word in both places. Collyer's
> emendation was repeated in other collections.

**726** C.M.
*Spiritual emotions.*

1 CALM me, my God, and keep me calm;
    Let Thine outstretchèd wing
Be like the shade of Elim's palm
    Beside her desert spring.

2 Yes, keep me calm, though loud and rude
    The sounds my ear that greet,
Calm in the closet's solitude,
    Calm in the bustling street,

3 Calm in the hour of bouyant health,
    Calm in my hour of pain,
Calm in my poverty or wealth,
    Calm in my loss or gain,

4 Calm in the sufferance of wrong,
    Like Him who bore my shame,
Calm 'mid the threatening, taunting throng
    Who hate Thy holy name.

5 Calm me, my God, and keep me calm,
    Soft resting on Thy breast;
Soothe me with holy hymn and psalm
    And bid my spirit rest.

*Horatius Bonar*, [1857]

**727** 7.7.7.7.
*Pleasures of religion.*

1 'TIS religion that can give
    Sweetest pleasures while we live;
'Tis religion must supply
    Solid comfort when we die.

2 After death, its joys will be
Lasting as eternity.
Be the living God my friend,
Then my bliss shall never end.

1-2.2 *Mary Masters*, 1755
[2.3-4 *John Rippon*, 1800]

# CHRISTIAN PRIVILEGES: ADOPTION.

## 728 S.M.
*Adoption.*

1 BEHOLD what wondrous grace
The Father hath bestow'd
On sinners of a mortal race,
To call them sons of God!

2 'Tis no surprising thing
That we should be unknown;
The Jewish world knew not their King,
God's everlasting Son.

3 Nor doth it yet appear
How great we must be made,
But when we see our Saviour here,
We shall be like our head.

4 A hope so much divine
May trials well endure,
May purge our souls from sense and sin
As Christ the Lord is pure.

5 If in my Father's love
I share a filial part,
Send down Thy Spirit, like a dove,
To rest upon my heart.

6 We would no longer lie
Like slaves beneath the throne;
My faith shall 'Abba Father' cry,
And Thou the kindred own.

*Isaac Watts*, [1707]

## 729 7.7.7.7.
*Sons of God blessed.*

1 BLESSÈD are the sons of God;
They are bought with *Jesus's* blood;
They are ransom'd from the grave;
Life eternal they shall have.
  With them number'd may *we* be,
  *Now*, and *through* eternity!

2 God did love them, in His Son,
Long before the world begun;
They the seal of this receive,
When on Jesus they believe.
  With them number'd may *we* be,
  *Now*, and *through* eternity!

3 They are justified by grace;
They enjoy a solid peace;
All their sins are wash'd away;
They shall stand in God's great day.
  With them number'd may *we* be,
  *Now*, and *through* eternity!

4 They produce the fruits of grace
In the works of righteousness;
Born of God, they hate all sin;
God's pure *Word* remains within.
  With them number'd may *we* be,
  *Now*, and *through* eternity!

5 They have fellowship with God
Through the Mediator's blood;
One with God, *through* Jesus one;
Glory is in them begun.
  With them number'd may *we* be,
  *Now*, and *through* eternity!

6 Though they suffer much on earth,
Strangers *to the worldling's* mirth,
Yet they have an inward joy,
Pleasure which can never cloy;
  With them number'd may *we* be,
  *Now*, and *through* eternity!

*Joseph Humphreys*, 1743
[*alt. John Rippon*, 1787, *rev. ca.* 1805]

**1.2:** *Christ's own*  **1.5, etc.:** *I*
**1.6, etc.:** *Here / in*  **4.4:** *seed*  **5.3:** *with*

**6.2:** *quite to this world's* **Ed:** The hymn was written in 8 sts. of 4 lines. Richard Conyers converted the hymn to 5 stanzas of 8 lines, using the the last two lines as a repeating refrain, in his *Collection* (1767). Augustus Toplady modified this arrangement to 6 sts. of 6 lines with the same refrain, in his *Psalms & Hymns* (1776); this was adopted into John Rippon's *Selection* (1787), with his alterations.

# UNCHANGING LOVE.

## 730
8.7.8.7.4.7.
*Praise to the God of love.*

1 FATHER, *'twas Thy love* that knew us
 Earth's foundation long before;
That same love to Jesus drew us
 By its sweet constraining pow'r,
  And will keep us
 Safely now and evermore.

2 God of love, our souls adore Thee!
 We would still Thy grace proclaim,
Till we cast our crowns before Thee,
 And in glory praise Thy name.
  Hallelujah!
 Be to God and to the Lamb.

*James George Deck*, [1838, *alt.*]

**1.1:** *'Twas Thy love, O God,*
**Ed:** Taken from the longer hymn, "Once we all were wretched strangers." This version appeared as early as 1856 in *A Few Hymns … for the Little Flock.*

## 731
C.M.
*The Refiner sitting by the fire.*

1 GOD'S furnace doth in Zion stand,
 But Zion's God sits by,
As the refiner views his gold
 With an observant eye.

2 *His* thoughts are high, His love is wise,
 His wounds a cure intend;
And though He does not always smile,
 He loves unto the end.

3 Thy love is constant to its line,
 Though clouds oft come between;
O could my faith but pierce these clouds,
 It might be always seen.

4 But I am weak and forced to cry;
 Take up my soul to Thee;
Then as Thou ever art the same,
 So shall I ever be.

5 Then shall I ever, ever sing,
 Whilst Thou dost ever shine;
I have Thine own dear pledge for this;
 Lord, Thou art ever mine.

*John Mason*, 1683 [*alt.*]

**2.1:** *God's* **Ed:** Taken from the longer hymn, "I that am drawn out of the depth." This minor variant dates to the mid 1700s, possibly earlier.

## 732
11.11.11.11.
*The firm foundation.*

1 HOW firm a foundation,
 ye saints of the Lord,
Is laid for your faith in His excellent Word;
What more can He say than
 to you He hath said,
You who unto Jesus for refuge have fled?

2 In every condition, in sickness, in health,
 In poverty's vale, or abounding in wealth,
At home and abroad, on the land,
 on the sea,
"As thy days may demand,
 shall thy strength e'er be.

3 "Fear not, I am with thee,
 O be not dismay'd!
I, I am thy God, and will still give thee aid;
I'll strengthen thee, help thee,
 and cause thee to stand,
Upheld by My righteous, omnipotent hand.

4 "When through the deep waters
 I call thee to go,
The rivers of *grief* shall not thee overflow:
For I will be with thee,
 thy troubles to bless,
And sanctify to thee thy deepest distress.

5 "When through fiery trials
 thy pathway shall lie,
My grace all-sufficient shall be thy supply;
The flame shall not hurt thee; I only design
Thy dross to consume,
 and thy gold to refine.

6 "E'en down to old age,
 all My people shall prove
My sovereign, eternal, unchangeable love;
And when hoary hairs shall
 their temples adorn,
Like lambs they shall still in
 My bosom be borne.

7 "The soul that on Jesus
 hath lean'd for repose,
I will not, I will not desert to his foes;
That soul, though all hell should
 endeavour to shake,
I'll never, no never, no never forsake!"

K— in John Rippon's *Selection*, 1787
[*alt. A Selection of Hymns for the Use of
Baptist Congregations*, 1838]

**4.2:** *woe* **Ed:** In the 1st ed. of our *OOHB*,
Sedgwick credited this hymn to "Kirkham or
Kennedy, 1787." Thomas Kirkham published
*A Collection of Hymns* in 1788, not including
"How firm." Kennedy's name appeared with this
hymn as early as 1826 in Nettleton's *Village
Hymns*; this person's identity is unknown. In
the 2nd ed. of *OOHB* (1867), the attribution
was changed to "K—", then changed again to
George Keith in 1873. Keith was son-in-law
of Rippon's predecessor, John Gill; Keith left
the church when Rippon was hired. In Julian's
*Dictionary* (p. 537), his examination of Sedgwick's manuscripts showed that the ascription
to Keith was "based upon nothing but the
statement of an old woman whom Sedgwick
met in an almshouse."
 The most likely author is actually Robert
Keene, Rippon's precentor, based on the testimony of Rippon's tune book editor Thomas
Walker. In the preface to his *Selection*, Rippon
wrote, the hymns "which have only a single
letter prefixed to them, were, many of them
composed by a person unknown, or else have

undergone some considerable alterations,"
thus Rippon likely deserves partial or substantial credit for the shape of the hymn in its
published form.

# 733  11.11.11.11.
   *"I will never leave thee."*

1 O ZION! afflicted with wave upon wave,
 *Whom* no man *can comfort*,
  whom no man can save,
 *With* darkness surrounded,
  by terrors *dismay'd*,
In toiling and rowing,
  thy strength *is decay'd*.

2 *Loud roaring, the billows
  now nigh* overwhelm,
But *skillful's the* Pilot *who* sits at the helm.
His wisdom conducts thee,
  His pow'r thee defends,
In safety and quiet thy warfare He ends.

3 "O fearful, O faithless!" in mercy He cries,
 *"My promise, My truth, are
  they light in thine eyes?*
 *Still*, still I am with thee,
  My promise shall stand;
Through *tempest and tossing*
  I'll bring thee to land.

4 "Forget thee I will not, I cannot; thy name
Engrav'd on My heart *doth
  forever* remain;
*The* palms of My hands *whilst
  I look on* I see
The wounds I received *when
  suffering* for thee.

5 "I feel at My heart all
  thy sighs and thy groans,
For thou art most near Me,
  My flesh and My bones;
In all thy distresses thy Head feels the pain,
Yet all are most needful, not one is in vain.

6 "Then trust Me, and fear not;
  thy life is secure;
My wisdom is perfect;

supreme is My pow'r;
  In love I correct thee, thy soul to refine,
To make thee at length in
  My likeness to shine.

7 "The foolish, the fearful,
    the weak are My care;
The *helpless, the hopeless,*
    I hear their sad pray'r;
From all their afflictions
    My glory shall spring,
And the deeper their sorrows,
    the louder they'll sing."

*James Grant,* 1784
[*alt. John Rippon,* 1800]

**1.2:** *By / comforted*  **1.3:** *By undone,*
**1.4:** *almost gone.*
**2.1:** *Thine en'mies are many, thy fears*
**2.2:** *thy blessèd / He*
**3.2:** *My kindness thou doubts of, my promise*
    *denies;*  **3.3:** *Yet*  **3.4:** *tossing and tempest*
**4.2:** *it does ever*  **4.3:** *On the / while looking*
**4.4:** *in dying*  **7.2:** *hopeless, the helpless*

# 734   10.10.11.11.
*Be gone, unbelief.*

1 BE gone, unbelief, my Saviour is near,
  And for my relief will surely appear;
By pray'r let me wrestle,
    and He will perform;
With Christ in the vessel,
    I smile at the storm.

2 Though dark be my way,
    since He is my guide,
'Tis mine to obey, 'tis His to provide;
Though cisterns be broken
    and creatures all fail,
The word He has spoken
    shall surely prevail.

3 His love in time past forbids me to think
He'll leave me at last in trouble to sink;
Each sweet Ebenezer I have in review
Confirms His good pleasure
    to help me quite through.

4 Determined to save,
    He watched o'er my path
When, Satan's blind slave,
    I sported with death;
And can He have taught me
    to trust in His name,
And thus far have brought me
    to put me to shame?

5 Why should I complain of want or distress,
Temptation or pain? He told me no less;
The heirs of salvation,
    I know from His Word,
Through much tribulation
    must follow their Lord.

6 How bitter that cup no heart can conceive,
Which He drank quite up,
    that sinners might live!
His way was much rougher
    and darker than mine;
Did Christ, my Lord, suffer,
    and shall I repine?

7 Since all that I meet
    shall work for my good,
The bitter is sweet, the med'cine is food;
Though painful at present,
    will cease before long,
And then, oh! how pleasant
    the conqueror's song!

*John Newton,* 1779

**EE:** Hymns, Set 1 (Jan./Nov.), 27th Eve,
  PORTUGAL NEW
**FPN:** 20 Oct. 1889 (No. 2341), HANOVER
**MM:** "In all places whithersoever we go, He has
  been our forerunner; each burden we have to
  carry has once been laid on the shoulders of
  Immanuel. 'His way was much rougher and
  darker than mine; Did Christ, my Lord, suffer,
  and shall I repine?' Take courage! Royal feet
  have left a blood-red track upon the road and
  consecrated thy thorny path forever" (Jan. 23).

# 735   7.7.7.7.
*"Lovest thou Me?"*

1 HARK, my soul! it is the Lord!
  'Tis thy Saviour, hear His word;

Jesus speaks, and speaks to thee;
"Say, poor sinner, lov'st thou Me?

2 "I deliver'd thee when bound,
And when bleeding, heal'd thy wound,
Sought thee wand'ring, set thee right,
Turn'd thy darkness into light.

3 "Can a woman's tender care
Cease toward the child she bare?
Yes, she may forgetful be,
Yet will I remember thee.

4 "Mine is an unchanging love,
Higher than the heights above,
Deeper than the depths beneath,
Free and faithful, strong as death.

5 "Thou shalt see my glory soon,
When the work of grace is done;
Partner of My throne shalt be;
Say, poor sinner, lov'st thou Me?"

6 Lord, it is my chief complaint
That my love is weak and faint,
Yet I love Thee and adore—
O for grace to love Thee more!

*William Cowper,* [1768, *rev.* 1788]

## 736  7.7.7.7.7.7.
*"Who shall separate?"*

1 HALLELUJAH! Who shall part
Christ's own church
from Christ's own heart?
Sever from the Saviour's side
Souls from whom the Saviour died?
Dash one precious jewel down
From Immanuel's blood-bought crown?

2 Hallelujah! Shall the sword
Part us from our glorious Lord?
Trouble dark or dire disgrace
E'er the Spirit's seal efface?
Famine, nakedness, or hate,
Bride and bridegroom separate?

3 Hallelujah! Life nor death,
Powers above nor powers beneath,

Monarch's might nor tyrant's doom,
Things that are nor things to come,
Men nor angels e'er shall part
Christ's own church
from Christ's own heart.

*William Dickinson,* 1846

# SECURITY IN CHRIST.

## 737  S.M.
*Saints' trial and safety.*

1 FIRM and unmov'd are they
That rest their souls on God;
Firm as the mount where David dwelt
Or where the ark abode.

2 As mountains stood to guard
The city's sacred ground,
So God and His almighty love
Embrace His saints around.

3 What though the Father's rod
Drop a chastising stroke,
Yet lest it wound their souls too deep,
Its fury shall be broke.

4 Nor shall the tyrant's rage
Too long oppress the saint;
The God of Israel will support
His children, lest they faint.

5 But if our slavish fear
Will choose the road to hell,
We must expect our portion there,
Where bolder sinners dwell.

*Isaac Watts,* [1707, *rev.* 1719]

## 738  L.M. Double
*Accepted and safe.*

1 A DEBTOR to mercy alone,
Of covenant mercy I sing;
Nor fear, with Thy righteousness on,
My person and off'ring to bring;
The terrors of law and of God,

With me can have nothing to do;
My Saviour's obedience and blood
Hide all my transgressions from view.

2 The work which His goodness began,
The arm of His strength will complete;
His promise is yea and Amen,
And never was forfeited yet:
Things future, nor things that are now,
Not all things below nor above,
Can make Him his purpose forego,
Or sever my soul from His love.

3 My name from the palms of His hands
Eternity will not erase;
Impress'd on His heart it remains
In marks of indelible grace:
Yes, I to the end shall endure,
As sure as the earnest is giv'n;
More happy, but not more secure,
The glorified spirits in heaven.

*Augustus Toplady*, 1771

**EE:** "Thou art no more in fetters as a bond-slave;
thou art delivered now from the bondage of
the law; thou art freed from sin, and canst
walk at large as a free man; thy Saviour's
blood has procured thy full discharge. . . . Oh!
how great the debt of love and gratitude thou
owest to thy Saviour!" (Feb. 13).

# FINAL PRESERVATION.

**739** C.M.
*Preserved in Jesus.*

1 REJOICE, believer, in the Lord,
Who makes your cause His own;
The hope that's built upon His Word
Can ne'er be overthrown.

2 Though many foes beset your road,
And feeble is your arm,
Your life is hid with Christ in God,
Beyond the reach of harm.

3 Weak as you are, you shall not faint,
Or fainting, shall not die;

Jesus, the strength of ev'ry saint
Will aid you from on high.

4 Though sometimes unperceived by sense,
Faith sees Him always near,
A guide, a glory, a defence;
Then what have you to fear?

5 As surely as He overcame
And triumph'd once for you,
So surely you that love His name
Shall triumph in Him too.

*John Newton*, 1779

**740** L.M.
*"My words shall not pass away."*

1 THE moon and stars shall lose their light;
The sun shall sink in endless night;
Both heav'n and earth shall pass away;
The works of nature all decay.

2 But they that in the Lord confide
And shelter in His wounded side
Shall see the danger overpast,
Stand ev'ry storm, and live at last.

3 What Christ has said must be fulfill'd;
On this firm rock believers build;
His Word shall stand, His truth prevail,
And not one jot or tittle fail.

*Joseph Hart*, 1759

**741** 8.7.8.7.4.7.
*He will keep us.*

1 SAVIOUR! through the desert lead us;
Without Thee we cannot go;
Thou from cruel chains hast freed us;
Thou hast laid the tyrant low;
Let Thy presence
Cheer us all our journey through.

2 With a price Thy love has bought us;
Saviour, what a love is Thine!
Hitherto Thy pow'r has brought us;
Pow'r and love in Thee combine.

Lord of glory!
Ever on *Thy household* shine.

3 Through a desert waste and cheerless,
Though our destined journey lie,
Render'd by Thy presence fearless,
We may every foe defy.
Nought shall move us,
While we see our Saviour nigh.

4 When we halt (no track discov'ring),
Fearful lest we go astray,
O'er our path Thy pillar hov'ring,
Fire by night and cloud by day
Shall direct us;
Thus we shall not miss our way.

5 When we hunger Thou wilt feed us;
Manna shall our camp surround;
Faint and thirsty, Thou wilt heed us;
Streams shall from the rock abound.
Happy Israel!
What a Saviour thou hast found!

*Thomas Kelly*, [1802]
[*alt. George Wigram*, 1838]

**2.6:** *Thine Israel*

# 742 C.M.
*Saints in the hands of Christ.*

1 FIRM as the earth Thy gospel stands,
My Lord, my hope, my trust;
If I am found in Jesus' hands,
My soul can ne'er be lost.

2 His honour is engaged to save
The meanest of His sheep;
All that His heavenly Father gave
His hands securely keep.

3 Nor death, nor hell, shall e'er remove
His favourites from His breast;
In the dear bosom of His love
They must forever rest.

*Isaac Watts*, 1709

# 743 C.M.
*Final perseverance.*

1 WHERE God begins His gracious work,
That work He will complete,
For round the objects of His love,
All power and mercy meet.

2 Man may repent him of his work
And fail in his intent;
God is above the power of change,
He never can repent.

3 Each object of His love is sure
To reach the heavenly goal;
For neither sin nor Satan can
Destroy the blood-washed soul.

4 Satan may vex, and unbelief
*The saved one may annoy,*
But he must conquer, yes, as sure
As Jesus reigns in joy.

5 The precious blood of God's dear Son
Shall ne'er be spilt in vain;
The soul on Christ believing must
With Christ forever reign.

*Albert Midlane*, [1861, *alt. C.H.S.*]

**4.2:** *May mar the saved one's joy;*

# SUPPORT IN AFFLICTION.

# 744 7.7.7.7.
*"As thy day, thy strength shall be."*

1 WAIT, my soul, upon the Lord;
To His gracious promise flee,
Laying hold upon His Word—
"As thy *day*, thy strength shall be."

2 If the sorrows of *thy* case
Seem peculiar still to *thee*,
God has promised needful grace;
"As thy *day*, thy strength shall be."

3 Days of trial, days of grief,
In succession *thou may'st* see;

*This is still thy sweet* relief—
"As thy *day*, thy strength shall be."

4 Rock of Ages, I'm secure,
With Thy promise full and free,
Faithful, positive, and sure—
"As thy *day*, thy strength shall be."

*William Freeman Lloyd,* [1831]

**1.4, etc.** *days* **2.1:** *my* **2.2:** *me* **3.2:** *I may*
**3.3:** *Daily, this is my*
**Ed:** This hymn appeared as early as 1831 in W.B.
Leach's *Selection of Hymns,* unattributed,
then found a wider audience via the works
of Thomas Hastings, starting with the 1833
ed. of *Spiritual Songs for Social Worship.*
Footnotes indicate Lloyd's revisions for his
*Thoughts in Rhyme* (1851), which were not
incorporated into *OOHB.*

# 745 L.M.
*"As thy day, thy strength shall be."*

1 AFFLICTED soul, to Jesus dear,
Thy Saviour's gracious promise hear;
His faithful Word declares to thee
That "as thy day, thy strength shall be."

2 Let not thy heart despond and say,
"How shall I stand the trying day?"
He has engaged by firm decree
That, "as thy day, thy strength shall be."

3 Should persecution rage and flame,
Still trust in thy Redeemer's name;
In fiery trials thou shalt see
That, "as thy day, thy strength shall be."

4 When call'd to bear the weighty cross,
Or sore affliction, pain, or loss,
Or deep distress, or poverty,
Still, "as thy day, thy strength shall be."

5 When ghastly death appears in view,
Christ's presence shall thy fears subdue;
He comes to set thy spirit free,
And "as thy day, thy strength shall be."

*John Fawcett,* 1782

# 746 C.M.
*Sweetness of gracious meditations.*

1 WHEN languor and disease invade
This trembling house of clay,
'Tis sweet to look beyond the cage
And long to fly away.

2 Sweet to look inward and attend
The whispers of His love;
Sweet to look upward to the place
Where Jesus pleads above.

3 Sweet to look back and see my name
In life's fair book set down;
Sweet to look forward and behold
Eternal joys my own.

4 Sweet to reflect how grace divine
My sins on Jesus laid;
Sweet to remember that His blood
My debt of sufferings paid.

5 Sweet in His righteousness to stand,
Which saves from second death;
Sweet to experience, day by day
His Spirit's quick'ning breath.

6 Sweet on His faithfulness to rest,
Whose love can never end;
Sweet on His covenant of grace,
For all things to depend.

7 Sweet in the confidence of faith,
To trust His firm decrees;
Sweet to lie passive in His hand
And know no will but His.

8 Sweet to rejoice in lively hope,
That, when my change shall come,
Angels will hover round my bed
And waft my spirit home.

9 There shall my disimprison'd soul
Behold Him and adore,
Be with His likeness satisfied,
And grieve and sin no more.

10 Shall see Him wear that very flesh,
On which my guilt was lain;

His love intense, His merit fresh,
  As though but newly slain.

11 Soon, too, my slumb'ring dust shall hear
  The trumpet's quick'ning sound,
And by my Saviour's power rebuilt
  At His right hand be found.

12 These eyes shall see Him in that day,
  The God that died for me,
And all my rising bones shall say,
  Lord, who is like to Thee?

13 If such the sweetness of the stream,
  What must the fountain be,
Where saints and angels draw their bliss
  Immediately from Thee!

*Augustus Toplady*, 1780 [*rev.* 1796]

  **Ed:** Published in 8 sts. in Huntingdon's *Collection* (1780); expanded to 15 sts. in the *Gospel Magazine* (1796).
  **MM:** "What seems to you a crushing burden, would be to Him but as the small dust of the balance. Nothing is so sweet as to 'Lie passive in God's hands, and know no will but His.' O child of suffering, be thou patient; God has not passed thee over in His providence" (Jan. 6).

# 747 C.M.
*Joy under losses.*

1 WHAT though no flow'rs the fig-tree clothe,
  Though vines their fruit deny,
The labours of the olive fail,
  And fields no meat supply,

2 Though from the fold, with sad surprise,
  My flock cut off I see,
Though famine pines in empty stalls,
  Where *herds were wont* to be,

3 Yet in the Lord will I be glad
  And glory in His love;
In Him I'll joy, who will the God
  Of my salvation prove.

4 God is the treasure of my soul,
  *The* source of *lasting* joy,

*A joy which want shall not impair,*
  Nor death itself destroy.

[1-3 *Hugh Blair*, 1756]
[4 *Philip Doddridge*, 1745]
[*alt. Church of Scotland*, 1781]

  **2.4:** *cattle used*  **4.2:** *A sacred*
  **4.3:** *Which no afflictions can controul,*
  **Ed:** Doddridge's text, when first printed in 1745, began, "Secure the saint's foundation stands." In 1756, it was combined with the text by Blair; st. 1 is arguably a recast of Doddridge's original st. 2. In Doddridge's manuscripts, the hymn is dated 1735. It also appeared in his 1755 *Hymns*, beginning, "So firm the saint's foundations stand."

# 748 8.7.8.7.4.7.
*Chosen in the furnace of affliction.*

1 SONS of God, in tribulation,
  Let your eyes the Saviour view;
He's the rock of our salvation;
  He was tried and tempted too,
    All to succour
  Ev'ry tempted, burden'd son.

2 'Tis, if need be, He reproves us,
  Lest we settle on our lees;
Yet, He in the furnace loves us;
  'Tis express'd in words like these:
    "I am with thee,
  Israel, passing through the fire."

3 To His church, His joy, and treasure,
  Ev'ry trial works for good;
They are dealt in weight and measure,
  Yet how little understood;
    Not in anger,
  But from His dear cov'nant love.

4 With afflictions He may scourge us,
  Send a cross for ev'ry day;
Blast our gourds, but not to purge us
  From our sins, as some would say;
    They were number'd
  On the Scape Goat's head of old.

5 If today He deigns to bless us
  With a sense of pardon'd sin,
He tomorrow may distress us,
  Make us feel the plague within,
    All to make us
  Sick of self and fond of Him.

*John Kent*, 1803 [*rev.* 1833]

# 749
8.7.8.7.4.7.
*Sweet affliction.*

1 IN the floods of tribulation,
  While the billows o'er me roll,
Jesus whispers consolation
  And supports my fainting soul;
    *Hallelujah!*
  *Hallelujah! praise the Lord.*

2 Thus the lion yields me honey;
  From the eater food is given;
Strengthen'd thus I still press forward,
  Singing as I wade to heaven—
    Sweet affliction!
  *And my sins are all forgiven.*

3 'Mid the gloom, the vivid lightnings
  With increasing brightness play;
'Mid the thornbrake beauteous flow'rets
  Look more beautiful and gay;
    *Hallelujah!*
  *Hallelujah! praise the Lord.*

4 So in darkest dispensations
  Doth my faithful Lord appear,
With His richest consolations
  To re-animate and cheer:
    Sweet affliction!
  Thus to bring my Saviour near!

5 Floods of tribulations heighten;
  Billows still around me roar;
Those that know not Christ, ye frighten,
  But my soul defies your pow'r:
    *Hallelujah!*
  *Hallelujah! Praise the Lord.*

6 In the sacred page recorded,
  Thus *the* word securely stands,

"Fear not, I'm in trouble near thee;
  Nought shall pluck you from My hands."
    Sweet affliction!
  *Every word my love demands.*

7 All I meet I find assists me
  In my path to heav'nly joy:
Where, though trials now attend me,
  Trials never more annoy.
    *Hallelujah,*
  *Hallelujah! Praise the Lord.*

8 *Blest there with* a weight of glory,
  Still the path I'll ne'er forget,
But, *exulting, cry*, it led me
  To my blessèd Saviour's seat;
    Sweet affliction!
  *Which has brought* to Jesus' feet.

*Samuel Pearce*, [1799]
[*alt. John Rippon*, 1800]

**1.5-6, 2.6, 3.5-6, 5.5-6, 6.6, 7.5-6:** Added by
  John Rippon  **6.2:** *His*  **8.1:** *Wearing there*
  **8.3:** *reflecting how*  **8.6:** *Haste! Bring more*
**Ed:** In Pearce's posthumous *Memoirs* (1800), p.
  226, Andrew Fuller indicated that the hymn
  was probably written around May 1799 and
  had "appeared in several periodical publications, but with many inaccuracies." It did
  appear in both *The Evangelical Magazine*
  and *The Missionary Magazine* in Nov. 1799.
  The original form was 4 sts. of 10 lines; it was
  recast by John Rippon for his *Selection* (1800).

# 750
7.7.7.7. Double
*Welcoming the cross.*

1 'TIS my happiness below
  Not to live without the cross,
But the Saviour's pow'r to know,
  Sanctifying every loss.
Trials must and will befall,
  But with humble faith to see
Love inscrib'd upon them all—
  This is happiness to me.

2 God in Israel sows the seeds
  Of affliction, pain, and toil;

These spring up and choke the weeds
    Which would else o'erspread the soil;
Trials make the promise sweet;
    Trials give new life to pray'r;
Trials bring me to his feet,
    Lay me low, and keep me there.

3 Did I meet no trials here,
    No chastisement by the way,
Might I not, with reason, fear
    I should prove a castaway;
Bastards may escape the rod,
    Sunk in earthly, vain delight,
But the true-born child of God
    Must not, would not, if he might.

*William Cowper*, [1774, rev. 1779]

**MM:** "Perhaps, O tried soul, the Lord is doing
this to develop thy graces. There are some of
thy graces which would never be discovered if
it were not for thy trials. . . . Besides, it is not
merely discovery; real growth in grace is the
result of sanctified trials" (Feb. 18).

**EE:** "Some plants die if they have too much sunshine. It may be that you are planted where
get but little; you are put there by the loving
Husbandman, because only in that situation
will you bring forth fruit unto perfection"
(Nov. 11).

# 751 L.M.
*The suffering people.*

1 "POOR and afflicted," Lord, are Thine,
    Among the great unfit to shine;
But though the world may think it strange,
    They would not with the world exchange.

2 "Poor and afflicted," 'tis their lot;
    They know it, and they murmur not;
'Twould ill become them to refuse
    The state their Master deign'd to choose.

3 "Poor and afflicted," yet they sing,
    For Jesus is their glorious King;
Through suff'rings perfect now He reigns
    And shares in all their griefs and pains.

4 "Poor and afflicted," but ere long
    They'll join the bright, celestial throng;

Their suff'rings then will reach a close,
    And heav'n afford them sweet repose.

5 And while they walk the thorny way,
    *They oft are* heard to sigh and say,
"Dear Saviour, come, O quickly come!
    And take thy mourning pilgrims home."

*Thomas Kelly*, 1804
[*alt. James Montgomery*, 1825]

    **5.2:** *They're often*

# 752 C.M.
*Affliction leading to glory.*

1 OFTEN the clouds of deepest woe
    So sweet a message bear;
Dark though they seem, 't were hard to find
    A frown of anger there.

2 It needs our hearts be wean'd from earth;
    It needs that we be driven
By loss of every earthly stay,
    To seek our joys in heaven.

3 *For* we must follow in the path
    Our Lord and Saviour run;
We must not find a resting place
    Where He we love had none.

*Caroline Fry*, [1821]
[*alt.* John Rippon's *Selection*, 1844]

    **3.1:** *No;* **Ed:** In Fry's original text, the penulti-
    mate stanza (omitted here) asked, "And shall
    the world that frowned on Him / Wear only
    smiles for us?" The question-and-answer struc-
    ture is lost in this reduction.

# 753 L.M.
*The grateful review.*

1 THUS far my God hath led me on
    And made His truth and mercy known;
My hopes and fears alternate rise,
    And comforts mingle with my sighs.

2 Through this wide wilderness I roam,
    Far distant from my blissful home;

Lord, let Thy presence be my stay
And guard me in this dang'rous way.

3 Temptations ev'rywhere annoy,
And sins and snares my peace destroy;
My earthly joys are from me torn,
And oft an absent God I mourn.

4 My soul, with various tempests toss'd,
Her hopes o'erturn'd, her projects cross'd,
Sees ev'ry day new straits attend,
And wonders where the scene will end.

5 Is this, dear Lord, that thorny road
Which leads us to the mount of God?
Are these the toils Thy people know,
While in the wilderness below?

6 'Tis even so, Thy faithful love
Doth thus Thy children's graces prove;
'Tis thus our pride and self must fall,
That Jesus may be all in all.

*John Fawcett*, 1782

**Ed:** Taken from the longer hymn,
"Dark was my soul, and dead in sin."

# 754
8.7.8.7.7.7.
*None shall pluck me from Thy hand.*

1 CLOUDS and darkness round about Thee
For a season veil Thy face;
Still I trust, and cannot doubt Thee;
Jesus! full of truth and grace,
Resting on Thy words I stand;
None shall pluck me from Thy hand.

2 Oh rebuke me not in anger;
Suffer not my faith to fail;
Let not pain, temptation, languor,
O'er my struggling heart prevail;
Holding fast Thy word I stand;
None shall pluck me from Thy hand.

3 In my heart Thy words I cherish;
Though unseen Thou still art near;
Since Thy sheep shall never perish,
What have I to do with fear?

Trusting in Thy Word I stand;
None shall pluck me from Thy hand.

*Charlotte Elliott*, [1841]

# 755
C.M.
*"Fear not, for I am with Thee."*

1 INCARNATE God! the soul that knows
Thy name's mysterious pow'r
Shall dwell in undisturb'd repose
Nor fear the trying hour.

2 Angels, unseen, attend the saints
And bear them in their arms,
To cheer *their* spirit when it faints
And guard *their* life from harms.

3 The angels' Lord Himself is nigh
To them that love His name,
Ready to save them when they cry
And put their foes to shame.

4 Crosses and changes are their lot,
Long as they sojourn here,
But since their Saviour changes not,
What have His saints to fear?

*John Newton*, 1779

**2.3-4:** *the* **Ed:** This minor variant appeared
posthumously in Newton's *Works* (1827) and
was repeated in other collections.

# 756
C.M.
*"It is I, be not afraid."*

1 WHEN waves of trouble round me swell,
My soul is not dismayed;
I hear a voice I know full well—
"'Tis I—be not afraid."

2 When black the threatening skies appear,
And storms my path invade,
Those accents tranquilize each fear;
"'Tis I—be not afraid."

3 There is a gulf that must be crossed;
Saviour, be near to aid!
Whisper when my frail bark is tossed,
"'Tis I—be not afraid."

4 There is a dark and fearful vale;
    Death hides within its shade;
  O say, when flesh and heart shall fail,
    "'Tis I—be not afraid."

*Charlotte Elliott*, 1834

# A HAPPY PORTION.

**757** L.M.
*The Christian's treasure.*

1 HOW vast the treasure we possess!
  How rich Thy bounty, King of grace!
  This world is ours, and worlds to come;
  Earth is our lodge, and heav'n our home.

2 All things are ours; the gift of God,
  *The purchase of a* Saviour's blood;
  While the good Spirit shows us how
  To use and to *improve* them too.

3 If peace and plenty crown my days,
  They help me, Lord, to speak Thy praise;
  If bread of sorrows be my food,
  Those sorrows work my real good.

4 I would not change my blest estate,
  *For* all that *earth* calls *good* or great;
  And while my faith can keep her hold,
  I envy not the sinner's gold.

5 Father, I wait Thy daily will;
  Thou shalt divide my portion still;
  Grant me on earth what seems Thee best,
  Till death and heav'n reveal the rest.

  *Isaac Watts*, [1729]
[*alt. John Rippon*, 1801]

> **2.1:** *And purchas'd with our*   **2.4:** *enjoy*
> **4.2:** *With / flesh / rich*
> **Ed:** Sts. 2-5 are from Watts' hymn "My soul,
> survey thy happiness," both hymns being
> from vol. 3 of Watts' *Sermons.* This conflation
> seems to have been the work of John Rippon,
> in his *Arrangement* of Watts' hymns.

**758** S.M. / *"Say ye to the righteous,
it shall be well with him."*

1 WHAT cheering words are these!
  Their sweetness who can tell?
  In time and to eternal days,
    'Tis with the righteous well;

2 Well when they see His face
  Or sink amidst the flood,
  Well in affliction's thorny maze
  Or on the mount with God.

3 'Tis well when joys arise,
  'Tis well when sorrows flow,
  'Tis well when darkness veils the skies,
  And strong temptations blow.

4 'Tis well when at His throne
  They wrestle, weep, and pray;
  'Tis well when at His feet they groan,
  Yet bring their wants away.

5 'Tis well when they can sing
  As sinners bought with blood,
  And when they touch the mournful string,
  And mourn an absent God.

6 'Tis well when on the mount
  They feast on dying love,
  And 'tis as well in God's account
  When they the furnace prove.

*John Kent*, 1803

**759** 8.7.8.7.4.7.
*The favoured saint.*

1 GRACIOUS Lord, my heart is fixèd;
  Sing I will, and sing of Thee;
  Since the cup that justice mixèd,
    Thou hast drank, and drank for me;
      Great Deliv'rer!
  Thou hast set the pris'ner free.

2 Many were the chains that bound me,
  But the Lord has loosed them all;
  Arms of mercy now surround me,
    Favours these, nor few nor small;

Saviour, keep me;
Keep Thy servant lest he fall.

3 Fair the scene that lies before me;
Life eternal Jesus gives;
While He waves His banner o'er me,
Peace and joy my soul receives;
Sure His promise!
I shall live because He lives.

4 When the world would bid me leave Thee,
Telling me of shame and loss,
Saviour, guard me, lest I grieve Thee,
Lest I cease to love Thy cross;
This is treasure;
All the rest I count but dross.

*Thomas Kelly*, 1806

# UNION TO CHRIST.

**760** 8.7.8.7.4.7.
*The reign of grace.*

1 SOVEREIGN grace o'er sin abounding,
Ransom'd souls the tidings swell;
'Tis a deep that knows no sounding;
Who its breadth or length can tell?
On its glories
Let my soul forever dwell.

2 What from Christ my soul shall sever,
Bound by everlasting bands?
Once in Him, in Him forever;
Thus th' eternal cov'nant stands;
None shall pluck *me*
From the strength of Israel's hands.

3 Heirs of God, joint heirs with Jesus,
Long ere time its race begun;
To His name eternal praises;
O what wonders love hath done!
One with Jesus,
By eternal union one.

4 On such love, my soul, still ponder;
Love so great, so rich, so free;
Say, whilst lost in holy wonder,

Why, O Lord, such love to me?
Hallelujah,
Grace shall reign eternally.

*John Kent*, [1799, *rev.* 1833], *alt.* C.H.S.

**2.5:** *thee*

**761** L.M.
*Union with Jesus.*

1 'TWIXT Jesus and the chosen race
Subsists a bond of sov'reign grace,
That hell, with its infernal train,
Shall ne'er dissolve, nor rend in twain.

2 Hail, sacred union, firm and strong,
How great the grace, how sweet the song,
That worms of earth should ever be
One with Incarnate Deity!

3 One in the tomb, one when He rose,
One when He triumph'd o'er His foes,
One when in heav'n He took His seat,
While seraphs sang all hell's defeat.

4 This sacred tie forbids their fears,
For all He is or has is theirs;
With Him, their head, they stand or fall,
Their life, their surety, and their all.

*John Kent*, 1803

**762** C.M.
*One with Jesus.*

1 LORD Jesus, are we ONE with Thee?
O height! O depth of love!
With Thee we died upon the tree;
In Thee we live above.

2 Such was Thy grace, that for our sake
Thou didst from heav'n come down;
*Thou didst of* flesh and blood partake
In all our *sorrows* ONE.

3 Our sins, our guilt, in love divine,
Confess'd and borne by Thee;
The gall, the curse, the wrath were Thine,
To set Thy *members* free.

4 Ascended now, in glory bright,
　　Still ONE with us Thou art;
　Nor life, nor death, nor depth, nor height
　　Thy saints and Thee can part.

5 O teach us, Lord, to know and own
　　This wondrous mystery,
　That Thou with us art truly ONE,
　　And we are ONE with Thee.

6 Soon, soon shall come that glorious day
　　When, seated on Thy throne,
　Thou shalt to wond'ring worlds display
　　That Thou with us art ONE!

*James George Deck,* [1838, *rev.* 1855, *alt.*]

　**2.3:** *Our mortal* **2.4:** *misery* **3.3:** *people* (1855)
　**Ed:** The alts. at 2.3-4 appeared as early as 1 June
　1863 in *The Evangelical Witness.*

# 763 S.M.
*Union to Christ.*

1 　*DEAR* Saviour, I am Thine
　　By everlasting bands;
　My name, my heart, I would resign;
　　My soul is in Thy hands.

2 　To Thee I still would cleave
　　With ever-growing zeal;
　If millions tempt me Christ to leave,
　　They never shall prevail.

3 　His Spirit shall unite
　　My soul to Him, my Head,
　Shall form me to His image bright,
　　And teach His path to tread.

4 　Death may my soul divide
　　From this abode of clay,
　But love shall keep me near *Thy* side
　　Through all the gloomy way.

5 　Since Christ and we are one,
　　*Why* should *we doubt or* fear?
　If He in heav'n hath fix'd His throne,
　　He'll fix His members there.

　*Philip Doddridge,* 1755
　[*alt. John Rippon,* 1787]

　**1.1:** *My* **4.3:** *His* **5.2:** *What / remain to*

# THE GOLDEN BOOK OF
# COMMUNION WITH JESUS.

# 764 C.M.
*Sweet communion.*

1 I WOULD commune with Thee, my God—
　　E'en to Thy seat I come;
　I leave my joys, I leave my sins,
　　And seek in Thee my home.

2 I stand upon the mount of God
　　With sunlight in my soul,
　I hear the storms in vales beneath,
　　I hear the thunders roll,

3 But I am calm with Thee, my God,
　　Beneath these glorious skies,
　And to the heights on which I stand,
　　Nor storms nor clouds can rise.

4 Oh, this is life! Oh, this is joy!
　　My God, to find Thee so!
　Thy face to see, Thy voice to hear,
　　And all Thy love to know!

*George Burden Bubier,* [1855]

# 765 L.M.
*Retirement and meditation.*

1 MY God, permit me not to be
　A stranger to myself and Thee;
　Amidst a thousand thoughts I rove,
　Forgetful of my highest love.

2 Why should my passions mix with earth
　And thus debase my heav'nly birth?
　Why should I cleave to things below
　And let my God, my Saviour go?

3 Call me away from flesh and sense;
　One sovereign word can draw me thence;
　I would obey the voice divine,
　And all inferior joys resign.

4 Be earth with all her scenes withdrawn;
　Let noise and vanity be gone;

In secret silence of the mind
My heav'n, and there my God, I find.

*Isaac Watts*, 1709

**TD:** "His Spirit attends us in various operations,
like waters—to cleanse, to refresh, to fertilize,
to cherish. They are 'still waters,' for the Holy
Ghost loves peace, and sounds no trumpet of
ostentation in His operations. . . . That silence
is golden indeed in which the Holy Spirit
meets with the souls of His saints. . . . He is a
dove, not an eagle; the dew, not the hurricane"
(Ps. 23:2; vol. 1, p. 400).

# 766 C.M.
*When wilt thou come?*

1 WHEN wilt Thou come unto me, Lord?
　　Oh come, my Lord, most dear!
Come near, come nearer, nearer still;
　　I'm *blest* when Thou art near.

2 When wilt Thou come unto me, Lord?
　　I languish for the sight;
Ten thousand suns when Thou art hid
　　Are shades instead of light.

3 When wilt Thou come unto me, Lord?
　　*Until* Thou dost appear,
I count each moment for a day,
　　Each minute for a year.

4 There's no such thing as pleasure here;
　　My Jesus is my all;
As Thou dost shine or disappear,
　　My pleasures rise or fall.

5 Come, spread Thy savour on my frame;
　　No sweetness is so sweet,
Till I get up to sing Thy name,
　　Where all Thy singers meet.

*Thomas Shepherd*, [1693, *alt. C.H.S.*]

**1.4:** *well*　**3.2:** *For till*
**Ed:** Taken from the longer hymn,
　"Alas, my God, that we should be."
**EE:** Hymns, Set 1 (Jan./Nov.), 9th Eve,
　EVAN / WARWICK. "Oh for an evening glimpse

of Him! Oh to sup with Him tonight! My Lord,
by all Thy love to me, deign at this hour to
visit me in Thy kindness and give me the dawn
of heaven in my soul. . . . Come, Lord Jesus,
and abide with me forever" (June 19).
**TD:** "We long for the favour of the Lord more
than weary sentinels long for the morning
light which will release them from their tedious watch. . . . He that has once rejoined in
communion with God is sore tired by the hid-
ings of his face, and grows faint with strong
desire for the Lord's appearing" (Ps. 130:6; vol.
7, p. 72).

# 767 7.7.7.7.
*Jesus only.*

1 EVER to the Saviour cling;
Trust in Him and none beside;
Never let an earthly thing
Hide from thee the Crucified.

2 Ever cast on Him thy care;
He invites thee so to do;
Never let Thy soul despair;
He will surely help thee through.

3 Ever live as in the view
Of the day of glory, near;
Never be to Christ untrue,
Thou shalt soon His glory share.

*Albert Midlane*, [1861]

**EE:** Hymns, Set 1 (Jan./Nov.), 10th Eve,
　RATISBON / HART'S
**Ed:** Taken from the longer hymn,
　"Ever let thy soul repose."

# 768 C.M.
*None but Jesus.*

1 O MIGHT this worthless heart of mine
　　The Saviour's temple be!
Emptied of ev'ry love but Thine
　　And shut to all but Thee!

2 I long to find Thy presence there;
　　I long to see Thy face;

Almighty Lord, my heart prepare
The Saviour to embrace.

*Augustus Toplady*, 1759

> **Ed:** Taken from the longer hymn,
> "Come from on high, my King and God."

# 769 L.M.
*Emptied of earth.*

1 EMPTIED of earth I fain would be,
Of sin, myself, and all but Thee;
Only reserv'd for Christ that died,
Surrender'd to the Crucified;

2 Sequester'd from the noise and strife,
The lust, the pomp, and pride of life;
For heav'n alone my heart prepare,
And have my conversation there.

3 Nothing save Jesus would I know;
My friend and my companion Thou!
Lord, seize my heart, assert Thy right,
And put all other loves to flight.

4 The idols tread beneath Thy feet,
And to Thyself the conquest get;
Let sin no more oppose my Lord,
Slain by the Spirit's two-edged sword.

5 Larger communion let me prove
With Thee, blest object of my love;
But oh, for this no pow'r have I;
My strength is at Thy feet to lie.

*Augustus Toplady*, 1759 [rev. 1771]

# 770 6.6.6.6.
*Go up, my heart.*

1 GO up, go up, my heart;
Dwell with thy God above;
For here thou canst not rest,
Nor here give out thy love.

2 Go up, go up, my heart;
Be not a trifler here;
Ascend above these clouds;
Dwell in a higher sphere.

3 Let not thy love flow out
To things so soiled and dim;
Go up to heaven and God;
Take up thy love to Him.

4 Waste not thy precious stores
On creature-love below;
To God that wealth belongs,
On Him that wealth bestow.

*Horatius Bonar*, [1857]

# 771 C.M.
*Jesus' presence desired.*

1 LORD! let me see Thy beauteous face!
It yields a heav'n below;
And angels round the throne will say
'Tis all the heav'n they know.

2 A glimpse—a single glimpse of Thee,
Would more delight my soul
Than this vain world, with all its joys,
Could I possess the whole.

John Rippon's *Selection*, 1800

> **Ed:** In the 1873 ed., Sedgwick credited this hymn
> to "Beddome and Rippon, 1800," but this text
> did not appear in Beddome's *Hymns* (1817),
> and his name was not credited by Rippon.

# 772 S.M.
*"They saw no man, save Jesus."*

1 O PATIENT, spotless One!
Our hearts in meekness train
To *bear* Thy yoke and learn of Thee,
That we may rest obtain.

2 Jesus! Thou art enough
The mind and heart to fill;
Thy life—to calm the anxious soul,
Thy love—its fear dispel.

3 O fix our earnest gaze
So wholly, Lord, on Thee,
That with Thy beauty occupied,
We elsewhere none may see.

*Hymns for the Children of God*, 1851
[alt. *One Hundred Select Hymns*, 1862]

**1.3:** *take* **Ed:** The first stanza is based closely on a stanza from the hymn "Father, make me Thy child" (*A Collection of Hymns … for the Use of … the Brethren's Church*, 1754), which is translated from the German, "Mein Vater! zeuge mich" by Christian Andreas Bernstein (Freylinghausen's *Gesangbuch*, 1704).

# 773 8.7.8.7.4.7.
*Take my heart.*

1 LOOK upon me, Lord, I pray Thee;
   Let Thy Spirit dwell in mine;
Thou hast sought me, Thou hast bought me;
   Only Thee to know I pine.
      Let me find Thee!
   Take my heart and own me Thine!

2 Nought I ask for, nought I strive for,
   But Thy grace so rich and free;
That Thou givest whom Thou lovest,
   And who truly cleave to Thee.
      Let me find Thee!
   He hath all things who hath Thee.

*Joachim Neander*, [1680]
*tr. Catherine Winkworth*, 1858

   **Ed:** From the longer hymn, "Here behold me, as I cast me," translated from the German, "Seih hier bin ich Ehren König."

# 774 S.M.
*God all, and in all.*

1   MY God, my life, my love,
      To Thee, to Thee I call;
   I cannot love if Thou remove,
      For Thou art all in all.

2   Thy shining grace can cheer
      This dungeon where I dwell;
   'Tis Paradise when Thou art here;
      If Thou depart, 'tis hell.

3   The smilings of Thy face,
      How amiable they are!
   'Tis heaven to rest in Thine embrace,
      And nowhere else but there.

4   To Thee and Thee alone,
      The angels owe their bliss;
   They sit around Thy gracious throne
      And dwell where Jesus is.

5   Not all the harps above
      Can make a heavenly place,
   If God His residence remove,
      Or but conceal His face.

6   Nor earth, nor all the sky
      Can one delight afford;
   No, not a drop of real joy
      Without Thy presence, Lord.

7   Thou art the sea of love,
      Where all my pleasures roll,
   The circle where my passions move,
      And centre of my soul.

8   To Thee my spirits fly
      With infinite desire,
   And yet, how far from Thee I lie;
      Dear Jesus, raise me higher.

*Isaac Watts*, [1707, *rev.* 1709]

   **MM:** "But let God come to His child, let Him lift up his countenance, and the mourner's eyes glisten with hope. Do you not hear him sing—'Tis paradise if Thou art here; If Thou depart, 'tis hell'? You could not have cheered him, but the Lord has done it; 'He is the God of all comfort'" (Feb. 20).

# 775 C.M.
*God my exceeding joy.*

1 WHERE God doth dwell,
      sure heav'n is there,
   And singing there must be;
Since, Lord, Thy presence
      makes my heav'n,
   Whom should I sing but Thee?

2 My God, my reconcilèd God,
      Creator of my peace,
Thee will I love, and praise, and sing,
   Till life and breath shall cease.

3 My soul doth magnify the Lord;
  My spirit doth rejoice;
 *To Thee*, my Saviour and my God,
  I *lift my* joyful voice.

4 I need not go abroad for joy,
  *I* have a feast at home;
 My sighs are turnèd into songs;
  *My heart has ceased to roam.*

5 Down from above the blessèd Dove
  Is come into my breast,
 To witness *Thine* eternal love,
  *And give my spirit rest.*

6 *My God, I'll* praise Thee while I live,
  And praise Thee when I die,
 And praise Thee when I rise again,
  And to eternity.

*John Mason*, 1683, alt. C.H.S.

> **3.3:** *In God*   **3.4:** *hear His*   **4.2:** *Who*
> **4.4:** *The Comforter is come.*   **5.3:** *God's*
> **5.4:** *This is my heavenly feast.*   **6.1:** *O let me*
> **EE:** Hymns, Set 1 (Jan./Nov.), 12th Eve,
> BELGIUM / ARNOLD'S
> **Ed:** Sts. 1-2 are from Mason's hymn, "My God,
> my reconcilèd God," sts. 3-5 from "My soul
> doth magnify the Lord," and st. 6 from "What
> shall I render to my God."

# 776 C.M.
*My sole delight.*

1 MY God, my God! who art my all,
  Where art Thou to be found?
 Thy presence is my sole abode;
  My comforts there abound.

2 My wishes terminate above;
  Thou art my whole delight;
 Why dost Thou hide Thy holy face
  And roll Thyself in night?

3 Nor friends, nor comforts shall I wish,
  Nor pleasures want to know;
 Thou art *the* source of perfect bliss;
  Thou art a heaven below.

4 More welcome would be Thy return,
  Of greater far delight
 Than to the pilgrim beauteous morn
  Who wander'd all the night.

*William Williams*, 1759 [*alt. C.H.S.*]

> **3.3:** *a*   **Ed:** Stanza 4 is from Williams' hymn
> "Would'st Thou divide the wat'ry clouds," also
> from 1759 and designated as the second part
> of "My God, My God."

# 777 8.8.6.8.8.6.
*Perfect happiness in the cross.*

1 LONG plung'd in sorrow, I resign
  My soul to that dear hand of Thine,
   Without reserve or fear;
 That hand shall wipe my streaming eyes,
 Or into smiles of glad surprise
   Transform the falling tear.

2 My sole possession is Thy love;
  In earth beneath or heav'n above
   I have no other store;
 And though with fervent suit I pray,
 And importune Thee night and day,
   I ask Thee nothing more.

3 Adieu! ye vain delights of earth;
  Insipid sports, and childish mirth,
   I taste no sweets in you;
 Unknown delights are in the cross;
 All joy beside to me is dross,
   And Jesus thought so too.

4 The cross! Oh ravishment and bliss—
  How grateful e'en its anguish is;
   Its bitterness, how sweet!
 There ev'ry sense and all the mind,
 In all her faculties refin'd,
   Taste happiness complete.

*Jeanne Marie Guyon*, [1722]
*tr. William Cowper*, 1801

> **Ed:** Translated from the French, "Mon cœur
> depuis longtems plongé dans les douleurs."
> These translations were made by Cowper in
> 1782 but were not published until 1801.

# 778 L.M.
*At home everywhere with Jesus.*

1 OH Thou by long experience tried,
Near whom no grief can long abide,
My Love! how full of sweet content
I pass my years of banishment!

2 All scenes alike engaging prove
To souls impress'd with sacred love;
Where'er they dwell, they dwell in Thee,
In heav'n, in earth, or on the sea.

3 To me remains no place nor time;
My country is in ev'ry clime;
I can be calm and free from care
On any shore, since God is there.

4 While place we seek or place we shun,
The soul finds happiness in none,
But with a God to guide our way,
'Tis equal joy to go or stay.

5 Could I be cast where Thou art not,
That were indeed a dreadful lot,
But regions none remote I call,
Secure of finding God in all.

*Jeanne Marie Guyon*, [1722]
*tr. William Cowper*, 1801

> **Ed:** Translated from the French, "Amour que
> mon ame est contente," in 1782, but not pub-
> lished until 1801.
> **TD:** "Fair days, now gone, ye have left a light
> behind you which cheers our present gloom.
> Or does David mean that even where he
> was he would bethink him of his God; does
> he declare that, forgetful of time and place,
> he would count Jordan as sacred as Siloa,
> Hermon as holy as Zion, and even Mizar, that
> insignificant rising ground, as glorious as the
> mountains which are round about Jerusalem!
> Oh! it is a heavenly heart which can sing— 'To
> me remains nor place nor time; my country is
> in every clime'" (Ps. 42:6; vol. 2, p. 303).

# 779 L.M.
*Perfect safety in Jesus.*

1 MY country, Lord, art Thou alone,
Nor other can I claim or own;

The point where all my wishes meet;
My law, my love; life's only sweet!

2 I hold by nothing here below;
Appoint my journey, and I go;
Though pierc'd by scorn,
  oppress'd by pride,
I feel Thee good—feel nought beside.

3 No frowns of men can hurtful prove
To souls on fire with heav'nly love;
Though men and devils both condemn,
No gloomy days arise from them.

4 Ah then! to His embrace repair;
My soul, thou art no stranger there;
There love divine shall be thy guard,
And peace and safety thy reward.

*Jeanne Marie Guyon*, [1722]
*tr. William Cowper*, 1801

> **Ed:** A continuation of hymn No. 778.

# 780 C.M.
*Jesus, our heart's theme.*

1 I THINK of Thee, my God, by night,
  And talk of Thee by day;
Thy love my treasure and delight,
  Thy truth my strength and stay.

2 The day is dark, the night is long,
  Unblest with thoughts of Thee,
And dull to me the sweetest song,
  Unless its theme Thou be.

3 So all day long, and all the night,
  Lord, let Thy presence be
Mine air, my breath, my shade, my light—
  Myself absorb'd in Thee.

*John S.B. Monsell*, 1863

> **EE:** Hymns, Set 1 (Jan./Nov.), 26th Eve,
>   DEVIZES / TIVERTON
> **EE:** Hymns, Set 2 (Feb./Dec.), 1st Eve,
>   STEPHENS / MAGNUS

# 781 L.M.
### Grief that others love not Jesus.

1 AH! reign wherever man is found,
My spouse, belovèd and divine!
Then I am rich, and I abound,
When ev'ry human heart is Thine.

2 A thousand sorrows pierce my soul,
To think that all are not Thine own;
Ah! be ador'd from pole to pole;
Where is thy zeal? Arise; be known!

3 All hearts are cold, in ev'ry place,
Yet earthly good with warmth pursue;
Dissolve them with a flash of grace,
Thaw these of ice and give us new!

*Jeanne Marie Guyon*, [1722]
*tr. William Cowper*, 1801

**Ed:** Translated from the French, "Ah! regnez sur
toure la terre," in 1782; not published until 1801.

# 782 L.M.
### The unsearchable love of God.

1 O LOVE of God, how strong and true!
Eternal and yet ever new,
Uncomprehended and unbought,
Beyond all knowledge and all thought.

2 We read Thee best in Him who came
To bear for us the cross of shame,
Sent by the Father from on high,
Our life to live, our death to die.

3 We read Thy power to bless and save,
Even in the darkness of the grave;
Still more in resurrection light,
We read the fullness of Thy might.

4 O love of God, our shield and stay,
Through all the perils of our way,
Eternal love, in Thee we rest,
Forever safe, forver blest!

*Horatius Bonar*, [1864]

# 783 7.6.7.6. / "My Spirit hath
### rejoiced in God my Saviour."

1 TO Thee, O dear, dear Saviour!
My spirit turns for rest,
My peace is in Thy favour,
My pillow on Thy breast.

2 Though all the world deceive me,
I know that I am Thine,
And Thou wilt never leave me,
O blessèd Saviour mine.

3 O Thou whose mercy found me,
From bondage set me free,
And then forever bound me
With threefold cords to Thee.

4 O for a heart to love Thee
More truly as I ought,
And nothing place above Thee
In deed, or word, or thought.

5 O for that choicest blessing
Of living in Thy love,
And thus on earth possessing
The peace of heaven above.

*John S.B. Monsell*, 1863

# 784 C.M.
### Condescending love.

1 OH see how Jesus trusts Himself
Unto our childish love,
As though by His free ways with us
Our earnestness to prove!

2 His sacred name, a common word
On earth, He loves to hear;
There is no majesty in Him
Which love may not come near.

3 The light of love is round His feet,
His paths are never dim,
And He comes nigh to us when we
Dare not come nigh to Him.

4 Let us be simple with Him, then,
Not backward, stiff, or cold,

As though our Bethlehem could be
    What Sina was of old.

*Frederick W. Faber*, 1852

    **EE:** Mar. 25; May 3; Hymns, Set 2 (Feb./Dec.),
    29th Eve, EVAN / LANCASTER
    **Ed:** In his *Hymns* (1861), Faber changed the first
    line to read "Think well how Jesus trusts Him-
    self." "Sina" (4.4) most likely refers to Sinai.

# 785   C.M.
*"Whom having not seen we love."*

1   JESUS, these eyes have never seen
    That radiant form of Thine!
The veil of sense hangs dark between
    Thy blessèd face and mine!

2   I see Thee not, I hear Thee not,
    Yet art Thou oft with me;
And earth hath ne'er so dear a spot
    As where I meet with Thee.

3   Like some bright dream
      that comes unsought
    When slumbers o'er me roll,
Thine image ever fills my thought
    And charms my ravish'd soul.

4   Yet though I have not seen, and still
    Must rest in faith alone,
I love Thee, dearest Lord! and will,
    Unseen, but not Unknown.

5   When death these mortal eyes shall seal,
    And still this throbbing heart,
The rending veil shall Thee reveal,
    All glorious as Thou art!

*Ray Palmer*, 1858

# 786   C.M. / *"Thy name is
is as ointment poured forth."*

1   *JESUS*, the very thought of Thee
    With sweetness fills my breast,
But sweeter far Thy face to see
    And in Thy presence rest.

2   Nor voice can sing, nor heart can frame,
    Nor can the memory find
A sweeter sound than Thy blest name,
    O Saviour of mankind!

3   O hope of every contrite heart,
    O joy of all the meek,
To those who fall, how kind Thou art!
    How good to those who seek!

4   But what to those who find? Ah! this
    Nor tongue nor pen can show;
The love of Jesus, what it is,
    None but His lov'd ones know.

5   *Jesus*, our only joy be Thou,
    As Thou our *crown* wilt be;
*Jesus*, be Thou our glory now
    And through eternity.

[*English Cistercian*, 12th century]
    *tr. Edward Caswall*, 1849 [*rev.* 1858, *alt.*]

    **1.1, 5.1, 5.3:** *Jesu!*   **5.2:** *prize*
    **EE:** Hymns, Set 1 (Jan./Nov.), 14th Eve,
    FRENCH / PRESTWICH
    **TD:** "The Lord may hide His face for a season
    from His people, but He never has utterly, fi-
    nally, really, or angrily forsaken them that seek
    Him. Let the poor seekers draw comfort from
    this fact, and let the finders rejoice yet more
    exceedingly, for what must be the Lord's faith-
    fulness to those who find, if He is so gracious
    to those who seek" (Ps. 9:10, vol. 1, p. 110).
    **Ed:** For many years, the Latin hymn "Jesu dulcis
    memoria" was attributed to Bernard of Clair-
    vaux, but the manuscript record points to an
    English member of the Order of Citeaux (Cis-
    tercians), a form of monasticism popularized
    in part by Bernard. The alteration at 5.2 dates
    as early as 1857 in *The Winchester Church
    Hymn Book*; 1.1 etc. appeared in *The Sabbath
    Hymn Book* (1858)

# 787   C.M.
*Most glorious King.*

1   O JESU, King most wonderful!
    Thou Conqueror renown'd!
Thou sweetness most ineffable!
    In whom all joys are found!

2 When once Thou visitest the heart,
    Then truth begins to shine,
    Then earthly vanities depart,
    Then *kindles* love divine.

3 O Jesu! light of all below!
    Thou fount of living fire!
    Surpassing all the joys we know
    And all we can desire:

4 *Jesu, may all* confess Thy name,
    *Thy wondrous love* adore,
    And seeking Thee, *themselves* inflame
    To seek Thee more and more.

5 Thee, *Jesu, may our voices* bless,
    Thee may we love alone,
    And ever in our lives express
    The image of Thine own.

[*English Cistercian*, 12th century]
*tr. Edward Caswall*, 1849 [*rev.* 1858]
[*alt. Hymns Ancient & Modern*, 1861]

> **2.4:** *wakens* (1858) **4.1:** *May every heart*
> **4.2:** *and ever Thee* **4.3:** *itself*
> **5.1:** *may our tongues forever*
> **Ed:** A continuation of No. 786.

# 788 C.M. / *"We love him because He first loved us."*

1 MY GOD, I love Thee, not because
    I hope for heaven thereby,
    Nor *yet because* who love Thee not
    Must burn eternally.

2 Thou, O my Jesus, Thou didst me
    Upon the cross embrace,
    For me didst bear the nails, and spear,
    And manifold disgrace,

3 And griefs and torments numberless,
    And sweat of agony,
    *Yea*, death itself—and all for *me*
    Who was Thine enemy.

4 Then why, O blessèd Jesu Christ,
    Should I not love Thee well?
    Not for the hope of winning heaven,

Nor of escaping hell,

5 Not with the hope of gaining aught,
    Not seeking a reward,
    But as Thyself hast lovèd me,
    O ever-loving Lord.

6 *So would* I love Thee, *dearest Lord*,
    And in Thy praise will sing,
    Solely because Thou art my God
    And my eternal King.

*Francis Xavier*, [16th century]
*tr. Edward Caswall*, 1849 [*alt.*]

> **1.3:** *because they* **3.3:** *E'en / one*
> **6.1:** *E'en so / and will love*
> **Ed:** From the Latin, "O Deus ego amo Te, Nec amo Te ut salves me," in turn based on a Spanish sonnet, "No me mueve, mi Dios, para quererte," attr. to St. Theresa of Spain. The alterations at 1.3 and 3.3 appeared in *The Sabbath Hymn Book* (1858), although the changes in that collection were far more extensive and given as "I love Thee, O my God, but not." The text as given above is from *Hymns Ancient & Modern* (1861).
> **MM:** "Yes, it is a Christian's duty to praise God. It is not only a pleasurable exercise, but it is the absolute obligation of his life. . . . You are bound by the bonds of love to bless His name so long as you live, and His praise should continually be in your mouth, for you are blessed in order that you may bless Him" (Sept. 30).

# 789 S.M. *We love Him for Himself.*

1 BLEST be Thy love, dear Lord,
    That taught us this sweet way,
    Only to love Thee for Thyself,
    And for that love obey.

2 O Thou, our souls' chief hope!
    We to Thy mercy fly;
    Where'er we are, Thou canst protect;
    Whate'er we need, supply.

3 Whether we sleep or wake,
    To Thee we both resign;
    By night we see, as well as day,

If Thy light on us shine.

4 Whether we live or die,
  Both we submit to Thee;
In death we live, as well as life,
  If Thine in death we be.

*John Austin*, 1668

> **EE:** Hymns, Set 1 (Jan./Nov.), 15th Eve,
> ARRAN / PRAGUE
> **Ed:** Taken from the longer hymn,
> "Lord, now the time returns."

# 790 7.6.7.6.
*Christ or nothing.*

1 IF my Lord Himself reveal,
  No other good I want;
Only Christ my wounds can heal
  Or silence my complaint.

2 He that suffer'd in my stead
  Shall my Physician be;
I will not be comforted
  Till Jesus comforts me.

*Augustus Toplady*, 1759

> **Ed:** Taken from the longer hymn,
> "Whom have I in heaven but Thee."

# 791 C.M.
*Jesus and His righteousness prized.*

1 THE more my conduct I survey,
  *Or Thee my Master* see,
My own sufficience dies away,
  I find my need of Thee.

2 Were I a martyr at the stake,
  I'd plead my Saviour's name,
Intreat a pardon for His sake,
  And urge no other claim.

3 If blest with that exalted love
  Which tunes a seraph's tongue,
Yet from the cross I would not move,
  For there my hopes are hung.

4 Could I get nearer to the throne
  Than is the common length,
My soul with gratitude should own
  'Tis done by borrow'd strength.

5 O Thou, the antidote of fear,
  The charmer of my heart,
My comforts bloom when Thou art near,
  And fade if Thou depart.

6 *Let others* boast whate'er they please;
  Their hopes *I'll not* contest;
Smile Thou, and I can live at ease
  Or die divinely blest.

*Thomas Greene*, 1780 [*alt. C.H.S.*]

> **1.2:** *Jesus, the more I* **6.1:** *Others may*
> **6.2:** *I won't* **Ed:** Taken from the longer hymn,
> "Did I the noblest gifts possess."
> **TD:** "'And redeem us for thy mercies' sake' [Ps.
> 44:26]. Here is the final plea. The favour is
> redemption, the plea is mercy; and this, too,
> in the case of faithful sufferers who had not
> forgotten their God. Mercy is always a safe
> plea, and never will any man find a better"
> (vol. 2, p. 341).

# 792 C.M.
*Christ is all.*

1 COMPAR'D with Christ, in all beside
  No comeliness I see;
The one thing needful, dearest Lord,
  Is to be one with Thee.

2 The sense of Thy expiring love
  Into my soul convey;
Thyself bestow; for Thee alone
  I absolutely pray.

3 Less than Thyself will not suffice,
  My comfort to restore;
More than Thyself I cannot *crave*,
  And Thou canst give no more.

4 Loved of my God, for Him again
  With love intense I burn;
Chosen of Thee ere time began,
  I choose Thee in return.

5 Whate'er consists not with Thy love,
    O teach me to resign;
  I'm rich to all th' intents of bliss,
    If Thou, O God, art mine.

*Augustus Toplady*, 1772
[*alt. John Rippon*, 1787]

**3.3:** *have*, **MM:** "He has chosen us for His
    portion, and we have chosen Him for ours. It
    is true that the Lord must first choose our in-
    heritance for us, or else we shall never choose
    it for ourselves; but if we are really called
    according to the purpose of electing love, we
    can sing—
        Loved of my God, for Him again
            With love intense I burn;
        Chosen of Him ere time began,
            I choose Him in return" (Nov. 16).

# 793 7.7.7.7.
*Idols destroyed and Jesus loved.*

1 SOON as faith the Lord can see
  Bleeding on a cross for me,
  Quick my idols all depart,
  Jesus gets and fills my heart.

2 None among the sons of men,
  None among the heav'nly train,
  Can with Jesus then compare;
  None so sweet, and none so fair!

3 Then my tongue would fain express
  All His love and loveliness,
  But I lisp and falter forth
  Broken words, not half His worth.

4 Vex'd, I try and try again;
  Still my efforts all are vain;
  Living tongues are dumb at best;
  We must die to speak of Christ.

*John Berridge*, 1785

# 794 C.M.
*Jesus our only care.*

1 CAN my heaven-born soul submit
    To care for things below?
  Nay, but never from the feet
    Of Jesus may I go.

2 Anxious, Lord, for nothing here,
    In ev'ry strait I look to Thee;
  Humbly cast my ev'ry care
    On Him that cares for me.

*Augustus Toplady*, 1759

# 795 C.M.
*Jesus, our chief delight.*

1 JESUS, my Lord, my chief delight,
  For Thee I long, for Thee I pray,
  Amid the shadows of the night,
  Amid the business of the day.

2 When shall I see Thy smiling face,
  That face which often I have seen?
  Arise, Thou Sun of Righteousness,
  Scatter the clouds that intervene.

3 Thou art the glorious gift of God
  To sinners weary and distress'd,
  The first of all His gifts bestow'd,
  And certain pledge of all the rest.

4 Could I but say this gift is mine,
  The world should lie beneath my feet;
  Though poor, no more would I repine
  Or look with envy on the great.

5 The precious jewel I would keep
  And lodge it deep within my heart;
  At home, abroad, awake, asleep,
  It never should from thence depart.

*Benjamin Beddome*, [1787, *rev.* 1817]

# 796 C.M.
*Desiring to abide with Jesus.*

1 OH, let my Jesus teach me how
    I may in Him abide;
  From wand'ring save my foolish heart,
    And keep it near Thy side.

2 Thy side is all the tow'r I have
    To screen me from my foes,
  And in that side a fountain is,
    Which healeth human woes.

3 Put round my heart Thy cord of love;
 It hath a kindly sway;
  But bind me fast and draw me still,
  Still nearer every day.

*John Berridge*, 1785

# 797   8.8.6.8.8.6. / *"Who loved me and gave Himself for me."*

1 O LOVE divine, how sweet Thou art!
 When shall I find my willing heart
  All taken up by Thee?
 I thirst, I faint, I die to prove
 The greatness of redeeming love,
  The love of Christ to me.

2 Stronger His love than death or hell;
 Its riches are unsearchable;
  The first-born sons of light
 Desire in vain its depths to see;
 They cannot reach the mystery,
  The length, and breadth, and height.

3 God only knows the love of God;
 O that it now were shed abroad
  In this poor stony heart!
 For love I sigh, for love I pine;
 This only portion, Lord, be mine,
  Be mine this better part.

4 O that I could forever sit
 With Mary at the Master's feet!
  Be this my happy choice;
 My only care, delight, and bliss,
 My joy, my heaven on earth, be this:
  To hear the Bridegroom's voice.

*Charles Wesley*, 1746 [*rev.* 1749]

# 798   8.8.8.8.8.8. *Rest in divine love desired.*

1 THOU hidden love of God, whose height,
 Whose depth unfathom'd no man knows,
 I see from far Thy beauteous light;
  Inly I sigh for Thy repose;
 My heart is pain'd, nor can it be
 At rest till it finds rest in Thee.

2 Is there a thing beneath the sun
 That strives with Thee my heart to share?
 Ah, tear it thence and reign alone,
  The Lord of every motion there;
 Then shall my heart from earth be free
 When it hath found repose in Thee.

3 Each moment draw from earth away
 My heart, that lowly waits Thy call;
 Speak to my inmost soul and say,
  "I am thy love, thy God, thy all!"
 To feel Thy pow'r, to hear Thy voice,
 To taste Thy love, be all my choice.

*Gerhard Tersteegen*, [1729]
*tr. John Wesley*, [1738, *rev.* 1739, 1780]

> **Ed:** From the German, "Verborgne Gottes Liebe du."
> **CUR:** "The second hymn was 'Thou hidden love
> of God,' to one of the old tunes, 'New Creation,'
> made up from Haydn's chorus, 'The heavens are
> telling.' This the people enjoyed, and sang as gen-
> erally as before" (p. 427, describing a service
> on 4 Jan. 1874). See also Nos. 46b, 818.

# 799   7.7.7.7. *Abide in me.*

1 THOU, who art th' incarnate God,
 In mine heart make Thine abode;
 Come, dear Lord, and come to stay,
 Not just smile and go away!

2 Let not clouds Thy face eclipse;
 Let not anger seal Thy lips;
 Thy fair count'nance let me see;
 With Thy sweet voice speak to me.

3 Rise then, Sun of Righteousness;
 Me with Thy sweet beamings bless;
 Winter then may stay or flee;
 Lord, 'tis all alike to me.

4 If in life I have Thy grace,
 And at death behold Thy face,
 Life may stay, or life may flee;
 Lord, 'tis all alike to me.

*John Ryland*, 1771

> **Ed:** Taken from the longer hymn, "Jesus, King of
> love and grace." Dated by Ryland as Jan. 1767.

# 800
8.7.8.7.
*Saviour, look on Thy beloved.*

1 SAVIOUR, look on Thy belovèd;
    Triumph over all my foes;
Turn to happy joy my mourning;
    Turn to gladness all my woes.

2 Live or die, or work, or suffer,
    Let my weary soul abide,
In all changes whatsoever,
    Sure and steadfast by Thy side.

3 Nothing will preserve my goings,
    But salvation full and free;
Nothing will my feet dishearten
    But my absence, Lord, from Thee.

4 Nothing can delay my progress,
    Nothing can disturb my rest,
If I shall, where'er I wander,
    Lean my spirit on Thy breast.

*William Williams*, 1772

> **Ed:** Sts. 3-4 are from a different hymn by Williams, "Saviour of the guilty sinner," also from 1772.

# 801
C.M.
*Jesus is enough.*

1 JESUS, my Saviour, is enough
    When all is gone and spent;
He fills and over-fills my soul,
    Thus I am pure content.

2 My covenant with flesh and blood
    And every sinful thing
Is broken, and is steadfast made
    With Jesus Christ, my King.

3 Vanish from me, ye objects vain,
    All scenes of lower kind;
A pleasure equal to my wish
    In God alone I find.

*William Williams*, 1759

> **EE:** Hymns, Set 2 (Feb./Dec.), 30th Eve,
> JACKSON'S / HENSBURY

# 802
8.7.8.7.4.7.
*Beauties of Jesus.*

1 WHITE and ruddy is my Belov'd;
    All His heavenly beauties shine;
Nature can't produce an object
    Nor so glorious, so divine;
      He hath wholly
    Won my soul to realms above.

2 Farewell all ye meaner creatures,
    For in Him is every store;
Wealth, or friends, or darling beauty
    Shall not draw me anymore;
      In my Saviour
    I have found a glorious whole.

3 Such as *find* Thee *find* such sweetness,
    Deep, mysterious, and unknown;
Far above all worldly pleasures,
    If they were to meet in one;
      My Belovèd,
    O'er the mountains haste away.

*William Williams*, 1772 [*alt. C.H.S.*]

> **3.1:** *found / found*
> **EE:** Hymns, Set 1 (Jan./Nov.), 16th Eve,
> MOUNT OF OLIVES / VESPER

# 803
8.7.8.7.
*Jesus, reign in us.*

1 JESUS, whose almighty sceptre
    Rules creation all around,
In whose bowels love and mercy,
    Grace and pity, full are found,

2 In my spirit rule and conquer;
    There set up Thy eternal throne;
Win my heart from every creature,
    Thee to love, and Thee alone.

3 In Thy bleeding wounds most happy,
    Nought will do for wretched me,
But a Saviour full of mercy,
    Dying, innocent, and free.

4 Climb, my soul, unto the mountain,
    Ever-blessèd Calvary;

See the wounded Victim bleeding,
   Nailèd to a cursèd tree.

5 Love to miserable sinners,
   Love unfathom'd, love to death,
Was the only end and motive,
   To resign His gracious breath.

*William Williams*, 1772

# 804
11.11.11.11.
*My Jesus, I love Thee.*

1 MY Jesus, I love Thee,
   I know Thou art mine;
For Thee, all the follies of sin I resign;
My gracious Redeemer,
   my Saviour, art Thou;
If ever I lov'd Thee, my Jesus, 'tis now.

2 I love Thee because Thou
   hast first lovèd me
And purchased my pardon
   on Calvary's tree;
I love Thee for wearing
   the thorns on Thy brow;
If ever I lov'd Thee, my Jesus, 'tis now.

3 I love Thee in life,
   I will love Thee in death,
And praise Thee as long as
   Thou lendest me breath,
And say when the death dew
   lies cold on my brow,
If ever I lov'd Thee, my Jesus, 'tis now.

4 In mansions of glory and endless delight,
I'll ever adore Thee in *heaven so bright;*
I'll sing with the glittering
   crown on my brow,
If ever I lov'd Thee, my Jesus, 'tis now.

[*William Featherston*, 1862]
[*alt.*] *London Hymn Book*, 1864

**4.1:** *the heaven of light;*
**Ed:** Line 3.1 originally contained an additional
word, "I *will* love Thee in life." Published
anonymously as early as October 1862 in *The
Primitive Methodist Magazine.* In Ira Sankey's

*My Life and Sacred Songs* (1906), p. 165, he
indicated that the hymn was written by William
Featherston in 1858 and the original manuscript was in the possession of the author's
aunt, E. Featherston Wilson. The first two lines
of the text are based an older, anonymous
hymn, "O Jesus, my Saviour, I know thou art
mine," first published in *The Christian Hymn-
Book* (1815).

# 805
L.M.
*Weaned from the world.*

1 I THIRST, but not as once I did,
   The vain delights of earth to share;
Thy wounds, Immanuel, all forbid
   That I should seek my pleasures there.

2 It was the sight of Thy dear cross
   First wean'd my soul from earthly things
And taught me to esteem as dross
   The mirth of fools and pomp of kings.

3 Dear fountain of delight unknown!
   No longer sink below the brim,
But overflow, and pour me down
   A living and life-giving stream!

*William Cowper*, 1779

**EE:** Hymns, Set 2 (Feb./Dec.), 31st Eve,
   MELCOMBE / WINCHESTER
**MM:** Hymns, Set 2 (Feb./Dec.), 24th Morn,
   HEBRON / CAPTIVITY

# 806
C.M.
*Longing to be with Jesus.*

1 MY soul amid this stormy world
   Is like some flutter'd dove,
And fain would be as swift of wing
   To flee to Him I love.

2 The cords that bound my heart to earth
   Are broken by His hand;
Before His cross I found myself
   A stranger in the land.

3 That visage marr'd, those sorrows deep,
   The vinegar and gall,

*These were His* golden chains of love,
   His captive to enthral.

4 My heart is with Him on His throne,
   And ill can brook delay,
Each moment listening for the voice,
   "Rise up and come away."

5 With hope deferr'd, oft sick and faint,
   "Why tarries He?" I cry;
*Let not* the Saviour chide my haste,
   *For then would I* reply:

6 "May not an exile, Lord, desire
   His own sweet land to see?
May not a captive seek release,
   A prisoner to be free?"

7 A child, when far away, may long
   For home and kindred dear,
And she that waits her absent Lord
   May sigh till He appear.

8 I would, my Lord and Saviour, know
   That which no measure knows,
Would search the mystery of Thy love,
   The depths of all Thy woes.

9 I fain would strike my *harp divine*
   Before the Father's throne,
There cast my crown of righteousness,
   And sing what grace has done.

10 Ah, leave me not in this base world,
   A stranger still to roam;
Come, Lord, and take me to Thyself,
   "Come, Jesus, quickly come!"

*Robert C. Chapman*, 1837 [*alt.*]

   **3.3:** *Were Jesus'* **5.3:** *And should*
   **5.4:** *Sure I could make* **9.1:** *golden harp*
   **Ed:** The alterations at 3.3 and 9.1 appeared in
   *The Wellington Hymn-Book* (1857); all four
   were in Roundell Palmer's *Book of Praise*
   (1862), a collection owned by Spurgeon.
   **MM:** "We remain on earth as sowers to scatter
   good seed, as ploughmen to break up the
   fallow ground, as heralds publishing salvation.
   We are here as the 'salt of the earth,' to be a
   blessing to the world. . . . Let us see that our

life answereth its end. . . . Meanwhile, we long
to be with Him, and daily sing—'My heart is
with Him on His throne, and ill can brook delay; each moment listening for the voice, "Rise
up, and come away"'" (June 10).

# 807    L.M.
*Jesus our choice.*

1 THOUGH all the world my choice deride,
   Yet Jesus shall my portion be,
For I am pleased with none beside;
   The fairest of the fair is He.

2 Sweet is the vision of Thy face,
   And kindness o'er Thy lips is shed;
Lovely art Thou, and full of grace,
   And glory beams around Thy head.

3 Thy sufferings I embrace with Thee,
   Thy poverty and shameful cross;
The pleasures of the world I flee,
   And deem its *treasures* only dross.

4 Be *daily* dearer to my heart,
   And *ever* let me feel Thee near;
Then willingly with all *I'd* part,
   Nor count it worthy of a tear.

*Gerhard Tersteegen*, [1745]
*tr. Samuel Jackson*, 1832 [*alt.*]

   **3.4:** *riches* **4.1:** *ever* **4.2:** *daily* **4.3:** *I'll*
   **Ed:** Jackson's translation begins, "The heart of
   man must something love," from the German,
   "Jedes Herz will etwas lieben." These alts.
   appeared as early as 1842 in John Leifchild's
   *Original Hymns.*

# 808    7.7.7.7.
*His name is lovely.*

1 OTHER name than my dear Lord's,
   Never to my heart affords
Equal influence to move
   Its deep springs of joy and love.

2 He from youth has been my guide,
   He to hoar hairs will provide,
Every light and every shade
   On my path His presence made.

3 He hath been my joy in woe,
Cheer'd my heart when it was low,
And with warnings softly sad,
Calm'd my heart when it was glad.

4 Change or chance could ne'er befall,
But He proved mine all in all;
All He asks in answer is
That I should be wholly His.

5 O that I may never prove
By a life of earnest love
How, by right of grace divine,
I am His and He is mine.

*John S.B. Monsell*, 1863

# 809 8.6.8.6.
*"I did know Thee in the wilderness."*

1 I KNEW Thee in the land of drought,
Thy comfort and control;
Thy truth encompass'd me about;
Thy love refresh'd my soul.

2 I knew Thee when the world was waste,
And Thou alone wast fair;
On Thee my heart its fondness placed;
My soul reposed its care.

3 And if Thine alter'd hand doth now
My sky with sunshine fill,
Who amid all so fair as Thou?
Oh let me know Thee still.

4 Still turn to Thee in days of light
As well as nights of care,
Thou brightest amid all that's bright!
Thou fairest of the fair!

5 My sun is, Lord, where'er Thou art,
My cloud, where self I see,
My drought in an ungrateful heart,
My freshest springs in Thee.

*John S.B. Monsell*, 1863

> **EE:** Hymns, Set 2 (Feb./Dec.), 8th Eve,
> ARNOLD'S / ANN'S. "When I was loathsome
> and self-abhorred, Thou didst receive me as Thy
> child, and Thou didst satisfy my craving wants.

Blessed forever be Thy name for this free,
rich, abounding mercy. Since then, my inward
experience has often been a wilderness, but
Thou hast owned me still as Thy beloved, and
poured streams of love and grace into me to
gladden me and make me fruitful. Yea, when my
outward circumstances have been at the worst,
and I have wandered in a land of drought, Thy
sweet presence has solaced me" (Oct. 31).

# 810 8.7.8.7.4.7.
*Hark, the voice of my Beloved.*

1 HARK! the voice of my Belovèd;
Lo, He comes in greatest need,
Leaping on the lofty mountains,
Skipping over hills with speed
    To deliver
Me unworthy from all woe.

2 In a dungeon deep He found me,
Without water, without light,
Bound in chains of horrid darkness,
Gloomy, thick, Egyptian night;
    He recover'd
Thence my soul with price immense.

3 And for this let men and angels,
All the heavenly host above,
Choirs of seraphims elected,
With their golden harps of love,
    Praise and worship
My Redeemer without end.

4 Let believers raise their anthems,
All the saints in one accord,
Mix'd with angels and archangels,
*Sing* their dear redeeming Lord;
    Love eternal,
Inconceivable, unknown.

*William Williams*, 1772 [*alt. C.H.S.*]

    **4.4:** *To*

# 811 L.M.
*The strength of Chris's love.*

1 O LET my name engraven stand,
*My Jesus, on Thy heart and hand;*

Seal me upon Thine arm, and wear
That pledge of love forever there.

2 Stronger than death Thy love is known,
Which floods of wrath could never drown,
And hell and earth in vain combine
To quench a fire so much divine.

3 But I am jealous of my heart,
Lest it should once from Thee depart;
Then let Thy name be well impress'd
As a fair signet on my breast.

4 Till Thou hast brought me to Thy home,
Where fears and doubts can never come,
Thy counten'nce let me often see,
And often Thou shalt hear from me.

5 Come, my belovèd, haste away,
Cut short the hours of Thy delay;
Fly like a youthful hart or roe
Over the hills where spices grow.

*Isaac Watts*, [1707, *alt. C.H.S.*]

**1.2:** *Both on Thy heart and on Thy hand;*
**Ed:** Taken from the longer hymn,
"Who is this fair one in distress."

# 812 C.M.
*On Jesu's heart and arm.*

1 I ASK my dying Saviour dear
To set me on His heart,
And if my Jesus fix me there,
Nor life nor death shall part.

2 As Aaron bore upon his breast
The names of Jacob's sons,
So bear my name among the rest
Of Thy dear chosen ones.

3 But seal me also on Thine arm,
Or yet I am not right;
I need Thy love to ward off harm
And need Thy shoulder's might.

4 This double seal makes all things sure
And keeps me safe and well;
Thy heart and shoulder will secure
From all the host of hell.

*John Berridge*, 1785

# 813 7.7.7.7.
*"To live is Christ, and to die is gain."*

1 CHRIST—of all my hopes the ground,
Christ—the spring of all my joy,
Still in Thee may I be found,
Still for Thee my pow'rs employ!

2 Fountain of o'erflowing grace,
Freely from Thy fullness give;
Till I close my earthly race,
May I prove it, "Christ to live."

3 Firmly trusting in Thy blood,
Nothing shall my heart confound;
Safely I shall pass the flood,
Safely reach Imanuel's ground.

4 When I touch the blessèd shore,
Back the closing waves shall roll;
Death's dark stream shall never more
Part fom Thee my ravish'd soul.

5 Thus, O thus, an entrance give
To the land of cloudless sky;
Having known it, "Christ to live,"
Let me know it "gain to die."

*Ralph Wardlaw*, 1817

# 814 L.M. / *Christ dwells in heaven,*
*visits His saints on earth.*

1 MY best-belovèd keeps His throne
On hills of light, in worlds unknown,
But He descends and shows His face
In the young gardens of His grace.

2 He has engross'd my warmest love;
No earthly charms my soul can move;
I have a mansion is His heart,
Nor death nor hell shall make us part.

3 He takes my soul ere I'm aware
And shows me where His glories are;
No chariot of Amminadab
The heavenly rapture can describe.

4 Oh, may my spirit daily rise
On wings of faith above the skies,

Till death shall make my last remove,
To dwell forever with my love.

*Isaac Watts*, [1707]

> **Ed:** Taken from the longer hymn,
> "When strangers stand and hear me tell."

# 815 7.7.7.7.
*"With Thee is the fountain of life."*

1 OBJECT of my first desire,
Jesus, crucified for me!
All to happiness aspire,
Only to be found in Thee:

2 Thee to please and Thee to know
Constitute our bliss below;
Thee to see and Thee to love
Constitute our bliss above.

3 Lord, it is not life to live,
If Thy presence Thou deny;
Lord, if Thou Thy presence give,
'Tis no longer death to die.

4 Source and giver of repose,
Singly from Thy smile it flows;
Peace and happiness are Thine;
Mine they are, if Thou art mine!

*Augustus Toplady*, 1774

> **Ed:** Taken from the longer hymn,
> "Happiness thou lovely name."

# 816 L.M.
*Love the source of love.*

1 WHAT wondrous *cause* could move
　Thy heart
To take on Thee my curse and smart?
When Thou foreknewest I should be
So cold and negligent *to* Thee?

2 The cause was love; I sink with shame
Before my sacred Jesu's name
That Thou shouldst bleed and
　slaughter'd be
Because, because Thou lovedst me.

3 Thou lovedst me; O boundless grace!
Who can such wondrous mercy trace?
I who unfaithful, foolish am,
Yet find Thee still a patient lamb.

*Clare Taylor*, 1742 [*alt.*]

> **1.1:** *thing* **1.4:** *t'wards*
> **Ed:** Taken from the longer hymn, "The cross,
> the cross, O that's my gain." The alteration at
> 1.1 appeared as early as 1754 in *A Collection
> of Hymns … for the Use of … the Brethren's
> Church*. Both alterations appeared together in
> C. Hull's *A Choice Collection of Spiritual and
> Divine Hymns* (1776). The first alteration is
> far more common than the second.

# 817 8.7.8.7.
*He is precious.*

1 PRECIOUS is the name of Jesus;
Who can half its worth unfold?
Far beyond angelic praises,
Sweetly sung to harps of gold.

2 Precious when to Calv'ry groaning,
He sustain'd the cursèd tree;
Precious when His death atoning
Made an end of sin for *me*.

3 Precious when the bloody scourges
Caused the sacred drops to roll;
Precious when of wrath the surges
Overwhelm'd His holy soul.

4 Precious in His death victorious,
He the host of hell o'erthrows;
In His resurrection glorious,
Victor crown'd o'er all His foes.

5 Precious, Lord! beyond expressing
Are Thy beauties all divine;
Glory, honour, power, and blessing
Be henceforth forever Thine.

*John Kent*, 1841 [*alt. C.H.S.*]

> **2.4:** *thee* **EE:** Hymns, Set 1 (Jan./Nov.),
> 13th Eve, BENEDICTION / ARNOLD'S

# 818 L.M.
*Beneath His cross.*

1 BENEATH Thy cross I lay me down
And mourn to see Thy bloody crown;
Love drops in blood from every vein;
Love is the spring of all His pain.

2 Here, Jesus, I shall ever stay
And spend my longing hours away,
Think on Thy bleeding wounds and pain,
And contemplate Thy woes again.

3 The rage of Satan and of sin,
Of foes without and fears within,
Shall ne'er my conq'ring soul remove
Or from Thy cross or from Thy love.

4 Secur'd from harms beneath Thy shade,
Here death and hell shall ne'er invade,
Nor Sinai, with its thund'ring noise,
Shall e'er disturb my happier joys.

5 O unmolested happy rest!
Where inward fears are all suppress'd,
Here I shall love and live secure,
And patiently my cross endure.

*William Williams*, 1772

> **MM:** Hymns, Set 2 (Feb./Dec.), 6th Morn,
> REST / CAPTIVITY
> **CUR:** "The third hymn was 'Beneath Thy cross I
> lay me down,' to the tune 'Rockingham,' which,
> of course, was a congenial melody. The people
> were warming to their work, and the volume
> of sound poured forth more solid and powerful
> than before" (p. 427, describing a service on 4
> Jan. 1874). See also Nos. 46b, 798.

# 819 L.M.
*Holy admiration of Jesus.*

1 JESUS, when faith with fixèd eyes
Beholds Thy wondrous sacrifice,
Love rises to an ardent flame,
And we all other hope disclaim.

2 With cold affections who can see
The thorns, the scourge, the nails, the tree,
Thy flowing tears and *purple* sweat,
Thy bleeding hands, and head, and feet?

3 Look, saints, *into His opening* side,
The breach how large, how deep, how wide!
Thence issues forth a double flood
Of cleansing water, pardoning blood.

4 Hence, O my soul, a balsam flows
To heal thy wounds and *cure* thy woes;
Immortal joys come streaming down,
Joys like His griefs, immense, unknown.

5 Thus I could *ever,* ever sing
The sufferings of my *heavenly* King;
With glowing pleasure spread abroad
The mysteries of a dying God.

*Benjamin Beddome*, [1782]

> **2.3:** *dewy*  **3.1:** *by faith, and view His*
> **4.2:** *ease*  **5.1:** *sit and* (1782)  **5.2:** *Lord and*
> **Ed:** Footnotes indicate Beddome's revisions for
> his *Hymns* (1817). His original version was ad-
> opted into Rippon's *Selection* (1787) and thus
> had proliferated more than his revisions.

# 820 L.M.
*Christ the eternal life.*

1 JESUS, our kinsman and our God,
Array'd in majesty and blood,
Thou art our life; our souls in Thee
Possess a full felicity.

2 All our immortal hopes are laid
In Thee, our surety and our head;
Thy cross, Thy cradle, and Thy throne
Are big with glories yet unknown.

3 *Oh* let my soul forever lie
Beneath the blessings of Thine eye;
'Tis heaven on earth, 'tis heaven above,
To see Thy *face and* taste Thy love.

*Isaac Watts*, 1734

> **3.1:** *But*  **3.4:** *face, to*  **Ed:** From the longer
> hymn, "Where all the tribes of Abraham find."
> These minor variants date to the late 1700s.

# DEATH.

## 821
8.7.8.7.4.7.
*Guide me, O Thou great Jehovah.*

1 GUIDE me, O Thou great Jehovah,
　　Pilgrim through this barren land;
I am weak, but Thou art mighty;
　　Hold me with Thy pow'rful hand;
　　　Bread of heaven!
Feed me *now and evermore.*

2 Open now the crystal fountain
　　Whence the healing streams do flow;
Let the fiery cloudy pillar
　　Lead me all my journey through;
　　　Strong deliv'rer!
Be Thou still my strength and shield.

3 When I tread the verge of Jordan,
　　Bid my anxious fears subside;
Death of deaths and hell's destruction,
　　Land me safe on Canaan's side;
　　　Songs of praises
I will ever give to Thee.

　*William Williams,* [1762]
　[1 *tr. Peter Williams,* 1771]
　[1.6, 2-3 *tr. William Williams,* 1772]

> **1.6:** *till I want no more* (1771)
> **Ed:** From the Welsh, "Arglwydd arwain trwy'r anialwch."

## 822
C.M.
*Victory over death.*

1 O FOR an overcoming faith
　　To cheer my dying hours,
To triumph o'er the monster, death,
　　And all his frightful pow'rs!

2 Joyful with all the strength I have,
　　My quivering lips should sing,
"Where is thy boasted victory, grave?
　　And where's the monster's sting?"

3 If sin be pardon'd, I'm secure;
　　Death hath no sting beside;

The law gives sin its damning pow'r,
　　But Christ, my ransom, died.

4 Now to the God of victory
　　Immortal thanks be paid,
Who makes us conq'rors while we die,
　　Through Christ our living head.

　*Isaac Watts,* [1707]

## 823
L.M.
*"The time is short."*

1 THE time is short ere all that live
　　Shall hence depart, their God to meet;
And each a strict account must give
　　At Jesu's awful judgment seat.

2 The time is short; oh who can tell
　　How short his time below may be?
Today on earth his soul may dwell,
　　Tomorrow in eternity.

3 The time is short; sinner, beware!
　　Nor squander these brief hours away!
O flee to Christ, by faith and prayer,
　　Ere yet shall close this fleeting day.

4 The time is short; ye saints, rejoice!
　　Your Saviour-Judge will quickly come;
Soon shall you hear the Bridegroom's voice
　　Invite you to His heavenly home.

5 The time is short, ere time shall cease,
　　Eternity be usher'd in,
And death shall die, and joy and peace
　　O'er the new earth benignant reign.

　*Joseph Hoskins,* 1789
　[*adapt.* John Rippon's *Selection,* 1844]

> **Ed:** Hoskins' text was originally in common metre, beginning "The time is short! the season near." It was almost completely rewritten for Rippon's *Selection.*

## 824
C.M.
*The solemn hour.*

1 THERE is an hour when I must part
　　With all I hold most dear,

And life, with its best hopes, will then
  As nothingness appear.

2 There is an hour when I must sink
  Beneath the stroke of death
And yield to Him, who gave it first,
  My struggling, vital breath.

3 There is an hour when I must stand
  Before the judgment seat,
And all my sins, and all my foes
  In awful vision meet.

4 There is an hour when I must look
  On one eternity,
And nameless woe, or blissful life,
  My endless portion be.

5 O Saviour, then, in all my need
  Be near, be near to me;
And let my soul, by steadfast faith,
  Find life and heaven in Thee.

*Andrew Reed*, 1842

**MM:** Hymns, Set 1 (Jan./Nov.), 15th Morn,
HELENA / NAOMI

# 825 C.M.
*Death and eternity.*

1 STOOP down, my thoughts,
    that used to rise,
  Converse awhile with death;
Think how a gasping mortal lies
  And pants away his breath.

2 His quiv'ring lip hangs feebly down,
  His pulses faint and few;
Then speechless, with a doleful groan,
  He bids the world adieu.

3 But O the soul that never dies!
  At once it leaves the clay!
Ye thoughts, pursue it where it flies,
  And track its wondrous way.

4 Up to the courts where angels dwell,
  It mounts triumphant there;
Or devils plunge it down to hell
  In infinite despair.

5 And must my body faint and die?
  And must this soul remove?
O for some guardian-angel nigh
  To bear it safe above!

6 Jesus, to Thy dear faithful hand
  My naked soul I trust,
And my flesh waits for Thy command
  To drop into *the* dust.

*Isaac Watts*, [1707, *rev.* 1709, *alt.*]

**6.4:** *my*  **Ed:** This common variant dates to the late 1700s.

# 826 L.M.
*Peace in the prospect of death.*

1 SHRINKING from the cold hand of death,
I *soon may* gather up my feet,
*May swift* resign this fleeting breath,
And die, my *fathers'* God to meet.

2 Numbered among Thy people, I
Expect with joy Thy face to see;
Because Thou didst for sinners die,
Jesus, in death, remember me.

3 O that without a lingering groan
I may the welcome word receive!
My body with my charge lay down,
And cease at once to work and live!

*Charles Wesley*, 1762 [*rev.* 1780], *alt. C.H.S.*

**1.2:** *too shall*  **1.3:** *Shall soon*  **1.4:** *father's*
**Ed:** This hymn was originally from two separate texts, "Shrinking from the cold hand of death," and "Happy, forever happy I," both in *Short Hymns* (1762). These three stanzas were combined for the 1780 *Collection*.

# 827 L.M.
*The tolling bell.*

1 OFT as the bell, with solemn toll,
Speaks the departure of a soul,
Let each one ask himself, "Am I
Prepar'd, should I be call'd to die?"

2 Only this frail and fleeting breath
    Preserves me from the jaws of death;
Soon as it fails, at once I'm gone,
    And plung'd into a world unknown.

3 Then, leaving all I lov'd below,
    To God's tribunal I must go,
Must hear the Judge pronounce my fate,
    And fix my everlasting state.

4 Lord Jesus! help me now to flee,
    And seek my hope alone in Thee;
Apply Thy blood, Thy spirit give,
    Subdue my sin, and let me live.

5 Then when the solemn bell I hear,
    If sav'd from guilt, I need not fear;
Nor would the thought distressing be,
    "Perhaps it next may tell for me."

6 Rather, my spirit would rejoice,
    And long, and wish, to hear Thy voice,
Glad when it bids me earth resign,
    Secure of heav'n, if Thou art mine.

*John Newton*, [1774, *rev.* 1781]

# 828 S.M.
*It is not death to die.*

1    IT is not death to die,
    To leave this weary road,
And 'midst the brotherhood on high,
    To be at home with God.

2    It is not death to close
    The eye long dimmed by tears,
And wake in glorious repose
    To spend eternal years.

3    It is not death to bear
    The wrench that sets us free
From dungeon chain, to breathe the air
    Of boundless liberty.

4    It is not death to fling
    Aside this sinful dust,
And rise on strong, exulting wing
    To live among the just.

5 Jesus, Thou Prince of Life,
    Thy chosen cannot die!
Like Thee, they conquer in the strife
    To reign with Thee on high.

*César Malan,* 1832
*tr. George W. Bethune,* 1847

**Ed:** From the French, "Non ce n'est pas mourir."

# 829 L.M.
*Christ's presence makes death easy.*

1 WHY should we start, *or* fear to die?
What timorous worms we mortals are!
Death is the gate of endless joy,
And yet we dread to enter there.

2 The pains, the groans, *the* dying strife,
Fright our approaching souls away;
Still we shrink back again to life,
Fond of our prison and our clay.

3 O if my Lord would come and meet,
My soul should stretch her wings in haste,
Fly fearless through death's iron gate,
Nor feel the terrors as she pass'd.

4 Jesus can make a dying bed
Feel soft as downy pillows are,
While on His breast I lean my head
And breathe my life out sweetly there.

*Isaac Watts,* [1707, *alt.*]

**1.1:** *and*   **2.1:** *and*   **Ed:** These minor variants
date to the early 1800s.

**TD:** "Many a holy man has slept the sleep of
death with the missionary [Henry] Martyn,
in a strange and inhospitable land, or with
the missionary [John] Smith, upon the floor
of a dungeon, and yet 'Jesus has made their
dying bed as soft as downy pillows are.' When
no other eye saw, when no other heart felt,
for these two never-to-be-forgotten martyrs,
murdered men of God, and apostles of Jesus,
then were they precious in God's sight, and
He was present with them. And so it is with all
His saints, who are faithful unto death" (Ps.
116:15; vol. 5, p. 307).

# 830
C.M.
*On a believer's death.*

1 IN vain my fancy strives to paint
   The moment after death,
   The glories that surround the *saint*,
   When yielding up *his* breath.

2 One gentle sigh the fetter breaks,
   We scarce can say, "They're gone!"
   Before the willing spirit takes
   Her mansion near the throne.

3 Faith strives, but all its efforts fail
   To trace her in her flight;
   No eye can pierce within the veil
   Which hides that world of light.

4 Thus much (and this is all) we know,
   They are completely blest;
   Have done with sin, and care, and woe,
   And with their Saviour rest.

5 On harps of gold they praise His name;
   His face they always view;
   Then let us follow'rs be of them,
   That we may praise Him too.

*John Newton*, 1779 [*alt.*]

   1.3: *saints*  1.4: *their*  **Ed:** This shift to singular
   dates to the 1790s.

# 831
Irregular.
*Victory over death.*

1 VITAL spark of heav'nly flame!
   Quit, oh quit this mortal frame;
   Trembling, hoping, ling'ring, flying,
   Oh the pain, the bliss of dying!
   Cease, fond nature, cease thy strife,
   And let me languish into life.

2 Hark! they whisper; angels say,
   Sister spirit, come away.
   What is this absorbs me quite,
   Steals my senses, shuts my sight,
   Drowns my spirit, draws my breath?
   Tell me, my soul, can this be death?

3 The world recedes; it disappears!
   Heav'n opens on my eyes! my ears
   With sounds seraphic ring;
   Lend, lend your wings! I mount! I fly!
   O grave, where is thy victory?
   O death, where is thy sting?

*Alexander Pope*, 1736

   **Ed:** Written in 1712, but not published until 1736.

# BURIAL HYMNS.

# 832
C.M.
*Burial of a saint.*

1 WHY do we mourn departing friends
   Or shake at death's alarms?
   'Tis but the voice that Jesus sends
   To call them to His arms.

2 Why should we tremble to convey
   Their bodies to the tomb?
   There the dear flesh of Jesus lay,
   And left a long perfume.

3 The graves of all His saints He blest,
   And softened every bed.
   Where should the dying members rest
   But with the dying Head?

4 Thence He arose, ascending high,
   And show'd our feet the way;
   Up to the Lord our flesh shall fly
   At the great rising day.

5 Then let the last loud trumpet sound
   And bid our kindred rise;
   Awake, ye nations, under ground;
   Ye saints, ascend the skies.

*Isaac Watts*, [1707, *rev.* 1709]

# 833
C.M. / *"Blessed are the
dead that die in the Lord."*

1 HEAR what the voice from heav'n proclaims
   For all the pious dead;
   Sweet is the savour of their names,
   And soft their sleeping bed.

2 They die in Jesus and are blest;
 How kind their slumbers are!
From suff'rings and from sins released,
 And freed from every snare.

3 Far from this world of toil and strife,
 They're present with the Lord;
The labours of their mortal life
 End in a large reward.

*Isaac Watts*, [1707]

# 834 L.M.
*The grave a bedchamber.*

1 UNVEIL thy bosom, faithful tomb;
Take this new treasure to thy trust,
And give these sacred relics room
To seek a slumber in the dust.

2 Nor pain, nor grief, nor anxious fear
Invades thy bounds; no mortal woes
Can reach the lovely *sleepers* here;
And angels watch *their* soft repose.

3 So Jesus slept; God's dying Son
Pass'd through the grave and blest the bed;
Rest here, dear saint, till from His throne
The morning break and pierce the shade.

4 Break from His throne, illustrious morn;
Attend, O earth, His sovereign Word;
Restore thy trust, a glorious form;
*He* must ascend to meet *his* Lord.

*Isaac Watts*, 1734 [*alt.*]

**2.3:** *sleepers*   **2.4:** *their*   **4.4:** *She / her*
**Ed:** These alterations appeared as early as ca.
1789 in *Psalmodia Evangelica*, vol. 2.

# 835 L.M.
*Housed and happy.*

1 O HAPPY they, who safely housed,
 To Jesus' bosom fly,
Before the storm of wrath is roused;
 Yes, happy they who die!

2 Care, pain, and grief, the wild array
 Of sorrows felt below,
The dread of trial's fiery day,
 Of persecution's glow—

3 All, all is o'er, with those at rest,
 For Jesus' sake forgiven!
No heavings of the anxious breast,
 No sickening fear in heaven!

4 Why linger then, with strange desire,
 Where reeks the deadly strife,
And shrink, unwilling to retire,
 To everlasting life?

5 Oh were it not for those he leaves
 Lone in a desert land,
'Tis wondrous when a Christian grieves
 To find his home at hand.

*Ann Gilbert*, 1842

# 836 C.M.
*Submission.*

1 PEACE, 'tis the Lord Jehovah's hand
 That blasts our joys in death,
Changes the visage once so dear,
 And gathers back *the* breath.

2 'Tis He, the Potentate supreme
 Of all the worlds above,
Whose steady counsels wisely rule,
 Nor from their purpose move.

4 Fair garlands of immortal bliss
 He weaves for ev'ry brow;
And shall tumultuous passions rise,
 If He corrects us now?

5 Silent I own Jehovah's name,
 I kiss the scourging hand,
And yield my comforts and my life
 To Thy supreme command.

*Philip Doddridge*, 1755
[*alt. John Rippon*, 1787]

**1.4:** *our*

# 837 C.M.
*Funeral of a young person.*

1 WHEN blooming youth is snatch'd away
    By death's resistless hand,
Our hearts the mournful tribute pay,
    Which pity must demand.

2 While pity prompts the rising sigh,
    O may this truth, impress'd
With awful pow'r—I too must die—
    Sink deep in ev'ry breast.

3 Let this vain world engage no more;
    Behold the gaping tomb!
It bids us seize the present hour;
    Tomorrow, death may come.

4 The voice of this alarming scene
    May ev'ry heart obey,
Nor be the heav'nly warning vain,
    Which calls to watch and pray.

5 O let us fly, to Jesus fly,
    Whose pow'rful arm can save,
Then shall our hopes ascend on high
    And triumph o'er the grave.

6 Great God, Thy sov'reign grace impart,
    With cleansing, healing pow'r;
This only can prepare the heart
    For death's surprising hour.

*Anne Steele*, 1760

# 838 C.M. / Consolation
*concerning a minister's death.*

1 NOW let our mourning hearts revive
    And all our tears be dry.
Why should those eyes be drown'd in grief,
    Which view a Saviour nigh?

2 What though the arm of conq'ring death,
    Does God's own house invade?
What though the prophet and the priest
    Be number'd with the dead?

3 Though earthly shepherds dwell in dust,
    The agèd and the young,
The watchful eye in darkness clos'd,
    And mute th' instructive tongue,

4 Th' eternal Shepherd still survives,
    New comfort to impart;
His eye still guides us, and His voice
    Still animates our heart.

5 "Lo, I am with you," saith the Lord,
    "My church shall safe abide;
For I will ne'er forsake My own,
    Whose souls in Me confide."

6 Through every scene of life and death,
    This promise is our trust,
And this shall be our children's song,
    When we are cold in dust.

*Philip Doddridge*, 1755

# RESURRECTION.

# 839 L.M.
*"I know that my Redeemer liveth."*

1 I KNOW that my Redeemer lives;
This thought transporting pleasure gives,
And standing at the latter day,
On earth, His glories *will* display.

2 And though this goodly, mortal frame
Sink to the dust, from whence it came,
Though buried in the silent tomb,
Worms shall my skin and flesh consume,

3 Yet on that happy, rising morn,
New life this body shall adorn;
These active powers refin'd shall be,
And God my Saviour I shall see.

4 Though perish'd all my cold remains,
Though all consum'd my heart and reins,
Yet for myself, my wondering eyes
God shall behold with glad surprise.

*[Joseph] Williams*, [1779]
*[alt. Edward Williams*, 1801]

> **1.4:** *shall*   **Ed:** Dated 1739 in his posthumous
> *Extracts* (1779). The first two lines were
> originally in the opposite order; that change
> seems to have come from Joseph Middleton's
> *Hymns* (1793).

# 840
L.M.
*"Behold, He cometh."*

1 THE time draws nigh when from the clouds
Christ shall with shouts descend,
And the last trumpet's awful voice
The heav'ns and earth shall rend.

2 Then they who live shall changèd be,
And they who sleep shall wake;
The graves shall yield their ancient charge,
And earth's foundations shake.

3 The saints of God, from death set free,
With joy shall mount on high;
The heav'nly hosts with praises loud
Shall meet them in the sky.

4 Together to their Father's house
With joyful hearts they go,
And dwell forever with the Lord
Beyond the reach of woe.

[*John Logan*, 1781]

**Ed:** Taken from the longer hymn, "Take comfort,
Christians! when your friends." See Julian's
*Dictionary of Hymnology*, pp. 187-189, for a
lengthy discourse regarding the proper attribution of this hymn.

# 841
C.M. / *Hope of heaven
by the resurrection of Christ.*

1 BLEST be the everlasting God,
The Father of our Lord;
Be His abounding mercy prais'd,
His majesty ador'd.

2 When from the dead He rais'd His Son
And call'd Him to the sky,
He gave our souls a lively hope
That they should never die.

3 What though our inbred sins require
Our flesh to see the dust,
Yet as the Lord our Saviour rose,
So all His followers must.

4 There's an inheritance divine
Reserv'd against that day;

'Tis uncorrupted, undefil'd,
And cannot *fade* away.

5 Saints by the pow'r of God are kept
Till the salvation come;
We walk by faith as strangers here
Till Christ shall call us home.

*Isaac Watts*, [1707, *alt.*]

**4.4:** *waste* **Ed:** This common variant appeared
in editions of Watts as early as 1771.

# 842
S.M.
*The hope of resurrection.*

1 AND must this body die?
This mortal frame decay?
And must these active limbs of mine
Lie mouldering in the clay?

2 Corruption, earth, and worms
Shall but refine this flesh
Till my triumphant spirit comes
To put it on afresh.

3 God my Redeemer lives,
And often from the skies
Looks down and watches all my dust,
Till He shall bid it rise.

4 Array'd in glorious grace
Shall these vile bodies shine,
And every shape, and every face
Look heavenly and divine.

5 These lively hopes we owe
To Jesus' dying love;
We would adore His grace below
And sing His power above.

6 Dear Lord, accept the praise
Of these our humble songs,
Till tunes of nobler sound we raise
With our immortal tongues.

*Isaac Watts*, [1707, *rev.* 1709]

**Ed:** In the 1st ed. of *OOHB*, 4.3 incorrectly read
*shade;* this was corrected to *shape* in 1869.

# 843
6.6.6.6.4.4.4.4.
*I shall arise.*

1 MY life's a shade, my days
 Apace to death decline;
 My Lord is life, He'll raise
 My dust again, even mine.
  Sweet truth to me!
  I shall arise,
  And with these eyes
  My Saviour see.

2 My peaceful grave shall keep
 My bones till that sweet day;
 I wake from my long sleep
 And leave my bed of clay.
  Sweet truth to me!
  I shall arise,
  And with these eyes
  My Saviour see.

3 *My Saviour's* angels shall
 Their golden trumpets sound
 At whose most welcome call
 My grave shall be unbound.
  Sweet truth to me!
  I shall arise,
  And with these eyes
  My Saviour see.

*Samuel Crossman*, 1664 [alt. C.H.S.]

 **3.1:** *My Lord His*

# 844
8.8.8.8.8.8.
*Death swallowed up in victory.*

1 WE sing His love, who once was slain,
 Who soon o'er death reviv'd again,
 That all His saints through Him might have
 Eternal conquests o'er the grave.
  Soon shall the trumpet sound, and we
  Shall rise to immortality.

2 The saints who now in Jesus sleep,
 His own almighty power shall keep
 Till dawns the bright illustrious day,
 When death itself shall die away.
  Soon shall the trumpet sound, and we
  Shall rise to immortality.

3 How loud shall our glad voices sing
 When Christ His risen saints shall bring
 From beds of dust and silent clay
 To realms of everlasting day.
  Soon shall the trumpet sound, and we
  Shall rise to immortality.

4 When Jesus we in glory meet,
 Our utmost joys shall be complete;
 When landed on that heav'nly shore,
 Death and the curse will be no more.
  Soon shall the trumpet sound, and we
  Shall rise to immortality.

5 Hasten, dear Lord, the glorious day,
 And this delightful scene display;
 When all Thy saints from death shall rise,
 Raptur'd in bliss beyond the skies.
  Soon shall the trumpet sound, and we
  Shall rise to immortality.

*Rowland Hill*, 1796

# ASPIRATIONS FOR HEAVEN.

# 845
C.M.
*"To be with Christ is far better."*

1 OH! how I long to reach my home,
 My glorious home in heaven!
 And wish the joyful hour were come,
 The welcome mandate given!

2 Oh! how I long to lay aside
 These worn out weeds of clay,
 And led by my celestial Guide,
 T' explore yon azure way!

3 Oh! how I long to be with Christ,
 Where all His glory beams!
 To be from this dark world dismiss'd,
 Which His dear name blasphemes.

4 Oh! how I long that world to hail,
 Where sin can ne'er defile!
 Where not a cloud shall ever veil
 From me my Saviour's smile.

5 Oh! how I long to join the choir
   Who worship at His feet!
Lord! grant me soon my heart's desire;
   Soon, soon Thy work complete.

*Charlotte Elliott*, 1834

# 846
S.M.
*"Forever with the Lord."*

1 "FOREVER with the Lord!"
   Amen, so let it be;
Life from the dead is in that word,
   'Tis immortality.

2 Here in the body pent,
   Absent from Him I roam,
Yet nightly pitch my moving tent
   A day's march nearer home.

3 My Father's house on high,
   Home of my soul, how near,
At times, to faith's foreseeing eye,
   Thy golden gates appear!

4 Ah! then my spirit faints
   To reach the land I love,
The bright inheritance of saints,
   Jerusalem above.

5 "Forever with the Lord!"
   Father, if 'tis Thy will,
The promise of that faithful word,
   Even here to me fulfill.

6 Be Thou at my right hand,
   Then can I never fail;
Uphold Thou me, and I shall stand;
   Fight, and I must prevail.

7 So when my latest breath
   Shall rend the veil in twain,
By death I shall escape from death,
   And life eternal gain.

8 Knowing as I am known,
   How shall I love that word,
And oft repeat before the throne,
   "Forever with the Lord!"

9 Then, though the soul enjoy
   Communion high and sweet,
While worms this body must destroy,
   Both shall in glory meet.

10 That resurrection word,
   That shout of victory,
Once more, "Forever with the Lord!"
   Amen, so let it be.

*James Montgomery*, 1835

> **Ed:** At the memorial service for C.H. Spurgeon,
> 4 Feb. 1892, held in Menton, France, where he
> had been staying during his last illness, "The
> hymn 'Forever with the Lord' was solemnly
> sung, and then all stood while the coffin was
> carried to the open hearse, … followed by
> probably a larger and sadder company of
> mourners than ever gathered for a Protestant
> funeral at Menton" (S&T, Mar. 1892, p. 136).
>
> The hymn was also sung to conclude the
> memorial service held at the Metropolitan
> Tabernacle, 11 Feb. 1892, following "a long and
> impressive prayer from Rev. Newman Hall"
> (see Nos. 163, 403; S&T, Mar. 1892, p. 151).

# 847
L.M.
*Let me be with Thee.*

1 LET me be with Thee where Thou art,
   My Saviour, my eternal rest!
Then only will this longing heart
   Be fully and forever blest.

2 Let me be with Thee where Thou art,
   Thy unveil'd glory to behold;
Then only will this wandering heart
   Cease to be faithless, treacherous, cold.

3 Let me be with Thee where Thou art,
   Where spotless saints Thy name adore;
Then only will this sinful heart
   Be evil and defiled no more.

4 Let me be with Thee where Thou art,
   Where none can die, where none remove,
Where life nor death my soul can part,
   From Thy blest presence and Thy love.

*Charlotte Elliott*, [1839, *rev.* 1842, 1844]

# 848
11.11.11.11.
*The Pilgrim's Song.*

1 MY rest is in heaven, my rest is not here;
Then why should I *tremble*
when trials are near?
Be hushed, my dark spirit!
the worst that can come
But shortens thy journey
and hastens thee home.

2 It is not for me to be seeking my bliss
*Or* building my hopes in a region like this;
I look for a city that hands have not piled;
I pant for a country by sin undefiled.

3 Afflictions may *press* me,
they cannot destroy;
One glimpse of His love turns
them all into joy,
And the bitterest tears,
if He smile but on them,
Like dew in the sunshine,
grow diamond and gem.

4 Let doubt, then, and danger
my progress oppose;
They only make heaven
more sweet at the close.
Come joy or come sorrow,
whate'er may befall,
An hour with my God will
make up for *them* all.

5 A scrip on my back and a staff in my hand,
I march on in haste
through an enemy's land;
The road may be rough,
but it cannot be long,
And I'll smooth it with hope,
*and* cheer it with song.

*Henry Francis Lyte,* [1833]
[*alt.* John Rippon's *Selection,* 1844]

**1.2:** *murmur*  **2.2:** *And*  **3.1:** *damp*
**4.4:** *it*  **5.4:** *and I'll*

# 849
8.7.8.7.
*"This is not your rest."*

1 THIS is not my place of resting;
Mine's a city yet to come;
Onward to it I am hasting,
On to my eternal home.

2 In it all is light and glory;
O'er it shines a nightless day;
Every trace of sin's sad story,
All the curse, *hath* pass'd away.

3 There the Lamb, our Shepherd, leads us,
By the streams of life along,
On the freshest pastures feeds us,
Turns our sighing into song.

4 Soon we pass this desert dreary,
Soon we bid farewell to pain;
Never more *are* sad or weary,
Never, never sin again.

*Horatius Bonar,* [1845]
[*alt. Sabbath Hymn Book,* 1858]

**2.4:** *has*  **4.3:** *be*

# 850
L.M.
*Rising to God.*

1 NOW let our souls on wings sublime
Rise from the vanities of time,
Draw back the parting veil and see
The glories of eternity.

2 Twice born by a celestial birth,
Why should we grovel here on earth?
Why grasp at transitory toys,
So near to heav'n's eternal joys?

3 Shall aught beguile us on the road,
When we are trav'lling back to God?
For strangers into life we come,
And dying is but going home.

4 Welcome, sweet hour of full discharge
That sets my longing soul at large,
Unbinds my chains, breaks up my cell,
And gives me with my God to dwell.

5 To dwell with God, to feel His love,
   Is the full heaven enjoy'd above,
And the sweet expectation now
   Is the young dawn of heav'n below.

*Thomas Gibbons*, 1762

# 851 C.M.
*"Present with the Lord."*

1 THERE is a house not made with hands,
   Eternal and on high,
And here my spirit waiting stands
   Till God shall bid it fly.

2 Shortly this prison of my clay
   Must be dissolv'd and fall;
Then, O my soul, with joy obey
   Thy heav'nly Father's call.

3 'Tis He, by His almighty grace,
   That forms thee fit for heav'n;
And as an earnest of the place,
   Has His own Spirit giv'n.

4 We walk by faith of joys to come;
   Faith lives upon His Word;
But while the body is our home,
   We're absent from the Lord.

5 'Tis pleasant to believe Thy grace,
   But we had rather see;
We would be absent from the flesh,
   And present, Lord, with Thee.

*Isaac Watts*, 1709

# 852 C.M.
*The church triumphant.*

1 GIVE me the wings of faith to rise
   Within the veil and see
The saints above, how great their joys,
   How bright their glories be.

2 Once they were mourning here below
   And wet their couch with tears;
They wrestled hard, as we do now,
   With sins, and doubts, and fears.

3 I ask them whence their victory came;
   They with united breath
Ascribe their conquest to the Lamb,
   Their triumph to His death.

4 They mark'd the footsteps that He trod,
   (His zeal inspired their breast,)
And following their incarnate God,
   Possess the promis'd rest.

5 Our glorious Leader claims our praise
   For his own pattern giv'n,
While the long cloud of witnesses
   Show the same path to heav'n.

*Isaac Watts*, 1709

> **Ed:** This hymn was sung at the memorial service
> for C.H. Spurgeon, 4 Feb. 1892, held in Men-
> ton, France, where he had been staying during
> his last illness (S&T, Mar. 1892, p. 134).

# 853 C.M.
*Longing to worship in Heaven.*

1 FATHER, I long, I faint to see
   The place of Thine abode;
I'd leave Thy earthly courts and flee
   Up to Thy seat, my God!

2 Here I behold Thy distant face,
   And 'tis a pleasing sight;
But to abide in Thine embrace
   Is infinite delight.

3 I'd part with all the joys of sense
   To gaze upon Thy throne:
Pleasure springs fresh forever thence,
   Unspeakable, unknown.

4 There all the heavenly hosts are seen;
   In shining ranks they move,
And drink immortal vigour in,
   With wonder and with love.

5 Then at Thy feet with awful fear
   Th' adoring armies fall;
With joy they shrink to nothing there,
   Before th' Eternal ALL.

6   There I would vie with all the host,
     In duty and in bliss,
    While less than nothing I could boast,
     And vanity confess.

7   The more Thy glories strike mine eyes,
     The humbler I shall lie;
    Thus while I sink, my joys shall rise
     Immeasurably high.

*Isaac Watts*, [1707]

## 854 L.M.
*"For here have we no continuing city."*

1   "WE'VE no abiding city here";
    This may distress the worldling's mind,
    But should not cost the saint a tear
    Who hopes a better rest to find.

2   "We've no abiding city here";
    Sad truth, were this to be our home;
    But let this thought our spirits cheer,
    "We seek a city yet to come."

3   "We've no abiding city here";
    Then let us live as pilgrims do;
    Let not the world our rest appear,
    But let us haste from all below.

4   "We've no abiding city here";
    We seek a city out of sight:
    Zion its name—the Lord is there;
    It shines with everlasting light.

5   O sweet abode of peace and love,
    Where pilgrims freed from toil are blest!
    Had I the pinions of the dove,
    I'd fly to thee and be at rest.

6   But hush, my soul, nor dare repine!
    The time my God appoints is best;
    While here, to do His will be mine,
    And His to fix my time of rest.

*Thomas Kelly*, [1802, *rev.* 1804]

## 855 L.M. / *The sight of God and Christ in heaven.*

1   DESCEND from heaven, Immortal Dove;
    Stoop down and take us on Thy wings,
    And mount and bear us far above
    The reach of these inferior things,

2   Beyond, beyond this lower sky,
    Up where eternal ages roll,
    Where solid pleasures never die
    And fruits immortal feast the soul.

3   Oh for a sight, a pleasing sight,
    Of our Almighty Father's throne!
    There sits our Saviour crown'd with light,
    Cloth'd in a body like our own.

4   Adoring saints around Him stand,
    And thrones and powers before Him fall;
    The God shines gracious through the Man,
    And sheds sweet glories on them all.

5   O what amazing joys they feel
    While to their golden harps they sing,
    And sit on every heavenly hill,
    And spread the triumphs of their King!

6   When shall the day, dear Lord, appear,
    That I shall mount to dwell above,
    And stand and bow amongst them there,
    And view Thy face, and sing, and love?

*Isaac Watts*, [1707, *rev.* 1712]

## 856 8.7.8.7.7.7.
*The soul's flight.*

1   WHAT is life? 'Tis but a vapour;
    Soon it vanishes away;
    Life is like a dying taper;
    O my soul, why wish to stay?
    Why not spread thy wings and fly
    Straight to yonder world of joy?

2   See that glory, how resplendent!
    Brighter far than fancy paints;
    There in majesty transcendent,
    Jesus reigns, the King of saints.
    Spread thy wings, my soul, and fly
    Straight to yonder world of joy.

3 Joyful crowds, His throne surrounding,
    Sing with rapture of His love;
Through the heav'ns His praises sounding,
    Filling all the courts above.
Spread thy wings, my soul, and fly
Straight to yonder world of joy.

4 Go and share his people's glory;
    'Midst the ransom'd crowd appear;
Thine a joyful, wondrous story,
    One that angels love to hear.
Spread thy wings, my soul, and fly
Straight to yonder world of joy.

*Thomas Kelly*, 1809

# 857
C.M.
*"I have fought a good fight."*

1 WITH heav'nly weapons I have fought
    The battles of the Lord,
Finish'd my course, and kept the faith,
    And wait the sure reward.

2 God hath laid up in heav'n for me
    A crown which cannot fade;
The righteous Judge at that great day
    Shall place it on my head.

3 Nor hath the King of grace decreed
    This prize for me alone,
But all that love and long to see
    Th' appearance of His Son.

4 Jesus the Lord shall guard me safe
    From ev'ry ill design,
And to His heav'nly kingdom keep
    This feeble soul of mine.

5 God is my everlasting aid,
    And hell shall rage in vain;
To Him be highest glory paid
    And endless praise—Amen.

*Isaac Watts*, [1707, *rev.* 1709]

> **Ed:** Taken from the longer hymn, "Death, I'm
> prepared to meet thee now," revised as "Death
> may dissolve my body now" in 1709.

# 858
C.M.
*Hopes of heaven our support.*

1 WHEN I can read my title clear
    To mansions in the skies,
I bid farewell to every fear
    And wipe my weeping eyes.

2 Should earth against my soul engage
    And hellish darts be hurl'd,
Then I can smile at Satan's rage
    And face a frowning world.

3 Let cares like a wild deluge come,
    And storms of sorrow fall;
May I but safely reach my home,
    My God, my heaven, my all.

4 There shall I bathe my weary soul
    In seas of heavenly rest,
And not a wave of trouble roll
    Across my peaceful breast.

*Isaac Watts*, [1707, *rev.* 1709]

# 859
C.M. / *"The whole family
in heaven and earth."*

1 COME, let us join our friends above
    Who have obtain'd the prize,
And on the eagle wings of love
    To joy celestial rise.

2 Let all the saints terrestrial sing
    With those to glory gone,
For all the servants of our King
    In earth and heaven are one.

3 One family we dwell in Him,
    One church above, beneath,
Though now divided by the stream,
    The narrow stream of death.

4 One army of the living God,
    To His command we bow;
Part of His host have cross'd the flood,
    And part are crossing now.

5 *What numbers* to their endless home
    This solemn moment fly,

And we are to the margin come,
And we expect to die.

6 E'en now by faith we join our hands
With those that went before,
And greet the blood-besprinkled bands
On the eternal shore.

7 O that we now might grasp our Guide!
O that the word were given!
Come, Lord of hosts, the waves divide,
And land us all in heaven.

*Charles Wesley*, 1759
[*alt. Hymns for the use of the Methodist
New Connexion*, 1836]

**5.1:** *Ten thousand* **EE:** "Our heaven-born
spirits should long for their native air. Yet,
should the celestial summons be the object of
patient waiting. Our God knows best when to
bid us 'Come up hither.' We must not wish to
antedate the period of our departure. I know
that strong love will make us cry, 'O Lord of
Hosts, the waves divide, and land us all in
heaven,' but patience must have her perfect
work" (Feb. 7).

# 860 6.6.8.6.4.7.
*The Christian's journey.*

1 FROM Egypt lately come,
Where death and darkness reign;
We seek our new, our better home,
Where we our rest shall gain.
Hallelujah!
We are on our way to God.

2 To Canaan's sacred bound,
We haste with songs of joy,
Where peace and liberty are found,
And sweets that never cloy.
Hallelujah!
We are on our way to God.

3 Our toils and conflicts cease
On Canaan's happy shore;
We there shall dwell in endless peace
And never hunger more.
Hallelujah!
We are on our way to God.

4 But hark! those distant sounds
That strike our list'ning ears,
They come from Canaan's happy bounds
Where God our King appears.
Hallelujah!
We are on our way to God.

5 There in celestial strains,
Enraptured myriads sing;
There love in every bosom reigns,
For God himself is King.
Hallelujah!
We are on our way to God.

6 We soon shall join the throng;
Their pleasures we shall share,
And sing the everlasting song
With all the ransom'd there.
Hallelujah!
We are on our way to God.

7 How sweet the prospect is!
It cheers the pilgrim's breast;
We're journeying through the wilderness,
But soon shall gain our rest.

*Thomas Kelly*, [1802, *rev.* 1826]

# HEAVEN.

# 861 8.7.8.7.
*The ascent to heaven.*

1 SEE! the Captain of salvation
Lead His armies up the sky,
Rise above the conflagration,
Leave the world to burn and die.

2 Lo! I see the fair immortals
Enter to the blissful seats;
Glory opes her waiting portals,
And the Saviour's train admits.

3 All the chosen of the Father,
All for whom the Lamb was slain,
All the church appear together,
Wash'd from ev'ry sinful stain.

4 His dear smiles the place enlightens
   More than thousand suns could do;
All around, His presence brightens,
   Changeless, yet forever new.

5 Blessèd state! beyond conception!
   Who its vast delights can tell?
*May it be my blissful portion,*
*With my Saviour there to dwell.*

*Richard Lee*, 1794
[*alt. John Dobell*, 1806]

**5.3-4:** *Far the muse's best description,*
*Far her brightest figures fail!*
**Ed:** Taken from the longer hymn, "Now, farewell
to faith and patience." Dobell's truncated and
altered version was adopted into Rippon's
*Selection* (1844) and other Baptist collections.

# 862  C.M.
*The blissful regions.*

1 FAR from these narrow scenes of night,
   Unbounded glories rise,
And realms of infinite delight,
   Unknown to mortal eyes.

2 Fair distant land! could mortal eyes
   But half its charms explore,
How would our spirits long to rise
   And dwell on earth no more!

3 No cloud those blissful regions know,
   Forever bright and fair!
For sin, the source of mortal woe,
   Can never enter there.

4 Prepare us, Lord, by grace divine,
   For Thy bright courts on high,
Then bid our spirits rise and join
   The chorus of the sky.

*Anne Steele*, 1760

**MM:** "Christian, meditate much on heaven; it will
help thee to press on, and to forget the toil of
the way. This vale of tears is but the pathway
to the better country; this world of woe is but
the stepping stone to a world of bliss. 'Prepare
us, Lord, by grace divine, for Thy bright courts
on high…'" (Feb. 7).

# 863  7.6.7.6. Double
*Jerusalem, the golden.*

1 JERUSALEM the golden!
   With milk and honey blest,
Beneath Thy contemplation
   Sink heart and voice oppress'd;
I know not, oh I know not
   What *joys await us* there,
What radiancy of glory,
   What bliss beyond compare.

2 They stand, those halls of Sion,
   Conjubilant with song,
And bright with many an angel,
   And all the martyr throng;
The Prince is ever in them,
   The *daylight is* serene;
The pastures of the blessèd
   Are decked in glorious sheen.

3 There is the throne of David,
   And there, from *care* released,
The song of them that triumph,
   The shout of them that feast;
And they, *who with* their leader
   Have conquered in the fight,
Forever and forever
   Are clad in robes of white.

[*Bernard of Cluny*, 12th century]
*tr. John Mason Neale*, 1851
[*alt. Hymns Ancient & Modern*, 1861]

**1.6:** *social joys are*  **2.6:** *light is aye*
**3.2:** *toil*  **3.5:** *beneath*
**Ed:** From the Latin, "Urbs Sion aurea," part of a
much longer text, "Hora novissima, tempora
pessima sunt, vigilemus." Neale translated 218
lines of the original text for his collection *The
Rhythm of Bernard* (1858).

# 864  7.6.7.6.
*O heavenly Jerusalem.*

1 O HEAVENLY Jerusalem,
   Of everlasting halls,
Thrice blessèd are the people
   Thou storest in thy walls!

2 Thou art the golden mansion
    Where saints forever sing,
The seat of God's own chosen,
    The palace of the King.

3 There God forever sitteth,
    Himself of all the crown,
The Lamb the light that shineth
    And never goeth down.

4 Nought to this seat approacheth
    Their sweet peace to molest;
They sing their God forever,
    Nor day nor night they rest.

5 Calm hope from thence is leaning;
    To her our longings bend;
No short-lived toil shall daunt us
    For joys that cannot end.

6 To Christ the Sun that lightens
    His church above, below,
To Father and to Spirit
    All things created bow.

[*Breviarium Parisiense*, 18th century]
    *tr. Isaac Williams*, 1839

**Ed:** From the Latin, "Coelestis O Jerusalem."

# 865 6.6.6.6.4.4.4.4.
*Jerusalem on high.*

1 JERUSALEM on high
My song and city is,
My home whene'er I die,
The centre of my bliss.
    Oh happy place!
    When shall I be,
    My God, with Thee,
    And see Thy face?

2 There dwells my Lord, my King,
Judged here unfit to live;
There angels to Him sing
And lowly homage give.
    Oh happy place!
    When shall I be,
    My God, with Thee,
    And see Thy face?

3 The patriarchs of old
There from their travels cease;
The prophets there behold
Their longed-for Prince of Peace.
    Oh happy place!
    When shall I be,
    My God, with Thee,
    And see Thy face?

4 The Lamb's apostles there
I might with joy behold;
The harpers I might hear
Harping on harps of gold.
    Oh happy place!
    When shall I be,
    My God, with Thee,
    And see Thy face?

5 The bleeding martyrs, they
Within those courts are found,
Clothèd in pure array,
Their scars with glory crown'd.
    Oh happy place!
    When shall I be,
    My God, with Thee,
    And see Thy face?

6 Ah me! Ah me that I
In Kedar's tents here stay!
No place like this on high;
Thither, Lord! guide my way.
    Oh happy place!
    When shall I be,
    My God, with Thee,
    And see Thy face?

*Samuel Crossman*, 1664

**Ed:** This text is part two of a longer hymn,
    "Sweet place, sweet place alone."

# 866 C.M.
*The heavenly Jerusalem.*

1 JERUSALEM! my happy home!
    Name ever dear to me!
When shall my labours have an end,
    In joy, and peace, and thee?

2 When shall these eyes thy
    heaven-built walls
  And pearly gates behold?
Thy bulwarks, with salvation strong,
  And streets of shining gold?

3 O when, thou city of my God,
  Shall I thy courts ascend,
Where congregations ne'er break up,
  And sabbaths have no end?

4 There happier bowers than Eden's bloom,
  Nor sin nor sorrow know:
Blest seats! through rude
    and stormy scenes
I onward press to you.

5 Why should I shrink at pain and woe?
  Or feel, at death, dismay?
I've Canaan's goodly land in view,
  And realms of endless day.

6 Apostles, martyrs, prophets there,
  Around my Saviour stand;
And soon my friends in Christ below
  Will join the glorious band.

7 Jerusalem! my happy home!
  My soul still pants for thee;
Then shall my labours have an end,
  When I thy joys shall see.

[*F.B.P.*, ca. 1593]
[*adapt. James Montgomery*, ca. 1796]

**Ed:** This hymn is related to an older Latin text,
"Mater Hierusalem, civitas sancta Dei," by Jean
of Fecamp (990-1078), from his *Supputationes*,
which was republished as Chapter XXV of the
spurious *Meditations of St. Augustine*. Sedgwick credited this English text to the *Eckington Collection*, which according to William T.
Brooke in Julian's *Dictionary*, p. 583, probably
refers to a small collection of hymns printed by
James Montgomery for the Eckington Parish
Church Choir, ca. 1796-1800. Montgomery's
adaptation was repeated in his *Psalms &
Hymns* (1802) and *Christian Psalmist* (1825).
The original text by F.B.P. is preserved in the
British Library, MS Add. 15225.

  Brooke noted how Sedgwick had supplied
the name "Francis Baker, Pater" [Priest] to

two other authors, J.M. Neale and Josiah Miller, without evidence:

  "From an intimate acquaintance with the
late Daniel Sedgwick, we are in a position to
state that what he contributed to Dr. Neale
was "Francis Baker, Pater," and that Dr.
Neale misread "Pater" as "Porter." J. Miller's
suggested reading was also from Sedgwick.
This reading by Sedgwick was a pure guess on
his part, and cannot be received. The writer,
probably a Roman Catholic, and possibly a
priest, remains unknown."

# 867 C.M.
*The heavenly Jerusalem.*

1 JERUSALEM, my happy home,
  When shall I come to thee?
When shall my sorrows have an end,
  Thy joys when shall I see?

2 O happy harbour of the saints!
  O sweet and pleasant soil!
In thee no sorrows may be found,
  No grief, no care, no toil.

3 Thy walls are made of precious stones,
  Thy bulwarks diamonds square,
Thy gates are of right orient pearl,
  Exceeding rich and rare.

4 Thy turrets and thy pinnacles
  With carbuncles do shine;
Thy very streets are paved with gold,
  Surpassing clear and fine.

5 O my sweet home, Jerusalem,
  Would God I were in thee!
Would God my woes were at an end,
  Thy joys that I might see!

[*F.B.P.*, ca. 1593]

**Ed:** See the notes for No. 866.
**TD:** "The Creator has not set His creatures down
in a dwelling place where the table is bare,
and the buttery empty; He has filled the earth
with food, and not with bare necessities only,
but with riches—dainties, luxuries, beauties,
treasures. In the bowels of the earth are
hidden mines of wealth, and on her surface
are teeming harvests of plenty. . . . If His house

below is so full of riches what must His house above be, where 'The very streets are paved with gold exceeding clear and fine'?" (Ps. 104:24; vol. 5, p. 10).

# 868 7.6.7.6.
*The paradise eternal.*

1 O PARADISE eternal!
     What bliss to enter thee,
 And once within thy portals,
     Secure forever be!

2 In thee no sin nor sorrow,
     No pain nor death is known,
 But pure glad life, enduring
     As heaven's benignant throne.

3 There all around shall love us,
     And we return their love;
 One band of happy spirits,
     One family above.

4 There God shall be our portion,
     And we His jewels be,
 And gracing His bright mansions,
     His smile reflect and see.

5 So songs shall rise forever,
     While all creation fair,
 Still more and more revealèd
     Shall wake fresh praises there.

6 O Paradise eternal,
     What joys in thee are known!
 O God of mercy, guide us,
     Till all be felt our own!

*Thomas Davis*, 1864

# 869 7.6.7.6.
*Oh for the robes of brightness!*

1 OH for the robes of whiteness!
     Oh for the tearless eyes!
 Oh for the glorious brightness
     Of the unclouded skies!

2 Oh for the no more weeping,
     Within that land of love,

The endless joy of keeping
     The bridal feast above!

3 Oh for the bliss of flying,
     My risen Lord to meet!
 Oh for the rest of lying
     Forever at His feet!

4 Oh for the hour of seeing
     My Saviour face to face!
 The hope of ever being
     In that sweet meeting-place!

5 Jesus! Thou King of Glory,
     I soon shall dwell with Thee;
 I soon shall sing the story
     Of Thy great love to me.

6 Meanwhile, my thoughts shall enter
     E'en now before Thy throne,
 That all my love may centre
     In Thee, and Thee alone.

*Charitie Lees Smith*, 1861

> **Ed:** Sedgwick dated the hymn 1861; Julian's *Dictionary*, p. 109, claims it was published as a leaflet in 1860; its first appearance in a hymnal was William Reid's *Praise of Jesus* (1863).

# 870 C.M.
*Spiritual and eternal joys.*

1 FROM Thee, my God, my joys shall rise
     And run eternal rounds
 Beyond the limits of the skies
     And all created bounds.

2 The holy triumphs of my soul
     Shall death itself outbrave,
 Leave dull mortality behind,
     And fly beyond the grave.

3 There, where my blessed Jesus reigns,
     In heaven's unmeasur'd space,
 I'll spend a long eternity
     In pleasure and in praise.

4 Millions of years my wond'ring eyes
     Shall o'er Thy beauties rove,

And endless ages I'll adore
  The glories of Thy love.

5 Sweet Jesus, every smile of Thine
    Shall fresh endearments bring,
  And thousand tastes of new delight
    From all Thy graces spring.

6 Haste, my Belovèd, fetch my soul
    Up to Thy blest abode;
  Fly, for my spirit longs to see
    My Saviour and my God.

*Isaac Watts*, [1707]

> **MM:** "Oh how sweet the prospect of the time
> when we shall not behold Him at a distance,
> but see Him face to face! When He shall not
> be as a wayfaring man tarrying but for a night,
> but shall eternally enfold us in the bosom of
> His glory! We shall not see Him for a little
> season, but:
>   'Millions of years our wondering eyes
>     Shall o'er our Saviour's beauties rove,
>   And myriad ages we'll adore
>     The wonders of His love'" (Dec. 10).

# 871 S.M.
*The contrast.*

1   THE people of the Lord
    Are on their way to heav'n;
  They there obtain their great reward;
    The prize will there be giv'n.

2 'Tis conflict here below;
    'Tis triumph there, and peace;
  On earth we wrestle with the foe;
    In heav'n our conflicts cease.

3 'Tis gloom and darkness here;
    'Tis light and joy above;
  There all is pure, and all is clear,
    There all is peace and love.

4   There rest shall follow toil
    And ease succeed to care;
  The victors there divide the spoil;
    They sing and triumph there.

5   Then let us joyful sing;
    The conflict is not long;

We hope in heav'n to praise our King
    In one eternal song.

*Thomas Kelly*, 1820

# 872 C.M.
*The everlasting song.*

1 EARTH has *engross'd my love too* long;
    *'Tis time I lift* mine eyes
  Upward, *dear* Father, to Thy throne,
    And to my native skies.

2 There the *blest* man, my Saviour, sits;
    The God, how bright He shines!
  And scatters infinite delights
    On all the happy minds.

3 Seraphs with elevated strains
    Circle the throne around,
  And move and charm the starry plains
    With an immortal sound.

4 Jesus, the Lord, their harps employs;
    Jesus, my Love, they sing;
  Jesus, the *life* of both our joys,
    Sounds sweet from ev'ry string.

5 Hark, how beyond the narrow bounds
    Of time and space they run,
  And *echo in* majestic sounds
    The Godhead of the Son.

6 And now they sink the lofty *tune*,
    And *gentler* notes they play,
  And bring *the Father's Equal* down
    To dwell in humble clay.

7 *But when to Calvary they turn,*
    *Silent their harps abide;*
  *Suspended songs a moment mourn*
    *The God that loved and died.*

8 Then, all at once, to living strains,
    They summon ev'ry chord,
  *Tell how He triumph'd o'er His pains,*
    And *chant the* rising Lord.

9 Now let me *mount,* and join their song,
    And be an angel too;

My heart, my hand, my ear, my tongue,
 Here's joyful work for you.

10 I would begin the music here,
 And so my soul should rise;
O for some heav'nly notes to bear
 My *passions* to the skies!

11 There ye that love my Saviour sit;
 There I would fain have place
Among your thrones or at your feet;
 So I might see His face.

 *Isaac Watts*, 1706
 [*alt. Augustus Toplady*, 1776]

 **1.1:** *detain'd me prisoner*
 **1.2:** *And upward glance*  **1.3:** *my*
 **2.1:** *dear*  **4.3:** *name*  **5.3:** *speak in most*
 **6.1:** *tone*  **6.2:** *milder*  **6.3:** *th' Eternal Godhead*
 **7.1-4:** *In the full choir a broken string*
  *Groans with a strange surprise;*
  *The rest in silence mourn their King*
  *That bleeds and loves and dies.*
 **8.3:** *Break up the Tomb, and burst his chains,*
 **8.4:** *show their*  **9.1:** *rise*  **10.4:** *passions*
 **TD:** "It would be a shameful crime, if, after
 receiving God's mercies, we should forget to
 praise Him. God would not have our tongues
 lie idle while so many themes for gratitude
 are spread on every hand. He would have no
 dumb children in the house. They are all to
 sing in heaven, and therefore they should all
 sing on earth. Let us sing with the poet:
  'I would begin the music here,
   And so my soul should rise;
  Oh for some heavenly notes to bear
   My passions to the skies'"
 (Ps. 30:12; vol. 2, p. 51).

# 873 L.M.
*The white-robed band.*

1 O HAPPY saints, who dwell in light
 And walk with Jesus, cloth'd in white,
Safe landed on that peaceful shore,
 Where pilgrims meet to part no more.

2 Released from sin, and toil, and grief,
 Death was their gate to endless life,
An open'd cage to let 'em fly,
 And build their happy nest on high.

3 And now they range the heav'nly plains
 And sing their hymns in melting strains;
And now their souls begin to prove
 The heights and depths of Jesu's love.

4 He cheers them with eternal smile;
 They sing hosannas all the while,
Or overwhelm'd with rapture sweet,
 Sink down adoring at His feet.

5 Ah! Lord, with tardy steps I creep,
 And sometimes sing, and sometimes weep,
Yet strip me of this house of clay,
 And I will sing as loud as they.

 *John Berridge*, 1785

 **Ed:** Berridge's hymn is essentially a recasting of
 Ralph Erskine's "Aurora veils her rosy face,"
 from his *Gospel Sonnets*, 2nd ed. (1726).

# 874 C.M.
*On Jordan's brink.*

1 ON Jordan's stormy banks I stand
 And cast a wishful eye
To Canaan's fair and happy land,
 Where my possessions lie.

2 O the transporting, rapturous scene
 That rises to my sight!
Sweet fields array'd in living green,
 And rivers of delight!

3 There generous fruits that never fail
 On trees immortal grow;
There rocks and hills, and brooks and vales
 With milk and honey flow.

4 All o'er those wide extended plains
 Shines one eternal day;
There God the Sun forever reigns
 And scatters night away.

5 No chilling winds or poisonous breath
 Can reach that healthful shore:
Sickness and sorrow, pain and death,
 Are felt and fear'd no more.

6 When shall I reach that happy place
 And be forever blest?

When shall I see my Father's face
And in His bosom rest?

7 Fill'd with delight, my raptur'd soul
  Can here no longer stay;
Though Jordan's waves around me roll,
  Fearless I'd launch away.

*Samuel Stennett, 1787*

## 875 C.M.
*Sweet fields.*

1 THERE is a land of pure delight
  Where saints immortal reign,
Infinite day excludes the night,
  And pleasures banish pain.

2 There everlasting spring abides,
  And never-withering flowers;
Death, like a narrow sea, divides
  This heav'nly land from ours.

3 Sweet fields beyond the swelling flood
  Stand dress'd in living green;
So to the Jews old Canaan stood,
  While Jordan roll'd between.

4 But timorous mortals start and shrink
  To cross this narrow sea,
And linger, shivering on the brink,
  And fear to launch away.

5 O could we make our doubts remove,
  Those gloomy doubts that rise,
And see the Canaan that we love
  With unbeclouded eyes.

6 Could we but climb where Moses stood
  And view the landscape o'er,
Not Jordan's stream nor death's cold flood
  Should fright us from the shore.

*Isaac Watts*, [1707]

## 876 C.M.
*Sweet fields.*

1 OUR journey is a thorny maze,
  But we march upward still,

Forget *the* troubles of the *way*,
  And reach at Zion's hill.

2 See the kind angels at the gates,
  Inviting us to come!
There Jesus the Forerunner waits
  To welcome trav'llers home!

3 There on a green and flow'ry mount
  Our weary souls shall sit,
And with transporting joys recount
  The labours of our feet.

4 No vain discourse shall fill our tongue,
  Nor trifles vex our ear;
Infinite grace shall fill our song,
  And God rejoice to hear.

5 Eternal glories to the King
  That brought us safely through;
Our tongues shall never cease to sing,
  And endless praise renew.

*Isaac Watts,* [1707, *rev.* 1740, *alt.*]

**1.3:** *these / ways*
**Ed:** Taken from the longer hymn, "Lord! what
a wretched land is this." The alterations at
1.3 and the truncation beginning as above
appeared as early as 1759 in Carl Bogatzky's
*Edifying Thoughts on God's Paternal Heart.*

## 877 7.7.7.7.
*The redeemed in heaven.*

1 WHO are these array'd in white,
Brighter than the noon-day sun,
Foremost of the sons of light,
Nearest the eternal throne?

2 These are they *who* bore the cross,
*Faithful to* their Master *died,*
*Suffer'd* in His righteous cause,
Followers of the *crucified.*

3 Out of great distress they came,
*And* their robes by faith below,
In the blood of *Christ the* Lamb
*They have wash'd as* white as snow.

4 More than conquerors at last,
Here they find their trials o'er;
They have all their sufferings pass'd,
Hunger now and thirst no more.

5 He that on the throne doth reign
Them *forever more shall* feed,
With the tree of life sustain,
To the living fountain lead.

6 *He shall all their griefs remove;*
*He shall all their wants supply;*
*God Himself, the God of love,*
*Tears shall wipe from every eye.*

*Charles Wesley,* 1745
[*alt. Samuel Wilberforce,* 1832]

> **1.1:** *What*  **2.1:** *that*  **2.2:** *Nobly for / stood*
> **2.3:** *Sufferers*  **2.4:** *dying God.*  **3.2:** *Wash'd*
> **3.3:** *yonder*  **3.4:** *Blood that washes*
> **5.2:** *the Lamb shall always*
> **6.1-4:** *He shall all their sorrows chase,*
> *All their wants at once remove,*
> *Wipe the tears from every face,*
> *Fill up every soul with love.*
> **Ed:** The alteration at 1.1 appeared as early as
> 1786 in Edward Smyth's *Choice Collection,* but
> the other changes can be traced to Wilber-
> force and were repeated in Rippon's *Selection,*
> Comprehensive Ed. (1844).
> **FPN:** 5 Aug. 1888 (No. 2037), NOTTINGHAM

# 878  7.7.7.7.
*Jesus adored in heaven.*

1 PALMS of glory, raiment bright,
Crowns that never fade away,
Gird and deck the saints in light,
Priests, and kings, and conquerors they.

2 Yet the conquerors bring their palms
To the Lamb amidst the throne,
And proclaim in joyful psalms
Victory through His cross alone.

3 Kings for harps their crowns resign,
Crying, as they strike the chords,
"Take the kingdom, it is Thine,
King of kings and Lord of lords!"

4 Round the altar priests confess,
If their robes are white as snow,
'Twas the Saviour's righteousness,
And His blood that made them so.

5 Who were these? on earth they dwelt,
Sinners once of Adam's race;
Guilt, and fear, and suffering felt,
But were saved by sovereign grace.

6 They were mortal, too, like us;
Ah! when we, like them, must die,
May our souls, translated thus,
Triumph, reign, and shine on high!

*James Montgomery,* 1829 [*rev.* 1853]

# 879  8.8.8.8.
*The realms of the blest.*

1 WE speak of the realms of the blest,
*That* country so bright and so fair,
And oft are its glories confess'd—
But what must it be to be there!

2 We speak of its pathways of gold,
Its walls deck'd with jewels so rare,
Its wonders and pleasures untold—
But what must it be to be there!

3 We speak of its freedom from sin,
From sorrow, temptation, and care,
From trials without and within—
But what must it be to be there!

4 We speak of its service of love,
The robes which the glorified wear,
The church of the first-born above—
But what must it be to be there!

5 Do thou, Lord, midst *gladness* or woe,
*For* heaven our spirits prepare,
And shortly we also shall know
And feel what it is to be there!

*Elizabeth Mills,* [1831], *alt.*

> **1.2:** *Of that*  **2.2:** *Of its*  **2.3:** *Of its*  **4.2:** *Of the*
> **4.3:** *Of the*  **5.1:** *pleasure*  **5.2:** *Still for*
> **Ed:** The 2nd ed. of Charles Rogers' *Lyra Britan-*
> *nica* (1868) described the origin and transmis-
> sion of this hymn:

"Mrs. Elizabeth Mills … died of consumption, in 1829, in her twenty-third year. She wrote the hymn a few weeks before her death, and presented a copy of it to her relative, Mrs. J. Carus Wilson. This excellent lady committed the verses to memory, and frequently repeated them during her last illness. In a memoir of his wife [1831], Mr. Carus Wilson inserted the hymn, which has led to the authorship being ascribed to her. Miss Maria Mills, the author's sister-in-law, has kindly furnished us with a transcript of the verses from the original MS."

In *OOHB* 1866, Sedgwick credited the hymn to "Mrs. Wilson, 1837?" This was corrected in the 1867 edition.

The hymn was inspired by Charles Bridges' *Exposition of Psalm CXIX*, verse 44, where he wrote, "We speak of heaven; but oh! to be there!" The hymn is often printed with the final punctuation of each stanza as a question mark rather than an exclamation point. The regularization of the meter to fit 8.8.8.8. appeared as early as 1844 in *Parish Hymns*; the change at 5.1 appeared as early as 1859 in *The Sabbath School Bell*.

# 880 C.M.
*Heaven anticipated.*

1 TOO long, alas! I vainly sought
 For happiness below,

But earthly comforts, dearly bought,
 No solid good bestow.

2 At length, through Jesu's grace, I found
 The good and promis'd land,
Where milk and honey much abound
 And grapes in clusters stand.

3 My soul has tasted of the grapes,
 And now it longs to go
Where my dear Lord His vineyard keeps,
 And all the clusters grow.

4 Upon the true and living vine
 My famish'd soul would feast,
And banquet on the fruit divine,
 An everlasting guest.

*John Berridge*, 1785

**Ed:** In the 1867 ed. of *OOHB*, Sedgwick added the note, "From John Cennick, 1744." If Berridge had based his hymn on one of Cennick's, that connection could not be determined by the present editor.

**EE:** "O my sweet home, Jerusalem, thou happy harbour of my soul! Thanks, even now, to Him whose love hath taught me to long for Thee; but louder thanks in eternity, when I shall possess Thee" (July 12).

# State of the Lost

# 881 L.M.
*Gratitude for escape.*

1 LOOK down, my soul, on hell's domains,
 That world of agony and pains!
What crowds are now associate there,
 Of widely different character.

2 Oh were it not for grace divine,
 This case so dreadful had been mine!
Hell gaped for me! but Lord, Thy hand
 Snatch'd from the fire the kindling brand.

3 And now, though wrath was my desert,
 I hope to share a better part,
But heaven must wonder sure to see
 A sinner enter, vile as me.

4 Oh grace, rich grace, delightful theme!
 All heaven shall echo with the same;
While angels greet a sinner thus—
 "Art thou become like one of us?"

*John Ryland*, 1777

**Ed:** The date assigned by Sedgwick suggests it was printed in *The Gospel Magazine*, but it did not appear in any issues in 1777. It was included in the 27th ed. of Rippon's *Selection* (1827), where it was credited to Ryland.

## 882 C.M. / *The everlasting absence of God intolerable.*

1 THAT awful day will surely come,
Th' appointed hour makes haste,
When I must stand before my Judge
And pass the solemn test.

2 Thou lovely chief of all my joys,
Thou sovereign of my heart,
How could I bear to hear Thy voice
Pronounce the sound, "Depart?"

3 O wretched state of deep despair
To see my God remove,
And fix my doleful station where
I must not taste His love!

4 Jesus, I throw my arms around
And hang upon Thy breast;
Without a gracious smile from Thee,
My spirit cannot rest.

5 O tell me that my worthless name
Is graven on Thy hands;
Show me some promise in Thy book,
Where my salvation stands.

6 Give me one kind, assuring word
To sink my fears again,

And cheerfully my soul shall wait
Her threescore years and ten.

*Isaac Watts*, [1707, *rev.* 1709]

## 883 S.M. *The second death.*

1 O WHERE shall rest be found,
Rest for the weary soul?
'Twere vain the ocean's depths to sound
Or pierce to either pole.

2 Beyond this vale of tears
There is a life above,
Unmeasured by the flight of years,
And all that life is love.

3 There is a death, whose pang
Outlasts the fleeting breath;
O what eternal horrors hang
Around "the second death"!

4 Lord God of truth and grace,
Teach us that death to shun,
Lest we be banish'd from Thy face
And evermore undone.

5 Here would we end our quest;
Alone are found in Thee,
The life of perfect love—the rest
Of immortality.

*James Montgomery*, [1818, *rev.* 1825]

# The Church

## 884
8.7.8.7. Double
*Glorious things spoken of Zion.*

1 GLORIOUS things of thee are spoken,
    Zion, city of our God!
He, whose word cannot be broken,
    Form'd thee for His own abode.
On the Rock of Ages founded,
    What can shake thy sure repose?
With salvation's walls surrounded,
    Thou may'st smile at all thy foes.

2 See! the streams of living waters,
    Springing from eternal love,
Well supply thy sons and daughters,
    And all fear of want remove.
Who can faint while such a river
    Ever flows their thirst t' assuage?
Grace, which like the Lord, the giver,
    Never fails from age to age.

3 Round each habitation hov'ring,
    See the cloud and fire appear!
For a glory and a cov'ring,
    Showing that the Lord is near,
Thus deriving from their banner
    Light by night and shade by day;
Safe they feed upon the manna,
    Which He gives them when they pray.

4 Blest inhabitants of Zion,
    Wash'd in the Redeemer's blood!
Jesus, whom their souls rely on,
    Makes them kings and priests to God.
'Tis His love His people raises
    Over self to reign as kings,
And as priests, His solemn praises
    Each for a thank-off'ring brings.

5 Saviour, if of Zion's city,
    I through grace a member am,
Let the world deride or pity;
    I will glory in Thy name;
Fading is the worldling's pleasure,
    All his boasted pomp and show;
Solid joys and lasting treasure,
    None but Zion's children know.

*John Newton, 1779*

## 885
C.M.
*Sinai and Sion.*

1 NOT to the terrors of the Lord,
    The tempest, fire, and smoke,
Not to the thunder of that word
    Which God on Sinai spoke,

2 But we are come to Sion's hill,
    The city of our God,
Where milder words declare His will
    And spread His love abroad.

3 Behold th' innumerable host
    Of angels clothed in light;
Behold the spirits of the just,
    Whose faith is turn'd to sight.

4 Behold the blest assembly there,
    Whose names are writ in heav'n,
And God, the Judge of all, declares
    Their vilest sins forgiv'n.

5 The saints on earth, and all the dead,
    But one communion make;
All join in Christ, their living head,
    And of His grace partake.

6 In such society as this
    My weary soul would rest;
The man that dwells where Jesus is
    Must be forever blest.

*Isaac Watts, 1709*

## 886
8.7.8.7.4.7.
*God's faithfulness to His church.*

1 ZION stands by hills surrounded,
    Zion kept by pow'r divine;

All her foes shall be confounded,
   Though the world in arms combine.
     Happy Zion!
   What a favour'd lot is Thine!

2 Ev'ry human tie may perish!
   Friend to friend unfaithful prove;
Mothers cease their own to cherish;
   Heav'n and earth at last remove;
     But no changes
   Can attend Jehovah's love.

3 Zion's Friend in nothing alters,
   Though all others may and do;
His is love that never falters,
   Always to its object true.
     Happy Zion!
   Crown'd with mercies ever new.

4 If thy God should show displeasure,
   'Tis to save, and not destroy;
If He punish, 'tis in measure;
   'Tis to rid thee of alloy.
     Be thou patient;
   Soon thy grief shall turn to joy.

5 In the furnace God may prove thee,
   Thence to bring thee forth more bright,
But can never cease to love thee;
   Thou art precious in His sight.
     God is with thee,
   God thine everlasting light.

*Thomas Kelly*, 1806

## 887 7.6.7.6.
*God's faithfulness to His church.*

1 O JESUS Christ, most holy,
   Head of the church, Thy bride,
Each day in us more fully
   Thy name be magnified.

2 O may in each believer
   Thy love its pow'r display,
And none among us ever
   From Thee, our Shepherd, stray.

*Nicolaus Ludwig von Zinzendorf*, 1737
*tr. C.G. Clemens*, 1789

**Ed:** Translated from stanza 4 of the longer German hymn, "Ruht aus von eurer Mühe."

# Christian Fellowship

## 888 7.7.7.7. Double
*The communion of saints.*

1 PARTNERS of a glorious hope,
Lift your hearts and voices up;
Jointly let us rise, and sing
Christ our Prophet, Priest, and King.
Monuments of Jesu's grace,
Speak we by our lives His praise,
Walk in Him we have receiv'd;
Show we not in vain believ'd.

2 While we walk with God in light,
God our hearts doth still unite;
Dearest fellowship we prove,
Fellowship in Jesu's love;

Sweetly each, with each combin'd,
In the bonds of duty join'd,
Feels the cleansing blood applied,
Daily feels that Christ hath died.

3 Still, O Lord, our faith increase;
Cleanse from all unrighteousness;
Thee th' unholy cannot see;
Make, O make us meet for Thee.
Every vile affection kill;
Root out every seed of ill;
Utterly abolish sin;
Write Thy law of love within.

4 Hence may all our actions flow;
Love the proof that Christ we know;

Mutual love the token be,
Lord, that we belong to Thee;
Love, Thine image, love impart,
Stamp it on our face and heart;
Only love to us be given;
Lord, we ask no other heaven.

*Charles Wesley*, 1740

**Ed:** Part 4 of a much longer hymn,
"Come, and let us sweetly join."

# 889 C.M.
*Fellow citizens with the saints.*

1 HAPPY the souls to Jesus join'd,
    And saved by grace alone;
Walking in all His ways, they find
    Their heav'n on earth begun.

2 The church triumphant in Thy love,
    Their mighty joys we know;
They sing the Lamb in hymns above,
    And we in hymns below.

3 Thee, in Thy glorious realm, they praise,
    And bow before Thy throne!
We in the kingdom of Thy grace;
    The kingdoms are but one.

4 Thee holy to the holiest leads;
    From thence our spirits rise;
And he that in Thy statutes treads
    Shall meet Thee in the skies.

*Charles Wesley*, 1745 [*rev.* 1780]

# 890 C.M.
*Saints on earth and in heaven.*

1 IN one fraternal bond of love,
    One fellowship of mind,
The saints below and saints above
    Their bliss and glory find.

2 Here, in their house of pilgrimage,
    Thy statutes are their song;
There, through one bright, eternal age,
    Thy praises they prolong.

3 Lord, may our union form a part
    Of that thrice happy whole,
Derive its pulse from Thee, the heart,
    Its life from Thee, the soul.

*James Montgomery*, [1822, *rev.* 1825]

**Ed:** Taken from the longer hymn,
"The glorious universe around."

# 891 7.7.7.7.
*Christians one family.*

1 LORD, we all look up to Thee
    As one flock, one family;
May all strife between us cease
    As we love Thee, Prince of Peace.

2 Make us of one heart and mind,
    Gentle, meek, forgiving, kind,
Lowly both in thought and word,
    Like Thyself, belovèd Lord.

3 Let us for each other care,
    Each the other's burden bear,
Each to each by love endear,
    One in faith, and hope, and fear.

4 Free from all that hearts divide,
    Let us thus in Thee abide;
All the depths of love express,
    All the heights of holinesss.

*Charles Wesley*, 1749
*adapt. Thomas Davis*, 1864

**Ed:** Wesley's original began, "Jesu, Lord, we look
to Thee." Davis' version is mostly a rephrasing
of the original text; a few lines from Wesley
were preserved intact (2.1, 3.1, 4.3-4.4).

# 892 S.M.
*Love to the brethren.*

1 BLEST be the tie that binds
    Our hearts in Christian love;
The fellowship of kindred minds
    Is like to that above.

2 Before our Father's throne
    We pour our ardent prayers;

Our fears, our hopes, our aims are one,
Our comforts and our cares.

3    We share our mutual woes,
Our mutual burdens bear,
And often for each other flows
The sympathizing tear.

4    When we asunder part,
It gives us inward pain,
But we shall still be join'd in heart
And hope to meet again.

5    This glorious hope revives
Our courage by the way,
While each in expectation lives
And longs to see the day.

6    From sorrow, toil, and pain,
And sin we shall be free,
And perfect love and friendship reign
Through all eternity.

*John Fawcett*, 1782

# 893 C.M.
*Receiving members.*

1 COME in, thou blessèd of the Lord!
Stranger nor foe art thou.
We welcome thee with warm accord,
Our friend, our brother, now.

2 The hand of fellowship, the heart
Of love, we offer thee;
Leaving the world, thou dost but part
From lies and vanity.

3 The cup of blessing which we bless,
The heavenly bread we break,
(Our Saviour's blood and righteousness,)
Freely with us partake.

4 Come with us, we will do thee good,
As God to us hath done;
Stand but in Him, as those have stood,
Whose faith the victory won.

5 And when, by turns, we pass away,
As star by star grows dim,

May each, translated into day,
Be lost and found in Him.

*James Montgomery*, 1836

# 894 8.7.8.7.4.7.
*Receiving members.*

1 NOW we'll render to the Saviour
Praise for all that He has wrought,
For the precious, full salvation,
Which has now to souls been brought.
Hallelujah,
Jesus shall have all the praise!

2 Heaven has rung with joy and transport,
While we here have been convened,
Over the returning sinner,
Numbered now with the redeemed;
Hallelujah,
Jesus shall have all the praise!

*Albert Midlane*, [1861, *rev.* 1865]

# 895 L.M.
*A welcome to Christian friends.*

1 KINDRED in Christ, for His dear sake,
A hearty welcome here receive;
May we together now partake
The joys which only He can give!

2 To you and us by grace 'tis giv'n,
To know the Saviour's precious name,
And shortly we shall meet in heav'n,
Our hope, our way, our end the same.

3 May He by whose kind care we meet,
Send His good Spirit from above,
Make our communications sweet,
And cause our hearts to burn with love!

4 Forgotten be each worldly theme,
When Christians see each other thus:
We only wish to speak of Him,
Who lived, and died, and reigns for us.

5 We'll talk of all He did, and said,
And suffer'd for us here below,
The path He mark'd for us to tread,
And what He's doing for us now.

6 Thus, as the moments pass away,
  We'll love, and wonder, and adore,
  And hasten on the glorious day
  When we shall meet to part no more.

*John Newton*, 1779

# 896
**7.7.7.7.**
*Meeting and parting.*

1 AS the sun's enliv'ning eye
  Shines on ev'ry place the same,
  So the Lord is always nigh
  To the souls that love His name.

2 When they move at duty's call,
  He is with them by the way;
  He is ever with them all,
  Those who go, and those who stay.

3 From His holy mercy-seat
  Nothing can their souls confine;

Still in spirit they may meet,
  *Still* in sweet communion join.

4 For a season call'd to part,
  Let us then ourselves commend
  To the gracious eye and heart
  Of our ever-present Friend.

5 Jesus, hear our humble pray'r!
  Tender Shepherd of Thy sheep!
  Let Thy mercy and Thy care
  All our souls in safety keep.

6 In Thy strength may we be strong;
  Sweeten every cross and pain;
  Give us, if we live, ere long
  Here to meet in peace again.

*John Newton*, 1779, *alt.*

> **3.4:** *And*  **Ed:** This minor variant appeared as
> early as 1823 in John Kempthorne's *Select
> Portions of Psalms.*

---

<h1 style="text-align:center">Pastors</h1>

# 897
**8.7.8.7.**
*Choosing a minister.*

1 LORD, Thy church, without a pastor,
  Cries to Thee in her distress;
  Hear us, gracious Lord and Master,
  And with heavenly guidance bless.

2 Walking midst Thy lamps all golden,
  Thou preservest still the light;
  Stars in Thy right hand are holden,
  Stars to cheer Thy church's night.

3 Find us, Lord, the man appointed
  Pastor of this flock to be,
  One with holy oil anointed,
  Meet for us, and dear to Thee.

4 Send a man, O King of Zion,
  Made according to Thine heart,

Meek as lamb, and bold as lion,
  Wise to act a shepherd's part.

5 Grant us now Thy heavenly leading;
  Over every heart preside;
  Now in answer to our pleading,
  All our consultations guide.

*Charles H. Spurgeon*, 1866

# 898
**C.M.**
*Watching for souls.*

1 LET Zion's watchmen all awake
  And take th' alarm they give;
  Now let them, from the mouth of God,
  Their awful charge receive.

2 'Tis not a cause of small import
  The pastor's care demands,

But what might fill an angel's heart
    And fill'd a Saviour's hands.

3 They watch for souls for which the Lord
    Did heav'nly bliss forego,
For souls which must forever live
    In raptures or in woe.

4 All to the great tribunal haste,
    Th' account to render there,
And shouldst Thou strictly mark our faults,
    Lord, how should we appear?

5 May they that Jesus, whom they preach,
    Their own Redeemer see,
And watch Thou daily o'er their souls
    That they may watch for Thee.

*Philip Doddridge*, 1755

**Ed:** Dated 21 Oct. 1736 in Doddridge's MSS.

# 899 L.M.
*Welcoming a new minister.*

1 WE bid thee welcome in the name
Of Jesus, our exalted head;
Come as a servant, so He came,
And we receive thee in His stead.

2 Come as a shepherd; guard and keep
This fold from hell, and earth, and sin;
Nourish the lambs and feed the sheep,
The wounded heal, the lost bring in.

3 Come as a teacher sent from God,
Charged His whole counsel to declare;
Lift o'er our ranks the prophet's rod
While we uphold thy hands with prayer.

4 Come as a messenger of peace,
Fill'd with the Spirit, fired with love;
Live to behold our large increase,
And die to meet us all above.

*James Montgomery*, 1825

# 900 L.M.
*Minister bold for his Lord.*

1 SHALL I, for fear of feeble man,
Thy Spirit's course in me restrain?

Or undismay'd, in deed and word,
Be a true witness for my Lord?

2 Awed by a mortal's frown, shall I
Conceal the Word of God most high?
How then before Thee shall I dare
To stand, or how Thy anger bear?

3 Shall I, to soothe th' unholy throng,
Soften Thy truths and smooth my tongue?
To gain earth's gilded toys, or flee
The cross endured, my God, by Thee?

4 The love of Christ doth me constrain
To seek the wandering souls of men;
With cries, entreaties, tears, to save,
To snatch them from the *fiery wave*.

5 My life, my blood, I here present,
If for Thy truth they may be spent:
Fulfill Thy sov'reign counsel, Lord!
Thy will be done! Thy name adored!

6 Give me Thy strength, O God of pow'r!
Then let winds blow, or thunders roar;
Thy faithful witness will I be—
'Tis fix'd! I can do all through Thee!

*Johann Joseph Winckler*, [1708]
*tr. John Wesley*, 1739 [*alt. C.H.S.*]

> **4.4:** *gaping grave*   **Ed:** Translated from
> the German, "Sollt ich aus Furcht vor
> Menschenkindern."

# 901 L.M.
*Prayer for a minister.*

1 WITH *heavenly* power, O Lord, defend
Him whom we now to Thee commend;
*His person bless, his soul* secure,
And make him to the end endure.

2 Gird him with all-sufficient grace;
*Direct his feet in* paths of peace;
Thy truth and faithfulness fulfill,
*And help him to obey Thy will.*

3 Before *him Thy* protection send;
O love him, save him to the end!
Nor let him as Thy pilgrim rove,
Without the convoy of Thy love.

4 Enlarge, inflame, and fill his heart;
   In him Thy mighty power exert,
   That thousands yet unborn may praise
   The wonders of redeeming grace.

Rowland Hill's *Collection*, 1774
[*alt. John Rippon*, 1787]

**1.1:** *all Thy*   **1.3:** *Our faithful minister*
**2.2:** *Give to his footsteps*
**2.4:** *Preserve him, Lord, from ev'ry ill.*
**3.1:** *his face*

# 902 L.M.
*Prayer for ministers.*

1 FATHER of mercies, bow Thine ear,
   Attentive to our earnest prayer;
   We plead for those who plead for Thee;
   Successful pleaders may they be!

2 Clothe Thou with energy divine
   Their words, and let those words be Thine;
   To them Thy sacred truth reveal;
   Suppress their fear; inflame their zeal.

3 Teach them aright to sow the seed;
   Teach them Thy chosen flock to feed;
   Teach them immortal souls to gain,
   Nor let them labour, Lord, in vain.

4 Let thronging multitudes around
   Hear from their lips the joyful sound,
   In humble strains Thy grace adore,
   And feel Thy new-creating power.

5 Let sinners break their massy chains,
   Distressèd souls forget their pains;
   *Let* light through distant realms be spread,
   Till Zion rears her drooping head.

*Benjamin Beddome*, [1787, *rev.* 1817]

**Ed:** The revised version at 5.3 reads *And*, but
Spurgeon has retained the older reading, *Let*.

# 903 L.M.
*Dangerous illness of a minister.*

1 O THOU, before whose gracious throne
   We bow our suppliant spirits down,

Avert Thy swift descending stroke,
Nor smite the shepherd of the flock.

2 Restore him, sinking to the grave;
   Stretch out Thine arm, make haste to save;
   Back to our hopes and wishes give,
   And bid our friend and father live.

3 Bound to each soul by tenderest ties,
   In every breast his image lies;
   Thy pitying aid, O God, impart,
   Nor rend him from each bleeding heart.

4 Yet if our supplications fail,
   And prayers and tears can nought prevail,
   Be Thou his strength, be Thou his stay,
   Support him through the gloomy way.

5 Around him may Thy angels wait,
   Deck'd with their robes of heavenly state,
   To teach his happy soul to rise
   And waft him to his native skies.

[*J—K—* in Evans & Ash *Collection*, 1781]

**Ed:** In the first ed. of *OOHB*, Sedgwick credited
the hymn to *K—* in Rippon's *Selection*; this
was changed to "George Keith, 1787" in the
6th ed. (1873). In Julian's *Dictionary*, p. 850:
"This uncertainty of authorship was increased
by D. Sedgwick's guesses at the meaning of
'K.' In one of his books annotated in MS we
find him giving it to 'John Kentish,' in another
to 'George Keith,' and so on, but in each case
confessing that it was a guess only."
   The hymn actually predates Rippon's *Selection*. It appeared in the 4th ed. of the Evans
& Ash *Collection*, unattributed, and was later
labeled "J—K—" in the 8th ed. (1801).

# 904 8.7.8.7.
*Deacons or elders.*

1 RISEN Lord, Thou hast receivèd
   Gifts to bless the sons of men,
   That with souls who have believèd,
   God might dwell on earth again.

2 Now these gifts be pleased to send us,
   Elders, deacons still supply,
   Men whom Thou art pleased to lend us,
   All the saints to edify.

3 Guide us while we here select them;
  Let the Holy Ghost be nigh;
Do Thou, Lord, Thyself elect them
  And ordain them from on high.

*Pause while the election is made.*

4 Lord, Thy church invokes Thy blessing
  On her chosen {elders / deacons} head,

Here we stand our need confessing,
  Waiting till Thy grace be shed.

5 Pour on them Thy rich anointing,
  Fill Thy servants with Thy power,
Prove them of Thine own appointing,
  Bless them from this very hour.

*Charles H. Spurgeon*, 1866

---

# The Lord's Day

## 905   7.7.7.7.7.7. / *Seeking a blessing on the coming Sabbath.*

1 SAFELY through another week
  God has brought us on our way;
Let us now a blessing seek
  On th' approaching Sabbath day;
Day of all the week the best,
Emblem of eternal rest.

2 Mercies multiplied each hour
  Through the week our praise demand,
Guarded by almighty pow'r,
  Fed and guided by His hand;
Though ungrateful we have been,
Only made returns of sin.

3 While we pray for pard'ning grace,
  Through the dear Redeemer's name,
Show Thy reconcilèd face,
  Shine away our sin and shame;
From our worldly care set free;
May we rest this night with Thee.

4 When the morn shall bid us rise,
  May we feel Thy presence near;
May Thy glory meet our eyes
  When we in Thy house appear!
There afford us, Lord, a taste
Of our everlasting feast.

5 May the Gospel's joyful sound
  Conquer sinners, comfort saints,
Make the fruits of grace abound,
  Bring relief for all complaints;
Thus may all our sabbaths prove,
Till we join the church above!

*John Newton*, [1774, *rev.* 1779]

## 906   L.M.   *Another Sabbath is begun.*

1 ANOTHER six days' work is done,
Another Sabbath is begun;
Return, my soul, *enjoy* thy rest;
*Improve* the day thy God has blest.

2 Come, bless the Lord, whose love assigns
So sweet a rest to wearied minds,
Provides an antepast of heaven,
And gives this day the food of seven.

3 O that *our* thoughts and *thanks* may rise
As *grateful incense to the* skies,
And *draw* from heaven that sweet repose
Which none but he that feels it knows.

4 This heavenly calm within the breast
Is the dear pledge of glorious rest,
Which for the church of God remains,
The end of cares, the end of pains.

5 In holy duties *let* the day,
In holy pleasures *pass* away;
How sweet a sabbath thus to spend
In hope of one that ne'er shall end!

1,3-5 *Joseph Stennett*, 1732 [*alt.* Evans, 1769]
[2 Evans & Ash *Collection*, 1769]

**1.3:** *unto* **1.4:** *Revere* **3.1:** *my / words*
**3.2:** *incense to propitious* **3.3:** *fetch*
**5.1:** *thus* **5.2:** *melts* **MM:** Hymns, 1st Lord's
Day, HEBRON / MEROE

# 907 S.M.
*Welcome, sweet day of rest.*

1 WELCOME, sweet day of rest
That saw the Lord arise;
Welcome to this reviving breast
And these rejoicing eyes!

2 The King himself comes near
And feasts His saints today;
Here we may sit and see Him here,
And love, and praise, and pray.

3 One day amidst the place
Where my dear God hath been
Is sweeter than ten thousand days
Of pleasurable sin.

4 My willing soul would stay
In such a frame as this,
And sit and sing herself away
To everlasting bliss.

*Isaac Watts*, [1707]

**MM:** Hymns, 8th Lord's Day,
SILVER STREET / ST. THOMAS

# 908 8.8.6.8.8.6.
*The joyful morn.*

1 THE festal morn, my God, *has* come,
That calls me to Thy honour'd dome,
Thy presence to adore;
My feet the summons shall attend,
With willing steps Thy courts ascend,
And tread the hallow'd floor.

2 Hither from Judah's utmost end,
The heav'n-protected tribes ascend,
Their offerings hither bring;
Here, eager to attest their joy,
In hymns of praise their tongues employ,
And hail th' immortal King.

3 Be peace by each implor'd on thee,
O Sion, while with bended knee,
To Jacob's God we pray;
How blest, who calls himself thy friend!
Success his labour shall attend,
And safety guard his way.

4 Seat of my friends and brethren, hail!
How can my tongue, O *Sion*, fail,
To bless thy lov'd abode?
How cease the zeal that in me glows,
Thy good to seek, whose walls enclose
The mansions of my God?

*James Merrick*, 1765, *alt.*

**1.1:** *is* **4.2:** *Salem* **Ed:** The change at 1.1
seems to be unknown prior to *OOHB*, but 4.2
appeared in the Evans & Ash *Collection* (1769)
and was repeated in Rippon's *Selection* (1787).

# 909 C.M.
*Hosanna.*

1 THIS is the day the Lord hath made;
He calls the hours His own;
Let heaven rejoice, let earth be glad,
And praise surround the throne.

2 Today He rose and left the dead,
And Satan's empire fell;
Today the saints His triumphs spread,
And all His wonders tell.

3 Hosanna to th' anointed King,
To David's holy Son;
Help us, O Lord! descend and bring
Salvation from Thy throne.

4 Blest be the Lord, who comes to men
With messages of grace,
Who comes in God His Father's name
To save our sinful race.

5 Hosanna in the highest strains
    The church on earth can raise;
The highest heavens in which He reigns
    Shall give Him nobler praise.

*Isaac Watts*, 1719

> **MM:** Hymns, 23rd Lord's Day,
>     WOODLAND / PETERBORO
> **FPN:** 10 Aug. 1890 (No. 2158), WINCHESTER
> **TD:** "We observe the Lord's day as henceforth
>     our true Sabbath, a day made and ordained
>     of God, for the perpetual remembrance of the
>     achievements of our Redeemer. Whenever the
>     soft Sabbath light of the first day of the week
>     breaks upon the earth, let us sing, 'This is the
>     day the Lord hath made; He calls the hours His
>     own'" (Ps. 118:24, vol. 5, p. 332).

# 910 S.M.
*Sweet day, so calm, so bright.*

1   SWEET is the task, O Lord,
    Thy glorious acts to sing,
To praise Thy name, and hear Thy Word,
    And grateful off'rings bring.

2   Sweet at the dawning hour,
    Thy boundless love to tell,
And when the night wind shuts the flower,
    Still on the theme to dwell.

3   Sweet, on this day of rest,
    To join in heart and voice
With those who love and serve Thee best
    And in Thy name rejoice.

4   To songs of praise and joy
    Be ev'ry Sabbath given,
That such may be our best employ
    Eternally in heaven.

[*Harriet Auber*, 1829]

> **Ed:** Sedgwick attributed this text to Henry
>     Lyte, 1834, in the 1st ed. of *OOHB*, then 1841
>     in subsequent eds., implying Lyte's *Spirit of
>     the Psalms*, 1st & 5th eds., respectively. The
>     confusion may have arisen from Auber's col-
>     lection having the same title, but with 18 other
>     texts elsewhere in *OOHB*, Sedgwick knew
>     Auber's work, making the error odd.

# 911 C.M.
*Jesus rose on the first day of the week.*

1 BLESS'D morning,
    whose young dawning rays
    Beheld our rising God,
That saw Him triumph o'er the dust
    And leave His dark abode.

2 In the cold prison of a tomb
    The dead Redeemer lay,
Till the revolving skies had brought
    The third, th' appointed day.

3 Hell and the grave unite their force
    To hold our God in vain;
The sleeping Conqueror arose
    And burst their feeble chain.

4 To Thy great name, almighty Lord,
    These sacred hours we pay,
And loud hosannas shall proclaim
    The triumph of the day.

5 Salvation and immortal praise
    To our victorious King;
Let heaven, and earth, and rocks, and seas
    With glad hosannas ring.

*Isaac Watts*, [1707]

# 912 L.M.
*The eternal Sabbath anticipated.*

1 LORD of the Sabbath, hear our vows
    On this Thy day, in this Thy house,
    And own, as grateful sacrifice,
    The songs which from the desert rise.

2 Thine earthly Sabbaths, Lord, we love,
    But there's a nobler rest above;
    To that our labouring souls aspire
    With ardent pangs of strong desire.

3 No more fatigue, no more distress,
    Nor sin nor hell shall reach the place;
    No groans to mingle with the songs
    Which warble from immortal tongues.

4 No rude alarms of raging foes,
    No cares to break the long repose,

No midnight shade, no clouded sun,
But sacred, high, eternal noon.

5 O long-expected day, begin;
Dawn on these realms of woe and sin;
Fain would we leave this weary road
And sleep in death, to rest with God.

*Philip Doddridge*, 1755

> **Ed:** In Doddridge's manuscripts, this hymn be-
> gan "O God of Sabbath, hear our vows"
> and was dated 2 Jan. 1736-7.
> **MM:** Hymns, 5th Lord's Day,
> BRATTLE STREET / ZEPHYR
> **FPN:** 5 Aug. 1888 (No. 2037), MONTGOMERY

# 913 6.6.6.6.8.8.
*Wake up, my heart.*

1 AWAKE, our drowsy souls,
Shake off each slothful band;
The wonders of this day
Our noblest songs demand;
Auspicious morn! thy blissful rays
Bright seraphs hail in songs of praise.

2 At thy approaching dawn,
Reluctant death resign'd
The glorious Prince of Life
*In* dark domains confin'd;
Th' angelic host around Him bends,
And 'midst their shouts the God ascends.

3 All hail, triumphant Lord!
Heaven with hosannas rings;
While earth, in humbler strains,
Thy praise responsive sings:
"Worthy art Thou, who once wast slain,
Through endless years to live and reign."

4 Gird on, great God, Thy sword;
Ascend Thy conquering car,
While justice, truth, and love
Maintain the glorious war.
Victorious Thou, Thy foes shalt tread,
And sin and hell in triumph lead.

5 Make bare Thy potent arm
And wing th' unerring dart

With salutary pangs
To each rebellious heart;
Then dying souls for life shall sue,
Numerous as drops of morning dew.

[*D.* in Evans & Ash *Collection*, 1769]
[*alt. John Dobell*, 1806]

> **2.4:** *Her*  **Ed:** Sedgwick credited the hymn to
> Elizabeth Scott, 1763, but this attribution rais-
> es a number of issues. In Scott's MSS at Yale
> (1740), she had penned a hymn beginning
> "Awake, my drowsy soul," in quatrains; this
> text has little in common with the text above
> and should not be considered the same hymn.
> Sedgwick's date, 1763, would imply (based on
> his index) that this hymn first appeared in *The
> Christian's Magazine*, yet it is not to be found
> in the 1763 issues, and it is not named among
> Scott's hymns in that magazine in Julian's *Dic-
> tionary*, pp. 1019-1020. This was likely a guess
> on Sedgwick's part.
>     William T. Brooke's article on this hymn in
> Julian's *Dictionary*, p. 103, ascribed it to Scott
> and gave the first printing as Evans & Ash,
> 1769. The first printing does indeed seem to be
> that collection, but there it was simply marked
> "D." The attribution to Scott started with John
> Dobell's *Selection* (1806) and spread from
> there. The real author is unknown.

# 914 8.7.8.7.4.7.
*Public worship.*

1 HAIL, ye days of solemn meeting!
    Hail, ye days of praise and prayer!
Far from earthly scenes retreating,
    In your blessings we would share;
        Sacred *seasons*,
    In your blessings we would share.

2 Be Thou near us, blessèd Saviour,
    Still at morn and eve the same;
Give us faith that cannot waver,
    Kindle in us heaven's own flame;
        Blessèd Saviour,
    Kindle in us heaven's own flame.

3 When the fervent prayer is glowing,
    Sacred Spirit, hear that prayer;

When the *joyous* song is flowing,
  Let that song Thine impress bear;
    Sacred Spirit,
  Let that song Thine impress bear.

4 Angel bands! these scenes frequenting,
    Often may your praises wake;
  Oft may joy o'er souls repenting
    From your harps melodious break;
      Oft may anthems
    From your harps melodious break.

[*Samuel Francis Smith*, 1832, *alt.*]

> **1.5:** *meeting*, **3.3:** *choral* **Ed:** Sedgwick
> credited this text as "American Hymn, 1840."
> The alteration at 1.5 is from Rippon's *Selection*
> (1844); 3.3 is by Spurgeon.

# 915 8.7.8.7.4.7.
*Divine worship.*

1 IN Thy name, O Lord, assembling,
    We, Thy people, now draw near;
  Teach us to rejoice with trembling;
    Speak and let Thy servants hear,
      Hear with meekness,
    Hear Thy Word with godly fear.

2 While our days on earth are lengthen'd,
    May we give them, Lord, to Thee!
  Cheer'd by hope and daily strengthen'd,
    May we run, nor weary be;
      Till Thy glory
    Without clouds in heav'n we see.

3 There in worship, purer, sweeter,
    *All* Thy people shall adore,
  Tasting of enjoyment greater
    *Than they could conceive* before;
      Full enjoyment,
    Full, unmix'd, and evermore.

*Thomas Kelly*, 1815

> **3.2:** *Thee* **3.4:** *Far, than thought conceiv'd*
> **Ed:** Footnotes here indicate revisions Kelly
> made in later editions of his *Hymns.*

# 916 7.7.7.7.
*Going to worship.*

1 TO Thy temple I repair;
  Lord, I love to worship there;
  When within the veil I meet
  Christ upon the mercy seat.

2 Thou, through Him, art reconciled;
  I, through Him, become Thy child;
  Abba! Father! give me grace
  In Thy courts to seek Thy face.

3 While Thy glorious praise is sung,
  Touch my lips, unloose my tongue,
  That my joyful soul may bless
  *Christ* the Lord, my Righteousness.

4 While the prayers of saints ascend,
  God of love! to mine attend;
  Hear me, for Thy Spirit pleads,
  Hear, for Jesus intercedes.

5 While I hearken to Thy law,
  Fill my soul with humble awe,
  Till Thy gospel bring to me
  Life and immortality.

6 While Thy ministers proclaim
  Peace and pardon in Thy name,
  Through their voice, by faith, may I
  Hear Thee speaking from *on high.*

7 From Thy house when I return,
  May my heart within me burn,
  And at evening let me say,
  "I have walk'd with God today."

*James Montgomery*, 1812 [*rev.* 1825]

> **3.4:** *Thee* **6.4:** *the sky* **Ed:** These alterations
> appeared in William Muhlenberg's *Church
> Poetry* (1823) and were repeated in other
> collections, then eventually incorporated into
> posthumous editions of Montgomery's works.
> **MM:** Hymns, 6th Lord's Day, MARTYN; 18th
> Lord's Day, HERNDON / PLEYEL'S HYMN

# 917
C.M.
*Sweet rest.*

1 MY Lord, my love, was crucified;
   He all the pains did bear;
   But in the sweetness of His rest
   He makes His servants share.

2 How sweetly rest Thy saints above
   Which in Thy bosom lie!
   The church below doth rest in hope
   Of that felicity.

3 Welcome and dear unto my soul
   Are these sweet feasts of love,
   But what a Sabbath shall I keep
   When I shall rest above!

4 I bless Thy wise and wondrous love,
   Which binds us to be free,
   Which makes us leave our earthly snares
   That we may come to Thee.

5 I come, I wait, I hear, I pray;
   Thy footsteps, Lord, I trace;
   I sing to think this is the way
   Unto my Saviour's face.

*John Mason*, 1683

# 918
S.M.
*Sabbath evening recollections.*

1 THE light of Sabbath eve
   Is fading fast away;
   What *pleasing* record will it leave
   To crown the closing day?

2 Is it a Sabbath spent
   Fruitless, and vain, and void?
   Or have these *precious* moments lent
   Been sacredly employ'd?

3 How dreadful and how drear,
   In yon dark world of pain,
   Will *Sabbath seasons* lost appear
   That cannot come again!

4 God of these Sabbath hours,
   Oh may we never dare

To waste, in *worldly* thoughts of ours,
   These sacred days of prayer!

*James Edmeston*, 1821
[*alt. John Rippon*, 1827]

   **3.3:** *Sabbaths*   **Ed:** Edmeston's hymn was written in 6.6.6.6; Rippon added one word to each
   stanza to make it fit common metre.

# 919
7.7.7.7. Double / *Abide with us,*
*for it is toward evening.*

1 HOLY Father! whom we praise
   With imperfect accents here,
   Ancient of eternal days!
   Lord of heaven and earth and air,
   Stooping from amid the blaze
   Of the flaming seraphim,
   Hear and help us while we raise
   This our Sabbath evening hymn.

2 We have trod Thy temple, Lord;
   We have joined the public praise;
   We have heard Thy holy Word;
   We have sought Thy heavenly grace;
   All Thy goodness we record;
   All our powers to Thee we bring;
   Let Thy faithfulness afford
   Now the shadow of Thy wing.

3 We have seen Thy dying love,
   Jesus! once for sinners slain;
   We would follow Thee above;
   We like Thee would rise and reign.
   Let revolving Sabbaths prove
   Seasons of delight in Thee;
   Let Thy presence, Holy Dove,
   Fit us for eternity.

*Thomas Binney*, 1857

# 920
7.7.7.7.
*The end of the Sabbath.*

1 ERE another *Sabbath* close,
   Ere again we seek repose,
   Lord! our song ascends to Thee;
   At Thy feet we bow the knee.

2 For the mercies of the day,
   For this rest upon our way,
   Thanks to Thee alone be given,
   Lord of earth and King of heaven.

3 Cold our services have been,
   Mingled every prayer with sin,
   But Thou canst and wilt forgive;
   By Thy grace alone we live.

4 Whilst this thorny path we tread,
   May Thy love our footsteps lead;
   When our journey here is past,
   May we rest with Thee at last.

5 Let these earthly Sabbaths prove
   Foretastes of our joys above;
   While their steps Thy pilgrims bend
   To the rest which knows no end.

[*O.P.* in *Missionary Minstrel*, 1826]

**1.1:** *Sabbath's* **Ed:** In the first ed. of *OOHB*,
Sedgwick credited the hymn to Edward
Bickersteth's *Christian Psalmody* (1833); by
1873, he had identified an earlier source, B.W.
Noel's *Selection of Psalms and Hymns* (1832).
William T. Brooke, in Julian's *Dictionary*, p.
352, found this 1826 source, which is likely the
original.

# Baptism

## 921
7.6.7.6. Double
*Buried with Him in Baptism.*

1 AROUND Thy grave, Lord Jesus!
   Thine empty grave, we stand,
   With hearts all full of praises
   To keep Thy bless'd command;
   By faith, our souls rejoicing
   To trace Thy path of love,
   Through death's dark angry billows,
   Up to the throne above.

2 Lord Jesus! we remember
   The travail of Thy soul,
   When in Thy love's deep pity
   The waves did o'er Thee roll;
   Baptiz'd in death's cold waters,
   For us Thy blood was shed;
   For us the Lord of glory
   Was number'd with the dead.

3 O Lord, Thou now art risen,
   Thy travail all is o'er,
   For sin Thou once hast suffer'd;
   Thou liv'st to die no more;
   Sin, death, and hell are vanquish'd
   By Thee, Thy church's Head,

And lo! we share Thy triumphs,
   Thou First-born from the dead.

4 Into Thy death baptizèd,
   We own with Thee we died;
   With Thee, our life, are risen,
   And in Thee glorified;
   From sin, the world, and Satan,
   We're ransom'd by Thy blood,
   And now would walk as strangers
   Alive with Thee to God.

*James George Deck*, [1842]

## 922
L.M.
*The place where Jesus lay.*

1 *COME, happy souls, adore the Lamb,*
   Who lov'd our race *ere* time *began,*
   *Who veil'd His Godhead in our clay,*
   And in the humble manger lay.

2 To Jordan's stream the Spirit led,
   To mark the path His saints should tread;
   *With joy they* trace *the* sacred way
   *To* see the place where Jesus lay.

3 *Baptized* by John in Jordan's wave,
*The Saviour* left His wat'ry grave;
Heav'n own'd the deed, approv'd the way,
And bless'd the place where Jesus lay.

4 Come, all who love His precious name;
Come, tread His steps and learn of Him;
Happy beyond expression they
Who find the place where Jesus lay.

*Thomas Baldwin*, [1808, *alt.*]

**1.1:** *Ye happy saints, the Lamb adore,*
**1.2:** *all / before!*
**1.3:** *Assum'd a body form'd of clay,*
**2.3:** *They love to / this* **3.1:** *Immers'd*
**3.2:** *Rising He* **Ed:** All of the alterations except 3.1 were made by James Winchell for the 2nd ed. of his *Arrangement of … Isaac Watts* (1820); that version was adopted into Stow & Smith (1843), plus the change at 3.1.

# 923 C.M.
*Praise to Jesus buried and risen.*

1 COME, ye who bow to sov'reign grace,
Record Immanuel's love;
Join in a song of noble praise
To Him who reigns above.

2 Once in the gloomy grave He lay,
But by His rising pow'r,
He bore the gates of death away;
Hail! mighty Conqueror!

3 Here we declare in emblem plain
Our burial in His grave,
And since in Him we rose again,
We rise from out the wave.

4 No trust in water do we place,
'Tis but an outward sign;
The great reality is grace,
The fountain, blood divine.

[1,2,4 *Maria de Fleury*, 1793]
3 *Charles H. Spurgeon*, 1866

**Ed:** Sedgwick incorrectly attributed this hymn to James Upton, 1814.

# 924 C.M.
*Dead with Jesus.*

1 O LORD! whilst we confess the worth
Of this, the outward seal,
Teach us the truths herein set forth,
Our very own to feel.

2 Death to the world we here avow,
Death to each fleshly lust;
Newness of life our portion now,
A risen Lord our trust.

3 And we, O Lord, who now partake
Of this eternal life,
With every sin, for Thy dear sake,
Would be at constant strife.

4 Baptized into the Father's name,
We'd walk as sons of God;
Baptized in Thine, with joy we claim
The merits of Thy blood.

5 Baptized into the Holy Ghost,
We'd prove His mighty power,
And making Thee our only boast,
Obey Thee hour by hour.

*Mary (Bowly) Peters*, 1842

# 925 C.M.
*The example of Jesus.*

1 BURIED beneath the yielding wave,
The dear Redeemer lies;
Faith views Him in the watery grave,
And thence beholds Him rise.

2 Thus it becomes His saints today,
Their ardent zeal t' express,
And in the Lord's appointed way,
Fulfill all righteousness.

3 With joy we in His footsteps tread
And would His cause maintain,
Like Him be numbered with the dead,
And with Him rise and reign.

4 His presence oft revives our hearts
And drives our fears away;

When He commands, and strength imparts,
  We cheerfully obey.

5 Now we, dear Jesus, would to Thee
  Our grateful voices raise;
With Wash'd in the fountain of Thy blood,
  Our lives shall all be praise.

*Benjamin Beddome,* 1817

# 926 C.M.
*Practical improvement of baptism.*

1 HEARKEN, ye children of your God;
  Ye heirs of glory, hear,
For accents so divine as these
  Might charm the dullest ear.

2 Baptiz'd into your Saviour's death,
  Your souls to sin must die;
With Christ your Lord ye live anew,
  With Christ ascend on high.

3 There by His Father's hand He sits,
  Enthroned divinely fair,
Yet owns Himself your brother still,
  And your forerunner there.

4 Rise from these earthly trifles, rise
  On wings of faith and love;
With Christ your choicest treasure lies,
  And be your hearts above.

5 But earth and sin will drag us down
  When we attempt to fly;
Lord, send Thy strong attractive force
  To raise and fix us high.

*Philip Doddridge,* 1755 [*rev.* 1839]

# 927 C.M. / *The believer constrained by the love of Christ to follow Him.*

1 DEAR Lord, and will Thy pard'ning love
  Embrace a wretch so vile?
Wilt Thou my load of guilt remove
  And bless me with Thy smile?

2 Hast Thou for me the cross endur'd
  And all the shame despis'd?

And shall I be ashamed, O Lord,
  With Thee to be baptiz'd?

3 Didst Thou the great example lead
  In Jordan's swelling flood?
And shall my pride disdain the deed
  That's worthy of my God?

4 Dear Lord, *the ardour of Thy* love
  Reproves my cold delays;
*And now my willing footsteps move*
  *In Thy delightful ways.*

*John Fellows,* 1773
[*alt. John Rippon,* 1787]

    **4.1:** *Thy condescending*
    **4.3-4:** *My wand'ring steps how slow they move,*
    *How careless in thy ways!*

# 928 C.M.
*"Hinder me not."*

1 IN all my Lord's appointed ways,
  My journey I'll pursue;
"Hinder me not," *ye much-loved saints,*
  For I must go with you.

2 Through floods and flames, if Jesus lead,
  I'll *follow where* He goes;
"Hinder me not," shall be my cry,
  *Though earth and hell* oppose.

3 Through duty and through trials *too*
  I'll go at His command;
"Hinder me not," for I am bound
  To my Immanuel's land.

4 *And when my Saviour* calls me home,
  Still this my cry shall be,
"Hinder me not," come welcome Death,
  I'll gladly go with Thee.

*John Ryland,* [1775]
[*alt. John Rippon,* 1787]

    **1.3:** *my brethren dear*   **2.2:** *go where'er*
    **2.4:** *Let whoso will*   **3.1:** *all*
    **4.1:** *When Christ's own servant*
    **Ed:** Taken from the longer hymn, "When Abram's
    servant to procure." For two different ac-

counts on how this hymn was composed, see Julian's *Dictionary*, p. 984, and Josiah Miller's *Singers and Songs of the Church* (1869), p. 313. Either way, Sedgwick's date of 1773 for the composition was correct, and it was first published in 1775.

Spurgeon quoted this hymn in his last sermon at the Metropolitan Tabernacle, 7 June 1891: "No other leader is worth following. We must follow the Son of David. Mutiny against Him is out of the question. 'Through floods or flames, if Jesus lead, we'll follow where he goes'" (MTP, vol. 37, p. 314).

**MM:** "Fear not, Christian; Jesus is with thee. In all thy fiery trials, His presence is both thy comfort and safety. He will never leave one whom He has chosen for His own. . . . Wilt thou not, then, take fast hold of Christ, and say, 'Through floods and flames, if Jesus lead, I'll follow where he goes'?" (Mar. 3).

# 929   8.7.8.7. / *"If ye love me,*
*keep my commandments."*

1 LORD, in humble, sweet submission,
   Here we meet to follow Thee,
Trusting in Thy great salvation,
   Which alone can make us free.

2 Nought have we to claim as merit;
   All the duties we can do
Can no crown of life inherit;
   All the praise to Thee is due.

3 Yet we come in Christian duty,
   Down beneath the wave to go;
O the bliss! the heavenly beauty!
   Christ the Lord was buried so.

4 Come, ye children of the kingdom,
   Follow Him beneath the wave;
Rise, and show His resurrection,
   And proclaim His power to save.

5 Is there here a weeping Mary,
   Waiting near the Saviour's tomb,
Heavy-laden, sick, and weary,
   Crying, "Oh! that I could come"?

6 Welcome, all ye friends of Jesus,
   Welcome *to* His church below;

Venture wholly on the Saviour;
   Come, and with His people go.

*Robert T. Daniel,* [1828*, alt.*]

   **6.2:** *in*  **Ed:** Sedgwick dated the hymn 1850 because he found it in Basil Manly's *Baptist Psalmody*, including this minor alteration.

# 930   8.7.8.7.
*Buried with Christ in baptism.*

1 JESUS, mighty King *in* Zion!
   Thou alone our guide shall be;
Thy commission we rely on;
   We would follow none but Thee.

2 As an emblem of *Thy* passion
   And *Thy* victory o'er the grave,
*We who* know *Thy* great salvation
   *Are baptiz'd beneath the* wave.

3 Fearless of the world's despising,
   We the ancient path pursue,
Buried with our Lord, *arising*
   To a life divinely new.

*John Fellows,* 1773
[*alt. John Rippon,* 1787, 1844]

   **1.1:** *of*  **2.1:** *His*  **2.2:** *His*  **2.3:** *They that / His*
   **2.4:** *Plunge beneath the sacred*  **3.3:** *and rising*

# 931   8.7.8.7.4.7.
*Taking up the cross.*

1 HAST Thou said, exalted Jesus,
   Take Thy cross and follow me?
Shall the word with terror seize us?
   Shall we from the burden flee?
      Lord, I'll take it,
   And rejoicing, follow Thee.

2 While this liquid tomb surveying,
   Emblem of my Saviour's grave,
Shall I shun its brink, betraying
   Feelings worthy of a slave?
      No! I'll enter;
   Jesus enter'd Jordan's wave!

3 Sweet the sign that thus reminds me,
   Saviour, of Thy love *to* me;

Sweeter still the love that binds me
   In its deathless *bond* to Thee.
      Oh, what pleasure,
      Buried with my Lord to be!

4 Should it rend some fond connection,
   Should I suffer shame or loss,
Yet the fragrant, blest reflection,
   I have been where Jesus was,
      Will revive me
      When I faint beneath the cross.

5 Fellowship with Him possessing,
   Let me die to all around,
So I rise t' enjoy the blessing
   Kept for those in Jesus found,
      When th' archangel
      Wakes the *sleeper* under ground.

6 Then baptized in love and glory,
   Lamb of God, Thy praise I'll sing;
Loudly with th' immortal story
   All the harps of heaven shall ring.
      Saints and seraphs
      Sound it loud from every string.

*John Eustace Giles*, 1837

**3.2:** *for*   **3.4:** *bonds*   **5.6:** *sleepers*
**Ed:** Written in 1830 for his congregation at
Salters' Hall, London, but not known to have
been published before 1837. These minor
changes appeared in the Comprehensive Ed.
of Rippon's *Selection* (1844), and may or may
not have been supplied by Giles himself.

# 932 S.M.
*Following Jesus.*

1 SAVIOUR, Thy law we love,
   Thy pure example bless,
And with a firm, unwavering zeal,
   Would in Thy footsteps press.

2 Not to the fiery pains
   By which the martyrs bled,
Not to the scourge, the thorn, the cross,
   Our favour'd feet are led.

3 But at this peaceful tide,
   Assembled in thy fear,

The homage of obedient hearts
   We humbly offer here.

*Lydia Huntley Sigourney*, [1832]

# 933 S.M.
*A doxology for Baptism.*

1 FATHER of all, to Thee
   Let endless praises rise,
Who for such rebel worms as we
   Salvation didst devise.

2 Incarnate Deity,
   Let all the ransom'd race
Render in thanks their lives to Thee
   For Thy redeeming grace.

3 Spirit of holiness,
   *Oh let us all* adore
Thy sacred energy, and bless
   Thine heart-renewing power.

4 Baptized into Thy name,
   Almighty One in Three,
Thy grace and goodness we'll proclaim
   Through all eternity.

1,4 John Rippon's *Selection*, 1827
2,3 *Charles Wesley*, 1747 [*alt. Rippon*]

   **3.2:** *Let all thy saints*   **Ed:** The stanzas by
   Wesley are from his hymn, "Father, in whom
   we live."

# 934 S.M.
*Death, burial, and resurrection.*

1 HERE, O ye faithful, see
   Your Lord baptized in woe,
Immersed in seas of agony,
   Which all His soul o'erflow.

2 Here we behold the grave
   Which held our buried Head;
We claim a burial in the wave
   Because with Jesus dead.

3 Here, too, we see Him rise
   And live no more to die;

And one with Him by sacred ties
 We rise to live on high.

*Charles H. Spurgeon*, 1866

# 935 C.M.
*Burial with Christ.*

1 SAVIOUR! we seek the watery tomb,
  Illumed by love divine;
 Far from the deep, tremendous gloom
  Of that which was once Thine.

2 Down to the hallowed grave we go,
  Obedient to Thy Word;

'Tis thus the world around shall know
 We're buried with the Lord.

3 'Tis thus we bid its pomps adieu
  And boldly venture in;
 O may we rise to live anew
  And only die to sin.

*Maria Grace Saffery*, 1828

> **Ed:** Julian's *Dictionary*, p. 1588, noted that this hymn "is attributed to 'Maria G. Saffery' on the authority of Mr. W.H.J. Page of Calne" in Sedgwick's manuscripts. Her authorship is also affirmed in the *Dictionary of National Biography* (1897), vol. 50, p. 114.

---

# The Lord's Supper

# 936 C.M.
*This do in remembrance of me.*

1 ACCORDING to Thy gracious Word,
  In meek humility,
 This will I do, my dying Lord;
  I will remember Thee.

2 Thy body, broken for my sake,
  My bread from heaven shall be;
 Thy testamental cup I take,
  And thus remember Thee.

3 Gethsemane, can I forget?
  Or there Thy conflict see,
 Thine agony and bloody sweat,
  And not remember Thee?

4 When to the cross I turn mine eyes
  And rest on Calvary,
 O Lamb of God, my sacrifice!
  I must remember Thee.

5 Remember Thee, and all Thy pains,
  And all Thy love to me;

Yea, while a breath, a pulse remains,
 Will I remember Thee.

6 And when these failing lips grow dumb,
  And mind and memory flee,
 When Thou shalt in Thy kingdom come,
  Jesus, remember me.

*James Montgomery*, 1825

# 937 S.M.
*The sorrows of our Lord.*

1   WE'LL praise our risen Lord
   While at His feast we sit,
 His griefs a hallow'd theme afford
   For sweetest music fit.

2   Such torments He endur'd
   As none e'er felt before,
 That joy and bliss might be secur'd
   To us forever more.

3   Hurried from bar to bar,
   With blows and scoffs abus'd,

Revil'd by Herod's men of war,
    With Pilate's scourges bruis'd.

4    His sweet and reverend face
      With spittle all profan'd;
That visage, full of heav'nly grace,
    With His own blood distain'd.

5    Stretch'd on the cruel tree,
      He bled, and groan'd, and cried,
And in a mortal agony,
    Languish'd awhile and died.

6    Then *up* to heav'n *He rose*,
      That we might thither go,
Where love and praises have no end,
    Where joys no changes know.

[1 *Charles H. Spurgeon*, 1866]
2-6 *Joseph Stennett*, [1697, *rev.* 1705]
*alt. C.H.S.*

> **6.1:** *did / ascend*   **Ed:** Stennett's hymn originally
> began "Immortal praise be given."

# 938   C.M.
*Jesu's love.*

1  GRACIOUS Redeemer, how divine,
    How wondrous is Thy love!
The subject of th' eternal songs
    Of *blood-wash'd hosts* above.

2  Join *all your* sacred harmony,
    Ye saints on earth below,
To praise Immanuel, from whose name
    All fragrant odours flow.

3  He left His crown, He left His throne
    By His great Father's side,
*He wore the thorn, He bore the* cross,
    Was scourged and crucified.

4  Behold how every wound of His
    A precious balm distills,
Which heals the scars that sin had made,
    *And cures all mortal ills.*

5  Those wounds are mouths that
      preach His grace;

The *ensigns of His* love;
    The seals of our expected bliss
      In paradise above.

6  We see Thee at Thy table, Lord,
      By faith, with great delight;
O how refin'd those joys will be
      When faith is turn'd to sight!

*Joseph Stennett*, [1697, *rev.* 1705], *alt. C.H.S.*

> **1.4:** *blessed spirits*   **2.1:** *sacred*
> **3.3:** *Wore thorns, sustain'd a heavy*
> **4.4:** *With joy the sinner fills.*   **5.2:** *characters of*
> **EE:** "Why should our exalted Lord appear in His
> sounds in glory? The wounds of Jesus are His
> glories, His jewels, His sacred ornaments. . . .
> Ah! if Christ thus loves to retain the thought
> of His sufferings for His people, how precious
> should His wounds be to us!" (Apr. 23).

# 939   L.M.
*Jesu's presence delightful.*

1  AMIDST us our Belovèd stands
    And bids us view His piercèd hands,
    Points to His wounded feet and side,
    Blest emblems of the Crucified.

2  What food luxurious loads the board,
    When at His table sits the Lord!
    The wine how rich, the bread how sweet,
    When Jesus deigns the guests to meet!

3  If now with eyes defiled and dim,
    We see the signs but see not Him,
    Oh may His love the scales displace,
    And bid us see Him face to face!

4  Our former transports we recount,
    When with Him in the holy mount,
    These cause our souls to thirst anew,
    His marr'd but lovely face to view.

5  Thou glorious Bridegroom of our hearts,
    Thy present smile a heaven imparts;
    Oh lift the veil, if veil there be;
    Let every saint Thy beauties see.

*Charles H. Spurgeon*, 1866

# 940
7.7.7.7.7.7.
*Heavenly bread and wine.*

1 BREAD of heav'n! on Thee I feed,
For Thy flesh is meat indeed;
Ever may my soul be fed
With this true and living bread;
Day by day with strength supplied,
Through the life of Him who died.

2 Vine of heav'n! Thy blood supplies
This blest cup of sacrifice;
'Tis Thy wounds my healing give;
To Thy cross I look and live.
Thou my life! Oh let me be
Rooted, grafted, built on Thee.

*Josiah Conder, 1824*

# 941
L.M.
*Enjoyment of Christ.*

1 FAR from my thoughts, vain world, be gone;
Let my religious hours alone;
Fain would my eyes my Saviour see;
I wait a visit, Lord, from Thee.

2 My heart grows warm with holy fire
And kindles with a pure desire;
Come, my dear Jesus, from above,
And feed my soul with heavenly love.

3 Blest Jesus, what delicious fare!
How sweet Thy entertainmnets are!
Never did angels taste above
Redeeming grace and dying love.

4 Hail, great Immanuel, all divine;
In Thee Thy Father's glories shine;
Thou brightest, sweetest, fairest One
That eyes have seen or angels known.

*Isaac Watts, [1707]*

**TD:** "Gospel provisions deserve every praise that
we can heap upon them; they are free, full,
and pre-eminent; they are of God's preparing,
sending, and bestowing. He is well fed whom
God feeds; heaven's meat is nourishing and
plentiful. If we have ever fed upon Jesus we
have tasted better than angels' food, for 'Never

did angels taste above redeeming grace and
dying love'" (Ps. 78; vol. 3, p. 440).

# 942
C.M.
*Christ's dying love.*

1 HOW condescending and how kind
Was God's eternal Son?
Our misery reach'd His heavenly mind,
And pity brought Him down.

2 When justice, by our sins provoked,
Drew forth its dreadful sword,
He gave His soul up to the stroke
Without a murmuring word.

3 He sunk beneath our heavy woes
To raise us to His throne;
There's ne'er a gift His hand bestows
But cost His heart a groan.

4 This was compassion like a God,
That when the Saviour knew
The price of pardon was His blood,
His pity ne'er withdrew.

5 Now though He reigns exalted high,
His love is still as great;
Well He remembers Calvary,
Nor lets His saints forget.

6 Here let our hearts begin to melt,
While we His death record,
And with our joy for pardon'd guilt,
Mourn that we pierc'd the Lord.

*Isaac Watts, [1707, rev. 1709]*

# 943
C.M.
*We are one bread, one body.*

1 HOW happy are Thy servants, Lord,
Who thus remember Thee!
What tongue can tell our sweet accord,
Our perfect harmony!

2 Who Thy mysterious supper share,
Here at Thy table fed;
Many, and yet but one we are,
One undivided bread.

3 One with the living Bread divine
    Which now by faith we eat,
Our hearts, and minds, and spirits join,
    And all in Jesus meet.

4 So dear the tie where souls agree
    In Jesu's dying love,
Then only can it closer be
    When all are join'd above.

*Charles Wesley,* 1745

# 944 C.M.
*The feast and the guests.*

1 HOW sweet and awful is the place,
    With Christ within the doors,
While everlasting love displays
    The choicest of her stores.

2 While all our hearts and all our songs
    Join to admire the feast,
Each of us cry with thankful tongues,
    "Lord, why was I a guest?

3 "Why was I made to hear Thy voice
    And enter while there's room,
When thousands make a wretched choice,
    And rather starve than come?"

4 'Twas the same love that spread the feast,
    That sweetly forc'd us in,
Else we had still refus'd to taste,
    And perish'd in our sin.

5 Pity the nations, O our God,
    Constrain the earth to come;
Send Thy victorious Word abroad,
    And bring the strangers home.

6 We long to see Thy churches full,
    That all the chosen race
May with one voice, and heart, and soul,
    Sing Thy redeming grace.

*Isaac Watts,* [1707]

# 945 C.M.
*Divine love remembered.*

1 IF human kindness meets return
    And owns the grateful tie,
If tender thoughts "within us burn,"
    When earthly friends are nigh,

2 Oh, shall not warmer accents tell
    The gratitude we owe
To Him who died our fears to quell,
    Our more than orphan woe!

3 While yet His anguished soul surveyed
    Those pangs He would not flee,
What love His latest words displayed—
    "Meet and remember me!"

4 Remember Thee! Thy death! Thy shame!
    Our hearts' sad load to bear!
Oh! memory, leave no other name
    But His recorded there!

*Gerard T. Noel,* [1810, *rev.* 1826]

# 946 C.M.
*The feast.*

1 IN mem'ry of *the Saviour's* love,
    *We* keep the *sacred* feast,
Where ev'ry *humble,* contrite heart
    Is made a welcome guest.

2 By *faith we* take the bread of life,
    With which *our* souls are fed,
And cup, in token of *His* blood
    *That was* for *sinners* shed.

3 *Under His banner thus we sing*
    The wonders of *His* love,
And thus anticipate, by faith,
    *The heav'nly feast* above.

*Thomas Cotterill,* [1805]
[*alt.*] *Richard Whittingham,* 1835

    **1.1:** *His dying*   **1.2:** *We'll / joyful*   **1.3:** *broken*
    **2.1:** *faith, come,*   **2.2:** *your*   **2.3:** *my*
    **2.4:** *Which is / many*
    **3.1:** *Lord! we accept Thy call; and muse*
    **3.2:** *Thy*   **3.4:** *Eternal joys*

**Ed:** Taken from Cotterill's longer hymn,
"Bless'd with the presence of their God."

## 947 L.M.
*Feeding in green pastures.*

1 THOU whom my soul admires above,
All earthly joy and earthly love,
Tell me, dear Shepherd, let me know,
Where doth Thy *choicest* pasture grow?

2 Where is the shadow of that rock
That from the sun defends Thy flock?
Fain would I feed among Thy sheep,
Among them rest, among them sleep.

3 The footsteps of Thy flock I see;
Thy sweetest pastures here they be;
A wondrous feast *of* love *appears*,
Bought with Thy wounds, and groans,
    and tears.

4 His dearest flesh He makes my *bread;*
*For wine His richest blood is shed;*
Here to these hills my soul will come,
Till my Belovèd lead me home.

*Isaac Watts,* [1707, *alt. C.H.S.*]

   **1.4:** *sweetest* **3.3:** *Thy / prepares* **4.1:** *food*
   **4.2:** *And bids me drink His richest blood;*

## 948 L.M.
*Christ the King at His table.*

1 LET Him embrace my soul and prove
Mine interest in His heavenly love;
The voice that tells me, "Thou art mine,"
Exceeds the blessings of the vine.

2 Jesus, allure me by Thy charms;
My soul shall fly into Thine arms!
Our wandering feet Thy favours bring
To the fair chambers of the King.

3 Though in ourselves deform'd we are,
And black as Kedar's tents appear,
Yet when we put Thy beauties on,
Fair as the courts of Solomon.

4 While at His table sits the King,
He loves to see us smile and sing;
Our graces are our best perfume,
And breathe like spikenard round the room.

5 As myrrh new bleeding from the tree,
Such is a dying Christ to me;
And while He makes my soul His guest,
My bosom, Lord, shall be Thy rest.

6 No beams of cedar or of fir
Can with Thy courts on earth compare;
And here we wait, until Thy love
Raise us to nobler seats above.

*Isaac Watts,* [1707]

## 949 C.M.
*Grace admired.*

1 LORD, at Thy table I behold
   The wonders of Thy grace,
But most of all admire that I
   Should find a welcome place:

2 I that am all defil'd with sin,
   A rebel to my God;
I that have crucified His Son
   And trampled on His blood.

3 What strange surprising grace is this,
   That such a soul has room!
My Saviour takes me by the hand;
   My Jesus bids me come.

4 Had I ten thousand hearts, dear Lord,
   I'd give them all to Thee;
Had I ten thousand tongues, they all
   Should join in harmony.

*Samuel Stennett,* [1782]

## 950 L.M.
*Delight in communion with Jesus.*

1 LORD, what a heaven of saving grace
Shines through the beauties of Thy face
And lights our passions to a flame!
Lord, how we love Thy charming name!

2 When I can say, "My God is mine,"
  When I can feel Thy glories shine,
  I tread the world beneath my feet,
  And all that earth calls good or great.

3 While such a scene of sacred joys
  Our raptur'd eyes and souls employs,
  Here we could sit and gaze away
  A long, an everlasting day.

4 Well, we shall quickly pass the night
  To the fair coasts of perfect light;

Then shall our joyful senses rove
O'er the dear object of our love.

5 There shall we drink full draughts of bliss
  And pluck new life from heav'nly trees,
  Yet now and then, dear Lord, bestow
  A drop of heaven on worms below.

6 Send comforts down from Thy right hand
  While we pass through this barren land,
  And in Thy temple let us see
  A glimpse of love, a glimpse of Thee.

*Isaac Watts*, [1707]

# Revivals and Missions

## 951
L.M.
*The presence of God desired.*

1 O THOU the hope of Israel's host,
  Their strength, their helper,
    and their boast,
  How oft their Saviour hast Thou been
  In times of trouble and of sin!

2 *And have not we beheld* Thy face?
  *Thy visits crown'd the means of* grace;
  O come *again, indulgent* Lord,
  With all the joy Thy smiles afford.

3 Enter our hearts, Redeemer blest;
  Enter, thou ever-honour'd Guest;
  *Enter, and make our hearts Thine own,*
  *Thy house, Thy temple, and Thy throne.*

4 And stay, not only for a night,
  To bless us with a transient sight,
  But with us dwell, through time, and then
  In heaven forever more. Amen.

[1,4 John Rippon's *Selection*, 1827]
  2,3 *Philip Doddridge*, 1755 [*alt. Rippon*]

  **2.1:** *Reveal the lustre of*

**2.2:** *And make us feel Thy vital*
**2.3:** *Thyself, most gracious*
**3.3-4:** *Not for one transient hour alone,*
    *But there to fix thy lasting throne.*
**Ed:** Sts. 2-3 are from Doddridge's "Come, our
  indulgent Saviour, come." Sedgwick originally
  credited this hymn to Rippon's *Selection*, 1829,
  but changed the attribution to "Doddridge and
  Gibbons, 1755–1784" in the 1873 ed. of *OOHB*.
  Julian's *Dictionary*, p. 851, repeated the attribution to Doddridge and Gibbons with more
  explanation, including the appearance in Rippon's 27th ed. The 1784 ed. of Gibbon's hymnal
  available to this editor does not include this
  text, nor could it be located in any hymnal
  prior to Rippon's ed., so without further evidence, the additional stanzas and alterations
  must be ascribed to Rippon's *Selection*.

## 952
L.M.
*Zion visited in grace.*

1 TRIUMPHANT Zion, lift thy head
  From dust, and darkness, and the dead;
  Though humbled long, awake at length,
  And gird thee with thy Saviour's strength.

2 Put all thy beauteous garments on,
  And let thy various charms be known;
  The world thy glories shall confess,
  Deck'd in the robes of righteousness.

3 No more shall foes unclean invade
  And fill thy hallow'd walls with dread;
  No more shall hell's insulting host
  Their vict'ry and thy sorrows boast.

4 God from on high thy groans will hear;
  His hand thy ruins shall repair;
  Rear'd and adorn'd by love divine,
  Thy tow'rs and battlements shall shine.

*Philip Doddridge*, 1755

# 953 C.M.
*The church awakened.*

1 NOW let the slumb'ring church awake
    And shine in bright array;
  Thy chains, O captive daughter, break,
    And cast thy bonds away.

2 Long hast thou lain in dust supine,
    Insulted by thy foes;
  "Where is," they cried, "that God of thine,
    And who regards thy woes?"

3 Thy God incarnate, on His hands
    Beholds thy name engrav'd;
  Still unrevok'd His promise stands,
    And Zion shall be sav'd.

4 He did but wait the fittest time
    His mercy to display,
  And now He rides on clouds sublime,
    And brings the promis'd day.

5 Thy God shall soon for thee appear
    And end thy mourning days;
  Salvation's walls around thee rear
    And fill thy gates with praise.

*John Ryland*, 1798 [*rev.* 1828]

# 954 7.7.7.7. Double
*Great events from small beginnings.*

1 SEE how great a flame aspires,
  Kindled by a spark of grace!
  Jesu's love the nations fires,
  Sets the kingdoms on a blaze;
  To bring fire on earth He came,
  Kindled in some hearts it is;
  O that all might catch the flame,
  All partake the glorious bliss!

2 When He first the work begun,
  Small and feeble was His day;
  Now the word doth swiftly run;
  Now it wins its widening way;
  More and more it spreads and grows,
  Ever mighty to prevail;
  Sin's strongholds it now o'erthrows,
  Shakes the trembling gates of hell.

3 Sons of God, your Saviour praise;
  He the door hath open'd wide;
  He hath giv'n the word of grace;
  Jesu's word is glorified;
  Jesus, mighty to redeem,
  He alone the work hath wrought;
  Worthy is the work of Him,
  Him who spake a world from nought.

4 Saw ye not the cloud arise,
  Little as a human hand?
  Now it spreads along the skies,
  Hangs o'er all the thirsty land!
  Lo! the promise of a shower
  Drops already from above;
  But the Lord will shortly pour
  All the Spirit of His love.

*Charles Wesley*, 1749

# 955 8.7.8.7.4.7.
*"There shall be showers of blessing."*

1 "SHOWERS of blessing," gracious promise,
    From the God who rules on high;
  From the everlasting Father,
    He will not, cannot lie.
      Showers of blessing,
    He has promised from the sky.

2 "Showers of blessing," joyful showers,
　　Making every heart rejoice;
Come, ye saints, and plead the promise,
　　Raise in faith the suppliant voice;
　　　Showers of blessing,
　　Oh, let nothing less suffice!

*Albert Midlane*, [1862]

# 956 L.M.
*"Awake, O arm of the Lord!"*

1 ARM of the Lord, awake, awake;
Thy power unconquerable take;
Thy strength put on, assert Thy might,
And triumph in the dreadful fight.

2 Why dost Thou tarry, mighty Lord?
Why slumbers in its sheath Thy sword?
Oh, rouse Thee, for Thine honour's sake;
Arm of the Lord, awake, awake!

3 Behold, what numbers still withstand
Thy sov'reign rule and just command,
Reject Thy grace, Thy threats despise,
And hurl defiance at the skies.

4 Haste then, but come not to destroy;
Mercy is Thine, Thy crown, Thy joy;
Their hatred quell, their pride remove,
But melt with grace, subdue with love.

5 Why dost Thou from *the* conquest stay?
Why do Thy chariot wheels delay?
*Lift up Thyself; hell's kingdom shake;*
Arm of the Lord, awake, awake!

*Henry March*, 1839 [*alt. C.H.S.*]

**5.1:** *Thy*　**5.3:** *Will God, the Lord, His cause
forsake?*　**Ed:** The change at 5.3 is actually a
transplanted line from another stanza in the
hymn that is not given here.
**TD:** "Wherefore this inaction, this indifference
for Thine own honour and Thy people's safety? How bold is the suppliant! Does He err?
Nay, verily, we who are so chill, and distant,
and listless in prayer are the erring ones. . . . It
is fit that we should enquire why the work of
grace goes on so slowly, and the enemy has so
much power over men: the inquiry may sug-

gest practical reflections of unbounded value"
(Ps. 74:11, vol. 3, p. 371).

# 957 S.M.
*Revival sought.*

1 REVIVE Thy work, O Lord;
　　Thy mighty arm make bare;
Speak with the voice that wakes the dead,
　　And make Thy people hear.

2 Revive Thy work, O Lord;
　　Disturb this sleep of death;
Quicken the smouldering embers now
　　By Thine almighty breath.

3 Revive Thy work, O Lord;
　　Create soul-thirst for Thee;
And hungering for the bread of life,
　　O may our spirits be.

4 Revive Thy work, O Lord;
　　Exalt Thy precious name,
And by the Holy Ghost, our love
　　For Thee and Thine inflame.

5 Revive Thy work, O Lord,
　　And give refreshing showers;
The glory shall be all Thine own;
　　The blessing, Lord, be ours.

*Albert Midlane*, [1858]

# 958 8.7.8.7.
*Give reviving.*

1 FATHER, for Thy promised blessing,
　　Still we plead before Thy throne;
For the times of sweet refreshing,
　　Which can come from Thee alone.

2 Blessèd earnests Thou hast given,
　　But in these we would not rest;
Blessings still with Thee are hidden;
　　Pour them forth and make us blest!

3 Prayer ascendeth to Thee ever;
　　Answer, Father, answer prayer!
Bless, O bless each weak endeavour,
　　Blood-bought pardon to declare!

4 Wake Thy slumbering children, wake them,
　　Bid them to Thy harvest go;
　Blessings, O our Father, make them;
　　Round their steps let blessings flow.

5 Give reviving—give refreshing—
　　Give the looked-for Jubilee;
　To Thyself may crowds be pressing,
　　Bringing glory unto Thee.

6 Let no hamlet be forgotten,
　　Let Thy showers on all descend,
　That in one loud blessèd anthem,
　　Myriads may in triumph blend.

*Albert Midlane*, [1860]

# 959　8.7.8.7.4.7.
*Prayer for a revival.*

1 SAVIOUR, visit Thy plantation;
　　Grant us, Lord, a gracious rain!
　All will come to desolation,
　　Unless Thou return again;
　　　Lord, revive us;
　　All our help must come from Thee.

2 Keep no longer at a distance;
　　Shine upon us from on high,
　Lest, for want of Thine assistance,
　　Ev'ry plant should droop and die.
　　　Lord, revive us;
　　All our help must come from Thee.

3 Surely, once Thy garden flourish'd,
　　Ev'ry part look'd gay and green;
　Then Thy Word our spirits nourish'd;
　　Happy seasons we have seen!
　　　Lord, revive us;
　　All our help must come from Thee.

4 But a drought has since succeeded,
　　And a sad decline we see;
　Lord, Thy help is greatly needed;
　　Help can only come from Thee.
　　　Lord, revive us;
　　All our help must come from Thee.

5 Dearest Saviour, hasten hither;
　　Thou canst make them bloom again;

Oh permit them not to wither;
　　Let not all our hopes be vain!
　　　Lord, revive us;
　　All our help must come from Thee.

6 Let our mutual love be fervent;
　　Make us prevalent in pray'rs;
　Let each one esteem'd Thy servant
　　Shun the world's bewitching snares.
　　　Lord, revive us;
　　All our help must come from Thee.

7 Break the tempter's fatal power,
　　Turn the stony heart to flesh,
　And begin, from this good hour,
　　To revive Thy work afresh.
　　　Lord, revive us;
　　All our help must come from Thee.

*John Newton*, 1779
alt. *John Ryland*, 1787

> **Ed:** The first four lines of each stanza are by
> Newton, the last two by Ryland. Newton's
> original text was grouped in sets of eight lines.

# 960　C.M.
*Prayer for quickening power.*

1 O THOU, our Head, enthroned on high,
　　By whom Thy members live!
　Wilt Thou not hear our fervent cry,
　　The holy unction give?

2 Arise, O Lord! send forth Thy Word;
　　Thy faithful heralds call;
　And while the gospel trump is heard,
　　Let Satan's bulwarks fall.

3 Breathe forth, O wind, and to new birth
　　Quicken the bones of death;
　Regenerate this wither'd earth;
　　Give to the dying breath.

*Josiah Conder*, 1856

# 961　L.M.
*Jesus, manifest Thy power.*

1 O JESUS, manifest Thy grace;
　　Scatter Thy mighty darts abroad;

Constrain the unbelieving race
To fall before a wounded God.

2 Thy hands, Thy side, Thy feet were pierc'd,
The most unholy to restore;
Thy blood was shed to heal the worst
And save the poorest of the poor.

3 Then let them taste Thy saving grace,
Be cleans'd and glorified by Thee,
And in the sacrifice of praise
Employ a blest eternity.

*Augustus Toplady*, 1759

**Ed:** Taken from the longer hymn,
"My yielding heart dissolves as wax."

# 962 L.M.
*Awake, all-conquering arm.*

1 AWAKE, all-conquering arm, awake,
And *Satan's mighty* empire shake;
Assert the honours of Thy throne
And *make* this ruin'd world Thine own.

2 Thine all-successful pow'r display;
*Convert* a nation in a day,
*Until the universe shall be*
*But one great temple, Lord, for Thee.*

*Philip Doddridge*, 1755
[*alt. Stow & Smith*, 1843]

**1.2:** *hell's extensive*   **1.4:** *call*   **2.2:** *Produce*
**2.3-4:** *For at Thy Word this barren earth*
*Shall travail with a gen'ral birth.*
**Ed:** From the longer hymn, "Behold, with pleasing extacy," dated 30 Oct. 1737 in Doddridge's
MSS. The last two lines in the altered version,
2.3-4, are transplanted from a hymn by William
Shrubsole Jr., "Bright as the sun's meridian
blaze," first published in *The Evangelical Magazine*, Sept. 1795.

# 963 C.M.
*God invoked for His church.*

1 AWAKE, awake! Thou mighty arm,
Which has such wonders wrought,

Which captive Israel freed from harm
And out of Egypt brought.

2 Art Thou not it which Rahab slew,
And crush'd the dragon's head?
Constrain'd by Thee, the waves withdrew
From their accustomed bed.

3 Again Thy wonted prowess show,
Be Thou made bare again,
And let Thine adversaries know
That they resist in vain.

*Benjamin Beddome*, [1800]

# 964 L.M.
*Awake, O arm of the Lord.*

1 ARM of the Lord! Awake! Awake!
Put on Thy strength, the nations shake,
And let the world, adoring, see
Triumphs of mercy wrought by Thee.

2 Say to the heathen from Thy throne,
"I am Jehovah, God alone!"
Thy voice their idols shall confound
And cast their altars to the ground.

3 No more let human blood be spilt,
Vain sacrifice for human guilt,
But to each conscience be applied
The blood that flow'd from Jesus' side.

4 Arm of the Lord, Thy power extend;
Let *Muhammed's* imposture end;
Break papal superstition's chain,
And the proud scoffer's rage restrain.

5 Let Zion's time of favour come;
Oh bring the tribes of Israel home,
And let our wondering eyes behold
Gentiles and Jews in Jesus' fold.

6 Almighty God! Thy grace proclaim
In every clime of every name;
Let adverse powers before Thee fall,
And crown the Saviour, Lord of all.

*William Shrubsole Jr.*, 1795

**4.2:** Spelled *Mahomet's* in OOHB. Many sources
report that the hymn was published in the

London Missonary Society's *Missionary Hymns* (1795); it was credited that way in John Dobell's *New Selection* (1806). One copy of the *Missionary Hymns* printed ca. 1801 does not contain this hymn; an alternate copy printed before 1806 could not be secured.

# 965
C.M.
*The church awakened.*

1 DAUGHTER of Zion, from the dust
    Exalt thy fallen head;
Again in thy Redeemer trust;
    He calls thee from the dead.

2 Awake, awake, put on thy strength,
    Thy beautiful array;
The day of freedom dawns at length,
    The Lord's appointed day.

3 Rebuild thy walls, thy bounds enlarge,
    And send thy heralds forth;
Say to the south, "Give up thy charge,
    And keep not back, O north!"

4 They come, they come; thine exiled bands,
    Where'er they rest or roam,
Have heard thy voice in distant lands
    And hasten to their home.

5 Thus, though the universe shall burn
    And God His works destroy,
With songs Thy ransom'd shall return,
    And everlasting joy.

*James Montgomery,* [1822, *rev.* 1825]

# 966
6.6.4.6.6.6.4.
*"Preach the gospel to every creature."*

1 SOUND, sound the truth abroad;
Bear ye the Word of God
    Through the wide world;
Tell what our Lord has done;
Tell how the day is won,
And from his lofty throne
    Satan is hurl'd.

2 Speed on the wings of love,
Jesus, who reigns above

Bids us to fly;
They who His message bear
Should neither doubt nor fear;
He will their Friend appear;
    He will be nigh.

3 When on the mighty deep,
He will their spirits keep,
    Stay'd on His Word;
When in a foreign land,
No other friend at hand,
Jesus will by them stand,
    Jesus their Lord.

4 Ye who, forsaking all,
At your lov'd Master's call,
    Comfort's resign;
Soon will your work be done;
Soon will the prize be won;
Brighter than yonder sun,
    Then shall ye shine.

*Thomas Kelly,* 1820

# 967
8.7.8.7.4.7.
*"Cry aloud, spare not."*

1 MEN of God, go take your stations;
    Darkness reigns throughout the earth;
Go proclaim among the nations
    Joyful news of heav'nly birth;
        Bear the tidings
    Of the Saviour's matchless worth.

2 Of His gospel not ashamèd,
    As "the power of God to save,"
Go, where Christ was never namèd,
    Publish freedom to the slave!
        Blessèd freedom!
    Such as Zion's children have.

3 What though earth and hell united
    Should oppose the Saviour's plan?
Plead His cause, nor be affrighted;
    Fear ye not the face of man;
        Vain their tumult;
    Hurt His work they never can.

4 When expos'd to fearful dangers,
　　Jesus will His own defend;
　Borne afar, midst foes and strangers,
　　Jesus will appear your Friend,
　　　And His presence
　Shall be with you to the end.

*Thomas Kelly*, 1806

# 968 L.M.
*Prayer to the Captain of the host.*

1 CAPTAIN of Thine enlisted host,
　Display Thy glorious banner high;
　*The summons send* from coast to coast,
　And call a num'rous army nigh.

2 A solemn jubilee proclaim;
　Proclaim the great sabbatic day;
　*Assert the glories of Thy name;*
　Spoil Satan of his wish'd-for prey.

3 Bid, bid Thy heralds *publish loud*
　*The peaceful blessings of Thy reign,*
　And when they speak of *sprinkled* blood,
　The myst'ry to the heart explain.

4 Chase the usurper from his throne;
　*Oh! chase him to his destined hell;*
　Stout-hearted sinners overcome,
　And *glorious* in Thy temple dwell.

5 Fight for Thyself, O Jesus, fight;
　The trevail of Thy soul regain;
　*To* each blind soul *make* darkness light;
　To all *let* crooked paths *be* plain.

*Christopher Batty*, 1757, *alt.*

> **1.3:** *Send the white horse*　**2.3:** *Let the year of
> release be seen;*　**3.1:** *cry aloud*
> **3.2:** *Aloud, thy honour to proclaim;*　**3.3:** *sprinkling*　**4.2:** *On each a show'r of grace
> distill;*　**4.4:** *peaceful*　**5.3:** *'Fore / makes*
> **5.4:** *make / quite*　**Ed:** The alterations in sts. 1-3
> are from Countess of Huntingdon's *Collection*,
> 3rd ed. (1770), and possibly as early as her
> first collection from 1764, which could not be
> located for verification. The alterations in sts.
> 4-5 are by Spurgeon.

# 969 7.6.7.6. Double
*The call of the heathen for help.*

1 FROM Greenland's icy mountains,
　From India's coral strand,
　Where Afric's sunny fountains
　Roll down their golden sand;
　From many an ancient river,
　From many a palmy plain,
　They call us to deliver
　Their land from error's chain.

2 What though the spicy breezes
　Blow soft o'er *Ceylon's* isle,
　Though every prospect pleases,
　And only man is vile,
　In vain with lavish kindness
　The gifts of God are strewn;
　The heathen, in his blindness,
　Bows down to wood and stone.

3 *Can* we, whose souls are lighted
　With wisdom from on high,
　*Can* we, to men benighted,
　The lamp of life deny?
　Salvation! oh salvation!
　The joyful sound proclaim,
　Till each remotest nation
　Has learnt Messiah's name!

4 Waft, waft, ye winds, His story,
　And you, ye waters, roll,
　Till, like a sea of glory,
　It spreads from pole to pole,
　Till o'er our ransom'd nature,
　The Lamb for sinners slain,
　Redeemer, King, Creator,
　In bliss returns to reign.

*Reginald Heber*, 1823 [*rev.* 1827]

> **2.2:** *Java's* (1827)　**3.1:** *Shall* (1823)
> **3.3:** *Shall* (1823)
> **TD:** "'Let the sinners be consumed out of the
> earth, and let the wicked be no more.' They are
> the only blot upon creation. 'Every prospect
> pleases, and only man is vile'" (Ps. 104:35; vol.
> 5, p. 13).

# 970

S.M.
*Arise, O God!*

1 O LORD our God, arise;
  The cause of Truth maintain,
And wide o'er all the peopled world
  Extend her blessèd reign.

2 Thou Prince of Life, arise,
  Nor let Thy glory cease;
Far spread the conquests of Thy grace,
  And bless the earth with peace!

3 Thou Holy Ghost, arise;
  Expand Thy quick'ning wing,
And o'er a dark and ruin'd world
  Let light and order spring.

4 All on the earth arise;
  To God the Saviour sing;
From shore to shore, from earth to heav'n,
  Let echoing anthems ring!

*Ralph Wardlaw,* [1800, *rev.* 1803]

# 971

8.7.8.7.4.7.
*Influences of the Spirit.*

1 WHO but Thou, Almighty Spirit,
  Can the heathen world reclaim?
Men may preach, but till Thou favour,
  Heathens will be still the same;
    Mighty Spirit!
  Witness to the Saviour's name.

2 Thou hast promis'd by the prophets
  Glorious light in latter days;
Come and bless bewilder'd nations,
  Change our pray'rs and tears to praise;
    Pormis'd Spirit!
  Round the world diffuse Thy rays.

3 All our hopes, and pray'rs, and labours
  Must be vain without Thine aid,
But Thou wilt not disappoint us;
  All is true that Thou hast said;
    *Gracious* Spirit!
  *O'er the world Thine* influence shed.

*Eriphus* in *Evangelical Magazine,* 1821, *alt.*

**3.5:** *Faithful*  **3.6:** *Soon thy gen'ral*
**Ed:** The alteration at 3.6 is from Asahel Nettleton's *Village Hymns* (1824); this was repeated
in James Winchell's *Arrangement* (1832) with
the additional change at 3.5.

# 972

L.M.
*The Holy Spirit invoked.*

1 O SPIRIT of the living God!
  In all Thy plentitude of grace,
Where'er the foot of man hath trod,
  Descend on our apostate race.

2 Give tongues of fire and hearts of love
  To preach the reconciling Word;
Give power and unction from above,
  Whene'er the joyful sound is heard.

3 Be darkness, at Thy coming, light,
  Confusion, order in Thy path;
Souls without strength, inspire with might;
  Bid mercy triumph over wrath.

4 O Spirit of the Lord! prepare
  All the round earth her God to meet;
Breathe Thou abroad like morning air,
  Till hearts of stone begin to beat.

5 Baptize the nations far and nigh;
  The triumphs of the cross record;
The name of Jesus glorify,
  Till every kindred call Him Lord.

*James Montgomery,* [1823, *rev.* 1825]

# 973

8.7.8.7.4.7.
*Longing for the spread of the gospel.*

1 O'ER *the* gloomy hills of darkness,
  Look, my soul; be still and gaze;
All the promises do *travail*
  *With* a glorious day of grace;
    *Blessed jubilee,*
  Let thy glorious morning dawn!

2 Let the Indian, let the Negro,
  Let the rude Barbarian see
That divine and glorious conquest
  Once obtain'd on Calvary;

Let the gospel
Loud resound from pole to pole.

3 Kingdoms wide that sit in darkness,
*Grant them, Lord, the saving* light;
And from eastern coast to western,
May the morning chase the night,
And redemption,
Freely purchas'd, win the day.

4 May the glorious day approaching,
*On their grossest* darkness dawn,
And the everlasting gospel
Spread abroad Thy holy name,
All the borders
Of the great Immanuel's land.

5 Fly abroad, *thou mighty* gospel,
Win and conquer, never cease;
May thy *lasting*, wide dominions
Multiply and still increase;

*Sway* Thy sceptre,
*Saviour, all the* world around.

6 Every creature, living, breathing,
In divinely grateful lays,
Father, Son, and Spirit, praising,
Magnify the God of grace;
Hallelujah!
Fill the universe with praise!

1-5 *William Williams*, 1772,
[*alt.* John Rippon, 1787, *ca.* 1805, 1828, 1844]
6 *John Rippon*, [1827]

**1.1:** *those*  **1.3:** *travel*  **1.4:** *On*  **1.5:** *Blessèd jubil*,
**3.2:** *Let them have the glorious*
**4.2:** *From eternal*  **5.1:** *eternal*  **5.3:** *eternal*
**5.5:** *May*  **5.6:** *Sway th' enlight'ned*
**Ed:** Rippon's version went through many changes, including some alterations and omissions
in the 27th ed. which were later reversed;
its final form in the Comprehensive Ed. was
adopted into *OOHB*.

# Prayer Meetings

# 974
S.M.
*Early morning prayer meeting.*

1 SWEETLY the holy hymn
Breaks on the morning air;
Before the world with smoke is dim,
We meet to offer prayer.

2 While flowers are wet with dews,
Dew of our souls descend;
Ere yet the sun the day renews,
O Lord, Thy Spirit send.

3 Upon the battlefield,
Before the fight begins,
We seek, O Lord, Thy sheltering shield
To guard us from our sins.

4 Ere yet our vessel sails
Upon the stream of day,

We plead, O Lord, for heavenly gales
To speed us on our way.

5 On the lone mountain side,
Before the morning's light,
The Man of Sorrows wept and cried
And rose refresh'd with might.

6 Oh hear us then, for we
Are very weak and frail;
We make the Saviour's name our plea
And surely must prevail.

*Charles H. Spurgeon*, 1866

**Ed:** In his *Treasury of David*, vol. 4, p. 134, Spurgeon provided two stanzas in this form:

Let prayer and holy hymn
Perfume the morning air;

Before the world with smoke is dim
    Bestir thy soul to prayer.

    While flowers are wet with dew
    Lament thy sins with tears,
And ere the sun shines forth anew
    Tell to thy Lord thy fears.

## 975 S.M.
*Evening prayer meeting.*

1  NOW from the world withdrawn,
    For intercourse with Thee,
May each, *O Lord*, before Thy throne
    From earthly cares be free.

2  Possess our ev'ry thought
    And teach our minds to pray;
Help us to worship as we ought,
    And thus conclude the day.

3  Our strength may we renew
    And lift our hearts above,
That while life's journey we pursue,
    We still may walk in love.

4  Then in our latter end,
    When death shall close our eyes,
Thy mercy will our souls attend
    And bear them to the skies.

*John Bulmer*, 1835, [*alt.* C.H.S.]

    **1.3:** *dear*

## 976 8.7.8.7.
*Evening prayer and praise.*

1  GRACIOUS Saviour, thus before Thee,
    With our varied want and care,
For a blessing we implore Thee;
    Listen to our evening prayer!

2  By Thy favour safely living,
    With a grateful heart we raise
Songs of jubilant thanksgiving;
    Listen to our evening praise!

3  Through the day, Lord, Thou hast given
    Strength sufficient for our need,

Cheered us with sweet hopes of heaven,
    Helped and comforted indeed.

4  Lord, we thank Thee and adore Thee
    For the solace of Thy love,
And rejoicing thus before Thee,
    Wait Thy blessing from above!

*Henry Bateman*, 1862

## 977 C.M.
*Prayer described.*

1  PRAYER is the soul's sincere desire,
    Utter'd or unexpress'd,
The motion of a hidden fire
    That trembles in the breast.

2  Prayer is the burden of a sigh,
    The falling of a tear,
The upward glancing of an eye,
    When none but God is near.

3  Prayer is the simplest form of speech
    That infant lips can try;
Prayer, the sublimest strains that reach
    The Majesty on high.

4  Prayer is the Christian's vital breath,
    The Christian's native air;
His watchword at the gates of death;
    He enters heaven with prayer.

5  Prayer is the contrite sinner's voice,
    Returning from his ways;
While angels in their songs rejoice,
    And cry, "Behold, he prays!"

6  The saints in prayer appear as one,
    In word, and deed, and mind;
While with the Father and the Son
    Sweet fellowship they find.

7  Nor prayer is made on earth alone;
    The Holy Spirit pleads;
And Jesus, on th' eternal throne,
    For mourners intercedes.

8  O Thou, by whom we come to God,
    The life, the truth, the way!

The path of prayer Thyself hast trod;
  Lord, teach us how to pray!

*James Montgomery*, [1818, *rev.* 1825]

> **MM:** Hymns, Set 1 (Jan./Nov.), 17th Morn,
> OLD HUNDREDTH
> **TD:** "When we are looking to the Lord in hope,
> it is well to tell Him so in prayer: the Psalmist
> uses his voice as well as his eye. We need not
> speak in prayer; a glance of the eye will do it
> all, for—
> > 'Prayer is the burden of a sigh,
> >   The falling of a tear,
> > The upward glancing of an eye
> >   When none but God is near'"
> > (Ps. 123:1; vol. 6, p. 444).

# 978 S.M.
*The throne of grace.*

1   BEHOLD the throne of grace!
    The promise calls me near;
There Jesus shows a smiling face
    And waits to answer pray'r.

2   That rich atoning blood,
    Which sprinkled round I see,
Provides for those who come to God,
    An all-prevailing plea.

3   My soul, ask what thou wilt;
    Thou canst not be too bold.
Since His own blood for thee He spilt,
    What else can He withhold?

4   Beyond Thy utmost wants
    His love and pow'r can bless;
To praying souls He always grants
    More than they can express.

5   Thine image, Lord, bestow
    Thy presence and Thy love;
I ask to serve Thee here below
    And reign with Thee above.

6   Teach me to live by faith;
    Conform my will to Thine;
Let me victorious be in death,
    And then in glory shine.

*John Newton*, 1779

# 979 7.6.7.6. / *"God be merciful unto us and bless us."*

1  LORD of the vast creation,
    Support of worlds unknown,
Desire of ev'ry nation,
    Behold us at Thy throne.

2  We come for mercy crying
    Through Thine atoning blood,
And on Thy grace relying,
    We seek each promis'd good.

3  O when shall Thy salvation
    Be known through ev'ry land,
And men in every station
    Obey Thy great command?

4  In God's own Son believing,
    From sin may they be free,
And gospel-grace receiving,
    Find life and peace in Thee!

*John Bulmer*, 1835

# 980 7.7.7.7.
*"Ask what I shall give thee."*

1  COME, my soul, thy suit prepare;
    Jesus loves to answer pray'r;
He Himself has bid thee pray,
    Therefore will not say thee nay.

2  Thou art coming to a King;
    Large petitions with thee bring,
For His grace and pow'r are such;
    None can ever ask too much.

3  With my burden I begin;
    Lord, remove this load of sin!
Let Thy blood, for sinners spilt,
    Set my conscience free from guilt.

4  Lord! I come to Thee for rest;
    Take possession of my breast;
There Thy blood-bought right maintain,
    And without a rival reign.

5  While I am a pilgrim here,
    Let Thy love my spirit cheer;

As my Guide, my Guard, my Friend,
Lead me to my journey's end.

*John Newton,* 1779

**MM:** Hymns, Set 1 (Jan./Nov.), 21st Morn,
NUREMBERG / HORNDON

# 981 7.7.7.7.
*Holy importunity.*

1 *LORD,* I cannot let Thee go
Till a blessing Thou bestow;
Do not turn away Thy face;
Mine's an urgent, pressing case.

2 Dost Thou ask me who I am?
Ah, my Lord, Thou know'st my name!
Yet the question gives a plea
To support my suit with Thee.

3 Thou didst once a wretch behold,
In rebellion blindly bold,
Scorn Thy grace, Thy pow'r defy;
That poor rebel, Lord, was I.

4 Once a sinner near despair,
Sought Thy mercy-seat by pray'r;
Mercy heard and set him free;
Lord, that mercy came to me.

5 Many *days* have pass'd since then,
Many changes I have seen,
Yet have been upheld till now;
Who could hold me up but Thou?

6 Thou hast help'd in ev'ry need;
This emboldens me to plead;
After so much mercy past,
Canst Thou let me sink at last?

7 No—I must maintain my hold;
'Tis Thy goodness makes me bold;
I can no denial take,
When I plead for Jesu's sake.

*John Newton,* 1779
[*alt. John Rippon,* 1787]

**1.1:** *Nay,*   **5.1:** *years*

# 982 7.7.7.7.
*A blessing requested.*

1 LORD, we come before Thee now;
At Thy feet we humbly bow;
Oh! do not our suit disdain;
Shall we seek Thee, Lord, in vain?

2 In Thy own appointed way,
Now we seek Thee, here we stay;
*Lord, from hence we would not go*
Till a blessing Thou bestow.

3 Send some message from Thy Word
That may joy and peace afford;
Let Thy Spirit now impart
Full salvation to each heart.

4 Grant that those who seek may find
Thee, a God *supremely* kind;
Heal the sick, the captive free;
Let us all rejoice in Thee.

*William Hammond,* 1745, *alt.*

**2.3:** *Lord, we know not how to go*
**4.2:** *sincere and*   **Ed:** The alteration at 2.3
appeared as early as 1776 in Rowland Hill's
*Collection;* 4.2 appeared as early as 1777 in
George Whitefield's *Collection,* 23rd ed. Both
were adopted into Rippon's *Selection* (1787).

# 983 7.7.7.7.
*"There am I in the midst of them."*

1 MET again in Jesus' name,
At His feet we humbly bow;
He is evermore the same;
Lo! He waits to meet us now.

2 In His name, if two or three
Meet, and for His mercy call,
There, the Saviour says, I'll be
In the midst to bless you all.

3 You shall never ask in vain,
Though your number be but few;
Firm the promise doth remain:
Lo, I always am with you.

4 Saviour, we believe Thy Word,
Calmly wait the promised grace;

Spirit of our risen Lord,
Holy Spirit, fill the place!

*John Pyer*, [1836]

# 984 L.M.
*I will pray.*

1 I WILL approach Thee—I will force
My way through obstacles to Thee;
To Thee for strength will have recourse,
To Thee for consolation flee!

2 Oh cast me, cast me not away,
From Thy dear presence, gracious Lord!
My burden at Thy feet I lay;
My soul reposes on Thy Word.

*Charlotte Elliott*, 1834

> **Ed:** Taken from the longer hymn,
> "Often, my God! when most I need."

# 985 C.M.
*Our advocate above.*

1 THOU Lamb of God, for sinners slain!
We glorify Thy love;
High Priest in heaven's eternal fane,
Our Advocate above.

2 Now, through Thy rended veil of flesh,
We dare the throne draw nigh,
And sprinkled with Thy blood afresh,
With boldness Abba cry.

*Josiah Conder*, 1856

> **Ed:** Taken from the longer hymn,
> "Substantial truth, O Christ, Thou art."

# 986 L.M.
*Answer by fire.*

1 LORD! with *Thy* grace our hearts inspire;
Answer our sacrifice by fire;
And by Thy mighty acts declare,
Thou art the God who heareth prayer.

2 Faith asks no signal from the skies
To show that prayers accepted rise;

Our Priest is in the holy place
And answers from the throne of grace.

*Josiah Conder*, [1836, *alt.*]

> **1.1:** *this*　**Ed:** Taken from the longer hymn,
> "O God, who didst Thy will unfold." This minor
> variant appeared as early as 1847 in Benjamin
> Clark's *The Domestic Sanctuary.*
> **MM:** "True, He regards not high looks and lofty
> words; He cares not for the pomp and pag-
> eantry of kings; He listens not to the swell of
> martial music; He regards not the triumph and
> pride of man; but wherever there is a heart big
> with sorrow, or a lip quivering with agony, or a
> deep groan, or a penitential sigh, the heart of
> Jehovah is open; He marks it down in the regis-
> try of His memory; He puts our prayers, like
> rose leaves, between the pages of His book of
> remembrance, and when the volume is opened
> at last, there shall be a precious fragrance
> springing up therefrom" (Nov. 3).

# 987 C.M.
*"Thy name's sake."*

1 LORD, for Thy name's sake! such the plea,
With force triumphant fraught,
By which Thy saints prevail with Thee,
By Thine own Spirit taught.

2 *Now*, for Thy name's sake, O our God!
Do not abhor our prayer,
But while we bow beneath Thy rod,
Thy chastened people spare.

3 Oh for Thy name's sake, richly grant
The unction from above;
Fulfill Thy holy covenant
And glorify Thy love.

*Josiah Conder*, 1836 [*alt. C.H.S.*]

> **2.1:** *Then*

# 988 L.M.
*Jesus present with two or three.*

1 "WHERE two or three, with sweet accord,
Obedient to their sovereign Lord,
Meet to recount His acts of grace
And offer solemn prayer and praise:

2 "There," says the Saviour, "will I be
Amid this little company;
To them unveil my smiling face
And shed my glories round the place."

3 We meet at Thy command, dear Lord,
Relying on Thy faithful Word;
Now send Thy Spirit from above;
Now fill our hearts with heavenly love.

*Samuel Stennett, 1787*

## 989 7.7.7.7.
*Pleading for power.*

1 LORD, our waiting spirits bow
In Thy blessèd presence now;
May the Holy Spirit be
Now our power to wait on Thee.

2 Power, O Lord, for power we cry!
Grant us each a rich supply,
That our longing souls may be
Fully satisifed by Thee.

3 Sweet the solemn hour of prayer,
Sweet to feed on heavenly fare,
Now let such our portion be,
Saviour, waiting upon Thee.

*Albert Midlane, 1866*

## 990 L.M.
*"Remember us, O Lord."*

1 APART from every worldly care,
We bow before Thee, Lord, in prayer;
And as our one, our only claim,
We lisp our blessèd Jesu's name.

2 May the blest Spirit, Father, now
Each heart in holy reverence bow,
And may our feeble breathings rise
To Thee, like holy sacrifice.

3 Our need Thou knowest; Thou art nigh,
And Thou canst every need supply;
Boundless, dear Fathers, is Thy store;
Remember us, we ask no more.

*Albert Midlane, 1866*

## 991 S.M.
*Confession of sin.*

1 ONCE more we meet to pray,
Once more our guilt confess;
Turn not, O Lord, Thine ears away
From creatures in distress.

2 Our sins to heaven ascend,
And there for vengeance cry;
O God! behold the sinner's Friend,
Who intercedes on high.

3 Though we are vile indeed
And well deserve Thy curse,
The merits of Thy Son we plead,
Who lived and died for us.

4 Now let Thy *bosom* yearn,
As *it hath* done before;
Return to us, O God, return!
And ne'er forsake us more.

[George Whitefield's *Collection*, 1798]
[*alt.* Stow & Smith, *The Psalmist*, 1843]

**4.1:** bowels   **4.2:** they have
**Ed:** In the first ed. of *OOHB*, Sedgwick had
attributed the hymn to "*Baptist Psalmody,
1843*" (referring to Stow & Smith); in the 1873
ed., he changed this to "Philip Doddridge,
1755, alt." The connection to Doddridge is
inexplicable. In the decades preceding Stow &
Smith, the hymn can be found exclusively in
copies of Whitefield's *Collection*, starting with
the 1798 ed. edited by Matthew Wilks, where it
was unattributed.

## 992 C.M.
*Prayer for unbelievers.*

1 THOU Son of God, whose flaming eyes
Our inmost thoughts perceive,
Accept the humble sacrifice
Which now to Thee we give.

2 We bow before Thy gracious throne
And think ourselves sincere,
But show us, Lord, is every one
Thy real worshipper?

3 Is here a soul that knows Thee not,
    Nor feels his want of Thee,
A stranger to the blood which bought
    His pardon on the tree?

4 Convince him now of unbelief,
    His desperate state explain,
And fill his heart with sacred grief
    And penitential pain.

5 Speak with that voice which wakes the dead
    And bid the sleeper rise,
And bid his guilty conscience dread
    The death that never dies.

*Charles Wesley*, 1767 [*rev.* 1781]

# 993 C.M.
*Divine sympathy.*

1 *THERE is no sorrow, Lord, too light*
    *To bring in prayer to Thee;*
*There is no anxious care too slight*
    *To wake Thy sympathy.*

2 Thou who hast trod the thorny road
    Wilt share each small distress;
*The love which* bore the greater load
    Will not refuse the less.

3 *There is no* secret sigh we breathe
    But meets *Thine* ear divine,
And every cross grows light beneath
    The shadow, Lord, of Thine.

4 Life's *ills* without, sin's strife within,
    The heart would overflow,
But for that love which died for sin,
    That love which wept with woe.

*Jane Crewdson*, 1860
*alt. Thomas Davis*, 1864

> **1.1-4:** *There's not a grief, however light,*
>     *Too light for sympathy!*
> *There's not a care, however slight,*
>     *Too slight to bring to Thee!*
> **2.3:** *For He who*   **3.1:** *There's not a*
> **3.2:** *the*   **4.1:** *woes*

# 994 L.M.
*Hindrances to prayer.*

1 WHAT various hindrances we meet
    In coming to a mercy seat!
Yet who that knows the worth of pray'r
    But wishes to be often there.

2 Pray'r makes the darken'd cloud withdraw,
    Pray'r climbs the ladder Jacob saw,
Gives exercise to faith and love,
    Brings ev'ry blessing from above.

3 Restraining pray'r, we cease to fight;
    Pray'r makes the Christian's armour bright;
And Satan trembles when he sees
    The weakest saint upon his knees.

4 While Moses stood with arms spread wide,
    Success was found on Israel's side,
But when through weariness they fail'd,
    That moment Amalek prevail'd.

5 Have you no words? Ah, think again;
    Words flow apace when you complain,
And fill your fellow-creature's ear
    With the sad tale of all your care.

6 Were half the breath thus vainly spent,
    To heav'n in supplication sent,
Your cheerful song would oft'ner be,
    "Hear what the Lord has done for me!"

*William Cowper*, 1779

> **MM:** "Prayer is the forerunner of mercy. Turn to
> sacred history, and you will find that scarcely
> ever did a great mercy come to this world
> unheralded by supplication" (Feb. 19).

# 995 L.M.
*The garden of Christ.*

1 WE are a garden wall'd around,
    Chosen and made peculiar ground,
A little spot enclosed by grace
    Out of the world's wide wilderness.

2 Like trees of myrrh and spice we stand,
    Planted by God the Father's hand,
And all His springs in Zion flow
    To make the young plantation grow.

3 Awake, O heavenly wind, and come,
　　Blow on this garden of perfume;
　Spirit divine, descend and breathe
　　A gracious gale on plants beneath.

4 Make our best spices flow abroad
　　To entertain our Saviour God;
　And faith, and love, and joy appear,
　　And every grace be active here.

*Isaac Watts*, [1707]

# 996 C.M.
*"Teach us to pray."*

1 LORD, teach us how to pray aright,
　　With reverence and with fear;
　Though dust and ashes in Thy sight,
　　We may, we must draw near.

2 We perish if we cease from prayer;
　　O grant us power to pray;
　And when to meet Thee we prepare,
　　Lord, meet us by the way.

*James Montgomery*, [1818, *rev.* 1825, 1853]

# 997 C.M.
*"I said not, seek ye me in vain."*

1 WE come, *blest* Jesus, to Thy throne,
　　To open all our grief;
　Now send Thy promised mercy down
　　And grant us quick relief.

2 Ne'er didst Thou say to Jacob's seed,
　　"Seek ye My face" in vain,
　And canst Thou now deny Thine aid
　　When burden'd souls complain?

3 The same Thy power, Thy love the same;
　　Unmoved the promise shines;
　Eternal truth surrounds Thy name
　　And guards the precious lines.

4 Though Satan rage and flesh rebel,
　　And unbelief arise,
　We'll wait around His footstool still,
　　For Jesus hears our cries.

*James Boden*, [1801, *alt. C.H.S.*]

**1.1:** *dear* **Ed:** Sedgwick dated the hymn 1777
in reference to several other hymns by "J—s
B—n" that had appeared in *The Gospel Magazine* that year, including No. 490, but this
hymn was not among them. See also Julian's
*Dictionary*, pp. 151-152.

# 998 C.M.
*"Prayer heard in heaven."*

1 WHEN God inclines the heart to pray,
　　He hath an ear to hear;
　To Him there's music in a groan
　　And beauty in a tear.

2 The humble suppliant cannot fail
　　To have his wants supplied,
　Since He for sinners intercedes,
　　Who once for sinners died.

*Benjamin Beddome*, 1817

**Ed:** Taken from the longer hymn,
　"Prayer is the breath of God in man."

# 999 8.7.8.7.
*"Let us pray."*

1 LET us pray! the Lord is willing,
　　Ever waiting, prayer to hear;
　Ready, His kind words fulfilling,
　　Loving hearts to help and cheer.

2 Let us pray! our God with blessing
　　Satisfies the praying soul,
　Bends to hear the heart's confessing,
　　Moulding it to His control.

3 Let us pray! though foes surrounding
　　Vex, and trouble, and dismay;
　Precious grace, through Christ abounding,
　　Still shall cheer us on our way.

4 Let us pray! our life is praying;
　　Prayer with time alone may cease;
　Then in heaven, God's will obeying,
　　Life is praise and perfect peace.

*Henry Bateman*, 1862

# 1000

L.M.
*Peace at the mercy-seat.*

1 FROM every stormy wind that blows,
From every swelling tide of woes,
There is a calm, a *safe* retreat;
'Tis found beneath the mercy seat.

2 There is a place where Jesus sheds
The oil of gladness o'er our heads,
A place than all beside more sweet;
It is the blood-stained mercy seat.

3 There is a spot where spirits blend,
Where friend holds fellowship with friend;
Though sunder'd far, by faith *we* meet
Around *our* common mercy seat.

4 Ah! whither could we flee for aid,
When tempted, desolate, dismay'd—
Or how the hosts of hell defeat,
Had suffering saints no mercy seat?

5 There, there, on eagle-wing we soar,
And time and sense seem all no more,
And heaven comes down our souls to greet,
And glory crowns the mercy seat.

6 Oh! *let* my *hands* forget *their* skill,
My tongue be silent, cold, and still,
This bounding heart forget to beat,
If I forget the mercy seat.

*Hugh Stowell*, 1832, *alt.*

**1.3:** *sure*  **3.3:** *they*  **3.4:** *one*
**6.1:** *may / hand / her*  **Ed:** These alterations
appeared as early as 1855 in John Leechman's
*Choral Book.*

# 1001

S.M.
*"Our Father which art in heaven."*

1 OUR Heavenly Father hear
The prayer we offer now:
Thy name be hallow'd far and near;
To Thee all nations bow.

2 Thy kingdom come, Thy will
On earth be done in love,
As saints and seraphim fulfill
Thy perfect law above.

3 Our daily bread supply,
While by Thy Word we live;
The guilt of our iniquity
Forgive, as we forgive.

4 From dark temptation's power,
From Satan's wiles defend,
Deliver in the evil hour,
And guide us to the end.

5 Thine, then, forever be
Glory and power divine;
The sceptre, throne, and majesty
Of heaven and earth are Thine.

*James Montgomery*, 1825

# 1002

7.7.7.7.
*Jesus met them.*

1 SWEET the time, exceeding sweet,
When the saints together meet,
When the Saviour is the theme,
When they join to sing of Him.

2 Sing we then eternal love,
Such as did the Father move;
*When He saw* the world undone,
Lov'd the world, and gave His Son.

3 Sing the Son's amazing love,
How he left the realms above,
Took our nature and our place,
Lived and died to save our race.

4 Sing we too the Spirit's love;
With our wretched hearts He strove,
*Turn'd our feet from ways of shame,
Made us trust in Jesu's name.*

5 Sweet the place, exceeding sweet,
Where the saints in glory meet,
Where the Saviour's still the theme,
Where they see, and sing of Him.

*George Burder*, [1779], *alt.*

**2.3:** *He beheld*
**4.3-4:** *Things of precious Christ he took,
Gave us hearts, and eyes to look.*

**Ed:** The alteration at 2.3 appeared as early as 1836 in *Christian Hymns … for the Christian Church at Tor* and was adopted into Rippon's *Selection* (1844); 4.3-4 are by Spurgeon.

# 1003
7.7.7.7.7.7.
*Sweetness of fellowship.*

1 IF 'tis sweet to mingle where
Christians meet for social prayer—
If 'tis sweet with them to raise
Songs of holy joy and praise—
Passing sweet that state must be
Where they meet eternally.

2 Saviour, may these meetings prove
Preparations for above;
While we worship in this place,
May we go from grace to grace,
Till we, each in his degree,
Meet for endless glory be.

*Ingram Cobbin*, 1828

# 1004
L.M. / *Joy in heaven over a repenting sinner.*

1 WHO can describe the joys that rise
Through all the courts of Paradise
To see a prodigal return,
To see an heir of glory born?

2 With joy the Father doth approve
The fruit of His eternal love;
The Son with joy looks down and sees
The purchase of His agonies.

3 The Spirit takes delight to view
The holy soul He form'd anew,
And saints and angels join to sing
The growing empire of their King.

*Isaac Watts*, 1709

# 1005
8.7.8.7.
*For a blessing.*

1 AS the dew, from heav'n distilling,
Gently on the grass descends,

*Richly unto all* fulfilling
What Thy providence intends,
*So may truth, divine and* gracious,
*To our waiting spirits prove;*
*Bless and make it* efficacious
*In the children of Thy* love!

2 Lord! behold *this* congregation;
*All Thy* promises fulfill;
From Thy holy habitation,
Let the dew of life distill;
Let our cry come up before Thee,
Sweetest influence shed around;
So Thy people shall adore Thee
And confess the joyful sound.

*Thomas Kelly*, 1804
alt. *John Bulmer*, 1835

> **1.3:** *And revives it, thus*
> **1.5:** *Let Thy doctrine, Lord, so*
> **1.6:** *Thus descending from above,*
> **1.7:** *Blest by thee prove* **1.8:** *To fulfill thy work of*
> **2.1:** *Thy* **2.2:** *Precious*

# 1006
L.M.
*National fast.*

1 OH may the pow'r which melts the rock
Be felt by all assembled here!
Or else our service will but mock
The God whom we profess to fear!

2 Lord, while Thy judgments shake the land,
Thy people's eyes are fix'd on Thee!
We own Thy just, uplifted hand,
Which thousands cannot, will not see.

3 The Lord, displeas'd, has rais'd His rod;
Ah! where are now the faithful few
Who tremble for the ark of God
And know what Israel ought to do?

4 Lord, hear Thy people ev'rywhere,
Who meet to mourn, confess, and pray;
The nation and Thy churches spare,
And let Thy wrath be turn'd away.

*John Newton*, 1779

**Ed:** In *Olney Hymns*, this was headed "Confession and Prayer. December 13, 1776."

# 1007
C.M.
*National fast.*

1 ETERNAL God! Before Thy throne,
　　Three nations prostrate fall;
　Their great, their numerous sins they own;
　　O Lord, forgive them all.

2 Burst, Lord, upon these mourning isles
　　With bright and gladdening rays;
　Turn grief to joy, and tears to smiles,
　　And prayer to grateful praise.

3 Oh sanctify the painful low,
　　Which justly Thou didst give;
　May we the Lord who smote us know,
　　And turn to Thee and live.

*James Edmeston*, [1866]

> **Ed:** Sedgwick dated the hymn 1847, which might
> imply that it was included in Edmeston's
> *Sacred Poetry*, but it does not appear there. In
> fact, this hymn could not be located in any col-
> lection outside of *OOHB*. It is named among
> Edmeston's works in Julian's *Dictionary*, p.
> 322, without a stated source. It seems, based
> on the original List of Works and Authors in
> *OOHB*, that Edmeston supplied some of his
> unpublished manuscripts to Spurgeon, dated
> 1837-1849, so for lack of any other explana-
> tion, this hymn had its first and only known
> publication in *OOHB*.

# 1008
7.7.7.7.
*National thanksgiving.*

1 MAY we, Lord, rejoicing say,
　Now Thine anger's turn'd away,
　Sheathed the sword that waved before,
　Mission'd to destroy no more.

2 Lord, accept our grateful praise;
　Just, yet kind, are all Thy ways,
　Ever ready to forgive,
　Bidding the repentant live.

3 In Thy courts would we appear,
　Mingling joy and praise with fear;
　Judgments past in memory bear,
　Yet thanksgiving offer there.

4 Grateful hearts we fain would bring;
　Pardoning mercy would we sing;
　We may now rejoicing say,
　Lord, Thine anger's turn'd away.

*James Edmeston*, [1866]

> **Ed:** Dated 1849 in Edmeston's manuscripts, and
> first published in *OOHB*. Like No. 1007, this
> hymn is not known outside of *OOHB*.

# 1009
C.M.
*Prayer for our country.*

1 SHINE, mighty God, on Britain shine
　　With beams of heavenly grace;
　Reveal Thy power through all our coasts,
　　And show Thy smiling face.

2 Amidst our isle, exalted high,
　　Do Thou our glory stand,
　And like a wall of guardian fire,
　　Surround *this favour'd* land.

3 When shall Thy name from shore to shore
　　Sound all the earth abroad,
　And distant nations know and love
　　Their Saviour and their God?

4 Sing to the Lord, ye distant lands,
　　Sing loud, with solemn voice,
　While British tongues exalt His praise
　　And British hearts rejoice.

5 Earth shall obey her Maker's will
　　And yield a full increase;
　Our God will crown His chosen isle
　　With fruitfulness and peace.

6 God, the Redeemer, scatters round
　　His choicest favours here,
　While the creation's utmost bound
　　Shall see, adore, and fear.

*Isaac Watts*, [1707, *rev.* 1719, *alt.*]

> **2.4:** *the favourite*

# Mothers' Meetings

## 1010
C.M.
*"Lord, have mercy on my Son."*

1 WITHIN these *peaceful* walls, O Lord,
    A fond parental band
Have met, Thy goodness to record,
    And seek Thy guiding hand.

2 If e'er a *parent's* prayerful strain
    Hath gain'd Thy listening ear,
O Saviour, now in mercy deign
    Our ardent cry to hear.

3 'Tis for our children, Lord, we plead,
    Dear objects of our care;
Dangers on every side are spread;
    Save them from every snare.

*Thomas Hastings*, 1834
[*alt. John Campbell*, 1837]

**1.1:** *quiet*   **2.1:** *mother's*

## 1011
C.M.
*Pleading for our children.*

1 O LORD, behold us at Thy feet,
    A needy, sinful band;
As suppliants round Thy mercy seat,
    We come at Thy command.

2 'Tis for our children we would plead,
    The offspring Thou hast giv'n;
Where shall we go in time of need,
    But to the God of heav'n?

3 We ask not for them wealth or fame
    Amid the worldly strife,
But in the all-prevailing name,
    We ask eternal life.

4 We crave the Spirit's quick'ning grace
    To make them pure in heart,
That they may stand before Thy face
    And see Thee as Thou art.

*Thomas Hastings*, 1834 [*rev.* 1836]

## 1012
7.7.7.7.
*Prayer to Jesus for our little ones.*

1 JESUS, Thou wast once a child,
Meek, obedient, pure, and mild;
Such may *our* dear children be!
Teach them, Lord, to follow Thee.

2 Thou didst grow in grace and truth
Up from infancy to youth;
May we, Lord, *our* children see
Striving thus to copy Thee!

3 Subject to Thy parents' word,
When their least command was heard,
May we, Lord, our children see
Thus obedient unto Thee!

4 At Thy heavenly Father's voice,
Thou in duty didst rejoice;
Changed by grace, O Lord, would we
See our children follow Thee!

*James Gabb*, 1864, *alt. C.H.S.*

**1.3:** *these*   **2.3:** *these*   **Ed:** Gabb revised his
hymn in 1875 for his *Welburn Appendix.*

## 1013
7.7.7.7. Double
*Not one left to perish.*

1 GRACIOUS Lord, our children see,
By Thy mercy we are free;
But shall these, alas! remain
Subjects still of Satan's reign?
Israel's young ones when of old
Pharaoh threaten'd to withhold;
Then Thy messenger said, "No,
Let the children also go."

2 When the angel of the Lord,
Drawing forth his dreadful sword,
Slew with an avening hand
All the first-born of the land,
Then Thy people's door he pass'd,
Where the bloody sign was plac'd;

Hear us now upon our knees;
Plead the blood of Christ for these!

3 Lord, we tremble, for we know
How the fierce malicious foe,
Wheeling round his watchful flight,
Keeps them ever in his sight;
Spread Thy pinions, King of Kings!
Hide them safe beneath Thy wings,
Lest the rav'nous bird of prey
Stoop and bear the brood away.

*William Cowper*, 1779

# 1014 C.M.
*Our Father, hear us.*

1 THOU, who a tender Parent art,
  Regard a parent's plea;
Our offspring, with an anxious heart,
  We now commend to Thee.

2 Our children are our greatest care,
  A charge which Thou hast given;
In all Thy graces let them share,
  And all the joys of heaven.

3 If a centurion could succeed,
  Who for his servant cried,
Wilt Thou refuse to hear us plead,
  For those so near allied!

4 On us Thou hast bestow'd Thy grace;
  Be to our children kind;
Among Thy saints give them a place
  And leave not one behind.

5 Happy we then shall live below,
  The remnant of our days,
And when to brighter worlds we go,
  Shall long resound Thy praise.

[George Whitefield's *Collection*, 1798]

> **Ed:** Sedgwick evidently had trouble tracing this
> hymn, first attributing it to John Campbell's
> *Comprehensive Hymn Book* (1839), then in

the 1867 ed. to Rowland Hill, 1808, but the
hymn is from Matthew Wilks' ed. of Whitefield's *Collection*.

# 1015 C.M.
*Save our children.*

1 GOD of mercy, hear our prayer
  For the children Thou hast giv'n;
Let them all Thy blessings share,
  Grace on earth and bliss in heav'n.

2 In the morning of their days,
  May their hearts be drawn to Thee;
Let them learn to lisp Thy praise
  In their earliest infancy.

3 Cleanse their souls from ev'ry stain,
  Through the Saviour's precious blood;
Let them all be born again
  And be reconcil'd to God.

4 For this mercy, Lord, we cry;
  Bend Thine ever-gracious ear;
While on Thee our souls rely,
  Hear our prayer, in mercy hear.

*Thomas Hastings*, 1834

# 1016 L.M.
*Parents pleading.*

1 FATHER of all! before Thy throne,
  Grateful but anxious parents bow;
Look in paternal mercy down,
  And yield the boon we ask Thee now.

2 'Tis not for wealth, or joys of earth,
  Or life prolonged, we seek Thy face;
'Tis for a new and heavenly birth,
  'Tis for the treasures of Thy grace.

3 'Tis for their souls' eternal joy,
  For rescue from the coming woe;
Do not our earnest suit deny;
  We cannot, cannot let Thee go.

*John Howard Hinton*, 1833

# Opening Places for Worship

## 1017
**L.M.**
*Opening or enlargement.*

1 JESUS, where'er Thy people meet,
 There they behold Thy mercy seat;
 Where'er they seek Thee, Thou art found,
 And ev'ry place is hallow'd ground.

2 For Thou, within no walls confin'd,
 Inhabitest the humble mind;
 Such ever bring Thee, where they come,
 And going, take Thee to their home.

3 Dear Shepherd of Thy chosen few!
 Thy former mercies here renew;
 Here, to our waiting hearts, proclaim
 The sweetness of Thy saving name.

4 Here may we prove the pow'r of pray'r
 To strengthen faith and sweeten care,
 To teach our faint desires to rise,
 And bring all heav'n before our eyes.

5 Behold! at Thy commanding word,
 We stretch the curtain and the cord;
 Come Thou, and fill this wider space,
 And bless us with a large increase.

6 Lord, we are few, but Thou art near,
 Nor short Thine arm, nor deaf Thine ear;
 Oh rend the heav'ns, come quickly down,
 And make a thousand hearts Thine own!

*William Cowper*, 1779

## 1018
**C.M.**
*Dedication of the house.*

1 SPIRIT of glory and of grace,
 Thy favour we entreat;
 Thou true Shekinah of the place,
 Where true disciples meet.

2 Oh! let the labour of our hands
 Be precious in Thy sight,

And long as this our temple stands,
 Thy presence be its light.

3 Here float the gospel's banner wide
 O'er faithful hearts and brave,
 And here, O Jesus crucified,
 Come forth in power to save!

*Joseph Tritton*, 1861

**Ed:** Composed for the opening of the Metropolitan Tabernacle, 18 Mar. 1861, and subsequently published in MTP, vol. 7, p. 168, in 6 sts., then adopted into *OOHB*, minus sts. 4-6:

> Make bare thine arm, thou King of saints,
>  To bring dead souls to life,
> And when Thy children's courage faints,
>  Renew them for the strife.

> No Bochim this—a place of woe—
>  But Pisgah's holy steep,
> Where dying ones their heaven shall know,
>  Ere yet they fall asleep.

> While we who live shall urge the race,
>  If Jesus be but here;
> Spirit of glory and of grace,
>  Revealing Christ, appear!

## 1019
**C.M.**
*"The glory of the Lord filled the house."*

1 LIGHT up this house with glory, Lord;
 Enter and claim Thine own;
 Receive the homage of our souls;
 Erect Thy temple throne.

2 We rear no altar—Thou hast died;
 We deck no priestly shrine;
 What need have we of creature-aid?
 The power to save is Thine.

3 We ask no bright shekinah cloud
 To glorify the place;
 Give, Lord, the substance of that sign—
 A plenitude of grace.

4 No rushing, mighty wind, we ask;
   No tongues of flame desire;
Grant us the Spirit's quickening light,
   His purifying fire.

5 Light up this house with glory, Lord;
   The glory of that love
Which forms and saves a church below,
   And makes a heaven above.

*John Harris*, 1859

# 1020
6.6.6.6.8.8.
*Opening a place of worship.*

1 *GREAT King of Zion now,*
   *Display Thy matchless grace;*
   *In love the heavens bow,*
   *With glory fill this place;*
Beneath this roof, O deign to show
How God can dwell with men below!

2 Here may Thine ears attend
   Our interceding cries,
   And grateful praise ascend
   All fragrant to the skies;
Here may Thy Word melodious sound
And spread celestial joys around.

3 Here may th' attentive throng
   Imbibe Thy truth and love,
   And converts join the song
   Of seraphim above,
And willing crowds surround Thy board
With sacred joy and sweet accord.

4 Here may our unborn sons
   And daughters sound Thy praise,
   And shine, like polish'd stones,
   Through long succeeding days;
Here, Lord, display Thy saving power,
Until the last triumphant hour.

1-2 *Benjamin Francis*, 1787, *alt. C.H.S.*
3-4 *Charles H. Spurgeon*, 1866

**1.1-4:** *Then, King of glory, come,*
*And with Thy favor crown*
*This temple as Thy dome,*
*This people as Thy own.*

**Ed:** Francis' original hymn begins, "In sweet exalted strains." A note in Rippon's *Selection* (1787) states, "Sung on opening the meeting house at Horsley, Gloucestershire, September 18, 1774, and also at the opening of the new meeting house at Downend, near Bristol, October 4, 1786."

# 1021
L.M.
*Thankfulness for the house.*

1 SING to the Lord with heart and voice,
Ye children of His sovereign choice;
The work achieved, the temple raised,
Now be our God devoutly praised.

2 For all the treasure freely brought—
For all the toil in gladness wrought—
For warmth of zeal and purpose strong—
Wake we today the thankful song.

3 Lord of the temple! once disowned,
But now in worlds of light enthroned—
Thy glory let Thy servants see,
Who dedicate this house to Thee.

4 Be Thy dear name, like ointment, shed
O'er every soul, on every head;
Make glorious, O our Saviour King,
The place where thus Thy chosen sing.

5 More grand the temple, and the strain
More sweet, when we Thy heaven
   shall gain;
And bid, for realms where angels dwell,
*Thy courts on earth, a glad* farewell!

*Joseph Tritton*, 1861 [*rev.* 1866]

**5.4:** *Our Tabernacles here,* (1861)
**Ed:** Composed for the opening of the Metropolitan Tabernacle, 18 Mar. 1861, and printed in "a penny hymn-book" made for the service, then adopted into *OOHB*. It was also sung at a special service for the contributors to the Building Fund, 26 Mar. 1861, and printed in MTP, vol. 7, p. 185, with an additional stanza (originally stanza 4):

What if the world still disallow—
Our corner and our top-stone Thou!
Thy shame, and death, and risen joy
Shall here our ceaseless thought employ.

## 1022 C.M.
*Re-opening.*

1 O GOD, before whose radiant throne
　　The heav'nly armies bend,
　Now graciously incline Thine ear
　　And to our suit attend.

2 Where our forefathers join'd in praise,
　　We meet to praise *Thy name;*
　*Where they Thy faithful promise proved,*
　　*We find Thee still the same.*

3 This house, these walls re-edified,
　　Are raisèd, Lord, for Thee;
　In all the plentitude of grace,
　　*In this assembly* be.

4 Here may the dead be made alive,
　　Backsliding souls return,
　More grace by gracious souls be felt,
　　And saints like seraphs burn.

5 Here build Thy church, maintain Thy cause,
　　Nor let it e'er decline,

But flourish *till the Lord descends*
　*In majesty divine.*

[John Rippon's *Selection,*] 1810, *alt.* C.H.S.

**2.2:** *Thee too;*
**2.3-4:** *For us and others here they pray'd;*
　　*We now their work renew.*
**3.4:** *Let this Thy temple*
**5.3-4:** *when the trumpet sounds—*
　　*The kingdoms, Lord, are Thine.*
**Ed:** Sedgwick attributed this hymn to John Rippon, based on its inclusion in the 1810 ed. of his *Selection.* In response, John Julian wrote, "We have seen no authority for attributing the original to Dr. Rippon. Its anonymous appearance in his *Selection,* in which the authors' names are usually given with the hymns, is no proof that he was the author" (*Dictionary of Hymnology,* p. 830).
　A note in Rippon's *Selection* says: "Sung July 22, 1810 at Uffculme, Devon, at the first administration of the Lord's Supper by Dr. R., after the meeting house had been rebuilt."

# Morning

## 1023 L.M.
*Morning.*

1 AWAKE, my soul, and with the sun,
　Thy daily stage of duty run;
　Shake off dull sloth, and joyful rise
　To pay thy morning sacrifice.

2 Thy precious time mis-spent, redeem;
　Each present day thy last esteem;
　Improve thy talent with due care;
　For the great day thyself prepare.

3 In conversation be sincere;
　Keep conscience, as the noon-tide, clear;
　Think how all-seeing God thy ways,
　And all thy secret thoughts, surveys.

4 Wake, and lift up thyself, my heart,
　And with the angels bear thy part,
　Who all night long unwearied sing
　High praise to the Eternal King.

5 I wake, I wake, ye heavenly choir;
　May your devotion me inspire,
　That I, like you, my age may spend,
　Like you, may on my God attend.

6 May I, like you, in God delight,
　Have all day long my God in sight,
　Perform, like you, my Maker's will;
　O may I never more do ill.

7 Lord, I my vows to Thee renew;
　Disperse my sins as morning dew;

Guard my first springs of thought and will,
And with Thyself my spirit fill.

8 Praise God from whom all blessings flow;
Praise Him all creatures here below;
Praise Him above, ye heavenly host;
Praise Father, Son, and Holy Ghost.

*Thomas Ken*, [1692, *rev.* 1695, 1709]

**MM:** Hymns, Set 1 (Jan./Nov.), 8th Morn,
DUKE STREET / ROTHWELL

# 1024 C.M.
*A hymn for morning or evening.*

1 HOSANNA, with a cheerful sound,
To God's upholding hand;
Ten thousand snares attend us round,
And yet secure we stand.

2 That was a most amazing power
That rais'd us with a word,
And every day, and every hour,
We lean upon the Lord.

3 The evening rests our *wearied* head,
And angels guard the room;
We wake, and we admire the bed
That was not made our tomb.

4 The rising morning can't assure
That we shall end the day,
For death stands ready at the door
To *take* our lives away.

5 Our breath is forfeited by sin
To God's *avenging* law;
We own Thy grace, immortal King,
In every gasp we draw.

6 God is our sun, whose daily light
Our joy and safety brings;
Our feeble flesh lies safe at night
Beneath His shady wings.

*Isaac Watts*, [1707, *alt.*]

**3.1:** *weary*  **4.4:** *seize*  **5.2:** *revenging*
**Ed:** The alterations at 4.4 and 5.2 appeared in
posthumous eds. of Watts starting in 1772; 3.1
in eds. of Watts as early as 1837.

# 1025 C.M.
*Keep us, O Lord, this day.*

1 NOW that the sun is *beaming* bright,
*Once more to God we pray*
That He, the uncreated light,
May guide *our souls this day.*

2 No sinful word, nor deed of wrong,
Nor thoughts that idly rove,
But simple truth be on our tongue,
And in our hearts be love.

3 And while the hours in order flow,
O Christ, securely fence
Our gates, beleaguer'd by the foe,
The gate of every sense.

4 And grant that to Thine honour, Lord,
Our daily toil may tend,
That we begin it at Thy Word,
And in Thy favour end.

[*Anonymous*, 5th Century]
[*rev. Charles Coffin*, 1736]
[*tr. John Henry Newman*, 1844, *alt.*]

**1.1:** *gleaming*  **1.2:** *Implore we, bending low,*
**1.4:** *us as we go.*  **Ed:** From the Latin, "Iam
lucis orto sidere." The hymn is sometimes
attributed to Ambrose of Milan, but modern
scholars do not count it among the hymns
officially credited to him. Sedgwick attributed
the Latin to Ambrose and its translation to
*Hymns for Public and Private Use* (1847).
Charles Coffin revised the Latin for the *Breviarium Parisiense* (1736); John Newman
republished texts from that collection in his
*Hymni Ecclesiae* (1838). Newman's translation was prepared in Feb. 1842 at the request
of Francis Palgrave, apparently for his essay
"The Conquest and the Conqueror" in *The
Quarterly Review* (1844), where it appeared
together with the Latin. See also Palgrave's
*History of Normandy and of England* vol. 3
(1864), p. 588.

In Newman's *Verses on Various Occasions*
(1868), the hymn appeared in a revised form,
beginning "Now that the day-star glimmers
bright," with an additional two stanzas.

The alterations are borrowings from John
Chandler's translation, "Once more the sun

is beaming bright," from his *Hymns of the Primitive Church* (1837). The origin of this juxtaposition of Chandler and Newman is unclear. It had appeared in 1865 in *Hymns for the Use of the Evangelical Lutheran Church*, which was part of Spurgeon's personal library.

# 1026 C.M.
*Thanks.*

1 LORD, for the mercies of the night,
  My humble thanks I pay,

And unto Thee I dedicate
  The first-fruits of the day.

2 Let this day praise Thee, O my God,
  And so let all my days,
And O let mine eternal day
  Be Thine eternal praise.

*John Mason*, 1683

**Ed:** Taken from the longer hymn,
  "My God was with me all this night."

# Evening

# 1027 8.7.8.7
*Seeking an evening blessing.*

1 SAVIOUR, breathe an evening blessing,
  Ere repose our spirits seal;
Sin and want we come confessing;
  Thou canst save, and Thou canst heal.

2 Though destruction walk around us,
  Though the arrow past us fly,
Angel-guards from Thee surround us;
  We are safe if Thou art nigh.

3 Though the night be dark and deary,
  Darkness cannot hide from Thee;
Thou art He who, never weary,
  Watchest where Thy people be.

4 Should swift death this night o'ertake us,
  And our couch become our tomb,
May the morn in heaven awake us,
  Clad in light and deathless bloom.

*James Edmeston*, 1820

**EE:** Hymns, Set 1 (Jan./Nov.), 1st Eve,
  MARINER'S / HAYDN'S. "God our Father is
  here, and will be here all through the lonely
  hours; He is an almighty Watcher, a sleepless
  Guardian, a faithful Friend. . . . Darkness is not
  too dark for Him" (Apr. 22).

# 1028 L.M.
*"Abide with us."*

1 SUN of my soul! Thou Saviour dear,
  It is not night if Thou be near:
  Oh may no earth-born cloud arise
  To hide Thee from Thy servant's eyes.

2 When the soft dews of kindly sleep
  My wearied eyelids gently steep,
  Be my last thought, how sweet to rest
  Forever on my Saviour's breast.

3 Abide with me from morn till eve,
  For without Thee I cannot live;
  Abide with me when night is nigh,
  For without Thee I dare not die.

4 If some poor wandering child of Thine
  Have spurn'd today the voice divine,
  Now, Lord, the gracious work begin;
  Let him no more lie down in sin.

5 Watch by the sick, enrich the poor
  With blessings from Thy boundless store;
  Be every mourner's sleep tonight,
  Like infant's slumbers, pure and light.

6 Come near and bless us when we wake,
  Ere through the world our way we take,

Till in the ocean of Thy love
We lose ourselves in heaven above.

*John Keble*, 1827

> **EE:** Hymns, Set 1 (Jan./Nov.), 3rd Eve,
> PASCAL / ROCKINGHAM
> **Ed:** Taken from the longer hymn,
> "'Tis gone, that bright and orbèd blaze."

# 1029 <small>7.7.7.7<br>*Prayer at eventide.*</small>

1 SOFTLY now the light of day
Fades upon my sight away;
Free from care, from labour free,
Lord, I would commune with Thee!

2 Thou whose all-pervading eye
Nought escapes, without, within,
Pardon each infirmity,
Open fault and secret sin.

3 Soon for me the light of day
Shall forever pass away;
Then, from sin and sorrow free,
Take me, Lord, to dwell with Thee!

4 Thou who, sinless, yet hast known
All of man's infirmity;
Then, from Thine eternal throne,
Jesus, look with pitying eye.

*George W. Doane*, [1824]

> **EE:** Hymns, Set 1 (Jan./Nov.), 4th Eve,
> KIEL / GERMAN HYMN

# 1030 <small>C.M.<br>*An evening song.*</small>

1 DREAD Sov'reign, let my evening song
Like holy incense rise;
Assist the offerings of my tongue
To reach the lofty skies.

2 Through all the dangers of the day
Thy hand was still my guard,
And still to drive my wants away,
Thy mercy stood prepar'd.

3 Perpetual blessings from above
Encompass me around,
But oh how few returns of love
Hath my Creator found!

4 What have I done for Him that died
To save my wretched soul?
How are my follies multiplied,
Fast as my minutes roll!

5 Lord, with this guilty heart of mine
To Thy dear cross I flee,
And to Thy grace my soul resign
To be renew'd by Thee.

6 Sprinkled afresh with pard'ning blood,
I lay me down to rest,
As in th' embraces of my God,
Or on my Saviour's breast.

*Isaac Watts*, [1707]

> **EE:** Hymns, Set 1 (Jan./Nov.), 6th Eve,
> STEPHEN'S / LONDON

# 1031 <small>L.M.<br>*Beneath the almighty wings.*</small>

1 *GLORY* to Thee, my God, this night,
For all the blessings of the light;
Keep me, oh keep me, King of Kings,
*Beneath Thine* own almighty wings.

2 Forgive me, Lord, for Thy dear Son,
The *ill that* I this day have done;
That with the world, myself, and Thee,
I, ere I sleep, at peace may be.

3 Teach me to live, that I may dread
The grave as little as my bed;
*Teach me to die, that so I may
Rise glorious at the judgment day.*

4 O may my soul on Thee repose,
And with sweet sleep mine eyelids close;
Sleep that may me more vig'rous make
To *serve* my God when I awake.

5 When in the night I sleepless lie,
My soul with heav'nly thoughts supply;

Let no ill dreams disturb my rest,
No powers of darkness me molest.

6 O when shall I, in endless day,
Forever chase dark sleep away,
And *endless praise with th' heav'nly* choir,
Incessant sing, and never tire?

*Thomas Ken*, [1692, rev. 1695, 1709], *alt.*

**1.1:** *All praise* (1692/1709)
**1.4:** *Under Thine* (1692); *Under Thy* (1695)
**2.2:** *ills which* (1692)
**3.3:** *To die that this vile body may* (1709)
**3.4:** *Triumphing rise at the last day* (1692/5);
   *Rise glorious at the awful day* (1709)
**4.4:** *praise* (1692)
**6.3:** *hymn with the supernal* (1709)
**EE:** Hymns, Set 1 (Jan./Nov.), 2nd Eve,
   EVENING HYMN / OLD 100TH
**Ed:** The 1695 and 1709 versions have both been
   widely adopted; here, they have been mixed.
   The change from *awful* to *judgment* in 3.4
   dates as early as 1827 in William Villers' *Selection of Psalms*. The first 5 sts. here appeared
   exactly as in Edward Bickersteth's *Christian
   Psalmody* (1833) and Josiah Conder's *Congregational Hymn Book* (1836), but both differ
   in the last stanza. Spurgeon's source for this
   6-staza version is unclear.

# 1032 C.M.
*An evening hymn.*

1 NOW from the altar of my heart,
   Let incense flames arise;
Assist me, Lord, to offer up
   Mine evening sacrifice.

2 Minutes and mercies multiplied
   Have made up all this day;
Minutes came quick, but mercies were
   More fleet and free than they.

3 New time, new favours, and new joys
   Do a new song require;
Till I should praise Thee as I would,
   Accept my heart's desire.

4 Lord of my time, whose hand hath set
   New time upon my score,
*Thee may* I praise for all my time
   When time shall be no more.

*John Mason*, 1683 [*alt.*]

**4.3:** *Then shall*   **Ed:** This minor variant ap-
   peared as early as 1753 in George Whitefield's
   *Collection*, except his version converted the
   text to first person plural.
**EE:** Hymns, Set 1 (Jan./Nov.), 7th Eve,
   FARRANT / MAGNUS
**MM:** Hymns, 21st Lord's Day,
   BALERMA / BROWN

# Harvest

# 1033 L.M.
*Harvest.*

1 GREAT God, as seasons disappear,
   And changes mark the rolling year,
   *Thy favor still has* crowned our days,
   And *we would celebrate Thy praise.*

2 The harvest song we would repeat:
   Thou givest us the finest wheat;

The joys of harvest we have known;
The praise, O Lord, is all Thine own.

3 Our tables spread, our garners stored,
   *Oh give us* hearts to *bless Thee*, Lord;
   Forbid it, Source of light and love,
   That hearts and lives should barren prove.

4 *Another* harvest comes apace;
   *Ripen our spirits by Thy* grace,

That we may calmly meet the blow
The sickle gives to lay us low.

5 That so, when angel reapers come
To gather sheaves to Thy blest home,
Our spirits may be borne on high
To Thy safe garner in the sky.

1,3,4.1-2 *Edmund Butcher*, 1796, *alt. J.C.*
2,4.3-4,5 *Josiah Conder*, 1836

> **1.3:** *Long has Thy favour*
> **1.4:** *summer shed again its rays.*
> **3.2:** *Where are our / praise the*
> **4.1:** *The moral*   **4.2:** *The closing day of life and*

# 1034 C.M.
*A harvest hymn.*

1 TO praise the ever-bounteous Lord,
My soul, wake all thy powers;
He calls, and at His voice come forth
The smiling harvest hours.

2 His covenant with the earth He keeps;
My tongue His goodness sing;
Summer and winter know their time;
His harvest crowns the spring.

3 Well-pleas'd the toiling swains behold
The waving yellow crop;

With joy they bear the sheaves away
And sow again in hope.

4 Thus teach me, gracious God, to sow
The seeds of righteousness:
Smile on my soul, and with Thy beams,
The ripening harvest bless.

5 Then in the last great harvest I
Shall reap a glorious crop;
The harvest shall by far exceed
What I have sown in hope.

6 Oh may the promised, *blissful* hour,
The welcome season come,
When all Thy servants shall unite
To shout the harvest home.

7 A joyful harvest they shall have
Who now in sadness sow,
And those shall live to sing above,
Who wept for sin below.

1-5 *John Needham*, 1768
[6-7 *Benjamin Beddome*, 1817]

> **Ed:** St. 6 is from Beddome's hymn, "The ripened grain appears," with the word *blissful* added to accommodate common metre. St. 7 is from Beddome's hymn "Fair spring, with all its beauties, yields." This combination of sts. is from Rippon's *Selection*, 27th ed. (1827).

# New Year

# 1035 8.7.8.7. Double
*Grateful recollection.*

1 COME, Thou fount of ev'ry blessing,
Tune my heart to sing Thy grace;
Streams of mercy, never ceasing,
Call for songs of loudest praise.
Teach me some melodious sonnet,
Sung by flaming tongues above;
Praise the mount—*oh fix me on* it,
Mount of God's unchanging love.

2 Here I raise my Ebenezer;
Hither by *Thine help* I'm come;
*And* I hope, by Thy good pleasure,
*Safely* to arrive at home.
Jesus sought me when a stranger,
Wand'ring from the fold of God;
He, to rescue me from danger,
Interpos'd *His* precious blood.

3 O! to grace how great a debtor
Daily I'm constrain'd to be;

Let that grace, now, like a fetter,
  Bind my wand'ring heart to Thee.
Prone to wander, Lord, I feel it,
  Prone to leave the God I love;
*Here's* my heart, O take and seal it,
  Seal it from Thy courts above.

[*Robert Robinson*, 1759, *alt.*]

**1.7:** *I'm fixed upon*  **2.2:** *thy grace*  **2.3:** *So*
**2.4:** *Shortly*  **2.8:** *with*  **3.7:** *Take*
**Ed:** The alterations at 2.2-2.4 are from Martin Madan's *Collection* (1760); these were
  repeated in the *Collection* (1764) of Selina, the
  Countess of Huntingdon, adding the others,
  except her version of 1.7 reads *oh fix us on it*,
  in the plural.
    Sedgwick attributed this hymn to the
  Countess of Huntingdon. John Julian, in his
  *Dictionary*, p. 252, described a manuscript
  containing this hymn, bound with a copy of
  Wesley's *Hymns and Sacred Poems* (1747).
  The title page bore the name "Diana Bindon,
  1759," and this hymn was labeled "Hymn by
  the Countess of Huntingdon." Julian noted:
  "Upon this evidence alone … Sedgwick
  carried on a long controversy in the *Notes
  and Queries*, and other periodicals, in 1858-9,
  contending that Diana Bindon was a personal
  friend of Lady Huntingdon's, and that she had
  made her MS copy direct from another MS by
  the Countess. And this he did not only upon
  the worthless evidence here given, but also
  whilst receiving, privately, direct testimony to
  the contrary, together with a positive denial
  made to him by Lady Huntingdon's biographer.
  His MSS show that having committed himself,
  he held it to be beneath him, and damaging to
  his reputation, to acknowledge his error."

# 1036 S.M.
*Ebenezer.*

1  LET hearts and tongues unite,
    And loud thanksgivings raise;
  'Tis duty, mingled with delight,
    To sing the Saviour's praise.

2  When in our blood we lay,
    He would not let us die,
  Because His love had fix'd a day
    To bring salvation nigh.

3  In childhood and in youth
    His eye was on us still;
  Though strangers to His love and truth,
    And prone to cross His will.

4  And since His name we knew,
    How gracious has He been!
  What dangers has He led us through,
    What mercies have we seen!

5  Now through another year,
    Supported by His care,
  We raise our Ebenezer here,
    "The Lord has help'd thus far."

6  Our lot in future years,
    Unable to foresee,
  He kindly to prevent our fears,
    Says, "Leave it all to Me."

7  Yea, Lord, we wish to cast
    Our cares upon Thy breast!
  Help us to praise Thee for the past,
    And trust Thee for the rest.

*John Newton*, 1779

# 1037 L.M.
*Another year.*

1  FATHER of mercies! God of love!
  Whose kind compassion still we prove,
  Our praise accept, and bless us here,
  As brought to this—another year.

2  We sing Thy goodness all divine,
  Whose radiant beams around us shine;
  'Tis through Thy goodness we appear
  *Preserved* to this—another year.

3  Our souls, our all, we here resign;
  Make us, and keep us ever Thine,
  And grant that in Thy love and fear
  We may begin—another year.

4  Be this our sweet experience still,
  To know and do Thine holy will;
  Then shall our souls, with joy sincere,
  Bless Thee for this—another year.

5 Still, Lord, through life Thy love display,
And then in death's approaching day,
We'll joyful part with all that's here,
Nor wish on earth—another year.

*Samuel Medley*, 1789 [*alt.*]

> **2.4:** *Spared* **Ed:** This alt. seems to be unknown
> prior to *OOHB* and is probably by C.H.S.

# 1038 L.M.
*Goodness sought.*

1 GREAT God, we sing that mighty hand,
By which supported still we stand;
The opening year Thy mercy shows;
Let mercy crown it, till it close.

2 By day, by night, at home, abroad,
Still are we guarded by our God,
By His incessant bounty fed,
By His unerring counsel led.

3 With grateful hearts the past we own;
The future, all to us unknown,
We to Thy guardian care commit,
And peaceful leave before Thy feet.

4 In scenes exalted or depress'd,
Thou art our joy, and Thou our rest;
Thy goodness all our hopes shall raise,
Adored through all our changing days.

5 When death shall interrupt these songs
And seal in silence mortal tongues,
Our helper God, in whom we trust,
In better worlds our souls shall boast.

*Philip Doddridge*, 1755

# 1039 L.M.
*God's help received.*

1 MY helper God! I bless His name;
The same His power, His grace the same;
The tokens of His friendly care
Open, and crown, and close the year.

2 I 'midst ten thousand dangers stand,
Supported by His guardian hand,
And see, when I survey my ways,
Ten thousand monuments of praise.

3 Thus far His arm hath led me on;
Thus far I make His mercy known;
And while I tread this desert land,
New mercies shall new songs demand.

4 My grateful soul, on Jordan's shore,
Shall raise one sacred pillar more:
Then bear, in His bright courts above,
Inscriptions of immortal love.

*Philip Doddridge*, 1755

# 1040 7.7.7.7.
*A birthday hymn.*

1 I MY Ebenezer raise
To my kind Redeemer's praise;
With a grateful heart I own
Hitherto Thy help I've known.

2 What may be my future lot,
Well I know concerns me not;
This should set my heart at rest;
What Thy will ordains is best.

3 I my all to Thee resign;
Father, let Thy will be mine;
May but all Thy dealings prove
Fruits of Thy paternal love.

4 Guard me, Saviour, by Thy pow'r,
Guard me in the trying hour;
Let Thy unremitted care
Save me from the lurking snare.

5 Let my few remaining days
Be directed to Thy praise;
So the last, the closing scene,
Shall be tranquil and serene.

6 To Thy will I leave the rest;
Grant me but this one request,
Both in life and death to prove
Tokens of Thy special love.

*John Fawcett*, 1782

# 1041 7.7.7.7.
*Shortness and uncertainty of life.*

1 WHILE with ceaseless course the sun
*Rolls along the passing* year,

Many souls their race have run,
Never more to meet us here.

2 Fix'd in an eternal state,
They have done with all below;
We a little longer wait,
But how little—none can know.

3 Swiftly thus our fleeting days
Bear us down life's rapid stream!
Upwards, Lord, our spirits raise;
All below is but a dream.

4 Bless Thy word to young and old,
Fill us with a Saviour's love,
And when life's short tale is told,
May we dwell with Thee above.

*John Newton*, [1774, *rev.* 1779]
[*alt.* John Rippon's *Selection*, 1844]

**1.2:** *Hasted through the former*

# 1042 7.7.7.7.
*Prospect of another year.*

1 FOR Thy mercy and Thy grace,
Faithful through another year,
Hear our song of thankfulness—
Father and Redeemer, hear!

2 In our weakness and distress,
Rock of strength, be Thou our stay;
In the pathless wilderness,
Be our true and living way.

3 Who of us death's awful road
In the coming year shall tread?
With Thy rod and staff, O God,
Comfort Thou his dying *bed.*

4 *Make* us faithful, keep us pure,
Keep us ever more Thine own;
Help, O help us to endure;
*Fit us for* the promised crown.

5 *So* within Thy palace gate
We shall praise, on golden strings,
Thee, the only Potentate,
Lord of Lords, and King of Kings!

*Henry Downton*, [1843, *alt.*]

**3.4:** *head* **4.1:** *Keep* **4.4:** *Till we take* **5.1:** *Till*
**Ed:** The alterations at 4.4 and 5.1 were made in
Arthur T. Russell's *Psalms and Hymns* (1851);
these were repeated in *Hymns Ancient &
Modern* (1861), plus 3.4 and 4.1 and others
that *OOHB* did not follow. Downton republished the hymn in his own collection, *Hymns
and Verses* (1873), incorporating the changes
at 4.4 and 5.1.

# 1043 6.6.6.6.8.8.
*Watchnight.*

1 YE virgin souls, arise;
With all the dead awake;
Unto salvation wise,
Oil in your vessels take;
Upstarting at the midnight cry,
Behold *your* heavenly Bridegroom nigh!

2 He comes, He comes to call
The nations to His bar,
And raise to glory all
Who fit for glory are;
Make ready for your full reward;
Go forth with joy to meet your Lord.

3 Go, meet Him in the sky,
Your everlasting Friend,
Your Head to glorify,
With all His saints ascend:
Ye pure in heart, obtain the grace
To see, without a veil, His face.

4 The everlasting doors
Shall soon the saints receive,
Above yon angel-powers
In glorious joy to live,
Far from a world of grief and sin,
With God eternally shut in.

5 Then let us wait to hear
The trumpet's welcome sound;
To see our Lord appear,
Let us be watching found;
When Jesus doth the heavens bow,
Be found—as, Lord, Thou find'st us now.

*Charles Wesley*, 1749 [*rev.* 1780]
[*alt.* John Rippon, 1787]

**1.6:** *the*  **Ed:** This minor variant first appeared in Rippon's *Selection*, but Rippon's changes were more extensive, not generally reflected here in *OOHB*.

**MM:** "Thou shalt soon be with the glorified, where thy portion is; thou art only waiting here to be made meet for the inheritance; and that done, the wings of angels shall waft thee far away to the mount of peace, and joy, and blessedness, where 'Far from a world of grief and sin, with God eternally shut in,' thou shalt rest forever and ever" (May 28).

---

## Marriage

## 1044
7.7.7.7.7.7.
*Marriage.*

1 DEIGN this union to approve,
And confirm it—God of love!
Bless Thy servants; on their heads
Now the oil of gladness shed;
In this nuptial bond, to Thee
Let them consecrated be.

2 In prosperity, be near,
To preserve them in Thy fear;
In afliction, let Thy smile
All the woes of life beguile—
And when every change is past,
Take them to Thyself at last.

*William Bengo Collyer,* 1837

## 1045
C.M.
*A wedding hymn.*

1 *SINCE* Jesus freely did appear
To grace a marriage feast,
O Lord, we ask Thy presence here
To make a wedding guest.

2 Upon the bridal pair look down,
Who now have plighted hands;
Their union with Thy favour crown,
And bless *their* nuptial bands.

3 With gifts of grace their hearts endow,
Of all rich dowries best;
Their substance bless, and peace bestow
To sweeten all the rest.

4 In purest love their souls unite,
*That they with Christian* care
*May make domestic* burdens light
By taking mutual share.

*John Berridge,* [1775, *rev.* 1785]
[*alt.* John Rippon, 1787, *rev.* 1800]

> **1.1:** *Our* (1785)  **1.3:** *And* (1785)  **2.4:** *the* (1775, 1785)  **4.2:** *And link in kindly* (1775); *And link'd in kindly* (1785)  **4.3:** *To render family* (1775, 1785)  **Ed:** Sedgwick gave the publication date for Berridge's *Sion's Songs* (1785), but the hymn had appeared ten years earlier in *The Gospel Magazine* (Aug. 1775).

## 1046
7.7.7.7.
*Truly One.*

1 FATHER of the human race,
Sanction with Thy heavenly grace
What on earth hath now been done,
That these twain be truly one.

2 One in sickness and in health,
One in poverty and wealth—
And as year rolls after year,
Each to other still more dear.

3 One in purpose, one in heart,
Till the mortal stroke shall part—
One in cheerful piety,
One forever, Lord, with Thee.

*William Bengo Collyer,* 1837

## 1047 8.7.8.7.4.7.
*"Show me a token for good."*

1 GRANT *us, Lord*, some gracious token
  *Of Thy love* before we *part;*
  *Crown* Thy Word which has been spoken,
  Life and peace to each *impart!*
    *And all blessings*
    *Which shall sanctify the heart.*

*Thomas Kelly,* [1802]
*alt. John Rippon,* 1827

> **1.1:** *Of Thy love* **1.2:** *Grant us Lord / go!*
> **1.3:** *Bless* **1.4:** *bestow!*
> **1.5-6 [7-10]:**
> *When we join the world again,*
> *Let our hearts with Thee remain!*
>   *O direct us,*
>   *And protect us,*
> *Till we gain the heav'nly shore,*
> *Where Thy people want no more.*

## 1048 8.7.8.7.4.7. / *"I will not let*
*Thee go except Thou bless me."*

1 GOD of our salvation, hear us;
  Bless, O bless us, ere we go;
  When we join the world, be near us,
  Lest Thy people careless grow;
    Saviour, keep us,
    Keep us safe from ev'ry foe.

2 As our steps are drawing nearer
  To *our best and lasting* home,
  May our view of heav'n grow clearer,
  Hope more bright of joys to come;
    And when dying,
    May Thy presence cheer he gloom.

*Thomas Kelly,* 1815
[*alt.* John Rippon's *Selection,* 1844]

> **2.2:** *the place we call our*

## 1049 6.6.6.6. Double
*Hymn and chorus parting.*

1 COME, *brethren, ere* we part,
  *Bless* the *Redeemer's* name;
  *Join every tongue and* heart
  T' *adore and praise the Lamb.*
    Jesus, the sinner's friend,
    Him whom our souls adore,
    His praises have no end;
    Praise Him forever more.

2 Lord, in Thy grace we came;
  That blessing still impart;
  We met in Jesus' name;
  In Jesus' name we part.
    Jesus, the sinner's friend,
    Him whom our souls adore,
    His praises have no end;
    Praise Him forever more.

3 If here we meet no more,
  May we, in realms above,
  With all the saints adore
  Redeeming grace and love.
    Jesus, the sinner's friend,
    Him whom our souls adore,
    His praises have no end;
    Praise Him forever more.

1 *Joseph Hart,* 1762 [*alt. J. Rippon*]
2 *Robert Hawker,* [1787]
[3 John Rippon's *Selection,* 1844]

> **1.1:** *Once more before* **1.2:** *We'll bless / Sav-*
>   *iour's* **1.3:** *Record His mercies, ev'ry*
> **1.4:** *Sing, ev'ry tongue, the same.*
> **Ed:** The refrain is by Hawker. For a more de-
>   tailed account of the evolution of this hymn,
>   see Julian's *Dictionary of Hymnology,* p. 869.
>   See also No. 1051.

## 1050 L.M.
*Dimission.*

1 COME, *Christian brethren,* ere we part,
  Join every voice and every heart;

One solemn hymn to God we raise,
*The closing* song of grateful praise.

2 Christians, we here may meet no more,
But there is yet a happier shore;
And there, releas'd from toil and pain,
*Dear brethren*, we shall meet again.

3 *And now* to God, the Three in One,
Be *everlasting* glory done;
*Raise, raise*, ye saints, the sound again;
Ye nations, join the loud Amen.

*Henry Kirke White*, [1812]
[*alt. John Rippon*, 1827]

**1.1:** *Christians! brethren!* **1.4:** *One final*
**2.4:** *Brethren*, **3.1:** *Now* **3.2:** *eternal* **3.3:** *Raise*,
**Ed:** Sedgwick dated the hymn 1806, likely
thinking that the hymn appeared in White's
*Remains*, but it first appeared in William
Collyer's *Hymns* (1812).

# 1051 S.M.
*Parting.*

1 ONCE more, before we part,
We'll bless the Saviour's name;
Record His mercies, ev'ry heart;
Sing, ev'ry tongue, the same.

2 Hoard up His sacred Word,
And feed thereon and grow;
Go on to seek to know the Lord,
And practice what you know.

*Joseph Hart*, 1762

**Ed:** The original version of No. 1049.

# 1052 8.7.8.7.4.7.
*At dismission.*

1 LORD, dismiss us with Thy blessing;
Fill our hearts with joy and peace;
Let us each, Thy love possessing,
Triumph in redeeming grace;
O refresh us!
*Trav'lling through this wilderness.*

2 Thanks we give, and adoration,
For Thy gospel's joyful sound;
May the fruits of Thy salvation
In our hearts and lives abound;
*May Thy presence*
*With us ever more* be found!

3 So whene'er the signal's given,
Us from earth to call away,
Borne on angel's wing to heaven,
Glad the summons to obey,
We shall *surely*
Reign with Christ in endless day!

[*John Fawcett*, 1773]

**1.6:** *In this dry and barren place*
**2.5-6:** *Ever faithful*
*To the truth may we* **3.5:** *ever*
**Ed:** Sedgwick attributed the hymn to Walter
Shirley. For a full discussion of the earliest
printings of the hymn and identification of its
author, see Julian's *Dictionary*, pp. 686-687.
The alteration at 1.6 is from Richard Conyers'
*Collection* (1774); the others are from Augus-
tus Toplady's *Psalms & Hymns* (1776).

# 1053 8.7.8.7. Double
*The benediction.*

1 MAY the grace of Christ our Saviour
And the Father's boundless love,
With the Holy Spirit's favour,
Rest upon us from above!
Thus may we abide in union
With each other and the Lord,
And possess, in sweet communion,
Joys which earth cannot afford.

*John Newton*, 1779

# 1054 C.M.
*Benediction.*

1 NOW may the God of peace and love,
Who from th' impris'ning grave
Restor'd the Shepherd of the sheep,
Omnipotent to save,

2 Through the rich merits of that blood,
Which He on Calv'ry spilt,

To make th' eternal cov'nant sure,
  On which our hopes are built,

3 Perfect our souls in ev'ry grace
  T' accomplish all His will,
And all that's pleasing in His sight
  Inspire us to fulfill!

4 For the great Mediator's sake,
  We for these blessings pray;

With glory let His name be crown'd
  Through heav'n's eternal day!

*Thomas Gibbons*, 1769

# Blessing and Thanks

## 1055 L.M.
*Before meat.*

1 OUR Father, bless the bounteous store
Wherewith Thou hast our table spread;
With grateful songs we all adore
And bless the hand by which we're fed.

*Charles H. Spurgeon*, 1866

## 1056 8.7.8.7.4.7.
*Before meat.*

1 HEAVENLY Father, grant Thy blessing
  On the food before us spread;
All our tongues are now confessing,
  By Thy hand alone we're fed,
    And Thou givest,
  Best of all, the living bread.

*Charles H. Spurgeon*, 1866

## 1057 L.M.
*Before meat.*

1 BE present at our table, Lord;
Be here and ev'rywhere ador'd;
*These mercies* bless, and grant that we
May feast in Paradise with Thee.

*John Cennick*, 1741, *alt.*

**1.3:** *Thy creatures*   **Ed:** This alteration appeared as early as 1842 in John Campbell's *Marrow of Modern Hymn-Books.*

## 1058 8.7.8.7.
*After meat.*

1 JOIN to bless the bounteous Giver
For the food He here bestows;
From His goodness like a river
Every earthly blessing flows.

*Charles H. Spurgeon*, 1866

## 1059 C.M.
*After meat.*

1 WE thank Thee, Father, for the love
  Which feeds us here below,
And hope in fairer realms above
  Celestial feasts to know.

*Charles H. Spurgeon*, 1866

## "OMITTED."

# 1060
L.M.
*Not ashamed of Jesus.*

1 JESUS! and shall it ever be,
A mortal man ashamed of Thee?
*Ashamed of Thee, whom angels praise,*
*Whose glories shine thro' endless days.*

2 Ashamed of Jesus! sooner far
Let ev'ning blush to own a star;
He sheds the *beams of light* divine
O'er *this benighted* soul of mine.

3 Ashamed of Jesus! just as soon
Let midnight be ashamed of noon;
'Tis midnight with my soul till He,
Bright Morning Star, bid darkness flee.

4 Ashamed of Jesus! *that dear* Friend
On whom *my hopes of heaven* depend!
*No; when I blush,* be this my shame,
That I no more revere His name.

5 Ashamed of Jesus! yes, I may,
When I've no *guilt* to wash away,
No tear to wipe, no *good* to crave,
No fears to quell, no soul to save.

6 Till then (nor is *my* boasting vain),
Till then I boast a Saviour slain.
And O may this my *glory* be,
That *Christ is* not ashamed of me!

1-2,4-6 *Joseph Grigg,* 1765, *alt. B. Francis*
3 *Benjamin Francis,* 1787

**1.3-4:** *Scorn'd be the thought by rich and poor;*
  *O may I scorn it more and more!*
**2.3:** *beam of noon*  **2.4:** *all this midnight soul*
**4.1:** *of that*  **4.2:** *for heaven my hopes*
**4.3:** *It must not be—*  **5.2:** *crimes*  **5.3:** *joy*
**6.1:** *the*  **6.3:** *portion*  **6.4:** *Saviour*

---

As the various versions of the Psalms amount to 70
more than the numbering indicates, there is a total
of 1130 psalms and hymns in this volume.

# How Shall We Sing?

COULD we rule the service of song in the house of the Lord, we should, we fear, come into conflict with the prejudices and beliefs of many most excellent men, and bring a hornet's nest about our ears. Although we have neither the will nor the power to become reformers of sacred music, we should like to whisper a few things into the ear of some of our Jeduthuns or Asaphs,[1] who happen to be "chief musicians" in country towns or rural villages. We will suppose the following words to be our private communication.

O sweet singer of Israel, remember that the song is not for your glory, but for the honour of the Lord, who inhabiteth the praises of Israel;[2] therefore, select not anthems and tunes in which your skillfulness will be manifest, but such as will aid the people to magnify the Lord with their thanksgivings. The people come together not to see you as a songster, but to praise the Lord in the beauty of holiness.[3] Remember also, that you are not set to sing for yourself only, but to be a leader of others, many of whom know nothing of music; therefore, choose such tunes as can be learned and followed by all, that none in the assembly may be compelled to be silent while the Lord is extolled. Why should so much as one be defrauded of his part through you? Simple airs are the best, and the most sublime; very few of the more intricate tunes are really musical. Your twists, and fugues, and repetitions, and rattlings up and down the scale, are mostly barbarous noise-makings, fitter for Babel than Bethel.[4] If you and your choir wish to show off your excellent voices, you can meet at home for that purpose, but the Sabbath and the church of God must not be desecrated to so poor an end.

True praise is heart work. Like smoking incense, it rises from the glowing coals of devout affection. Essentially, it is not a thing of sound: sound is associated with it very properly for most weighty reasons, but still the essence and life of praise lie not in the voice, but in the soul. Your business in the congregation is to give to spiritual praise a suitable embodiment in harmonious notes. Take care that you do not depress what you should labour to express. Select a tune in accordance with the spirit of the psalm or hymn, and make your style of singing suitable to the words before you. Flippantly to lead all tunes to the same time, tone, and emphasis, is an abomination; and to pick tunes at random is little less than criminal. You mock God and injure the devotions of his people if you carelessly offer to the Lord that which has cost you no thought, no care, no exercise of judgment. You can help the pious heart to wing its way to heaven upon a well-selected harmony, and you can, on the other hand, vex the godly ear by inappropriate or unmelodious airs,

---

1.  1 Chronicles 15-16
2.  Psalm 22:3
3.  1 Chronicles 16:29

4.  Genesis 11 / Genesis 35

adapted rather to distract and dishearten than to encourage intelligent praise.

The time is a very primary consideration, but it is too often treated as a matter of no consequence. Large bodies move slowly, and hence the tendency to drawl out tunes in numerous assemblies. We have heard the notes prolonged till the music has been literally swamped, drenched, drowned in long sweeps and waves of monotonous sound. On the other hand, we cannot endure to hear psalms and solemn hymns treated as jigs, and dashed through at a gallop. Solemnity often calls for long-drawn harmony, and joy as frequently demands leaping notes of bounding delight. Be wise enough to strike the fitting pace each time, and by your vigorous leadership inspire the congregation to follow *en masse*.

May we in the very gentlest whisper beg you to think very much of God, much of the singing, and extremely little of yourself. The best sermon is that in which the theme absorbs the preacher and hearers, and leaves no one either time or desire to think about the speaker; so in the best congregational singing, the leader is forgotten because he is too successful in his leadership to be noticed as a solitary person. The head leads to the body, but it is not parted from it, nor is it spoken of separately; the best leadership stands in the same position. If your voice becomes too noticeable, rest assured that you are but a beginner in your art.

One of your great objects should be to induce all the congregation to join in the singing. Your minister should help you in this, and his exhortations and example will be a great assistance to you; but still as the Lord's servant in the department of sacred song,

you must not rely on others, but put forth your own exertions.

Not only ought all the worshippers to sing, but each one should sing praises with understanding,[5] and as David says, "play skillfully" unto the Lord.[6] This cannot be effected except by instructing the people in public psalmody. It is not your duty to institute classes for young and old? Might you not thus most effectually serve the church and please the Lord? The method of Mr. Curwen,[7] and the use of his Sol-fa Notation, will much aid you in breaking ground, and you can in after years either keep to the new method, or turn to the old notation as may seem best to you. Thousands have learned to sing who were hopelessly silent until the Sol-fa system was set on foot.

The institution of singers, as a separate order, is an evil, a growing evil, and ought to be abated and abolished, and the instruction of the entire congregation is the readiest, surest, and most scriptural mode of curing it. A band of godless men and women will often install themselves in a conspicuous part of the chapel and monopolise the singing to the grief of the pastor, the injury of the church, and the scandal of public worship; or else one man, with a miserable voice, will drag a miserable few after him in a successful attempt to make psalms and hymns hideous or dolorous. Teach the lads and lasses and their seniors to run up and down the Sol-fa Modulator, and drill them in a few good, solid, thoroughly musical tunes, and you, O sons of Asaph, shall earn yourself a good degree.

C.H. Spurgeon
*The Sword and the Trowel*
1 June 1870

---

5.  Psalm 47:7, 1 Corinthians 14:15
6.  Psalm 33:3
7.  John Curwen (1816-1880)

# Editorial Notes

*Our Own Hymn-Book* was first published in 1866 in two versions: a pocket-size edition (13cm), released in September of that year, and a large-type edition (19cm), released in December. The larger edition had more features than the smaller one, such as an Index of Subjects, a List of Works (authors and sources), and a General Index (first line of every stanza). The first edition contained 1059 hymns (1129 counting multiple versions of the Psalms).

The following account describes the official unveiling of the hymnal on 14 Sept. 1866:

"On Friday, the 14th inst., the new hymn-book, so long promised to the congregation of the Metropolitan Tabernacle, was introduced by Mr. C.H. Spurgeon. The rev. gentlemen stated that he had adopted for the title, *Our Own Hymn-Book,* and though this title was objected to by some persons, he thought it a good one, as most possessers of the book would like to call it their "own hymn-book." . . . He then referred to the *Union Tune Book[1]* as being the most serviceable selection of melodies extant. Several tunes, with which Mr. Spurgeon thought the congregation might not be acquainted, were sung by the 'leaders,' Messrs. Hale and Turner. It is a sign of the smallness of the selection of tunes used at the Tabernacle that such tunes as 'Abbotsford,' 'Bradford,' and 'Darwell's' were described as being new to the congregation.

"Mr. Spurgeon concluded by stating that he did not intend to appoint any trustees to the new hymn-book fund—he thought he should make a sufficiently good trustee. If there were any profits, the first appropriation would go towards the almshouses, and any future profits would be given to such objects as he should determine, but he should not take a farthing of the profits for himself."[2]

An early review of the hymnal described how the project had been in gestation for some time, then completed in earnest in 1866:

"The task at first appeared so formidable that, after more than one attempt, it was laid aside to be again resumed; and when, during last year, considerable progress was believed to have been made, it was again allowed to rest, partly owing to the care and responsibility it involved, when other duties were pressing heavily on the pastor's attention. With the opening of the year 1866, the hymn-book was again taken in hand, this time with a purpose and resolve to allow no other duties to hinder its progress. Six months, we believe, were allotted to the task of its compilation, but it has required nearly eight to complete the book, with all the help which could be obtained from every available and reliable source."[3]

The 2nd ed. (1867) added hymn no. 1060 (curiously titled "Omitted"), for 1130 total, and corrected some authorship attributions.

---

1. *Union Tune Book: A Selection of Psalm and Hymn Tunes.* Arranged by J.I. Cobbin, 1854.

2. "Mr. Spurgeon's New Hymn Book," *The South London Chronicle,* 22 Sept. 1866, p. 6.

3. *The Wesleyan Times,* 10 Sept. 1866.

More corrections followed, mostly to issues of authorship, in the 3rd (1868), 4th (1869), 5th (also 1869), and 6th (1873) eds. The corrections ceased after 1873, but further numbered editions followed, including a 10th ed. (1882), and the hymnal was printed until at least 1908.

The Burke Library at Union Theological Seminary holds copies of the first five editions, at least one of which (1867) belonged to Daniel Sedgwick, and it contains his handwritten corrections, some of which were applied to subsequent editions (Fig. 1).

The church published a supplement in 1898, adding Nos. 1061-1363, including some additional hymns by Charles Spurgeon which he had written in the intervening years since the original hymnal. His son Thomas, who was pastor of the church at the time, also contributed hymns to the supplement.

The present edition retains the hymns as they appeared in the original editions, consistent with how they were learned and used at the Metropolitan Tabernacle, with added footnotes indicating Spurgeon's textual alterations, Sedgwick's hymnological methods, and other insights on the hymns.

## Editorial Considerations

Spurgeon, assisted by Daniel Sedgwick, preferred to use accurate versions of hymns from the original authors, whenever possible. Similarly, all the hymns in this edition have been checked against primary sources, with variants noted in detail. This edition takes into account the original authors' preferences for contractions ("heav'n" vs. "heaven"), punctuation, and vocatives ("O" / "Oh"). *Our Own Hymn-Book* did not have strict standards for contractions or vocatives, thus we have also not applied overarching standards on these issues and have allowed for variation between authors.

This edition makes some minor adjust-

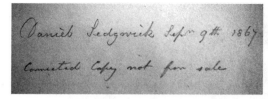

**Figure 1.** Inscription inside an 1867 ed. of *Our Own Hymn-Book*, formerly belonging to Daniel Sedgwick, now held at The Burke Library, Union Theological Seminary. Image courtesy of Eric Stedfeld.

ments to punctuation for the purposes of grammatical clarity. Metre designations were often abbreviated in the original hymnal ("7s," "148th"); they have been expanded in this edition ("7.7.7.7"), except for common metre, long metre, and short metre. The footnotes and cross references in this volume are entirely by the present editor, as are all editorial brackets. Where the Psalms are given in multiple versions, this edition assigns letters to each version (100a, 100b, etc.).

In the attributions, Sedgwick sometimes reported the date of authorship from the writer's manuscript or some attested date of composition, if prior to the earliest publication. This edition always gives the date of earliest publication in the attribution and the index, while providing an earlier date of manuscript composition in the footnotes, if applicable.

This edition preserves the capitalization of divine pronouns ("Thee," "His") and names of God. Spurgeon often did not capitalize "word" in referring to Scripture; this edition does, in keeping with the prevailing modern practice.

The hymn titles in this volume reflect what was given in *Our Own Hymn-Book* and generally do not reflect the titles bestowed by the original authors. Scripture references in the original sources are reflected in the Index of Scriptures.

Spurgeon omitted stanzas from long hymns, as is common in hymn collections;

**Figure 2.** One of Spurgeon's pulpit notes (sermon outlines) from 21 Dec. 1884, showing the hymn numbers for the week and Spurgeon's preferred tunes. Image courtesy of The Spurgeon Library, Midwestern Baptist Theological Seminary.

his abridgments are not indicated in this edition, except if the original first stanza has been omitted or if the abridgment is notable in some regard. Readers are advised to consult the original sources for full, unabridged versions of these hymns.

Spurgeon made some deliberate alterations and repeated alterations from other collections; those alterations are set apart by italics; the original form of the text is given in footnotes. Alterations which are known or believed to be by Spurgeon himself are marked with his initials. None of the textual alterations should be attributed to Daniel Sedgwick, since Sedgwick's role was to ensure accuracy, whereas Spurgeon frequently altered or loosely quoted hymns across his corpus of printed works.

In his preface, Spurgeon lamented over the "mangling of hymns," a practice "to be most heartily deprecated." Nonetheless, in spite of his and Sedgwick's best attempts, a great number of alterations were repeated in his hymnal, sometimes from long or seemingly obscure chains of variation (such as 264 or 307). Many hymns in this collection reflect the long legacy of John Rippon's cultivation of texts and his editorial hand, as indicated in the Index of Authors and Sources.

Hymnal editors understand how hymns are endlessly tweaked from collection to collection in order to reflect the doctrinal or linguistic preferences of the compilers, so a certain amount of meddling is to be expected. Spurgeon should be applauded for at least attempting to work from undoctored versions, even if he ultimately perpetuated the "system," as it were, of unwittingly repeating someone else's changes.

### Spurgeon's Tunes

Spurgeon did not indicate tunes in his hymnal, but he did make tune recommendations in other sources, such as in *Morning by Morning* and *Evening by Evening*. J. Spencer Curwen, in a visit to Metropolitan Tabernacle on 4 January 1874, observed the use of three hymns and tunes and recorded his observations in his *Studies in Worship Music*. Spurgeon provided tune names in some of his manuscript sermon outlines; some of these were given in his *Fac-Simile Pulpit Notes*, others are held in collections at Midwestern Baptist Theological Seminary (Fig. 2). These various resources yielded the tune footnotes and the Index of Tunes, new features for this edition. The collection of pulpit notes at Spurgeon's College in London was not accessible for the purposes of this edition; this is a treasure trove of research for future study.

Spurgeon is known to have used at least six different tunebooks, as described by Curwen and as stated in the preface to Spurgeon's own *Tabernacle Tune Book* (*ca.* 1869): *The Union Tune Book* (1837, 1854), *The Bristol Tune-Book* (1864, 1881, 1891), *Hymns Ancient & Modern* (1861, 1868, 1875, 1889, etc.), *The Congregational Psalmist* (1858, 1860, 1872, 1879, etc.), and *The Psalmist* (1835, 1863).

### Daniel Sedgwick's Involvement

Daniel Sedgwick (1814–1879) was a self-made hymnologist, a bookseller who developed a specialty for collecting and reselling hymnals. An anonymous account in 1893 described the man and his unique store at 93 Sun Street in London:

"[His] dingy shop in London used to be sought out by lovers of hymnology from all parts of Great Britain and America. There was a little back room or 'parlor' to his shop, just large enough to hold the tiny grate, table, and a stool or two. The walls were lined with hymn books and hymnological works, two or three deep, and engravings of famous old hymn writers in worn black frames hung over the books. Seated on a three-legged stool, unkempt, unshaven, in much soiled shirtsleeves, with a stumpy black pipe in his mouth, Mr. Sedgwick would discourse of his books, catalogs, indexes, and work."[4]

He ventured into publishing by reprinting the works of notable hymn writers, including William Williams' *Hosannah* and *Gloria in Excelsis* (1859), Augustus Toplady's *Hymns and Sacred Poems* (1860), *Hymns and Verses* by John Ryland (1862), and *Hymns, Psalms, and Poems* by Anne Steele (1863).

In 1860, he published his *Comprehensive Index . . . of Authors and Translators*; this was revised in 1863.

His efforts in assisting other hymnal compilers and editors began with Roundell Palmer's *Book of Praise* (1862), and continued with Spurgeon's *Our Own Hymn-Book* (1866), and Josiah Miller's *Our Hymns: Their Authors and Origin* (1866; revised as *Singers and Songs of the Church*, 1869). He is credited with providing valuable assistance to the editors of *Hymns Ancient & Modern* (1861). His manuscripts, after his death, were acquired by John Julian and referenced during the production of the *Dictionary of Hymnology* (1892, with suppl., 1907).

Sedgwick's work on Palmer's and Spur-geon's collections is significant because up until that time, some hymnals did not credit authors at all; in fact, many of Spurgeon's other works did not credit the hymns he used. In addition to attempting to identify all the authors, Sedgwick also gave the date of composition, a feature which is common today but unique in his time. If the timeline of publication for *OOHB* was indeed squeezed into the first nine months of 1866, the gathering of all this data would have been a Herculean effort, even by modern standards. Granted, he continued to edit his work over several editions, but for comparison, the vetting of that same data for this edition took well over a year, even with the benefit of digital books, OCLC, and a long hymnological paper trail.

Sedgwick is thus often called the Father of English Hymnology. As one late admirer put it, "Without exception, the hymn books in use in every religous denomination during the last thirty years were directly indebted to the aid of a man whom many people would have been ashamed to speak to in the public streets on account of his seedy appearance."[5]

Nonetheless, some of his work was deserving of further scrutiny. His biggest critic was probably Julian, whose blunt correctives are noted throughout this edition. He lamented Sedgwick's "worthless" guesses at the authorship of No. 366 ("When thou, my righteous judge, shall come"), and noted how Sedgwick had refused to admit his error on the authorship of No. 1035 ("Come, thou fount of every blessing").

William T. Brooke's biography of Sedgwick in Julian's *Dictionary*, pp. 1036-1037, weighed the good and the bad, and ultimately conceded that for all his "dogmatic ignorance and want of power to balance evidence," his sometimes "baseless sugges-

---

4. "Hymns, Their History and Development" [review], *The Independent*, 13 Apr. 1893, p. 24.

5. "Daniel Sedgwick, Hymnologist," quoting the *Manchester Evening News* of 18 Aug. 1892, in *Notes & Queries*, 19 Nov. 1892, p. 409.

tions and erroneous conclusions, . . . with all drawbacks of education, temperament, and narrow theological prepossessions, he, by the collection and comparison of hymns and hymnological literature, and by careful annotation, made it possible for others to reap a rich harvest."

## The Design of the New Edition
This edition was designed as an homage to the style of Spurgeon's published works. The original hymn and body text were printed in a classic typeface designed by Giambattista Bodoni (1740–1813); here we have used ITC Century Std., a modern descendant, updated by Morris Fuller Benton (1872–1948). Hymn numbers in this edition match the Clarendon typeface originally designed by Robert Besley (1794–1876). Headings are set in Linotext by Morris Fuller Benton, a close approximation to the distinctive Old English typeface used by Passmore & Alabaster. Subheading text is Latin MT Std., also a close approximation to the all-caps typeface found in many of Spurgeon's works.

## Acknowledgements
This project would not have been possible without the gracious assistance of many people. Eric Stedfeld (Elmer Holmes Bobst Library, New York University) contributed valuable research on Daniel Sedgwick, examined rare hymnals in libraries across New York City, and helped clarify the revision history of *Our Own Hymn-Book*. Dr. V. Erika Smith (PhD, Case Western Reserve University) provided information and resources related to her 2006 dissertation on Spurgeon.

Jennifer Taylor and Rachel Cohen provided assistance with the Spurgeon collection at Samford University. The professional staff at Midwestern Baptist Theological Seminary provided assistance with their extensive Spurgeon collection.

Dr. Esther Crookshank (The Southern Baptist Theological Seminary) provided her hymnological expertise and editorial eye. Dr. Joe Herl (Concordia University, Nebraska) provided hymnological primary source materials and valuable feedback.

Emilee Smith (SBTS) provided patient assistance in acquiring materials through interlibrary loan. Adam Winters (SBTS) examined some materials while visiting Emory University. June Can (Beinecke Library) assisted with the Elizabeth Scott manuscripts at Yale. Helen Weller (Westminster College, Cambridge) graciously provided images from Thomas Gibbons' 1769 collection.

This project also would not have been possible without the wealth of digital resources available at a scholar's fingertips, including Google Books, Internet Archive, HathiTrust, Hymnary.org, Early English Books Online, Eighteenth Century Collections Online, The Gospel Magazine, and others. The online editions of the hymns of Charles and John Wesley, hosted by Duke Divinity School and edited by Randy Maddox, were a valuable resource for clarifying the revision histories of those texts. The British Library's digital scanning service was an asset in many cases. The James P. Boyce Centennial library at The Southern Baptist Theological Seminary served as a hub for access to these and other digital resources, and it contains its own storehouse of rare, original materials related to Charles Spurgeon and Christian hymnody.

*Chris Fenner*
The Southern Baptist Theological Seminary
Louisville, KY

*Matt Boswell*
The Trails Church
Prosper, TX

# Known Revisions in Our Own Hymn-Book

No. 100B
1866: John Hopkins, 1562
1868: William Kethe, 1562

No. 160
1866: Josiah Conder, 1837
1867: Josiah Conder, 1824

No. 170
1866: Thomas Marriott, 1825
1867: John Marriott, 1813

No. 172
1866: Richard Mant, 1824
1867: Richard Mant, 1809

No. 176
1866: Sabbath Hymn Book, 1858
1869 (5th): Edwards A. Park, 1858

No. 178
1866: Anna Shipton, 1865
1867: Anna Shipton, 1855

No. 195
1866: Frederick William Faber, 1852
1869 (4th): Frederick William Faber, 1849

No. 216
1866: James Hervey, 1763
1867: James Hervey, 1745, a.

No. 222
1866: Frederick William Faber, 1852
1869 (4th): Frederick William Faber, 1849

No. 254
1866: Samuel Medley, 1789
1867: Samuel Medley, 1787

No. 264
1866: James Montgomery, 1819
1867: James Montgomery, 1808

No. 278
1866: Frederick William Faber, 1852, a.
1869 (4th): Frederick William Faber, 1849, a.

No. 292
1866: James Montgomery, 1825
1867: James Montgomery, 1812

No. 301
1866: Canterbury Hymnal, 1863
1867: Hymns and Poetry for Schools, 1840

No. 309
1866: Thomas Kelly, 1809, a.
1867: Thomas Kelly, 1804, a.

No. 311
1866: William Howes Groser, 1853
1867: — Groser, 1844
1868: William Groser, 1838

No. 318
1866: Society Hymns, 1853, a.
1867: Cecil Francis Alexander, 1852, a.

No. 320
1866: Thomas Kelly, 1809
1867: Thomas Kelly, 1804

No. 323
1866: John Bakewell, 1760
1873: John Bakewell, 1757

No. 333
1866: Thomas Kelly, 1809
1873: Thomas Kelly, 1806

No. 338
1866: Thomas Kelly, 1809
1867: Thomas Kelly, 1806

No. 344
1866: James Kelly, 1850
1867: James Kelly's Collection, 1849

No. 351
1866: James Kelly, 1850
1867: Edward Denny, 1837

No. 356
1866: Edward Denny, 1848
1867: Edward Denny, 1839

No. 358
1866: Thomas Kelly, 1809
1867: Thomas Kelly, 1806

No. 363
1866: John Cennick, 1752;
U— in Rippon's Selection, 1787
1867: John Cennick, 1752;
Caleb Evans' Collection, 1769

No. 392
1866: W— in Rippon's Selection, 1787
1873: John Wingrove, 1785

No. 396
1866: Nettleton's Village Hymns, 1825
1867: Jonathan Evans, 1803
1868: Jonathan Evans, 1784

No. 402
1866: M—L—, 1853
1868: Jane E. Leeson, 1842

No. 415
1866: John Cennick, 1743
1867: John Cennick, 1742

No. 419
1866: John Bakewell, 1760
1873: John Bakewell, 1757

No. 420
1866: John Cennick, 1743
1873: John Cennick, 1742

No. 440
1866: William Langford, 1760
1867: Madan's Collection, 1763

No. 443
1866: Rippon's Selection, 1844
1873: Richard Cope, 1813

No. 446
1866: Thomas Kelly, 1809
1867: Thomas Kelly, 1806

No. 460
1866: Andrew Reed, 1842
1867: Andrew Reed, 1817

No. 463
1866: Rippon's Selection, 1829, a.
1873: Beddome and Rippon, 1800

No. 500
1866: F.D. Huntingdon, 1843
1867: Baptist Psalmist, 1843

No. 502
1866: Ambassador's Hymn Book, 1862
1869 (4th): William Freeman Lloyd, 1835

No. 507
1866: Frederick Wenzel Neisser
1873: Nicholas Louis Zinzendorf, 1736

No. 516
1866: Mrs. A.B. Hyde, 1825
1867: Ann Beadley Hyde, 1825

No. 518
1866: Jonathan Allen, 1803?
1869 (5th): Jonathan Allen, 1801, a.

No. 524
1866: William Urwick's Collection, 1829
1867: Charlotte Elizabeth Tonna, 1829, a.

No. 527
1866: — Waterbury, 1844
1867: Jared Bell Waterbury, 1844

No. 528
1866: Isaac Watts, 1706, a.
1873: Watts and Rippon, 1706-1787

No. 541
1866: Count Zinzendorf, 1739
1873: Count Zinzendorf, 1736

No. 548
1866: Mary Jane Deck, 1845
1867: Mary Jane Deck, 1847

No. 549
1866: Edward Mote, 1836, a.
1873: Edward Mote, 1825

No. 555
1866: Isaac Watts, 1709
1869 (4th): Isaac Watts, 1706

No. 557
1866: Richard Parkinson, 1845
1867: Richard Burnham, 1796, a.

No. 567
1866: Cherrie Smith, 1863
1867: Charitie Lees Smith, 1863

No. 576
1866: Presbyterian Psalms and Hymns, 1843
1868: Mrs. J.L. Gray, 1843

No. 580
1866: from the Italian, 1769
1870: tr. R.A. Coffin, 1854

No. 602
1866: Anna Shipton, 1865
1867: Anna Shipton, 1855

No. 626
1866: Josiah Conder, 1856
1867: Josiah Conder, 1836

No. 628
1866: Philip Doddridge, 1755
1873: Watts and Rippon, 1706-1787

No. 629
1866: Rippon's Selection, 1800
1873: Beddome and Rippon, 1800

No. 653
1866: Charitie Smith, 1861
1867: Charitie Lees Smith, 1861

No. 659
1866: Henry Francis Lyte, 1833
1873: Henry Francis Lyte, 1825

No. 663
1866: James George Deck, 1845
1867: James George Deck, 1837

No. 668
1866: Hymns for the Children of God, 1851
1867: Mary Bowly, 1847

No. 673
1866: Henry Kirke White, 1807
1867: Henry Kirke White, 1806;
    Fanny Fuller Maitland, 1827

No. 680
1866: Samuel W. Gandy, 1842
1867: Samuel W. Gandy, 1837

No. 684
1866: John Andrew Rothe, 1731
1867: John Andrew Rothe, 1728

No. 687
1866: (5.2) And that none …
1867: (5.2) And none …

No. 691
1866: From the Latin,
    W. Reid's Hymns of Praise, 1865
1867: Frederick Wiilliam Faber, 1852
1869 (4th): Frederick Wiilliam Faber, 1849
1873: Frederick Wiilliam Faber, 1835

No. 701
1866: Hymns for the Poor of the Flock, 1842
1867: Hymns for the Poor of the Flock, 1837
1869 (4th): William Freeman Lloyd, 1835

No. 730
1866: Hymns for the Poor of the Flock, 1842
1867: James George Deck, 1837

No. 732
1866: Kirkham or Kennedy, 1787
1867: K— in Rippon's Selection, 1787
1873: George Keith, 1787

No. 735
1866: William Cowper, 1779
1869 (4th): William Cowper, 1771
1870: William Cowper, 1779
1873: William Cowper, 1771

No. 741
1866: Thomas Kelly, 1809
1867: Thomas Kelly, 1804

No. 744
1866: Hasting's Spiritual Songs, 1833
1869 (4th): William Freeman Lloyd, 1835

No. 751
1866: Thomas Kelly, 1809
1867: Thomas Kelly, 1804

No. 759
1866: Thomas Kelly, 1809
1867: Thomas Kelly, 1806

No. 760
1866: John Kent, 1803, a.
1867: John Kent, 1827

No. 761
1866: John Kent, 1803, a.
1873: John Kent, 1827

No. 762
1866: James George Deck, 1855
1867: James George Deck, 1837

No. 771
1866: Rippon's Selection, 1800
1873: Beddome and Rippon, 1800

No. 777
1866: Jeanne Marie Guyon, 1790
1869 (4th): Jeanne Marie Guyon, 1722

No. 778
1866: Jeanne Marie Guyon, 1790
1869 (4th): Jeanne Marie Guyon, 1722

No. 781
1866: Jeanne Marie Guyon, 1790
1869 (4th): Jeanne Marie Guyon, 1722

No. 784
1866: Frederick William Faber, 1852
1869 (4th): Frederick William Faber, 1849

No. 798
1866: G. Tersteegen and P. Gerhardt
1867: G. Tersteegen and P. Gerhardt, 1731
1873: Gerhard Tersteegen, 1731

No. 807
1866: Gerard Tersteegen, 1731
1867: Gerhard Tersteegen, 1731
      tr. Samuel Jackson, 1832

No. 831
1866: Alexander Pope, 1720
1869 (4th): Alexander Pope, 1736

No. 839
1866: John Williams, 1810
1867: John Williams, 1801

No. 840
1866: L.M.
1868: C.M.

No. 842
1866: (4.3) "every shade"
1869 (5th): (4.3) "every shape"

No. 854
1866: Thomas Kelly, 1809
1867: Thomas Kelly, 1804

No. 869
1866: Cherrie Smith, 1861
1867: Charitie Lees Smith, 1861

No. 878
1866: James Montgomery, 1853
1868: James Montgomery, 1829

No. 879
1866: Mrs. Wilson, 1837? a.
1867: Elizabeth Mills, 1829, a.

No. 880
1866: John Berridge, 1785, a.
1867: John Berridge, 1785, a.
      from John Cennick, 1744

No. 886
1866: Thomas Kelly, 1809
1867: Thomas Kelly, 1806

No. 887
1866: John Swertner's Collection, 1789
1873: tr. C.G. Clements, 1789

No. 893
1866: James Montgomery, 1825
1869 (4th): James Montgomery, 1836

No. 903
1866: K— in Rippon's Selection, 1787
1873: George Keith, 1787

No. 910
1866: Henry Francis Lyte, 1834
1867: Henry Francis Lyte, 1841

No. 916
1866: James Montgomery, 1812
1868: James Montgomery, 1821

No. 919
1866: Thomas Binney, 1857
1867: Thomas Binney, 1825

No. 920
1866: Edward Bickersteth's Collection, 1833
1873: B.W. Noel's Selection, 1832

No. 924
1866: Psalms, Hymns, and Spiritual Songs, 1845
1867: Mary Bowly, 1845

No. 931
1866: J.E. Giles, 1844
1867: John Eustace Giles, 1837

No. 933
1866: Rippon's Selection, 1829
1867: Charles Wesley, 1747, a.

No. 935
1866: Baptist Selection, 1828
1867: Maria Grace Saffery, 1828

No. 951
1866: Rippon's Selection, 1829
1873: Doddridge and Gibbons, 1755-1784

No. 957
1866: Albert Midlane, 1865
1868: Albert MIdlane, 1861

No. 962
1866: Baptist Psalmody, 1843
1867: Baptist Psalmist, 1843
1868: Philip Doddridge, 1755, a.

No. 964
1866: William Shrubsole, 1794
1869 (4th): William Shrubsole, 1795

No. 967
1866: Thomas Kelly, 1809
1867: Thomas Kelly, 1806

No. 971
1866: Nettleton's Village Hymns, 1825
1867: Eriphus, Evangelical Magazine, 1821

No. 991
1866: Baptist Psalmody, 1843
1867: Baptist Psalmist, 1843
1873: Philip Doddridge, 1755, a.

No. 993
1866: Hymnologia Christiana, 1863;
        Hymns Old and New, 1864
1867: Jane Crewdson, 1860
        Benjamin Hall Kennedy, 1863

No. 1005
1866: W.S. DuSautoy's Selection, 1818
1867: Thomas Kelly, 1804
        John Bulmer, 1825

No. 1014
1866: Comprehensive Hymn Book, 1839
1867: Rowland Hill (?) 1808

No. 1016
1866: Rippon's Selection, 1844
1868: John Howard Hinton, 1833

No. 1023
1866: Thomas Ken, 1709
1870: Thomas Ken, 1697

No. 1025
1866: St. Ambrose, Third Century
1870: St. Ambrose, Fourth Century

No. 1033
1866: Edmund Butcher, 1798
1868: Edmund Butcher, 1768, a.
1869 (4th): Edmund Butcher, 1796

No. 1042
1866: Henry Downton, 1851
1867: Henry Downton, 1843

No. 1047
1866: Thomas Kelly, 1809
1867: Thomas Kelly, 1804; John Rippon, 1829

No. 1060
1866: [Hymn not printed]
1867: [Hymn added]

# Resources for Further Study

## Life and Hymns of Charles Spurgeon

Brown, Donald C. "Spurgeon's Hymnals." *The Hymn.* Vol. 30, No. 1 (Jan. 1979), pp. 39-48.

Curwen, J. Spencer. "Metropolitan Tabernacle." *Studies in Worship Music.* 1st Series. 3rd ed. Enl. & Rev. London: J. Curwen & Sons, 1901.

Drummond, Lewis A. *Spurgeon: Prince of Preachers.* Grand Rapids: Kregel, 1992.

Fullerton, W.Y. *C.H. Spurgeon: A Biography.* London: Williams & Norgate, 1920.

Morden, Peter J. *Communion with Christ and His People: The Spirituality of C.H. Spurgeon.* Oxford: Regent's Park College, 2010.

Nettles, Tom. *Living by Revealed Truth: The Life and Pastoral Theology of Charles Haddon Spurgeon.* Scotland: Christian Focus Publications, 2013.

Pike, G. Holden. *From the Pulpit to the Palm Branch.* London: Passmore & Alabaster, 1892.

Pike, G. Holden. *The Life and Work of Charles Haddon Spurgeon.* 6 vols. London: Cassell & Company, [n.d.].

Rhodes, Ray Jr. *Susie: The Life and Legacy of Susannah Spurgeon.* Chicago: Moody Publishers, 2018.

Shindler, Robert. *From the Usher's Desk to the Tabernacle Pulpit.* London: Passmore & Alabaster, 1892.

Smith, Veneenea Erika. *Dinna Forget Spurgeon: A Literary Biography.* Dissertation. Case Western Reserve University, 2006.

Spurgeon, Susannah, and Joseph Harrold. *The Autobiography of Charles H. Spurgeon, Compiled from His Diary, Letters, and Records.* 4 vols. London: Passmore & Alabaster, 1898-1900.

## Related Publications by Charles Spurgeon

*Evening by Evening, or Readings at Eventide for the Family or the Closet.* London: Passmore & Alabaster, 1868.

*Fac-Simile Pulpit Notes.* London: Passmore & Alabaster, 1894.

*The Interpreter, or Scripture for Family Worship.* London: Passmore & Alabaster, 1874. The hymns were also published separately as *The Interpreter Hymn Book.*

*Metropolitan Tabernacle Pulpit.* 57 vols. London: Passmore & Alabaster, 1861-1917.

*Morning by Morning, or Daily Readings for the Family or the Closet.* London: Passmore & Alabaster, 1865.

*New Park Street Pulpit.* 6 vols. London: Passmore & Alabaster, 1855-1860.

*Supplement to Our Own Hymn Book.* London: Passmore & Alabaster, 1898.

*The Sword and the Trowel.* 101 vols. London: Passmore & Alabaster, 1865-1966. The series was resumed under Peter Masters in 1980.

*Treasury of David.* 7 vols. London: Passmore & Alabaster, 1870-1886.

## Charles Spurgeon and Hymn Tunes

*The Bristol Tune-Book: A Manual of Tunes and Chants.* Novello & Co., 1863; 2nd ed. 1881; 3rd ed. 1891.

*The Congregational Psalmist.* Edited by Henry Allon and Henry J Gauntlett. London: Ward & Co., 1858; 2nd part, 1860; 3rd part, 1872; 4th part, 1879.

"The Congregational Psalmist Hymnal" [review]. *The Sword and the Trowel.* Vol. 22 (Nov. 1886), pp. 597-598.

*Hymns Ancient & Modern.* Edited by H.W. Baker and W.H. Monk. London: Novello, 1861; with appendix, 1868; rev. and enl. 1875; with appendix, 1889; etc.

*The Psalmist: A Collection of Psalm and Hymn Tunes.* Edited by Vincent Novello. London: J. Haddon, 1835; revised by Henry C. Lunn, 1863.

"The Psalmist" [review]. *The Sword and the Trowel.* Vol. 16 (Jan. 1880), p. 33.

*Union Tune Book: A Selection of Psalm and Hymn Tunes.* Arranged by John Peck. London: Sunday School Union, 1837; arr. Thomas Clark, 1842; and J.I. Cobbin, 1854.

Spurgeon, C.H. *The Tabernacle Tune Book: A Companion to Our Own Hymn Book.* London [ca. 1869].

## About Daniel Sedgwick

"A Hymnologist." *The Independent.* Vol. 19 (14 Feb. 1867), p. 2.

Bird, Frederick M. "Hymn Notes and Queries." *The Independent.* Vol. 32 (10 June 1880), p. 6.

[Bird, Frederick M.] [Obituary of Daniel Sedwick.] *The Independent.* Vol. 31 (1 May 1879), p. 15.

Boase, G.C. "Sedgwick, Daniel." *Dictionary of National Biography.* Vol. 51. New York: The MacMillan Co., 1897.

"Hymns, Their History and Development in the Greek and Latin Churches, Germany, and Great Britain" [review]. *The Independent.* Vol. 45 (13 Apr. 1893), p. 24.

Julian, John. "Sedgwick, Daniel," *A Dictionary of Hymnology.* Rev. ed. with Supplement. London: J. Murray, 1907.

Miller, Josiah. *Our Hymns: Their Authors and Origin.* London: Jackson, Walford & Hodder, 1866. See the preface, p. x.

Palmer, Roundell. *The Book of Praise.* London: The MacMillan Co., 1862.

Sedgwick, Daniel. *A Comprehensive Index of Names of Original Authors and Translators of Psalms and Hymns.* London: Daniel Sedgwick, 1860; 2nd ed., 1863.

# Index of Tunes

# Index of Authors and Sources

*Originally compiled by Daniel Sedgwick, newly revised.*
*Numbers refer to hymns in this volume.*

**Ed:** In Julian's *Dictionary*, pp. 734-5, 957, and 1562, the above resource is described both as *British Messenger* and *London Messenger*. The staff at the British Library were unable to locate any of these hymns in either of these publications, nor in *Baptist Messenger*. The run of *London Messenger* in the BL begins with 1 Jan. 1862, but the first issue indicates it had a predecessor: "At the commencement of a New Year we introduce ourselves in a new form, and at a lower price. . . . We need not remind our readers that, although we assume a new form, we abide to the old Truth." The previous form of the newspaper could not be located by the BL staff. The citations by Julian are probably genuine, and are repeated here, but could not be verified for this edition.

# Index of Subjects

*As originally compiled for Our Own Hymn-Book*

# Index of Scriptures

*Scripture references as given by the original authors in their
published works, newly compiled for this edition.*

## In Order by Number

# Index of First Lines

*Italics indicate alternate and foreign language first lines.*

## Spurgeon's Sorrows

Realistic Hope for those who Suffer from Depression

Zack Eswine

Christians should have the answers, shouldn't they? Depression affects many people both personally and through the ones we love. Here Zack Eswine draws from C.H Spurgeon, 'the Prince of Preachers' experience to encourage us. What Spurgeon found in his darkness can serve as a light in our own darkness. Zack Eswine brings you here, not a self–help guide, rather 'a handwritten note of one who wishes you well.'

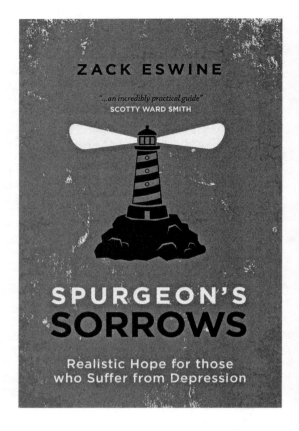

*Eswine's work demonstrates the value of reading biographies, old books, and sermons. Interacting with godly men and women from church history can be a vital aid to Christian maturity. He handles Spurgeon carefully, yet provocatively at points, and produces a volume that promises to help pastors and laypeople confront the sad terror of the dark night of the soul.*

The Gospel Coalition

978-1-7819-1538-7

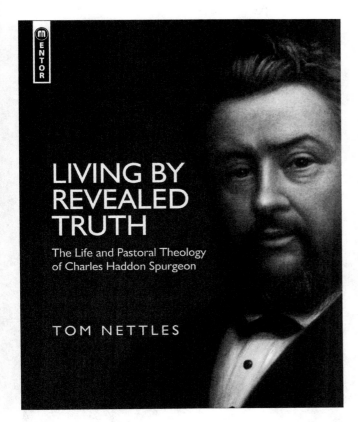

Living by Revealed Truth

The Life and Pastoral Theology of
Charles Haddon Spurgeon

TOM J. NETTLES

Tom Nettles has spent more than 15 years working on this magisterial biography of Charles Haddon Spurgeon, the famous 19th century preacher and writer. More than merely a biography, it covers his life, ministry and also provides an indepth survey of his theology.

*... takes us into the heart of Charles Spurgeon's conviction and his pastoral theology. This is a book that will encourage, educate, and bless its readers.*

R. Albert Mohler
President, The Southern Baptist Theological Seminary, Louisville, Kentucky

*Despite his ongoing popularity, Charles Spurgeon has only recently begun to attract the serious attention he deserves. Tom Nettles' work now makes a major contribution to this growing appreciation of the man and his ministry. Mining neglected but important sources, he has given sharper definition to our picture of Spurgeon, and produced a highly stimulating and readable account.*

Michael Reeves
President and Professor of Theology, Union School of Theology, Oxford, England

978-1-7819-1122-8

## Cheque Book of the Bank of Faith

### C. H. SPURGEON

A short reading for every day. Spurgeon wrote this selection of readings to encourage believers to enter into the full provision that their relationship to Jesus entitled them to realise, on a daily basis. He explains we have to present the promises of Scripture to God in prayer and faith, anticipating that he will honour what he has said. Available in a variety of colours.

978-1-8455-0071-9

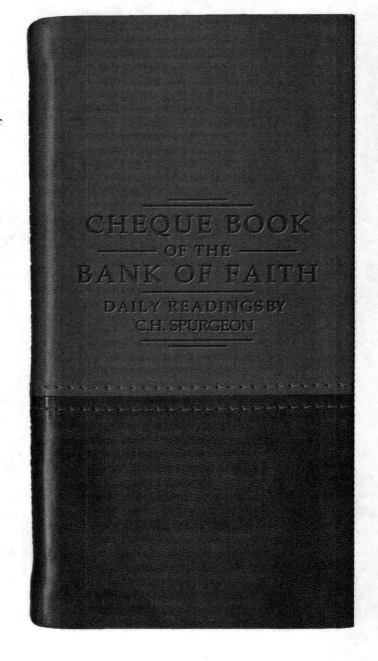

## Morning and Evening

### C. H. SPURGEON

A wealth of Biblical meditations from Spurgeon with applications that are relevant for contemporary Christians. Spurgeon's characteristically pithy comments hit home with a wit and elegance rarely found in other writing. Christians young and old will find his words challenging and stimulating. Complete and unabridged, available in a variety of colours.

978-1-8455-0014-6

# Christian Focus Publications

Our mission statement —

STAYING FAITHFUL

In dependence upon God we seek to impact the world through literature faithful to His infallible Word, the Bible. Our aim is to ensure that the Lord Jesus Christ is presented as the only hope to obtain forgiveness of sin, live a useful life and look forward to heaven with Him.

Our books are published in four imprints:

### CHRISTIAN
## FOCUS

Popular works including biographies, commentaries, basic doctrine and Christian living.

### CHRISTIAN
## HERITAGE

Books representing some of the best material from the rich heritage of the church.

## MENTOR

Books written at a level suitable for Bible College and seminary students, pastors, and other serious readers. The imprint includes commentaries, doctrinal studies, examination of current issues and church history.

## CF4•K

Children's books for quality Bible teaching and for all age groups: Sunday school curriculum, puzzle and activity books; personal and family devotional titles, biographies and inspirational stories — because you are never too young to know Jesus!

Christian Focus Publications Ltd,
Geanies House, Fearn, Ross-shire,
IV20 1TW, Scotland, United Kingdom.
www.christianfocus.com
blog.christianfocus.com